Phyllis Schlafly and Grassroots Conservatism

POLITICS AND SOCIETY IN TWENTIETH-CENTURY AMERICA

SERIES EDITORS

William Chafe, Gary Gerstle, Linda Gordon, and Julian Zelizer

A list of titles

in this series appears

at the back of

the book

Phyllis Schlafly and Grassroots Conservatism

A WOMAN'S CRUSADE

Donald T. Critchlow

PRINCETON UNIVERSITY PRESS   PRINCETON AND OXFORD

Library of Congress Cataloging-in-Publication Data

Critchlow, Donald T., 1948-
Phyllis Schlafly and grassroots conservatism : a woman's crusade / Donald T. Critchlow.
p. cm.—(Politics and society in twentieth-century America)
Includes bibliographical references and index.
ISBN-13: 978-0-691-07002-5 (cloth : alk. paper)
ISBN-10: 0-691-07002-4 (cloth : alk. paper)
1. Schlafly, Phyllis.   2. Conservatives—United States—Biography.   3.
Conservatism—United States.   4. Republican Party (U.S. : 1854-)   5. Women political
activists—United States—Biography.   6. Political activists—United States.   I. Title.
II. Series.

JC573.2.U6C75 2005
320.52'092—dc22
[B]
2004062469

British Library Cataloging-in-Publication Data is available

This book has been composed in Palatino
Printed on acid-free paper. ∞
pup.princeton.edu

Printed in the United States of America
10 9 8 7 6 5 4 3 2 1

To those I owe so much,
my wife Patricia, my uncle Tom Critchlow,
and three friends
Bill Rorabaugh, Tom Shippey, and John Garrison

Contents

Acknowledgments

In researching my previous book, *Intended Consequences: Birth Control, Abortion, and the Federal Government* (1999), I became keenly aware of the political influence exerted by grassroots conservatives on public policy in the United States. This awareness aroused my interest in the history of grassroots conservatism. The political career of Phyllis Schlafly, which began in the late 1940s and continues today, provided a conduit to understanding the methods and ideology of a movement that has transformed American politics. In the process of writing this book, I relied on a number of people whom I would like to thank.

This book would not have been possible without Phyllis Schlafly's granting me complete and unrestricted access without editorial control to her extensive personal files, as well as the exceedingly rich records of the Eagle Forum. She provided me a desk for work at Eagle Forum while I conducted research in what turned out to be unprocessed, but well-organized, archival collections that extended over 175 linear feet. What was remarkable about this access is that I had never met Phyllis Schlafly until I approached her about writing a political biography of her. Her decision was based only on reading the book proposal, which I told her my agent had submitted to Princeton University Press. Although she sometimes expressed wonder at the amount of time I spent researching the book and occasionally asked me what files I was looking at, she never sought to impose her perspective on my work. Although I pursued this project as a scholar and never as a partisan, I suspect that there is much she will like about this book, but also parts that she will disagree with. Phyllis Schlafly is a woman of strong views, but I have also learned that she is a gracious woman with a good sense of humor. This explains much about her political fortitude and my relationship with her. This book is based on my original research in archival materials, however, not on personal interviews with Phyllis Schlafly or other prominent conservatives who appear in this book, except for a handful duly noted in the footnotes.

I reinforced my research in Mrs. Schlafly's papers with research in more than 50 other archival collections. In the process, I incurred other debts of thanks to many archivists across the country. I especially want to thank David Wigdor and John Earl Haynes at the Library of Congress

Manuscript Division who directed me, respectively, to the ERAmerica Papers and the newly acquired Herbert Philbrick Papers, as well as other important collections there. Also, I want to thank the archivists at the Bentley Library at the University of Michigan and the Gerald Ford Presidential Library who arranged for me to see the Elly Peterson papers while the Bentley was undergoing renovation. The many archivists I worked with at the Ronald Reagan Library and the John F. Kennedy Library deserve acknowledgment. Archivists at the University of Oregon, the University of Arkansas, and the Chicago Historical Society were also extremely helpful in directing me to the right spots in their collections. I want to thank my long and dear friends Elizabeth and James Mohr of the University of Oregon for their hospitality while I worked in Eugene. Research assistance was provided by John Korasick, Andrew Ayers, and Matthew Sherman. Mr. Sherman assisted in reproducing the illustrations and he indexed the book. Staff members at the Eagle Forum—Julia Algya, Gwen Kelley, and Patrick Ertmann—helped me find library materials, while providing conversation during my escape from the lower depths of the archives in the basement. Saint Louis University provided me with a year's sabbatical leave to write this book.

A number of people read the manuscript in its various drafts. When Thomas LeBien left Princeton University Press, Brigitta von Rhineberg took over editorial oversight of this book. If this book enjoys success, it will be largely due to her splendid editorial hand. She insisted on reading early drafts of chapters, gently prodding me to set a judicious tone for a controversial subject, while keeping the general reader in mind. Brigitta's editorial assistant, Alison Kallet, kept the production process on schedule and gave me good advice on photographs for the book.

Early drafts of this book were read by Christopher Gray, John Earl Haynes, and Gregory Schneider, who brought their extensive knowledge of conservatism and communism to the manuscript. A later and completed draft of the manuscript was read by my friend William Rorabaugh and by William Rusher. Mr. Rusher, long-time publisher of the *National Review*, was especially important in developing my thinking about the relationship between conservative intellectuals and grassroots conservatives. Readers for the Princeton University Press, Paula Baker and Leo Ribuffo, who both identified themselves in their reports, led me to trim and tighten the focus of the book. Julian Zelizer read the revised manuscript and his comments provided opportunities for final polishing. After discussing the manuscript with other editors of a series he edits for Princeton—Politics and Society in Twentieth-Century America—Julian invited me to include this book in the series, even though it was already under contract with Princeton University Press. I accepted his invitation.

I did not count the many drafts of this manuscript that my wife Patricia read. This is my thirteenth book and her patience and endurance continue to amaze me. My appreciation of her, as she knows, is deep.

Phyllis Schlafly and Grassroots Conservatism

Introduction

ONE OF THE most remarkable features of American politics in the late twentieth century is that while governmental responsibilities and obligations to its citizens increased, and democratic rights and civil protections were extended to new groups and classes of people, liberalism was perceived to be a failure. With this failure, many social commentators remarked on the electorate's notable shift to the right. This shift was far from universal; voters, largely in urban areas along the East and West coasts and in a few Midwestern industrial cities, erected impenetrable fortresses of support for liberal candidates. At the same time, much of the electorate simply did not vote, reflecting both apathy and a deep mistrust of the two major parties, political leaders, and political institutions. Yet, few doubt that a dramatic shift in American politics occurred over the last four decades of the twentieth century. This was evidenced in the increased number of voters willing to identify themselves as "conservative," by the takeover of the Republican party by the Right, and by the shifting of political debate to issues once considered the exclusive domain of the Right—fiscal responsibility, returning power to the states, peace through military strength, and the importance of individual responsibility in maintaining civil society. At the start of the twenty-first century, an undeniable sense prevailed among many observers of the American political scene that conservatism in America was ascendant and New Deal liberalism on the decline.

This turn in American politics was of historic proportions. The liberal vision, which had dominated American politics at least since the early twentieth century, appeared spent, exhausted by campus protests, urban riots, a war in Vietnam in the 1960s, inept political leadership in the 1970s, and anxious attempts to graft conservative rhetoric onto a hybrid liberalism in the 1990s. Long-time liberal fears that the American Right might gain political power had become reality. Conservatism had become a badge of respectability for many voters, while public officials were running away from the label "liberal." Whether middle-class Americans were actually more conservative in 2000 than they were in 1956 is debatable. What is important is that more Americans called themselves conservatives than did those who proclaimed themselves liberal. Furthermore, many of those calling themselves conservative proudly declared themselves evangelical Christians or traditionalist Jews, Protestants, or Catholics. This was an extraordinary reversal from fifty years, or even thirty years, earlier when being called a conservative was an opprobrium often associated with "little old ladies in tennis shoes" searching for communists at their local school board meeting. By the twenty-first century, average Americans, blue collar and white collar workers, middle-class husbands and wives, white Southerners, and many college students across the country proudly proclaimed themselves to be conservative. Conservatism in the twenty-first century implied opposition to the status quo, rebellion against the establishment, a democratic faith in the people, and a deep suspicion of the wisdom of the liberal elites in government, the media, and academia. "I am a conservative," the newly elected U.S. Senator Roger Jepsen declared in 1980, "because I am for change."

This shift to the right was reflected in the transformation of the Republican party into a voice of conservatism. This transformation was neither inevitable nor smooth, but came through fierce factional and ideological warfare within the party as liberals, moderates, and pragmatists battled to defeat the GOP's rightwing. At any number of times, the GOP Right looked as though it had been defeated for good. Following conservative Barry Goldwater's defeat for the presidency in 1964, his followers were purged from party leadership. Richard Nixon's election in 1968 did little to resuscitate the GOP Right, even though many conservatives had rallied to his campaign for the presidency. When Nixon left office in disgrace, the Republican Right was isolated and demoralized. Only the emergence of cultural issues—abortion, feminism, prayer-in-school, and homosexual rights—revived the Right, and in doing so, set the stage for Ronald Reagan, an avowed conservative, in 1980. The GOP became a party dominated by religious and cultural traditionalism, as evidenced by the party platforms of the 1980s. A survey of delegates attending the 1992 Republican National Convention found that "over 22 percent of the convention delegates identified themselves as fundamentalists, while 66 percent attended worship services regularly, and 52 percent were either members of or were sympathetic to the political movement known as the Christian Right."[1]

While the Democratic National Convention meeting in New York that same summer of 1992 nominated a Southern Baptist and a New Democrat centrist, William Clinton, the delegates attending the convention contrasted sharply with their Republican counterparts. Those declaring themselves atheists, agnostics, or individuals not affiliated with any religion accounted for 19 percent of all delegates, while 55 percent of the delegates said they rarely attended worship services. The Democratic party had become a party of secular and religious progressives who, while not abandoning religious commitment, rejected the moral dictates of the orthodox camp. The divide between the two parties extends beyond political ideology to a deeper cultural and religious chasm that encourages heated partisanship and disallows easy political compromise. This religious and cultural divide emerged at a time when New Deal economic liberalism, the glue which had held the Democrats together since the 1930s, began to be repudiated by the American electorate.

How had a small movement, consisting of a few conservative intellectuals and grassroots anticommunist activists in the 1950s, become so powerful as to radically change American politics in ways arguably comparable to Jacksonian democracy in the 1830s or the Republican party in the 1860s? What transpired in the last half century to change America as a beacon of liberalism at the end of World War II to a voice of conservatism as the century drew to a close? Why did liberalism come to be seen by so many Americans as a failed experiment by the end of the twentieth century, even though it had fulfilled its promise to create the modern welfare state in the 1930s, had created a new international order after World War II, and had extended new rights and civil liberties to Americans in the 1960s?

This book offers insight into this transformative upheaval in American politics through the political career of Phyllis Schlafly, whose involvement in the Republican Right began in the immediate aftermath of World War II and extended into the twenty-first century. Schlafly's political activities impart their own intrinsic interest, but the importance of Schlafly lies in what her career tells us about the remarkable changes that took place in the larger politics of the last half of the twentieth century. Never elected to political office, although she ran twice for Congress, Schlafly rose to prominence in conservative politics not as a philosopher or intellectual, but as an organizer. Her Eagle Forum, the organization she founded in the early 1970s, today claims a membership of 50,000 women who can be mobilized for conservative causes and candidates. Her career as an anticommunist crusader in the 1950s, her book *A Choice Not an Echo* that sold over three million copies in 1964 and helped secure Barry Goldwater's presidential nomination, her campaign against the SALT Treaties and for American strategic superiority, her commitment to defeat the Equal Rights Amendment (ERA), her two campaigns for Congress, and her leadership in the pro-family movement personified the rise of the Right in contemporary United States.

Schlafly is best known to those over the age of forty for her *A Choice Not an Echo* and her campaign to defeat ERA, which drew thousands of women into an antifeminist, pro-family crusade. Both these were catalysts that propelled a resurgent Right and made her a heroine of the Right. Since the 1960s she has been a regular radio and television commentator, beginning with her fifteen-minute Daughters of the American Revolution "America Wake Up" radio program. This was followed by her CBS Spectrum radio commentaries and televised debates (1973–78), her syndicated three-minute daily commentaries (1983–present), and live interviews on hundreds of television and radio programs. Her one-hour weekly live-broadcast is heard regularly on Christian radio today. Her *Phyllis Schlafly Report*, begun in 1967, is read by 30,000 subscribers for its essays on politics, education, national defense, feminism, the judiciary, and immigration. Through these activities Schlafly tapped into the anxieties of traditional-minded Middle Americans concerned about changing social and cultural mores in America. Schlafly helped organize the grassroots movement in churches and local communities that eventually became a major player in the Republican party. At the same time, these activities unleashed an intense and seemingly irrepressible culture war. The election of Ronald Reagan in 1980 intensified debates over gender, abortion, and cultural issues, and, twenty-five years later, this debate is as vigorous as ever.

Schlafly's life presents a fascinating story in itself, but her importance—at least for the purposes of this book—rests in what her political activities tell us about the transformation of the Republican party from moderate/liberal to conservative. (Readers interested in a more personal biography of her are referred to Carol Felsenthal, *The Sweetheart of the Silent Majority: The Biography of Phyllis Schlafly*, published in 1981.) Through her political career, three themes emerge. First, this study constructs an alternative narrative to other histories of the Republican Right in America. Previous studies have tended to assume a sequence of events that culminated with the election of Ronald Reagan. That linear story usually begins with a small number of conservative intellectuals who became prominent in the post–World War II period.

They prepared the ground for Goldwater's nomination in 1964, and although he was defeated, conservatives returned home to build an elaborate network of conservative organizations and programs. Conservatives endowed foundations such as the Bradley Foundation, the Olin Foundation, and the Richard and Helen DeVos Foundation; built policy centers such as the Heritage Foundation; and funded educational programs through such groups as the Institute for Humane Studies, the Liberty Fund, and the Intercollegiate Studies Institute. This network prepared the ground for Ronald Reagan's election in 1980.

The problem with linear history is that the conservative triumph was not a straight march from Point A to Point B, nor was the arrival at Point B at all certain. The history of the Republican Right as illustrated through the political career of Schlafly was an interrupted tale of fits and starts, in which conservatives were often defeated in political fights with the Left and within the Republican party. The history of the Republican Right is episodic, a dramatic story of defensive battles and losing campaigns—foot-soldiers driven by concerns about communism and the subversion of the American Republic, often isolated by charges of extremism. Defeated in the presidential election of 1964, purged from leadership positions in its aftermath, and then betrayed by Richard Nixon in the 1970s, conservatives were demoralized and uncertain of their future in the 1970s. Arguably, if Ronald Reagan had won the Republican nomination in 1976 against incumbent Gerald Ford, he would have been defeated by Jimmy Carter in the general election. Yet another setback would have been difficult for the Right to overcome. Conservatism as an ideology would have remained, but as a major political force it might have been spent. Of course, this is conjecture, but it makes the point that the triumph of the Republican Right was certainly not inevitable.

Until recently, much of the history of the conservative movement has focused largely on the conservative intellectuals and writers, while ignoring the importance of grassroots conservatism. Those histories portrayed a small group of writers and intellectuals, articulating an antistatist philosophy that deeply resonated with the republican tradition in America—its distrust of centralized government and political elites, and its fear of corruption. From these intellectual seeds, it was assumed that a grassroots political movement sprang forth, but nature knows that seed dropped on barren soil does not grow. A few fringe groups sprang up that were given to conspiratorial views of history, which allowed liberals to hang extremist labels on the grassroots Right. Those groups were subsequently marginalized within the larger conservative movement.[2]

This study of the postwar Republican Right finds that the foundation of the Republican Right was laid in grassroots anticommunism that paralleled the development of an intellectual movement that sought to educate the general public, especially young people, about the principles of conservatism. At the same time, grassroots anticommunist organizations in the late 1950s educated large numbers of Americans through hundreds of often obscure publications, local seminars, lectures, film strips, study groups, and educational campaigns. Radio programs such as the Dan Smoot Report and the Manion Forum reached tens of thousands of listeners, while Dr. Fred C. Schwarz's Christian Anti-Communism Crusade organized training schools and rallies that attracted thousands of participants. These grassroots anticommunist activities were often conducted through local groups and organizations that were tied together only by their cause and by national speakers and writers who attended local events. Without belying the importance of intellectuals such as Friedrich von Hayek, Leo Strauss, Eric Voegelin, Ayn Rand, William F. Buckley, Jr., or Russell Kirk, grassroots activists were reading books such as Barry Goldwater's best-seller *The Conscience of a Conservative* (1960), John A. Stormer's *None Dare Call It Treason* (1964), Phyllis Schlafly's *A Choice Not an Echo* (1964), and eye-witness reports by ex-communists. Without intellectual foundations, the modern conservative movement might have gone the way of earlier grassroots movements that rebelled against the established order, for example, the Anti-Masons in the 1840s and the Populists in the 1890s. Yet without grassroots activists to give political substance and energy to conservative ideas, conservatism as political movement would have remained largely the province of a handful of writers. Schlafly's talent, in part, was her ability to translate conservative ideas to grassroots activists and motivate them to achieve political goals.[3]

The second theme emerges from the first: Conservative intellectuals and grassroots activists waged war on New Deal liberalism, but conservatism triumphed only when New Deal liberalism was perceived as a failure by the American people. Writing in 1959, William F. Buckley, Jr., the founding editor of the newly established *National Review*, declared, "We must bring down the thing called Liberalism, which is powerful, but decadent; and salvage a thing called conservatism, which is weak but viable."[4] Through a well-organized grassroots campaign, conservatives were able to nominate Barry Goldwater as the Republican presidential candidate in 1964, but Goldwater's subsequent overwhelming defeat, followed by factionalism within the Republican party kept conservatism weak and perhaps not viable, either.

Four years later in 1968, America appeared to many on both the Left and the Right to be a nation in inner turmoil—economic, spiritual, and cultural. The nation had become mired in an interminable war in Vietnam, torn apart by internal dissent and racial violence, its economy bloated with inflation, and its military power and prestige in the world in decline. Liberalism took much of the blame. By the 1970s, liberalism fell into further disrepute for not upholding values of responsibility for one's actions: that work is better than public assistance, that having children in marriage is better than out-of-wedlock, and that freedom and authority are not opposite values. "Liberal" became a label to be avoided. Running for the presidency in 1988, Michael Dukakis was branded with the "L" word and it cost him the election. Liberal had become a tarnished word to many Democratic politicians by 1992.

Perhaps this caricature of liberals was unfair, but liberalism was increasingly placed on the defensive. Liberal Democrats continued to control Congress, and the Democratic party elected two presidents to office after 1968, but both Jimmy Carter in 1976 and Bill Clinton in 1992 and 1996 ran as centrists. The last liberal elected to the presidency was forty years ago, Lyndon Johnson in 1964. Liberalism appeared to become little more than a boiling cauldron of identity politics that pandered to the jealousies of ethnic and minority groups. Liberal candidates were elected to local and state office, but by the late 1960s liberalism as an intellectual force was placed on the defensive and appeared to have run out of fresh ideas, living on by wrapping itself in the legacy of the New Deal of the 1930s. Only then, as economic liberalism declined, did conservatism as an ideology and a movement become a powerful force in American politics.

The final theme in this study is the importance of women in the emergence of the grassroots Right, and the unique sensibility that they brought to the movement. Of course, men played an important role as leaders and grassroots activists, but women were especially important in organizations such as the National Federation of Republican Women and the Daughters of the American Revolution, organizations in which Phyllis Schlafly held high office. The discovery of conservative, antifeminist women has attracted serious attention by scholars, and this study could not have been written without the rich literature that has developed in this area. This is not a study of gender politics, but gender played an essential role in the triumph of the Right. While recognizing the importance of women in the conservative movement, this study is primarily concerned about the political effects of grassroots conservatism on American politics in general. In understanding the motivation of the grassroots Right and the individuals involved, I came to the conclusion that sociological interpretation based on status anxiety, gender privilege, class interest, or misplaced maternalism was inadequate to explain the grassroots Right, especially the women of the Right.

Instead, this study places the women of the Right within a deeply rooted ideological sensibility that combines a libertarian espousal of the virtues of small government and individual responsibility with a faith in traditional values and divine moral authority. These two strains—libertarianism and religious traditionalism—were embodied in a sentiment that created an uneasy, and even at times a volatile, tension. In the late eighteenth and early nineteenth centuries, this sentiment found expression in a religious morality and political outlook that abhorred the excesses of the French Revolution, moral decay in antebellum politics, and, later, intemperance in late nineteenth-century society. In the twentieth century, this sentiment, although not clearly articulated in a systematic political ideology, resisted the secularization of society with its reliance on expertise, government bureaucracy, and commitment to progress through centralized government. By synchronizing religion and politics, this moral sensibility assumed that free government rested upon a moral or religious citizenry whose principal civil responsibility was the protection of public virtue. The sensibility upheld the belief that ultimately republican government rested on moral foundations that, if eroded, would lead to the collapse of the polity.[5]

This view of the world assumed that the American republic was founded on God's grace and flourished with His blessing. Although opponents charged evangelical and traditional Christians with wanting to erect a theocratic state, this sensibility adhered to deeply held republican values. Indeed, some within this tradition went so far as to claim that the Israelite theocratic state was actually a republic. For example, writing in 1892, two Presbyterian theologians, Rev. John Hall and Rev. William E. Moore declared, "The Christian Church in its earliest organization was a republic. Its rulers under Christ were the elders of the people of God. The doctrine, like the polity, is drawn from the Bible. There is no necessary connection between government by chosen representation and the doctrines of grace; but the affinity between them is so close that, given one, we naturally expect the other."[6]

By the late twentieth century, this kind of theological discussion became less prevalent, but this view that Judeo-Christian morality provided the foundation of the American republic remained. At the root of the anti-communism, anti-feminism, and pro-family movements in post-World War II America remained a conviction that the nation must not stray from its religious foundations and values lest society collapse into anarchy. As sociologist Rebecca Klatch summarizes this view, "While America was founded with God's grace and has flourished with His blessing, an historical shift has occurred that threatens America's standing. Of chief concern, America has moved away from God. Pleasure and prosperity have replaced biblical principles as the priority of the nation. . . . the moral absolutes that govern the nation are in disarray."[7]

This moral republican sentiment, while not leading every evangelical and traditional-minded Christian and Jew into active politics, nonetheless inspired many to become politically involved throughout the nineteenth and early twentieth centuries. Religious republican values were not necessarily associated with any particular political party, and at times, these sentiments manifested strikingly illiberal tendencies apparent to contemporaries and later historians. In the nineteenth century, for example, this moral republicanism found expression in nativist anti-immigrant and anti-Catholic political movements. Still, the fear that the nation was in moral decline persisted in the twentieth century and ultimately drew evangelical Protestants, Roman Catholics, and Mormons together. A precarious alliance between these religious traditions gave a potent political impetus to grassroots conservatism in the late twentieth century.

Once on the fringe of American politics, the grassroots Right entered into American politics with a suddenness and force that stunned both the Left and the Republican establishment. When the Right gained control of the Republican party, its opponents were frightened and angered by this movement that left the politics of old in ruins. The mentality of the Republican Right seemed unfathomable to those who believed that social justice, social equality, and social progress were attainable through the action of state power. Of course, not all members of the Republican Right were religious and cultural traditionalists. Some were motivated by secular beliefs in small government, opposition to welfare liberalism, equal opportunity rather than preferential rights, and a strong national defense. The mindset of the Right that spoke of the fundamental right to life of the fetus, biblical teachings about the proper family structure and sexual relations, the sin of homosexuality, and the need to restore prayer in school was so removed from the modern sensibilities that it appeared nearly incognizable to many on the Left. They spoke a different language, understood the world differently, and brought different cultural values and social visions to the political arena.

This book seeks to understand the Republican Right by placing its emergence within a political context of the day. To accomplish this, I entered into the world of the grassroots Right through an extensive reading of private correspondence, speeches, leaflets, pamphlets, newspapers, and books. I also benefited from access to Phyllis Schlafly's extensive archives at the headquarters of the Eagle Forum and her personal papers. These unpublished sources and archival records were supplemented through research in many other archives, including papers of her opponents, as well as other conservatives. In addition, I undertook research in pertinent presidential libraries and the collections of major political leaders of the twentieth century.

Phyllis Schlafly granted me access to her papers with the understanding that this book was not to be an authorized account of her political career, and that I would bring the critical skills of a professional, independent-minded historian to this project. I relied primarily on printed and archival sources for this book, using only a handful of interviews. I wanted this book to be history, not journalism. On a few occasions when I was working in the archives at the Eagle Forum headquarters, I caught Schlafly unannounced with a specific document and found that it triggered memories that she relayed to me, often with great excitement. Following these conversations, I immediately typed my notes from memory for later use.

What emerged from this research was a political world quite remote from my own experiences. In writing about this world, I sought to capture the outlook of the grassroots Right, while representing it accurately. At the same time, I placed the Republican Right in a critical perspective by relating how differently its opponents saw events. In doing this,

I hope I convey the high drama of a political contest that so profoundly transformed American politics in the last half of the twentieth century. I leave the reader to judge whether I have succeeded in my purpose, with the caveat made by eighteenth-century historian and philosopher David Hume that authors will also be judged by "the few [who are] apt to form to themselves systems of their own, which they resolve not to relinquish."[8] This is what makes writing and reading history so rewarding.

CHAPTER ONE

The Making of a Grassroots Conservative

"I'D LIKE TO BURN you at the stake!" an exasperated Betty Friedan, the coryphaeus of feminism, blurted out in a debate with Phyllis Schlafly at Illinois State University in the spring of 1973. Friedan expressed the sentiments of most feminists who saw Schlafly as the person most responsible for stalling progress of the Equal Rights Amendment (ERA) that only a year before appeared to be on its way to victory. Denouncing the ERA as radical, unnecessary, and a threat to legal rights of women and the American family, Schlafly mobilized tens of thousands of women across the nation to block the proposed twenty-seventh amendment to the United States Constitution. In the years that followed, Schlafly emerged as the most prominent opponent of modern feminism and as a major spokesperson for a powerful conservative movement that would lead to the election of Ronald Reagan, an avowed conservative, as President of the United States in 1980. Feminists, from their perspective, had every reason to despise Schlafly. Most galling, perhaps, was the fact that Schlafly had discovered a genuine populist sentiment in a large female population that opposed the ERA, feminism, and modern liberalism with the same intensity of emotion that feminists brought to their cause. In doing so, Schlafly emerged a heroine of the Right. By mobilizing these women—joined by others disenchanted with the liberal welfare state that had been erected in the twentieth century—Schlafly tapped a wellspring of resentment that transformed the Republican party into a party of conservatism that changed American politics as the century drew to a close.

Friedan and Schlafly symbolized this political and cultural divide. At the heart of this division were irreconcilable visions of what makes for a good and just society. For those who like their history delivered in didactic doses, it is easy, although inaccurate, to view Friedan, the feminist, as the conveyer of political values of liberation, social progress, and cultural liberation, while seeing Schlafly, the conservative, as the defender of reaction, the status quo, and the patriarchal oppression of women. Any characterization of Schlafly must be qualified with the recognition that she, and the other grassroots conservatives who joined her, opposed the political status quo. They waged a protracted struggle against the liberal welfare state, with its reliance on centralized government, bureaucratic expertise, judicial activism, and distrust of popular democracy, traditional values, and patriotism.

To understand the values that Schlafly carried into her crusade against the feminists and her struggle to make the GOP into a conservative party, a brief biographical chapter sketching her childhood and coming of age is in order. Her political views, which contrasted sharply with her opponents on the Left, came from the values she learned as a child growing up in a Catholic family hard hit by the Great Depression of the 1930s. From this same economic crisis, others became supporters of New Deal liberalism, but for Schlafly it cemented her faith in God, country, and family.

Parallel Spheres

Betty Friedan's and Phyllis Schlafly's childhood backgrounds bear a striking resemblance: Both were born in the Midwest in the 1920s into middle-class families, with strong mothers who emphasized the importance of education and supported their intellectually gifted children going to college. Both reflected the emergence of women as major political leaders in the postwar period, by no means a new phenomenon in American history, but one that gained new significance as the role of women changed in society. Friedan and Schlafly accepted the challenge of destiny and emerged as leaders of transformative female social movements that changed American society and politics in the last half of the twentieth century. Yet, no two women could have taken different paths in their lives. Friedan became a feminist who saw history as having imbued women with a role that kept them entrapped, frustrated, and oppressed by the myth of the traditional family. Schlafly became an antifeminist who saw history as having fulfilled the promise of womanhood by allowing women to choose to become wives and mothers in traditional families, the cornerstone of civilized society. Their choices became symbols for other women who made similar choices in their own lives during an unsettled time in America when the meaning of the family, the place of women, and the nature of rights were opened to argument.

When Friedan and Schlafly met on the stage at Illinois State University in 1973, their arguments and the political forces they represented were already being felt in politics, but few people sensed that reverberations of their clash and what it symbolized were about to shake both main political parties from their moorings. Feminists gained many of their goals through legislation and shifting the Democratic party to the left. Yet, feminists lost their battle for the ERA, and that struggle enabled conservatism to emerge victorious. How one saw the Friedan-Schlafly debate largely depended on the predisposition brought into the auditorium, just as Betty Friedan and Phyllis Schlafly had reached different conclusions about their lives despite their many similarities on the surface. So dissimilar were these conclusions, however, that an outsider might conclude that these two women had grown up on separate planets.[1]

Friedan's career course from a child growing up in the Midwest during the Depression to becoming an activist closely aligned with the Communist party and then a feminist leader differs considerably from Phyllis Schlafly's path to the Republican Right.[2] Both drew different lessons from their childhood experiences during the Depression and from their families, teachers, and friends. As both women matured, each made choices that determined the paths they would pursue as female leaders. Step by step, Friedan followed a path as a progressive activist until she emerged as a radical feminist. Similarly, Schlafly made specific decisions that set her on the road to becoming an anti-feminist conservative. They were predisposed toward the choices that they made: Friedan was Jewish, growing up in a small Midwestern town in an affluent family, with a mother who felt frustrated by giving up a career. Schlafly, raised in a strong Roman Catholic family that voted Republican in a predominantly Democratic city, St. Louis, was imbued with values of hard work, education, and family—just as was Friedan. Both women passed these values to their children, and one of the strange coincidences of life occurred when their sons, Roger Schlafly and Daniel Friedan, were doctoral students together, with the same faculty adviser, mathematician Isadore M. Singer, at the University of California, Berkeley, in the late 1970s.

In making their choices, Friedan and Schlafly emerged as important leaders, representative in their different ways of the increasing power of women in America after World War II. In the postwar period, women entered the workforce in large numbers, enrolled in higher education, gained entry into once male-dominated professions, and increased their economic and financial power. These changes challenged gender roles, the traditional family, and the cultural and political mores of American society. Carrying the banner for women's liberation, Friedan and other feminists allied themselves with the Left and soon gained unprecedented influence in the Democratic party. Changes also occurred in the Republican party, beginning with the nomination of Barry Goldwater in 1964. Despite his crushing defeat in November of that year, Republican conservatives continued to gain strength, culminating with the election of Ronald Reagan in 1980.

The emergence of the Left within the Democratic party and the Right within the Republican party marked an ideological polarization of American politics unseen since the Populist upheaval of the 1890s. Political and cultural fissures became evident in America as it entered the twenty-first century. Conservatives, led by such people as Phyllis Schlafly, tapped into the anxieties of Middle Americans and their disappointment with the liberal welfare state by organizing grassroots movements in churches, local communities, and local and state Republican party organizations over a range of social issues—the Equal Rights Amendment, abortion, feminism, prayer in school, homosexual rights—as well as national defense and economic policies. The pro-family movement initiated by Schlafly during the ERA fight marked the beginning of an intense and seemingly irrepressible cultural confrontation. The transformation of the Republican party into a conservative party and the shift in the national political climate to the Right intensified ideological debates over gender, abortion, and cultural issues. Twenty-five years later, this debate is as pronounced as ever.

In their struggle to overturn the liberal order inherited from the New Deal, Schlafly and other conservative activists were not given to subtle complaint or understated rhetoric, and they were just as anxious for political transformation as were their political counterparts. Schlafly and other conservatives believed that the free market brings affluence and social progress to society, while providing a foundation for democratic governance. They believed the regulated domestic economy and the international global economy—the new world order, as George Herbert Walker Bush labeled it—was supported by large corporate interests, and they certainly were not apologists for corporate privilege, excess, or closed-door influence in government. Indeed, Republican conservatives saw their enemies within the GOP as the party's Eastern financial wing ("Wall Street"). Grassroots conservatives were involved in politics to protect the political values of a free Republic, not to reestablish the golden age of a previous time—a mythic era of nineteenth-century laissez-faire capitalism or an idealized patriarchal order that subordinated women and racial minorities. Republican conservatives battled the liberal political establishment in the Democratic party just as aggressively as the liberal-moderate political establishment within their own party, the Republican party. They believed political change could be accomplished through the electoral system and democratic political activity, and they abhorred undemocratic groups found on both the Left and the Right.

Women such as Schlafly played a significant role in challenging the liberal New Deal order and in forcing a shift to the Right in the GOP. It is arguable whether these women have been given credit or recognition by their male counterparts in the conservative movement, but nonetheless, their participation in conservative politics fell within an established Anglo-American tradition of women's involvement in conservative political causes and polemics. While many of the women in this tradition remain obscure and its full history has yet to be written, women polemicists contributed in important ways to Tory political theory and social vision in late seventeenth-century and early eighteenth-century England. For example, Mary Astell (1666–1731), joined by other Tory male and female writers, took issue with English political philosopher John Locke's contractual theory of natural rights through a series of erudite writings that upheld a divinely ordained hierarchy.[3] The concept of the divinely ordained family took on a distinct, broadly conceived, republican character in revolutionary America. Drawing upon a group of Enlightenment theorists in Scotland including Adam Smith, David Hume, Henry Home, William Robertson, and John Miller, new notions of the role and status of women gained acceptance in the early American Republic that removed barriers between public and private life. These Scottish Enlightenment thinkers promulgated a view of civil society that perceived women acting as both the means and the beneficiaries of social progress within the hierarchical family. In an age of commerce, women acting as wives and mothers within the hierarchical family tempered the adverse effects of trade that encouraged luxury, promoted avarice, and spread vice, thereby subverting virtue and sapping the martial spirit necessary to the preservation of a republic. The hierarchical family in which the wife and mother was the cornerstone became the primary conveyer of tradition and custom, morals, and civil habits and manners.[4]

This socially conservative notion of the divinely ordained hierarchy also allowed women to participate in American politics through the Federalist party and the Whig party in the early nineteenth century.[5] For example, evangelical Christian women became actively involved in Whig politics by supporting party candidates and actively participating in campaigns to control local school boards and to enact and enforce local ordinances intended to uphold the moral order through Sabbath and temperance laws.[6] This Anglo-American conservative vision, as expressed in the Federalist and Whig parties, embodied eighteenth-century republican political thought and an absolutist Christian moral vision that created permeable spheres of private and public life, even while ensuring a distinct place for women in the hierarchical family. At the basis of female and Christian involvement in the public sphere was an assumption that the Divine Creator had endowed humans with certain inalienable rights, but it was up to a virtuous citizenry, a religious and educated citizenry, to protect individual liberty and the spiritual interests of the nations. The belief common to citizens in the nineteenth century was that Americans were a religious people whose institutions presuppose a Supreme Being. This Anglo-American conservative sensibility, from which twentieth-century female activists such as Schlafly drew, emphasized the importance of the nation's place in fulfilling a divine promise for moral redemption and salvation. Thus, as Christians, they saw themselves as the moral guardians of the nation. Without this spiritual protection, republicanism as a form of government would perish and its citizens would be destroyed by the anarchy that would follow. As one evangelical Christian involved in Whig politics declared, "A republic is the body, Christianity is the soul."[7]

This Christian involvement in politics derived not from a well-defined or systematically developed ideology, but from a set of political and religious assumptions that expressed itself as a sensibility about the world. Schlafly and like-minded female conservative activists in the late twentieth century were direct descendants of this sensibility developed earlier. Integral to what might be called this Christian-republican sensibility was a belief that there is a Supreme Being whose divine law is absolute and provides the foundation necessary for a republican government to survive. Ultimately, if the citizens are corrupt, public virtue dissipates; the republic weakens and then collapses. Thus, while partaking of a tradition that upheld divinely ordained natural rights, this Christian-republican outlook rejected radical Enlightenment concepts of rationalism, secularism, and relativism—all of which linked progress to a new faith in humanity. This political sensibility presented a kind of counter-Enlightenment perspective that progress was not found in the advance of scientific knowledge that replaced revealed religion; nor was progress found in philosophies that placed mankind at the center of the universe; nor would progress be found in modern values which assert that all religions, moral beliefs, and cultural customs have equal value. Indeed, this sensibility tended to view history as a struggle between the forces of good versus evil, light versus darkness, Christianity versus paganism.

Women were integral to upholding these conservative political principles in the nineteenth and early twentieth centuries.[8] Within this sensibility, the primary concern was to maintain the family and protect and educate children. At the same time, this moral vision called on women to participate in public life as the guardians of a republican political order that placed a greater reliance on individuals to maintain social order and improve society than on centralized government. Even while participating in public life, conservative women held an inherent distrust of centralized government intrinsic to republican ideology. Their volunteer work through women's clubs, civic organizations, and churches was primarily aimed at improving society within the context of a relatively weak central government. In the American republican tradition, governmental power was seen as a potential threat to liberty. The legitimate function of government was to protect the nation from its external foes, maintain public order through the rule and enforcement of law, and remove obstacles to the free exchange of goods. Because power tends to corrupt, governmental power must be restrained.

For the generation of social conservatives that emerged following the Second World War, represented by women such as Phyllis Schlafly, the Christian tradition remained the principal foundation for preserving the Republic because the breakdown of social morality led inevitably to political disorder. Believing this, Schlafly assumed a religious-political sensibility that had deep roots in the Anglo-American political culture, even though she was unfamiliar with the female social conservative movements prior to the Second World War, as well as acrid anti-Roosevelt sentiment that found expression in the decades of the 1930s and 1940s. As a devout Roman Catholic and a young girl who while growing up did not pay much attention to politics, Schlafly was unaware of the long Protestant tradition of female involvement in moral reform in American history. Ironically, Schlafly played a critical role in bringing traditionalist-minded women from different faiths—Protestant, Roman Catholic, Mormon, and Jewish—together in a united grassroots movement.[9] This uneasy cooperation between these religious traditions imparted a potent political impetus to moral conservatism in the late twentieth century.

GROWING UP IN THE GREAT DEPRESSION

The values that Phyllis Schlafly carried with her into adulthood reflected her experiences as a child and a young woman. Unlike many people who develop political awareness in high school or in college, Schlafly's political education as a conservative came only after she left graduate school. The conservatism she encountered fit with her own life experiences and the religious values she had learned at home and in school. These childhood values did not lead inexorably to political conservatism, but Schlafly did not have to undergo apostastic conversion when she declared herself a conservative. Raised in St. Louis during the Great Depression of the 1930s, she was influenced by two strong women—her mother and grandmother. They taught Phyllis and her younger sister Odile the importance of education, cultural refinement, and family.[10]

Phyllis Schlafly's mother grew up on the then fashionable West Pine Avenue, the daughter of Ernest Cole Dodge, a former assistant city attorney and a relatively prominent attorney in St. Louis. Known as Dadie, she graduated from the Sacred Heart Academy in St. Charles, Missouri, and received her Bachelor's degree from Washington University in 1920. Following college, she took a two-year course in Library Science. In 1921, she met and married John Bruce Stewart, a heavy-equipment salesman of steam engines and generators, recently transferred to St. Louis by Westinghouse. He was seventeen years her senior. Three years later, on August 15, 1924, their first daughter, Phyllis, was born, followed six years later by a second daughter, Odile. Both parents, although traditional in their views of the family that derived from their religious faith, believed their daughters should not be any less ambitious or educated than boys. Both parents emphasized education and culture. Politically, the parents were Republican, and later anti-New Deal, but Phyllis Schlafly did not remember her family talking much about politics at home.[11]

From family letters and interviews conducted by Phyllis Schlafly's first biographer, Chicago journalist Carol Felsenthal, three general observations can be made about Phyllis and her family: Phyllis was an intellectually precocious and well-adjusted child; her mother Dadie was a strong, loving mother who was ambitious for her daughters, both of whom graduated from Washington University, completed postgraduate work at Radcliffe College, and pursued independent professional careers; and the Stewart family was quiet and well mannered. No tensions between the parents were evident to their children or revealed in correspondence or diaries.[12] Dadie Stewart was an attractive woman devoted to her family.

Until 1930, the Stewart family enjoyed the fruits of life in a prospering city. St. Louis City reached its population height at 820,000 residents. (Seventy years later, its population had declined by a half million.) In the fifteen years following the St. Louis World's Fair in 1904, the city had boomed as a manufacturing and transportation city. It fell behind its rival Chicago, but it was an attractive city with tree-lined streets and brick buildings mandated by city regulations. In 1924, the city voted Republican, giving its votes to Calvin Coolidge, and in 1928 it went for Herbert Hoover. When financial disaster struck with the Great Depression in 1929, the Stewarts were personally affected. Bruce Stewart lost his job as a sales engineer for Westinghouse in 1930. Fifty-one at the time and without a pension, he was unemployed with a wife and two children. Dadie and the two children spent the year 1932 in Los Angeles with Dadie's well-to-do uncle, W. Pratte Layton. Bruce Stewart stayed in St. Louis, living with Dadie's parents, each day seeking work, unsuccessfully. In 1932, there was not much need for a fifty-one-year-old heavy-equipment salesman.

Phyllis Stewart was in fourth grade. Too young to realize her family's financial problems, her diary records the thrill of the three-day, un-airconditioned, train trip from St. Louis to Los Angeles and the sights of Los Angeles. Dadie and the girls returned to St. Louis and moved in with Dadie's parents. The following year the entire family moved into a rented house in the St. Louis suburb of Normandy. There the two children attended Roosevelt Public School, where Phyllis Stewart wrote, typed, and mimeographed the school newspaper, *The Roosevelt Rocket*.

Dadie Stewart took a job for $12 a week selling yard goods and draperies at Famous-Barr, a St. Louis department store. She worked nine hours a day, traveling by streetcar an hour each way. Dadie's friends from the Academy of the Sacred Heart could not understand a woman taking a job outside the home, but if Dadie was embarrassed by having to support her family she did not show it. Indeed, she used her time on the streetcar to start writing a cultural history of St. Louis.

After several years, Dadie secured a job teaching English in a public elementary school. Finally, in 1937 she became Librarian of the St. Louis Art Museum, where she worked until she retired, creating an outstanding collection of art books. Dadie's job at the Art Museum required her to live in the city, so the family made its last move to a modest apartment in the Central West End, where Phyllis Stewart spent her high school years. By the time she was thirteen the family had lived in six different places, but now they were settled. The Stewarts never owned their own home and Dadie never learned to drive a car. Intent on making sure that her daughters had the best education possible, Dadie approached the Mother Superior of the Academy of the Sacred Heart and offered to catalogue and maintain the school's library in exchange for free tuition for her daughters. She devoted Mondays to the Sacred Heart school library, while working the other six days (including Sundays) at the Art Museum. Bruce Stewart worked intermittently until World War II, when he finally secured a job as an electrical engineer with the War Production Board, and after the war as a technical expert for the Reconstruction Finance Corporation engaged in the disposal of surplus mechanical equipment.

Even though the Stewarts' life had been turned upside down by the Depression, there remained a normality to their lives. Later, Dadie Stewart revealed that her husband had been shocked and hurt by losing his job with Westinghouse, after working for the company for twenty-five years, and he never had the zest for life he once had. Still, he remained a man with a good sense of humor, always devoted to his family. He was an avid reader, given to quoting Shakespeare, and he worked for seventeen years to invent a rotary gasoline engine, which he was able to patent. Both he and his wife remained committed Republicans who heartily disliked Franklin Roosevelt and the New Deal. Bruce refused to go on the dole, because his grandchildren would have to pay for "Roosevelt's war on the free-enterprise system, this planned economy, and the welfare state he was building."[13] In a city in which nearly half the population identified themselves as Roman Catholic, and where Franklin Roosevelt's winning vote margins were substantial over Wendell Willkie in 1940 and over Thomas Dewey in 1944, it was unusual to find many Catholic Republicans.[14] In the evenings, Dadie worked on her cultural history of St. Louis, while Bruce worked on the design of his rotary engine. Dadie's mother, Bertha Dodge, made clothes for the children (Phyllis did not have a store-bought dress until she could buy it with her own money), and the children did their homework.

Phyllis Stewart proved to be a meticulous, ambitious student, well liked by her peers. "All my school years were most happy and most full," the sixteen-year-old Stewart recorded in her diary.[15] The Academy of the Sacred Heart, located in a three-story building of imposing brick on a tree-lined street, emphasized daily Mass, Christian doctrine, strict discipline, and a classical education. Classes were small and she strove to be the best student in her class, lamenting in her sophomore year that she lost the prize for the highest average "because of the absence caused by my measles."[16] Phyllis Stewart was studious, but clearly enjoyed her high school years. She was a Girl Scout, earning nine merit badges, including homemaking, cooking, and needlework. She always attended student concerts performed by the St. Louis Symphony. She worked during the summers—one summer earning $25 which she used for Girl Scout equipment. When she won one dollar for a joke she sold to the *St. Louis Post-Dispatch*, she used it to attend a Nelson Eddy concert. Her senior year was filled with concerts, plays, parties, and teas at her classmates' homes. For a class ring, she wore her mother's. The school year ended with Phyllis Stewart graduating valedictorian of her class, receiving top honors in classical languages and French. She recorded in her diary, "I've been very lucky in being in such a class at such a school, where the girls were not only gifted, and really nice, but who came from the good, long standing St. Louis families, whose homes I was always proud to visit."[17]

Upon graduation, Phyllis Stewart received a four-year scholarship on the basis of a competitive examination to Maryville College, a local Catholic school run by the Religious of the Sacred Heart. At the end of the first year, she concluded that Maryville was not challenging enough for her academically. She decided to enroll in Washington University with the understanding that she would have to pay her own tuition. This was a bold decision on Phyllis Stewart's part because it meant not only giving up a four-year scholarship, but having to go to work full-time to earn her way through university. It also meant leaving her friends at Maryville College. When she told Sister Mouton that she had decided to transfer to Washington University, "she was great," but the other nuns gave her the cold shoulder. She wrote in her diary, "I will be sorry to lose the girls and all the lovely traditions. It has been a very happy year, but after all it was just an anti-climax to life" in high school.[18]

World War II was on, so Phyllis Stewart found a full-time job at the St. Louis Ordnance Plant testing ammunition by firing rifles and machine guns. Her salary was $1,250 per year. She usually worked the night shifts, either 4 P.M. to midnight, or midnight to 8 A.M., so she could take morning classes at Washington University. This rigorous schedule determined which classes she could take, and Political Science became her major. She recorded in her diary that 100 percent of her time was taken up with working and school. Entertainment was limited to a "poor Faust" play and one movie. "The world is upside down this year, and I am too, but I hope all this is worth something."[19]

She worked an eight-hour shift, testing ammunition for accuracy, velocity, penetration, and machine gun and aircraft function. It was a physically and mentally demanding job for which the uniform was navy slacks, blue shirt, safety shoes, and ear plugs. Meanwhile she continued her studies, consistently receiving mostly "A"s with an occasional "B." By taking summer courses, she was able to finish her degree in three years, graduating Phi Beta Kappa. Encouraged by Professor Arnold Lien, the head of the Political Science department, she applied for fellowships to Radcliffe College, Columbia University, and Wellesley College.[20] (She wrote on the receipt for Wellesley College that she pasted in her scrapbook, "This was $10 thrown after a dream, when money was far too scarce.") She received a $700 fellowship from Columbia University and a $500 fellowship from Radcliffe University, whose graduate school was coed with Harvard University. "It was a hard choice," she confided in her diary, "but Harvard won."[21] June 27, 1944 was her last day on the job. Her last entry for the summer of 1944 read, "The most wonderful 2 years of my life, a beautiful experience."[22] Her hard work had paid off and now she was off to Harvard University, the daughter of two proud parents who had seen their baby grow into a mature, self-confident young woman.

Radcliffe proved to be an ideal choice for Stewart. She excelled there, receiving her Master's degree in June 1945, earning "A"s in all her classes. At Radcliffe, she considered herself a Republican, having worn a campaign pin for Wendell Willkie in 1940, but her career plan, to the extent she had one, was to secure a job working for the federal government.[23] She went to Radcliffe because she believed it would open doors for her professionally. In her scrapbook for her year at Harvard University there was no mention of politics, not even that she heard visiting professor Friedrich von Hayek, whose *Road to Serfdom*, published in 1944, had become a best-seller, serialized in *Reader's Digest* and selected as a Book of the Month Club offering.[24] Her term papers at Harvard reflected her career ambitions and reveal a gifted graduate student who wrote well-researched, well-argued, and academically objective papers, often on narrow administrative or constitutional topics.[25]

Her essays in graduate school also reflected an idealism shared by many young Americans as the World War II drew to a close. In a term paper on the Dumbarton Oaks proposal for the establishment of the United Nations, she wrote that national military forces under United Nations command "must be ready for simultaneous, decisive movement at the beginning of hostilities, not after a territorial change . . . To be effective, the joint use of contingents of national forces on the basis of a multilateral agreement must be made available for policy work in sufficient strength to deter a would-be aggressor."[26] A few years later, such prescriptions for an international order would have been seen by her as shibboleths of a naïve idealist, but in 1945, she was caught up in faculty and student euphoria about building a more peaceful world through international cooperation. In any case, she impressed her professors with her obvious intelligence, so much so that one of her Government professors encouraged her to pursue doctoral work in Political Science or a degree in law. She declined his offer. She was out of money and needed a job.[27] This did not mean returning to St. Louis, however. Still, there was good news in St. Louis. Shortly before Christmas, 1945, her father Bruce sent his daughter a lengthy article from *Southern Power and Industry*, announcing the "Stewart Rotary Engine."[28]

THE MAKING OF A CONSERVATIVE

When Phyllis Stewart left Radcliffe at the end of the spring term of 1945, she decided that she wanted a job in government, and the best place to use her expertise was in Washington, D.C. This was another bold move for a shy, young, twenty-one year old from the Midwest, but Phyllis Stewart was ambitious. She arrived in the nation's capital on September 2, 1945, right after V-J Day, in a city where she did not know a soul. Her Harvard University professors personally wrote to friends at the Bureau of the Budget and the Tennessee Valley Authority recommending her for any position that was open. With the end of the Second World War, as wartime agencies began to dismantle, finding work in the federal government was difficult, made even more so by preferential hiring for veterans for the few jobs that were open. In November 1945, Phyllis Stewart won a readers' essay contest sponsored by the *Washington Daily News*, declaring, "The cards are stacked against the enterprising and ambitious person and in favor of the mediocre adults or the unqualified veteran."[29] Finally, she turned to a private employment firm that found her a position as a researcher for the newly organized American Enterprise Association, later the American Enterprise Institute.

Established in 1943 by the president of Johns Manville Corporation, Lewis H. Brown, the American Enterprise Association (AEA) was the first glimmer of the emergence of an organized modern conservatism. Prior to the Second World War there was no conservative *movement*, but various anti-New Deal groups and organizations existed without a shared political philosophy or even much communication with each other. This menagerie included agrarians opposed to industrialized capitalism, nationalists, anticommunists, corporatists, single-taxers, anti-Semites, anti-Catholics, Coughlinites, and New Humanists.[30] The American Liberty League was established in 1934 by members of the DuPont family, John K. Raskob, Alfred E. Smith and other anti-New Dealers, plus conservative Democrats such as John W. Davis and Governor Eugene Talmadge (D-Georgia). It challenged Roosevelt's third term, but it failed to get off the ground. With the outbreak of European hostilities that started the Second World War, a powerful grassroots anti-interventionist movement produced such groups as the America First Committee, as well as a variety of conservative antiwar women's groups, the so-called mothers' antiwar movement. Some of the leaders of these female antiwar groups, which drew tens of thousands of women into their cause, tended toward anti-Semitism by seeing Communism as part of an international Jewish conspiracy.[31] Yet, as vehement as these expressions were, Stewart knew nothing of them. Indeed, in her senior year in high school she had worn a Vote for Willkie button after attending a Republican rally in 1940. Phyllis Stewart had not been particularly political in high-school or college and her awareness of preceding political movements was not high. Through her work at the American Enterprise Association she was introduced to prewar ideological opposition to the New Deal and to modern conservatism.

The American Enterprise Association marked a break with the prewar Right, although some of its board members had been involved in the America First Committee. Unlike the prewar Right, the AEA was concerned with policy analysis from a conservative business point of view. The AEA's "Statement of Purpose" warned "The tide of radicalism may be receding momentarily, but this certainly does not mean that America has returned to sound fiscal policies, put an end to deficit financing, to economic experimentation, and stopped making utopian plans for the future."[32] Lewis H. Brown represented a shift in business thinking that had occurred during the New Deal. He considered himself a new breed of corporate leader, an industrial statesman, distinguished from those "antediluvian" self-centered and supremely individualistic businessmen who sought to return to a golden age of laissez-faire capitalism. On the other hand, he warned against what he saw as the liberal tendency for government to "enter into direct competition with its citizens, and that government of a representative democracy [can] do everything for everybody." He condemned deficit spending and redistributive income programs, and he warned that America could not possibly "reconcile the principle of democracy, which means cooperation, with the principle of government omniscience under which everyone waits for an order before doing anything. In that way lies loss of freedom and dictatorship."[33] Brown personally selected members of the board, including economic journalist Henry Hazlitt; Charles C. Abbott, dean of the Harvard Business School; and Harvard University legal scholar Roscoe Pound. With a staff of five based in Washington, the AEA conducted research for legislative analyses and broader studies of national economic problems, hundreds of pamphlets by well-known conservative scholars on fiscal policy, antitrust issues, farm price supports, natural resources, social welfare, and Social Security.[34]

Phyllis Stewart worked only a year at AEA, but in this short time she received her first education as a political conservative. When she first arrived at AEA, she disliked Franklin Roosevelt, but did not fall into the category of a "Roosevelt-hater." In Washington, she joined the local chapter of the United Nations Association, a social group supportive of the United Nations organization. She attended their meetings and lectures and won first prize in a public speaking course offered by the club.[35] But, as she worked at AEA, read its literature, and worked on legislative analysis, her political views changed. Working as a researcher for the small staff at AEA, Stewart imbibed the philosophy of conservatism. She read Henry Hazlitt criticizing Keynesianism, John T. Flynn lambasting the New Deal and Roosevelt, and Friedrich von Hayek on the liberal state's drift toward socialism; she worked with Senator Kenneth Wherry (R-Nebraska) on opposing an American loan to Britain; and she began to read *Human Events* founded by Felix Morley and Frank Hanighen a year earlier in the AEA offices. When the year was over she emerged as a conservative, devoted to free-enterprise and the preservation of American liberty. She wrote two articles against New Deal agencies that she submitted to *Redbook Magazine* and *American Magazine*, but they were rejected.[36] Her religious faith, now combined with a well-formed conservative ideology, created a formidable political outlook.

Equally important, Stewart learned from her work experience at AEA how to articulate complex issues and arguments into a simplified form easily understood by an average reader. Much of her early political writings and speeches were derivative, based on extensive reading of conservative books and periodicals, government reports, and liberal newspapers; her originality lay in the way she framed issues. Having developed these skills, she decided in 1946 to return to St. Louis, much to the excitement of her parents. "Dear Baby," her mother wrote, "Daddy and I are pleased that you are coming home. . . . You have no idea how much we have missed you. I have been looking to get you into Junior League and I have reason to believe that our friends will do everything they can for you."[37] Before she returned home she sought a teaching position in the School of Business and Public Administration at Washington University, but was turned down when the dean warned that she would not be able to "handle a bunch of tough-minded, battle scarred GIs. We have some men teachers who are having difficulties and embarrassments in the course of their tasks. Your personality is attractive, but you would face great problems . . . Believe me, it is difficult enough for a man."[38] Instead, a local employment agency found her a position divided half-time as research assistant for Towner

Phelan, who wrote a monthly newsletter for the St. Louis Union Trust Company, and as the librarian for its affiliate, the First National Bank in St. Louis.

While she waited to hear about this position, she took the initiative and contacted Claude Bakewell, a St. Louis lawyer, who was running for Congress as a Republican in the 11th district against a popular incumbent Democrat, John Sullivan. Bakewell was well-established in St. Louis. He was a Navy veteran, a member of the American Legion and the Veterans of Foreign Wars, and had graduated from Georgetown University in 1932 and St. Louis University School of Law in 1935. During the World War II he had been elected to the Board of Aldermen, serving from 1941–45. Ready to move to higher office, Bakewell was looking for a campaign manager when he was contacted by the twenty-two year old Phyllis Stewart. Bakewell recalled, "I was impressed by her incredible knowledge of the most nitty-gritty details of St. Louis ward politics . . . she had so much plain good political sense, I had to keep looking at her to remind myself I was not talking to a fat, old cigar-chomping ward heeler."[39] She was hired on the spot and went to work as his campaign manager. Stewart's knowledge of ward politics was actually limited to a close reading of the local newspaper. Nonetheless she was a quick learner and soon mastered the politics of the district.

Working out of Bakewell's downtown law office, she wrote press releases and the candidate's speeches, and scheduled his events. Running in a district with a heavy labor vote and black vote, Bakewell attacked the Democratic administration for its failure to provide housing to veterans; called for the end of price controls; spoke of the need for a volunteer army to replace conscription; championed free enterprise; and warned of the dangers of centralized, bureaucratic government in Washington. In one of his set speeches written for him by Stewart, he called for racial tolerance, declaring that "Religious and racial intolerance is the very antithesis of the principles on which this great American Republic was founded. . . . No man is either good or bad because of the color of his skin or the Church he attends. . . . There is a decency and a fineness of character in every man, which recognized and given a chance to develop, will grow and expand, not only throughout our country, but throughout the world." Bakewell did not make anti-Communism a central theme of his campaign, but he warned of "moral laxness" in the nation and charged the Democratic administrations of Roosevelt and

Truman with allowing Communist infiltration into government.[40] In a fiercely fought election, Bakewell won 41,202 to 39,879 votes. He profusely thanked Stewart for the essential role she played in his victory.

Meanwhile, Towner Phelan at the St. Louis Union Trust Company received a personal phone call from the head of the American Enterprise Association recommending Phyllis Stewart to him. A few weeks before Election Day, she went to work for the St. Louis Union Trust Company and the First National Bank, splitting her time between the two institutions. When she left her job three years later, she wrote in a memorandum to her replacement, "The small salary connected with my job was somewhat compensated for by the fact that I had two titles, which I could use alternately." Her duties as the bank's librarian began with the creation of a library. Prior to Stewart's arrival most of the literature the bank received was sent to a warehouse, where it was not properly catalogued. She organized the library and set up a filing system for the ninety periodicals to which the bank subscribed.[41]

As she grew into the job, she was giving Phelan ideas for pieces as well as drafts for essays. Phelan, the St. Louis Union Trust Company's vice president for advertising, produced a monthly newsletter on the premise that the prosperity of the company's clients depended on the maintenance of the private enterprise system and the rejection of socialism. His four-page *St. Louis Union Trust Company Letter* expounded the virtues of free enterprise, criticized "creeping welfarism" in the federal government, and warned of Communist espionage in Washington and the external Soviet threat.[42] The Phelan newsletter was conservative, but not an apologist for big business. Indeed, Phelan parsed the difference between "antimonopoly" bigness and conservative complaints against "big government" and "big business." "Left wing 'antimonopoly' sentiment," he declared, "is directed against big business and concentration. But it favors price-fixing under 'fair trade' laws and farm prices and subsidies in order to shelter marginal farmers and retailers from competition." Nonetheless, he maintained that the objections to big business should be social and political. Industrial concentration affects, he wrote, "the location of political power and the character and size of pressure groups." Conservatives distrusted "big government" and "big business," Phelan concluded, but "objections to industrial concentration are not sufficient to make us willing to give up the material benefits which an industrialized big business economy provides."

Phelan was a well-read, articulate conservative intent on extending conservative ideas to a larger audience. By working with him over the next three years, Stewart furthered her philosophical education as a conservative. Probably at no other point in her life would she spend as much time engaged with the abstract, theoretical ideas of conservatism. Through Phelan she learned how to write, produce a newsletter, and convey conservative ideas to a larger public. Stewart developed an understanding of the intellectual conservative tradition, although she had little knowledge or interest in the organizational history of conservatism or rightwing women's movements prior to the Second World War.[43] In her three years at the bank, Stewart assumed more and more responsibilities, writing speeches for the president and vice presidents of the bank.[44] In addition, she initiated an educational program for women to provide information on financial problems such as wills, trusts, inheritance taxes, and property conservation. The trust company assigned her to give lectures to various women's groups on the importance of estate planning and financial investment. Reporting on one of her speeches before a women's club, the *St. Louis Globe-Democrat* described her as a "blonde banking expert" and a "forceful speaker." The message Stewart conveyed in her speeches was direct and encouraging: "When women have been able to get adequate information and experience in investing, they have done as well as men." She urged wives to be involved in estate planning, because too often, a poor widow has been forced to "remarry because the share that the law allowed her when her husband died leaving no will was simply not sufficient."[45] Her talks were so well received that she became a featured speaker before women's groups throughout the city, lecturing on trusts, estate planning, marital taxes, and financial planning for women.

Through the Junior League, she became involved in the St. Louis community, devoting volunteer time to the problem of low-income housing. The population of St. Louis during the Second World War had increased 16 percent, but housing had not kept pace with this growth. It was estimated that of the 251,610 dwellings in the city, at least one-third were substandard, 33,000 had outside privy vaults, and 25,000 had toilets shared by several families.[46] By late 1945, the growth of slums in St. Louis became such a problem that the city's mayor created an Anti-Slum Commission later renamed the St. Louis Reorganization Commission. Citizen participation was welcomed through the Citizen's

Council on Housing and Community, a local community group of ministers, businessmen, and civic officials. As a member of the Junior League with connections in the banking community, Phyllis Stewart was asked to participate in writing the Council's housing proposal. In October 1948, she made the front page of the *St. Louis Post-Dispatch* as the author of the report that proposed a $16 million bond issue for urban renewal between Market and Olive streets. In order to halt white urban flight to the suburbs, she called for the public funding of apartments, hotels, public buildings and parks. The report declared, "There are 280,000 residents of St. Louis living under slum conditions. They account for crime and disease out of all proportion to their numbers and depreciate property values in the rest of the city." Opposed by an alliance of conservative businessmen concerned about the cost of the project and a group of black ministers who felt that the African-American community had been excluded in the process, the bond issue failed in the November election.[47]

STEWART BECOMES A SCHLAFLY

In 1949, Phyllis Stewart was twenty-four, unmarried, and independently supporting herself. She dated frequently, but had not found a man who met her high expectations. Then she met Fred Schlafly, a thirty-nine-year-old attorney from Alton, Illinois, an industrial town across the river from St. Louis. Fred came from a distinguished family in the St. Louis area that reflected another American success story. Fred's grandfather, August Schlafly, came to America with his family from Switzerland in the early 1850s. He received only a sixth-grade education before he had to go to work in a country store in western Illinois. By the late 1800s he had established six banks in the area, including one in Alton. To ensure the future of his four sons, he established each of his sons in a business of his own. John Fred Schlafly (Fred's father) received the Mountain Valley Water Company, which allowed him to support his four children: Fred (who married Phyllis Stewart), two other sons, Daniel and Robert, and his daughter Eleanor. Fred, Jr. and his brother Robert went to Harvard Law School and became attorneys. Daniel went into business, took over the Mountain Valley Water Company, and married an oil heiress, Adelaide Mahaffey. He served twenty-five years on the St. Louis School Board, leading efforts at school desegregation before the Supreme Court's *Brown* decision, and became in 1967 the first lay chairman of a major Catholic college, St. Louis University.

After graduating from Georgetown University with his bachelor's degree and his law degree from Harvard University, Fred Schlafly Jr. accepted a position in the leading law firm in Alton, Illinois, Green and Verlie, which represented many of the leading businesses in town, including the bank owned by Fred's uncle, Louis Schlafly, the First National Bank in Alton. Fred Schlafly was politically conservative and a devout Roman Catholic. Most people believed he was a confirmed bachelor, but then he met Phyllis Stewart, whose politics, religion, and intelligence caught his attention when he visited Phelan one day to discuss politics. He had heard about Phyllis Stewart and wanted to meet her. What followed was a rather unusual courtship in which they usually saw each other once a week on the weekends, while the rest of the time they exchanged poetry and letters. These letters were intellectual exchanges about political and theological questions, written as much to display the author's intelligence as to convey knowledge.[48] Fred and Phyllis Schlafly married on October 20, 1949, in a ceremony at the St. Louis Cathedral, duly reported on the society pages of the local newspapers. On their honeymoon in Mexico, they took an extra suitcase full of books. Their shared faith and political ideology bound the couple from the outset of their marriage. Later, Phyllis Schlafly told a reporter, "We have a happy intellectual partnership. One of the reasons I have been able to do so much is that he and I have constant brainstorming sessions that go from early in the morning until late at night."[49]

Phyllis Schlafly moved across the Mississippi River to Alton, Illinois to begin a new life as a homemaker. Located on the bluffs of the Mississippi River, Alton was an industrial city of 35,000 people, best known as the place where a mob murdered abolitionist editor Elijah Lovejoy in 1837. In the early 1950s, Alton was a bustling town, home to Owens-Illinois, the largest glass manufacturer in the United States; enormous Shell Oil and Standard Oil refineries; the Olin Corporation; Mississippi Lime Company; Russell-Miller Milling Company; and Laclede Steel Company. In Alton, Phyllis Schlafly realized the postwar American dream—a handsome, devoted, successful and prominent husband; a small but attractive home (with a white picket fence); a healthy family that would grow to six children (four boys and two girls), summer vacations at the Schlafly family summer house in Harbor Point, Michigan;

and entrance into the small and unpretentious but wealthy social circle in the small Illinois river town. Within the year, Phyllis Schlafly joined her husband as an active volunteer in community activities. She became a board member of the YWCA, president of the St. Louis Radcliffe Club, and volunteer for various fund drives. She also became active in the Illinois Federation of Republican Women and the Daughters of the American Revolution.

Even with civic activities, home remained the primary focus of Phyllis Schlafly's life. Her family life in Alton reinforced her social conservative views about the importance of family and the joys of marriage and motherhood. The Schlafly's first son, John, was born on November 25, 1950, followed by Bruce in 1955, Roger in 1956, Liza in 1958, Andrew in 1961, and Anne in 1964. She breastfed each of her children until they were at least six months, fed them healthy foods, and, after reading Rudolf Flesch's bestseller *Why Johnny Can't Read* (1955), taught them all to read using phonics before they entered school. John, Liza, and Andrew became lawyers, Bruce an orthopedic surgeon, Roger a mathematician, and Anne a successful businesswoman. All remained conservative in their political outlook. While Phyllis Schlafly managed the family, Fred Schlafly's law practice prospered, enabling the family to move in 1962 to Fairmount, an enclave of beautiful homes on the bluffs of the Mississippi River. They bought a mansion owned by Spencer T. Olin of the Olin Corporation. Life for Phyllis Schlafly in these years was nearly perfect, and it reinforced her own conservative values and developing political education as a conservative.

The Faith of the Schlaflys

Imbued with a conservative political perspective that came from an extensive reading of conservative literature and modern history, as well as daily reading of the anti-New Deal *Chicago Tribune*, Fred Schlafly furthered his wife's political education.[50] Fifteen years his wife's senior, Fred Schlafly brought to the marriage an astute mind of a Jesuit-educated and Harvard-trained lawyer. His influence further informed his wife's conservative politics, adding depth to her understanding of how communism, internationalism, and liberalism were intrinsically linked, not by an organized conspiracy or by a shared ideology, but by a common faith in social panacea and anointed leaders. An obsessive letter writer—despite the heavy duties of his legal practice—he corresponded regularly with historian Charles Tansill about America's entrance into the Second World War, author George N. Crocker about Roosevelt's "betrayal" at Yalta, and conservative columnist William Henry Chamberlin about individual liberties. He exchanged lengthy letters discussing politics with U.S. Senator Everett Dirksen (R-Illinois), General Robert E. Wood of Sears Roebuck, Clarence Manion former dean of the University of Notre Dame Law School, and nearly every well-known conservative anti-Communist writer. He was on a first-name basis with Vice President Richard Nixon, whom he had met in the Pacific during the war. He kept a running correspondence with five college roommates from Georgetown who had also roomed together at the Harvard Law School. He wrote authors, journalists, and newspaper columnists across the country praising or criticizing their pieces or asking the sources of their reports.[51]

Fred Schlafly was not active in conservative politics before the war, but it is evident from his later correspondence that he was closer to the Old Right (anti-New Deal, non-interventionist conservatism) than the postwar conservative movement that would emerge under William F. Buckley, Jr. and the *National Review*. William F. Buckley, Jr. accepted an internationalist foreign policy and took great cautions against anti-Semitism in the movement.[52] Yet whatever their differences, prewar conservatives and postwar conservatives shared much in common—promotion of private enterprise, espousal of individual responsibility, absolute opposition to communism, and distrust of centralized government.

The Old Right was not so much a rigorous political philosophy—those associated with it were too disparate ideologically—but a frame of mind that despised two *isms*: socialism and internationalism.[53] For the prewar Right, Franklin D. Roosevelt represented both these ideological conceits, based on the illusion of a false equality—economic equality among people, international equality among nations. Both meant the ultimate subversion of the rule of law, civil liberties, property rights, and national sovereignty. Critics of Roosevelt argued that the New Deal had already taken the first steps toward socialism and the subrogation of constitutional principles to executive powers. Behind socialism and internationalism lurked Bolshevism. Although some cranks such as Elizabeth Dilling, author of *The Red Network*, indiscriminately made accusations of communist affiliation based on the flimsiest of evidence (later documents from the Soviet Union revealed she and other red-hunters were looking at the wrong people), most Old Right critics of the New Deal did not accuse Roosevelt of being an agent of the Soviet Union or a fellow traveler secretly worshipping the Soviet "economic miracle." Nonetheless, in Hayek's phrase, the New Deal had set the nation on the road to socialist serfdom, and internationalism played directly into the hands of the Bolsheviks under Soviet tyrant Joseph Stalin.

With the outbreak of war in Europe in September 1939, Roosevelt's critics demanded American neutrality and nonintervention in the European war. For most anti-interventionists, the Soviet Union presented the gravest danger to the world, not Germany. Journalist Freda Utley, a former communist, maintained in 1940 that "The Russian brand of National Socialism is even more oppressive and far more destructive of life and material prosperity."[54] Ideology, not class interest or social anxiety, separated noninterventionists from interventionists. Indeed, many of those opposed to U.S. involvement in a European war tended to see international financial interests at work. Some spoke of a Wall Street-Downing Street Axis. This distrust of Eastern financial interests and London took multiple forms. The hydra of interventionism appeared to be headed by British lions, emblazoned with dollar and pound signs on their foreheads. Behind this talk of "perfidious Albion" lay a fear of economic and political concentration.[55]

Fred Schlafly shared this distrust of Eastern financial influence, even though he represented some of the nation's largest corporations.[56] Anti-elitist and anti statist views lay at the heart of his opposition to liberalism. In a letter to D. M. Ellinwood at Moody's Investor's Service, Fred Schlafly expressed this opposition when he declared that "the fallacy of progressivism is that it replaces the fundamentals of natural law, or personal responsibility and faith in the individual, with the fundamentalism of statism."[57] Progressivism, he believed, manifested the ideology of collectivism, found in the *isms* of the left: communism, socialism, liberalism, one-worldism, internationalism, and welfarism. These *isms* were not all the same, but old-school conservatives such as Schlafly perceived them as sharing a belief in the importance of the bureaucratic state over individual rights.

Phyllis Schlafly agreed, having asserted in 1949 that liberals believed that "individual liberty should be restricted by the State in order to achieve 'social justice,' that is, to equalize possession and incomes."[58]

Ultimately, she declared individual rights rested not on the state, but on a virtuous citizenry willing to protect their rights from coercion and regimentation by the state. As a result, she said, the social welfare state seeks to coerce and regiment man for the welfare of society. Indeed, much of the Old Right's criticism of the welfare state, liberalism, and collectivism offered a reminder of an earlier tradition that proclaimed the necessity of a literate, well-informed, and uncorrupted citizenry. Such an outlook imparted a moral impetus to the Old Right and its offspring, the postwar grassroots Right. She, like other grassroots conservative activists who would begin to appear on the political stage, carried this anticollectivist, moral outlook into battle.

CHAPTER TWO

Ideology and Politics in 1952

SHORTLY AFTER CHRISTMAS day in 1951, Charles Thomae, Madison County Republican Central Committee Chairman, phoned Fred Schlafly and asked if he could come to the Schlafly home to discuss "something important" about the approaching Republican congressional primary. A couple of days later, he showed up with a small delegation of leading Republicans in the county. They came to persuade Fred Schlafly to enter the Republican primary for Congress. They told him that they would back him as Madison County's candidate against the East St. Louis Republican machine headed by Dan McGlynn and James McRoberts. Schlafly's response was immediate: he told them "No. I am not your guy." Finally, somebody in the room blurted out—"How about Phyllis?" By the time the evening was over, it was agreed that Phyllis Schlafly, the twenty-seven year old housewife, would run for Congress. Her race for Congress in 1952 was a fluke—the fortunes of a meeting held in her house in late December 1951 with Republican officials—but her activism within the Republican party was not. Throughout her fifty-year career as a political activist, she remained a Republican. Her loyalty to the party, which combined both ideology and practical politics, is essential to understanding Phyllis Schlafly and other like-minded activists. Schlafly's activism reflected an ideological commitment derived from her faith as a conservative anticommunist, but this ideology was tempered—perhaps gently—by the reality of practical politics. This balance between ideology and pragmatic politics, while not always in equilibrium, characterized Schlafly and other grassroots Republican conservatives. Through political work within the Republican party, grassroots conservative activists—many of them women, mostly based in the Midwest and Far West—began to shape a distinct ideological faction within the GOP aimed at taking control of the party from moderates and liberals who, in their opinion, were too ready to accept New Deal policies.

Typical of thousands of conservative women across the country, Schlafly saw in the Republican party an instrument to redeem the nation from what they perceived as its rapid drift toward collectivism and statism that had begun under Franklin Roosevelt in the 1930s and continued under his successor Harry Truman. By working at the grass-roots, these activists learned politics—how to organize, how to run political campaigns, and how to wage ideological war against opponents, both within the Republican party and in independent campaigns. When combined with ideological fervor, these organizing skills, learned through the hard knocks of politics, proved critical in sustaining grass-roots conservatism for the next half century. During the first decade, they remained for the most part unsuccessful, if only because there was no nationally organized political movement and much of this activism was directed toward anticommunism. Grassroots activists were united principally by an ideological hostility to liberalism, but conservatism in these formative years had not coalesced into a well-organized political movement. The world of the conservative in the immediate decade after the Second World War was best described by Ronald Reagan after he became President, when he told a conservative audience that "Ever since F.D.R. and the New Deal, the opposition party [the Democrats], and particularly those of a liberal persuasion, have dominated the political debate. Their ideas were new; they had momentum; they captured the imagination of the American people. The left held sway for a long time. There was a Right, but it was, by the '40s and '50s, diffuse and scattered, without a unifying voice."[1]

The Moral Passion of a Grassroots Conservative

Long before Phyllis Schlafly became a nationally known figure, she worked in the trenches of the Republican party, serving as a campaign worker for a congressional candidate, precinct committeeman, poll watcher, national convention party delegate, and officer in the state GOP women's organization. She was like other grassroots conservative party activists, but she was exceptional in one important regard: she had won the nomination as the Republican candidate for the 21st Congressional District in Illinois in 1952. It was an extraordinary event. In winning the primary election, she ran against the East St. Louis Republican political machine and became the first female candidate in the district ever to win nomination to a high office. How this twenty-seven year-old woman, a new mother, and an Illinois resident for less than three years, became a candidate reveals how conservative Midwestern Republicanism was in the 1950s.

During her race to win the GOP nomination and her challenge to the Democratic incumbent, Schlafly displayed the ideological intensity of the grassroots Right as it waged ideological war against New Deal liberalism at home and international Communism abroad. Yet, Schlafly showed another tendency not noted by contemporaries at the time or later by scholars of American conservatism: Work within the Republican party—a political party intent on winning on Election Day—tempered ideological doctrinarianism in quite important ways. Nonetheless, ideas drove grassroots conservatives to become involved in politics and sustained them in battle. The formation of a conservative faction within the Republican party emerged from the confluence of two streams: a popular anticommunist movement on the grassroots level and the writings of a group of intellectuals and writers who articulated a philosophy of conservatism challenging New Deal big-government ideology. Grassroots anticommunism was populist in both its appeal against the elites and its projections of fears that the communist conspiracy, centered in the Kremlin, had infiltrated its agents into the highest circles of American government. Grassroots anticommunism found expression in an extensive, popular literature that offered a careful study of communist goals, strategy, and tactics. This literature rallied everyday people to the struggle against domestic and international communism.

Phyllis Schlafly played an important role in introducing this literature to a larger American audience when she produced a small pamphlet, *A Reading List for Americans*, a brief bibliographical guide to important anticommunist books. First printed in 1957, it gained in popularity when it was recommended by the *American Legion Magazine* and the national Catholic weekly *Our Sunday Visitor* in 1958. In subsequent years it sold tens of thousands of copies.[2] The titles of the books on the list reveal the emotion that nourished the movement: *I Led Three Lives: Citizen, "Communist," Counterspy* (1952); *The Web of Subversion (1954); Masters of Deceit* (1958); *No Wonder We Are Losing* (1958); and *Seeds of Treason* (1962).[3] The books themselves varied in intellectual quality, but many offered sober analysis of the history and ideology of communism. She also included on her list congressional documents that could be purchased through the Government Printing Office. Some books on the list emphasized the Soviet Fifth Column aspect of the U.S. communist party, while others portrayed the party as an agency of political subversion and ideological influence rather than a classic Fifth Column prepared for industrial and military sabotage in support of overt military

action. For example, the party's role in the labor movement was sometimes portrayed in anticommunist literature and in numerous congressional hearings as preparation for industrial sabotage. J. Edgar Hoover,
director of the Federal Bureau of Investigation (FBI), tended to emphasize the Fifth Column view of the party because that fell within his
agency's jurisdiction. He was joined by other popular anticommunist
writers such as Herbert Philbrick who tended to present this same
perspective.[4] On the other hand, James Burnham's *Web of Subversion*
presented something like a legal brief against communist subversion,
while carefully delineating between Soviet espionage and day-to-day
Communist party political work. Schlafly admired Burnham's book
and believed that it was perhaps the best popular study of Soviet spy
activities in the federal government.

Her list fed popular anticommunist passions, but many of the books
had enduring intellectual value. For example, Elinor Lipper's *Eleven
Years in Soviet Prison Camps* (1949), a powerful and haunting memoir,
frames an existential tale of finding the meaning of life in a world in
which all signs of humanity are lost.[5] The most widely read book on
her list was Whittaker Chambers's *Witness* (1952), which surpassed
any other anticommunist memoir in drama, psychological insight, and
literary quality. *Witness* is similar in outline to Benjamin Gitlow's *I Confess* (1940), another memoir that described an idealistic young man's
passage into the communist movement, only to discover a cynical world
in which avaricious power consumes human decency. Chambers' account brought a deeper psychological dimension to how a young man
relinquished his soul as he willingly betrays his country to serve the interests of Soviet espionage. In this respect, *Witness* presents a kind of
modern day morality play of a man seeking truth through reason only
to discover that real truth is revealed in a higher transcendent faith of
Christianity. *Witness* became an instant best-seller.[6]

Literature such as *Witness* inspired a large anticommunist movement that emerged in local communities across the nation, where individuals met in study groups to study the nature of communism and
address local issues that revealed subversive influences. This popular
anticommunist literature inspired grassroots activists, but it alone could
not have maintained a larger political movement. Critical to the success of the GOP Right in the next two decades was the emergence of a
group of intellectuals and authors who appeared on the American scene
in these years. As a consequence, this renaissance in intellectual thought

added substance to a popular grassroots anticommunist movement that laid the foundation for the conservative movement that later emerged. Grassroots anticommunism was not an hysterical reaction caused by political and social anxiety, as some historians have suggested, but was a heady brew that gained political substance through an intellectual ferment produced by authors such as Ludwig von Mises, Friedrich von Hayek, Ayn Rand, James Burnham, Richard Weaver, William F. Buckley, Jr., Russell Kirk, Frank Meyer, Leo Strauss, Eric Voegelin, and Robert Nisbet.[7] These writers, often differing among themselves as to the meaning of conservatism (some even denying they were conservatives), enunciated a distrust of centralized government and political elites, and a fear of moral and political corruption within the Republic. Without the two—grassroots anticommunist activity and intellectual conservative writing—the conservative movement would have languished without a coherent alternative to the liberal regime.

Phyllis Schlafly's importance in grassroots conservatism came because she helped translate the ideas of intellectuals and anticommunist authors to the grassroots, while at the same time providing leadership to activists who eventually came to identify themselves as conservatives. With her background at the American Enterprise Association and the St. Louis Union Trust Company, Phyllis Schlafly acted as a conduit linking this intellectual movement and grassroots anticommunism. Her importance came because she helped evangelize the ideas of intellectuals and anticommunist authors to grassroots conservatives. It was within the Republican party that she translated her knowledge into political action. Her mental world was that of a partisan and a polemist, not that of an intellectual who carefully delineated subtleties of logic and gradations of argument. She was a partisan who engaged equally partisan opponents.

Like thousands of other white middle- and upper-class women, Schlafly turned to conservative politics within the Republican party as part of a larger, historic struggle to preserve freedom through constitutional government. Her involvement brought acrimony and unrewarded hard work. As did many conservative women who came of age in the Great Depression and the Second World War, Schlafly was driven by a deep inner moral compass that pointed her toward political life. Schlafly conveyed this moral passion and sense of righteousness when she exhorted her fellow anticommunists in the early 1960s, "Good Americans must accept their moral obligation to participate in the political life of our country. . . . Do not be intimidated by the smear words 'political' and 'controversial.' Nearly every man and woman in history who accomplished anything was controversial at the time: St. Peter, St. Paul, Joan of Arc, Christopher Columbus, Louis Pasteur, George Washington, Thomas Jefferson, and the women suffragettes."[8] This sense of public morality led these women to join the struggle against the forces of communism, an insidious evil that threatened to subjugate all free peoples.

A deep religious faith prevailed in much of the grassroots Right, and clearly Phyllis Schlafly, as well as her husband Fred, were motivated by their shared faith in the Catholic Church and its teachings. During times of stress, both would kneel and recite the rosary. At the basis of their religious faith was a belief in an omniscient and omnipresent God. This all-forgiving God had given his only begotten Son, Jesus Christ, for the redemption of the faithful, and this all-knowing God had designed a well-ordered universe from which rational men and women of faith could derive social and political principles. Finally, this all-loving God had provided faith and reason to humanity. From this ability to reason, enlightened men and women were able to discern nature's physical and social laws. These laws laid the foundation for the American Republic, based on the principles of limited government, the rule of law, and inalienable individual rights. It was these principles the Schlaflys struggled to preserve. They brought to their politics a moral sensibility, a righteousness that did not allow easy compromise over principle, and an inner tenacity beneath their well-spoken words.

Fred and Phyllis Schlafly believed it was one's duty to become involved in politics. In a draft of a brochure urging Catholics to join the grassroots anticommunist movement, Phyllis Schlafly declared, "As Catholic Americans, we are proud of our heritage and believe that our Republic offers the greatest opportunity for individual freedom and the pursuit of happiness." She easily reconciled her Republican values with Catholicism. The brochure continued, "We wish to insure for ourselves and future generations the God-given rights proclaimed by the Declaration of Independence and guaranteed by the United States Constitution. We acknowledge Almighty God as the Author of all rights, and we pledge ourselves to expose and oppose atheistic Communism and its collaborators, who are conspiring to destroy our church and subvert our country."[9] As this language suggests, the Schlaflys were not defensive about their Catholicism. Americanism and Catholicism were integrally linked.[10]

THE GOP RIGHT TAKES SHAPE

Driven by moral passion derived from their faith as Christians, the Schlaflys joined other grassroots conservative activists vigilantly defending liberty against forces that threatened individual rights and the Constitution. These threatening forces were the collectivists and internationalists in their many forms: the communists in Moscow; the internationalists who promoted the United Nations and its agenda; and the Eastern clique that controlled the Republican party and thwarted the GOP rank and file by placing Wendell Willkie on the ticket in 1940 and Thomas Dewey in 1944 and 1948.[11]

Internationalism and the Eastern establishment were linked in the minds of conservatives such as the Schlaflys.[12] Opposition to internationalism and the Eastern establishment defined Midwestern Republicanism in the early 1950s. They found their leader in United States Senator Robert A. Taft (R-Ohio), whose loyalty to the GOP and steadfast defense of conservative principles earned him the honorific title "Mr. Republican," but whose unspoken title might have been "Mr. Midwestern, pro-American and anti-internationalist." The son of President William Howard Taft, he was the symbol and leader of Midwestern Republicanism that stood in opposition to the liberal Eastern internationalist wing of the party. As a Taft Republican, Phyllis Schlafly believed that a small clique of Eastern financiers had through guile, intimidation, and media and money power personally imposed their candidates on the Republican party ticket every four years beginning with Alf Landon in 1936. Republican activists such as Schlafly believed that *they* represented the majority of the party against a willful minority. Still, it did not matter whether she was in the majority or the minority on a political issue, or standing with or against the party. She entered the battles confident that she was right and would prevail because her opponents were ill-informed, misled, or, in the case of communists, agents of subversion.

The election of 1948, in which Harry Truman thrashed Republican challenger Thomas Dewey, proved especially sour for grassroots conservatives. "Snatching defeat from the jaws of victory" expressed the sentiments of many Republican conservatives about Dewey's lackluster campaign. Taft Republicans looked on Dewey's nomination as having been foisted on the party through political chicanery at the 1948 convention. Conservatives believed that the Eastern internationalists would rather lose the election than see Taft win the nomination and become president. The expectation of Republican victory in 1948 was formed in the mid-term elections two year earlier when Republicans won control of Congress by assailing sixteen years of Democratic rule. The slogans "Had enough?" and "To err is Truman" captured the public's discontent with wage and price controls, rationing, and corruption in the Truman administration. This discontent handed Republicans a spectacular congressional victory that went unmatched until 1994. The Republican 80th Congress carried out an authentic conservative agenda: cutting taxes, balancing the budget, passing the Taft-Hartley Act, which outlawed the closed shop and secondary boycotts, over Truman's veto, and passing the 22nd Amendment to the U.S. Constitution, which rebuked Franklin D. Roosevelt's four terms by limiting future Presidents to two terms.[13]

In 1948 the Republican convention met in Philadelphia and on the third ballot, Thomas Dewey, governor of New York, the favorite of the Eastern establishment, won the nomination. Grassroots conservatives cried foul, claiming that Taft had been blocked from the nomination by the internationalists including Harold Stassen, Earl Warren, and Arthur Vandenberg. Taft complained privately that he could provide a list of people who double-crossed him in Philadelphia. Yet, even some of Taft's friends pointed out that Dewey had lined up powerful right-wingers such as Representative Charles Halleck of Indiana, Speaker of the House Joseph Martin of Massachusetts, and Senator James Kem of Missouri. Whatever the case, Robert Taft simply could not persuade the delegates that he could beat Truman, although he had won election as Senator in the industrial state of Ohio.[14] Truman acknowledged Taft's campaign ability when he confided that "[Taft] has plenty of labor support when he runs and wins in Ohio for the Senate. He would be a very much tougher opponent for me than Governor Dewey."[15]

Taft supporters wanted a knock-down, hard-driving presidential campaign that confronted the Democrats on big issues. They did not want a "me-too" Republican who accepted the New Deal welfare state, especially now that it was, in their view, globalized through the Marshall Plan and foreign assistance to every country in the world. They wanted a campaign that pressed the Democrats about recent charges by two former communist agents—Whittaker Chambers and Elizabeth Bentley—about Soviet espionage involving Harry Dexter White, a key official in the Treasury Department during World War II and then head of the International Monetary Fund; Lauchlin Currie, a presidential assistant to Roosevelt; and Alger Hiss, an important State Department official until 1947, head of the American delegation to the founding conference of the U.N., and then president of the Carnegie Endowment for International Peace. Taftites did not get that campaign or that candidate in Thomas Dewey or his running mate, the liberal governor of California, Earl Warren.

The 1948 election results were decisive: Truman received over two million more votes than Dewey out of 26.1 million cast, winning 303 electoral votes, 37 more than needed to win the presidency, and the Democrats regained control of the House. It was no consolation to Republicans that this election was the closest since 1912. A small shift of votes in Ohio, Illinois or California would have swung the election to Dewey. Taft supporters exclaimed: We told you so; 1952 is our turn. As one man in Houston wrote his local newspaper, "The Republicans lost in 1940, 1944, 1948 three times—with candidates other than Senator Taft. Yet they have the unmitigated gall to spread the sing-song statement: Taft cannot win."[16] Taft supporters responded that 1952 was to be Taft's year.

The 1952 election marked an important juncture for Taft supporters, grassroots conservatives, and Phyllis Schlafly. Republican conservatives had waited with growing impatience for the GOP to nominate Robert A. Taft, the one man they argued who offered a real choice between restoring constitutional government or continuing along the road to socialism. Typical of the high regard grassroots conservatives held for Taft, the Schlaflys enlisted early in the campaign. Taft and his staff invited Fred Schlafly and a select group of supporters to meet with him at the Statler Hotel in St. Louis to discuss strategy for winning Illinois.[17] When Taft addressed a huge crowd in Alton on April 4, the party chose Phyllis Schlafly to introduce him.

Taft supporters thought their candidate was on his way to victory when charges were raised by the Dwight Eisenhower campaign that Taft had "stolen" the Texas Republican primary. For their part, Taft supporters saw the Eisenhower campaign as "engineered by John Foster Dulles and his associates" in order to assure "the continuance of present policies which have been shaped by Mr. Dulles and his internationalist group."[18] Taft confidentially told Ohio conservative and the state's perennial national committeewoman, Katharine Kennedy Brown, "if we get Eisenhower we will practically have a Republican New Deal Administration with just as much spending and socialism as under Mr. Truman."[19]

By the time the 1952 Republican National Convention opened in Chicago, emotions ran high on both sides.[20] Fred Schlafly was a member of the Illinois delegation and Phyllis had a ring-side seat to watch the machinations. When Eisenhower partisans challenged the seating of Taft delegates from Texas and Louisiana, the stakes got higher. Speaking on behalf of the Taft delegates, Illinois Senator Everett Dirksen reminded the convention how loyally he and other Taft delegates had supported candidate Thomas Dewey in 1944 and 1948. Dirksen then warned, "we followed you before and you took us down the road to defeat."[21] Commotion erupted on the floor. Later that night, the convention voted to seat Eisenhower delegates from Texas and Louisiana. Eisenhower won on the first ballot by a handful of votes.[22] Once again grassroots Republicans saw the nomination stolen by the Machiavellian Eastern establishment. Two years after the election, a Taft supporter wrote to Fred Schlafly that he still regretted that his candidate had not won the nomination at Chicago. "Had he been," he felt, "we would at least have had a showdown between the America First nationalists and the internationalists, do-gooders, and the 'mutual security' boys," those who supported the concept of mutual defense embodied in the North Atlantic Treaty Organization (NATO).[23]

As a Taft Republican, Phyllis Schlafly viewed the 1952 convention as the betrayal of a true Republican by the liberal Eastern establishment of the GOP. As a result, the 1952 convention took on mythic proportions. The GOP Right firmly believed that insider forces at work denied the democratic expression of the party faithful in order to promote an internationalist agenda that served the interests of Wall Street. This interpretation of events bore striking similarity to the Populist movement of the late nineteenth-century and it elicited similar anger. Such rhetoric in 1952 expressed genuinely believed and sincerely felt hostility to the Eastern financial interests. The populist attacks on the Eastern establishment in 1952 came not from agrarian interests that distrusted industrial capitalism but from middle-class Republicans who distrusted centralized government and wanted free enterprise to be unshackled. This was also true for Republicanism in the South, where the GOP began to revive first in suburban areas outside large metropolitan areas.[24]

Still, both populist versions of history mixed fact with hyperbole. In fact, Taft was a more accomplished politician than his opponents portrayed him, but it was also true that Taft often came across to crowds as too reserved. His relations with the press were poor, and newspaper reporters often enlarged incidents in order to cast Taft in a poor light. (Most reporters favored New Deal liberalism, even though their editors and newspaper owners tended to be Republican in those years.) Taft was a conservative Republican, but he was hardly a purist. He supported federal aid to both public housing and education, and when push came to shove he voted for the Marshall Plan and foreign aid programs. Furthermore, while arguably the Texas and Louisiana delegations were stolen from him at the convention, thereby costing him the nomination, there is little doubt that the Taft Republicans in Texas played hardball as tough as the Eisenhower Republicans. The importance of the defeat in 1952, much like other lost causes, lay in its capacity to engender future battle cries.

SCHLAFLY RUNS FOR CONGRESS

While Republican presidential politics was being played out on the national stage, Phyllis Schlafly had her own race to run in the 21st District. In this campaign, she revealed her now well-developed conservative ideology, tempered by political instincts for compromise. She also showed an independent streak and an inner fortitude to stand up against her opponents in both parties. It was an upset when Phyllis Schlafly won the GOP primary in the 21st Congressional district against the Republican machine in East St. Louis. The race was based on issues, not personalities. In filing for the primary, she declared, "As a housewife, I am greatly concerned about the fact that we have the highest prices and highest taxes in our country's history—caused by wasteful government spending, graft, and a policy of betraying our friends and arming our enemies."[25] She stressed the importance of virtue in politics and the role women could play in bringing clean government to the people. "I am a candidate for Congress," she declared, "because I feel very disturbed about the corrupt situation in politics.

I think that women should get into politics and do something about it."[26]

The image of a small-town Illinois housewife challenging the male-dominated political machine was quickly picked up by the press and became national news. The oddity of a housewife running for Congress hit the newspapers, as Fred Schlafly put it, "like a man biting a dog, and her picture in an apron cooking breakfast was printed in newspapers coast to coast."[27] In 1952 twenty-nine women sought congressional seats, but Phyllis Schlafly, "the average housewife," caught the press's attention. Headlines across the nation read "Powder-Puff In." Throughout the primary and the general election, Schlafly was portrayed as the "Alton housewife" who had decided to enter politics to bring virtue to government. Schlafly continued to stress this theme—that women had a moral responsibility to restore virtue to politics. Her rhetoric echoed an earlier time when women saw themselves not as men's equals, but as their moral superiors—the moral guardians of the nation. For example, Schlafly urged voters, "Turn out of office the men who openly boast that governments are not bound by moral law.... Since women have always been the guardians of morality in the home, our country would benefit if women exercised their voting rights to restore morality to our federal government."[28] She was not asking for the liberal moral principles that led to the growth of the welfare state or to international collectivism. That, she claimed, was "immoral morality."[29] Such rhetoric was good politics for the first woman candidate to run in the 21st District; it also expressed a belief in her role and women's role in maintaining public virtue in a republic.

Labeled the "powder-puff " candidate by the press, she faced three tough male opponents in the primary: a landscape engineer, a former congressional candidate, and her chief rival—John T. R. Godlewski, an East St. Louis attorney backed by the St. Clair County Republican machine.[30] The two leaders of the East St. Louis Republican machine, James McRoberts and Dan McGlynn, had fallen out when McGlynn made a bid to become mayor of the city in 1951. Subsequently, McRoberts declared for Eisenhower while McGlynn backed Taft, but both came out for Godlewski against the upstart from Alton, Phyllis Schlafly.[31] Their endorsements played into Schlafly's strategy of presenting the image of an average housewife who had entered the race because she was concerned with corruption in politics. She told the press she was "pleased" that the machine was backing Godlewski. "This confirms my claim that I am not under obligation to any small faction or pressure group." A Republican candidate wearing the label "Approved by Your Local Political Machine" was not the best kind of endorsement for Godlewski during an election year in which the strategy of the national GOP was to attack Democrats on "Corruption, Communism, Korea," the so-called C2 K1 formula. One Schlafly supporter observed, "Her skirts are clean."[32] Reformers in the party touted her as "a natural new face with an immaculate background, something other than a party war-horse." Old-time Republican politicos saw her as a "political fledging" out of her depth. Innuendo circulated that a women's place was at home, not in the political arena.[33]

Thin, with angular features and a receding hairline made more prominent by his thick mustache, Godlewski contrasted sharply to Schlafly, whom a local St. Louis newspaper described as "a tallish, blue-eyed young woman with light brown curly hair."[34] She was the first female candidate ever to seek the Republican nomination in the 21st district, so local newspapers followed her campaign closely. At the same time she produced her own media campaign by launching a daily barrage of press releases to local newspapers. Without a campaign manager or staff, Schlafly wrote, typed, and distributed her own press releases. Her energy amazed her supporters, opponents, and the press. She wrote her own speeches; arranged speaking engagements; and drove herself around the district, but always returned for dinner at home. She spoke before any group that would hear her—women's groups, school associations, church gatherings, social clubs. It was one of the most vigorous primary campaigns ever seen in the 21st District. Godlewski could hardly keep up with his rival. She was quick-witted, well spoken, and the sharpest debater he had ever encountered. After debating her one morning, he felt prepared for that afternoon's debate a few hours later in another town. Schlafly astounded him by giving an entirely different speech.

Throughout the primary campaign, Schlafly projected a persona as an average housewife who happened to have the political expertise and moral character to be in Congress. Background pieces on her in the local newspapers, often taken verbatim from her press releases, typically mentioned that she had a graduate degree in Political Science from Radcliffe, had worked in Washington, D.C. at the American Enterprise Association, and was a "housewife who did her own shopping and most of the housework." Feature stories commented on her intelligence and knowledge of the issues, noting she had not "read a novel since college."[35] She was a local girl who had made good; a housewife concerned about the moral side of the issues; and a candidate who would rather read dry government documents than fiction.

She was a reformer who promised to refurbish the image of a tired Republican party; she was a political novice tired of Big Government interference in her life. She was a new political voice that was sick of the old politics. She told voters they needed to throw out those "political leaders who have adopted the immoral doctrines of expediency and the end-justifies-the-means philosophy." She told the Washington School Mothers Club in Alton that "religious training to develop honor and spiritual values in our youth is more necessary than ever before. Morality without intelligence may be useless, but intelligence without morality is highly dangerous." Look at Alger Hiss, she said, a man of high intelligence who willingly betrayed his country. Referring to the scandals in the Truman administration, she said, "Until we make morality the prime requisite for public leadership, we will continue to be plagued by vicuña coats, five percenters, and the betrayal of our military secrets."[36]

She was young, vivacious, and not afraid to state her mind. Against a seasoned politician such as Godlewski, this made for good politics. Godlewski had served in the army from 1940 to 1946 and had earned a law degree from Saint Louis University, a Jesuit college. He had been the mayor of Pearl, Illinois. Schlafly compensated for her general lack of political experience by offering clear-cut political opinions. When the League of Women Voters sent questionnaires on critical issues of the day to all the congressional candidates, the responses showed sharp differences. Asked about their positions on the United Nations, the incumbent Democrat, Mel Price, answered banally that the U.N. was the "hope for peace in the world"; Godlewski recommended revisiting the veto power of permanent members of the Security Council. Schlafly minced no words: "expel nations that consistently violate international law such as Russia" which had seized eight countries since the U.N. was established. On Korea, both Price and Godlewski spoke in generalities calling for support of U.S. troops. Once again, Schlafly was blunt. She felt Korea was "an unnecessary war" into which the Soviet Union had lured the United States, but now that American troops were militarily engaged, the war should be carried into border regions in China through strategic bombing raids.[37]

Such militant talk was completely agreeable to local Republicans. Talk of expelling the Soviet Union from the U.N. and carrying the air war to the Chinese side of the Yalu River might be strong medicine back east, but it was ordinary Republican rhetoric in Illinois in 1952. As one editorial remarked of her performance before 500 party faithful at the Madison County Lincoln Day Dinner, "Schlafly stole the show. Yep, the nearest thing to an ovation that anybody received was given to Mrs. Phyllis Schlafly of Alton." She was "like a welterweight boxer in good trim flaying the hide off " her opponents. The editor added that her speech was "delivered in a forthright manner, without the corny overtones of the usual male political dissertation."[38] By the time of the primary election, local newspapers reported that most precinct committeemen in both counties had endorsed Schlafly. After what the press called one of the "liveliest campaigns" in years, Schlafly easily defeated Godlewski by 4,000 votes out of approximately 26,000 cast. She swept her own Madison County, winning 7,800 votes to Godlewski's 1,900 votes. She took the majority of St. Clair County with the exception of East St. Louis.[39] "I never ran out of ammunition," she told the press.

Phyllis Schlafly was then pitted against Melvin Price, a fifth-term incumbent, in a heavily Democratic district. Price fit the district well and had the common touch. A bachelor, he lived with his widowed mother in East St. Louis and had a small efficiency apartment in Washington, D.C. As one newspaper described him, he was a politician whose "personal contacts far outshine his stage impact. . . . He is not tall and is slightly balding." But he had the ability to "be a good listener" and gives the impression that what his constituents tell him is "considered to be even more enlightening that it could possibly be."[40] Every time there was a birth, death, or wedding anniversary in his district, Price sent a personal note. He presented himself as a "man of the people," whose father had been a railroad worker in East St. Louis for 40 years. He entered politics in 1933 after covering the 1931 election as a reporter for the *East St. Louis Journal*, taking a staff position with long-time Democratic Representative, Edwin M. Schaefer. When Schaefer retired, Price made an unsuccessful bid for the seat. He went to work for the *St. Louis Globe-Democrat*. In a clever political maneuver, Price entered the army in October 1944 and then ran for election to Congress as an enlisted man. He won, gained an honorable discharge, and then used his position to gain a seat on the Armed Services Committee and the Committee on Atomic Energy. On these committees, he directed federal funds for projects in his district that included Scott Air Force base. He was a pro-labor Democrat who deviated little, if at all, from the party. Fred Schlafly described him as "not a doctrinaire socialist, but a man who simply wants to stay in office."[41]

Price had won his previous bids for reelection easily, but this was the toughest fight of his career. Schlafly's eloquence contrasted sharply with Price's faltering style on the stump. He was ill at ease on the stage and often spoke in banalities. As the race progressed, Price became increasingly frustrated by his opponent's unrelenting campaign against his record. Following the script she developed in the primary, Schlafly's campaign strategy was to try to place Price on the defensive by painting him as a liberal who was weak on communist subversion in government, a supporter of a corrupt administration, and a toady of Truman's stalemated war in Korea. In pursuing this strategy, she needed to tack a fine course of being aggressive in her attacks on Democratic policies, while making sure she did not come across as a know-it-all trying to make Price look stupid. She stuck to the issues, while at the same time generating enough excitement to keep her name in the newspapers.

She had a message, but getting that message to the voters remained a persistent problem in a poorly financed campaign. Indeed, her campaign was low-budget, even by the standards of the days before television inflated campaign costs. From the time she won the nomination, she placed twenty-five political advertisements in local newspapers including the *East St. Louis Journal*, *Alton Evening Telegraph*, and *Belleville Daily Advocate*. She also placed one ad in the *CIO Labor News Review* and *The Messenger*, an East St. Louis African-American weekly. The total cost of her campaign, including $1,250 spent on stationery, gasoline, telephone, envelopes, stamps and miscellaneous items, was $2,889.44 spread over three months. Her contributions came from leading citizens of Alton such as John M. Olin and Spencer T. Olin, who each gave her $500. Most of the contributions were $10, $25, or $50 donations. Her only sizeable donation from outside the state came late in the campaign from rightwing Texas oil billionaire H. L. Hunt, who contributed $500, possibly after hearing about Schlafly's campaign from conservative commentator Clarence Manion, a close friend of the Schlaflys.[42]

To compensate for a low-budget campaign, Schlafly barraged local newspapers with press releases announcing her speaking engagements and her positions on the issues. Each press release was personally typed by her on a standard Royal typewriter with a dozen carbon copies made on onion-skin paper. Direct attacks on Price's political positions helped ensure newspaper space, so Schlafly kept on the offensive throughout most of the campaign. She also garnered publicity by inviting outside speakers to the district, including a visit by vice-presidential candidate Richard Nixon, who concluded his tour of southern Illinois at a packed rally in East St. Louis. Drawing a crowd of 3,000, Nixon caught the excitement of the crowd and broke from his set speech to urge the crowd to vote for Schlafly; her election, he exclaimed, would add "some charm and beauty to Washington. And believe me we can stand it."[43]

Speakers such as Nixon drew crowds, but Schlafly shrewdly targeted outside speakers at groups she thought could be won over to the Republican ticket. For example, she arranged to have Representative Charles J. Jenkins, the African-American chairman of the Illinois House Appropriations Committee, make speeches in her district. When the Republican National Committee offered to sponsor one national speaker for her, she requested Arthur Bliss Lane, former United States Ambassador to Poland. Lane, who had served in Poland from 1945 to 1947, had emerged as one of the nation's foremost critics of the Roosevelt-Truman-Acheson foreign policy. His sentiments were captured in the title of his 1948 book, *I Saw Poland Betrayed.* Schlafly arranged for Lane to speak at a series of events in heavy Polish-American districts in Granite City and East St. Louis, which drew sizeable crowds. Lane urged Polish-Americans to cut their roots with the Democratic party, charging that Truman and Secretary of State Dean Acheson had appeased the communists by providing a $90 million loan to the Polish government in 1946, even though Lane recommended against the loan until free elections were held. It is not clear whether Lane won over many Polish-Americans for Schlafly. Indeed, Fred Schlafly observed that Lane, even though well known for his bluntness, might not have been strong enough to persuade voters that Democratic foreign policy had allowed Poland to come under control of the Soviet Union.[44]

Lane's appearances reinforced Schlafly relentless attacks on the Democrats for allowing communists to infiltrate the government. The charges tended to border on the sensational. She told the Belleville Republican Club, another sympathetic audience, "The New Deal party was extremely slow in realizing the dangers of Communism, but my opponent, Melvin Price, was even slower than most of his party." Of course, she did not accuse Price of being a communist. In fact, she said he was "a loyal American. But his voting record shows he does not realize the dangers of Communism."[45] These kinds of attacks led later critics to associate Schlafly with Senator Joseph McCarthy (R-Wisconsin) and McCarthyism. For years afterwards, opponents raised the ridiculous charge that Schlafly had worked for McCarthy, when in fact she lived in Illinois and had never met McCarthy in person. Schlafly's anticommunist rhetoric resonated well with Midwestern Republicans, but she was anxious to be linked to Eisenhower during the campaign. When she was asked by a reporter about a rumor that Joe McCarthy was coming to speak on her behalf, she turned the question around to strengthen her association with Eisenhower by replying, "Do I welcome him [McCarthy]? Well, I guess I should be glad to have anyone speak for me. I asked for Eisenhower."[46] When she joined other Republican candidates invited to a meeting with Eisenhower during the campaign, Schlafly made sure that the photograph of her with the General appeared in local newspapers around the district. Whatever reservations she might have had about Eisenhower, she knew a good photo opportunity when she saw one.

Schlafly carefully delineated between what she described as Truman's "unconstitutional" war in Korea and her proposal to expand the war; her call to strengthen the American military and her opposition to the draft; and her support for a balanced budget and tax cuts and her insistence that defense expenditures should be increased. Schlafly believed that the Korean War was unconstitutional and mistaken, yet should be won after America decided to enter it. Her position on Korea foreshadowed her later positions on military intervention abroad, including the Vietnam War. Only Congress can declare war, she declared, but "Truman made the decision to go to war in Korea alone, while flying in his plane from Missouri." Having made this decision, she continued, Truman did not seek a declaration of war through Congress, but instead went to the United Nations for its approval. As a result, Truman had been lured into a war designed by Stalin to distract the United States from communist activities in Europe. Meanwhile, he had fired Douglas MacArthur, the one general who had called for military victory in Korea, and entered into negotiations with the communists that were going nowhere. "Truce talks," she told her audiences, "are always a Red trap—a stall for time to build up their air force and to bring up artillery, fresh troops and supplies. During the sixteen months of negotiations, we have made all the concessions."[47] She continued to remind her audiences that Price had told voters that he supported the war, but did not have any idea of how to end it.[48]

Schlafly had ideas on how to end it: She called for the use of Japanese troops in Korea, blockading the coast of China, bombing the bridges across the Yalu River, and bombing the hydro-electric plants at the Chosin, Yalu and Changjin reservoirs.[49] Intensifying the war was the real way to force serious negotiations on the Chinese. This strategy followed closely what General MacArthur had called for before he was relieved of command by Truman. This call for intensifying the war also fit into her insistence that defense spending should be increased and made more efficient. She noted that $246 billion had been spent for defense since the end of World War II, but "our poor foot soldiers are being sent into battle with weapons inferior to the Chinese." Typically, she gave exact figures to prove she knew what she was talking about. Chinese small mortars, she claimed, outranged our small caliber mortars by a half-mile, while the large 1220 Chinese mortar fired a full mile farther than our largest caliber mortar. Our lack of firepower, she claimed, had led to 122,000 causalities.[50] She held Price, a member of the House Armed Services Committee, responsible for this neglect of American troops.

Her call for an increase in defense expenditures reflected her belief that American troops in Korea needed better equipment, but this demand also fit into her view that a strong defense was necessary to prevent war with the Soviet Union, the main enemy that faced the nation. The Korean War was only a peripheral war that America had been drawn into by the Soviet Union in order to detract attention from Soviet aggression in Europe. Such peripheral wars, she maintained, were part of a Soviet strategy to drain American resources, while the Soviet Union launched a major defense buildup. This became a common theme in her writings on defense until the collapse of the Soviet Union forty years later. At the same time, she worried that these peripheral wars were used by liberals to take away individual rights from American citizens and to extend government influence in the economy.

Of particular concern was Truman's insistence on military conscription. She called for an end of the draft and the creation of a volunteer army. "I do not believe," she told a cheering Republican rally, "that our economy should be built on war, or that full employment should be based on a peacetime draft. The best way to prevent permanent conscription, higher taxes, higher prices, and future Koreas all over the world is to vote the straight Republican ticket." At a smaller gathering of women, she argued that women had a moral responsibility to prevent a militarized society. "Time is running out," she warned. "We women must work together if we are to safeguard our homes from continued invasion by the New Deal war party. We must vote together . . . to restore to our people that fundamental American freedom—freedom from the draft."[51] Ending the draft was necessary to the preservation of the American home. Conscription, she declared, was an assault on the American home. In her view, women had a special obligation to oppose the draft and protect the American home. "In former years," she observed, "a woman's place was in the home. Today, American women must stand together if we are to protect our home."[52] Schlafly continued to oppose conscription into the Vietnam War era and welcomed the introduction of a volunteer army. It is worth nothing, however, that given the nature of land warfare in the 1950s and the slight qualitative edge of American land force weapons over Soviet weapons, conscription appeared necessary to field a land force that could credibly deter a Soviet attack on Western Europe.

Schlafly's opposition to conscription appeared to some to be inconsistent with her call for maintaining American military superiority as a means of deterring war with the Soviet Union. At the same time, her position that America should maintain a strong defense, yet not become a militarized society also appears contradictory. This position that the United States remain militarily superior, yet not become a militarized society with a conscripted army, echoed the noninterventionist prewar Right that called for a "fortress America," while keeping the United States out of foreign entanglements.[53] Prewar and postwar conservatives feared that unrestrained government spending would increase inflation and labor unrest, as well as leading to high levels of taxation needed to finance a fully militarized economy.[54]

As might be expected given this line of thought, Schlafly called for a reduction of the income tax, a balanced budget, and an end to foreign aid. Nevertheless, there was a pragmatic side to Schlafly's fiscal conservatism, which was most readily apparent when she attacked Price's left flank by calling for the expansion of Social Security and veterans' benefits. She refused to be caught flat-footed on social policy, calling for the doubling of old-age assistance, aid to dependent children, and aid to the blind. She declared that "all of these payments could easily be doubled by squeezing the waste and graft out of New Deal foreign giveaway programs."[55] Nor was she going to be outbid by Price on veterans' benefits. When Price issued a press release taking credit for a new federal loan program for veterans, Schlafly retorted that the program was stingy, pointing out that the amount set aside for home loans was "pitifully small, while not providing direct business, farm or occupation loans to veterans."[56] Obviously, she would do better, if elected. Her most audacious assault came when she accused the Democrats of "betraying labor." Noting that Truman had threatened to draft strikers into the army in 1946 and had tried to seize the steel industry in 1952, she charged that these policies guaranteed that "labor will be taxed and taxed, drafted and drafted, and expended and expended."[57] She did not hesitate to tell labor audiences that she favored the Taft-Hartley Act because it "protects the working man" from the barons of organized labor, but she also declared that she believed that "labor's right to strike should be protected."[58]

Schlafly's endorsement of expanding Social Security, veterans' benefits, and other social welfare programs stood in lockstep with mainstream Republican policy in the immediate aftermath of the Second World War. Entitlement programs such as Social Security and health care simply did not have the budgetary magnitude that they acquired two decades later. For example, when Schlafly called for the doubling of aid to dependent children, out-of-wedlock births (which accounted for only 4 percent of births) were not a major social problem. While Republicans opposed extending the welfare state through the establishment of new programs called for under Truman's Fair Deal, most Republicans supported, if only for political reasons, the incremental growth of established programs. Thus Republicans called for a balanced budget, but they did not demand that the Social Security Act be repealed or that agricultural subsidies established in the 1930s be ended. Broadly, the GOP opposed further advances in the New Deal revolution—national health insurance, government guaranteed full-employment, and cradle-to-grave welfare—but for the most part, accepted the New Deal programs enacted during the Depression. For all their rhetoric, Republicans were not counterrevolutionaries; they just wanted to prevent the revolution from going further. Schlafly, although to the right of the moderate Eisenhower wing of the GOP, was not an exception.

Schlafly's ability to bob and weave ideologically made her a hard target to hit, especially by an opponent not conditioned to a tough fight. At the start of the race, Price pretended not to take Schlafly seriously. Price maintained this strategy throughout most of the first half of the campaign. Price refused to debate her, publicly claiming that debates in the district were not part of the "Illinois tradition"—a patently absurd position given that Alton, Illinois was the site of one of the Lincoln-Douglas debates.[59] As the campaign proceeded, however, Price found himself appearing frequently, usually inadvertently, on the same stage as Schlafly, so a debatelike format was created contrary to Price's strategy.[60] In these appearances, Schlafly cut a sharp contrast to her opponent, as one friendly newspaper reported when it observed that "Mrs. Schlafly had the edge on Price for looks. She is an attractive, neat woman who wore a gray business suit, black high heel pumps, pearl earrings, and who offset the distracting influence of her femininity by . . . speaking with conviction as she exhibited various charts and maps."[61] Even unfriendly newspapers noted that Schlafly was a more forceful speaker and received "more applause" than her opponent. While addressing domestic issues, she continued to warn that the United States was becoming militarized by the draft, the Korean War, and commitments abroad. "I believe," she declared at the conclusion of one debate, "that America can achieve real prosperity without a war and without a militaristic philosophy that inevitably leads to war. We must not let it be said than any country in the world affords its citizens more freedom than does the United States."[62]

Schlafly's eloquence and mastery of the facts made Price's practice of speaking without notes and in broad generalities look amateurish. Schlafly had self-assuredness and sometimes an underlying tone of self-righteousness that tended to exasperate opponents. In part this was a reflection of her personality, but to a great extent it also expressed her deep political convictions and her view that women have a moral obligation to be involved in civic affairs and politics. (It is no small irony that two decades later, feminists, who shared a similar belief that women had a special role to play in politics, experienced the same frustration that Price felt in 1952 when it came to debating Schlafly.) She was ironclad in her views and gave no ground to her opponents in a debate. She did not try to soften her tone with such phrases as "that is an interesting point you make" or "I understand your position, but don't you think. . . ." Instead, she rebutted her opponents directly and without qualification. In doing so, her arguments were directed to rally her supporters and persuade those who might be persuaded. To Price, and to her later opponents, she appeared doctrinaire, intolerant, and self-righteous; to her supporters she said what they would have liked to have said. She was logical, morally passionate, and spoke on the behalf of average Americans.

As Price became increasingly frustrated in his encounters with Schlafly, he turned to personal attacks, accusing her of representing the forces of reaction that sought to end Social Security and take away the rights of labor. He warned his constituents of the "danger of military control by a group of retired Republican generals, including Dwight D. Eisenhower, Douglas MacArthur, Albert Wedemeyer and others."[63] By the time of their final meeting, Price simply could not abide Schlafly on the same stage and publicly refused to shake her hand. In the meanwhile, newspaper editorials also became more acerbic and personal in their criticisms of Schlafly as the campaign drew to a close. While on the whole the press reported the campaign fairly, the editorial pages and columnists in this heavily Democratic district clearly supported Price. For example, James O. Monroe, a regular columnist for the *Collinsville Herald*, criticized "our effervescent young Republican candidate for Congress," who has been able to criticize the Democrats for the Korean War, but does not tell us what the Republicans are going to do about Korea. It would be informative, he wrote, "if the ebullient Phyllis would give us a blueprint of just what she proposed to do about Korea come next January." He asked, "Does she want to withdraw our troops, send more there, or leave the situation as it is? Does she want to confine the war to Korea, or invade Manchuria?" Or does she want to attack "Communism at its heart—in Moscow?" He concluded, "Phyllis is a smart girl, but perhaps a little immature."[64] As the campaign drew to a close, this line of criticism was again taken up by the *Collinsville Herald* editors who accused Schlafly as being "the best twister of facts who has appeared on the local political scene . . . during the last thirty-five years." She speaks "half truths to her wide-eyed followers."[65]

This kind of criticism by the press was unnecessary because most observers believed that the outcome of the election was a forgone conclusion. That proved to be the case when Price won in a landslide, swamping Schlafly even in Madison County. A few days after the election, a reporter asked Schlafly if she would have won if her name had been "Phillip" and not "Phyllis." Schlafly replied, "No," adding that she lost because she was a Republican in a Democratic district. The nationally popular Eisenhower lost the district by the same margin. Schlafly expected to lose the election, so she saw the campaign as a way of serving the party. She proved to be a fierce debater and an articulate speaker for Republican positions. As one local newspaper noted at the time, her campaign had "rocked Madison and St. Clair Counties like a minor tremor" and in doing so she had "given the lie to all the tired old axioms about politics, masculine prerogatives and the so-called 'weaker sex.' "[66] Even the Democratic-oriented *East St. Louis Journal* noted she had "conducted the most vigorous campaign any opponent Mr. Price ever has faced, awakening him to the evils of being a rubber stamp for the Democratic party leadership. In salute to Mrs. Schlafly, we thank her for that."[67]

As a result of her vigorous campaign style, Schlafly gained attention from the press and she earned recognition by state Republicans for her speaking ability. News of Schlafly's ability to deliver hard knock-out speeches led to an unexpected invitation for her to deliver the keynote address at the Illinois Republican State Convention in June, 1952. Delegates to the convention did not know what to expect when they heard that the keynote speaker was going to be a twenty-seven-year-old woman from Alton, Illinois. At the convention, 5,000 Republicans in Springfield "sat at rapt attention in torrid temperatures reaching close to 100 degrees in a non-air conditioned assembly hall to hear Phyllis Schlafly flay Democrats"—as one newspaper reported. She brought to her audience the political enthusiasm of a young woman and the moral passion of a person committed to the spiritual rejuvenation of the nation, which would come with the election of Republicans to office. As she spoke, the crowd became caught up in her passion and stood again and again to applaud her. "The women of this nation," she said, "are truly aroused by the New Deal's invasion of the American home. The New Deal administration has been demoralizing our children by bad example, drafting our men and confiscating the family income."[68] The United States, she declared, was bogged down in a land war in Korea because government in Washington, D.C. was run by a "self-anointed minority of men without moral principle." If the Democrats were elected for another term, she added, "We can expect socialized agriculture, socialized medicine—and a scarcity of both food and doctors." The problems within the administration were not just problems of misguided policies, but a reflection of "moral corruption." There was only one conclusion to be reached: "Only a Republican victory will end the striped pants diplomacy of the New Deal, including the vertical stripes worn by Dean Acheson and the horizontal strips now worn by his good friend Alger Hiss."[69] When she finished the crowd rose to give her a standing ovation. A new face, a new voice, had arrived in the Republican party.

This young woman, married only three years earlier, a housewife and mother with one young child, emerged as the favorite female speaker in Illinois Republican circles. She stood next in popularity to U.S. Senator Everett Dirksen, who was known for his deep-throated oratorical eloquence. Speaking to groups throughout the state, to local Republican clubs, to the Daughters of the American Revolution, to state conventions, and later through a weekly radio program, Schlafly brought a basic moral message to the grassroots: "America cannot save the free world from Communism until our leaders learn that a Communist is a conspirator against Christianity and democracy."[70]

The battle against communism, she believed, was not just a military struggle or a competition between two economic systems, but a moral confrontation between two diametrically opposed world views. At stake was the civilized world that had been created by Western Christendom, and the United States needed to be prepared politically, militarily, and morally to maintain its resolve. Victory lay in sound leaders and a sound citizenry. For Schlafly and other grassroots Republican activists, victory also meant transforming the GOP into a party opposed to collectivism and internationalism in its many guises, a party that stood for those values necessary to the preservation of a Judeo-Christian Republic. She called for an insurrection within the party against the Eastern wing of the party.

Victory against the forces that sought to accommodate the party to New Deal collectivism would not come overnight. But in 1952, Phyllis Schlafly had taken what she believed to be the first small step to transform the GOP into an instrument necessary to preserve constitutional government, protect the Republic, and defeat the forces of internationalism and collectivism.

CHAPTER THREE

Anticommunism: A Young Woman's Crusade

SPEAKING BEFORE THE Illinois Daughters of the American Revolution in early 1960, Phyllis Schlafly appealed to Christian women to fulfill their obligation to serve their communities. She suggested that one of the most important ways of doing so would be to enter the fight against communism. She reminded her audience, "God told Abraham that the cities of Sodom and Gomorrah would be spared from His wrath if only ten just men could be found in each city. Fire and brimstone descended on these cities when ten could not be found. Our Republic can be saved from the fires of Communism which have already destroyed or enslaved many Christian cities, if we can find ten patriotic women in each community."[1]

For anticommunist activists such as Schlafly, the struggle against communism dictated all aspects of political life from the local to the national level. The foundation of the GOP Right was laid in grassroots anticommunism in the 1950s, although that was not its only issue of concern. The GOP Right pursued other goals such as federal budget restraint, a strong military defense, regulatory reform, tax cuts, and ending foreign aid programs, but anticommunism provided the glue that held the conservative wing of the Republican party together. It tethered the Republican party to a foreign policy and it motivated anticommunist activists to resist control of the party by the liberal, internationalist wing. The Republican Right, made up of grassroots activists such as Schlafly, opposed the liberal wing of the Republican party because it was viewed as not placing high enough priority on the communism issue and because of its willingness to promote collectivist social programs in order to win elections.

Furthermore, postwar conservatives showed far *more* concern with communism, in general, than they did with race relations. There were anti-Semites and segregationists on the Right, but such prejudices were more often found in the South and would intensify in this region with the growth of militant civil rights activities. Southern anti-Semitism and racism were not integral to conservative thought in the South, nor were these prejudices closely associated with the Republican party in the South, which saw its first political inroads in the postwar era in white middle-class suburbs. Poor rural white and working class urban white voters provided the fodder for racial extremist groups that emerged in response to the black civil rights movement. Moreover, whatever the association with segregation and anticommunism in the South during the 1950s, most anticommunist conservative leaders in the North frequently pointed out that it was a common ploy of the communists to play on racial and social divisions in American society. As a consequence they warned that the promotion of anti-Semitic and racist views played into the hands of the communists. Anticommunist lecturers warned that racial and religious division in the world was often stirred up by the Reds as a means of weakening civil society. A graphic lesson of communist diversionary tactics came in the form of a 42-page comic book, "Is This Tomorrow America Under Communism," published by the Guild Education Society. In this futuristic tale about a Communist seizure of power in the United States, an early frame shows a heavy-mustached communist leader telling his followers, "We have done an exceptional job of making different classes and religions hate one another."[2] The GOP Right in the 1950s and 1960s can be faulted for ignoring race problems in the 1960s, but to understand the growth of conservatism in these decades, it is essential to understand the overriding importance of the issue of communism.[3]

The communist issue dominated debates in the GOP Right about defense policy, cultural exchanges, trade with Eastern bloc countries, and arms control treaties with the Soviet Union. Indeed, all social, cultural, and moral issues seemed to converge in the confrontation with communism—education, modern art, Hollywood films, pornography, civil liberties, libraries, and even mental health. "Whether we like it or not," Phyllis Schlafly wrote, "we are already engaged in Total War that the Communists are waging on every front: spiritual, political, economic, cultural, military, psychological, and in every other way they can think of. And it is time we realize it is a war to the death—our death if we don't win it."[4]

SPIES IN GOVERNMENT FUEL THE ANTICOMMUNIST MOVEMENT

The anticommunist mindset of the Republican Right cannot be grasped without understanding the shock waves that followed the news of communist spy rings deep inside the American government.[5] Set within the context of Soviet domination of Eastern and Central Europe, the revelations of communist infiltration in high posts in the United States government heightened public anxieties about national security. The first case broke in the summer of 1945 when six people, including a State Department Asian expert, John Stewart Service, were arrested for giving classified government documents to the left-leaning journal, *Amerasia*, edited by Philip Jaffe, a friend of Communist party chieftain Earl Browder. Further evidence of communist infiltration of the federal government came directly from American and Canadian government interviews with Elizabeth Bentley, an American courier for a Soviet spy network; an intelligence officer working in the Soviet Embassy in Canada, Igor Gouzenko; and Whittaker Chambers.[6] These reports revealed the existence of an atomic spy ring led by Julius and Ethel Rosenberg, as well as two major spy rings operating in Washington, D.C. that implicated major figures in the New Deal administration, including Assistant Secretary of the Treasury Harry Dexter White and White House aide Lauchlin Currie. It was a sensation when former communist spy and *Time* magazine editor Whittaker Chambers charged Alger Hiss, a former high State Department official in the Roosevelt and Truman administrations, with being a communist agent.[7]

These security fears intensified with the fall of China to the communists and the Soviet explosion of an atomic bomb in 1949. In early 1950, the Republican National Committee issued a "Statement of Republican Principles" charging that communists and fellow travelers had been employed to "a dangerous degree" in important government positions.[8] At Lincoln Day dinners, Republican speakers openly accused the Truman administration of allowing communists to continue serving in government. The junior Republican Senator from Wisconsin, Joseph R. McCarthy, gained immediate national attention when he declared in a Lincoln Day speech to a Republican women's club in Wheeling, West Virginia in February 1950 that communists were employed in the State Department.[9] McCarthy's influence and popularity with the general American public grew rapidly after the Korean War broke out in June 1950.[10] McCarthy provided a national voice for anticommunism, and his speeches supporting Eisenhower during the 1952 campaign were well received by Republicans. His influence largely came to an end after he was censured by the U.S. Senate in a 65 to 22 vote in December 1954.[11] Many Americans, including Fred and Phyllis Schlafly, continued to view him favorably.[12] While McCarthy became a national symbol of anticommunism, it was already well rooted in American culture and did not need his encouragement to grow. As the leading historian of this movement noted, "a vital civic culture of anti-communism" prevailed in America.[13]

These revelations created the climate in which Schlafly and other grassroots anticommunists operated in the 1950s.[14] In the aftermath of a world war in which the United States had suffered over one million casualities and in the new world created by the atomic bomb, Americans were understandably anxious that their government appeared to be riddled with enemy spies. Even though they were called hysterical, compared with Salem witch hunters, and denounced for creating an atmosphere of fear, grassroots anticommunist activists refused to believe that every communist agent working in the U.S. government had been caught. Women played an especially important role in this grassroots anticommunist movement. Typical of this activity, Phyllis Schlafly wrote and delivered dozens of articles and lectures on the topic, often tying the issue of communist infiltration into government to the Roosevelt and Truman administrations and Democratic party foreign policy. For example, speaking at the Alton Women's Republican Club, she declared, "Ever since Soviet agents such as Alger Hiss and Harry Dexter White began running the New Deal, the Communists have had far more to gain by voting the Democratic ticket." A couple of weeks later she told the Alton Travel Club, "The success of the Communist spies in stealing our secrets is exceeded by their success in influencing our foreign policy."[15]

Schlafly was certainly not a lone voice in the 1950s. Anticommunist activities were promoted by city officials, businessmen, fraternal organizations, and churches. The United States Chamber of Commerce, through its Committee on Socialism and Communism, provided a forum for speakers, while providing anticommunist educational material of its own to local businesses. In the late 1940s, Fr. John F. Cronin, a Baltimore Catholic priest, was hired to write a report on Communist party activities, "Communist Infiltration in the United States." Appearing under the byline of Chamber official Francis P. Matthews, the first printing of the report ran to 400,000 copies.[16] In local communities across the country, anticommunist investigations, petitions, and rallies were held. In Baltimore, the local bar association, the Kiwanis, Optimist, and Rotary Clubs appointed anticommunist committees in the late 1940s, and in 1951, 50,000 Roman Catholics gathered in Memorial Stadium to pray for the conversion of Russia from "godless communism" to Christianity. In the blue-collar neighborhood of South Gate in Los Angeles, local merchants brought flags in 1954 to line Tweedy Boulevard as a display of patriotism, and the following year the suburb held a "Loyalty Day Parade" against the "Red Menace." Throughout ethnic neighborhoods in industrial Pennsylvania, campaigns were undertaken to eliminate communist influence in ethnic and fraternal organizations.[17]

The image of communist spies and agents in the United States became imbedded in the public consciousness. Popular anticommunist themes were found in movies such as *The Iron Curtain* (1948), which related Igor Gouzenko's defection in Canada, and *I Was a Communist for the FBI* (1951) based on a *Saturday Evening Post* story by former agent Matt Cvetic. Other anticommunist films included *Walk East on Beacon* (1951) and *My Son John* (1952), which told the story of a family ripped apart when a son was revealed to be a communist. There was even an anticommunist comedy in 1939, *Ninotchka*, starring Greta Garbo (her only movie in which she laughed). Television viewers watched *I Led Three Lives*, a syndicated series that ran from 1953 through 1956, and for years afterward as reruns, based on Herbert Philbrick's best-selling book about infiltration into the Communist party in the Boston area. Popular magazines such as *Reader's Digest*, edited by Eugene Lyons, and the *Saturday Evening Post* carried strong anticommunist messages. All major religious denominations conducted anticommunist educational programs. In 1948, New York Rabbi Benjamin Schultz started the American Jewish League against Communism that attracted much national attention when it attacked communist influence among Catholic, Protestant, and Jewish clergy.

This was the popular culture in which Phyllis Schlafly and other grassroots anticommunists worked. Like other grassroots anticommunists, Schlafly's religious views reinforced her political views. The importance of the Christian faith cannot be overstated in explaining how Schlafly and others reacted to the facts of communist infiltration in America. There were exceptions to the rule—Ayn Rand was notable in this regard—but Christian faith inspired many anticommunist activists. Christian doctrine, as it was interpreted by grassroots anticommunist writers and speakers, magnified the fight against communism into a historic battle between the forces of good and evil, light and darkness, Christianity and paganism. Driven by this apocalyptic vision of a world at war, grassroots anticommunist Protestants and Catholics joined forces in an uneasy alliance to battle their common enemy—communism.

Evangelical Protestants denounced communists in the nation's churches, schools, and government. Leading evangelist Billy Graham tied individual redemption to national redemption, declaring, "Only as millions of Americans turn to Jesus Christ at this hour and accept him as Savior can this nation possibly be spared the onslaught of demon-possessed communism."[18] At the same time, unreconstructed Protestant fundamentalists saw the hand of Satan in the communist advance. The Reverend Carl McIntyre used his American Council of Christian Churches, founded in 1941, to campaign against communism, the United Nations, and declining national morals. Harding College in Searcy, Arkansas, under its vigorous president Dr. George S. Benson, launched a national campaign against communism in 1948 through its National Education Program. It produced radio broadcasts, pamphlets, brochures, and school study outlines to protect American citizens against communist infiltration and propaganda. Billy James Hargis established the Christian Crusade in 1950 from Tulsa, Oklahoma, integrating anticommunism into a "fire and brimstone" Christian message, and opportunistically making large sums of money.

Arguably the most influential anticommunist evangelical Christian was Dr. Fred C. Schwarz. An Australian Jewish physician, Dr. Schwarz's conversion to Christianity led him to anticommunism. In 1953 he launched the Christian Anti-Communism Crusade. While Schlafly never had any contact with McIntyre or Hargis, in 1957 and 1958 she invited Schwarz to her anticommunism schools in St. Louis. This gave Schwarz one of his first opportunities to bring his message to a larger public. It also gave him the model for setting up his own anticommunism schools, one-day to five-day programs in local communities that proved immensely popular throughout the 1950s.[19]

The belief that Christianity remained the bulwark against communist subversion found ready acceptance among Roman Catholics. The Vatican strenuously opposed socialism and communism throughout the nineteenth and twentieth centuries. The church's anticommunist message was expressed in homilies, church newspapers, parish newsletters, and Catholic schools and universities throughout the country. In 1950, the Blue Army of Fatima (based on an appearance to three peasant children in Fatima, Portugal by the Virgin Mary, who asked them to pray for the conversion of Russia) was organized by a New Jersey priest to initiate prayer among Catholics for this cause. Within a year, the organization's magazine had a circulation of 70,000.[20] New York's Francis Cardinal Spellman promoted the cause within the Catholic Church. The Catholic lay association, the Knights of Columbus, rallied to the defense of countries behind the Iron Curtain and prevented Yugoslavian communist dictator Tito from visiting the United States in 1957. Catholics played an important role in supporting a successful national campaign that led Congress in 1954 to include "under God" in the official Pledge of Allegiance to the Flag. Catholics were also the major supporters of a campaign to enact legislation designating the third week of July as Captive Nations Week, which criticized communist domination over Catholic countries of Eastern Europe.[21]

As supporters of Captive Nations Week, Fred and Phyllis Schlafly believed that in fighting communism they were helping to fulfill God's mission for America.[22] The Lord's hand was evident in the course of the nation's history—its laws and institutions; its material and technological progress; and its standing as a Republic and a pluralistic society. Writing to Vincent P. Ring of the Knapp Monarch Company, Phyllis Schlafly warned that the struggle today was not between communism and capitalism, but between communism and Christianity.

THE WORLD OF PHYLLIS SCHLAFLY

Most of Phyllis Schlafly's political activity in the 1950s remained on the local level. As concerned as Schlafly was with national and international issues, her political and social world remained primarily the local community and Illinois. Along with her involvement in the Daughters of the American Revolution and the Illinois Federation of Republican Women, she served on the board of the local YMCA and the budget committee of Community Chest, the predecessor to United Way. For years she headed the annual St. Louis Radcliffe Alumnae House Tour fundraiser. She wrote a newsletter for the National Conference of Christians and Jews, organized to promote better understanding between these groups. Still, life in Alton and St. Louis remained largely parochial. This is evident from a letter she wrote to T. Coleman Andrews, who had been invited to speak to a monthly conservative dinner club, the

Discussion Club. She and a small group of conservatives and libertarians organized the club in 1955 to hear speakers on a range of topics. (That this group identified itself as libertarian and conservative reveals much about the nature of the conservative movement in the 1950s, as well as the nonsectarian nature of conservatives in the outback—at least in places such as St. Louis.) Andrews was worried about receiving unfavorable publicity in St. Louis, after his unsuccessful run for the presidency as a third-party candidate in 1956. Schlafly wrote that he should not fret about bad publicity: "Don't worry about publicity—we never have any. In brainwashed St. Louis, we are practically a pro-American underground." She added, "Things are so bad in St. Louis that the public library deliberately hides the *National Review*, that the *Post-Dispatch* buys Westbrook Pegler [a rightwing columnist] and files him in the wastebasket so no other newspaper can publish him, that Fulton Lewis [a conservative radio broadcaster] is barred from the air, and that one of the leading banks balked at opening an account for the Manion Forum. It is rare that anyone of your political persuasion speaks in St. Louis."[23] This was the insular world in which grassroots conservatives and anticommunists lived in the 1950s.

Through her anticommunist work, Schlafly became part of a larger movement that was for the most part diverse, decentralized, and composed of disparate organizations operating locally with little or no coordination or contact. Her political activities reflected an anticommunist movement that remained organizationally and politically fragmented. As a consequence, she was a member of a movement that was little more than local groups reading the same books, newsletters and congressional reports, hearing the same speakers, and listening to Clarence Manion and Fulton Lewis on the radio, but had little contact with one another. Long-distance telephone calls were expensive, the U.S. mail was slow, and fax machines and the Internet did not exist. For somebody living on the East Coast in 1951, St. Louis was remote. Even as late as 1957, the St. Louis Cardinals were the westernmost and southernmost of any major league baseball team. America's national pastime was not yet national; neither was grassroots anticommunism.[24] Fred Schwarz's Christian Anti-Communism Crusade operated through separate local meetings and schools, but its national operation consisted of Schwarz and one assistant.[25] Billy Hargis's Christian Crusade, based in Tulsa, never organized local chapters. Harding College in Searcy, Arkansas, a small Church of Christ school, produced literature and films, but its work remained on a small scale. Other groups included Kent and Phoebe Courtney's Conservative Society of America; Major Edgar C. Bundy's Wheaton, Illinois-based Church League of America; the Circuit Riders in Cincinnati, Ohio, headed by Myers G. Lowman; and LifeLine Foundation sponsored by H. L. Hunt in Texas. These organizations produced newsletters and pamphlets, but they never reached a significant circulation even among the grassroots and none developed national memberships. Contact between these organizations was at best occasional and mostly nonexistent.

The number of people like Phyllis Schlafly involved in the grassroots conservative or anticommunist organizations (the two were often synonymous) is not known. One report written by a conservative in 1955 estimated that there were some 185 organizations and 135 publications "on our side," with "about 100 that have as their objective the fight against communism, socialism, internationalism, and one-worldism." The report noted that these organizations "lacked coordination at the top."[26] Regardless whether these figures were accurate, there is little to suggest that large numbers of Americans were actually involved in organized anticommunist groups. The John Birch Society grew rapidly in membership after its founding by candy-manufacturer Robert Welch in 1958, but its financial statement to the Attorney General of Massachusetts in 1962 reported a national membership of no more than 24,000 people.[27] Grassroots anticommunist organizations reached large numbers of Americans through their publications, seminars, lectures, study groups and educational campaigns, but even this audience was quite limited. Radio programs such as the Dan Smoot Report from Texas and the Manion Forum from Indiana reached tens of thousands of listeners.

Still, a common complaint in anticommunist publications was that average Americans were anticommunist and supported the Cold War, but this opinion did not necessarily lead to accepting the urgency of the threat or the extent of communist infiltration in the United States. Furthermore, diversity of anticommunist groups and organizations imparted at times a sectarian image to the cause. What unified these diverse grassroots groups was the belief that communism was a conspiracy directed by the Soviet Union and this threat was imminent. Yet this agreement on the conspiratorial nature of communism did not stop bickering and the expression of harsh differences of opinion among anticommunist leaders and groups, which Schlafly stayed clear of. For example, Fred Schwarz believed that Robert Welch did a disservice to anticommunism for a variety of reasons, including his suggestions that Eisenhower was soft on communism. Not all accepted at face value Major George Racey Jordan's story that while he was in the Army Air Corps during the Second World War, he discovered a conspiracy led by Harry Hopkins to ship enriched uranium and cobalt to the Soviet Union.[28] Furthermore, grassroots anticommunists differed in political affiliation. Some, such as Fred Schwarz claimed to be nonpartisan. Many of the anticommunist activists in the South remained Democrats, while others such as Kent and Phoebe Courtney sought to form a third party and later became supporters of George Wallace. Phyllis Schlafly was typical of many women in the Midwest and West who combined their anticommunist activities with active involvement in the Republican party.

Through her anticommunist work and her activities in the Republican party, especially the Illinois Federation of Republican Women (IFRW), as well as her involvement in the Daughters of the American Revolution (DAR), Schlafly was gradually introduced to a larger national audience of like-minded activist women. Long before she appeared on the scene with her best-seller *A Choice Not an Echo* (1964), she had developed a network of friends across the country. In the course of the decade, Phyllis Schlafly became a favorite speaker before community women's groups, DAR chapters, and local Republican clubs. In the DAR, Schlafly found an organization that meshed with her patriotic, anticommunist, Christian values. In the *DAR Yearbook* (1957), she reported her first year's activities as Regent: the Alton chapter established a community-wide observance of Constitution Week by sending three lawyers to speak at local high schools; heard a report by the member of the Midwest Residential Seminar on Techniques of Communism, which Schlafly had organized at Pere Marquette Lodge (an Illinois state park); presented Good Citizens Pins to high schoolers and American History Medals to middle schoolers; and donated 197 pounds of clothing to needy children.[29]

The DAR was not allied with other organizations, but DAR members were staunchly anticommunist and anti-internationalist. As such, the DAR was another segment of the insular world of grassroots anticommunism. Schlafly served two terms as state chairman of National Defense, then as state recording secretary for the Illinois organization, and then served five terms as the DAR National Chairman of National

Defense. In that capacity, she wrote an article for every issue of the monthly *DAR Magazine*, wrote a newsletter called *The National Defender*, and selected and introduced speakers—all conservatives and anticommunists—for the annual DAR National Defense Night at Constitution Hall, the DAR headquarters in Washington, D.C. In 1962, the Illinois Daughters of the American Revolution decided to sponsor a weekly syndicated radio program. Heard on twenty-five Illinois stations, this syndicated 15-minute program called "America Wake Up" featured Schlafly speaking on national security issues of the day and occasionally interviewing a prominent conservative guest. The program functioned solely on volunteer labor. A DAR member and owner of radio station WSDR in Sterling, Illinois donated tapes for the 15-minute public service program, while another volunteer, Betty Shaw, took on the time-consuming task of duplicating and mailing reel-to-reel tapes to station subscribers.[30]

At the same time, Schlafly produced a steady barrage of polemics for newsletters and magazines. She wrote and spoke on a wide breadth of topics including Republican politics, art, education, civil liberties, defense, foreign policy, and the role of women in politics and society, as well as communism. Nearly every subject she spoke about in later decades had been researched for her speeches and writings in the 1950s. Most of her speeches and writings were derivative, but she showed considerable talent for making abstruse arguments understandable to the average reader or listener. This allowed her critics to accuse her of simplifying complex problems.

To many liberals in the 1950s, the intensity which grassroots conservatives brought to their fight appeared an obsession. It was one thing, liberals said, to realize that the Soviet Union was a serious rival of the United States and the West, but it was another when conservatives kept up an unabated and vituperative attack on the Soviet Union, refusing to accept trade and cultural exchanges with Eastern-bloc countries or arms control agreements with the Soviet Union. Liberals did not disagree that the Communist party in the United States parroted the Soviet line and that Soviet agents had infiltrated the government in the 1930s and 1940s, but the American Right held a Manichean world view that did not allow for improving relations between the two countries. Unless relations improved, liberals warned, the outcome could only be a prolonged, never-ending Cold War or, possibly, a nuclear holocaust brought about by a hot war. Furthermore, liberals feared that the Right's fear of domestic communists threatened civil liberties. And, as Daniel Bell observed in his edited volume, *The Radical Right*, the ultra-radical right's "identification of Communism with liberalism" was even more threatening. With the authoritative voice of the postwar social scientist, Bell wrote, "What the right wing is fighting, in the shadow of Communism, is essentially 'modernity.' "[31] Liberals believed that what actually bothered conservatives was not really communism per se, but anxiety about a changing world introduced by post-industrialism.

While impugning the motives of the anticommunist Right, these social scientists were correct in finding anticommunist ideology at the core of grassroots conservatism in the aftermath of World War II.[32] Grassroots anticommunist activists such as Schlafly believed that Soviet communism was the most important problem facing America. Schlafly believed that the Soviet Union and the United States were engaged in a life-and-death struggle, so it was reasonable that anticommunist conservatives within the Republican party would give this issue priority. It followed that anticommunist conservatives would find themselves opposed to people whom they considered too willing to compromise with such a deadly opponent without seeking any guarantees that peace was at hand.

Schlafly abhorred communism because in her eyes it was an ungodly, collectivist ideology. Like other conservatives, Schlafly feared America was marching down the road to collectivism, or as Austrian economist Friedrick von Hayek declared, "the road to serfdom."[33] Conservatives believed American liberals were socialists at heart—historian Arthur Schlesinger, Jr. and economist Kenneth Galbraith had said as much—but conservatives such as Schlafly believed that this did not make them communists or communist sympathizers. In fact, grassroots anticommunists such as Phyllis Schlafly were always careful to warn fellow anticommunists not to accuse liberals of being communists. The GOP Right did believe, however, that liberals and socialists suffered from a false political assumption that the responsibility of government was to grant rights to its citizens. For Schlafly, individual rights were "natural," endowed by God and only preserved by a vigilant citizenry. The purpose of government was to uphold the rule of law and to protect the nation from internal disorder and external threats from its foreign enemies. Power tends to corrupt, and therefore, the power of government must be limited, otherwise it would deprive citizens of liberty.

Conservatives did not deny that liberals professed to be anticommunists, nor did they deny that liberals had played an essential role in driving communists out of organized labor and the Democratic party. Conservatives did maintain, however, that liberals misunderstood the tactics and strategy of the communists. Fundamentally the difference between conservatives and liberals lay in the liberals' view that the best approach to fighting communism lay in progressive social reform.[34] Historian Arthur Schlesinger, Jr. articulated the principles of liberal anticommunism in his 1949 book, *The Vital Center*. The "vital center" as he described it was liberalism prescribing progressive economic and political reform as the best means of protecting democracy from the false promises of communism. As an anticommunist liberal, Schlesinger did not doubt that the Soviet Union was imperialistic and a threat to the United States. Yet, he maintained that this threat was primarily external, not internal. He believed that domestic communism needed to be confronted through "debate, identification, and exposure," and he rejected the argument that the Communist party should be outlawed. Moreover, he accused the House Committee on Un-American Activities of threatening civil liberties by its "promiscuous and unprincipled attack on radicalism." In foreign policy, Schlesinger held that international communism needed to be fought with political and economic weapons, not military ones, and he called for political alliances with the noncommunist socialists in Europe, "the strongest bulwarks in Europe against Communism."[35]

Despite their commonalities, grassroots conservatives such as Phyllis Schlafly never accepted liberals as allies in the fight against communism. When push came to shove, she maintained, liberals clung to their belief in the expansion of government in order to address domestic problems, and in her mind they would always advocate a foreign policy based on accommodation with the Soviet Union. While she never suggested liberals were the same as communists, she still maintained that conservatives and liberals differed fundamentally as to the meaning of liberty. For Schlafly and other conservatives, liberty meant limited government, property rights, and personal freedom. Because liberals sought government solutions for every problem, Schlafly remained suspicious of their ability to understand the problems of statism and collectivism, and this blindness had led liberals to allow communists into government and liberal organizations in the 1930s and 1940s. She agreed with other anticommunist conservatives in excoriating what columnist James Burnham called "that jelly-fish brand of contemporary liberalism—pious, guilt-ridden, and do-good."[36]

Simply put, the difference between liberal anticommunists and conservative anticommunists such as Schlafly came down to the question of whether the communists could be trusted at all. For grassroots activists like Schlafly, that answer was a resounding, NO—period. Similarly, they held that liberals were too anxious to trust the communists. For the Republican Right, communism was an attack directed by the Soviet Union on American values of religion, patriotism, independence, family, and local civic society. Liberal anticommunists believed that, while the American Communist party remained an enemy of democracy, repressive legislation would drive the Communist party underground, fostering a witch hunt that could be turned against liberals and the Democratic party.[37] Liberal anticommunists defined their opposition to communism in terms of intellectual freedom, and liberals viewed conservative adherence to religion and tradition as a restriction on cultural freedom.[38]

Through her writings and speeches, Schlafly painted a detailed portrait of communism, one that differed sharply from the liberal view. To begin with, she dismissed the idea that communism was caused by poverty. This was a "common fallacy," she declared; actually "the experience of every country under Communist rule proves that it is the reverse which is true: Communism causes poverty."[39] She pointed out that the most vigorously anticommunist countries in Europe were the poorest: Ireland, Spain, and Portugal. "Communism," she wrote, "had its greatest appeal to the financial, educational, and social beneficiaries of capitalism."[40] While it appealed to the idealistic youth and the cynical intellectual, communism as a political movement remained, in her words, an "international criminal conspiracy founded on atheism, materialism, and economic determinism, organized with the dictatorship of the Party as its central feature and dedicated to use any illegal and immoral means toward the achievement of its goals." "We are engaged," she warned, "in a life-and-death struggle with the criminal underground whose leaders confidently expect to destroy our Church, our country, our freedom, the institution of the family, and everything else we hold dear."[41]

This view was widely shared by grassroots anticommunists. "Knowledge and moral strength have always been the guardians of freedom,"

Schwarz advised his audiences. "Without these, military and economic programs will be futile" was a sentiment that was widely shared by grassroots anticommunists over the country.[42] Fearing moral decline, grassroots conservatives emphasized moral education, traditional family values, and the importance of religious expression in public. As such, moral conservatism and political conservatism became integrally linked. E. Merrill Root, a professor at Earlham College in Indiana and author of a number of widely read books about the decline of education in America, warned "We don't have to fear nuclear fallout as much as a moral fall down." Root emphasized, "A conservative is a conservationist of the inner life, of moral virtues, of spiritual and patriotic values."[43]

REDEEMING AMERICA'S YOUTH

Grassroots anticommunist conservatives lamented that Americans had become too materialistic, too self-absorbed, and morally soft. Worse yet, American youth were being affected by a declining moral climate, abetted by an educational system that failed to imbue students with patriotic values or a sense of right or wrong. Instead of being taught values, students were being taught vague, righteous-sounding sentiments without meaning. Fred Schwarz constantly warned his audiences, "We see a breakdown in moral values, debunking of patriotism, and the transformation of students into lovers of mankind, so nothing is worth fighting for."[44] In his mind, undermining traditional values opened the door for communism. Conservative author Taylor Caldwell, in her novel plotted around a communist takeover of America, had one character declare, "The teachers of America, as a class, are very docile, and always eager to serve the most powerful master. You know how their so-called 'liberalism' helped to enslave the people several decades ago."[45]

It was this fear of corrupting American youth and the assumption that education should not be left just to the educators that led many grassroots conservatives such as Phyllis Schlafly to become active in their local school districts."[46] Educational experts, Schlafly claimed, prided themselves on undermining traditional values held by students. The very words *Christian*, *patriotic*, and *nationalism* denoted bigotry to the "liberal"-minded educational establishment. She recalled the words of C. S. Lewis who wrote in *The Screwtape Letters* that modern man has been "accustomed, ever since he was a boy, to having a dozen incompatible philosophies dancing about together inside his head. He doesn't think of doctrines primarily as 'true' or 'false,' but as 'academic' or 'practical,' 'outworn' or 'contemporary,' 'conventional' or 'ruthless.' "[47] In her opinion, this was a direct result of "the John Dewey school of education, which taught that there is no such thing as right or wrong, there are no absolutes, and no standards of achievement." Instead, she continued, the Dewey theory offered "life adjustment" education, meaning that "no matter how decadent the community morals or irreligious its atmosphere, the chief purpose of education is to accommodate the child to the group."[48]

Throughout her speeches on education in the 1950s, she repeated to audiences that the problems with American education were not "poor teachers or inadequate schools"; instead the "two main evils in today's education were bad methods and bad textbooks." Instead of being taught phonics in the first grade—as she had taught her own children—children were "subjected to a lot of boring, unnecessary, and repetitious exercises" in which they were taught to memorize a few dozen words by guessing at them from the pictures on the page. Through this whole-word method, "the poor child is inflicted with endless pages of 'Look up, Look down,' and 'Quack, Quack said the duck.' "[49] The teaching of phonics became a life-long passion of Schlafly, leading her to develop her own reading program for children in 1994. Behind her concern with phonics, however, lay a belief that children absolutely must be literate in order to protect the American republic.

Schlafly shared with other grassroots anticommunists the belief that without proper education, American youth were vulnerable to communist propaganda. When writing about education, Schlafly often mentioned the frequently cited figure that "one out of every three Americans" taken prisoner during the Korean War succumbed to communist brainwashing, probably because of "their confusion concerning American history and our political and economic system." Her figures came from a speech by Major William E. Mayer, the U.S. Army psychiatrist who examined the American POWs of the Korean War. Dr. Fred Schwarz said that tapes of William E. Mayer's speech "have been reproduced and used more often than any other tape recordings of my knowledge and experience."[50]

Other conservatives joined her in blasting what they perceived as the breakdown of American public education. In late 1950, the Daughters of the American Revolution undertook a survey of American history textbooks and found a "very scant number" were satisfactory.[51] This DAR report circulated throughout the 1950s. E. Merrill Root's *Brainwashing in the High Schools* received even wider distribution when Major Edgar C. Bundy made the paperback edition available for $1.00 a copy and $.80 if a hundred or more were ordered. This literature repeated a common theme: schools were miseducating American youth by failing to teach patriotic values or in many cases demeaning patriotism. Schwarz noted that "Schools are making 'capitalism' a cuss-word. An entire generation has been trained to have trigger-reaction emotion against capitalism."[52] Roy R. Friday, writing in the *American Mercury*, chimed in with a heated attack on *Scholastic Magazine* for each week "brainwashing" youngsters into "one-worldism and socialism ideas and ideals."[53] These jeremiads expressed a single concern, expressed succinctly by Schlafly who warned, "The result of a generation's training in relativism is the inability of many leaders to chart a national course which will bring victory over communism."[54]

The issue that divided grassroots conservatives such as Schlafly and liberal educators was the meaning of patriotism. For liberal educators, patriotism meant instilling in students humanistic values of freedom, civic obligation, and social responsibility. Patriotism, they believed, should be imbued with values of universal human rights and social justice. Unthinking loyalty to government held within it the seeds of despotism, liberals argued, so students should learn critical thinking. Grassroots conservatives, on the other hand, believed a proper education should begin with instruction in basic skills, reading, writing, and arithmetic, and lessons in individual responsibility and virtue, and the teaching of the principles and the history that made America "the city on the hill." Her view of patriotism was straightforward. "It is part of the Communist strategy," Schlafly lectured the Daughters of the American Revolution, "to destroy the feeling of pride we have when we see the Stars and Stripes unfurled." But, she declared, there was nothing wrong with being labeled a "flag-waver" in this war against communism. "In order to save our religion, our freedom, and our Constitution, we need the alertness of vigilantes, the fidelity of 100 percent Americans, the spirit of the flag-waver, the fervor of the nationalists, and the courage of our super-patriots."[55]

Saving the Constitution and the Church

Patriotism, religious faith, and anticommunism led Fred and Phyllis Schlafly to become involved with the American Bar Association's Committee on Communist Tactics, Strategy, and Objectives in 1957, which gained national press attention for its criticism of the Earl Warren Supreme Court. Appointed to this commission at the recommendation of Clarence Manion, Fred Schlafly played an important role in writing the committee's 1957 report.[56] Manion and Schlafly shared a consistent political outlook—limited government, American sovereignty, and anticommunism.[57]

Phyllis worked closely with Fred in writing the first drafts of the *American Bar Association's Report on Communist Tactics, Strategy, and Objectives*.[58] Written under the direction of the chairman of the committee, former U.S. Senator Herbert R. O'Conor (D-Maryland), the report was submitted to the ABA House of Delegates at its annual meeting held in London in the summer of 1957. The report caused an immediate sensation by criticizing fifteen Supreme Court decisions of the Warren Court pertaining to communism.[59]

After listing fifteen Warren Court decisions in favor of the communists and adverse to the U.S. government since 1955, the report advised Congress to enact remedial legislation.[60] Public criticism of the Warren Court by the ABA drew immediate press attention, beginning with the publication of the full report in the *New York Herald Tribune* and major excerpts in the *New York Times* and *U.S. News and World Report*. Senator Strom Thurmond (D-South Carolina) placed much of the report in the *Congressional Record*. After the report appeared, Chief Justice Warren cancelled his engagement to deliver a keynote address at the annual ABA convention in London.[61] Many believed that the report led the Warren Court to retreat from its restrictive decisions concerning Congress's authority to investigate and restrict communist activities.[62]

The 1958 ABA *Report on Communist Tactics, Strategy and Objectives* (a slightly expanded version of the 1957 report) became not only one of the most widely read documents ever produced by the ABA, it was probably the single most widely read publication of the grassroots anticommunist movement. It was entered into the *Congressional Record* by Senator Styles Bridges (R-New Hampshire), and then (after his death) reentered by Senator Everett Dirksen (R-Illinois). Anticommunist groups across the country distributed copies to the grassroots by the hundreds of thousands. While people involved in the writing or distributing of the ABA Report did not support the call to impeach Earl Warren, which emerged at this time, the report encouraged those who did by suggesting that the Warren Court was allowing communists to abuse civil liberties.[63]

When Fred and Phyllis Schlafly returned from the ABA meeting in London that summer of 1957, they decided to undertake an even larger project—the establishment of a new anticommunist organization, designed with the single purpose of educating Roman Catholics about the threat of communism. The new organization was to be named after the imprisoned prelate of Hungary, Joseph Cardinal Mindszenty. In May 1958, following five days of speeches at a seminar attended by 130 people in St. Louis, the keynote speaker, Dr. Fred Schwarz, sat down with a small group including Father Stephen Dunker, a former missionary in China, Fred and Phyllis Schlafly, and Fred's sister, Eleanor Schlafly. They had asked to meet with Schwarz, the founder of the Christian Anti-Communism Crusade, to propose a united Protestant-Catholic organization to combat communism. The Schlaflys were convinced that Catholics could provide a major force in such an organization because of the Church's historically strong position against communism. Schwarz did not take long to think about forming such an alliance; his answer was a vehement "No." He told the group that much of his support came from evangelical Protestants, and he believed that a formal alliance with Roman Catholics might "be suspect in certain circles." He urged the group to form their own separate organization. Following his advice, the Cardinal Mindszenty Foundation (CMF) was established in 1958 to serve as a Catholic counterpart to Schwarz's organization.[64]

Inspired by Pope Pius XI's encyclical *Divini Redemptoris* (1937) condemning "Atheistic Communism" and named for Cardinal Mindszenty, a Hungarian cleric imprisoned for years by the communists, the Cardinal Mindszenty Foundation became the focus of much of Schlafly's political activity for the next several years.[65] The Foundation was organized under of the leadership of Fred's younger sister, Eleanor Schlafly, and Father Stephen Dunker, a Vincentian who had had first-hand experience under the communists as a missionary in China. Phyllis Schlafly took on the role of research director, writing the monthly *Mindszenty Reports* until she stepped down in 1964 to devote herself to direct political organizing for the Goldwater campaign.

Although not officially endorsed by the Roman Catholic Church, the foundation's advisory council was composed exclusively of Catholic clerical missionaries who had been imprisoned by communist governments in Asia, Eastern Europe, and Cuba. These priests came from different backgrounds, religious orders, and political beliefs. What united them was their first-hand experience with Communism and their missionary efforts to work with the poor, orphans, and the ill throughout the world.[66] A typical CMF Council member was Fr. Harold W. Rigney, author of *Four Years in a Red Hell* (1956). Arrested in 1951 while he was serving as president of Fu Jen Catholic University in Beijing, Rigney suffered fifty months of torture by the Chinese Communists. His book conveyed a strong spiritual faith that resonated with his Christian readers. When asked what he learned from his terrible ordeal, he wrote, "I did suffer with my Divine Savior. I was granted a deeper insight into the bitter suffering of Our Blessed Lord in His Holy Passion."[67] His message was clear to his readers: if Christ could endure suffering for the salvation of mankind, the faithful must be ready to suffer in combat against the communists.

The Cardinal Mindszenty Foundation operated entirely on donations and volunteer workers. There was no paid staff. Eleanor Schlafly, having worked in New York City for the American Committee for the Liberation of Russian Peoples, a CIA-funded broadcast operation to the Soviet Union, served as CMF's director, a position she still holds forty-seven years later. Phyllis Schlafly wrote the educational materials including the *Mindszenty Report,* a four-page monthly newsletter, and *The Red Line,* a report on what was currently discussed in Communist party publications such as *Political Affairs* and the *Daily Worker.* The Mindszenty programs were developed to educate average Catholics about the tactics and strategies of the communists so they could become vocal anticommunist activists in their local communities.

A typical line from CMF literature read, "If you would like to help yourself and others to recognize what the Holy Father called the 'diabolical' nature of communist propaganda, organize a Cardinal Mindszenty Study Group so you will be informed on summit conferences and other Communist tactics."[68] Initiated in the spring of 1959, the CMF anticommunist study program for small groups, designed by Phyllis

Schlafly, consisted of ten weekly meetings, with each session focusing on a congressional committee document on communism. This emphasis on education—know thy enemy approach—was typical in the grass-roots anticommunist movement. The aim was to train average Americans to recognize communist propaganda and not be fooled by communist rhetoric. Anticommunist activists spent hours in study—much of it extremely academic.[69] Despite the tedium of much of this reading, the technique of organizing small discussion groups proved remarkably successful. By 1962, the Foundation claimed to be sponsoring more than 3,000 study groups in 48 states, every Canadian province, Caribbean countries, and Mexico.

The Mindszenty Foundation also launched a larger and equally successful seminar program that targeted large public assemblies at civic centers and churches. These seminar programs also found their way into college, seminary, and high school courses, as well as classes sponsored by individual parishes and Catholic lay organizations. These seminars ran for from one to four days covering specific subjects such as Marxist dialectics, the theory and history of communism, techniques and tactics of communists, communist propaganda, psychological warfare and agitprop, legislation and court decisions, and Soviet foreign policy. Often these day-long public seminars utilized stars of the movement such as Madame Chiang Kai-Shek, author Herbert Philbrick, former counsel to the Senate Internal Security Committee Robert Morris, former Douglas MacArthur aide General Charles Willoughby, and John Noble, author of *I Was a Slave in Russia*.

Through these seminars the Mindszenty Foundation sought to activate the average American to join in the battle against communism. As Schlafly declared in one of her speeches, "Communism can only be stopped by the individual actions of little people." She reprimanded people who excused their failure to act by saying, "if only I was a President, a King, a General, or the head of some large organization!" Instead, she invited people to become "a Freedom Fighter in your own sphere of influence. You, too, can do big things if you have faith and dedication."[70] Attendance at these seminars varied from fewer than a hundred to thousands of participants. Total attendance at a Houston seminar in late 1960 totaled over 10,000, with the final session drawing 4,000 people. Over 20,000 pieces of free literature were distributed, 1,600 books and pamphlets were sold, and the seminar was broadcast over the radio. The following spring in Milwaukee, a Mindszenty seminar co-sponsored by the American Legion and the Catholic War Veterans attracted over 10,000 participants.[71]

By the time John F. Kennedy became President, the Mindszenty Foundation was reaching tens of thousands of Americans through its educational programs. In 1961 the Mindszenty Foundation began sponsoring a 15-minute syndicated radio program called "Dangers of Apathy," featuring Phyllis Schlafly interviewing leading conservative speakers. It ran in twenty cities coast to coast (and was still running in 2005, although Schlafly was no longer associated with it). At the same time, publications went to colleges and universities, seminaries, and high schools, including such titles as "Inside the Communist Conspiracy," "Teach about Communism in Catholic Schools," and "Handbook to Combat Communism." In 1961 alone the Foundation distributed over 125,000 copies of the American Bar Association's report, *Communist Tactics, Strategy, and Objectives.* The *Mindszenty Report* reached a circulation of nearly ten thousand at its height, providing Phyllis Schlafly an opportunity to share her views on a variety of subjects. These publications tapped into a deep religiosity that brought thousands of Roman Catholics into the anticommunist cause.[72] Since it was not endorsed by the Church, the Mindszenty Foundation carefully cultivated relations with sympathetic bishops, inviting them to speak or to offer opening prayers at the start of their programs.[73] Mindszenty Foundation programs often highlighted speakers who were not Catholics. In addition to Dr. Fred Schwarz, an evangelical Protestant, Herbert Philbrick, a devout Baptist, often spoke at Mindszenty events. Such inclusion enabled Foundation activities to draw large audiences, while it integrated the Schlaflys into a larger, although loosely defined, network of grassroots anti-communist leaders.

Eisenhower Confronts Grassroots Anticommunism

The growth of a grassroots anticommunist movement in the 1950s constrained the Eisenhower administration in improving relations with the Soviet Union. Any move toward better relations with the Soviet Union by the administration—whether it be a proposal for trade with Yugoslavia, foreign loans to Poland, cultural exchanges with Hungary, or an arms control agreement—might and often did spark massive protest against appeasement of communists.

While Eisenhower, especially in his second term, sought to improve U.S. relations with the Soviet Union, he faced a wing of his party that was haunted by the continuing advance of communism—its physical advancement in Eastern Europe and Asia and its ideological advancement in democratic countries. "The plain facts are," Schlafly said, "that Communism is advancing over the surface of the globe with such rapidity that if it continues at the same rate for the next 13 years that it has been advancing during the past 13 years, America will be Communist by 1970."[74] Movies and filmstrips shown by the Mindszenty Foundation at its seminars—"Communism on the Map," "Communist Encirclement of America," "Red Nightmare," and "Red Map"—captured this foreboding that the communists were winning.

The fear among grassroots conservatives that the communists might win the Cold War came from at least two sources: a belief that the United States was growing morally weak and that government leaders would be misled by Soviet offers of peace. The anticommunist Right feared that the American people had become so intoxicated by a hedonistic materialism that they had grown morally soft. Contrary to Marx's dictum, religion was not "the opiate of the masses," consumerism was. The second source of American weakness followed from the first. Because Americans had lost their moral bearings, communism took advantage of this disorientation through disinformation campaigns that promoted peace on communist terms, nuclear disarmament, peaceful coexistence, cultural exchanges, and East-West trade. Such disingenuous slogans were designed to appeal to soft-minded liberals and to deceive the uninformed.[75]

Schlafly's views reflected those of most grassroots anticommunists, for whom there was one basic truth: The Soviet Union could not be trusted. Its history was a record of broken treaties, betrayal, and subversion. After all, this had been the experience of Eastern and Central European countries that had fallen to communism, and this had been the American experience in negotiating with Stalin at Yalta at the end of World War II and with the communists in Korea. Such beliefs were reinforced by authors such as Admiral C. Turner Joy, a member of the American negotiating delegation during the Korean War, who declared in *How Communists Negotiate* (1955) that "The measure of expansion achieved by Communism through negotiations is impossible to disassociate from what they have achieved by force, for the Communists never completely separate the two methods."[76]

Behind this lack of confidence in U.S. negotiating skills lay a belief that top echelons of the State Department, having been recruited out of the Eastern establishment, were internationalists more interested in creating structures for international cooperation, if not world governance, than they were with protecting the sovereignty of the American nation. An early indication of problems Eisenhower faced with the GOP Right came in the fight over the Bricker Amendment in 1954. Introduced in the Senate by John W. Bricker (R-Ohio), who had run for vice-president with Dewey in 1944, and co-sponsored by sixty-two other senators from both parties, this constitutional amendment declared that any part of an international treaty that conflicted with the U.S. Constitution would be invalid and that congressional legislation would be needed to validate any treaty affecting U.S. law. The Bricker Amendment gained widespread, popular support. Conservatives rallied to support the amendment through organizations such as Vigilant Women for the Bricker Amendment, led by Winifred Barker in Chicago and Ruth Murray in Oshkosh, Wisconsin. This group mobilized women across the country to gather a half-million signatures in support of the amendment. The American Bar Association and the American Medical Association both endorsed the amendment.[77]

One of the Vigilant Women for the Bricker Amendment was Phyllis Schlafly. The Vigilant Women for the Bricker Amendment found its way into churches, American Legion women's auxiliaries, conservative organizations such as the Committee for Constitutional Government, and ad hoc committees. Her first lobbing trip to Congress was with a contingent of Vigilant Women working for the Bricker amendment.[78] Her articulate support of the Bricker amendment drew speaking invitations, where she warned that the amendment was necessary to prevent "the United Nations from infecting our free American system with world government and international socialism by the devious device of treaty law." She warned that the "international socialists" were seeking treaties that would undermine individual freedom, trial by jury, and private property.[79] Such rhetoric was commonplace in conservative Republican circles.

Eisenhower, acting on the advice of his Secretary of State, John Foster Dulles, opposed the Bricker amendment, even though most of his cabinet supported it.[80] Dulles in a memorandum to the president warned that if this proposed amendment passed the Senate, "it would be taken by our friends, and by our enemies, as foreshadowing a revolutionary change in the position of the United States."[81] Eisenhower prevailed, but barely; the modified version of the amendment fell a single vote short of the two-thirds necessary for Senate passage of a constitutional amendment.

The defeat of the Bricker Amendment embittered its supporters, many of whom were convinced that United States had placed itself on the losing side of an historic battle. The general counsel of Humble Oil wrote Clarence Manion, "The public simply does not know what had been going on and by what a slender thread a sword is hanging over our heads."[82] For some conservatives, the defeat of the Bricker Amendment showed that Eisenhower and the GOP could not be trusted. One long-time conservative activist bluntly told Manion, "It seems to me that the leftwing element in both political parties, including various socialists, liberals, and New Dealers and Fair Dealers of every stripe, are making steady gains. . . . The country is sliding slowly into International Socialism. Those responsible for it include many capable businessmen who somehow have been sold on internationalism."[83] For many conservatives, the struggle over the Bricker Amendment was one of those defining moments in the history of the struggle against internationalism and big government. Even in the late 1970s John Bricker continued to insist that if his amendment had been ratified, the United States would not have become involved in wars in Korea or Vietnam.[84]

The Bricker Amendment was only the first in a series of battles Eisenhower faced against the right wing of his party. Although the Republican Right hesitated to criticize Eisenhower publicly, the brutal suppression of the Hungarian Revolution by Soviet tanks in 1956 angered many conservatives who felt that the United States should have aided Hungarian freedom fighters. The Soviet invasion to suppress the Hungarian uprising occurred after the February 1956 Twentieth Party Congress in the Soviet Union in which Nikita Khrushchev in a six-hour speech denounced the Stalin personality cult and enumerated its horrors to loyal Communist party members.[85] The military suppression of the Hungarian uprising led to approximately 2,900 deaths, the destruction of 4,000 buildings, and largescale deportation of dissident Hungarians to the Soviet Union. American conservatives were haunted by cries from the freedom fighters pleading for Western assistance.[86] Grassroots anticommunists did not expect America to go to war to save the freedom fighters, but they believed that if Eisenhower had immediately granted diplomatic recognition to the new free government of

Hungary, Khrushchev would not have dared to roll his tanks into Budapest. The attitude of the GOP Right was captured in the title of an unsigned editorial written by Phyllis Schlafly that appeared in a national conservative Catholic newspaper, "Right or Wrong: Our Share in Hungary's Tragedy."[87]

The suppression of the Hungarian revolt was further proof for the GOP Right that the Soviet Union was evil and that the U.S. State Department could not be trusted. Eisenhower continued to face pressure from the right wing of his party over his overtures to improve relations with the Soviet Union. Conservatives protested Eisenhower's invitation to Nikita Khrushchev to visit the United States in 1959. Letters, telegrams, and petitions flooded into Congress opposing the visit, while conservative periodicals lashed out against the visit of Stalin's former lieutenant, the man who had starved and arrested millions in the Ukraine and the man who had sent troops into Budapest. Schlafly reported in 1959 that DAR members in Illinois wrote over 290 letters to Congress against Khrushchev's proposed visit to the United States.[88] Schlafly used Khrushchev's visit to denounce cultural exchanges by directing readers to the recent Senate testimony of Peter Deriabin, a former high Soviet intelligence officer, who told how Red agents invariably headed religious, trade, and scientific delegations.[89]

Similarly, grassroots conservatives denounced the proposed Eisenhower-Khrushchev summit meeting in 1959. Schlafly reported that through her efforts over 200 letters and petitions from the Illinois Federation of Republican Women had been sent to the White House opposing the summit. These efforts were joined by DAR chapters, Republican women's clubs, and ad hoc antisummit groups. Behind this opposition lay a deep fear among grassroots anticommunists that American officials especially in the State Department might be fooled into nuclear disarmament with the Soviet Union. Given conservatives' distrust of the State Department, such fears were inevitable. Conservatives' fears had been heightened when Eisenhower imposed a unilateral ban on atmospheric nuclear bomb testing in 1958.[90] While not attacking Eisenhower directly, most hardcore anticommunists agreed with Phyllis Schlafly who wrote in the *Mindszenty Report* that the ban on atomic testing was a "victory for appeasement-minded politicians and pacifists over our military advisors who urged resumption of tests for our national survival. . . . An agreement with the Russians will not stop Red aggression any more than disarming our local police will stop murder, theft, and rape."[91] As negotiations between the United States and the Soviet Union continued in Geneva, Schlafly continued her attacks on U.S. foreign policy, carefully not blaming Eisenhower personally. She declared, "It was not an armament race, but a disarmament race, which caused World War II."[92]

Phyllis Schlafly's warnings about the growing Soviet military threat were typical of the views of thousands of Americans on the Right. The continued growth of grassroots anticommunism, even after the Senate censure of Joseph McCarthy, worried liberals. This heated rhetoric and activism of the Right, liberals believed, threatened to undermine progress with the Soviet Union in lessening Cold War tensions. Most upsetting for them was what appeared to be the eager acceptance by many average Americans of hard-line anticommunist warnings and criticisms of the United Nations, world government, and international socialism.[93] Grassroots conservatives, on the other hand, were just as worried about the need to protect individual liberty from the all-powerful pagan state and the subversion of the American Republic from communism's deceit. These two perspectives of the world—liberal and conservative—were not reconcilable and clashed in a world threatened by nuclear war.

CHAPTER FOUR

The Republican Right Under Attack

IN 1962, PHYLLIS SCHLAFLY lashed back at an attack on the Cardinal Mindszenty Foundation by the Reverend John F. Cronin, Assistant Director of Social Action at the National Catholic Welfare Conference, whose recently published booklet, "The Communist Threat in America," accused most anticommunist organizations of being "financial rackets" that should have desisted their activities once the domestic communist threat had been thwarted in the Truman administration. Cronin's pamphlet revealed an important shift both in Catholic circles and American public opinion away from the intense anticommunism of the previous decade. In the late 1940s, Cronin had made a national reputation as an anticommunist crusader, having organized workers against communists in the Baltimore shipyards and served as adviser to the Catholic hierarchy, Senators Joseph McCarthy, and Richard Nixon on the communism issue.

Cronin's apparent reversal came in a general climate in which the grassroots anticommunist Right was coming under attack as extremist. Magazine articles, academic books, and state and federal government reports disclaimed what was called the "Extremist Right." Ironically, these attacks on the Far Right came at the moment when the grassroots anticommunist Right was about to nominate a conservative, U.S. Senator Barry Goldwater, to head the GOP ticket in 1964. On the verge of success, the grassroots anticommunist Right was left reeling as the label "anticommunist activist" became pejorative. Under attack on the communist issue, grassroots conservatives turned to national defense and the military threat posed by the Soviet Union, while also criticizing the over-extension of federal powers at the expense of the states, and the erosion of individual liberty and traditional values. The shift was subtle, but important for the future development of the GOP Right.

The growth of grassroots anticommunism in the 1950s and its heated rhetoric against the Soviet Union and communist infiltration and influence in government genuinely alarmed liberal Democrats, who convinced themselves that rightwing activists were reminiscent of pre–World War II fascist movements where charismatic demagogues of small extremist parties were able to gain mass followings by playing on the worst fears of the people.[1] By the late 1950s, liberals had become convinced that grassroots anticommunist organizations and their leaders needed to be unmasked as "extremists" lest they gain too much political power. Articles and books began to appear denouncing the extremism of the anticommunist Right. These the attacks on the grassroots anticommunist Right took a toll and put the political Right on the defensive. This became evident to Phyllis Schlafly in the early 1960s, when orders stopped coming from study groups and activists clubs for her *Reading List for Americans.* "Suddenly, one day," she recalled, "the orders stopped. It was if a curtain had descended on grassroots anticommunism."[2] Other anticommunists experienced a similar decline in public interest.[3]

CHANGING PERCEPTIONS ABOUT THE COMMUNIST THREAT

By the early 1960s the general American public had modified its views on domestic communism and the Soviet Union. Domestic communism no longer seemed a significant threat, but the threat of a nuclear attack remained, suggesting that improving relations with the Soviet Union, which had emerged as a nuclear superpower, should be given a high priority.

In 1947, the Communist party membership stood at above 60,000 members, but by 1960 it was barely over 3,000. Not only was the Communist party's membership small, it had been demoralized by Khrushchev's secret speech denouncing Stalinism, as well as by Western reaction to the Hungarian revolution in 1956. The domestic communist problem in 1960 was very different from what it had been in 1947–48, and the American public knew it.[4] Furthermore, after a decade of the Cold War, American attitudes toward the Soviet nuclear threat began to soften, as captured in the slogan, "Better Red than Dead." By the early 1960s, polls revealed that the majority of Americans supported a policy of improving relations with the Soviet Union, although they continued to support a strong national defense and military intervention against communist insurrection when necessary.

A series of books and movies captured these popular fears of nuclear holocaust. Rightwingers saw these books and movies as "creating the climate" (to use Phyllis Schlafly's phrase) to support a campaign to disarm America. A few conservatives went so far as to believe that this campaign for arms control was being coordinated by the Soviet Union, but most conservative activists saw these books and films as manifestations of a naive mindset that unconsciously played into the hands of extreme liberal ban-the-bomb types found in the National Committee for a Sane Nuclear Policy (SANE). These liberals included Freudian psychiatrist Erich Fromm, child psychologist Benjamin Spock, Nobel-prize winner Linus Pauling, English philosopher Bertrand Russell, and historian H. Stuart Hughes. Conservatives such as Schlafly argued that these liberals had been taken in politically by an act of faith that war could be prevented through arms reduction.

Schlafly pointed to a series of books and movies that had first appeared in the late 1950s warning of nuclear war. One of the first novels that came under criticism from Schlafly, as well as other conservatives, was Nevil Shute's *On the Beach* (1957), a frightening fictional account of the last days on earth as a radioactive cloud produced by a nuclear exchange descends on a community. Schlafly was unsparing of the movie that followed, denouncing it as "morally and scientifically false." She said that after the production of this movie Americans are asking if "Hollywood is ripe for another period of Red penetration." Later, when the movie was shown on television in 1962, she called it a "prime vehicle" of the Communist propaganda which persuaded the U.S. unilaterally to stop the testing of nuclear weapons, and which will be used on TV to spread the " 'rather red than dead' psychology." She warned that television had become a "battleground of the Cold War."[5] (Unbeknownst to the American Right was the fact that Shute was so vociferously antisocialist and anticollectivist that he left his native England to emigrate to Australia.)[6] America conservatives had good reason, however, for distrusting *Two Hours to Doom* (1958) by British novelist and nuclear disarmament activist Peter Bryant. This novel created a picture of nuclear doom caused by a renegade air force general. Later, film director Stanley Kubrick translated this novel into the dark comedy *Dr. Strangelove: Or How I Learned to Stop Worrying and Love the Bomb* (1964).

Other books also warned of accidental nuclear war. Fletcher Knebel's *Seven Days in May* (1962) kept readers spellbound with a plot centered around an attempted military coup d'état led by the Chairman of the Joint Chiefs of Staff, Air Force General James Mattoon Scott, who is fearful of an impending arms treaty with the Soviet Union. Scott (played by Burt Lancaster) was modeled on the blunt speaking Air

Force General Curtis LeMay, and the movie's depiction in 1964 of a U.S. Senator from California who joins the conspiracy reminded viewers of U.S. Senator William Knowland (R-California). After a kidnapping, murder, and the discovery of a secret military base set up by the conspirators, the story climaxes when the President skillfully defeats the plotters. At the movie's conclusion, the President addresses the American people with these ringing words, "Our country is strong—strong enough to be a peacemaker." In 1962, *Fail-Safe* introduced readers to an even more frightening scenario in which the President of the United States is forced to order a nuclear bomb dropped on New York after a computer error had led to bombing Moscow.[7] The audiences who saw the movie *Fail-Safe* (1964) could not help but be shaken. A public debate broke out in the newspapers and magazines as to whether *Fail-Safe* could in fact occur.[8] These antinuclear books and movies contributed to the growing feeling among the American public that the world would be better off with improved relations with the Soviet Union.[9] For Schlafly these books and films served a Soviet propaganda effort to "brainwash" the American people into accepting arms control with the Soviet Union, a regime that could not be trusted to live up to any peace treaty. Whether we have arms control or not, she wrote, "will not stop Red aggression any more than disarming our local police will stop murder, theft, and rape."[10] Grassroots conservatives believed that it was not any accident that the national attack on anticommunists and what they perceived as the widespread propaganda to promote better relations with the Soviet Union coincided with the election of President John F. Kennedy in 1961.

JOHN F. KENNEDY AND THE AMERICAN RIGHT

Kennedy's campaign captured a feeling of a large segment of the electorate that America was entering a period of dramatic change.[11] Few realized that these changes would be as tumultuous as they were. Although his ambitious liberal domestic program became stalled in Congress, Kennedy offered the nation a new vision of its future. Despite his projection of energy and youth, John F. Kennedy stood between two worlds—the older world of defined social parameters and an age of new racial and sexual identity, expanded rights, and an unsettled egalitarianism.[12] Kennedy's public pronouncements on communism reflected the ambiguities of a world in transition as Kennedy looked to improve relations with the Soviet Union, while facing an aggressive Nikita Khrushchev. During the 1960 campaign, Kennedy declared to an audience in Salt Lake City, "The enemy is the Communist system itself—implacable, insatiable, increasing in its drive for world domination. . . . This is not a struggle for supremacy of arms alone. It is a struggle for supremacy between two conflicting ideologies: freedom under God versus ruthless, godless tyranny."[13]

Grassroots conservatives distrusted Kennedy's resolve from the outset of his administration. Within days after the election, Phyllis Schlafly issued a press release warning that Kennedy should be prepared for the building of a Red missile base in Cuba. "Our goal," she declared, "must be victory—not containment, coexistence, disengagement, or stalemate."[14] Schlafly's warning reflected a growing anxiety among conservatives that the new administration intended to pursue a policy of accommodation with the Soviet Union. In their view, the Eisenhower administration had already laid the foundation for this policy by agreeing to summit meetings with Khrushchev, cultural exchanges with the Soviet Union, and, unforgivably, the unilateral stopping of nuclear weapons testing in 1958. Schlafly and other conservatives warned that any permanent test-ban treaty would be impossible to monitor because the Soviet Union has a vast, isolated land mass to test nuclear weapons and because instrument test detection was virtually impossible.

Schlafly joined other grassroots conservatives in their certainty that peaceful coexistence, cultural exchanges, and trade agreements played into the hands of Kremlin leaders, who had never relinquished Lenin's missionary zeal to bring communism to the world. While liberals tended to see Soviet premier Nikita Khrushchev as a symbol of de-Stalinization in the Soviet Union and a leader who might thaw U.S.-Soviet relations, conservatives denounced Khrushchev as a hard-liner who had threatened to "bury" the United States. Conservatives such as Schlafly were unwilling to forget that Khrushchev had been Stalin's viceroy who directed massive repression in the Ukraine and Byelorussia between 1939 and 1941. In this two-year period, 1.25 million people, or nearly 10 percent of the total population, were deported, and approximately a half million people were imprisoned. Some 50,000 people were executed or tortured in prison, while 300,000 died in exile. The boss in charge of this brutality was Nikita Khrushchev, personally picked by Stalin to Sovietize the Ukraine.[15] Schlafly and other conservatives refused to see Khrushchev as anything other than a representative of a brutal and imperialistic one-party state. The Republican Right, in short, believed that Soviet communism was intrinsically incapable of substantive change. Liberals, as well as political moderates in the Republican party, while wary of Soviet intentions, held that the post-Stalin regime under Khrushchev opened the way for better relations between the two countries. Conservatives rejected the possibility of détente, while liberals welcomed it. In the early 1960s, given the closed nature of the Soviet Union it was difficult to discern which view was correct.[16]

Schlafly gave voice to conservative fears that Khrushchev's peace initiative was intended to distract the West from Khrushchev's continued commitment to the Bolshevik mission of world domination. Through her radio program, America Wake Up, and her speeches to Republican groups in Illinois, Phyllis Schlafly pressed the theme that the Soviets had undertaken a clever campaign to convince the world that they wanted peace and nuclear disarmament. "Today," she told her listeners, "under the slogans of 'peace' and 'peaceful coexistence,' we are witnessing . . . this Communist peace offensive." Yet, what did they mean by "peace"? she asked. For her it meant that "they [the Soviets] will take a peaceful gun, containing a peaceful bullet, and kill you peacefully and put you in a peaceful grave." For Schlafly and other conservatives, events in Hungary and Cuba belied all sweet talk of peace. "When the Russian tanks rolled into Budapest to butcher and destroy, it was a glorious peace," she declared.[17]

The establishment in 1959 of a communist government in Cuba led by Fidel Castro—a revolutionary who never hid his intense hatred of America—was unforgivable in the eyes of conservatives. A Soviet-aligned, communist government only ninety miles off Florida's coast brought out the worst fears of the anticommunist Right, who saw yet another step being taken in communism's quest for world domination. Conservatives had warned as early as 1959 that the Soviet Union would establish missile bases in Cuba, and Schlafly, who shared this fear, believed that Castro's next target would be Panama.[18] Indeed, Schlafly and other conservatives believed that Castro was a communist long before he announced in August 1960 that Cuba was entering into a "new stage" of revolution, explaining that the revolutionary movement was to be led by "new communists."[19]

The announcement by Castro that the revolution in Cuba was communist came as no surprise to conservatives. Headlines in conservative newspapers and magazines said it all: "Castro: In the Image of

Lenin-Marx," "Cuba—Reds' New Colony," "Publisher Says Castro Is Out and Out Red," and "Cuba Air Force Chief Describes Castro, Brother, and Others as Communists."[20] In a book often recommended by Schlafly in her speeches and writings, Nathaniel Weyl, a former Communist turned anticommunist, maintained in his widely-read *Red Star over Cuba* (1960) that "as early as 1949, Fidel Castro was not merely an implacable enemy of the United States, but a trusted Soviet agent." It was public knowledge that Castro's brother Raul had been a member of the Communist party since 1953. Others such as Thomas Freeman in *The Crisis in Cuba* maintained that Castro, because of his intense anti-Americanism, had aligned himself with the Soviet Union and had undermined his own independence.[21] Moreover, conservatives were certain that the U.S. State Department had helped Castro to come to power by refusing to denounce him beforehand. They pointed to the favorable treatment that Castro received from *New York Times* reporter Herbert Matthews in a series of interviews with the guerrilla leader, as well as the "almost universal adulation" (to quote Phyllis Schlafly) he received from Edward R. Murrow and Ed Sullivan. William Buckley, Jr. was so irate that he accused Matthews of having done more "than any other single man to bring Fidel Castro to power. . . . [Matthews] is a man whose loyalty to his misjudgments renders him a stubborn propagandist and an easy mark for ideologues on-the-make."[22] In an attempt to counter State Department subversion, conservatives sought to rally the American people against the Castro regime by organizing grassroots groups such as such the Committee to Defend Cuba and the Committee for the Monroe Doctrine.[23]

The failure of the CIA-backed landing of the anti-Castro Cuban exiles at the Bay of Pigs in Spring 1961 led Schlafly and other critics to further denounce President Kennedy as a weak-kneed leader.[24] Following the failed Bay of Pigs invasion, Schlafly and other conservatives watched in horror as Castro consolidated his power in Cuba. The invasion provided him an excuse for the mass arrests of thirty-thousand persons suspected of antirevolutionary sentiments, including Havana's Roman Catholic auxiliary bishop.[25] Then, shortly following the failed Bay of Pigs invasion, U.S.-Soviet tensions deteriorated further when Khrushchev demanded that the long-standing problem of a divided Berlin be resolved by the end of the year and, to show he meant business, he announced that he was increasing his armed forces by one-third. In July 1961, Khrushchev further raised the ante in this diplomatic showdown by declaring, "If you want to threaten us from a position of strength, we will show you our strength. You do not have 50- and 100-megaton bombs. We have stronger than 100-megaton bombs." He made his point by resuming atmospheric nuclear testing, exploding a 30-megaton bomb followed by a 50-megaton bomb at the Soviet nuclear testing site.[26]

The immediate Berlin crisis tapered off in the fall of 1961, but within a year the world was brought to the brink of war in a showdown in October 1962 between Kennedy and Khrushchev over the installation of Soviet missiles in Cuba. When the crisis was over, Kennedy stood triumphant, privately crowing at his victory. Conservatives were less indulgent, however. For them, Khrushchev had come out ahead. Schlafly declared in her radio broadcast following the crisis that "Cuba is now the headquarters of the Communist conspiracy in the Western hemisphere. . . . Our policy should be to liberate Cuba."[27] Schlafly accused Kennedy of having capitulated, in effect, by removing the Jupiter missile bases in Turkey in exchange for the Soviets' offer to remove missiles in Cuba. The Kennedy administration claimed that Jupiter missiles were obsolete, an assertion denied by Schlafly and other conservative hardliners. Writing in 1964, Schlafly summarized the GOP Right's view of the events when she declared that "the Kennedy administration presented the Cuban crisis to the American people as a great victory and as evidence that we made Khrushchev back down!—whereas the truth is that the deal was a defeat for the United States, binding us to give up our bases in Turkey and Italy, guarantee Castro against any invasion, and accept Khrushchev's word on how many missiles he withdrew."[28] Witnessing the events in Cuba, as well as the growing American involvement in Vietnam, Schlafly and others on the GOP Right were convinced that the United States had been placed on the defensive and that, at the current rate of advancement, the Soviet Union would soon be the world's number-one superpower. Dr. Fred Schwarz predicted that by 1973 the Soviet Union would dominate the world, with the United States becoming a third-rate power.[29]

Kennedy Launches a Counterattack against the Right

Liberalism was ascendant in the 1960s, but its rise was paralleled by a growing conservative movement that was beginning to take a distinct, although not uniform, shape. Indeed, there is some irony in that the formation of a conservative movement occurred precisely at a time when national politics swung to the left with the election of John F. Kennedy. The decade of the 1960s was characterized by campus upheaval and student protest, but the first signs of ferment on campus came from the Right, not the Left, when Young Americans for Freedom (YAF) formed chapters across the country. YAF was a conservative youth group organized under the direction of William F. Buckley, Jr. and William Rusher.[30] Inspired by books such as Hayek's *Road to Serfdom*, Ayn Rand's *Atlas Shrugged*, and William F. Buckley's magazine, *National Review*, YAFers, as they were called, were not old mossback conservatives, but rebels against the Liberal Establishment.[31] This ferment became so noticeable that *Life* magazine devoted a feature story to the new rebels on campus, and the twenty-seven-year-old editor of the *Indianapolis News*, M. Stanton Evans, produced a book called *Revolt on the Campus*—an ironic title, given leftist student strikes and riots later in the decade.[32]

While Young Americans for Freedom was considered a mainstream organization, essentially a youth branch for conservative Republicans, the John Birch Society (JBS) was seen as a different kind of organization by its friends and opponents on the Right and the Left. Organized by Massachusetts candy-manufacturer Robert Welch in 1958, the JBS brought a militant anticommunist message that attracted tens of thousands of businessmen and grassroots conservatives who believed that the communist threat—through influence and infiltration at home and Soviet imperialism aboard—was immediate and advancing. If one group could be singled out as representative of what the left called the "Far Right," it was the JBS. Like no other group, the JBS embodied the pessimism and passion of anticommunist fervor: Although the Soviet Union appeared to be winning, members of the Society pronounced that its members would battle on until the last American patriot had died with a sword in hand. Named after an American soldier killed by Chinese communists during the Second World War—"the first death of the Cold War"—the JBS brought intensity to the anticommunist movement not seen since the first days of the Cold War, and perhaps not even then. JBS founder Welch viewed every aspect of American foreign policy through the lens of anticommunism, declaring, "A patient gradualism has been key to the Communists' overwhelming success" in the Soviet Union's march toward world control.[33] The JBS resonated with many grassroots conservatives including Fred and Phyllis Schlafly when it emerged as the first viable national anticommunist organization with a national membership and chapters throughout the country.[34] Although the membership of the JBS never reached the 100,000 feared by its critics, it exerted considerable influence on grassroots conservatism.

Because of Welch's charge that Eisenhower was a communist agent (an accusation Welch himself later publicly retracted), many conservatives kept their distance from the JBS lest they be painted with the extremist label.[35] As conservative Clare Boothe Luce told William F. Buckley, Jr., "Birchers refuse to believe that sheer stupidity and ignorance of history have an enormous amount to do with our foreign policy, and that the increasing secularization of a pluralistic society naturally favors the Left."[36] Phyllis and Fred Schlafly never denounced the Society. They agreed with the urgency of the communist threat, although they had a fundamental disagreement about the source of the threat. By the early 1960s, Schlafly saw the primary threat not as internal subversion, but as the growing Soviet nuclear arsenal. Welch believed that the Soviet Union was too economically backward to pose a military threat to the United States, and that the communist strategy was to take over countries through internal subversion. It came as a considerable annoyance to Schlafly when she was attacked in JBS publications for her views on the Soviet missile threat. Nevertheless, the Schlaflys did not criticize Welch or his organization because of their respect and friendship for many JBS members, such as Clarence Manion. Fred Schlafly declined Robert Welch's personal invitation to become a member of the JBS Council. Because the Schlaflys did not join in the objurgation of the John Birch Society, both Schlaflys were accused of being members—a charge in Phyllis Schlafly's case that would haunt her for years after Robert Welch (who boasted that he always kept his membership confidential), declared that she was "one of our most loyal members."[37] Phyllis Schlafly arguably encouraged such accusations through her unwillingness to criticize Robert Welch and the John Birch Society.

In 1962, William F. Buckley, Jr., editor of the *National Review*, leveled his first public criticism of Welch by describing the leader of the John Birch Society as a "likeable, honest, courageous, energetic man" who nevertheless, "by silliness and injustice of utterance" has become "the kiss of death" for any conservative organization. In 1963, Buckley excommunicated Welch and the JBS from the conservative movement by declaring that "in joining the Society some members may indeed have partaken of the fantasies of Mr. Welch, but the overwhelming majority no more believe that Eisenhower is a Communist than they believe Mr. Welch is a Communist." He was joined in his condemnation of Welch and his organization by Walter Judd, Fulton Lewis, Jr., Fred Schwarz, and Frank E. Holman.[38]

While liberals hurled charges of racism against the grassroots Right and the John Birch Society, race was not prominent in the thinking of most northern conservative anticommunists in this period. A substantial body of material about race did appear in the late 1950s and 1960s in the South, coinciding with the struggle for black civil rights.[39] Welch realized that he had become an easy target for leftist critics who were anxious to tar every conservative with ugly epithets. He warned that the primary goal of the communists was to create dissension in the United States, especially racial and ethnic tensions. "The Communists," he declared, "use race hatred to stir up trouble among good Americans. These people are not Jews but Communist troublemakers."[40]

Liberals watching the rise of groups such as the John Birch Society, as well as more militant groups, such as Robert DePugh's armed militia group the Minutemen, said they feared for the state of democracy in America, although they were probably more afraid of the political activism that could defeat liberal candidates for public office. To guard against this, some liberals tried to associate the Right with the political irrationality that swept Germany and Europe into the fascist maelstrom of the 1930s.[41] Fred J. Cook warned in his thirty-page jeremiad in *The Nation*, "The Ultras," that the "portrait of the Radical Right" is not the "face of fascism as we have known it in Europe. But unmistakably it is a face bearing the marks of a sickness that could develop into fascism."[42] Negative labels such as the "Extremist Right," the "Far Right," and the "Radical Right" entered the political vocabulary. Writing in the *New York Times Magazine*, liberal academic Alan Barth noted that "one of the common denominators characterizing the Right-Wing groups is a deep distrust of democratic institutions and of the democratic process—a distrust, in short, of the people."[43] Frightened about the insurgence of what they saw as a populist antidemocratic movement, academics and popular authors tended to lump all groups on the Right together.[44] For example, authors Arnold Forster and Benjamin R. Epstein, in their widely read *Danger on the Right* (Random House, 1964), placed William F. Buckley, Jr. with segregationists, paramilitary anticommunists, and conspiracists who "tear at the fine fabric of this democratic Republic by their fevered fancies and false counsels of fear, hatred, confusion, and suspicion."[45] Forster and Epstein called this a witch's brew whose very vapors threatened democracy.[46]

The Kennedy administration did not believe a fascist takeover was imminent, but as rightwing attacks became shriller, fears arose that a populist backlash against U.S. foreign policy would prevent any chance to improve relations with the Soviet Union.[47] Especially worrisome to administration officials was a belief that the U.S. Armed Forces were being politicized by rightwing anticommunist propaganda. Specifically, they feared that some conservative military officers had joined with civilian anticommunist organizations such as the John Birch Society to indoctrinate American troops with hard Right political propaganda.[48] In March, 1961, Roswell L. Gilpatric, Deputy Secretary of Defense, issued a memorandum to the Secretaries of the Army, Navy, and Air Force declaring that the Defense Department had established a new office for "evaluating materials designed for indoctrination of personnel." In addition, the memorandum ordered that the popular anticommunist film *Operation Abolition* was not to be used by the military. Shortly afterward an order was issued by the Defense Department that the filmstrip *Communism on the Map* was not to be purchased by military training personnel.[49] (These films were popular among grassroots anticommunists, and the Schlaflys entertained friends in their home with after-dinner showings.) The issue heated up when the *New York Times* carried a front page story headlined, "Right-Wing Officers Worrying Pentagon" that reported on a "score" of military-sponsored anticommunist programs and "extremist" oriented seminars.[50]

Contained in the article was a report that Major General Edwin A. Walker, commander of the Twenty-Fourth Infantry Division in Germany, had been officially "admonished" for conducting a troop education program in which he had extolled the John Birch Society and criticized Harry S. Truman, Eleanor Roosevelt, and Dean Acheson as "definitely pink."[51] In June 1961, a Kennedy-ordered investigation by the Army concluded that General Walker's anticommunist education program was "not attributable to any program of the John Birch Society," but that the general had been "injudicious" in "making derogatory public statements about prominent Americans." Walker resigned his commission, protesting that he "must be free from the power of little men" who had questioned his loyalty to his country.

With Walker's resignation, the Right began to claim that a program of what they called "Muzzling the Military" had been initiated by the

Kennedy administration. The Right's worst suspicions were confirmed when it was discovered that Senator William Fulbright (D-Arkansas), at the urging of Secretary of Defense Robert McNamara, had sent a long memorandum to President Kennedy condemning "radical extremism" in the military's educational programs. The Fulbright Memorandum urged the Department of Defense to take swift action to correct this problem in order to protect the administration's foreign policy and address a "dangerous development."[52] When word of the memorandum leaked out, Senator Strom Thurmond (D-South Carolina) launched a congressional investigation that forced a reluctant Fulbright to reveal the contents of his memorandum.[53] Revelations that the speeches of other top military leaders, including General Arthur Trudeau and Admiral Arleigh Burke, had been censored ignited the rightwing.[54] Strom Thurmond wrote in his constituent newsletter that "one of the most disturbing and potentially disastrous conspiracies being conducted today is the movement to discredit and discourage our military leaders" in their efforts to expose the dangers posed by the "insidious forces of world communism." He added for good measure that the Kennedy administration did not want the American people to face up to the grave threat of world communism or "the internal threat of subversion and gradually falling under the spell of domestic socialism and welfare statism."[55]

The Walker episode and the Fulbright Memorandum sparked a firestorm of protest in Fulbright's home state of Arkansas and in Washington, D.C. Hundreds of letters poured into Fulbright's office in support of Walker.[56] The Walker affair allowed grassroots conservatives to launch a counter-offensive against their liberal critics. Leading conservative publications blasted the Kennedy administration for suppressing anticommunist education in the military—all for the sake of laying the ground for appeasing the Soviet Union. Radio commentator Dan Smoot in Texas asked, "What Price Glory: Major General Edwin A. Walker." Clarence Manion defended Walker in a radio broadcast entitled "Complete Disarmament of American People Now Planned through U.N." The American Security Council, a Chicago based conservative organization influenced by Nancy Reagan's father, Dr. Loyal Davis, in its *Washington Report* provided a somewhat more tempered assessment of the strategic consequences of the Fulbright Memorandum, but it also concluded that the Memorandum reflected a "no-win" foreign policy pursued by the Kennedy administration.[57] Schlafly, who was the president of the Illinois Federation of Republican Women, joined the defense of the anticommunist Right by declaring that the Fulbright Memorandum was "another appeasement act of the Kennedy adminis- tration. It is an attempt to gag the military and prevent our patriotic military leaders from defending us against Communism." She reprinted the Hinsdale Women's Republican Club Newsletter which concluded that the real fear was not that military personnel would learn about the nature of communism, but that the "American people themselves" would. The Illinois Federation passed a resolution calling for an investi- gation of "muzzling the military" and for "all citizen groups to carry on the program of patriotic, anti-Communist education." Walker's former military aide Major Arch Roberts sent Schlafly a personal note thanking her for efforts on behalf of Walker.[58]

However there was one insurmountable problem in rallying conser- vatives to Edwin Walker's defense—the general himself. Behind the emotion over Walker's leaving the military and the Fulbright Memo- randum lay a man who did not fit the image created by the rightwing press. When Walker testified at congressional hearings on muzzling the military, he rambled, seemed disorganized, and at times incoher- ent. His speech before an overflow audience in Chicago in early 1962, "The American Eagle Is Not a Dead Duck," was prolix and his inflated language landed on the audience like the Hindenberg dirigible.[59]

Although Walker failed to rally the Right, Kennedy worried about the growing strength of what he considered extremist anticommunist groups and their influence among the American public. As a result, Kennedy launched a counter-offensive against the Right in the Fall of 1961.[60] The counterattack began when Kennedy ordered a White House aide to prepare monthly reports on the Right and asked the director of audits at the Internal Revenue Service to gather data on conservative organizations that held tax-exempt status.[61]

In November 1961, Kennedy journeyed into a hotbed of rightwingers when he traveled to Southern California to deliver a major speech at the Hollywood Palladium. Here, he openly ridiculed the Right as a fringe movement by parodying the rightwing view of history: "It was not the presence of Soviet troops in Eastern Europe that drove it to communism; it was the sellout at Yalta. It was not a civil war that removed China from the free world; it was treason in high places." He continued, "At times these fanatics have achieved a temporary success among those who lack the will or the vision to face unpleasant tasks or unsolved problems." He told his audience not to heed "these counsels of fear and suspicion."[62] As he spoke to a cheering crowd of Democratic loyalists in the Palladium, nearly 3,000 conservative protesters paraded outside carrying signs that read "Clean Up the State Department," "Disarmament is Suicide," and "CommUNism is our Enemy." Later that evening in a speech at a Democratic Party dinner, Kennedy again denounced the right wing in America as a threat to liberty.

As 1961 drew to a close, Kennedy unleashed further attacks on the GOP Right. In December, the administration leaked sections of a lengthy report on the threat of the Right in America produced by Victor and Walter Reuther and Joseph L. Rauh, Jr., both founders of the Americans for Democratic Action. The Reuther Memorandum had been requested by U.S. Attorney General Robert Kennedy, and the report urged the administration to "shift the battleground to an offensive posture." Shortly after the release of the Reuther report, the United Auto Workers Union organized Group Research, a left wing investigative organization, to track and report on rightist groups. This research organization kept the extreme Right in the news by releasing press releases and studies showing the growing strength of the Far Right. These reports often did not distinguish between conservative groups that operated within the democratic system and extremist groups that believed that democratic, electoral politics was a charade because the federal government was already controlled by alien forces, whether Communist, Jewish, or Wall Street. Three months before Kennedy's death in November 1963, Presidential aide Myer Feldman wrote the President that "the radical right-wing constitutes a formidable force in American life today," and he urged a federal investigation into the John Birch Society and other extremist groups.[63] Feldman suggested that such an investigation be timed to coincide with the approaching presidential election. He quoted U.S. Senator Gale McGee (D-Wyoming) who had sent him a memorandum warning, "A wide open investigation in the Congress of right wing groups now might have the effect of killing them dead before next fall [the presidential election]. I am personally convinced that the issue is such a good one that we need to keep the villain alive and kicking for a year from now. . . ."[64]

THE CARDINAL MINDSZENTY FOUNDATION UNDER FIRE

While the White House plotted its campaign strategy targeting the Far Right, the popular press through a plethora of books and magazine articles maintained a steady barrage of attacks on the Right. The *New York Times Magazine* in 1961 had set the tone of political reporting when it predicted that Barry Goldwater, "the darling" of the Right, will be "obliged" to "choose between the support of the Right and the support of real Republicans who will not care to forsake the traditions of their party for a forlorn kind of fascism."[65] Two years later in 1963, *Look* magazine spoke of "a fierce new breed of political activists" who call themselves conservatives in public, but in private they "put on another label: Right Wing."[66]

In this atmosphere it was inevitable that the Cardinal Mindszenty Foundation would also come under fire from the liberals. Liberal Catholics took the lead in criticizing the Cardinal Mindszenty Foundation, beginning with an attack by the Assistant Director of Social Action at the National Catholic Welfare Conference (NCWC), Rev. John F. Cronin, in "The Communist Threat in America." In this eighty-eight page booklet, Cronin warned about the "hysteria and fanaticism" being generated by right-wing Catholic groups such as the Cardinal Mindszenty Foundation. In an NCWC press release of March 1, 1962 announcing the book, Cronin labeled anticommunist Catholic organizations as "financial rackets" that were keeping up an unnecessary stream of anticommunist vitriol that should have ended in 1950 when the fight against the "menace of communism had been substantially accomplished."[67] He suggested in private conversations that got back to Phyllis Schlafly that the Mindszenty Foundation was "the Catholic" counterpart to the John Birch Society. Because Cronin had written the booklet under the auspices of the National Catholic Welfare Conference, the national organization of Catholic bishops in America, Cronin's opinion achieved widespread coverage including a report in the *New York Times*, as well as diocesan newspapers throughout the country. Shortly after the release of Cronin's booklet, Reverend Edward Duff, a Jesuit and former editor of *Social Order*, joined in criticism of the Cardinal Mindszenty Foundation with his booklet "There Is a Conspiracy," distributed in Catholic parishes in the summer of 1962. This conspiracy, he wrote, was "the activities of the self-appointed anti-Communists who are busily wrecking the structures of American society by undermining our political institutions." After warning that, at the present rate of screening, more people will have seen the anticommunist film *Operation Abolition* than had seen *Gone with the Wind*, Duff singled out for scorn the Mindszenty Foundation with its 2,000 study groups.[68]

Outraged by these attacks on the Mindszenty Foundation, Phyllis Schlafly responded by working late into the night typing dozens of letters to editors of Catholic newspapers across the country rebutting charges raised by Cronin and Duff. Writing a letter signed by her friend Janet S. McLaughlin, she reviewed Cronin's booklet for *The Tablet* of Brooklyn, N.Y.[69] Other conservative Catholic newspapers, including *The Wanderer* and *Our Sunday Visitor* and the magazine *The Priest*, also ran columns and editorials defending the Mindszenty Foundation against Cronin, often at the urging of Schlafly.[70] *National Review* editorialized that Cronin's position reflected a "new social gospel" in the Church that "we can beat the Communists by burnishing our own souls," by being honest, moral, and tolerant.[71] In this campaign, Phyllis Schlafly systematically answered the charges raised by Cronin: that the Mindszenty Foundation was associated with the John Birch Society (it was not, although it did on occasion recommend a JBS publication); that the Schlaflys were financially profiting from the anticommunist movement (all work at the Mindszenty Foundation was done by volunteers); and that the foundation had falsely accused people of being communists (the purpose of the organization was not to seek out communists in America, and no one was referred to as a communist unless that fact was verified in government documents, which were the primary sources for foundation education programs).[72]

In responding to the Catholic critics, Phyllis Schlafly was not content to defend the Mindszenty Foundation, but instead went on the attack, by taunting her critics about their denial in the late 1950s that Castro was a communist. The liberal Catholic press was not alone in this mistake, but given the subsequent persecution of Catholic priests and bishops by Castro, many Catholic newspapers were especially vulnerable to this "soft on communism" charge. Dale Francis, columnist for *Our Sunday Visitor*, felt the full brunt of her fire. In a series of op-ed pieces and letters to the editor appearing in conservative Catholic newspapers, *The Wanderer* and *The Tablet*, Schlafly charged that Francis had repeatedly told his readers in columns published in 1959 through 1961 that there was no need to worry about Castro's being a communist.

In substantiating her charges, she cited a series of columns that appeared in *Our Sunday Visitor* in which Francis had defended Castro from charges of being a communist, including one in August 10, 1959, favorably quoting a priest saying, "If this Castro's revolution is Communism, then Christ was a Communist."[73] Schlafly argued that liberal Catholics such as Francis had betrayed Catholic moral principles by defending Castro and his regime. While Francis was busy excusing Castro's excesses, she wrote, Catholic anticommunists such as herself were being denounced as "extremists," but unlike Francis, they had "accurately foretold the fate that would befall Cuba under Castro."[74]

Under fire from Schlafly, both Cronin and Francis beat a hasty retreat. In a letter to the Catholic magazine, *Ave Maria*, Cronin declared that he was not speaking for the Catholic bishops when he denounced Catholic anticommunist organizations as "financial rackets," and moreover, he did not mean to include the Cardinal Mindszenty Foundation in this group.[75] After a public exchange with Phyllis Schlafly, Dale Francis admitted that he had arrived late in deciding Castro was a communist, but once he reached this conclusion he had published a series of articles in the spring of 1959 warning that Castro was betraying the revolution.[76]

At the core of the controversies—aside from the false innuendo that the Schlaflys had a pecuniary interest in the anticommunist campaign—lay a fundamental difference as to how to combat communism. Phyllis Schlafly consistently refused to accept the liberal Catholic position that the eradication of poverty would eliminate the threat of communism. She wrote one Monsignor that every "right thinking person should be concerned with poverty, just as we are concerned about cancer. We should do all to reduce poverty and cancer in this world," she said. "Yet I know that physical disease does not cause Communism any more than poverty does, because Communism is a disease of the mind and soul, not of the stomach or body."[77]

ON THE EDGE OF THE 1964 ELECTION

Schlafly gained considerable attention in her controversies with Cronin and Francis, but her reputation still remained primarily regional. From 1959 to 1962 she received on average twenty-five invitations each year from local Republican groups, women's organizations, religious conventions, DAR chapters, Rotary Clubs, high schools and colleges, and trade associations such as the Illinois Retail Farm Equipment Association. Her ability to generate excitement increased her reputation throughout the state. Her power lay in her message and her ability to frame issues in a clear manner easily grasped by her audiences. After hearing her, one couple wrote, "We are also thankful that God has given you the strength and courage to carry on despite the many obstacles that face the faithful today." Another woman wrote, "I shall never forget the impact of your talk on all of us present that evening and I wished so much that many more people could have heard the talk."[78]

While her debates with Cronin and Francis brought Schlafly to a larger audience, the controversy over extremism inflicted great damage on the grassroots anticommunist movement. Furthermore, having a Catholic president in the White House who proposed arms control contributed to a diminution of the communist issue among the general public. The public realization that the Soviet Union had become a nuclear superpower led many Americans to believe that détente with the Soviet Union was an acceptable alternative to blowing up the world. Grassroots anticommunism did not vanish from the political scene, but it became subsumed in the larger issue of national security. The ideology of anticommunism remained, but soon would be expressed through the language of national defense.

Revealing of this shift away from explicit anticommunism to national security issues was the American Security Council, which was started initially to help corporations avoid communist influence in their companies. The ASC maintained the largest private files on communism in the country with a central index of over 2 million entries. In the early 1960s, however, the ASC under its director John M. Fisher shifted its attention to national defense issues by establishing an office in Washington, D.C. and appointing Stefan Possony and Rear Admiral Chester Ward, U.S.N. (Ret.) as research directors.[79] Phyllis Schlafly drew some of her speech material from American Security Council literature, and through the organization she became acquainted with leading defense experts on the Right. Schlafly's own speeches in the early 1960s began to reflect her growing technical knowledge of defense issues.[80]

As her knowledge of national defense increased, Schlafly began to articulate a clear position of defense that rested on two core principles: 1) The Soviet military threat is real and inescapable, so United States must have superior military strength to *avoid* war; 2) The Soviet Union seeks to bleed the resources and morale of the United States through satellite wars of attrition, while Russia tests its weapons and bides its time to confront a weakened United States. When she called on the United States to have a "first strike" capability, the purpose was to *avoid* war, not start one. Joining other conservatives who warned against disarmament (typified in Robert Morris's widely distributed 1963 book, *Disarmament: Weapon of Conquest*), Schlafly called for the United States to maintain "superiority of military striking power."[81] In 1963, she appeared before the Senate Foreign Relations Committee to testify against the Limited Test Ban Treaty proposed by the Kennedy administration. (Her testimony so impressed the *St. Louis Globe-Democrat* that the editors presented Phyllis Schlafly with its Woman of Achievement Award, the first time the award was given in public affairs.)[82] Two years later, Barry Goldwater was even blunter when he issued his foreign policy declaration, *Why Not Victory?* The theme that the United States could *and should* win the Cold War remained an article of faith for conservatives throughout the Cold War.

As the election of 1964 approached, Phyllis Schlafly stood on the verge of national visibility. In 1964, Phyllis Schlafly resigned as research director of the Cardinal Mindszenty Foundation in order to become more involved in Republican politics. She believed that grassroots conservatives stood on the cusp of a major political realignment in America that could be achieved through the nomination for President of Barry Goldwater, the U.S. Senator from Arizona in 1964. She was convinced that the Republican party could be transformed into a party of conservatism and through this the nation could be redeemed to fulfill its mission as a protector of liberty and freedom.

Liberal attacks on grassroots anticommunists had done nothing to diminish Schlafly and other activists in their belief that they were right. The grassroots Right had been bloodied, but stood unbowed.

CHAPTER FIVE

The Goldwater Campaign

FOLLOWING ATTENDANCE at the Republican National Convention in San Francisco in 1964, Phyllis and Fred Schlafly boarded a plane with their conservative friends Patrick Frawley and his wife, and comedian Bob Hope and his wife, for a brief holiday in Canada. At a refueling stop in Seattle, the pilot announced that a crowd at the gate wanted autographs from one of the passengers. Bob Hope stood up, straightened his tie, and started to the door when the pilot apologetically told him the crowd wanted Phyllis Schlafly to come out and autograph her book, *A Choice Not an Echo*, the bestselling political book of the year and a book to which many attributed Goldwater's winning the California primary. In the crowd was Mrs. Edgar Eisenhower, the former President's sister-in-law, who had come from Tacoma to see Phyllis at the airport. She expressed the sentiments of Goldwater activists when she told Schlafly, "You gave us a tool when we needed it most."[1]

Phyllis Schlafly's campaign book *A Choice Not an Echo* (1964) sold millions of copies in the six months before the general election. The book was a no-holds-barred attack on the liberal Eastern wing of the GOP and "me-too" Republicanism. Goldwater's triumph at the Republican National Convention in San Francisco introduced Schlafly for the first time to a national audience as a leading voice of the Republican Right. After years of being vilified as "extremist" by liberal journalists and academics, grassroots conservatives found their beliefs articulately expressed by a little-known activist from Alton, Illinois. Carrying this book in hand, grassroots conservatives nominated a conservative to head the GOP presidential ticket in 1964. In doing so, they learned an important and inspiring lesson: by mobilizing the grassroots, a conservative could win the Republican nomination. The first step toward taking control of the Republican party was accomplished. Grassroots activists began to believe that they could take the next step and elect a conservative as president. Perhaps 1964 was not the year, but it would come. The future was theirs; it was only a matter of time. In actuality, grassroots conservatives were too optimistic in their political projections. The Right's takeover of the Republican party eventually required skillful ex-Democrat political leaders from the Sunbelt such as Strom Thurmond, Jesse Helms, and Ronald Reagan, who tapped into the wellspring of grassroots activism.

1960: GOLDWATER FOR PRESIDENT

Schlafly never abandoned her loyalty to the GOP as a vehicle for restoration of the Republic, but other conservatives were considerably more ambivalent. Dissatisfaction among the GOP Right extended back to the Eisenhower presidency.[2] For many on the Right the problems with the GOP were deeper than Eisenhower's failure to roll back New Deal programs at home and communism abroad. William A. Rusher, publisher of the *National Review*, confided to William F. Buckley, Jr. that he believed "both major parties, as presently constituted, are simply highly efficient vote-gathering machines. It is pointless to upbraid such a machine for failing to concern itself with principles—just as it would be pointless to reproach a pear tree for failing to bear plums."[3] Conservatives believed both parties felt compelled to expand the welfare state in order to appease the electorate. As a result, Republicans and Democrats were just the same, "Socialist Party A and Socialist Party B," as one disgruntled right winger called them.[4]

As Eisenhower's second term drew to a close, conservatives felt considerable ambiguity about the prospect of Richard Nixon succeeding to the presidency in 1960. Neither liberal Republicans nor the right wing were enthralled by the prospect of a Nixon candidacy. Many liberal Republicans distrusted his anticommunist role in the Alger Hiss case, while many Taft conservatives disliked Nixon for helping to deliver the California delegation to Eisenhower at the 1952 Republican National Convention. Still, Nixon enjoyed general widespread support among regular Republicans. Evangelist Billy Graham told his congregation, "Dick Nixon is the best trained man for the job of president in American history."[5]

While GOP conservatives were unsure about Nixon, they openly despised Nelson Rockefeller. He was the Eastern Liberal Establishment and symbolized everything that was wrong with the Republican party. Conservatives faulted what they saw as the "internationalist" wing of the party for promoting the United Nations, trade with the Soviet bloc, foreign aid to communist countries, and an interventionist foreign policy. As one conservative wrote in 1959, the "country is sliding slowly, but steadily, into International Socialism."[6] Agreeing with this sentiment, conservatives across the country were asking a single question: Who could carry the banner for conservatism?

In South Bend, Indiana, Clarence Manion decided to recruit the second-term U.S. Senator from Arizona, Barry Goldwater. Manion knew that Goldwater was not interested in a run for the presidency in 1960, but Manion had the connections to organize a presidential movement that would bring the reluctant senator into the race. Manion had extensive contacts with conservatives across the country; he was a popular speaker at conservative gatherings, and he maintained frequent correspondence with conservative leaders. His book, *The Key to Peace* (1950) had sold extremely well, and his weekly 15-minute nationally aired radio program enjoyed a sizeable audience.[7] Through these contacts, Manion assembled the first Draft Goldwater Committee in mid-1959, a virtual Who's Who of the American Right, including Fred Schlafly.[8] He persuaded the committee members to go along with a two-stage plan. Stage one was to publish a campaign book by Barry Goldwater outlining his conservative philosophy, then organize a grassroots campaign around this book to make Goldwater a nationally known conservative leader. Stage two was to win the Republican party presidential nomination for Goldwater.

One large problem remained: Goldwater did not want to dance this two-step and cozy up to what appeared to be a far-fetched scheme. Working through intermediaries such as Arizona conservative Frank Brophy, Manion spoke several times to Goldwater about the project, but Goldwater remained adamant he was not the right choice.[9] Finally, in late 1959, Goldwater consented to have a book written using his name. Manion persuaded Brent Bozell, William F. Buckley's brother-in-law, to write the book, which Manion entitled *The Conscience of a Conservative*. Manion believed that the book would provide Goldwater an "authentic platform" to win conservative support and make a fight for the nomination at the 1960 convention. Manion secretly believed Goldwater would fail to get the nomination, as he confessed to William F. Buckley, Jr. Most likely, he said, Rockefeller stood a good chance and "if Rockefeller gets the nomination (as I honestly think he will), Hell will pop, I hope."[10]

Yet, as Manion worked to promote Goldwater as an "authentic voice of conservatism," he discovered that many Republicans were not all that excited about a Goldwater candidacy. Instead, they thought Nixon deserved the nomination and had the best chance of winning the general election. In Manion's own state of Indiana, the former conservative Senator William Jenner came out in support of Nixon.[11] Conservative Illinois power broker General Robert E. Wood told Manion straight-out that Nixon had the support of the whole party.[12] Columnist Fulton Lewis, Jr. tried to reassure Manion that once Nixon got the nomination he would dissociate himself from the bankrupt policies of the Eisenhower administration. Although William F. Buckley told Manion that while he believed Nixon was an "unreliable auxiliary of the Right," he was convinced that Nixon had the nomination sewn up.[13] While facing a Nixon juggernaut, Manion also confronted stirrings on his right when states-righters Kent Courtney of Louisiana and Dan Smoot of Texas called for a national convention in Chicago to form a new third party that would break with the GOP entirely. While this movement never got off the ground, this quixotic idea suggested that not even the hardcore Right was unified on a Goldwater candidacy.[14]

Manion, a man of tenacious views, remained convinced that a Goldwater movement would emerge once *The Conscience of a Conservative* appeared.[15] When the book appeared in March 1960, it quickly became a runaway best seller, aided by a pledge by members of Manion's Committee to place bulk orders for the book at $1 and sell them at $3, with the difference going into distribution costs and Goldwater's candidacy. For many Americans, this book was their first introduction to conservative political thought. *The Conscience of a Conservative* transformed Goldwater's image from a U.S. senator from a Western state then of little political importance into a principled statesman who stood up for what he believed. Goldwater became the acknowledged leader of the conservative movement. The 127-page book sought to "bridge the gap between theory and practice" by showing how basic conservative principles applied to domestic and foreign policy.[16] The book made clear that the foundation of conservative policies was a philosophy upholding the dignity of the human being. "The conscience of the conservative," the book declared, "is pricked by *anyone* who would debase the dignity of the individual human being." Therefore, the conservative is "at odds with dictators who rule by terror, and equally those gentler collectivists who ask our permission to play God with the human race."[17]

The book was a best-seller, but that was not enough to stop the Nixon bandwagon. Even Goldwater spoke highly of Nixon, much to Manion's dismay. As the Republican convention approached, Nixon appeared to have his party's nomination locked up.[18] Rockefeller had appeared to be out of the running by not entering any Republican primaries to challenge Nixon, but on May 1960, he suddenly reentered the scene following the failure of the Eisenhower-Khrushchev summit and the shooting down of the U-2 spy plane flown by U.S. pilot Francis Gary Powers. On June 8, Rockefeller proclaimed that the time for "plain talk" had come. "I am deeply convinced and deeply concerned," he said, "that those now assuming control of the Republican party have failed to make clear where this party is heading and where it proposes to lead the nation." He intimated that Eisenhower had not shown enough strength in dealing with the Soviets and that Richard Nixon, the leading Republican contender to succeed Eisenhower, was devoid of vision in foreign policy.[19] His statement threw top Republicans into a frenzy. *U.S. News & World Report* columnist David Lawrence called the Rockefeller statement "the suicide of his own party. . . . His statement would appear to make him a more logical contender for the Democratic nomination."[20] By early July, Rockefeller appeared to be at war with the entire Republican party. He had refused to challenge Nixon in the Republican primaries, but now he was on the attack as the convention was about to open. Rockefeller's scorched earth policy convinced many within the party that he was a poor loser, a spoiler, a rich kid demanding his own way.

Matters worsened when Rockefeller issued a press statement on July 20, 1960 asserting that the Republican platform lacked strength. He told the press he was going to fight for stronger civil rights and defense planks at the Republican national convention while delegates were already starting to arrive in Chicago. Fearing a full-blown platform fight that could boil over onto the convention floor, Nixon phoned Attorney General Herbert Brownell to arrange a meeting with Rockefeller. Approached by Brownell, Rockefeller struck a tough stance: He was willing to meet with Nixon, but he insisted the meeting be held in New York City, that it must remain secret, and any press release following the meeting must state that Nixon had requested the meeting. Nixon arrived in New York City on the evening of July 22, 1960 and went directly to Rockefeller's penthouse apartment at 810 Fifth Avenue. After dinner, a four-way telephone hook-up enabled Nixon and Rockefeller to talk with Charles Percy, chairman of the Platform Committee and then president of Bell and Howell, in Chicago's Blackstone Hotel and with Rockefeller associate Emmett Hughes at the nearby Chicago Sheraton. After an extended conversation, the two parties reached what became known as the "Compact of Fifth Avenue." The 14-point compact included seven points on foreign policy and seven points on civil rights. Rockefeller got what he wanted. Nixon swallowed his pride and accepted Rockefeller's demands for changes in the platform.

Rockefeller announced the 14-point agreement to the press the following morning. The news rocked the convention as talk of the "Fifth Avenue Sellout" spread through the convention. An irate Goldwater, who had been planning to announce that he was withdrawing his name from the nomination, told a breakfast meeting of Republicans, "Early today came the disturbing news that Mr. Nixon himself has felt it necessary to make overture and concession to the liberals. . . . I believe this to be immoral politics. I believe it to be self-defeating." Goldwater called the Compact the "Munich of the Republican Party."

Angry delegates, including Phyllis Schlafly representing her district, decided to rebel by not accepting the Nixon-Rockefeller deal. At the platform committee, conservative delegates confronted Rockefeller over his civil rights plank that demanded "aggressive action to remove the remaining vestiges of segregation or discrimination in all areas of national life." Delegates rallied behind John Tower of Texas in supporting the original civil rights plank—the one rejected by Rockefeller—that called for orderly progress toward full rights for black Americans, while opposing a permanent Federal Employment Practices Commission. The difference between the Rockefeller plank and the original civil rights plank actually was not very much, and probably most Republicans agreed with the sentiments expressed in the Rockefeller proposal. The fact was, however, that conservatives were going to oppose whatever Rockefeller proposed. The actual issue was not the civil rights plank, but control of the convention and the future of the party.

With Rockefeller supporters and conservatives at loggerheads over the civil rights plank, Nixon intervened to save face for Rockefeller. While a compromise measure on the defense plank was rejected by conservatives, Nixon persuaded conservatives to accept Rockefeller's civil rights plank.[21] Nixon's intervention, though, further angered conservative delegates who did not like the compromise civil rights plank being rammed through the convention. At this point rumors became rampant that Barry Goldwater was going to lead a revolt against both Nixon and Rockefeller by declaring he was willing to accept the GOP nomination. This announcement, it was whispered, would be made by Goldwater at his keynote speech at the Illinois Federation of Republican Women luncheon that had been organized by its new president, Phyllis Schlafly.[22] With everyone interested in what Goldwater had to say, tickets to the IFRW luncheon on July 26 became the hottest in town.[23]

When Schlafly first planned the luncheon she expected an attendance of about a thousand people who could fit into the ballroom of the Palmer House, but by the day of the luncheon the expected attendance had almost doubled. To seat the overflow, Schlafly arranged with the Palmer House for a second banquet hall to be opened to accommodate the guests. She convinced Goldwater to give his keynote speech a second time for the overflow crowd. Introducing Goldwater, Schlafly captured the enthusiasm of the audience. "Senator Goldwater," she said, "is a living lesson in the virtue of standing firm on principle, even if you are a minority of one."[24] Goldwater's speech repeatedly brought the audience to their feet for standing ovations, but those expecting a call for an uprising against the forces that had imposed the "Fifth Avenue Sellout" were disappointed. The long anticipated Goldwater revolt fizzled, but Goldwater nevertheless confirmed his place as a hero of the GOP Right.

By the next day it was clear that Nixon had the nomination sewn up. Still boiling from the Nixon-Rockefeller deal, however, Goldwater allowed his name to be placed in nomination for President of the United States just to show he represented a force within the party that could not be ignored. When Goldwater stepped to the podium, his supporters began an enthusiastic demonstration. Phyllis Schlafly nudged the delegate next to her, an Illinois state representative, to grab the Illinois standard and join the march around the convention hall. Goldwater watched silently as the demonstrators refused to be quieted. Finally, after a prolonged demonstration, Goldwater began his speech by announcing he was withdrawing his name from nomination. Shouts of "No, No!" came from the floor. Goldwater again quieted the crowd and then in a firm voice declared, "We had our chance. . . . Now, let's put our shoulders to the wheel for Dick Nixon and push him across the line." Then in words that would be remembered by everyone attending the convention, Goldwater declared, "This country is too important for anyone's feelings. . . . Let's grow up, conservatives. If we want to take this party back—and I think we can someday—let's get to work."[25] Goldwater's message to his supporters in the GOP Right was clear: Campaign for Nixon, support the Republican ticket on behalf of a better America, and show that conservatives can be responsible leaders of the GOP. His message also said that if Nixon lost in 1960, it would be the conservatives' turn in 1964 and Goldwater would run. Goldwater lived up to his promise to campaign for Nixon.[26]

Following the convention, Manion returned to South Bend where he continued to broadcast his nationally syndicated radio program until his death in 1979. His work on behalf of Goldwater paid off. *The Conscience of a Conservative* made the Goldwater name recognizable to millions of Americans. Manion had conceived of the book, arranged to have it written, published, and distributed—even the title was his. He remained a prominent voice in American conservatism, but his role in the GOP diminished as a new generation of conservatives stepped onto the stage, including Phyllis Schlafly. Following the convention, she returned to Alton, Illinois to continue her work as president of the Illinois Federation of Republican Women. She was elected to two more terms, and then in 1964 became vice-president of the national organization. Like other hard-core conservatives, she, too, was outraged by the "Fifth Avenue Compact" between Nixon and Rockefeller. Once again the Eastern wing of the party had exerted its power behind closed doors. Rockefeller and his minions showed that they had no scruples when it came to protecting their interests. If the Republican Right were to nominate Goldwater in 1964, convention delegates needed to be alerted to the dirty tactics the Eastern wing had employed since 1936 to secure the nomination for their candidates. Schlafly planned to do her part to make sure that the forces of good—the Republican Right—would win in 1964.

Schlafly Writes *A Choice Not an Echo*

When John F. Kennedy barely won the 1960 presidential election in one of the closest votes in American political history, conservatives charged that the election had been stolen through voter fraud in Illinois. By not challenging the election result, Richard Nixon was seen as a statesman who placed the interests of the nation above partisan politics.

Nonetheless, conservative Republicans were intent on winning the next presidential election, and they felt Goldwater was the candidate who could lead them to victory. Critical to his nomination would be the ability of activists to mobilize the grassroots, so it fell upon leaders such as Phyllis Schlafly to inspire the troops. Schlafly spoke as the face of the new woman in the Republican party, young, vivacious, and conservative. Speaking to Republican women's clubs throughout Illinois following the election of 1960, she carried a message of reassurance, telling her audiences that conservatism was the future of the GOP. She pointed out that Republicans had increased their numbers in the Illinois state legislature and that most of the new Republicans elected to Congress were conservatives. Furthermore, Nelson Rockefeller's own state of New York had fallen to the Democrats, thereby showing that liberal Republicanism was not the way to win elections. The key to the success of the party, she advised, lay in securing the nomination of Barry Goldwater by blocking the Rockefeller forces within the party from controlling the next convention. She warned conservatives not to be taken in by Rockefeller's attempt to court conservatives, as he appeared to be doing by attacking Kennedy's proposal for a new federal department of urban affairs and by denouncing Kennedy's proposed nuclear test ban treaty.

Schlafly's warnings were assisted on May 4, 1963, when Rockefeller married Margaretta (Happy) Murphy, a mother of four children who had recently divorced her husband. Neither the general public nor the Republican faithful received this news well. Rockefeller appeared to be a home-wrecker who divorced his own wife and mother of his children for a younger woman and broke up another home with four children. The erosion of Rockefeller's support within the GOP was evident in the polls. Before the marriage announcement, the Gallup poll found Rockefeller leading Goldwater 43 to 26; after the marriage, the poll reported Goldwater ahead by about 20 points. Goldwater became the man to beat, as other liberal-to-moderate candidates stepped forward to try to halt the conservative juggernaut.[27]

"Rocky" Rockefeller was not the kind to give up without a fight. In the late summer of 1963, Rockefeller reentered the race with a vengeance. This time he positioned himself not as a party unifier but as its savior from extreme right-wing forces that were about to seize control of the party. He hired congressional insider and former legislative counsel Graham T. Molitor to prepare a campaign strategy labeling Goldwater an

extremist. Molitor advised Rockefeller to attack Goldwater as a dangerous anticommunist who might blow up the world if he were elected
president and to hammer Goldwater hard on his failure to "acknowledge the possibility that Marxism may be modified by a process of evolution and humanization."[28] In July 1963 Rockefeller lashed out publicly
at the Right. It's time to wake up, he declared to Republican gatherings.
The party is in "real danger of subversion by a radical, well-financed,
and highly disciplined minority." He accused the Young Republican
convention that summer of being taken over by "extremist groups" in
a "coup" that used "tactics of ruthless, roughshod intimidation." He
warned that "the leaders of the Birchers and others of the radical Right
lunatic fringe" were moving to "subvert the Republican party itself."[29]

Rockefeller had shifted from attacking Eisenhower in 1960 for not
being tough enough on the Soviet Union to the position that communist regimes were evolving and economically beneficial for their people.
Rockefeller's jeremiads against extremists in the party revealed an opportunistic streak—a willingness to do anything to advance his career—
that put off many within regular Republican ranks. For the Republican
Right, though, the issue was not opportunism, but Rockefeller's big
government and internationalist policies. Rockefeller personified the
Eastern business and political elite. For the Republican Right, Rockefeller's shift to the left put him where he really stood all along—an
internationalist willing to accommodate Communist regimes and a
liberal who would perpetuate big-spending Democratic programs.

The assassination of John F. Kennedy in November 1963 all but assured that the Democrats would keep the White House under Lyndon
Johnson. Furthermore, after Kennedy's death, Goldwater's heart was
no longer in the race.[30] As he hesitated to declare his candidacy, Goldwater began receiving hundreds of letters from supporters urging him
to challenge Kennedy's successor, Lyndon Baines Johnson, for the
good of the party and the nation. Typical of these supporters was Phyllis
Schlafly who wrote Goldwater shortly after the Kennedy assassination,
"I believe that our country's situation is so desperate that 'the conscience of a conservative' will tell you that you have but one course of
action—to run."[31] She predicted that Johnson would prove easier to beat
than Kennedy, but first he needed to win the nomination against Nelson
Rockefeller, his primary challenger. Finally, in early January 1964, Goldwater wired his principal supporters including Phyllis Schlafly that he
had decided to enter the race formally. Upon receiving the telegram,

Schlafly decided to volunteer full time for Goldwater. A month earlier Schlafly had organized the Madison County Volunteers for Goldwater Committee, which had hosted its first meeting at Schlafly's home with Patricia Hutar, Illinois state co-chair of the Draft Goldwater Committee. Furthermore, Schlafly declared that she was running as a convention delegate from her district as a Goldwater supporter, which she would eventually win. Still, Schlafly thought she could do more for Goldwater's campaign by writing a campaign book that would inform Goldwater supporters how the Eastern wing of the party, represented by Nelson Rockefeller, had repeatedly placed their "me-too" candidates on the Republican presidential tickets.

In addition, this was to be a manifesto against the moderate-liberal wing of the party. These moderates and liberals within the party, contrary to Schlafly's depiction, did not constitute a coherent faction within the party and differed considerably over policy issues. Moderate and liberal Republicans, however, did share a general openness to accept the expansion of the New Deal welfare state and more readily entertained notions of winning African Americans to the GOP. As the conservative faction within the party took shape, moderate and liberal Republicans gained greater coherence in their opposition to the threat. They found agreement on a single point: The Right must be stopped.[32]

Developed from a stump speech she had begun using following Kennedy's assassination, "How Political Conventions Are Stolen," the book told the history of GOP presidential conventions from the point of view of the Republican Right—the Taft wing of the party.[33] Entitled *A Choice Not an Echo* (a phrase Goldwater used when announcing his candidacy), the 128-page book taught a single message to delegates who would attend the presidential nominating convention in 1964: We have been tricked, cajoled, and imposed upon by the Eastern wing of the GOP to accept candidates who were closer to the Democratic party philosophy than to "authentic" Republicanism, and each time we lost; this must not happen again in 1964; we need to nominate a principled conservative who stands for true Republican principles and this candidate must be Barry Goldwater.

The book was a clear articulation of the Republican Right's view of GOP convention history. Schlafly told how "from 1936 through 1960 the Republican presidential nominee was selected by a small group of secret kingmakers who are the most powerful opinion makers in the world." The kingmakers—a term popularized by Schlafly—had "dictated the choice of the Republican presidential nominee just as completely as the Paris dressmakers control the length of women's skirts."[34] Schlafly's book maintained that Republican candidates since 1936, when Alf Landon was nominated, had avoided critical issues that could have led to victory. In 1940 Wendell Willkie refused to challenge Roosevelt's acceptance of "Stalin's invasions of Poland, Finland, Latvia, Lithuania, and Estonia, while committing American boys to fight Hitler." Thomas Dewey in 1944 never mentioned how Roosevelt had "invited the disaster at Pearl Harbor" by maneuvering the Japanese into firing the first shot. (While noting that George Marshall had persuaded Dewey not to reveal that Japanese military telegrams had been intercepted before Pearl Harbor, Schlafly did not mention that Marshall was concerned that such information would show the Japanese that the United States had broken their codes.) In 1948, the Dewey-Warren ticket avoided the communism issue, especially the exposure of Alger Hiss, Harry Dexter White, and other communists in government.[35] In the chapter, "The Big Steal," Schlafly presented a scathing account of how the kingmakers had stolen the 1952 nomination from Bob Taft and handed it to their "long time favorite" Eisenhower. She recounted how the kingmakers had promised Earl Warren an appointment to the Supreme Court and Richard Nixon the Vice Presidency in order to lock up the California delegation for Eisenhower. She detailed how a Pennsylvania delegate on the Credentials Committee, after awarding contested delegates to Taft, reversed his vote the following day under intense pressure from Governor John S. Fine, who was promised he could dispense all federal patronage in his state.

In this highly ideological account of Republican conventions, she revealed her pragmatic side by not accusing Eisenhower of complicity in stealing the nomination. His operatives were responsible, and Eisenhower was only a tool for them to defeat Taft. Indeed, Schlafly specifically noted, "Eisenhower was not responsible for any of the vicious tactics used to win the nomination." Yet, she added, after winning the nomination, Eisenhower equivocated on the issues. Schlafly maintained that only after accepting Taft's advice to campaign on the solid Republican issues of communism and corruption in government and ending the Korean War did Eisenhower pull ahead of his Democratic opponent, Adlai Stevenson. "To the dismay of the kingmakers, as well as of the liberals and Democrats, the Republican Party closed ranks" and Eisenhower won the election.[36]

While she was ambivalent about Eisenhower, she was not reserved when it came to the kingmakers—the Eastern power elite—who forced their candidates on the Republican party. She identified men such as Nelson Rockefeller, Henry Cabot Lodge, investment banker C. Douglas Dillon, State Department official Arthur Dean, former Studebaker president and U.N. official Paul G. Hoffman, and Eisenhower's Secretary of the Treasury, Robert B. Anderson. These kingmakers exercised their influence in both the Republican and the Democratic parties. They were internationalist-minded and pursued what she called "an America Last foreign policy." What motivated the kingmakers? Schlafly told her readers the kingmakers held a financial stake in the welfare state, deficit spending, foreign giveaway programs, and an internationalist foreign policy. "Since the New York kingmakers dominate the consortium which fixes the interest rate the Government has to pay on its obligations, they have no incentive to see deficit financing stop." The only way to defeat the kingmakers was to vote for "candidates not controlled by the kingmakers."[37]

This was strong medicine, even for a campaign book intended to stir up the Republican grassroots. Schlafly told the story as she understood it; and this perception was shared by most grassroots activists, who believed that an Eastern elite of internationalists was shaping American policy for the benefit of their own economic interests. Conservative publications—pamphlets, newspaper and magazine articles, and private correspondence—were full of talk about the Eastern elite. When the *National Review* was founded, William Buckley identified the liberal establishment as the major target. A long history of denunciations of Eastern financial interests existed in conservative literature, at least dating back to the 1920s. The message was populist—the people versus power elites, who often worked in secret. American political history is replete with anti-elitist rhetoric. Schlafly was in this tradition, but she inverted the message of nineteenth-century radicalism so that it became a defense of capitalism, free market economics, and antistatism.[38] Populist rhetoric suggested conspiracies afoot, and Schlafly's message was not an exception.[39]

She devoted the second-to-last chapter of *A Choice Not an Echo* to describing the Bilderberg group, an annual meeting organized by Prince Bernhard of the Netherlands beginning in 1954 to bring together leaders from the United States, Canada, and Western Europe to talk about ways of mutually understanding one another. Prince Bernhard, concerned about a growing rift between the United States and Western Europe, believed that an annual meeting of leaders would ease tensions. Schlafly offered the Bilderberg group as an example of the fact that "powerful men actually do meet to make plans which are kept secret from American citizens."[40] Her chapter on the Bilderbergers was clearly an add-on and not relevant to her thesis about how Republican party candidates were chosen because she did not make the claim that Bilderbergers were involved in selecting Republican presidential candidates.[41] In writing about the Bilderbergers, Schlafly walked a delicate line between suggesting conspiracy by a well-organized, all-powerful group and illustrating how the rich and powerful, sharing a similar internationalist mindset, came together to discuss world affairs.[42]

The Bilderberg meetings were intended to be secret to facilitate frank discussion. Schlafly was not wrong on this score; the meetings were closed to the public. What fascinated Schlafly was not merely that the Bilderberg meetings were secret, but the super-extraordinary measures that were taken to keep the meetings secret. She was also fascinated that the list of attendees at the St. Simon's Island meeting in 1957 included men whose names were unknown to the American people at that time, but who subsequently rose to the most powerful positions in government: McGeorge Bundy, Dean Rusk, George Ball, Paul Nitze, and Henry Kissinger. Where she was wrong was seeing a uniformity of ideological agreement and economic interest in the group. She was unwilling to take Prince Bernhard at his word that the meetings were kept secret so differences could be expressed by the participants. Memoranda and position papers generated by the Bilderbergers show deep differences over a range of issues. The exchanges were polite, high toned, not personal, but clearly opposed. There were differences over monetary policy, U.S.-European trade, the strategic balance, and the Middle East. The clearest difference between the Europeans and the Americans came over policies toward domestic communist parties and Soviet communism. American representatives argued communist parties should be outlawed, while Europeans argued that Americans exaggerated the communist threat.[43] Similarly sharp differences were expressed over the recognition of mainland China, peaceful coexistence, disarmament, maintaining U.S. nuclear superiority, and the increased threat of regional wars.

Members of the Bilderberger group, however, shared an internationalist perspective and accepted, at least in principle, open markets, free trade, international cooperation, and mutual defense between the United States, Canada, and Western Europe. Prince Bernhard brought the rich and powerful together, and their meetings were secret, but there was a routine quality to the discussions. William F. Buckley, Jr. told William Rusher after attending one of their conferences in the mid-1970s that Bilderberg meetings were "boring." Buckley did not want this repeated, he told Rusher, because it would be "unconscionable if my hosts should hear about this." Nevertheless, Buckley added, he knew how disappointing his report on the Bilderbergers would be in some right-wing circles, but his conclusion remained: Not much really happened at the meetings that he could see.[44]

No doubt Schlafly would have found the papers presented by the Europeans boring, too. What excited her was the camaraderie of the celebrity American attendees and the fact that noncelebrity attendees subsequently rose to powerful positions. Schlafly's targeting of the Bilderbergers, Barry Goldwater's targeting of the Council of Foreign Relations, and the later targeting of the Trilateral Commission, provided a shortcut for the GOP Right to explain the nature of the grassroots conservatives' political enemy, the Eastern Establishment. Furthermore, Schlafly knew that her listeners and readers expected this kind of ex-posé writing. "This is the sort of thing that our people lap up and love," she told a friend.[45]

Schlafly genuinely believed the Eastern Establishment was real and exerted influence on both political parties through political, financial, and media connections. She held it was internationalist in outlook, dis-trusted nationalism, and always worked for bigger, more expensive government. Furthermore, she believed people in the Eastern Estab-lishment shared strategies to expand their political and financial influ-ence. What she avoided was equally important: She never postulated that a single group conspired to direct American and European gov-ernmental policies, and she never identified Jews as part of any con-spiracy. She focused the attention of her readers on the immediate fight confronting grassroots Republicans, not on the megahistorical forces that many conspiracy theorists saw as fundamental. The sole purpose of *A Choice Not an Echo* was to win votes for Goldwater and the book proved remarkably successful in this goal.

Early in the project Schlafly decided to self-publish the book, after witnessing the success of two other self-published books, *The Con-science of a Conservative* and John Stormer's *None Dare Call It Treason*

(1964). Stormer published *None Dare Call It Treason* under his own imprint, Liberty Bell Press, with a post office box address in Florissant, Missouri. Within a month of its publication in February 1964, Stormer's paperback had sold 100,000 copies. By August 1964, it was in its thirteenth printing, having sold 2.2 million copies.[46] Using these two books as models, Schlafly produced the first press run of 25,000 copies of *A Choice Not an Echo* in April. The day they arrived at her garage, she sent a mimeographed letter with a complimentary copy of the book to one hundred friends she had met through her Republican and anticommunist activities. Her letter asked them to read the enclosed book which "exposes the secret tricks being used by a few New Yorkers" to control the GOP and then "find an angel who will underwrite the cost of as many thousand copies as are needed to cover active Republicans in your state. Find a small team of volunteers who will handle the direct distribution to your state delegates and alternates to the Republican National Convention, county chairmen, state central committeemen, and prominent Republicans in your state. The time is NOW."[47] At the same time Fred Schlafly wrote about the book to friends across the country including San Francisco lawyer and author of *Roosevelt's Road to Russia*, George Crocker; Ohio Congressman John Ashbrook; Los Angeles businessman Patrick Frawley; Chicago businessman Rogers Follansbee; and California businessman Henri Salvatori, later a key supporter of Ronald Reagan whom Schlafly had met at Frawley's home the year before.[48] Manion ordered additional books to send to state delegations in California, Wisconsin, and Oregon.

Schlafly was soon overwhelmed with orders coming from all over the country from local activists whom she described as "having just run across the book and who frantically needed thousands of copies in order to win delegation contests."[49] As the orders flooded in, Schlafly, now pregnant with her sixth child who would be born shortly after the November election, found she could hardly keep her head above water.[50] She put the entire family to work; her children and their friends helped pack the boxes that Fred Schlafly loaded into the family station wagon and drove to the airport for air-freight shipping. As the Goldwater movement spread, Republican delegates snatched up copies of the books to give to their friends and neighbors. The book became a rallying cry for Goldwater Republicans to take control away from the Eastern liberal wing of the party. Typical was a Republican delegate from Iowa who wrote that he had heard most of what Schlafly had written about, but she had given substance to how the Eastern wing had controlled the party. Another delegate declared, "Through the years I can recall much of the material in the book, but this is the first time to read so much concentrated in one book." Another gushed, "This book points out facts which I had suspected. . . . I am convinced that we must nominate Barry Goldwater at the forthcoming convention."[51] The first edition sold 600,000 copies; the second edition published in May sold another 1 million copies. The third edition, published after the national convention, warned against "the kingmakers continuing propaganda against Senator Goldwater."[52] By November, *Choice* had sold 3.5 million copies.

CONSERVATIVES CAPTURE THE NOMINATION

Schlafly's book fell on receptive ears because most delegates attending the 1964 convention had never before attended a national party convention. Furthermore, the Republicans were dismayed because they had lost strength at every level beginning in 1954 through the 1960 election.[53] There were signs of growth in the South, but many Southern Republicans remained "palace" politicians interested in maintaining their positions in the state party. The one bright spot of Southern Republican politics was the election of John Tower to the Senate from Texas in 1961, when Texas liberals voted for Tower to prevent a conservative Democrat's election. Goldwater's strategy depended on winning Western and Southern delegates, but some advisers felt he needed to prove his popularity by winning outside the West and the South by entering the New Hampshire primary, even though they knew this was a dicey state because the death of conservative Republican Senator Styles Bridges had left the GOP deeply divided. Even though most Republicans were generally conservative, it was feared that if Goldwater lost New Hampshire, it might breathe new life into the Rockefeller campaign. In November 1963, Phyllis Schlafly was nearly beside herself that Goldwater might run in New Hampshire. She wrote Goldwater imploring, "Please, Please do Not enter the New Hampshire primary. . . . This step would be as fatal to you as it was to Bob Taft in 1952. It is too easy for the 'big boys' to buy up a little state like New Hampshire."[54]

Goldwater ignored this advice and entered, but the internal problems within the state GOP soon paled in comparison to troubles caused by Goldwater's tendency to speak his mind. In Portsmouth, New Hampshire he told the crowd that America's long-range missiles were not dependable. In a speech in New York City he said he believed that "most people who have no skills have no education for the same reason—low intelligence or low ambition." In Washington, D.C. he told a crowd of Young Republicans that "at best, political platforms are a packet of misinformation and lies."[55] Meanwhile, Nelson Rockefeller put together a well-organized campaign and began to project an empathetic appeal to voters. He attacked Goldwater's proposal that Social Security should be privatized and the income tax abolished. Passing under the radar screens of both Goldwater and Rockefeller, another campaign was quietly organized for an establishment favorite, Henry Cabot Lodge. The Lodge forces possessed an old Eisenhower mailing list of 95,000 New Hampshire Republicans and used it to send out instructions on how to write in Lodge's name on the ballot. On election day in New Hampshire, Lodge received 35.5 per cent of the vote, while Goldwater got 23.2 and Rockefeller 21.0 per cent. Granite State voters repudiated both Goldwater and Rockefeller.

The New Hampshire results threw the GOP race wide open, even to the point where some moderate insiders began talking about Governor William W. Scranton of Pennsylvania as a possibility. After having served a single term in Congress, Scranton won election as governor in 1962 by a good margin, so he looked like a vote-getter. Richard Nixon appeared ready to declare his availability, despite the fact that he had lost the California governor's race in 1962. Fears that the kingmakers were being given an opportunity to put their man—whether Rockefeller, Lodge, Scranton, or even Governor George Romney of Michigan—on the ballot worried Goldwater conservatives across the country. The Lodge campaign continued to pick up steam, winning respectable write-in votes in Nebraska, New Jersey, and Massachusetts. Lodge, instrumental in defeating Taft in 1952, appeared to be the leading candidate, but when he decided to remain in his post as ambassador to South Vietnam, which precluded active campaigning, the Lodge bandwagon broke down. After Rockefeller won the Oregon primary, all eyes turned to California. Whoever won this decisive primary would be the next Republican presidential nominee.

Grassroots conservatives had steadily increased their strength in California after the 1960 election. They had won control of the California Young Republicans and the California Federation of Republican Women. They had established their own organization, the United Republicans of California (UROC), which had a heavy John Birch Society influence.[56] The Birch issue put the Goldwater campaign in a difficult situation. As one confidential memorandum reported, "Fortunately or unfortunately, the Birchers are contributing a substantial portion of our workers and some of our leaders in important areas . . . the Society does, in fact, harbor some of the soundest conservatives and some of the wildest extremists."[57] The old-line moderate Republicans who had controlled California for many years, former Governor Goodwin Knight, Senator Thomas Kuchel, and San Francisco Mayor George Christopher, rallied around Nelson Rockefeller.

Rockefeller's strategy was to drive up Goldwater's negatives. Pouring money and organization into the state, the Rockefeller campaign mailed thousands of fliers asking voters if they wanted Goldwater in the same room with the H-bomb button, a theme later invoked by Lyndon Johnson against the Arizonan. The Goldwater campaign responded by taking to the streets, canvassing nearly 600,000 homes in one day in Los Angeles alone. Everywhere precinct workers went, they carried with them *A Choice Not an Echo*, which was being distributed by Gilbert Durand, who had volunteered to handle the job because he had a loading dock at his door manufacturing plant in Glendale, California. Republicans across the state seemed to lap up the book's message. Were not the kingmakers up to their old tricks by denouncing Goldwater as an extremist who could not be let near the H-bomb? Didn't Rockefeller represent everything wrong with the Eastern wing of the Republican party, as witness his epithets about extremists, his coziness with liberal domestic policies, and his accommodation with the Soviet Union? The turnout of grassroots conservatives ensured that the election would be close, but when a few days before the primary Rockefeller's new wife Happy gave birth to a daughter, the entire state of California was again reminded that Rockefeller was a home-breaker. On primary day, Goldwater squeaked through to victory. Rockefeller did well enough in the San Francisco Bay area, in farm and mountain regions of the state, and among minority voters, but not well enough to make up for Goldwater's staggering 207,000 vote majority in Los Angeles County. Goldwater's campaign manager declared, "All those little old ladies in tennis shoes that you called right wing nuts and kooks, they're the best volunteer political organization that's ever been put together, and they proved it today."[58]

There was little doubt in the Goldwater campaign that *A Choice Not an Echo* played a critical role in mobilizing those little old ladies in tennis shoes, as well as thousands of average Republicans to vote for Goldwater. Stephen Shadegg, the western states coordinator for the Goldwater campaign, later observed that the California campaign had an official policy of not endorsing or recommending *A Choice Not an Echo*, or the other two widely distributed right-wing books, Stormer's *None Dare Call It Treason* and J. Evetts Haley's *A Texan Looks at Lyndon*, but nonetheless Schlafly's book became the most widely distributed book during the primary race. In an unauthorized campaign, Goldwater supporters targeted distribution of the book in districts where Rockefeller was strong, and this campaign inflicted serious damage on Rockefeller on election day. A survey conducted by the United Republicans of California (UROC), as reported by Shadegg, showed that in precincts that were targeted with distribution of *A Choice Not an Echo*, the vote for Goldwater was 20 percent higher than in nonbook precincts. How accurate the UROC poll was is arguable, given the conservative bias of the organization. A survey of the 1,308 official delegates to the Republican convention by Shadegg following the election revealed that an extraordinary 92.8 percent had read the book and 25.6 said it influenced them to support Goldwater. Perhaps even more important was the perception that *Choice* had won the nomination for Goldwater. Manion wrote Fred Schlafly that when he was first shown *Choice* and told it was going to "secure the nomination for Goldwater," he had dismissed this as hyperbole, but "subsequent events proved that she was entirely right. It was a brilliant conception and its execution was magnificent."[59]

Back in Illinois, Fred and Phyllis Schlafly anxiously followed the California primary race. Fred Schlafly wrote his friend Patrick Frawley that on election night Phyllis and he were "so busy saying the Rosary the latter part of Tuesday night that when the returns came in, we did not have time to phone our friends." He added, "Phyllis and I think the California election will rank as one of the most important elections in all of American history. It is no exaggeration to say that the fate, not only of our country, but the whole free world, was riding on the results."[60]

As the convention approached, anti-Goldwater forces mounted yet another attack when, in a nationally televised address on June 28th, William Scranton of Pennsylvania declared that this was "an hour of crisis for the Republican party and for our nation." Scranton singled out Goldwater's vote against the Civil Rights Act of 1964, portraying it as supporting racial segregation. That unfair attack failed to persuade Republican delegates to switch to Scranton, but it was a foretaste of the kind of attacks to come in the general election. In fact, Goldwater had belonged to the NAACP, had integrated his family's department store in Phoenix, and had played a leading role in integrating the Arizona Air Force Reserve. He voted against the 1964 legislation because he felt it was unconstitutional, declaring that the measure would "embark the Federal Government on a regulatory course of action" in public accommodations and employment.[61]

Scranton was aware of Goldwater's record, but he was persistent in his efforts to prevent Goldwater from winning the nomination. He went so far as to arrange to meet with the Illinois delegation at Chicago's O'Hare airport on June 30th, just as it was about to depart for the convention in San Francisco. Phyllis Schlafly was a member of the 48-member delegation. She had won a hotly contested race for convention delegate, receiving the highest vote for delegate in the 24th Congressional District.[62] At the O'Hare meeting, Scranton lashed out at Goldwater for his vote on civil rights, but the delegates turned a deaf ear to his tirade. The chairman of the Illinois delegation, U.S. Senator Everett Dirksen, whose support of the Civil Rights Act was essential to its passage, responded that Goldwater's vote was consistent with his constitutional principles. Goldwater, he said, had "earned his spurs" as a Republican and deserved the nomination. Even Republican moderate Charles Percy refused to stray from the Illinois delegation to endorse Scranton.[63]

When the Illinois delegation arrived in San Francisco, Schlafly discovered she had become a celebrity. She played upon her prominence by hosting a splendid buffet at the Fairmont Hotel to promote the Goldwater campaign, funded by a $3000 gift from a Goldwater supporter in Greenwich, Connecticut.[64] Schlafly had become a hero to the GOP Right and her predictions of kingmaker treachery seemed to have been borne out during the primaries and even as the convention convened. In fact, the Goldwater campaign staff had sent out warnings of "1952 tricks" such as "whispering campaigns" and "threats and cajolery."[65]

On the Friday before the convention opened on Monday, a 40,000-strong civil rights march took over the City Hall Plaza with signs reading "Goldwater for Führer" and "Defoliate Mississippi." On Saturday, CBS reporter Daniel Schorr reported from Munich that he had discovered that, if Goldwater won the nomination, he planned to start "his campaign here in Bavaria, the center of Germany's right wing." He said that Goldwater had accepted an invitation to visit Berchtesgaden, "once Hitler's stamping ground, but now an American recreational center." In an interview with *Der Spiegel*, Schorr concluded Goldwater was making an explicit "appeal to [German] right-wing elements."[66] The next morning delegates awoke to copies of the Schorr transcript placed under their hotel doors by Scranton and Rockefeller aides. Other magazines joined in portraying the convention as a right-wing takeover of the party. *Life* magazine reported the Republican party was seized by the "unyielding right wing" and a "tide of zealotry." An editorial in *The Reporter* condemned the "conquest" of the GOP by fanatics. Drew Pearson, already despised by the grassroots Right, wrote that the "smell of fascism has been in the air at this convention."[67]

Rambunctious delegates for Goldwater did not help much by telling reporters that they were witnessing a revolution in the Republican party. On average, Goldwater delegates were under fifty years old, mostly male, middle and upper middle-class, and for most this was their first convention. They were not used to journalists anxious to get the most outrageous quotation to win a headline in the next day's edition. Goldwater delegates often accommodated the reporters by providing jarring statements. They had read *A Choice Not an Echo* and after five years of being vilified in the press as anticommunist "fanatics," they were filled with a mixed sense of celebration, determination, and resentment. Goldwater's platform reflected the moralistic fervor of the movement. Johnson was scourged for encouraging communist aggression in South Vietnam while reducing America's strategic power. On the domestic front, the platform promised the full implementation of the Civil Rights Act of 1964, but opposed federally sponsored "reverse discrimination." Republicans promised to balance the budget, lower taxes, and retire the national debt—standard Republican boilerplate language—but the platform also spoke about a "leadership grown demagogic and materialistic through indifference to national ideals." To help restore the moral fiber of the nation, Republicans called for curbing the flow of pornography through the mails and passing a constitutional amendment to restore prayer in schools and other public places.[68]

The 1964 platform represented a clear break with the party's 1960 platform, seen by Goldwater supporters as a Rockefeller-imposed document. Goldwater supporters, certain of their moral superiority over Rockefeller, were in no mood for compromise this time round. Nevertheless, the Rockefeller-Scranton-Romney forces, now united in an axis of opposition to Goldwater, made a last ditch effort by waging a floor fight on the evening of July 14th in support of planks repudiating the John Birch Society, supporting nuclear arms control, and strengthening civil rights. The Rockefeller planks were intended to deepen the rift about "extremism" in the party, but Goldwater delegates beat back every plank presented to the convention. Finally, when a defeated Rockefeller came to the podium, he was booed. He made one last plea to have his amendments accepted; he began talking about the "goon squads, bomb threats . . . and Nazi methods" he said he had seen used by his opponents. As he spoke, shouts of "We Want Barry" drowned him out. In response, Rockefeller played to the television camera by opining, "This is still a free country, ladies and gentlemen."[69] The image of Rockefeller being shouted down, even though he clearly had baited the delegates, was not the way to alleviate fears about extremism among the viewing public.

Accusations of extremism in the GOP intensified when Goldwater declared in his acceptance speech: "Extremism in the defense of liberty is no vice. Moderation in the pursuit of justice is no virtue." The phrase was allegedly borrowed from the ancient Roman orator Cicero, but in the context it gave the appearance that Goldwater was defending extremists. Goldwater spent valuable weeks after the convention apologizing for the statement, but Lyndon Johnson would not let Goldwater escape those words.

GOLDWATER LOSES THE ELECTION

For Phyllis Schlafly the convention was a total success. Only forty years old, she had become a star in the Republican Right as author of *A Choice Not an Echo*. Given her new status in the party, rumors circulated that Goldwater intended to invite Schlafly to join his national campaign staff. Many were surprised when he did not. In part, this was the result of Goldwater's decision to keep key staff positions controlled by his close political friends from Arizona, Denison Kitchel, Richard Kleindienst, and Dean Burch. Still, he did make room for others, including Buckley's Yale friend and Goldwater consultant, Charles Lichenstein, American Enterprise Institute president William Baroody, and former Eisenhower aide Ed McCabe. Under William Baroody's direction, the campaign sought to develop a moderate image for Goldwater aimed at winning the center. This meant staying away from certain issues such as Social Security, Vietnam, and civil rights. In the summer of 1964, racial riots exploded in Harlem, Brooklyn, and Rochester in New York; Jersey City, Paterson, and Elizabeth, New Jersey; Toledo, Ohio; and Philadelphia, Pennsylvania. Goldwater met with President Johnson in late July to tell him he was not going to make an issue out of racial riots. He also suggested he would hold his fire on Vietnam in order to maintain a united front against communism. Goldwater took this course of action primarily out of a sense of patriotism, but it also fit into a strategy of projecting moderation.

This strategy of trying to win the center meant distancing the campaign as far as politically possible from the grassroots Right. In January 1962, Goldwater and his staff had met with a group of leading conservatives including Russell Kirk, William Baroody, Stephen Shadegg, and William F. Buckley in Palm Beach, Florida to discuss how to address the liability posed by Robert Welch and the John Birch Society. Following this meeting, the editors of the National Review denounced Robert Welch for injuring the cause of "responsible conservatism." In 1964, the Goldwater campaign further distanced itself from the Birchers by instructing campaign workers to reject help from volunteers who identified themselves as Birchers.[70]

It was unlikely that Schlafly was going to be given a position in the campaign, although it appears some consideration was given to such an appointment. The Goldwater campaign solicited confidential reports on Phyllis Schlafly, but they were mixed. She was well respected for her organizational and leadership skills, but some felt she was too conservative. For example, a delegate report quoted Patricia Hutar, the co-chair of the Illinois Goldwater Committee, saying she was an "excellent speaker and well known conservative." The report went on to say some observers [not named] felt that she was "too adamant" to be an effective leader. Yet elsewhere the report described her as "qualified to lead" Goldwater forces. The report concluded, "The Schlaflys incidentally bought their present 6-bedroom, pool-equipped house from the Spencer Olins [major Republican contributors]."[71] Schlafly probably was not aware of any discussion about her. In any case she would have been unable to work full time on any political campaign because she was expecting her sixth child the week of the November election.

She was anxious to contribute to a Goldwater victory any way she could, while at the same time promoting the Right's agenda by urging the campaign to focus on the Soviet threat, foreign policy and national security issues. Indeed, in early January 1964, after watching Goldwater on a Sunday news program, Schlafly sent him a lengthy letter critiquing his performance. She told him that he appeared to be on the defensive throughout the program about his opposition to the 1964 Civil Rights Act and that he should have turned the tables on the interviewers by attacking the Democrats on foreign policy. "It is better," she lectured, "to talk about disarmament, Cuba, the wheat deal, or how faith in the American system" is important to our national defense.[72] As the campaign progressed, Schlafly became increasingly frustrated that Goldwater was not focusing enough on the Soviet arms buildup, which she believed should be hammered home to the American public in order to win the election. Further, she believed the Johnson administration was taking America deeper into a war in Vietnam, draining resources away from our nuclear defense. She warned that American boys were "fighting and dying in Vietnam with little hope under the policies of the present administration."[73] She feared the United States was on the verge of another no-win war like Korea.

Given her fears of the Soviet buildup, she jumped at a chance to coauthor a book with Rear Admiral Chester Ward (U.S.N. Ret.), when he approached her to write a book with him on national defense for the average American. As research director for the American Security Council, a conservative group concerned with communism and national defense issues, Ward was convinced that Secretary of Defense Robert S. McNamara's strategic policies were undermining U.S. national security and this needed to be brought to the attention of the general public.

In August 1964 Ward phoned Schlafly from his home in Honolulu and asked her to join him in bringing the military issue to the public before the November election.[74] They had met only once before, so the call came as a surprise. Then he asked her if she would co-author a book on national security aimed at the average American to be published before the November election. This meant that the book needed to be written immediately if it were going to have any effect on the election. What emerged was *The Gravediggers*, which took a month to write and less than a month to print. Following on the heels of *A Choice Not an Echo*, the book became an instant success and sold 2 million copies. While feverishly working on *The Gravediggers*, Phyllis Schlafly joined with Hollywood documentary filmmaker Raymond H. Wagner in trying to produce a film on Otto Otepka, the State Department security officer fired by the Kennedy administration. Wagner wanted Schlafly to narrate a film that could be shown throughout the country to discredit the current administration. The script had Schlafly saying, "Since our State Department seems to want the establishment of world government as the supreme authority, the firing of Mr. Otepka for failing to maintain this authority . . . could be expected."[75] Although Wagner approached the Goldwater campaign committee to find financial backing for the film, it never got off the ground.

Between writing *The Gravediggers*, working on a film, and giving dozens of speeches for Goldwater up and down Illinois, Schlafly conducted a campaign for vice president of the National Federation of Republican Women. She was unanimously elected at the NFRW convention in Louisville, Kentucky, on September 25, 1964. This presented a hellish work schedule for Schlafly, but her energy seemed unlimited. In early October, a group of California women approached Schlafly with a proposal to fund an address by her on behalf of Goldwater to be shown on television stations across the country. Her twenty-minute speech was filmed in a studio rented from Channel 4 in St. Louis. The set looked like the living room of an average American home. Seated in the background was Fred Schlafly reading to six-year-old Liza. To the side stood thirteen-year-old John playing the Notre Dame Victory March on his accordion. In the foreground were nine-year-old Bruce and eight-year-old Roger dressed in football uniforms tossing a football, while three-year-old Andrew looked on, wanting to play with his older brothers. In a mishap, the ball flew out of Bruce's hands, missed Roger, but was caught by Fred. He laughed and handed the ball back to the boys. The scene was wholly natural. The camera then shifted to Phyllis Schlafly seated behind a desk hiding her eight-month pregnancy.

Smiling she began, "These are the six reasons I am voting for Barry Goldwater this November." Speaking in a reassuring voice, she laid out the case for voting for Goldwater, or more accurately, the case for voting against Johnson. She did not speak from notes or a teleprompter. She had given the speech dozens of times and had put it in the *The Gravediggers*. She warned that under cover of increased military expenditures, the American people were being "gypped" by Robert Strange McNamara's cancellation of missile programs and new bombers such as the B-70, and cutbacks on B-52 production. McNamara had closed down naval bases in the Mediterranean and air force bases in Turkey. She accused the Johnson administration of gambling the nation's security on a belief that accommodation with the Soviet Union was possible. Yet, even the record of Soviet actions during the previous four years belied the assumption that the Kremlin leaders could be trusted; they broke the voluntary test ban in 1961 and lied about their missiles in Cuba. Peace comes through military strength. Concluding, she asked, as her family surrounded her, "Do you want to risk your family and children on the Johnson-McNamara policies?" The speech was powerful, both in its presentation and in its substance. It was delivered in a matter-of-fact way by a woman with a natural presence for the camera. While the production quality, especially with its use of charts and tables, was mediocre, its substance was informative and appeared authoritative. In short, it was a performance, comparable in many ways to Ronald Reagan's "A Time for Choosing" televised address a week before the election. Supporters bought time for Schlafly's address to appear on dozens of stations throughout the nation.

While Schlafly worked full steam for Goldwater, thousands of other volunteers threw themselves into the Goldwater campaign. These volunteers came from the grassroots Right, Young Republicans, Young Americans for Freedom, local Republican clubs, and individuals who had been motivated by Goldwater's *The Conscience of a Conservative* or Schlafly's *A Choice Not an Echo*. This was the first political experience for many, including William Rehnquist, Robert Bork, Antonin Scalia, and Edwin Meese. It marked the beginning of a coherent conservative movement. Yet for all their efforts, the race was over even before it began. Polls immediately after the San Francisco convention showed that Johnson had an insurmountable lead. Later, secret polls taken by the Goldwater staff during the campaign showed their candidate was fighting a lost cause.[76]

On election night November 3, NBC predicted a landslide for Johnson even before the polls closed. The other networks followed shortly afterward with similar projections. When the returns were finally counted, Johnson won by over 16 million votes, receiving 43 million votes to 27 million, a 61 to 39 percent victory. The electoral vote was even worse; Johnson received 486 votes to Goldwater's embarrassing 52. Johnson did well in all regions, including the Midwest where he won 61 percent of the vote. Outside of his home state, Goldwater did well only in the Deep South, winning Mississippi, Alabama, South Carolina, Georgia, and Louisiana. Goldwater's Southern vote portended well for the future but presented a thin silver lining at the time. Republican victories were few and far between. In the Senate, George Murphy won in California and Roman Hruska in Nebraska. Liberal Republicans did somewhat better. John Lindsay held onto his New York seat in the House. George Romney won reelection as governor in Michigan. After absorbing the full consequences of the loss, Goldwater apologized, "I'm sorry I couldn't produce better results. I'm sorry that so many good men . . . went down with me."[77]

The Goldwater debacle was costly to the Republican party and would not go unchallenged. Behind closed doors and in secret meetings, discussions were held on the need to purge party leadership of conservatives. The moderates were out for revenge, and Phyllis Schlafly naturally came into the cross-hairs of those seeking to regain control of the party. For those Republican moderates who sought to turn the party away from its rightward swerve, Phyllis Schlafly symbolized the GOP Right that had come out of nowhere to become a force in the Republican party. In what she later described as the most productive year of her life, she emerged as a nationally known author of two best sellers and a voice representing the conservative movement, won a contested election as a delegate to the Republican National Convention, served as president of one of the largest women's Republican organizations in the country, and won election as vice-president of the National Federation for Republican Women, with the expectation that she would become the organization's next president. If Goldwater's critics were to restore the party to the political mainstream, the GOP Right would have to be purged. Schlafly became a natural target in this purge. Phyllis Schlafly was about to find that the nastiness of the Goldwater campaign did not end on November 3, 1964.

CHAPTER SIX

The Establishment Purges Schlafly

AFTER THE 1964 ELECTION, Phyllis Schlafly wrote to a supporter, "I am a prime target of the rule-or-ruin bunch who want to purge every pre-convention Goldwater backer from the Party. It certainly isn't any fun to stand up to the hostile press, as I have been doing for the past month, and see the venom drooling from their faces. But I am not going to turn and run—now that the heat is on. Too many people have put their faith in me, and I am not going to abandon them."[1]

Schlafly was fully aware that the disaster of the 1964 election led Establishment Republicans to conclude that the party needed to be moved back to the center and reestablish a reputation of moderation. The first step in this counter-revolution began when Republican National Committee Chairman Dean Burch, a Goldwater supporter, was dumped and replaced with moderate Ray Bliss, who openly attacked "extremists" in the GOP when he assumed his post as RNC chairman.[2] Bliss was a pragmatist and an efficient organizational man who had been chair of the successful Ohio Republican Party (1949–54), where he pioneered Republican direct-mail lists. As national chair he was intent on removing what he considered conservative ideologues from party positions. Having taken control of the Republican National Committee, the moderate-liberal-pragmatic wing targeted the Young Republicans, whose organization had been seized by conservative activists, and the National Federation of Republican Women, which was poised to elect Phyllis Schlafly as president in 1966. Moderate-pragmatic Republican leaders and operatives believed that if the party were to stand any chance of regaining the White House in 1968, it could not go into the election with Phyllis Schlafly, the author of *A Choice Not an Echo*, as president of the NFRW with its membership of 500,000 women. In these circumstances, the presidential election of this Republican women's organization took on an importance not seen in previous NFRW elections and soon involved the entire Republican party.

SCHLAFLY BUILDS A RÉSUMÉ IN THE ILLINOIS FEDERATION OF REPUBLICAN WOMEN

Unanimously elected vice-president of the National Federation of Republican Women in 1964, most members saw Phyllis Schlafly as the natural choice to succeed incumbent Dorothy Elston as president of this large and prestigious Republican organization. Phyllis Schlafly was arguably the best known member of the NFRW and she was popular among much of its rank and file. Elected president of the Illinois Federation of Republican Women (IFRW) in 1960, she had built it into one of the largest state organizations. She was a popular leader and when she considered stepping down as president in 1962, there was a groundswell of support for her to serve another term. A delegation drove 300 miles from DuPage County to Alton to persuade Fred Schlafly to allow his wife to serve another term. She did, and IFRW membership increased another 10,000 members, or over 46 percent. Illinois claimed over 50,000 members with over 140 chapters located throughout the state.[3] Membership had nearly doubled since she took office in 1960 and over thirty new clubs had been added. This was accomplished on an annual budget of approximately $7,000 and an all-volunteer staff.[4]

Schlafly's success lay in her ability to inspire the rank and file and her skills as an organizer and speaker. Most women in the Illinois Federation considered themselves conservative Republicans, so there were no real ideological divisions in the organization. There was competition, however, between northern chapters around Chicago and downstate chapters. As a resident of Alton, Schlafly was definitely downstate, but in her three terms in office she faced no opposition from northern clubs. Schlafly instilled in Federation members a belief that they, too, should be leaders in the struggle for a better America. In order to instill a sense of confidence, Schlafly asked each IFRW chapter to develop study programs in which rank and file women learned to debate political issues and speak in public.

One training technique she recommended was for chapters to set aside time at meetings to educate members to respond to Democratic party arguments on current issues. In these sessions, the president would toss out a series of Democratic arguments on current issues to which club members were challenged to give short, effective answers.

Schlafly urged chapters to designate a part of each meeting to a book review. "Book reviews," she told chapter members, "are a perennial favorite program for all women's groups." Instead of having pro–New Deal or pro-socialist books, however, she said "pro-American books" are "virtually an untapped field" for review, and she provided a list of recommended books.[5] She recommended books on current issues such as the Cuban Revolution, liberal bias in the classroom, the Supreme Court, communists in government, Franklin D. Roosevelt, and Yalta. These were books for women who were politically involved—books useful in political debate, not books for the intellectual salon. Through these efforts, Schlafly developed a cadre of well-informed activists.

Schlafly understood that activists need to be inspired to remain committed over the long haul. There was a tendency within political groups such as the IFRW to become lethargic in off-election years. Schlafly kept the fires burning by reminding her members that their's was a moral mission—the preservation of American freedom. Writing shortly before Christmas of 1962, she said that the "Four Freedoms" needed to be protected. Her Four Freedoms were different from Roosevelt's. As she saw it, the IFRW was involved in a fight for the Freedom to Keep Our Religious Heritage, Freedom from Obscenity, Freedom from Criminal Attack, and Freedom from the Communist Conspiracy. "Clever campaigns," she said, have been conducted to "remove all acknowledgment of God from our public institutions and official life." While public displays of religious faith are taken out of public life, obscenity and pornography are legalized, even though the men who wrote the First and Fifth Amendments to our Constitution did not intend to make obscenity a civil right. An enervated national spirit prevented opposing social decay at home and the advance of communism aboard.[6]

"Each member a leader" was the motto Schlafly projected. In doing so, women could become leaders within the GOP. "The time is past," she declared, "when the women of the Republican party are merely doorbell pushers. We have earned our right to participate in the making of policies at the top which spell the difference between defeat and victory."[7] Schlafly projected the image of the new breed of Republican woman who sought more from political work than serving as volunteer labor for election campaigns. In "Women in Politics," an article written for the national magazine of Phi Gamma Nu, Schlafly expressed her conviction that "for many years, women have been carrying the major burden of the precinct work and doorbell pushing which win elections."[8] Now, she said, women within the party are winning strength in Party machinery and are "becoming more important in their own right, and not merely as the mirrored reflection of their masculine counterparts." This demand for power was not just a call for women to have power for the sake of power. Underlying her conviction that women should achieve prominence within the party was an understanding that NFRW members were *conservative* women who were part of a larger movement of conservatives who sought control of the Republican party. Conservative ideology united women and their male counterparts in the conservative movement, but women activists believed they had a special role to play as women.

Schlafly made women proud to be members of the IFRW. As one member wrote her following the IFRW 1960 convention, "You made me feel quite important. My importance would have been nil, if I had not surrounded myself with loyal friends. Many of them had never heard of the Illinois Federation of Republican Women, but they know all about it now."[9] Young mothers and career women were equally inspired by this mother of (then) five children.[10] For example, one young mother from Arlington Heights, a Chicago suburb, wrote Schlafly after hearing her speak before a women's Republican club at the Drake Hotel, "Your ability and enthusiasm really did inspire us in our local efforts. The example of your busy schedule leaves little alibi for us young mothers to shirk the responsibility of safeguarding our freedom."[11] These young women formed the basis of Schlafly's political support in the following decades. She elicited from her followers a loyalty rare in politics. They saw in her, as one member wrote her, the "demonstration of fearlessness and candor of women." She spoke and acted on their behalf. "Many times you are putting into words my very thoughts. . . . I am proud to be a member of an organization of which you are president and such an articulate spokesman. Don't ever let anyone persuade you to 'tone down.' "[12]

Schlafly's message resonated with the rank and file of the NFRW because she was in tune with their conservative politics and their sense of themselves as political volunteers trying to make America a better place for their children. Most women in the National Federation of Republican Women in 1964 were very conservative, and through leaders such as Phyllis Schlafly and Katharine Kennedy Brown in Ohio, they were inspired to become political activists. Most were not feminists, incipient feminists, or even feminist minded, but women who enjoyed working together as women. Schlafly stood with them, in political commitment, ideological belief, and moral outlook. For this reason, Republican women loved to hear Schlafly speak, so that by the early 1960s she had become one of the most popular speakers in the state. In 1960 alone, she made over 98 public appearances. Four years later as her term as president was drawing to a close, she had trekked thousands of miles throughout Illinois, lecturing to small groups, local chapters, and state conventions. Schlafly never seemed to tire. As she wrote one Federation member, "This is my 18th year working for the Republican party," and during this time "I have given thousand of hours of dedicated work for the cause of good government through the medium of the Republican party. I have traveled the length and breadth of our very large state of Illinois hundreds of times over in order to speak to small groups and large, help little clubs, build stronger Republican organizations, inject enthusiasm, inspire and persuade women to work for the Party . . . I have done this at my own expense and at great sacrifice on my part and on the part of my family—for one purpose, because I believe in working for good government."[13]

Schlafly brought an ideological message to her followers and for this reason she developed a deserved reputation as a fiercely committed conservative, certain of her own moral outlook and principles. Less noticed by her friends and enemies was the practical side of her political work and her ability to combine political principle and pragmatic politics, albeit within the confines of a well-defined conservatism that appeared narrowly ideological. A case in point was her relations with her home state U.S. Senator, Everett Dirksen. Both Fred and Phyllis Schlafly were on a first name basis with Dirksen and corresponded periodically with him about political matters. Dirksen supported strong anticommunist legislation and a strong military defense program—two areas which most concerned the Schlaflys. It was disappointing to Phyllis and other members of the Illinois Federation when Dirksen came out in support of President Kennedy's Nuclear Test Ban Treaty. Schlafly testified before the Senate Foreign Relations Committee against the treaty, reciting the history of treaties broken by the Soviet Union. The IFRW passed a resolution and organized a petition drive against the treaty. Some women in the IFRW wanted to censure Dirksen. This effort boiled over in late May 1962 at an IFRW training conference for the upcoming congressional elections. One young woman rose to present a censure motion, but Phyllis Schlafly ruled her out of order.

Following the meeting, Schlafly wrote the woman she was willing to debate the issue of the Test Ban Treaty, but she scolded the woman for not supporting Dirksen. "He does not always vote the way I would like," she wrote, "but he gets an 80 percent rating from the ACA, this is a passing grade. . . . Were you there in 1952 when Dirksen fought for the nomination of Bob Taft, a man who would have cleaned out the State Department, balanced the budget, and turned out of Washington the hoards of international socialists who control our government to this day?"[14] Moreover, Schlafly remained an adamant supporter of Dirksen when he played a critical role in the Senate in enacting the Civil Rights Act of 1964, another sign that Schlafly's conservatism was not driven by race or opposition to black civil rights.

On the other hand, her relations with liberal Republican Charles Percy, a rising star in Illinois, were more ambiguous. She endorsed Percy when he ran for U.S. Senator, but Percy blocked Schlafly's attempt to serve as the Illinois representative on the Platform Committee at the 1968 Convention. Differences with Percy, however, were symptomatic of festering problems within the Republican party between the conservative wing represented by Schlafly and Dirksen and the moderate wing represented by Percy.

THE BATTLE LINES ARE DRAWN IN THE FEDERATION

OF REPUBLICAN WOMEN

Fears that the Republican party was on its way to returning to its status during the 1930s of a minor, opposition party haunted the Republican Establishment following the Goldwater debacle of 1964. There was no doubt that liberalism was on the ascendance. The Republican party chanting "this is socialism" was not going to win elections. Even many of those who had supported Goldwater in 1964 were persuaded that ideological conservatism needed to be replaced by realistic pragmatism. Within the Republican leadership there was a growing belief that a more centrist course needed to be pursued by preventing Phyllis Schlafly from becoming the next president of the National Federation. Elly Peterson, Michigan Republican State Chairman and a Romney supporter, took it upon herself to organize against Schlafly, even before it was clear that Dorothy Elston, the current president, would support an anti-Schlafly movement. Elston had endorsed Goldwater in 1964, and although she did not like Schlafly, the two women seemed to get along quite well in public.[15]

Peterson was convinced that Schlafly and her followers needed to be defeated in the National Federation if the Republican party were to move forward. Her party position put her in close contact with other moderate-liberal Republicans in the state and nationally. Peterson made it clear that she wanted the Goldwater faction removed from the NFRW, the Young Republicans, and GOP leadership positions generally. She stood for giving the GOP a new look by supporting people such as John Lindsay, Edward Brooke, and Charles Percy.[16] In 1965, Peterson moved to take control of the Michigan Federation of Republican Women by running Ruth Hobbs against Goldwater supporter Bernice Zilly. Peterson described the state convention fight in September as "vicious," but by controlling the parliamentarian who continued to rule in favor of the Hobbs faction, Hobbs and her slate won 159–90. Following the victory, Peterson sent a letter to members of the anti-Schlafly coalition that was beginning to emerge nationwide describing how they had won in Michigan and how these same tactics could be used to win in other states. Peterson observed that there were five to seven states whose current presidents are "against us" but could be turned into "our column."[17]

As Peterson extended her network of anti-Schlafly women in the National Federation, she found others who shared her concern about what they considered extremists in the party. Typical was Katherine K. Neuberger, a Republican national committeewoman, who wrote Peterson to tell her she was glad she was "taking the leadership in the National Federation struggle." She agreed, "It is something that has got to be done and if we just drift on and hope it will all go away we will wake up some morning and find out that the Federation has been taken over by the extreme right wing which will be a catastrophe for the entire party." She mentioned that in her state of New Jersey they confronted "disciples of Phyllis Schlafly" whom she suspected of being Birchers. She warned that she had a distinct feeling, "although no proof, that she [Schlafly] is going to work this thing [the election] through the John Birch Society" and she believed that Schlafly was giving instructions to her Birch followers on "how to further infiltrate party machinery and clubs."[18] Neuberger was not the only Republican leader worried about a takeover of the party by the Right. Indeed, Peterson reported that talks had been held with Ray Bliss at the Republican

National Committee offices about the "Schlafly situation" and that Bliss was also opposed to Schlafly, but he doubted her strength in the Federation. Peterson was told that Bliss believed that "we would have to settle for a 'conservative' as president." Peterson agreed with this assessment and added that if electing a conservative was necessary to stop Schlafly, then "we should look at the least bad" conservative.[19] After much searching, it was decided that the NFRW board should run Gladys O'Donnell of California for president. Elston let it be known that she liked the idea of O'Donnell and would work behind the scenes to support her, but would not publicly endorse her until after she had received the official nomination by the Federation board.[20]

O'Donnell had never been elected to any NFRW office, but she was a long-time Republican activist with a reputation of being an independent-minded, although not terribly intellectual woman. She was an early female pilot, having won several transcontinental air races in the 1930s. During the Second World War she trained 8,000 cadets at a flight training school in Southern California. She was a Republican National Convention delegate in 1940, 1952, and 1956. She had worked in the gubernatorial campaigns of William Knowland and Richard Nixon and in the Senate campaign of George Murphy. An NFRW campaign letter offered this description of her: "She is a woman who has always worked to keep the party in the mainstream of American life. Her philosophy is one which embraces the conservative and moderate points of view and which recognizes the danger and futility of extremism."[21]

O'Donnell's reputation as an opponent of extremism within the NFRW came in the summer of 1965 when she sponsored a California Federation Board of Directors resolution against political extremism in California. Prior to this, O'Donnell had kept quiet about the strength of the grassroots Right, especially the John Birch Society, within the California Federation. In 1965, as the NFRW presidential campaign began to shape up, she publicly endorsed this resolution condemning a one-minute telephone message which callers heard when they dialed "Let Freedom Ring," a program sponsored by the John Birch Society. One dial-a-message program was critical of Eisenhower's foreign policy and allegedly urged listeners to purchase Robert Welch's *The Politician* and Phyllis Schlafly's and Admiral Ward's *The Gravediggers*. The resolution was clearly aimed at Phyllis Schlafly and was widely and favorably reported in newspapers throughout the state.[22]

Schlafly was shocked by the charges, describing them as utterly "false and treacherous propaganda." Upon reading the transcript of the telephone message, she discovered the *The Gravediggers* was not even mentioned. She wrote O'Donnell accusing her of participating in "defamatory attacks" that were "widely emotional and inflammatory." She pointed out Eisenhower was only mentioned once in *The Gravediggers*, where he was commended for his firm stand in defense of Quemoy and Matsu. Furthermore, Schlafly asked O'Donnell, "Do you really think it is 'constructive and objective' to draft a resolution attacking *The Gravediggers* when you admit you have not read the book and have no evidence that it was being promoted in the telephone message?"[23] Chapters throughout California passed counter-resolutions in support of Schlafly. O'Donnell tried to downplay the ideological differences, telling the press that "we are conservatives, not nuts."[24] Schlafly supporters saw the issue differently. As one woman from San Marino wrote Schlafly, "Our problem as you know is terrific personal ambition in certain leaders. . . . This leads to opportunism and a loosening of standards and principles. There is a great desire to be in the good graces of our party men."[25] When Schlafly came to California to speak to the Commonwealth Club in San Francisco later that fall, she drew an overflow crowd of women who turned out to show their support for her.

As Peterson set about organizing for O'Donnell, she discovered that the support Schlafly enjoyed in California was found in other states as well. An anti-Schlafly supporter in Delaware reported to Peterson that Elston's behind-the-scenes maneuvering for O'Donnell was having an opposite effect than intended. Many of the Delaware women, the report declared, were not "very impressed with Gladys" and "some of the clubs are so kooky" it is unlikely that they could be won for her. The best thing to do was to reorganize the state Federation along different geographical lines and start clubs with "a different point of view." Peterson found similar problems in other states—or as she put it, "the nut fringe is beautifully organized." She feared that the Schlafly forces had moved heavily into the South and "it is bad medicine in Southern California." Given the popularity of Schlafly, Peterson advised that "the only thing we can do is pray that Pennsylvania and New York and others in the East can control their delegates there." The situation was so dire that "I think it is time the men realized the seriousness and helped us and so I have moved in that field to discuss with some of the leaders on the National Committee, State Chairmen, etc., so they are with us."[26]

These reports indicated that Schlafly enjoyed national support in the rank and file of the Federation. When she won election as First Vice President of the Federation, Schlafly believed she was the odds-on favorite to become its president at its next biennial convention in 1966. Traditionally, women elected as vice-president were elected president in the following election. Schlafly was hesitant, however, to become president of the Federation because it meant spending large amounts of time in Washington, D.C. In late December, Schlafly wrote confidentially to her friend Chester Ward, "I would hate the cocktail party circuit there [Washington, D.C.]. I'd be delighted if I never had to sit at another head table. Enough of the thrills of politics will come my way regardless of whether or not I have any title."[27] Schlafly hoped that if she did become president an arrangement could be made for her to spend one or two days a week in Washington, D. C., returning home to spend most of her time in Alton. The plan was probably unrealistic, but living arrangements turned out to be the least of Schlafly's problems.

Schlafly realized that trouble was afoot when the Federation Executive Board decided in late August 1965 to change the biennial convention from its traditional even-dated year to 1967.[28] The ostensible reason given for the change was that it allowed more women to attend the convention since it did not conflict with congressional midterm or presidential elections. Few believed, however, that was the reason for the change. The national convention had been scheduled to be held in Los Angeles, a stronghold of Goldwater conservatives within the Federation. The previous year, conservatives had won major victories in Federation elections, taking control of most of Southern California, as well as many chapters in Northern California. Some NFRW members had previously suggested the national convention site be held in Hawaii, but that was defeated at a board meeting. Schlafly, in fact, spoke against the proposal declaring most Republican women "just don't travel by air. They go by bus, they share cars, and you just can't go to Hawaii that way." She added they often stay with relatives and friends, and this left Hawaii out.[29]

The Executive Committee decided that the national convention would be held in Washington, D.C. in 1967, a move Schlafly saw as benefiting her opponents who had strength on the East Coast. Schlafly could do nothing about the decision to postpone the convention and change the meeting site.[30] Privately she wrote the NFRW Executive Committee to say that the proposal to change the biennial from even to odd years had been "repeatedly explored, studied, and debated . . . and repeatedly voted down." She added she was refused the courtesy of being informed about the decision until two days after the vote, when she received a phone call from "one of the extreme left-wing newspapers in the United States [the *Washington Post*]." She told the board that once this report appeared, she was pursued with "relentless vigor" by "metropolitan newspapers in Washington, D.C., Detroit, Chicago, St. Louis, wire services, *Newsweek*, *The Saturday Evening Post*, and *Look*."[31] While Schlafly privately complained about the convention change, her supporters across the country mounted a protest campaign to persuade the NFRW national leadership to reverse course. Hundreds of women wrote to the national office complaining about what appeared to be a conscious move to prevent Schlafly from winning election to the presidency.

Most of those protesting the change were from the rank and file; Schlafly received little support from state presidents. There were some notable exceptions, however; Katharine Kennedy Brown, president of the Ohio Federation of Republican Women, openly protested the convention change. She was told by the national office that changing the date of the convention had not been aimed at Schlafly. "[T]his was the farthest thing from my mind," executive committee member Lahoma Dennis wrote, but her next words belied this assertion. She claimed that Schlafly was too controversial to become Federation president and that even Goldwater had refused to appoint her to a position on his national campaign staff. "Unfortunately," Dennis added, lest the point be missed, "many of our emotional federation members do not possess this quality of making a realistic choice either way." Dennis concluded her letter by stating that a stormy 1966 convention would be "very harmful to the official party. If you are successful in stirring up the trouble you appear to be trying to, you will be successful in dividing our party more and playing right into the Democratic hands."[32]

The stop-Schlafly forces revealed their plans in late January 1967 when the sixty-nine member Federation board met in New Orleans to choose a seven-woman nominating committee hostile to a Schlafly presidency. Schlafly did not have many supporters on the Federation's national board—her strength lay in the rank and file of the 4,200 individual clubs, especially those in California, the Midwest, and the South—so there was not much Schlafly or her supporters could do to change the nomination process. Schlafly decided to bring the issue to the press.

Prior to the board meeting, she gave a *Chicago Tribune* reporter a list of seven names who would be elected to the nominating committee—and each of the seven was subsequently elected.[33] She also told the reporter that this nominating committee would select a "liberal" candidate such as Mrs. Gladys O'Donnell to become the next president of the Federation. At the same time, Schlafly supporters charged in press reports that Winthrop Rockefeller, Governor of Arkansas and Nelson's brother, had sent eight paid members of his staff to lobby the Federation board meeting in New Orleans to ensure that Schlafly did not get the nomination. In addition, Schlafly supporters charged that Governor George Romney of Michigan also had sent political operatives to work the conference to ensure that the selection of the nominating committee went his way. Elly Peterson's name was not mentioned specifically, but it is evident that they had her in mind as a Romney operative.

Emotions were already charged on both sides when Schlafly told the *Chicago Tribune* that the Federation was trying to purge Goldwater supporters. Elston reported that Schlafly's charges revealed "her political immaturity, which is one reason the nominating committee now feels she is not the person to fill that sensitive charge" of being president of the NFRW.[34] O'Donnell then told the *Chicago Tribune* that a woman who is the mother of six children wouldn't have time to devote to the national presidency of the federation.[35] Charges about her six children continued to be heard throughout the fight.[36] One NFRW member wrote, "In reference to the 'child neglect' [accusation] the only thing I hear was that Mrs. Schlafly has six children, teenagers through 2 years old. It was just left for each individual to form her own opinion."[37] Such remarks ensured that the fight for the presidency was going to be a nasty, no-holds-barred contest, and it was by no means certain who was going to emerge as victor.

The nomination of Gladys O'Donnell was a clear slap in the face to Schlafly. O'Donnell's attack on extremists in the California Federation prior to her nomination was taken as evidence by Schlafly supporters that ideological warfare had been declared against Goldwater conservatives in the NFRW and the Republican party. In these circumstances, Schlafly was not about to run away from a fight, and it is doubtful that her supporters would have allowed her to do so. On April 5, 1967, Schlafly declared her candidacy at a joint press conference with Maureen Reagan, Governor Ronald Reagan's daughter and president of the Orange County Federation. The twenty-six-year-old Maureen Reagan became president of the Orange County Federation in 1966 in what the *Los Angeles Times* called "a coup d'état." Maureen Reagan opened the press conference by declaring Phyllis Schlafly was not "an extremist." If she were an extremist, Reagan asked, why had Schlafly been elected unanimously to the first vice-presidency of the organization? When Schlafly stepped forward to talk, she artfully ignored the issue of extremism and instead focused her remarks on the need to recruit youth into the federation. "It is high time that the Federation has a president who is a wife and a mother. . . . We must attract youth."[38] In doing so, Schlafly aimed to emphasize a single theme: the current NFRW leadership were old party hacks, who while proclaiming themselves "conservatives" were willing to do the bidding of party insiders seeking to purge the party of Goldwater Republicans. As Schlafly portrayed her opponents, patronage and power brought the NFRW leadership and the GOP moderate establishment together in a campaign against the new breed of Republican woman for whom principle ranked higher than patronage or power.

Schlafly proclaimed it a fight over the future of the Republican party. At issue was not just the NFRW presidency, but the desire of the Eastern Establishment to purge the Goldwater wing of the party from all positions of power, even one as humble as the NFRW presidency. Her rhetoric was populist; her appeal was "us against them"; and her message was "This is a fight for the integrity of the GOP." Schlafly cast the election in moral terms—principle versus self-aggrandizement; democratic expression against rule by an insider political clique; the rank and file against the kingmakers. She accused her opponents of being Rockefeller liberals who wanted to purge the NFRW of conservatives. She maintained that this was part of a larger strategy by the Republican establishment to drive out Goldwater Republicans. Actually, it was not just the Rockefeller wing of the party that opposed Schlafly, but also party operatives driven by the desire to win elected office. Nonetheless, Schlafly's ideological message inspired her followers by what they saw as Schlafly's unselfish tenacity in fighting for political principle. They were emboldened by recognizing they were taking on the entire Republican establishment.

Political observers at the time also saw the fight as a struggle over control of the Republican party between the moderates and the conservatives whom Rockefeller labeled "extremists." William Rusher warned in a widely distributed pamphlet that the liberal-Eastern wing of the party was attempting to sneak in the back door by gaining control of the NFRW.[39] Political columnist David Broder, writing in the *Washington Post*, declared that the temptation to dismiss the NFRW as "Mickey Mouse politics played with exaggerated emotion for minimal stakes is an error. . . . Their internal battles historically have proved accurate forecasts of succeeding convention fights. And, increasingly, senior party officials and even presidential prospects have been drawn into the fray."[40] Writing in the *St. Louis Post-Dispatch*, long-time Schlafly critic and journalist Richard Dudman reported "moderates" within the party did not want to be "saddled" with a Schlafly presidency in the 1968 election. One "informed Republican source" told Dudman, "This will keep her out of the presidency during the 1966 elections and give them [GOP leaders] a chance to find someone to run against her if she is a candidate a year later."[41]

Schlafly played upon this theme that the future of the party was at stake. The question she posed was whether the Republican party should stand for conservative principles or opportunistically pursue whatever best wins elections. In framing the issue this way, Schlafly saw the campaign as a struggle against a liberal takeover of the GOP. At the same time she wanted to project an image of the campaign as the young against the old, Insurgents against the Old Guard. There was much truth to this picture. Schlafly appeared to attract younger women who had recently come into the Federation through the Goldwater campaign, and these women were attracted to Schlafly as representing a new breed of Republican women—activists who were young, energetic, and well informed about domestic issues and international events. They were not willing to take a back seat any more in the party—just going to luncheons and teas to raise money for candidates, stuffing envelopes, and doing the menial work for political campaigns. During the campaign much of Schlafly's political rhetoric called for women to exert more political power as women within the GOP.[42] This special place Schlafly reserved for women—in the home and in politics—perplexed her liberal opponents then and later.

This message resonated well with her supporters. They had beaten the Eastern Establishment at the San Francisco GOP convention in 1964; they could do it again. This conviction was expressed in a Schlafly speech that was reprinted and widely circulated by the Glen Park Chapter in Gary, Indiana. Schlafly declared, "The millions of Republicans who worked for Goldwater resent being told they are second-class citizens and cannot hold high office no matter how well qualified. This is most divisive." At the bottom of the reprint was a printed hand-written note, "The liberal rats are out again. Support Phyllis Schlafly; she worked for Goldwater as we did." Over 50,000 copies of the speech were published and sent to congressmen, senators, governors, and chapter presidents.[43]

This theme was picked up in other mass mailings. In one campaign letter, a Midwestern Republican woman equated the established NFRW leadership with the kingmakers: "This same dictatorial group is attempting to regain control of the party by beginning with grassroots organizations. This is the time for us in the Midwest to make our voices heard with courage and forthrightness, so the party will remain a party of the people and one that truly offers us 'a choice, not an echo.' "[44] NFRW insiders were accused of having nominated Gladys O'Donnell in "perfume-filled rooms" behind closed doors.[45]

While many Republicans declared their neutrality in the NFRW fight, hard-core conservatives outside the NFRW rallied to Schlafly's cause. Representative John Ashbrook of Ohio actively solicited support for the Schlafly campaign. New Hampshire newspaper publisher William Loeb raised money from his friends to support Schlafly's campaign.[46] Similarly, other conservative editors came to Schlafly's support, seeing the election as part of a scheme by liberal Republicans to oust conservatives in the GOP. The editor of the Illinois *Dixon Telegraph*, Sanford J. Bowyer, wrote in an editorial, "Yes, the Eastern Kingmakers are at it again. These left wing, liberal, or moderate groups (take your choice) who cry for party unity—if it is on their terms—are out to eliminate Phyllis Schlafly one way or another."[47] Bowyer sent his editorial to leaders in the Republican party. Writing on behalf of Schlafly, General Thomas Lane declared in his weekly column, "The Left is doing in the Federation what it would like to do in the Party. It must be stopped if the party is ever to become an effective political body."[48]

The national NFRW officers under Dorothy Elston threw their full support behind O'Donnell, refusing to release delegate lists to Schlafly and issuing press statements in support of O'Donnell.[49] Both sides spent ten of thousands of dollars, while exchanging bitter accusations of unfair campaign tactics and allegations. Rumors spread that Phyllis Schlafly was a member of the John Birch Society and even a member of the militant Minutemen.[50] Much of the criticism leveled against Schlafly by her opponents focused on her allegedly divisive nature. A female critic in Louisiana wrote that Schlafly lacked "the ability to work harmoniously with people of different views." While she turns her "charm and graciousness on and off at will," often becoming "cold and curt," Schlafly would drive out opponents in the NFRW who disagreed with her.[51]

Both sides believed the stakes were high in what normally would be a routine election. The NFRW split along ideological lines, which tended to fall into regional patterns: the West, Midwest, and South threw its support to Schlafly, while the Northeastern states of Pennsylvania, New York, and New Jersey supported O'Donnell. The rapid expansion of clubs in those three states led to allegations by the Schlafly forces that they were "cooking" their membership lists. Schlafly accused Pennsylvania of claiming an increase from 10,743 members in 1965 to 45,024 in 1967, and New York claimed a membership of 65,000 members in 1967, but paid dues on only 46,752 members that year. Schlafly noted that ten Missouri clubs were denied the right to vote because the state treasurer was one day late in forwarding their dues to Washington. Schlafly concluded, "The point is that it was grossly unfair and illegal to disfranchise small clubs all over the country for trivial reasons, while New York and Pennsylvania were allowed such irregularities."[52] Factionalism was especially fierce in Michigan where Elly Peterson actively worked against Schlafly.[53] Schlafly enjoyed deep support in Michigan among the rank and file.

To counter this support, Elly Peterson began organizing new NFRW clubs, especially in urban black areas of Detroit. When the Michigan Federation tried to deny charters to these new chapters because of irregularities in their applications, Elly Peterson raised the race issue. She wrote the board of the state Federation, "I am told there are those who wish to deny Negro clubs admission—I positively refuse to believe this, even if there are not Negroes on your Board or in positions of authority. . . . Now, I understand much of the fear is because new clubs may have the strength to run people for office. Is there to be no broadening of the base within the Federation leadership?"[54] An irate board member responded to these charges of racism, "I resent having my integrity and honesty questioned. . . . Under great stress and duress, we have been asked to take these clubs into our membership so that they can vote at our convention, which they know absolutely nothing about." She added that "we have never discriminated against any woman, regardless of race, creed or color."[55] But Peterson's tactics prevailed. In the spring election for Michigan Federation officers in 1966, conservative leaders were ousted by a slate of moderates headed by Ruth Hobbs, later nominated for treasurer of the national organization. Peterson claimed that if moderates could reclaim the Michigan Federation, Governor George Romney could reclaim the GOP in 1968.[56]

Meanwhile, in other states pro-Schlafly chapters were expelled or denied charters by state organizations. Typical was the experience of the Nashville Robert Taft Republican Women's Club with a membership of 100 women which was denied membership in the Tennessee Federation of Republican Women. When it petitioned the national office, its petition was denied without a hearing. Elston told the group the fact your group was denied membership in the first place "would indicate to me that somewhere the Robert Taft Club did not qualify in some area."[57] In Wisconsin, the attack on pro-Schlafly supporters came under the guise of ousting members of the John Birch Society. At the same time, there were reports that the state organization was allowing new members to join the NFRW for one dollar apiece.[58] By January 1967, divisions within the states became a major problem for the national office. Elston announced she was deeply concerned over the reports of paper clubs being formed and large clubs being broken into small clubs for the purpose of creating more delegates.[59]

Emotions ran so high in California that lawsuits for libel were threatened as accusations were hurled back and forth in the battle to control the state with the largest membership in the NFRW. Schlafly had strong support in California. Maureen Reagan played an important role in organizing the state; and the president of the southern division of the California Federation, Grace Thackeray, was a Schlafly booster. Schlafly and Thackeray bore the brunt of the attack against extremism. Schlafly wrote Thackeray urging her to stand fast against the campaign of political slurs and not let political insults get her down. "Those who work in politics for material rewards," Schlafly wrote, "mistakenly think that others have the same objectives. There are fortunately many, such as you and me, who work in politics purely and simply to do our duty, as God gives us the light to see that duty, to help guarantee that our children grow up in a land that is free and independent."[60]

At the national office, Dorothy Elston supported the attempts to isolate and discredit Schlafly supporters in California. For example, Lucile Hosmer, a Schlafly supporter in Northern California, was surprised to find her regular legislative report was not sent to other NFRW members because of Elston's veto. Furthermore, Elston refused to pay for travel expenses when Hosmer was invited to speak at a regional NFRW meeting. Elston said it was NFRW policy not to fund talks by those who were not "standing chairs." But Hosmer pointed out she previously spoke at two other regional conferences, and the national office had paid for those trips. Hosmer charged that the national office had implemented a "ruthless" policy to "force conformity" to the point "where no one dares to disagree with the hierarchy for fear of being smeared as an extremist before her co-workers."[61]

Acrimony within the NFRW spilled over to the mainstream of the Republican party. Shortly before she declared that she was running for the presidency, Schlafly made a bold move to point an accusing finger at Ray Bliss: On March 23, 1967, Schlafly "invaded," as one newspaper described it, the Republican National Committee headquarters, leaving the staff "reeling." The *Washington Evening Star* reported "GOP Chairman Ray Bliss, Michigan Governor George Romney and other party moderates are privately opposed to her election because they fear it would blur the 'moderate' party image they have been so carefully cultivating since the Goldwater fiasco in 1964." Schlafly went to the National Federation suites at the GOP headquarters to demand the delegate list, a right of every candidate running for office. What ensued was a 2-hour "verbal battle between Schlafly and Mrs. Elizabeth Fielding, public relations director for the Federation." On the way out, Schlafly bumped into Ray Bliss at the elevator. The newspaper accounts did not describe the reaction of the two when they met, but it was not necessary. Behind any polite exterior, Bliss and Schlafly saw themselves as combatants.[62] Meanwhile, Congressman John Ashbrook (R-Ohio) denounced Bliss for trying to purge the party of conservatives by supporting O'Donnell.

As the campaign heated up, the RNC reported its office was flooded with mail, running sixty to seventy letters a day, plus phone calls. One national committee member working in the national office lamented, "it is a sad thing that this break had to come when we have an excellent chance to win in 1968. This fight is tending to split our party again." In April, an irate Goldwater telephoned the RNC claiming this fight was "so bitter in Arizona" it might cost him winning the Senate race.[63] In Arizona charges were made that because Goldwater had taken a neutral stand in the election, Schlafly supporters in the state were secretly supporting a more conservative candidate in Goldwater's bid to regain his Senate seat.[64] Matters with Goldwater became more complicated when NFRW President Dorothy Elston released a letter from Goldwater appearing to endorse O'Donnell. The letter stated "for over thirty years I have known, admired, and worked with Gladys O'Donnell in Republican politics." In the letter, Goldwater denied the contest was between "so-called liberal eastern wing and the western conservatives." This letter was sent to NFRW members and major newspapers across the country. It turned out that Dorothy Elston had cropped out a section favorable to Schlafly in which Goldwater said, "Anyone who is familiar with politics at all must be familiar with the fantastic work done by this fine lady [Schlafly]."[65] Proclaiming his neutrality, Goldwater sent a copy of his letter directly to Schlafly, who was able to release the full text to the press.

Meanwhile Schlafly supporters raked up old charges that O'Donnell had thrown the California delegation to Eisenhower, away from Taft, in 1952. These charges became so widespread that Senator George Murphy released a press statement from his hospital bed where he was recovering from surgery declaring O'Donnell was a true Republican conservative. In Illinois Everett Dirksen released a statement saying that while he did not wish to intrude in the internal politics of the Federation, he believed "Phyllis Schlafly does have real ability. . . . She can be quite eloquent and she does have administrative ability."[66] Other letters from Illinois state legislators and congressional representatives were released to the press supporting Schlafly for the presidency.[67] The rank and file of the Illinois Federation enthusiastically supported Schlafly. Some moderates, however, came out against her, among them Pat Hutar, a former national vice chairman of Young Republicans.

SCHLAFLY LOSES AN ELECTION

When the convention opened in Washington, D.C. on May 5, 1967, emotions ran high on both sides. Schlafly's supporters wore eagle pins to clearly identify themselves among the thousands of women who came to D.C. to fight for the soul of the GOP. These eagle pins symbolized the righteousness of their cause, being inspired by a Biblical verse in Isaiah 40:31, "They that wait upon the Lord shall renew their strength. They shall mount up with wings as eagles; they shall run, and not be weary; and they shall walk and not faint." (The eagle pin is still

Schlafly's insignia.) The NFRW leadership excluded conservatives from the platform and filled the program with so-called "unity" speeches from nearly every moderate-liberal Republican available, including Rep. Margaret Heckler of Massachusetts, Senators Mark Hatfield of Oregon, Charles Percy of Illinois, and Howard Baker of Tennessee, and Governors George Romney of Michigan, John A. Love of Colorado, and Walter Hickel of Alaska. The candidates were not permitted to address the convention.

There is evidence, although it remains inconclusive, that Elston and O'Donnell packed the convention with their delegates, while trying to exclude delegates identified as Schlafly supporters. A number of Schlafly supporters reported on the Saturday morning of the voting that they saw several buses from New York, New Jersey, and Pennsylvania unloading women at the rear of the convention hotel. "Each woman was given a packet, a badge, and told to say they were from Rochester," one woman informed Schlafly.[68] Typical of the many reports coming to Schlafly telling her about convention irregularities was a letter sent by two Ohio supporters who discovered expense money was available for O'Donnell supporters. When they arrived at the convention they were directed to contact Mrs. Robert Low Bacon, a prominent New York delegate, whom they found at the O'Donnell campaign suite. "We posed as O'Donnell fans," they wrote, "but shy on funds." They were surprised when they were offered "free quarters in lieu of cash to defray our expenses," but they were even more surprised to "wind up at the home of Rep. George H.W. Bush of Texas!" At the Bush home, they wrote, "we were really given the works—breakfast by a Mexican cook—and extended such courtesies as to embarrass us." At the convention, "we got through the voting line in a hurry too, and we are still wondering about that," given the huge voting delays Schlafly supporters endured. They concluded their letter by telling Schlafly that shenanigans were evident at the convention; then they asked "if there's any way the Americans in the Houston area can retire him [Mr. Bush]—we assume he is a fair-haired boy" of the Republican establishment.[69]

On the first evening of the convention, both sides threw receptions for their followers. The reception for O'Donnell, sponsored by the national headquarters, was elaborate. After being greeted by a reception line of NFRW officers—excluding First Vice President Phyllis Schlafly—guests were directed toward the bar. The Schlafly reception, sponsored by Californians for Schlafly, was more modest in its arrangements, but more spirited. The overwhelming majority of California delegates supported Schlafly rather than the Californian O'Donnell. The *Washington Post* reported some 1,500 noisy supporters of Schlafly packed into the Cotillion Room creating "an atmosphere more akin to a party convention than an internal battle for the presidency of the National Federation of Republican Women." Delegates from Illinois, Ohio, Missouri, Alabama, Mississippi, and Wisconsin wore "blue ribbons in their hair lettered with, 'P.S. I love you.' At the reception guests consumed 45 gallons of fruit punch and 1,500 cookies." A weary eyed but brightly smiling Phyllis Schlafly appeared to the applause of the crowd. She received endorsements from Maureen Reagan, Edith Kermit Roosevelt (granddaughter of Theodore Roosevelt), and Ruth Brennan, wife of the Hollywood actor Walter Brennan. Also speaking on her behalf were General Thomas A. Lane, General Albert Wedemeyer, Senator Strom Thurmond (R-South Carolina), and Rep. John Ashbrook (R-Ohio).

Schlafly supporters met open opposition from the credentials committee. The *Washington Post* reported, "Mutiny was in the air in the corridors of the Sheraton Park Hotel . . . as delegate after delegate found herself barred from the NFRW convention. . . . Delegates from Missouri, Oklahoma, Florida, Tennessee, and Ohio whose credentials were not accepted muttered they would desert the Republican party."[70] Other allegations were made that Schlafly delegates were left standing in long lines, while O'Donnell delegates from Pennsylvania and New York were allowed to vote as soon as they appeared at the polls.[71] Katharine Kennedy Brown, president of the Ohio Federation, reported later that Ohio delegates were told they needed to hand in their credential slips to get convention badges, but when they appeared to vote, they were told delegates needed both badges and credential slips (even though they were already handed in to the credentials committees). Brown said six of the Ohio clubs were denied voting, but in some states 30 to 40 delegates were thrown out.[72]

Elston responded to these charges: Of the 4,000 delegates and 1,100 alternates, only 200 had been found unacceptable. She added, "Many club presidents missed their deadlines or did not send in the lists of their delegates."[73] The stage was set for an open floor fight over credentials. Soon after the chair of the credentials committee began reading her official report, it became clear she had listed the wrong figures for the state-by-state breakdown of the delegates and the reading was discontinued. At that point, an attempt was made to present the minority credentials report, but the convention chair ruled this out of order. A partial credentials report was given, but a full report was never presented. In addition, Schlafly insisted the voting machines be inspected before the official voting began. She hired two voting machine inspectors to test the machines before the balloting began, but before they got a chance to inspect the machines, Elston ordered the machines sealed. Later, Elston denied she had agreed with Schlafly's insistence that the machines be inspected by independent auditors. In the most hotly contested election in the history of the Federation, O'Donnell won by 416 votes, 1910 to 1494. Later, Schlafly claimed the New York vote was decisive; that state's representation was at least 10 times larger than the usual New York representation in past conventions and the president of the New York Federation was a well-known Rockefeller Republican operative.[74] In the end, Schlafly conceded defeat gracefully and without recrimination.

Schlafly's supporters at the convention were stunned by the defeat. As one Schlafly delegate later remembered, "As we started out of the Convention Hall, brokenhearted and mad clearly through—a fantastic thing happened." Word spread they were to convene in the Cotillion Room. "Determined women, so tired they could drop, but so angry, came from everywhere," filling the stairways and the balconies. "Finally, Phyllis appeared, poised and gracious." When Schlafly stepped into the room, the crowd applauded. Here was their leader, smiling—not just smiling, but cheerful. How she "could even be on her feet, let alone smile, was beyond us." She stepped up on a table so the crowd could hear her. The speech sounded like a victory speech. She told the crowd they had campaigned with integrity and that they should be proud of what they had accomplished given the odds. Schlafly declared, "I have always said that loyalty is a two way street—from the grassroots to the top and from the top down to the grassroots. I will never compromise my principles for political expediency. You believe in the same things that I believe in, and we have just begun to fight to make those principles a reality in the Republican party. I will do anything you want me to do."[75] Then Schlafly affirmed the fight for the soul of the Republican party had just begun. She would continue this struggle against the corrupt forces within the Republican party. She closed by saying "The principles I work for will not die—constitutional government, individual freedom, dignity and morality, and American freedom."[76] The crowd of conservative women answered with wild cheering.

Following the election, Schlafly moved to shore up her support. Schlafly began by attacking Ray Bliss for what she considered his intervention into the NFRW election. There were too many reports of staff members from the Republican National Committee working behind the scenes on O'Donnell's behalf. Angered by this involvement, Schlafly publicly released a letter she wrote to Bliss stating, "I know that your office was *not* neutral before or during the Convention, but I had hoped that you would close ranks and promote harmony after the Convention." I have discovered, she wrote, your office has been releasing "hurtful stories" about me, including one coming from a paid employee of the RNC that "even accused me of causing cockroaches in the national headquarters." She demanded the RNC "open its financial books to see the portion of salaries being paid by the RNC for the time they spent campaigning against me." Representative John Ashbrook inserted Schlafly's letter in the *Congressional Record*.[77] Dorothy Elston denied Bliss intervened on behalf of O'Donnell. In a bitter reply to those who charged the election was rigged, Elston declared, "This is subversive." Elston added that while it was true that Bliss provided 15 people from his staff to help with the convention, Schlafly's charges were unfounded.[78] In a report circulated to Federation clubs, Elly Peterson, state chairwoman of the Michigan GOP, joined Elston in defending the integrity of the NFRW election. She claimed only ninety-five delegates were denied credentials. Moreover, responding to the charge that Nelson Rockefeller paid the expenses of some delegates, she answered, "So let us assume that both forces raised money from friends rather than from Nelson Rockefeller, the John Birch Society, and the Liberty Lobby." And while it was true busloads of women from New York, Pennsylvania, and New Jersey did not arrive until Friday night, the fact is "many women" did not want to be absent from their homes for an extra day. She concluded her report claiming the road ahead for the NFRW will be "rocky." Some members in the Federation will "prefer to be dissidents" and will take pleasure in it.[79]

Despite protestations that the election was fair and square, the NFRW was a severely wounded organization. In the next three years, membership fell from half a million members to less than half that number. After stepping down as president, Dorothy Elston announced she was eager to work for the nomination of Nelson Rockefeller in 1968.[80] For her part, the new president of the NFRW, Gladys O'Donnell called for party unity, "The Republican party needs conservatives, moderates, liberals. Welcome them all; accommodate them and show tolerance in this field and we will win."[81] O'Donnell's presidency was uninspired and by its end, both friends and critics believed that the NFRW had declined. Most revealing in this regard was a story brought to Schlafly in January 1974, by a man identifying himself as Frederick Sontag of Maine Public Broadcasting. Sontag told Schlafly that he was a liberal who did not agree with her on anything. He said that in 1967 he had been a reporter for a New Jersey newspaper and he had ridden in a bus to the NFRW convention that was filled with crooked delegates. He revealed to Schlafly that he had argued vigorously with George Hinman, Republican State Chairman of New York, and with Elly Peterson, telling them that they would "lose more by stealing it in a crooked election" than if Schlafly won. He added Elly Peterson had only recently admitted to him that she and others had in fact lost more than they gained. When Schlafly asked him why he did not write up the story, he replied, "I did, but my newspaper did not print it." The story remained in the realm of hearsay, but Schlafly found it credible.[82]

Schlafly sought to turn the election to her advantage. After the NFRW convention, her followers were disappointed and bitter. They had waged an emotional six-month campaign against great odds, only to lose at what they believed was a rigged convention. Hundreds of letters flowed into Schlafly's campaign headquarters at her home in Alton expressing outrage at how the convention was conducted, while pledging their admiration to her. One supporter from Leland, Mississippi wrote Schlafly, "I have literally been sick ever since the convention. I just could not have believed such unfairness and cruelty could exist." Another woman reported her club members were "shocked and horrified by the gross irregularities of the convention." In response to these letters, Schlafly deemed it important to bolster the morale of her followers. In a "Dear Friend" letter, she declared the recent NFRW election had "separated the patriots from those seeking payola of one kind or another." The election, she said, revealed all too clearly that "if anyone thinks those disloyal Republicans who deserted the ticket in 1964 have mended their ways and believe in the "unity" they preach, you had better dispel those illusions right now." The election showed that the "liberals are not even willing for our side to have anything at all—not even the crumb of a non-paid woman's position with practically no power." Schlafly pledged to carry on the fight, announcing that she was establishing an office in her home to provide education to

Republican women reflecting "a strong pro-American viewpoint, and advocate morality in government, constitutional government, a strong national defense, and free enterprise." She proclaimed her intention "to build an army of dedicated women wearing eagles as the symbol of American freedom."[83]

In August 1967 the first issue of the *Phyllis Schlafly Report* appeared as a four-page monthly newsletter. During the interim period, groups of women began withdrawing from the NFRW. For example, in Omaha, Nebraska, three women's clubs withdrew from the NFRW, while maintaining ties with each other. In Champaign, Illinois, six officials of the Federation quit, calling for a new organization. Columbus, Ohio reported twelve "Schlafly Clubs" were formed.[84] Declarations such as "Why We Need a New Organization" and "Against Remaining in the National Federation" circulated throughout the country, one drawing from the Bible by asking "Be ye not unequally yoked together with unbelievers: for what fellowship hath righteousness with unrighteousness? And what communion hath light with darkness?" The answer was rhetorical: "Why dissipate one's energies in a constant battle, when these same hours could be concentrated for a common goal— that of saving America from more liberalism, socialism, and eventually Communism?"[85]

In this sense, the election of NFRW proved to be a victory for Schlafly after all. She gathered a core of supporters who adhered to her in future political campaigns. Their loyalty to her was undeniable. One supporter told her, "I was always so proud of the way you were able to smile and conduct yourself. I just do not have that kind of strength and courage, so I followed you off in tears. . . . We shall appreciate any direction or leadership from you any time."[86] A Christian woman worried about the moral state of the nation was so inspired by Schlafly that she would continue the battle to redeem the nation: "I wish I could share your optimism. I think the Church and the country are in a woeful state. But I'm still in there fighting."[87]

In a broader perspective, the NFRW fight deepened the wounds left by the Goldwater campaign of 1964. The GOP remained a deeply divided party; the bitterness of the NFRW election played out in subtle ways. *Washington Post* political columnist David Broder declared that Sen. John Tower, William A. Rusher, and F. Clifton White were "responsible conservatives" who wanted to swing the NFRW away from the extremists.[88] Yet, there is no concrete evidence any of these men were involved in the election, and Rusher stated publicly he did not "have a dog in the fight." In *The Plot to Steal the GOP*, Rusher warned of an impending purge within the party. The NFRW election reinforced the view among conservatives that Republican insiders had undertaken a campaign to purge the party of conservatives.[89] Could conservatives regain what they won when Goldwater was nominated? Some conservatives began to see Richard Nixon as their next best hope for preserving Republican principles; others turned to California's governor, Ronald Reagan.

CHAPTER SEVEN

Confronting the Soviets in a Nuclear Age

IN 1968 PHYLLIS SCHLAFLY declared herself in support of Richard Nixon's bid to become President of the United States. Her endorsement surprised conservatives who were supporting Ronald Reagan for the GOP presidential nomination, but Schlafly and many other conservatives had been won over by Richard Nixon's strong pledge to restore America's nuclear superiority over the Soviet Union and to build an antiballistic missile (ABM) system. There were ample reasons for conservatives to support Nixon in 1968—his pledge to restore "law and order" to the streets and college campuses, his promise to end the Vietnam War costing hundreds of American lives each day in the jungles of Southeast Asia, his opposition to court-ordered busing, and his assurance "to clean up the welfare mess." Nonetheless, for many grassroots conservatives such as Schlafly, the major issue of the day remained the threat posed by the Soviet Union's continued rapid nuclear buildup. National security trumped every other issue in their minds, so Nixon's promise to reverse Democratic defense policies, which conservatives believed had enabled the Soviets to gain strategic superiority over the United States, was enough to win their support.

National defense—specifically, strategic nuclear policy—lay at the heart of Schlafly's worldview in the 1960s. Although an extension of anticommunist ideology, it had replaced the issue of domestic communism, which had been uppermost in concerns of many conservatives in the early Cold War years. Throughout the Kennedy-Johnson years, conservatives watched, at least as they saw it, the steady erosion of American nuclear capacity, making the nation unconscionably vulnerable to nuclear attack or blackmail from the Soviet Union. Eight years of witnessing what they perceived as a steady decline in American nuclear power left conservatives frustrated, fearful, and angry. For eight years they systematically critiqued and fought against Democratic nuclear policy implemented by Secretary of Defense Robert S. McNamara.

THE WORLD IN 1968 ACCORDING TO PHYLLIS SCHLAFLY

Joined by other conservatives such as Senator Strom Thurmond (R-South Carolina), Schlafly saw her battle to promote American strategic defense as a moral imperative because the nation's security was at stake. The moral energy that had given impetus to her anticommunist activities in the 1950s remained the driving force in her defense work. This apprehension that America could be defeated, or even destroyed, drove Phyllis Schlafly, just as it did grassroots conservative activists throughout the country. She conveyed this deep moral impulse in an eight-page letter written to a friend in June 1966. "There are only a pitiful few like you . . . Fred and me, who devote our whole lives to fighting Communism—because we know what the stakes are, and we are determined to save our country in spite of the apathy and indifference of our friends, and in spite of the obstacles that are thrown in our way. With God's help, I pray we can succeed."[1]

This moral imperative led Schlafly to co-author three major books on national defense in the 1960s, which sold over 2.5 million copies. Asked by a reporter writing a feature interview in the *St. Louis Globe-Democrat* in 1965 how a "housewife from Alton could know so much about national defense and nuclear warfare?" Schlafly attributed her knowledge of defense to her co-author, naval officer Rear Admiral Chester C. Ward, who had retired in Honolulu but stayed in daily communication with her, largely by letter.[2] She also noted that she subscribed to 100 magazines and relied extensively on congressional reports, the American Security Council newsletter, and various newspapers including the *New York Times*, the *Chicago Tribune*, and the *St. Louis Globe-Democrat*.

Phyllis Schlafly and Chester Ward constituted a unique and prolific team. From 1964 through 1968 they co-authored *The Gravediggers* (1964)—2 million copies; *Strike from Space* (1965)—250,000 copies; and *The Betrayers* (1968)—150,000 copies. In 1967 she also published a collection of essays called *Safe—Not Sorry*, which was bought by 100,000 readers. During the 1970s, Schlafly and Ward wrote two more books: *Kissinger on the Couch* (1975), an 846-page hardback, which sold 25,000 copies, and the paperback *Ambush at Vladivostok* (1976), which sold 100,000.[3]

Schlafly did most of the writing while Ward brought technical expertise learned during a distinguished career as a naval officer. Born in

1907, he was seventeen years older than his co-author. He completed naval cadet training at Pensacola in 1927. After his military service, he graduated with honors from Georgetown University in 1931 and completed his law degree at George Washington University in 1936. He did graduate work at American University, then became an Associate Professor of Law at George Washington University Law School, where he published leading articles in the law reviews of Harvard, Yale, Vanderbilt, and George Washington. He returned to active duty in June 1941. Following the end of the Second World War, he served as legal staff officer under Admirals Arthur Radford and Felix Stump. In 1956, he became Judge Advocate General of the Navy with the rank of Rear Admiral. Retiring in 1960, he turned to writing and speaking on defense matters.[4] Although he was trained as a lawyer, he was a member of the Council of Foreign Relations (CFR), a prestigious organization that attracted influential Americans, and he maintained a strong interest in defense and foreign policy issues.

Ward's reputation on defense issues was well established before he began working with Schlafly. Although he had written many articles and reports, his own writing tended to be too abstruse for the general public. He recognized this when he turned to Schlafly as a co-author. Ward's long-time membership in the Council of Foreign Relations led some on the Right to criticize the Schlafly-Ward books. For example, the John Birch Society openly attacked their books, *The Gravediggers* and *Strike from Space*, for their emphasis on the *external* threat posed by the Soviet Union. The JBS refused to believe that the Soviet economy was capable of creating advanced technology necessary for a large-scale missile program. The JBS noted that Ward was a member of the CFR, thus raising serious suspicions about him—and by association, Phyllis Schlafly.

Although the John Birch Society was critical of Ward, he was actually more to the right politically than Schlafly and leaned to George Wallace in 1968, even though Schlafly persuaded him to end *The Betrayers* (1968) with an endorsement of Richard Nixon. Ward tended to view the world through a highly interpretative lens, seeing Soviet machinations to deceive the United States in every pronouncement coming out of the Moscow. He refused, for example, to believe the Sino-Soviet split was real, believing such talk was communist disinformation designed to cause the West to let down its guard. Ward did have a solid knowledge of the technical aspects of defense, which was apparent in his voluminous correspondence with Schlafly. For her part, Schlafly moderated many of Ward's views in their books, and Fred Schlafly, who did some of the fact checking, provided an additional filter.

The Schlafly-Ward books were anything but moderate in tone and anything but tempered in their attack on the Kennedy-Johnson administration's defense policy. Their books were written for a popular audience of conservative activists (and read by Republican party leaders), and therefore were designed to arouse the grassroots to pressure their elected representatives to stand strong on defense. Schlafly and Ward timed the publication of their books to appear during election years. Books such as those written by Schlafly and Ward were part of a larger defense literature coming from the Right. In 1967, Senator Strom Thurmond, by then a Republican, devoted much of his *The Faith We Have Not Kept* (1967) to criticizing the Johnson-McNamara defense policy.[5] Also, in 1967, a committee of the American Security Council issued *ABM and the Changed Strategic Military Balance U.S.A vs. USSR*, a report signed by influential hawks in the defense community including Dr. Edward Teller, General Albert Wedemeyer, General Bernard A. Schriever, Lewis Strauss, Stefan Possony, Admiral Robert L. Dennison, General Nathan F. Twining, Dr. William J. Thaler, Dr. Willard Libby, and Rear Admiral Chester C. Ward. Although ostensibly nonpartisan, the American Security Council expressed the hard Right's views within the Republican party.

Schlafly and Ward exhorted grassroots conservatives to press forward in the fight to maintain a strong strategic defense. Theirs was a fight that could not be delayed, even though the leaders in the Kremlin had cleverly persuaded many world leaders and people that they desired peaceful coexistence with the United States. The concept of peaceful coexistence, Schlafly continued to say, did not mean the same thing to the Soviet leaders as it meant to Americans. For the Soviet communists, "peaceful coexistence" meant avoiding nuclear conflict with the United States, but it did not mean that the Soviet Union had given up its ambitions for world domination through nuclear superiority. Peaceful coexistence, she wrote, did not mean that the Soviet Union had relinquished its policy of developing a first-strike capability. Liberals, she warned, were being taken in by Soviet rhetoric.

"On all fronts," she declared, "the cry is peace." She warned that the belief Soviets have given up their desire to "bury" us has permeated the thinking of our national political leaders and church leaders.[6]

"America," she extolled, "will never have peace and security in the world until our people, especially our leaders, face the awful truth about the hideous cruelty, inhumanity, and immorality of the Communists."[7] Schlafly was particularly shocked by what she perceived as the susceptibility of Christian leaders to communist propaganda. A good example was a column written by Msgr. Charles Owen Rice in the *Pittsburgh Catholic* in October 6, 1966 calling for Catholics to "pray for the survival of the present government of China." Schlafly found the column typical of the fuzzy-mindedness permeating liberal thought, particularly in the hierarchy of the Catholic Church. In his column, Rice declared the current Red Guard campaign initiated by Mao was not "foolish." "The masses of China," he wrote, "must sacrifice for the sake of the nation, and they are willing to bear the great burden, but not bear it alone. Any development of a superior class to ride on the shoulders of the masses must be rooted out with periodic ruthlessness, if Peking's program is to have any chance of success. . . ." He added, "Mao Tse-tung and his followers have changed China utterly, and the change has been for the better. It is almost certain that, if the administration of Mao were to collapse, all of China would suffer grievously. . . . We all know that China puts the people first, ahead of even the program for national power, because badly needed capital is spent in the outside world for food so that no one will starve." Schlafly helped produce a newspaper ad that reprinted Rice's column in its entirety, with a rejoinder declaring "Communism and Christianity *are* irreconcilable" and "we know that the facts of history prove that every Communist government in the world controls the people *only* by terror, and the only kind of peace under Communism is the peace of the firing squad and the secret police."[8]

From the beginning of her career Schlafly was critical of liberals in the Democratic party. By the late 1960s, however, she began to develop a more systematic critique of liberalism and its "incapacity" to confront the Soviet threat.[9] At the core of this critique was a belief that liberals were vulnerable to communist peace rhetoric because they presumed that communists acted rationally. The leaders in the Kremlin were motivated by "simply a naked lust for power over all men." The lust for power stemmed from their ideology and also their need to maintain themselves in power in the Soviet Union.[10] Schlafly believed an even greater problem lay behind these problems with modern day liberals: Liberals believed international organizations could, and would, maintain peace. Deep in their hearts, she argued, liberals "desire world government, or a reasonable facsimile thereof, such as an all powerful U.N., or a NATO expanded into an Atlantic Community."[11]

For Schlafly and other grassroots conservatives, this willingness to trust the Soviet Union to uphold a treaty was more than naïve—it not only drastically weakened national security, it was dangerous because it invited war. Liberals misunderstood, Schlafly argued, what the leaders in the Kremlin meant by peaceful co-existence. By using the language of peace, she asserted, the Soviet Union sought to weaken the resolve of the American people and its leaders to prevent the Soviet Union from world domination. She observed that Khrushchev had publicly announced in January 1961 that the Soviet strategy was to support liberation movements in developing nations. At the same time, Moscow privately sought through its own technological advancements and favorable arm-reduction treaties to achieve military and nuclear superiority. Once having achieved this power, the Soviet Union, through the threat of nuclear war, would be able to intimidate a militarily inferior and spiritually weakened United States. Furthermore, conservatives feared that an eviscerated America would be vulnerable to outright nuclear attack.

Schlafly and Ward used forceful language to convey their sense of urgency about the Soviet threat. The very titles of their books projected crisis and personalized the debate: *The Gravediggers, Strike from Space,* and *The Betrayers.* They wanted to arouse mainstreet Republicans and grassroots conservatives to face the immediate danger posed by the Soviet missile buildup. Through these inexpensive paperbacks, they translated highly technical debates about the strategic balance found in journals such as *Orbis* and *Foreign Affairs* into a language understood by average Americans. Schlafly and Ward believed they were acting out of a moral and patriotic duty to warn that the nation was at risk. Through the use of passionate language, Schlafly and Ward helped embed the strategic issue deep within the conservative consciousness. They established a clear line separating conservatives and liberals on defense policy.

FEARS OF LIBERAL APPEASEMENT AND THE TEST BAN TREATY

Schlafly and Ward were convinced that liberals in the Kennedy and Johnson administrations had decided that the United States could not win a nuclear war with the Soviet Union and that, win or lose, a nuclear war would destroy America. Furthermore, they were certain that liberals placed too much faith in the ability of the Soviet Union's centralized economy to overtake America's decentralized economy.[12] Liberals believed (or so said Schlafly and Ward) that an arms race with the Soviet Union was insane and would lead to nuclear holocaust for both nations and the world. The only way to avoid calamity was to establish nuclear parity between two superpowers and even allow the Soviets to gain nuclear superiority in some areas in order to lessen Soviet paranoia.

Furthermore, Schlafly and Ward claimed that many liberals had reached the conclusion the United States was losing the arms race to the Soviet Union.[13] Schlafly and Ward feared that this sentiment was widespread in the Kennedy administration. This did not mean that liberals favored unilateral disarmament, but it did mean they wanted to shift American foreign policy in radical new directions toward accommodation with the Soviet Union.[14] What most concerned them was how the Kennedy defense team was comprised of all liberals, many of them brought from academia. Schlafly and Ward asserted that these Kennedy appointees had developed their accomodationist views toward the Soviet Union in a series of foreign policy seminars and conferences held throughout the 1950s, such as the annual Pugwash conferences. They were initiated by leftist millionaire Cyrus Eaton in 1955 as a means of bringing humanist scholars, scientists, and policy leaders from all over the world to discuss international relations. Among those participating were Soviet nuclear scientists. These conferences drew the attention of the right wing, leading to a barrage of pamphlets, newspaper and magazine articles, and speeches attacking Pugwash as a forum to promote disarmament and Soviet peace propaganda. These attacks gained respectability when U.S. Senator Thomas Dodd (D-CT) gave a speech on the floor of the Senate on August 8, 1961 attacking the Pugwash conferences. His three-page speech was widely distributed in conservative circles.

Of particular importance to conservatives was a speech given by Paul Nitze at the Sixth Army National Strategy Seminar at Asilomar, Pacific Grove, California in 1960. Nitze and Dean Acheson had written the foreign policy plank for the Democratic platform in 1956. The speech Nitze gave at the seminar would be cited time and again in conservative defense literature as an example of the disarmament mindset. To the consternation of his audience of some 500 military planners and strategists, government policymakers, and academics, Nitze asserted the United States should "multilateralize the command of our retaliatory systems by making SAC [Strategic Air Command] a NATO command. He argued that the United States should inform the United Nations that NATO will turn over ultimate power of decision on the use of these systems to the General Assembly of the United Nations.[15] Following widespread criticism of his Asilomar speech, Nitze later wrote in his memoirs that he was only playing a "mind-game" for thinking about strategy—that he was "dubious of its soundness," but this "foray into the 'wild blue yonder' haunted" him for years afterwards. Nitze was a young man trying to make a name for himself by throwing out a daring idea. Still, he and others, including John F. Kennedy and Robert McNamara, had become convinced that a nuclear war was not winnable.[16]

Sitting in Nitze's audience at Asilomar in 1960 was Admiral Chester Ward. He recognized in these words everything that the conservatives were saying, namely that liberals believed America could not compete with the Soviet Union in an arms race, and that liberals distrusted American power. In *The Gravediggers*, Schlafly and Ward devoted an entire chapter to the "Nitze Axis" as an example of how liberals were risking nuclear war through their disarmament policies. Schlafly and Ward wrote that "under the Nitze Asilomar Proposal, the United States would deliberately leave itself *no choice but surrender, no effective deterrent to* destruction. Everything would be staked on the 'hope' that the Soviets would disarm *after we* do [italics original]." They accused the Kennedy administration of seizing on the Asilomar proposals like "hungry flies on syrup." Schlafly and Ward declared, "Nitze's unique contribution was that he took the wildest notions of the most radical world-government pacifist disarmers, and he provided a practical plan to make these schemes work—and then he covered it with all the semantic camouflage needed to fool Congress and the public."[17] In making this argument, Schlafly and Ward rejected the image of John F. Kennedy as a cold-warrior, anxious to avoid nuclear war with the Soviet Union, but willing to militarily confront the Soviet Union and communist expansion. Furthermore, by highlighting Nitze in their criticism of Kennedy's foreign policy, they imparted to Nitze more influence in the Kennedy administration than arguably he had at the time.

Behind these hyperbolic accusations about Nitze and others in the Kennedy administration lay profound differences over the nature of the

Soviet Union. Conservatives such as Schlafly and Ward held that the liberal premise behind détente, based on a misunderstanding of the nature of the Soviet system, was that "the Russian people will love affluence so much that they won't let their leaders start a war." Instead, Schlafly and Ward saw the Soviet Union as a totalitarian system controlling every aspect of society. Moreover, the Soviet Union could never achieve affluence so long as it was a socialist economy. Trade with the West propped up the system, but was incapable of changing it.[18] Schlafly and Ward believed peaceful coexistence should be rejected in favor of a policy of nuclear superiority. Immediately following Kennedy's election, Schlafly urged him to be prepared for Soviet aggression and not fall for the peace rhetoric of détente. Writing in November 1960, she warned Kennedy to be prepared for a revolt behind communist lines, an attack on Quemoy and Matsu, the closing of Berlin, and even "a Red missile base being constructed in Cuba." "Our goal," she wrote, must be victory—not containment, coexistence, disengagement, or stalemate."[19]

The Kennedy administration brought into its policies a different set of assumptions. There was a sense that the Soviet economy and military were making rapid progress, which meant that the Soviet Union must be recognized as a superpower equal to the United States. The Kennedy administration believed that power between the two countries had changed in 1957 when the Soviets tested its first ICBM and launched its space satellite *Sputnik*, which had so shaken the American establishment. Furthermore, Kennedy experts placed importance on the Soviet Union's deployment in 1959 of its new military missile, the SS-4 MRBM, as a means of delivering atomic weapons. So powerful were Soviet long-range missiles that Khrushchev warned the Soviet Union might even discontinue bomber production.[20] Although Kennedy officials agreed that the United States had considerably more weapons than the Soviet Union, most in the administration agreed with National Security Adviser McGeorge Bundy's assessment that "Soviet military strength is formidable." Still, Bundy thought Khrushchev wanted some diplomatic success, so "there may be progress toward disarmament."[21] While Schlafly and Ward, as did other conservatives, lumped Kennedy's national security advisers together, there were differences within the administration about the extent to which meaningful arms control could be achieved. Nonetheless, there was considerable talk in the administration about the possibilities of nuclear disarmament.[22]

One of the clearest enunciations for arms control came when the U.S. Disarmament Agency, established by an executive order shortly before Eisenhower left office, released its *Freedom from War: The United States Program for General and Complete Disarmament in a Peaceful World* in 1961. This official publication outlined a detailed proposal for nuclear disarmament under which the United States would turn control of its weapons over to an international police force under the auspices of the United Nations. This publication set off a firestorm of protest from conservatives who widely distributed it as an example that the Kennedy administration was intent on a policy of unilateral disarmament policy. Defenders of the administration claimed that this document was only intended as Cold War propaganda and that the United States had no intention of disarming, but Schlafly cited the document time and again in her writing and speeches as an example of the administration's appeasement policy.[23] Conservatives refused to believe this message was a propaganda ploy by the United States merely intended to portray the United States as a peace-loving nation. Instead, conservatives such as Schlafly and Ward were convinced *Freedom from War* was a blueprint for disarmament. Thus, when the Kennedy administration in 1963 proposed a test ban treaty with the Soviet Union, conservatives saw this as the first stage in a utopian scheme to bring about universal disarmament—a dream bound to fail.

Shortly after John F. Kennedy entered the White House, and following a failed summit meeting in Vienna between Kennedy and Khrushchev, the Soviet Union resumed large-scale atmospheric testing in August 1961. On September 5, 1961, a reluctant Kennedy responded with the announcement that the United States was resuming underground testing. Two months later on November 2, the Soviet Union exploded a 58-megaton nuclear bomb, thereby confirming that it had developed heavy megaton nuclear bombs. After tensions between the two countries died down, in the course of the next two years the United States and the Soviet Union entered into intense negotiations to ban nuclear testing. From the outset, the Kennedy administration saw a test ban treaty as important politically for the administration and an important step in bettering relations between the two countries.[24] On June 25, 1963, the United States, the United Kingdom, and the Soviet Union entered into a partial test ban on nuclear testing in the atmosphere, outer space, and underwater. The treaty allowed for underground testing.[25] By negotiating the test ban treaty, the Kennedy administration took credit for having achieved the first major arms control treaty in the nuclear age.

Fearing the worst, grassroots conservatives mobilized to prevent the Test Ban Treaty from being ratified by the U.S. Senate. In Illinois, Schlafly organized a statewide letter-writing campaign by the Illinois Federation of Republican Women against the treaty and testified against the treaty before the U.S. Senate Foreign Relations Committee.[26] Senator Everett Dirksen's Washington office was flooded with letters urging him to vote against the treaty. Grassroots conservatives from all over the country called for the treaty to be rejected. The liberal *New York Post* editorialized, "The enemies of the treaty have begun to fight."[27]

The Kennedy administration responded with a national campaign to support ratification. Business support was rallied in New York and Washington, and local ads supporting the treaty were placed in Chicago, St. Louis, Des Moines, and Atlanta newspapers. The Farmers Union and the Grange were called on to rally farmers, who were concerned about radioactivity in milk due to nuclear tests; the administration contacted national church representatives to encourage "sermons throughout the country" on behalf of the treaty. The administration arranged for a petition signed by thirty-five Nobel prize-winning scientists calling for endorsement of the test ban treaty. Radio and television ads appeared in key areas.[28] Opponents of the treaty hoped a coalition to prevent ratification would emerge in the Senate led by Henry Jackson (D-Washington), Richard Russell (D-Georgia), and Barry Goldwater (R-Arizona), but when Dirksen, the Republican leader, announced he was supporting the treaty, ratification became certain. The treaty was ratified 80–19.[29]

The image of President Kennedy as the Cold Warrior who sought to beat swords into plowshares was confirmed in the public's mind. The treaty marked a turning point in the politics of defense. Although conservatives lost their fight against ratification, they staked out an important political position on the strategic question. Yet, even while the hard Right became increasingly vocal on maintaining American military superiority, the defense issue did not divide simply along partisan lines. Democratic Senators such as Senators Henry Jackson and Richard Russell, as well as a number of policy experts aligned with the Democrats, remained important voices within their party for maintaining a strong national defense. Their influence within the party became increasingly isolated, however, especially in the 1970s, while the Right's influence on military affairs grew.

DEBATING STRATEGIC BALANCE IN THE KENNEDY ADMINISTRATION

The debate over the Limited Test Ban Treaty set the context for a larger debate over strategic policy that followed. The Kennedy administration exuded supreme confidence in its willingness to embrace new ideas about defense policy and nuclear strategy.[30] From a series of RAND commission reports, Democratic defense strategists concluded American nuclear defenses were vulnerable to surprise attack from the Soviet Union because of an inadequate radar warning system and because funds for missile development had been diverted to bomber production. They argued that missile development should be accelerated and bases hardened for intercontinental ballistic missiles. The administration's new approach to strategic balance became evident under Secretary of Defense Robert S. McNamara. A few conservatives such as James Burnham defended McNamara, but for many grassroots conservatives, especially Phyllis Schlafly and Admiral Chester Ward, McNamara personified everything that was wrong with American nuclear strategy. Particularly disturbing to them was McNamara's belief that greater emphasis should be placed on having both sides, the Soviet Union and the United States, achieve second-strike parity. This meant that both sides should have enough nuclear capacity to launch second strikes following a devastating first strike that killed millions of people. McNamara and other Democratic strategists believed that such capacity ensured both sides would be deterred from launching first strikes. McNamara assured newspaper columnist Stewart Alsop in 1962 that "a nuclear exchange confined to military targets seems more possible, not less, when both sides have a more stable balance of terror."[31] McNamara argued in favor of allowing the Soviets to strengthen their arsenal because, if both sides realized that the other side could retaliate after a nuclear strike, then they would not be tempted to launch a preemptive strike. He feared that the Soviet Union was too weak, not too strong.[32]

Translated into specific defense policies, McNamara's program called for the rapid increase of Minuteman launchers, and accepted the building of forty-one Polaris submarines with nuclear launch capability and the hardening of missile silos. McNamara's defense strategy placed less reliance on a bomber force, the end of new bomber development, and the phase-out of heavy missiles in favor of the more accurate, lighter Minuteman missile. He dismantled Thor and Jupiter missiles and abandoned the Atlas and Titan missiles.[33] Instead, McNamara placed full reliance on the Minuteman, a solid-fuel propelled rocket that was small, accurate and light. Its payload was much smaller than the Titan, but it better fit the shift in policy to flexible response away from massive retaliation.[34]

Schlafly and Ward concluded that McNamara was deliberately dismantling American's nuclear arsenal to gain arms control treaties that would lead to complete nuclear disarmament. This was an alarmist view, but they claimed that the Soviets were pursuing a first-strike capability through the development of heavier and heavier missiles able to carry huge payloads. Furthermore, they joined other conservative hawks in warning that the Soviets had launched a massive nuclear buildup at a time when McNamara was abandoning a number of weapons systems.[35] Both sides in the debate—defenders and his critics such as Ward and Schlafly—agreed that in the 1960s the exuberant Soviet missile buildup was impressive in quantitative terms. Ward and Schlafly watched with horror as the United States abandoned its policy of nuclear superiority.[36] Warning that the McNamara policy was deliberately dismantling America's nuclear arsenal in order to allow the Soviets to attain superiority, all the while claiming the goal of parity through arms control treaties, they believed this would lead to nuclear blackmail or even surrender by the United States. Schlafly and her co-author called for a massive nuclear buildup to restore nuclear superiority over the Soviet Union, a policy repeatedly endorsed in all the Republican National Platforms of the 1960s.[37]

Schlafly and Ward perceived the McNamara strategy as a loss of nerve on the part of the American establishment and a willful relinquishing of nuclear superiority in the face of an aggressive opponent intent on world domination. Schlafly and Ward did not believe those who pursued this policy were conspiring with the Soviets to disarm the United States, or that it was a communist plot, or that McNamara and his Whiz Kids were communists. The McNamara policy was a deliberate weakening of American power because these liberal policymakers not only feared growing Soviet nuclear power, they also *feared American power.* McNamara sought accommodation with the Soviet

Union, but Schlafly and Ward warned that the Soviet Union was not accommodating itself to the United States. If there were any doubt of this, they said, just study the massive and continuing Soviet missile buildup. In making this argument, they refused to accept McNamara's arguments that the United States could be defended by targeting Soviet sites with smaller, more accurate missiles, while heavy missiles and bombers could be phased out because they were ineffective and antiquated.

At the outset of their collaboration, Schlafly and Ward agreed that their mission was to "change American defense philosophy, so it was not dictated by supersophisticates" who lacked the common sense of the average American.[38] They believed that common sense required maintaining nuclear military superiority, repudiating Mutual Assured Destruction (MAD), and building an antiballistic missile defense. Schlafly and Ward believed American nuclear superiority was the best way to prevent war. Schlafly and Ward as well as other defense hawks did not propose that the United States launch a surprise nuclear attack on the Soviet Union. Instead, they called for a U. S. nuclear strategy based on a first-strike capability that they believed would *prevent war*. Superior nuclear capability, they argued, protected the United States from a surprise Soviet attack. This strategy assumed that the United States could and would win an arms race against the Soviet Union.[39]

Schlafly and Ward cited figures showing the United States falling behind the Soviet Union. They observed that McNamara had cancelled the Nike-Zeus antiballistic missile, the Skybolt missile, and the Pluto missile; he maintained that these heavy missiles either did not work or were vulnerable to Soviet attack and counter-measures. In addition, believing that bombers were out of date because of Soviet counter-measures, McNamara stopped production on the B-70 bomber, scrapped 1,400 B-47s, and eliminated 30 B-52s. Schlafly and Ward accused him of "slashing" the heavy Atlas and Titan missiles from 203 to 54, and destroying the launching pads and guidance controls of these scrapped missiles.[40] While canceling these weapons, they asserted, "McNamara has not authorized or developed a single new strategic weapon system."[41]

In many ways, the debate was over apples and oranges when it came down to specific numbers and weapons. The debate between the two sides was highly technical, with differences often based on different assumptions brought to the table. For critics, such as General Curtis LeMay and the Joint Chiefs of Staff, superiority meant first-strike capability, while those in the Kennedy and Johnson administrations believed superiority meant better retaliatory, second-strike capacity.[42] Schlafly and Ward measured superiority, in part, on the total megatons of weapons available to each side and the megaton-load carried by weapons.

Still, evaluating specific weapons systems allowed much room for honest disagreement on both sides. For example, supporters of the Nike-Zeus program that McNamara had canceled pointed out that it was the only ABM missile we had and it might improve with further development. As supporters of the Nike-Zeus program, Schlafly and Ward were adamant in urging the necessity of developing an antiballistic missile system, arguing that this was the single most important issue facing Americans.[43]

The ABM Debate in the Johnson Administration

Criticisms of American strategic policy intensified in the Johnson administration as McNamara continued reorienting American nuclear strategy. At odds were two irreconcilable strategies: Kennedy-Johnson-McNamara sought nuclear parity between the Soviet Union and the United States, and the conservative Republican view demanded American nuclear superiority. One side was amenable to negotiations with the Soviet Union and the other side was not, unless the Soviet Union abandoned its first-strike nuclear policy and was willing to enter into verifiable arms control treaties. These two views inevitably clashed over policy, causing heated charges on both sides. This became all too evident in the debate over the antiballistic missile system during the Johnson administration and continued to appear in policy debates even after the breakup of the Soviet Union in the 1990s. The nature of the debate was highly technical and complex. While an ABM appeared defensive in nature, an effective missile defense against incoming enemy missiles had dangerous implications for first-strike capability. If a nation possessed the capability through an effective ABM system to protect itself against attack, it created uncertainty on both sides. An enemy without an effective ABM system might decide to launch an attack to knock out the other side before it had an opportunity to strike first, or the side with an effective ABM system might decide it could afford a first strike without fear of serious reprisal.

In the 1960s, the Soviet Union built an ABM system around Moscow, while a high-performance air defense system was positioned around the country's perimeter.[44] The Soviet ABM system was not effective, but this was not known for certain, although some experts doubted its effectiveness when the Johnson administration came into office after Kennedy's assassination in November 1963. Sizeable pressure began to build for the United States to develop its own ABM system. Among those calling for America to develop an ABM system were Phyllis Schlafly and Chester Ward. *Strike from Space* (1965) focused on the need to counter the Soviet Union's ability to develop a defense against an American missile strike. In *Safe—Not Sorry* (1967), Schlafly continued the argument that an ABM system was critical to U.S. strategic policy.

Fearing that the development of an ABM system would trigger another cycle in the arms race, Robert McNamara initially opposed the demand that America build an ABM system because he felt that ABMs were too inaccurate to work well enough to justify the cost, and that any antiballistic missile system was technologically unfeasible because an opponent could swamp any defense system with more missiles or dummy missiles. Closely tied to the ABM debate was the issue over MIRVs (multiple independently targeted re-entry vehicles). The technology behind MIRVs was astonishing and deadly: a single missile could release a payload of multiple warheads and, presumably, MIRVs could overwhelm an ABM system. The development of ABMs and MIRVs confronted the McNamara Defense Department with critical strategic decisions, and the continuing Soviet nuclear buildup placed them in a dangerous context. By 1967, the Soviets had reached near parity with the United States in missiles—and some conservatives argued that the Soviet Union had moved ahead in the arms race. Finally, already overwhelmed by the cost of the Vietnam War, McNamara announced that he had decided to give the go-ahead for MIRV testing, but balked at a go-ahead for the ABM, which he claimed would be expensive and unreliable.[45] President Johnson shared McNamara's concern about the ABM, but when Soviet Prime Minister Aleksei Kosygin rejected Johnson's call for both sides to limit ABM development— shouting at Johnson that "Defense is moral, offense is immoral"— Johnson gave his approval for the development of an ABM system. In

Phyllis Schlafly with her mother. Phyllis came from a family of strong women. Her mother, Odile Stewart, graduated from Washington University in 1920 and supported the family during the Depression as the librarian at the St. Louis Art Museum. Courtesy of Eagle Forum Archives

In 1941, Phyllis Schlafly graduated at the top of her high school class from the all-girls Academy of Sacred Heart in St. Louis. Courtesy of Eagle Forum Archives.

As a supporter, Schlafly welcomed Senator Robert Taft (Ohio) when he visited Alton, Illinois in his campaign for the Republican nomination in 1952.

In her 1952 congressional race, Schlafly proved herself to be an able debater against opponent Mel Price, seen in the background.

After Eisenhower won the nomination, she ran as an Eisenhower Republican. Courtesy of Eagle Forum Archives.

CLINIC ON COMMUNISM

DIAGNOSIS, PATHOLOGY and TREATMENT

Conducted by

FRED C. SCHWARZ, M.D.

Surgeon and Psychiatrist

from
SYDNEY, AUSTRALIA
Leading World Authority On Communism
Now On His Sixth World Lecture Tour

1. The Mind, Morals and Motives of Communism .... Tues., April 30
2. Communism In Economics, Industry and Government .... Tues., May 7
3. The Communist Party, Its Fronts and Captive Organizations ...... Tues., May 14
4. The International Communist Conspiracy .... Tues., May 21

TICKETS: $1.50 PER LECTURE IF PURCHASED SEPARATELY
$5.00 FOR THE SERIES OF FOUR LECTURES
For tickets, please make check payable to "Clinic On Communism", and
mail with self-addressed, stamped envelope to any one of the following:

Dr. R. Bruce McCloskey, 745 East Big Bend Bl., Webster Groves 19, Mo. ... WO 1-7881
Mr. Peter Steele, 2031 Railway Exchange Bldg., St. Louis 1, Mo. .... GA 1-3895
Mrs. William Dougherty, 7131 Westmoreland Dr., University City 5, Mo. ... PA 1-3157
Miss Eleanor Schlafly, 5 Edgewood Rd., Clayton 24, Mo. .... WY 3-1249

ALL SESSIONS BEGIN PROMPTLY AT 8:00 p.m. at the

ST. LOUIS MEDICAL SOCIETY

3839 LINDELL BOULEVARD

This 1957 leaflet announced a Clinic on Communism featuring Fred C. Schwarz,
organized by Phyllis Schlafly and held at the St. Louis Medical Society.

YOU ARE
CORDIALLY INVITED
TO SEE AND LEARN —

Narrated by **Ronald Reagan**

"the TRUTH about communism"

A new, full length feature film narrated by Ronald Reagan, produced in Hollywood by Documentary Films, Inc.

"**NOW,** in this film, the American people have the opportunity of viewing in its stark, horrible and frightening nakedness, the whole scope of Communism's history and the continuing threat it poses to the free world. "The Truth About Communism" should be a MUST for viewing by every American of high school age and older."

Dr. George S. Benson
President, Harding College

FREE — OPEN TO THE PUBLIC — TO BE SHOWN

This leaflet announced a popular anticommunist film narrated by Ronald Reagan. Grassroots anticommunist activists frequently gathered in one another's homes to view such films (circa 1950s). Courtesy of Eagle Forum Archives.

A CHOICE NOT AN ECHO

by Phyllis Schlafly

"the inside story of how American Presidents are chosen."

A Choice Not an Echo sold millions of copies and was credited with helping Senator Barry Goldwater win the critical 1964 California primary against Nelson Rockefeller. Courtesy of Eagle Forum Archives.

STRIKE FROM SPACE

HOW THE RUSSIANS MAY DESTROY US

STRIKE FROM SPACE

DEVIN·ADAIR

SCHLAFLY ★ WARD

PHYLLIS SCHLAFLY

★

CHESTER WARD
Rear Admiral, U.S. Navy (Ret.)

In 1965, she published *Strike from Space*, one of five books on defense written with Rear Admiral (ret.) Chester Ward. These books also sold millions of copies and gained wide circulation among the grassroots Right. Courtesy of Eagle Forum Archives.

September 1967, McNamara, who was about ready to leave office, announced the United States was developing a "thin" ABM system to defend itself against Chinese missiles.

Schlafly and other conservatives attacked the notion of a "thin" ABM defense as nearly useless. Writing in *Safe—Not Sorry*, Schlafly accused McNamara's proposal of being nothing more than a *political* response to a recent report issued by the American Security Council, *The Changing Strategic Military Balance: U.S.A. vs. the U.S.S.R.* Released in mid-July 1967, the so-called Schriever Report, named after its chairman, General Bernard A. Schriever, USAF (Ret.), warned that the Soviet Union was about to gain nuclear superiority over the United States. The report, prepared at the request of U.S. House Armed Services Committee Chairman A. Mendel Rivers (D-S.C.), was published as an official government document.[46] The panel drafting the report included a prestigious group of hawks, including General Curtis E. LeMay, USAF (Ret.), Professor Stefan T. Possony, General Thomas S. Power, USAF (Ret.), Dr. Edward Teller, and Rear Admiral Chester Ward. Given the composition of the panel, the report represented the armed services point of view.[47]

Schlafly employed the report to support her argument that McNamara's policies had allowed the United States to fall behind the Soviet Union in weapons development. She referred to charts in the report showing the strategic balance favored the Soviet Union; the intermediate and medium-range ballistic missile balance favored the Soviet Union; the ICBM balance favored the Soviet Union; and total megatonnage of available weapons favored the Soviet Union. In some categories, such as the number of submarine-launched weapons, the United States was barely ahead. Much of the evidence for this argument emphasized megatonnage rather than the accuracy and efficiency of weapons.[48] Based on the numbers, Schlafly concluded that if one of the first responsibilities of government is to protect the homeland, "the present Johnson-Humphrey-McNamara Administration has failed in this essential duty—and 1968 gives the voters their *last* chance to remedy the situation."[49]

Throughout their books, Schlafly and Ward pressed for a major American strategic buildup. Much of what they requested echoed demands being made by the Armed Forces. Schlafly and Ward supported the development of a new bomber, the expansion of the Polaris fleet, the development of new air-to-ground missiles, and nuclear powered aircraft. They declared that America needed to be fortified by orbital nuclear bombs, neutron bombs, and antimissile and antisatellite defense systems. They translated highly technical arguments into understandable language for their readers. They were perspicacious in their presentation, but behind this clarity was a toughness—some would say a bellicosity—that conveyed a sense of urgency in meeting the Soviet challenge. In order to defend the United States against a Soviet first strike, they argued, an executive order should be issued commanding the Polaris fleet in the event of a nuclear attack on the United States "not to return to port until they have fired all their missiles at their assigned Soviet targets." This order, irrevocable in event of a nuclear strike by the Soviet Union, served "the highly rational purpose of deterrence. We would convince the Soviets they could not escape the 'automatic' response to strike."[50] Yet, it was exactly this sort of "automatic" response proposal that was behind much of the era's nuclear anxiety, including the film *Dr. Strangelove*, based on a "Doomsday Machine." Schlafly inadvertently played into these fears with her calls for a first-strike capability.

These books were not intended to convert liberal opinion but to rally the conservative grassroots to organize politically to support a policy of "peace through strength." In posing the issue, as they put it, "Grassroots vs. Gravediggers," they asked what Americans could do to confront the nuclear challenge. They answered, most importantly, "our faith in God, faith in America, and in the ideals that made this great nation" must be "nourished and sustained." They urged grassroots activists to educate themselves about defense, work to change public opinion in order to reverse the "gravediggers' policies," and to work "with fidelity and devotion to assure the election of congressional candidates and other government and party officials on every level who support keeping America strong."[51]

The Schlafly-Ward books were read by millions of Americans. The literature that poured forth was intended to inform Republican leaders, but more significantly to arouse average Americans to place pressure on Congress to support strong defense policies. Hundreds of letters flowed into the White House, Congress, and the Defense Department complaining that America was pursuing a no-win defense policy. One correspondent wrote to Paul Nitze complaining that the proposal he presented in 1960 that SAC be placed under NATO command meant that "our hands [would be] tied so the Communists could blow us to bits." Another wrote, "I honestly trust that you will come to believe, as many Americans do, that national sovereignty is no more obsolete than the word of God."[52]

Officials in the Defense Department undertook efforts to defend themselves from such attacks.[53] Yet the pressure from the grassroots Right was felt in Congress. The flood of letters that flowed into the office of U. S. Senator Stuart Symington (D-MO) when President Lyndon Johnson nominated Paul Nitze Secretary of the Navy led Symington to request that Nitze answer the charges raised in Phyllis Schlafly and Chester Ward's *The Gravediggers*. In response to this request, Nitze provided a thirty-page "paragraph by paragraph" analysis of what he referred to as one of "the far Right books circulated during last Fall's [1964] campaign" that had "received considerable attention." He denied that he had called for unilateral disarmament in his Asilomar speech and instead claimed he called for "building a variety of secure, purely retaliatory systems, preferably those exploiting mobility and concealment." The speech, he declared, had proposed the scrapping of fixed, land-based vulnerable systems only for consideration and that we "multilateralize the command of our retaliatory systems by making SAC a NATO command" with the intention of eventually bringing NATO under the command of the United Nations, provided that our allies assume continuing responsibility for manning, maintaining, and improving the systems. The main point, he said, was that under his watch as Deputy Secretary of Defense since 1961, the United States had attained a 150 percent increase in nuclear warheads, a 200 percent increase in total megatonnage, a 60 percent increase in tactical nuclear forces in Western Europe, a 45 percent increase in tactical fighter squadrons, a 75 percent increase in aircraft capability, a 100 percent increase in ship construction, and a 800 percent increase in special forces.[54] This memorandum satisfied Symington, but Nitze's confirmation hearings as Secretary of the Navy were, as he recalled in his memoirs, "dominated by grueling interrogations" and he failed to win the votes of Senators Strom Thurmond of South Carolina, Barry Goldwater of Arizona, or Harry Flood Byrd of Virginia.[55]

While rightwing literature on nuclear balance did not directly influence defense policy, the steady stream of books, pamphlets, and magazine articles that spewed forth from Schlafly and others contributed to building a large majority within the Republican party that demanded strong defense policies. This constituency encouraged defense hawks in Congress to support increased expenditures for U.S. strategic defense and tough, verifiable provisions in arms control treaties. This message defined a conservative position on military defense, while inspiring conservatives to act on their belief that America was endangered by the allegedly soft policies pursued by the Kennedy-Johnson-McNamara administration. Nixon captured this constituency when he declared for the presidency in 1968.

CHAPTER EIGHT

Nixon Betrays the Right

SPEAKING BEFORE A group of 300 conservative women who had gathered in St. Louis at Phyllis Schlafly's invitation in the spring of 1969, Congressman John Ashbrook (R-Ohio) proclaimed that the election of Richard Nixon as President the previous November proved how "completely correct" conservative Republicans had been by remaining in the party. Through persistence, he declared, a conservative had been elected to the White House. "One of the pluses we have had since the Nixon Administration took office," he said in closing, "is the character of the President. . . . We now have a much more dedicated, a much higher character, a much more morally-inclined man in the White House than we did before. This is good."[1] Two and a half years after this speech, however, this praise of Nixon as a man of high moral character had soured; Ashbrook took the floor of the House to charge that "the Nixon administration has continued and even accelerated the drift of national policies to the left in many areas. . . . One sad consequence has been the effective silencing of all but a small handful of conservative spokesmen in Congress."[2] The Republican Right across the country joined in a chorus denouncing Nixon as a liberal who had dressed in conservative clothing to win their support in 1968, but once in office threw off these garments to reveal himself as a promoter of big government at home and appeasement abroad.[3]

Schlafly's disappointment in the Nixon administration was especially acute because she played a critical role in helping Nixon win election in 1968 by persuading many conservatives that Nixon was one of them. Indeed, she had run as a delegate for Nixon at the 1968 Republican National Convention and for Congress in 1970 as a Nixon Republican. In 1972, however, she and other faithful conservatives believed they had been betrayed by Nixon on both domestic and foreign policy.

NIXON RUNS FOR PRESIDENT AMID THE COLLAPSE
OF THE DEMOCRAT PARTY

What was especially disappointing to conservatives in Nixon's failure to fulfill the conservative promise was their belief that liberalism was collapsing under its own weight. Never before had the time seemed so auspicious for conservative resurgence, but Nixon's opportunism ruined any chance of political realignment. The nation was in social and political turmoil, and not since 1896 was the Democratic party so divided.[4] By the end of the decade, the potential for party realignment was openly discussed by Kevin Phillips in *The Emerging Republican Majority* (1969) and by Ben Wattenberg in *The Real Majority* (1970). Phillips and Wattenberg showed that discontent among blue-collar ethnic voters in the industrial Northeast and Midwest, and white voters in the South, threatened to undermine the New Deal Democratic party coalition. As one historian of the period observes, liberalism seemed no longer to "protect, or even sanction, the institutions and ideals of the urban white working class."[5]

For many white voters, race riots became a symbol of liberalism's failed promise. In 1966 alone, there were thirty-eight riots that killed seven people and injured 500. In the first nine months of 1967 there were 164 riots, thirty-three of these so violent that they required intervention by the state police, and eight riots led to calling out the National Guard. In Detroit federal troops were called out to suppress the rioting. Moreover, these riots occurred amidst a frightening rise in crime. From 1960 to 1966, the crime rate rose 60 percent while the population grew only 10 percent. In the following five years the crime rate shot up another 83 percent. For many Americans, the rising crime rate seemed linked to the failure of liberal government.

For many working Americans there was growing resentment that political leaders had abdicated their responsibilities to ensure public order by not demanding responsible behavior from all Americans.[6] While some historians and journalists later found this reaction shaped primarily by racial fears on the part of the white working class—and exploited by the Right in America—the roots of this revolt lay in a deeper discontent based on the belief that political leaders had deserted them and government was the enemy. As one woman in Baltimore put it in a letter to a local Baltimore newspaper, the "cry of citizens about crime is drowned out by the louder voices of our elected officials who cry 'More Taxes!'"[7] This populist impulse manifested itself in the 1960s and set the stage for a political realignment that was fundamentally conservative in that it championed existing American institutions while rebuking the liberal elite establishment.[8] Grassroots activists such as Schlafly took up the cry for law and order, which for liberals were code-words for white racism. Yet, Schlafly did not speak or write against busing, a hot button issue involving race in many northern and southern cities at the time. Furthermore, in her call for law and order, Schlafly included not only street crime but riots on college campuses.[9] Race issues appear to have intensified extremist opinion among white supremacists in the late 1960s and 1970s, but these forces were directed largely outside the electoral process, although some of this element was attracted to George Wallace's third-party presidential campaign in 1968. Few grassroots conservatives deserted the GOP to support Wallace, however.[10]

When Lyndon Johnson declined to run for a second term, a bitter primary in which Robert Kennedy was assassinated left the party divided. Hubert Humphrey won the Democratic party nomination, but riots outside the convention hall and Humphrey's initial unwillingness to criticize the war in Vietnam alienated Democratic voters on the left. Under the circumstances, Republicans sniffed victory. From the outset of the primaries, Richard Nixon was the frontrunner, but George Romney and Nelson Rockefeller were also in the race. Rockefeller's refusal to support Goldwater in 1964 earned him the wrath of the Republican Right.[11] Romney gained the support of liberal Republicans including Senator Jacob Javits (New York) and Senator Hugh Scott (Pennsylvania), but such support came at a cost.[12] On the campaign trail, Romney proved to be thin-skinned, arrogant, and politically tone-deaf. His undoing came when he announced that he had been "brainwashed" by the State Department into supporting the Vietnam War. After he lost the New Hampshire primary, Romney withdrew from the race.[13] Rockefeller once again played a cat and mouse game, finally declaring he was in the race on April 30, but Nixon handily won the Oregon primary 65 to 20 percent—a state Rockefeller had won in 1964. Once Nixon won in Oregon, his march to the nomination seemed likely, but not certain. Republicans were anxious to win the presidency and Nixon made a natural appeal to this ambition. Still many on the grassroots Right did not fully trust Nixon.[14]

Nixon knew if he were going to win the nomination, he needed the support of the Republican Right. Therefore he courted Senator Strom Thurmond (R-SC) and Phyllis Schlafly, among others. Sixty-five-year-old Strom Thurmond symbolized the emergent Republican party in the South. In his early political career as a judge and governor of South Carolina, Thurmond had distinguished himself for his liberal views on race by opening his courtroom to black lawyers and calling for dramatically increased funding for black schools in his state. In 1948, however, he broke with the national Democratic party and became the States' Rights presidential candidate. Elected to the U.S. Senate in 1954 as a Democrat, he switched parties in 1964 to support Goldwater. Thurmond endorsed Nixon after he was given assurances that Nixon would appoint "strict constructionist" judges to the courts and ease up on, although not abandon, civil rights enforcement. As one of the most admired politicians in the South, Thurmond's endorsement proved important when Reagan operatives urged Southern delegates to abandon Nixon.

Nixon also sought the endorsement of Phyllis Schlafly, who had emerged as an important voice in the GOP Right. After Nixon personally promised Schlafly that his administration would restore nuclear superiority over the Soviet Union, Schlafly publicly endorsed Nixon. For her, rebuilding America's nuclear forces was the primary issue of the day, even more important than the Vietnam War or civil rights. During this period she was speaking on a range of subjects, but she considered the strategic balance to be the overriding issue in the 1968 election.[15] For Schlafly this was a principled issue: There could be no compromise on the need for the United States to establish itself as the supreme nuclear power in the world in order to protect Americans from attack or blackmail by another nuclear power. She was convinced that "the bomb in the hands of America can mean world peace and the lasting freedom and independence of our people. Nuclear weapons are the best friends we've got—perhaps our only friends—certainly more reliable than our so-called friends who are trading with the enemy."[16] For her, the Vietnam War was a "Communist diversionary tactic" intended to "induce the United States to spend as much as possible on conventional weapons (which cannot protect us from a nuclear attack)—but spend as little as possible on strategic and defense forces." As a consequence she was less concerned about the war in Vietnam than the Soviet military buildup. She saw America's intervention in

Vietnam as another no-win war like Korea, a tactical war instigated by the communists, a war the Johnson administration was not willing to win. She did not publicly oppose the war, nor did she explain how having nuclear superiority would effectively counter the Soviet strategy of supporting Third World revolutions.

By emphasizing the strategic balance, conservatives projected a world view sharply at odds with the liberal mindset of the day. For liberals, poverty, urban violence, crime, education, social problems, and eventually the war in Vietnam were subsumed under the problem of race in America. For conservatives, the threat of communism subsumed all other issues in the 1950s, and in the 1960s this preoccupation was replaced by a Soviet military threat. Schlafly lived in western Illinois and race was never an issue in any of her races for Congress.[17] A survey of Schlafly's correspondence, speeches, and articles turned up only one short passage about race. She maintained that the 1967 race riots did not just happen, but were "organized by outside agitators and armed guerrillas, by various civil rights and New Left groups saturated with Communists and pro-Communists, by publicity-hunters who think violence is the quickest way to glory, by professional revolutionaries filled with a hatred of Western civilization, and by federally financed poverty workers and assorted do-gooders who think the only way to solve the problems of the 'ghetto' is to burn it down."[18]

Schlafly was attracted to Nixon not because of his call for law and order, but by his pledge to rebuild the nation's nuclear defenses, which he made both in public speeches and privately to her. Her enthusiastic support of Nixon surprised many on the Right, including her friend and co-author Admiral Chester Ward. After the election she wrote Chester Ward, "I am sure you think, or thought [that she decided to support Nixon] in order to protect my personal status in the Republican party. This was not the case." She told Ward that she had supported Nixon for two reasons: his stance on defense and because most of her supporters came out for Nixon. She told Ward that of the nearly 3,000 women who had supported her at the NFRW convention, only four women had come out for Wallace and only a dozen supported Reagan.[19] Furthermore, she said, the Midwest was solidly behind Nixon and there was no active campaign for Reagan in Illinois. She noted that the loss of Illinois cost Nixon the election in 1960, so Republicans in Illinois felt an obligation to Nixon.[20]

SCHLAFLY IN THE 1968 ELECTION

Having declared for Nixon, Schlafly threw herself into the campaign in typical fashion. She announced she was running for delegate to the Republican National Convention pledged to Nixon, and she set out to write a new book with Chester Ward to aid the Republican effort.[21] Published in the summer of 1968, *The Betrayers* repeated many of the themes found in their previous books, *Strike from Space* and *The Gravediggers*. Written for the ordinary citizen, it was also intended to provide defense hawks such as Admiral Arleigh Burke, General Bernard Schriever, General Thomas S. Power, and Steve Possony, as Ward put it, "with ammunition to overwhelm the pseudo-intellectuals, hoards of whom, like lemmings, blindly spout the propaganda of the gravediggers."[22] Ward initially wanted to subtitle the book, *Traitors or Dupes?*, but Schlafly vetoed the suggestion. She explained to Ward that "I am just plain 'chicken' about the use of that flamboyant and provocative word 'traitor.' . . . I am constantly on the firing line, on television, on radio, and in press conferences, and I just was not brave enough to add that word to the things that I must defend against attack." Nevertheless, she believed that one of the major purposes of the book was to "expose to the American people, especially to the South, that the Democratic Party has become the party of traitors." She added that she meant only the "ruling clique" of the party, and that their policies had the effect of being traitorous, although this was not their intention.[23] Schlafly hoped that *The Betrayers* might accomplish for the Nixon campaign what *A Choice Not an Echo* did for the Goldwater campaign in 1964. The book won the endorsement of military hawks such as Admiral Ben Morell and received a wide readership among grassroots conservatives. One admirer told Schlafly that she thought the book was "the most important book in the world next to the Bible."[24] In the end, *The Betrayers* did not reach the sales of *A Choice Not an Echo*. Although Nixon told Schlafly that he had received and read the book, his campaign did not promote it.[25] It appeared that the Nixon campaign wanted to keep its distance from the book, which Ward took as another sign of Nixon's disingenuousness on defense.[26]

While Schlafly was writing *The Betrayers*, she also conducted a campaign to be elected as a delegate to the national convention. Her congressional district had been reapportioned to include fifteen counties running from the Missouri border on the west to Indiana on the east. During the campaign, she drove over 10,000 miles and spent over $5,000. She gave Ward her typical schedule: "Monday night, Taylorville, 2 hours drive each way; Tuesday night, Olney, 3 hours drive each way; Wednesday night, Mt. Olive, one hour drive; Thursday night, Salem, 2 hours each way; Friday night, Hillsboro, 1.5 hours each way; Saturday night, Lawrenceville, 3.5 hours drive each way. It is absolutely dreadful. Two men and myself running for two spots."[27]

Schlafly's hard work paid off when she won the election on June 11, receiving the highest vote among the three candidates. For the fourth time, she was elected a delegate to the Republican National Convention. This victory was more of an accomplishment than she realized at the time, because Senator Charles Percy (R-Illinois) was working behind the scenes to prevent her election.[28] Percy, the father-in-law of John D. Rockefeller 4th, had instructed his political operatives to phone the county chairmen in her district to defeat Schlafly. There was no love lost between Schlafly and Percy, although Schlafly had supported him for his successful Senate race in 1966.[29]

Percy's machinations failed, but he was not through with Schlafly quite yet. When the Illinois delegation gathered to choose its representative for the Platform Committee, Percy spoke against electing Schlafly. Her supporters initiated a letter-writing campaign to elect her to the Platform Committee. Typical of these mailings, a "Dear Republican Friend" letter declared, "Rules say that a woman must be elected to the Platform Committee, so write Dirksen, Percy, and Governor Richard Ogilvie, telephone your delegates, and contact at least ten friends in your area and ask them to do the same this week."[30] When the Illinois caucus convened, however, Percy stood up and said, "Phyllis Schlafly is too conservative to represent the State of Illinois on the platform committee." With Percy in opposition, Schlafly was defeated 42 to 14 by Audrey Peak, a delegate at large. Schlafly put the best light on her defeat, telling friends that she guessed winning "25 percent of the vote was a lot when I had two U.S. Senators, the gubernatorial nominee, and the state chairman in a solid phalanx against me." She drew the obvious conclusion: "This is simply one more proof that liberals expect conservatives to be content with second-class citizenship in the Republican party. Conservatives are expected to 'know their place' when it comes to policymaking decisions of the Party."[31] The vote at the Illinois caucus reinforced her view that "the liberals in the Republican party are never going to give conservatives their fair share of positions as a matter of fair play, or seniority, or experience, or ability. Conservatives must fight for their principles and their candidates every step of the way."[32] Instead of the Platform Committee, Schlafly was elected to the Credentials Committee and Senator Dirksen invited her to testify on national defense at the Platform Committee hearings in July.

Phyllis Schlafly arrived in Miami on Sunday, July 28, a week before the convention opened, accompanied by Fred and their six children. The next day she testified on the strategic balance at the Republican National Convention Platform hearing. As Fred and Phyllis began to circulate among the delegates, they became increasingly confident that Nixon would win on the first ballot, although a big push was on for the recently elected governor of California, Ronald Reagan, as well as for the ubiquitous Nelson Rockefeller. Rockefeller had 300 delegates, but 667 were needed to receive the nomination. Pro-Rockefeller favorite sons George Romney and Ohio Governor James Rhodes were ready to swing their 182 delegates to Rockefeller, but he needed to prevent Nixon from winning on the first ballot. This placed Nixon primarily in a defensive position trying to protect his majority from jumping ship.[33] Ronald Reagan showed the most potential to increase his delegate support as the convention opened. As a result Rockefeller instructed his operatives to join forces with Reagan in the search for delegates. There was a fundamental flaw in Reagan's strategy, however. Acting on the advice of Clifton White, his campaign manager, Reagan refused to declare he was a candidate for the Republican nomination; White hoped for a deadlocked convention so Reagan could step forward as a compromise candidate. Schlafly pointed out that it was hard to round up delegates for a "non-candidate"; Douglas MacArthur had used a similar strategy in 1952, and failed.[34]

While not worried about a Reagan or Rockefeller threat, Phyllis Schlafly was concerned that Nixon planned to put a liberal on the ticket to shore up his support on the Left. Rumors circulated that Nixon wanted Charles Percy on the ticket to help win Illinois, the state that had cost him the presidency in 1960. Fears of a Percy candidacy were heightened when she learned that Illinois gubernatorial candidate Dick Ogilvie and Illinois attorney general candidate Bill Scott had come out for Percy for vice-president. As Schlafly talked to other delegates, she heard that Nixon had narrowed his choice of a running mate to John Lindsay of New York, Mark Hatfield of Oregon, and Percy—all aligned with the liberal wing of the party. To block such a nomination, Phyllis and Fred Schlafly concocted a plan to organize a conservative caucus to demand that Nixon place a conservative on the ticket under the threat that 50 to 100 delegates would desert Nixon for Reagan. After unsuccessfully trying to sell the plan to Katharine Kennedy Brown of Ohio and Evetts Haley of Texas, they arranged a meeting through their friend Bobbie Ames of Alabama with Strom Thurmond on Sunday, August 3rd at the Versailles Hotel where he was staying. When Schlafly proposed that Thurmond threaten to hold Southern delegates back unless Nixon agreed to a conservative running mate, they were surprised to hear Thurmond reply that he did not think of convention politics in this way, and he had pledged to support Nixon without asking or receiving any favors, so he was not going to demand concessions now. The meeting broke up with the Schlaflys having concluded, as Phyllis Schlafly later wrote a friend, "conservatives are such individualists" that they don't easily fall into line behind a strategy.

Nevertheless, the Schlaflys had set into motion a series of events that had significant consequences. Two days after meeting with Thurmond, Phyllis Schlafly paid a visit to the South Carolina delegation hospitality suite. As soon as she stepped into the room, Harry Dent, the South Carolina Republican state chairman, told her that by late Monday the "slippage" from Nixon to Reagan had become so bad that Nixon had sent for Thurmond. At the meeting was Nixon's campaign manager John Mitchell. "We got everything we wanted, and more," Dent said. "The Nixon people were worried," so they gave us a veto over the vice-president slot" with the understanding that it would not be Lindsay, Rockefeller, Hatfield, or Romney. In addition, Dent continued, we asked and received the say-so on the Supreme Court and Attorney General positions and a promise to block busing of schoolchildren in the South. Dent then asked Schlafly to draw up a list of acceptable and unacceptable choices for vice president to give to Thurmond, Roger Milliken, and himself to take to the upcoming meeting on the vice-presidential selection.

After Nixon clinched the nomination, he went into the traditional midnight session to choose his running mate. At four o'clock Thursday morning, a "very groggy" Phyllis Schlafly was wakened by a phone call from Strom Thurmond who told her that the meeting to select the vice-presidential nomination had been brutal, but they had gotten their way. Ohio Governor James Rhodes, whom Thurmond described as "a terrible man," would not hear of anyone but Rockefeller or Lindsay, while Goldwater argued for Reagan. Finally, after hours of debate, it was agreed to select Spiro Agnew, the Governor of Maryland, as the vice-presidential nominee.[35] Schlafly was not overjoyed with the choice; she had listed Agnew as a "doubtful, but acceptable" choice. Agnew had been elected governor in 1966. Only nine years before, his highest political ambition had been to win a seat on the Loch Raven Community Council. Because of his lukewarm acceptance of open housing in Maryland, he was characterized in the 1966 election as a "liberal," but he turned out to be no liberal, either as governor or as Vice President.

Following the convention, an elated Phyllis Schlafly returned home to spend the Fall campaigning for the Nixon-Agnew ticket by speaking at large Republican rallies throughout Wisconsin, Minnesota, Missouri, Texas, and Illinois. In addition, the Nixon campaign used Schlafly to serve as an unofficial liaison to the Right. Throughout the campaign Schlafly kept in close touch with Nixon's campaign manager, John Mitchell, and his aide Maurice Stans, keeping them updated on the mood of the meetings she attended with other conservatives.[36] To emphasize the point, she enclosed a letter (with the name removed) that had been sent to her after the election that read: "Some of us feel 'we wuz robbed' at the Republican National Convention when you took a stand for Richard Nixon over Ronald Reagan. We felt betrayed by some people such as you and Strom Thurmond and Senator Tower from Texas. . . . After reading *A Choice Not an Echo* and digesting your comments on Nixon, I cannot understand the complete switch."[37] Having committed herself to Nixon, she remained unwavering in her support for him and urged conservatives not to be led astray by the Wallace campaign.[38]

When Nixon barely won the election by getting 43.5 percent of the vote to Humphrey's 42.7 percent and Wallace's 13.5 percent, Schlafly boldly declared that Nixon "owes his victory to conservatives." She noted that Rockefeller, Lindsay, and Javits had failed to carry New York for Nixon, Romney failed to carry Michigan, Senator Hugh Scott, Governor Ray Shafer, and William Scranton had not carried Pennsylvania, and Senator Edward Brooke and Governor John Volpe failed to carry Massachusetts. (She failed to mention that Rhodes' state of Ohio and Percy's home state of Illinois went for Nixon.) Now, she concluded, conservative Republicans needed to work to get principled Republicans appointed to the administration.[39] While Schlafly did not seek a full-time appointment for herself, she did ask to be placed on the Foreign Intelligence Advisory Board. Instead, Nixon appointed Nelson Rockefeller to the board. While Nixon appointed some conservatives to his administration, he made it clear from the outset that he saw the key to reelection as beating liberal Democrats at their own game by enacting welfare, environmental, civil rights, and women's rights legislation.[40] This legislation was to be balanced by appeals to Catholic voters in the North and white voters in the South, whom he believed could be recruited into the Republican party. Watching Nixon during the campaign and his first days in office, William Rusher confided to a friend that Schlafly and Thurmond had persuaded many on the Right to support Nixon, although he doubted "whether their choice was a wise one."[41]

Although conservative Republicans played a critical role in nominating Nixon, once in office President Nixon did not pursue a conservative agenda. One of the problems he faced was that the Democrats controlled the Senate, 57-43. This was the most Republicans in the Senate since the Eisenhower years, but liberals had become dominant in the Senate, as older Southern conservatives dwindled and Northeastern liberals rose in seniority. In the House, conservatives chaired key military and foreign policy committees, but liberals were on the rise there, too. In special elections in 1969, liberal Democrats won in Wisconsin, Massachusetts, and Montana. Conservatives took some joy in the slim victory of Barry Goldwater, Jr. in California and the grassroots anti-establishment victory of Philip Crane to fill the North Shore Chicago suburban district that opened up when Donald Rumsfeld resigned to join the Nixon administration. Crane, who was enthusiastically backed by Schlafly and her supporters, ran as a free-market conservative. His victory attracted national attention and offered a glimmer of hope to the conservative movement.[42]

As the 1970 elections approached, Republicans hoped to reverse the liberal gains in Congress. Polls showed the electorate to be generally conservative on social and cultural issues and hawkish on defense issues. Although this boded well for the reelection of Richard Nixon, liberals made steady gains in the midterm congressional elections, especially as sentiment against the Vietnam War became pronounced in northern urban districts. The only major political setback for liberals in 1969 was a fatal automobile accident near Martha's Vineyard, where Senator Edward Kennedy's car rolled off a bridge in Chappaquiddick, Massachusetts, drowning Mary Jo Kopechne.[43] Chappaquiddick occurred within

a growing counter-culture that called for the rejection of materialistic values and sought an intensity of experience through drugs, mysti-
cism, and sexuality. Somehow in the minds of many on the Right, Chappaquiddick, counter-culture, the sex-revolution, and the collapse of
liberalism were all related.

SCHLAFLY RUNS FOR CONGRESS IN 1970

By 1970, America appeared to be polarized politically and culturally—
a phenomenon that would characterize political life through the end of
the century. Republicans, certain that the majority of Americans were
made silently angry by student protesters, long-haired, unwashed hip-
pies living off the fat of the land, and urban crime, sought to mobilize
this polarization through a "law and order" theme in the congressional
elections of 1970. This theme had a natural appeal to Phyllis Schlafly,
who as a conservative believed that this sense of disorder felt by the
majority of Americans could work to the advantage of the GOP. Thus
when fifteen county chairmen in Illinois's 23rd District approached her
to run for Congress, informing her that she had been unanimously endorsed at a secret caucus, Schlafly decided to take the challenge and
declared herself a congressional candidate. She ran unopposed in the
Republican primary, which allowed her to focus her speeches on incumbent George Shipley. Political experts saw Shipley, a seven-term
Democrat, as a "top priority," a coveted category that directed national
funding to the district. Only 10 percent of the 435 congressional districts
received this designation.

Republican strategists believed the district especially important because the Illinois congressional delegation was divided 12 Democrats
to 12 Republicans. State GOP strategists believed this was the only district in the state that had a chance of switching columns, and a Schlafly
victory would mean a realignment of a major state delegation in Congress. Schlafly's opponent looked vulnerable, having won in 1968 by
only 15,000 votes when Republicans had swept the races for president,
senate, and governor. Two-thirds of the counties in the 23rd district
regularly elected Republican candidates. The 23rd district, spanning
from the Mississippi River on the west to the Wabash River on the east,
remained in economic decline, even after fourteen years of Democratic
representation in Congress. The district was composed of small towns

surrounded by dwindling farms, played-out coal mines, depleted oil fields, and few sources of employment. If Schlafly could mobilize voter discontent, she stood a chance of beating Shipley. Politically, the district was conservative and tended to vote Republican, but the district tended toward political apathy.[44] There were signs of political volatility within the district. In 1968, George Wallace received close to 20,000 votes, primarily concentrated in seven of the fifteen counties. Also, the district was 15 to 20 percent Catholic, which favored Schlafly, and had few African Americans.

In order to win, Schlafly needed to excite the voters in the district to break out of this complacency and vote out the incumbent. This could be accomplished, Schlafly felt, by portraying Shipley as a liberal who supported big-government programs that did not benefit his own district. Shipley, on the other hand, counted on voters sticking with what they knew—a down-to-earth representative, regular in his appearance, unexciting in his presentation. Politically, he projected himself as a moderate, fending off Schlafly's criticism that he was a liberal, but he claimed that the real difference between his challenger and himself was one of style. He emphasized that Schlafly had gone to Harvard, married a Harvard-trained lawyer, and lived in Alton, the largest city in the district with 35,000 people, and she had grown up in St. Louis. In contrast, Shipley crafted a persona as a down-home folksy guy, best known, as one local newspaper put it, for performing "a consistent role as primer of pork barrel for federally funded projects."[45] He had been born and raised in Olney, Illinois, and spoke with a thick southern Illinois twang, closer to what could be heard in Kentucky than in central Illinois. "There are more than 400,000 voters in the district," Shipley said, "and I'll bet I've personally met half of them. That's what wins elections down here."[46]

Shipley was cut from the same cloth as Melvin Price, who had beaten Schlafly earlier, but unlike her 1952 race, this time Schlafly's campaign was well financed and managed by a professional staff. At the outset of the race, Schlafly estimated that the race would cost $100,000 to $150,000; in the end, it cost $250,000. To manage her campaign she contracted with a Chicago public relations firm, Campaign Group, Inc., a division of the James and Thomas Agency. Campaign Group assigned James Brady, later press secretary to Ronald Reagan, to work on the campaign three days a week, up to 125 days, for a flat fee of $26,000. The firm developed a strategy that relied heavily on radio, billboard, and some television advertising, while calling on the candidate to attend on average two or three coffee parties a day during the campaign, as well as delivering speeches to local groups and attending county fairs and local events such as the Demolition Derby. By the end of the campaign, Schlafly had attended several hundred coffee parties and fifteen county fairs and had driven over 50,000 miles.

Schlafly's campaign drew great enthusiasm from local Republicans, especially in the large network of women supporters she had developed over the years. Over 4,000 people volunteered for the campaign, which enabled Brady to organize a house-to-house literature distribution throughout the fifteen counties in the district. Women volunteers were given bright red and blue campaign aprons, imprinted with Phyllis Schlafly's name, elephants, and eagles. In an age of mini-skirts and blue-jeans, these aprons clearly identified Schlafly's female volunteers as Republicans in a traditional-minded district in middle America. Directing these activities were six full-time staff who worked at her campaign headquarters in her house. Fundraising was essential to maintain this high-cost operation. James Brady persuaded Americans for Constitutional Action, a conservative political action committee chaired by Charles McManus, to contribute $2,500. After a Chicago fundraiser, sponsored by James Kemper, failed to get off the ground, Schlafly accepted an offer by California Federation of Republican Women vice-president Ann Bowler to host a large fundraising luncheon on Friday, April 10, 1970 in Los Angeles. This was followed Saturday evening with a smaller private dinner hosted by Patrick Frawley. The California fundraiser was a big success. Bowler sent a mass mailing directed to Schlafly supporters in the California Federation of Republican Women, declaring, "It is our duty as responsible women leaders and volunteers to help elect women to public office. . . . It's a man's world only because women permit it to be. We are the majority." Over a hundred women turned out for the luncheon at the Los Angeles Marriott. At the luncheon, the audience of primarily women heard from the handsome, bright young star of the Republican Right, the newly elected Congressman Philip Crane and local television commentator Robert Dornan, who would soon make a run for Congress himself. The Frawley dinner the following evening proved equally successful when Henri Salvatori gave $3,000 to the campaign.

Meanwhile, a direct-mail fundraising appeal was organized through a Washington, D.C. firm. The disappointing returns to the first national letter were attributed to a postal strike and the enclosure of a brochure that featured a photo of Richard Nixon. Many conservatives responded that they would support Schlafly, but not Nixon. That was a harbinger of tensions between Nixon and conservatives that would become increasingly apparent after the 1970 election.[47] A second mailing was sent with a letter from Barry Goldwater, but it too, failed to pay for itself. However, contributions did come in from all over the United States. Most of these contributions ranged from $50 to $200, but a couple of donors gave over $10,000. The Republican Congressional Booster Club gave $10,000 and a luncheon in Rockford, Illinois, netted $3,600.[48] Other fundraisers were hosted for her by prominent Illinois, Republicans. Over the course of the campaign, a little less than $150,000 would be raised, with Fred Schlafly contributing close to $50,000 (which Phyllis Schlafly later complained to television pollster and campaign contributor Arthur C. Nielson was "vastly greater than we can afford").[49]

Following a week-long campaign training session in Washington, D.C., sponsored by the Republican Congressional Committee, Schlafly returned to the district ready to do battle. The national GOP congressional campaign instructed its candidates to focus on the "law and order" issue, especially campus protest. This issue appeared to gain traction when student protests broke over the U.S. invasion of Cambodia in April 1970. Over 400 university and colleges campuses shut down, and 100,000 students marched on Washington. On May 4, four students were killed by National Guardsmen at Kent State University. Eleven days later, state police killed two black students and wounded 11 at Jackson State College in Mississippi. Most campus demonstrations remained nonviolent, but the Cambodian invasion encouraged ultraradicals to undertake acts of violence. There were fire bombings on at least ten campuses, including Schlafly's alma mater, Washington University in St. Louis, where the ROTC building was burned to the ground on May 5th.

National Republican strategists instructed candidates to take advantage of this violence by denouncing student demonstrators. Schlafly followed suit in her campaign, declaring in a letter to voters, "Around our country are those who curse America and desecrate the flag. Instead of Old Glory, they wave the black flag of anarchy, the clenched-fist of hate, the Viet Cong flag of oppression."[50] She called for an end to the draft (a position she had held since the 1940s). In general, she shied away from the war in Southeast Asia, other than saying that she supported the president's goal to "end the war honorably." An early campaign brochure directed to youth described her as being "thumbs up for peace and promises to work as a congressman to see that U.S. never again involves itself in another Vietnam or Korea."[51] The fact of the matter was that despite the violence, the law and order issue simply did not have much appeal in her economically depressed district. The closest university was a branch of Southern Illinois University in Edwardsville, which was not a hotbed of radicalism.[52] While Schlafly tried to press the law and order issue, she quickly learned that voters were concerned about one issue: jobs.[53]

What voters were interested in was how the candidates were going to address national and local economic problems. By 1970, inflation had risen to an annual rate of more than 5 percent and was still growing, while unemployment—partly caused by the winding down of the war's defense contracts—reached 6 percent. The 23rd District was especially hard hit, as plant closings in 1970 left thousands without jobs. In East Alton the Olin plant laid off 3,000 workers and International Shoe laid off 700 employees. The Oliver Plow Company closed down leaving 1,000 unemployed. Schlafly discovered that the primary issue facing voters was "unemployment, plant-closings, tight money, high interest rates, in other words, the so-called Republican recession."[54]

Schlafly warned the national Republican leadership in the spring when she attended the Candidates' Conference in Washington that not addressing the economy was a "fatal mistake," but she had been reassured that the economy was expected to turn around by the fall. The national Republican strategy was to bypass the economic issue by focusing on law and order, but a candidate running for office in the summer of 1970 could not ignore the economic issue with unemployment figures rising. As she complained after the election, "There was no way that I, as a Republican congressional candidate, could escape the blame for this when my President and my Senator ignored the issue and kept talking about law and order, which was not the issue voters were interested in." Schlafly tried to approach the economic issue by arguing that when the Federal Reserve Board raised interest rates, it had unnecessarily slowed the economy and made money tight. She blamed the six Kennedy-Johnson Federal Reserve appointees who voted to raise interest rates, but she realized that this was not much of an argument given that Arthur Burns and David Kennedy, Republican appointees to the board, had also voted in favor of raising interest rates.[55]

Campaigning under the slogan, "We've Been Shortchanged Too Long," Schlafly promised that "as your representative in Congress, I will work for immediate tax relief, lower interest rates, improved Social Security benefits . . . and better roads at home." She criticized Shipley for voting against the automatic cost-of-living increase in Social Security benefits, while he accepted "a whopping 41 percent pay increase for himself and asked the rest of us to tighten our belts."[56] Schlafly scored Shipley for supporting foreign aid legislation that included road construction in Indonesia, while roads in the 23rd district continued to deteriorate. These themes were dramatically presented in two television spots, "Roads" and "Social Security." The roads spot simply pictured a car tire moving into a pothole while the voice-over declared, "While Congressman Shipley votes millions for new roads in Asia, our roads are going to pot—Vote Phyllis Schlafly for Congress in November." The social security spot was even harder in its message. The spot opened with an old woman sitting and rocking on a porch. As the camera moved in slowly with a plaintive harmonic solo of "Old Folks" playing in the background, a soft voice-over said, "Many of our neighbors live on fixed incomes. They're elderly. Or disabled. And they really feel the pinch of rising prices. Know what Congressman Shipley did about it? He voted against the automatic cost of living increase in Social Security benefits. Then he accepted a forty-one percent increase himself. Phyllis you can trust."[57] In many ways, Schlafly's proposals for cutting taxes and raising social security benefits were themselves inflationary, but her opponent generally ignored her attacks until the last few weeks of the campaign.

With close to $50,000 budgeted for advertising, she pursued an aggressive radio and limited television campaign. In one live broadcast she opined, "Women do the family spending. They are more careful with other people's money and better at getting a dollar's value for every dollar spent. If we can stop the runaway spending by Congress, we can stop inflation."[58] Billboards and radio were extensively utilized to repeat the message that a new face was needed in Congress. Voters saw billboards blaring, "We've been shortchanged too long." Over 100 billboards were rented throughout the district at a cost of $16,000. On the radio, voters heard Schlafly endorsed by celebrities such as John Wayne, George Murphy, Gerald Ford, Edgar Bergen, and Tony Martin.[59] When voters read their daily newspapers, there were stories of Schlafly having attended a coffee party with a group of women in their district. Every house in the district found a "Vote for Schlafly" hanger on the front doorknob. Three mass mailings were sent to district voters, as well as specialized mailings to young voters, doctors, dentists, and farmers. The Schlafly name appeared everywhere. The only voters Schlafly failed to reach were the Wallace supporters; they seemed a world apart and she never made contact with them.

These campaign efforts appeared to be paying off and newspapers were soon reporting that the race was a toss-up. The *Chicago Tribune* reported that Schlafly had "carried on a whirlwind campaign since last spring." As one Schlafly supporter told the *Tribune* reporter, "We may not beat Shipley, but we'll give him nightmares."[60] The *St. Louis Globe-Democrat*, which endorsed her, reported that the race had tightened after Schlafly began talking more about roads and higher social security payments. The *Globe-Democrat* noted, "Women have played an important part, many of them taking an active role in Mrs. Schlafly's campaign. Among some voters, however, there is still the view that a woman's place is in the home."[61] Yet behind the scenes, the Schlafly campaign was experiencing problems. In mid-August, Schlafly broke her contract with the James and Thomas Agency, complaining that the agency was devoting only one-and-a-half days a week to the campaign, leaving the rest of the "campaign staff demoralized," and its work was "of poor quality, always late, extravagant, and generally lacking imaginative ideas and organizational follow-through."[62] She was especially irate that the firm had placed a logo of "red hot lips" on a campaign button and produced a campaign card declaring that "Schlafly leads a revolt." "If anything," she said, "people in this district are against a revolt." Perhaps most damaging was the missed opportunity to challenge Shipley to a debate until after the congressional recess ended September 8.[63]

Although some critics charged that the problems were due to Schlafly's micro-management style, the failure to draw Shipley into a debate hurt Schlafly. It allowed Shipley to keep the campaign on the issue of personalities, while talking in vague generalities about issues. He told the press, "I don't have a public relations firm working out of my campaign. I don't have that kind of money." He then added, further contrasting his image of the down-home boy with the effete outsider, "These people know me. They're not going to believe the things she says about me."[64] He said that he used to be a hawk on Vietnam, but now believed that America should get out of the war as fast as it can and save lives. "If our experience in the last ten years in Southeast Asia has taught us anything at all," he declared, "it is that the philosophy of additional military force and the introduction of sophisticated weaponry and its employment will not and cannot bring about a resolution of problems."[65] Shipley also took issue with Schlafly's criticism of his "No" vote on automatic social security benefits. Such a cost-of-living proposal ultimately short-changed beneficiaries. He calculated that if this cost-of-living provision had been in effect since 1940, benefits would have increased only 166 percent, but instead Congress increased benefits 234 percent.[66]

In the final weeks of the campaign, Shipley sharpened his criticisms of Schlafly as a political outsider. Initially, he used humor, which fitted the image he wanted to project as a plain-talking country man. Shipley portrayed Schlafly as a rich dilettante who did not know much about the average person just scraping by. He pointed out that Schlafly had written twice to the newspaper editor in Breese, Illinois, but twice spelled the town's name Breeze.[67] In contrast, Shipley portrayed himself as a man of the people who respected the wisdom of his constituents, while Schlafly was a "know it all." Interviewed by the *Alton Evening Telegraph*, Shipley observed, "She gives the impression she's an expert on military affairs and foreign affairs," he said. "I say I'm not an expert on any of these things, that I need the guidance of the people of my district."[68]

As the race tightened, Shipley played to his constituents' base prejudices against electing a woman to Congress. There was widespread sentiment in the district that "a woman's place is in the home."[69] In his speeches, Shipley began to point out that his opponent's campaign literature failed to note that she was the mother of six children. An Associated Press reporter quoted one unidentified man saying, "She's got six kids, hasn't she? You'd think that would give her enough to do."[70] This was an easy line of attack against a female opponent running in 1970, but Shipley's campaign took a nastier turn in the final five days when bumper stickers began appearing, "Vote for a Worker, Not a John Bircher." Schlafly responded to these ad hominem attacks through a series of radio spots telling voters that Shipley had stepped beyond the pale by attacking her children and refusing to debate the issues.[71]

The election results suggest that Shipley's negative campaigning was unnecessary. Schlafly lost by about 13,000 votes, 46 to 54 percent, approximately the same number of votes the losing Republican candidate in 1968 had received. But Schlafly was not alone in her defeat; Republican candidates throughout the state went down, including favorites Ralph Smith for the U.S. Senate and Harold Clark for the Illinois Supreme Court. Post-election analysis showed that the imposition of a Illinois state income tax by Governor Richard Ogilvie, a Republican, had led to an immense voter backlash. The income tax plus the poor state of the economy was used against every Republican candidate, which resulted in the loss of the governor's mansion, the state legislature, and even the state supreme court. Given these economic and political circumstances of Illinois in 1970, it is difficult to see how Schlafly could have won her race. She ran against an incumbent in an off-presidential election year at a time when the economy was in recession. Perhaps the more prudent course would have been to decline the invitation to run when she was approached by the party, but after having encouraged women to run for office, she felt compelled to take up the Republican party banner. In doing so, Schlafly made it a genuine race and up until the very end, many believed that the election was a toss-up.

The campaign showed Schlafly's political ability to talk about bread and butter issues. Only on occasion did she raise ideological issues. For example, she criticized the report of the President's Commission on Pornography, which was released during the campaign, for not taking a tough stand on pornography, but she did not dwell on the issue. She spoke out against the legalization of abortion, but kept the focus of the campaign on local issues. Although she was attacked by her opponent as an extremist, she ran as a Nixon Republican and was able to tap national sources to finance her campaign. Her campaign literature gave little indication that she was to the right of Richard Nixon. At that time, few women could claim the honor of having been nominated to run for Congress in two different districts, but nevertheless, her defeat marked a low point in Schlafly's political life. Only three years before, she had lost the NFRW presidency. Now, in November 1970, she was defeated again. She confided to pollster Arthur Nielson, Sr., that her disappointment was "acute." She said she felt that the campaign had been beautifully organized and she had "the finest team of staff and volunteers, the best advertising I have ever seen for any candidate, and I could not improve anything if I had to do it all over again."[72]

THE GOP RIGHT IN REVOLT IN 1972

Although not expressed in the 1970 campaign, Schlafly had reached the conclusion that not only was the country marching down the wrong path, Richard Nixon was leading the parade. Contrary to campaign rhetoric, Nixon was not dismantling the welfare state. He had not abolished the Office of Economic Opportunity or even ordered the Model Cities Program disbanded. Instead, under his administration the welfare state grew. In his State of the Union speech in 1970, which could have been written by a liberal Democrat, he called for a guaranteed national income for all Americans. Although this legislation, called the Family Assistance Plan (FAP), failed in the Senate, federal programs continued to expand. In 1970, the Family Planning Services Act was enacted, expanding the federal government's role in family planning. Growing federal expenditures worsened inflation, and in 1971 Nixon imposed wage and price controls. The growth of federal domestic expenditures bitterly disappointed conservatives.[73] Social expenditures under Nixon rapidly increased, even though he had campaigned on the promise to "clean up the welfare mess."[74] By the time Nixon left office, social expenditures totaled approximately $338.7 billion, which covered an estimated 72.7 percent of all social welfare expenditures in the nation. The expansion of the welfare state under Nixon coincided with the regulatory state and the rights revolution. With Nixon's support, the Equal Employment Opportunity Commission (EEOC) began imposing targets for the hiring of minorities and women on federal projects.[75] Then, in March, 1972, Congress passed the Equal Rights Amendment (ERA) to the Constitution. The innocuous sounding amendment declared, "Equality of rights under the law shall not be denied or abridged by the United States or by any State on account of sex." Although privately Nixon's support for the amendment was lukewarm, publicly he endorsed the amendment to appease liberals in his own party.[76]

If conservatives were upset by Nixon's domestic program, his foreign policy put them in a state of agitation. His appointment of Henry Kissinger, a long-time associate of Nelson Rockefeller, was taken as an insult by conservatives such as Schlafly. It did not take long for conservatives to blame Nixon for prolonging the war in Southeast Asia and then opening negotiations with North Vietnam. Although conservative organizations such as the Young Americans for Freedom had held patriotic rallies to support the war, many conservatives thought Vietnam was a mistake that played into the hands of the Soviet Union, which was rapidly building its nuclear arsenal.[77] By 1970, conservatives were tiring of the war and were shocked by atrocities such as Lieutenant William Calley's massacre of 400 Vietnam civilians, mostly old men, women, and children, in the village of My Lai. Schlafly observed, "While we cannot judge all the facts about My Lai, it must be stressed that Lieutenant Calley was brought to trial for doing something the United States does not condone as part of our policy in Southeast Asia." Nonetheless, the My Lai incident placed conservatives on the defensive and provided further ammunition to those urging the withdrawal of American troops from Vietnam.[78]

By the spring of 1971, the Republican Right erupted in full anger when Nixon revealed that he was opening relations with mainland China. On April 14th, Nixon removed restrictions on travel, communication, and shipping with mainland China. For two decades, conservatives had crusaded against recognition of Red China and supported the nationalist government of Taiwan. Phyllis Schlafly wrote, "Civilized people don't dine with murderers and criminals. Communists have liquidated 20 million Chinese." But more than principle was at stake. Conservatives such as Schlafly believed accommodation with communist regimes, whether it be with the Soviet Union, North Vietnam, or China, threatened the security of the United States. Communist nations were intent on destroying capitalism and replacing it with communism. These nations were the sworn enemy of the United States. The favorable pictures and news stories coming out about life in China, she declared, might "erase history from the memories of the ignorant and naïve, but such deliberate self deception is dangerous for America."[79] She believed that an emergent China would pose a major threat to the United States in the future, and she continued to hold this belief even after China became one of America's largest trading partners.

By the fall of 1971, conservative Republicans were in open revolt. Schlafly polled 5,000 readers of the *Phyllis Schlafly Report*, and over a third who had voted for Nixon in 1968 planned not to vote for him in 1972. She concluded that "the Nixon administration is not listening to grassroots Republicans in 1971 any more than it did in 1970." Schlafly denounced Nixon for betraying the promises he made in 1968 to restore American nuclear superiority. She was scathing in her attack on

Nixon, comparing his policies to the appeasement policies of the former administration: "The Nixon administration has continued the Robert McNamara policy of military inferiority—even in the face of the tremendous Soviet missile and naval buildup—thereby abandoning the traditional Republican policy of military superiority. The Nixon administration has done nothing to change the disastrous course of nuclear disarmament carried out for seven years by McNamara." To accuse the Nixon administration of replicating the Johnson administration marked her complete break with Nixon.

In November, 1971, Phyllis Schlafly and a group of conservatives met with Barry Goldwater to convey a single message: "The strategic threat to America is so serious that something must be done to force the Nixon administration to take action." The meeting had been arranged with much difficulty by Congressman John Ashbrook. Attending the meeting were conservative U.S. Representatives Philip Crane (R-Illinois), John Schmitz (R-California), and John Rousselot (R-California), joined by General Thomas Lane, Admiral Arleigh Burke, and Phyllis Schlafly. At the meeting Goldwater defended Nixon, arguing that if conservatives deserted him it would only mean the election of Edward Kennedy or Edmund Muskie. Furthermore, he agreed that the Soviet Union was "still bent on world conquest," but he had absolute confidence in and agreed totally with Nixon's foreign policy. He added, to the surprise of the group, that Kissinger was more conservative than anyone in the room. Schlafly replied that the Nixon proposal at the current arms control negotiations with the Soviet Union called for maintaining only two antiballistic missile system sites, while Johnson had proposed twelve sites. Goldwater ignored the ABM issue, but denied categorically that Nixon had given up on a defense policy built around nuclear superiority. Following the meeting, the general agreement was that Goldwater simply lacked "the intellect to understand how silly and inconsistent his statements were. Goldwater is simply tired of fighting."[80] Nonetheless, without Goldwater's support, the group felt there was little they could do to restrain the Nixon administration from entering into an arms control treaty with the Soviet Union.[81]

Schlafly was convinced that Nixon had accepted the liberal line that arms control should be an end in itself, not tied to forcing the Soviet Union to stop supplying North Vietnam, or to demand withdrawal from Eastern Europe, or to stop supporting Third World revolutions.[82] Yet while having concluded that Nixon was following the same path of arms control negotiations set by Robert McNamara, Schlafly and other conservatives rallied behind Nixon's call for the development of an ABM system called Safeguard, especially when it drew immediate opposition from liberals in Congress and antinuclear peace groups.[83] The ABM issue erupted into partisan warfare, as opponents spent over $3 million in a public relations campaign to pressure Congress. In response, conservatives including Phyllis Schlafly fought back with their own grassroots campaign in support of the ABM. By the winter of 1970, Schlafly was devoting full time to the ABM to "put out the word to thousands of my political activist friends." Working closely with the American Security Council, which contributed ideas and money for mailings, Schlafly mobilized her extensive connections of Republican women across the country. She told supporters that they were up against "the most massive, well-coordinated, and well-financed campaign on any issue in 20 years."[84]

"The delusion that America can be defended by treaties instead of by weapons," Schlafly declared in her newsletter, "is the most persistent and pernicious of all liberal fallacies." The United States needed the ABM, and the belief that it would be perceived by the Soviet Union as provocative is "mischievous doubletalk originated by Jerome Wiesner and Roswell Leavitt Gilpatric." She asked how it could be provocative when the Russians were deploying their own antimissile system.[85] In the summer of 1969, Schlafly was invited to testify before the Senate Armed Services Committee in support of the ABM. Her testimony drew praise from Republicans supporting the ABM, including Senator Dirksen who wrote Schlafly to inform her that he had read her testimony on his way into work and found it one of the most concise and pointed arguments against Edward Kennedy and other critics of ABM. He was so enthusiastic about the testimony that he had it placed in the *Congressional Record*.[86] In the end, Nixon won the ABM vote, but only with Vice President Agnew cast the deciding vote to break the 50–50 deadlock.[87] Little did Schlafly realize that her support of the ABM was providing, in effect, a bargaining chip to be played by Nixon in an arms control treaty with the Soviet Union, which she would condemn as another Munich.

Schlafly's worst fears were realized in the summer of 1972 when Nixon met with Soviet premier Leonid Brezhnev to sign the Strategic Arms Limitation Treaty (SALT I) and a separate ABM Treaty limiting each side to the building of ABMs to protect two cities. When the treaty was announced, Schlafly counter-blasted, "For the first time in history," she wrote, "a great nation, at the peak of its economic and military strength, surrendered its military leadership without even a whimper. . . . The SALT pact is the obituary of the United States strategic power." She warned that the treaty rewarded the Soviets for their rapid missile buildup in the past three and half years. She quoted Senator Henry Jackson, "Simply put, the agreement gives the Soviets more of every-thing; more light ICBMs, more heavy ICBMs, more submarine launched missiles, more submarines, more payload, even more ABM radars. In no area covered by the agreement is the U.S. permitted to maintain parity with the Soviet Union."

Invited to testify before the Senate Foreign Relations Committee on June 29, 1972, about the SALT I treaty, her views remained adamant. She implored the Senate to reject the treaty because it "does not stop the spiraling arms race. This one-sided pact freezes the United States, but gives the Soviets written authorization to continue their nuclear building program for the next 5 years."[88] In her testimony, she pointed out that SALT I froze the ICBMs in favor of the Soviet Union, 1,054 U.S. missiles to 1,518 Soviet missiles. The treaty placed no limits on the pay-load of missiles. The treaty, she continued, allowed the United States 710 ballistic missile launchers on submarines and no more than 44 mod-ern ballistic submarines, but permitted the Soviet Union to have 950 ballistic missile launchers and 62 modern ballistic missile submarines. She maintained the American people were being told that the United States had more warheads than the Soviets, but the difference was that the Soviets had larger warheads that could inflict more damage. She added that the belief that the United States was ahead in MIRVs was grossly exaggerated because the Soviets could catch up. "We have been deceived," she declared.[89]

Schlafly placed the primary blame for the treaty on the Henry Kissinger-Paul Nitze crowd. She did not know that behind the scenes, Paul Nitze, who had been involved in the negotiations with the Soviets in Vienna, privately was dissociating himself from SALT. Nitze was an-gered when he learned that Nixon and Kissinger went behind the backs of the U.S. delegation to conclude the SALT treaty and the ABM treaty directly with Brezhnev in Moscow. Nitze believed, as he later wrote in his memoirs, that the ABM "tended to accentuate the asymmetries that already existed in favor of Soviet land-based missiles."[90] Publicly, Nitze's position was different. When SALT I came before the Senate, he supported it with reservations, which helped overcome the fierce opposition organized by grassroots conservatives such as Schlafly.

In Schlafly's view, this treaty, as well as the later SALT II agreement, jeopardized the national security of the United States; this was far more serious than "me-too-Republicanism" or the manifestation of some illusion Nixon might have about being a Disraeli conservative. Conservatives might have tolerated Nixon's domestic program if he had taken a tough stance toward the Soviet Union, but the administration's failure to live up to its promise to restore nuclear superiority was seen as an unconscionable act of betrayal. By this time there was open talk about challenging Nixon, either through Republican primaries or through a new third party effort. Few conservatives spoke of supporting George Wallace in 1972, but the GOP Right agreed that Nixon must go.[91]

Placing great stock in their influence in the party, many conservatives including Phyllis Schlafly believed, incorrectly as it turned out, that Nixon was vulnerable for reelection. Thus when Rep. John Ashbrook (R-Ohio) announced he was a candidate for president, Schlafly joined with other conservatives in the campaign to topple Nixon. Ashbrook, the conservative movement's favorite Congressman, expressed the deep feelings of the Republican Right that the Nixon administration had squandered a great opportunity. One sad consequence of the administration's policies, Ashbrook declared, had been the loss of "a major opportunity presented to the Republican party and the conservative cause" to have replaced failed liberal policies with principles of conservative government. Instead, Nixon followed the downward path of liberalism. Ashbrook accused Nixon of expanding government, failing to support U.S. military superiority, and ignoring the threat of world communism.[92]

On the campaign trail, Ashbrook confronted the reality of running against an incumbent president. Richard Viguerie's efforts at fundraising did not attract the kind of money necessary to run an effective campaign, although he received a few large donations from donors in the West and Southwest. Average Republican voters stuck with Nixon. As Ashbrook campaigned in New Hampshire hoping to pull off an upset, television viewers watched Richard Nixon in China, the first American president to go there since Herbert Hoover. On election day, Ashbrook received only 9.7 percent of the vote. Antiwar Republican Pete McCloskey won 19.8 percent and since he had set a goal of 20 percent, he announced he was withdrawing from the race. This left Nixon with

68 percent of the vote. The highest percent Ashbrook received in any primary was in California where he received 9.8 percent. So disheartening were the results that Ashbrook refused to have his name placed in nomination at the convention. Attending the convention as an observer, Schlafly watched Nixon easily win the party's nomination. The best conservatives could do was to defeat resolutions that would have established proportional representation of minorities and women for delegates, but there was no opposition to the Nixon juggernaut. In the general election that fall, Nixon trounced antiwar Democrat George McGovern in one of the largest landslide elections in American history. Nixon won without the right wing of his party.

Nixon's victory in 1972 was short-lived. In August 1974, a disgraced President Richard Nixon announced he was resigning from office after two years of political turmoil created by the Watergate scandal. Nixon left a shattered Republican party. Its liberal wing was atrophying and conservatives were generally demoralized.[93] Two years before Nixon's resignation, William Rusher assessed the languid state of the conservative movement, which he told William F. Buckley, Jr. was "not in good health, to be sure, but at least it is alive and capable of being fought for." Two years later, even this pessimistic assessment seemed overly rosy. William Rusher lamented the fallen state of conservatism in America: The Young Americans for Freedom was in factional disarray; subscriptions to *National Review* were down and the magazine's deficits were the biggest ever, and the conservative movement as a whole was dispirited.[94]

Rusher's assessment was widely shared. The Republican Right appeared to be in a state of rapid decline as a political force within the GOP and American politics. Its mark on American life at this point had been minimal: it had contributed to a disastrous defeat for the GOP in 1964 and it had served as a useful foil for liberal Democrats. Its obituary in the history books at this point would have been brief. Yet, even as conservatives were stunned into silence by the events that had led to Nixon's resignation, there were some signs of life suggesting that it was too early to issue a death certificate. Significantly, the American Conservative Union (ACU), formed shortly after the 1964 election, had continued to grow during the Nixon years. In 1971, the ACU had wisely distanced itself from the Nixon administration when it released its *Declaration Relating to President Nixon* labeling Nixon's policies an "anathema to conservatives." While the ACU's support of Ashbrook in 1972 proved quixotic, its membership climbed to 45,000.[95]

Nixon's resignation in 1974 left every Republican organization tarnished. For most Americans, Richard Nixon was the Republican party, and he symbolized its right wing. To have tried to convince the average American that Nixon was actually a liberal operating under the guise of a conservative would have been greeted with derision. Liberals trumpeted Nixon's resignation as a defeat of the Republican Right, even though conservatives such as Phyllis Schlafly rejected Nixon. Instead of burying Great Society liberalism, Nixon had isolated the conservatives and had revived the Left by his abuse of power. Howard Phillips, a former administration official and conservative activist, summarized the feelings of conservatives when he told the press, "Under Richard Nixon, our ideological opportunity has been squandered, our loyalties have been unreciprocated, and our party's reputation for integrity has been virtually destroyed."[96] Taking advantage of the post-Watergate revulsion and the anger created by Gerald Ford's full pardon of Nixon on September 8, the Democrats swept the 1974 congressional elections. Republicans were stunned by the size of their defeats. When the results were tallied, the Democrats controlled the House 290–145. In the Senate the Democrats picked up four seats to further extend their control. Thus, Watergate contributed to the revival of the Democratic party, but Nixon's resignation had an unexpected consequence. The politics of polarized ideology replaced the politics of opportunism, as both the Democratic party and the Republican party swung further apart—the Democrats to the left and Republicans to the right.[97] Ironically, this swing to the left within the Democratic party benefited the Republican Right and injected new life into a faction that had been weakened considerably during the Nixon years.

In office Nixon kept the Republican Right at bay. Once he left office, ideological politics within the Republican party was unleashed with a fury unexpected by Nixon's successor in the White House. The embattled Republican right wing began to put into place the instruments to challenge the party's moderate-liberal wing. In 1974, Paul Weyrich organized the Committee for the Survival of a Free Congress, which became a major instrument in the establishment of what would be called the "New Right." A year later in 1975, Terry Dolan established the National Conservative Political Action Committee, a PAC aimed at electing conservatives and defeating liberals.

The stage was set for a revival of the Republican Right.[98] It would be sparked, however, not by "me-too Republicanism," but by the emergence of the feminist movement and a growing cultural divide in America.[99] The feminist movement, to paraphrase a leading feminist historian, marked American's longest revolution and would subvert "authority and transform society in dramatic and irrevocable ways," but it also produced an unintended backlash. As Democrats relished the removal of their nemesis Richard Nixon and welcomed the feminist revolution, and as moderate Republicans led by Gerald Ford assumed control of the White House and the GOP, a thousand miles away, Phyllis Schlafly prepared to lead a counterattack against the feminist movement. In doing so, she paved the way for the Republican Right to triumph in retaking control of the party.

CHAPTER NINE

The ERA Battle Revives the Right

ON FEBRUARY 25, 1973, one year after Phyllis Schlafly had declared war on the Equal Rights Amendment (ERA) with the publication of "What's Wrong with 'Equal Rights' for Women," she confronted Representative Patricia Schroeder (D-Colorado) on the ABC Sunday news program, *Issues and Answers*. There was one point in the exchange between Schlafly and Schroeder in that winter of 1973 that seemed to crystallize the differences between the Left and the Right, both of substance and style:

> SCHLAFLY: The point is if we have ERA, we have this constitutional millstone around our neck, whereby if we have a national emergency, we then are saddled with social upheaval. And we do not want women serving in combat and on warships on an equal basis with men. . . . We have had a draft for 33 years and we have had three bloody wars that nobody expected, and most of the time the politicians were promising peace.
>
> SCHROEDER: Right now Congress could draft women anyway. They have that right in case of a national emergency. In World War II in England they drafted women. The draft is going out. She is correct about the voluntary status but the other thing that I think we keep overlooking too is that we are entering a new phase because of technology in the whole fighting of wars. It is more a push-button type of war. But when you boil all of that down, we still have had different kinds of deferment, etc, within the draft. . . .
>
> SCHLAFLY: This matter of technology, tell that to the POWs just coming back from Vietnam or tell that to the 45,000 men we lost in Vietnam. . . . But the point is, under the ERA, Congress will no longer have the option. Congress will be constitutionally required to draft women on the same basis as men.
>
> MODERATOR: Do you agree that you will have no option if the Equal Rights Amendment—
>
> SCHROEDER: That is right. We will have to put laws in that apply to males and females equally.

SCHLAFLY: Do you want to draft women?

SCHROEDER: That you can only draft women for combat duty if they can perform the same functions, and men and women would have to be equal.

MODERATOR: Do you think that is desirable?

SCHROEDER: Yes, I think that is all right.

MODERATOR: That a woman in combat is a desirable thing?

SCHROEDER: I think it [combat] is brutalizing. It is brutalizing to any human being. You know. I certainly don't wish that anyone has to put themselves in that situation. But I think that all of us have, you know, we are all Americans down under the skin and we all have certain rights and responsibilities and I think that the Congress can deal with that. I think we can still make it so we are not tearing up families.[1]

There was nothing inherently inconsistent in Schroeder's argument that women should be accorded equal treatment to be sent into military combat, while noting that war is brutalizing, but such an argument struck an odd note in a political debate by suggesting that feminists wanted equality at any cost, even if it was brutalizing, as Schroeder conceded would be the consequence of gender equality in combat. Yet, many supporters of ERA were uneasy with this position. For example, Hollywood actor Alan Alda was ridiculed when, appearing before the Illinois State Senate to testify on behalf of ERA, he echoed Schroeder's sentiments in support of female conscription. Asked by a hostile State Senator if he would support his two daughters being drafted during a war, Alda emphatically answered, "Yes," but then added that his daughters would not enter into the military even if drafted because they were pacifists who opposed all war and would declare themselves to be conscientious objectors.[2]

Such arguments appeared not only to suggest that equality was a goal in itself for liberals, but that it need not come with obligations to the nation.[3] In this way, the Equal Rights Amendment, through its succinct declaration, "Equality of rights under the law shall not be denied or abridged by the United States or by any State on account of sex," confronted the fundamental meaning of equality in American society. ERA gave new impetus to the movement for total equality in American political, social, and cultural life. In the aftermath of the civil rights struggle in the 1960s, speech against unqualified equality and in favor of hierarchy, authority, or privilege appeared to be a declaration against social and political progress. So widely shared was this effort to take equal rights beyond its traditional and narrow political moorings in classical liberalism that both political parties, Democratic and Republican, endorsed the Equal Rights Amendment. For supporters of the ERA, opposition to the amendment appeared to be little more than a defense of privilege.

For conservatives, this drive for equality threatened conventional culture, established institutions, and customary social roles. Feminists, on the other hand, believed that these institutions and social roles evolved or were created historically as instruments of oppression, and should be transformed. Yet, even as this revolution began in the late 1960s and early 1970s, it provoked a backlash unanticipated in its religious and political ferocity, and led to a shift to the Right by the end of the decade. Thus, while American culture in the 1970s accentuated personal liberation, American politics experienced a conflagration on the Right sparked by these cultural and social changes. The paradox of the decade was this: If this was the age of liberation, it was equally the age of reaction.

The Strange Career of ERA

The career of the ERA captured this strange twist of political fate. Ironically, the ERA helped revive the GOP Right and the GOP generally. After Nixon resigned from office, the Republican party stood arguably at its lowest point in its 120-year history, even lower than when Hoover left office in 1933. In 1974, only 18 percent of voters identified themselves as Republican. Yet within six years, many voters came to see the GOP not as a party of big business and the wealthy, but as a party of the little guy, the regular American Joe and his wife, while the Democratic party belonged to elitists who imposed schemes of social engineering, social privilege, and special interest—all at the expense of the hard-working middle-class. The catalyst for this transformation was found in the grassroots reaction against feminism, legalized abortion, ERA, and the ban on prayer in school. Writing after the ERA had been lost, feminist Sylvia Ann Hewlett observed, "It is sobering to realize that the ERA was defeated not by Barry Goldwater, Jerry Falwell, or any combination of male chauvinist pigs, but by women who were alienated from a feminist movement the values of which seemed elitist and disconnected from the lives of ordinary people."[4]

When ERA passed Congress in 1972, nobody expected it would have such strange political repercussions or become the epicenter of a political earthquake. The proposed amendment made its first appearance in Congress soon after the adoption of the Nineteenth Amendment enfranchising women in 1920. In July 1923 the ERA was unanimously endorsed by the National Woman's Party at a convention in Seneca Falls, New York, but feminists divided over the amendment because some feminists such as the National Consumer League's Florence Kelley believed it would undermine legislation protecting female workers.[5] The amendment gained momentum when the 1940 Republican platform endorsed the ERA, and four years later the Democratic party platform endorsed the ERA. When reintroduced in Congress in 1947, support for the ERA extended across party lines. Conservative New York Republican James W. Wadsworth (R-New York), for example, opposed the ERA, while conservative Republican Senator Robert Taft (Ohio) and liberal Democrat Helen Gahagan Douglas (California) supported the ERA.

In 1947, opposition arose immediately to the proposed amendment from conservative women's groups, a point sometimes neglected by historians who have tended to look only at divisions within the feminist movement. Representative James Wadsworth's office, for example, received many petitions and letters from women in his state opposing the ERA. Many of the arguments raised would be echoed in the 1970s, although Schlafly was unaware of this earlier opposition. Typical of this opposition was Cecilia Yawman, representing the Rochester Diocesan Council of Catholic Women, who wrote Wadsworth that 20,000 Catholic women in her city opposed ERA because "great danger lies in it. We do not confuse equal rights with identical rights." Jane Todd sent Wadsworth resolutions passed by the Federation of Women's Republican Clubs, representing 55,000 women, against the proposed ERA because it was deemed "retrogressive." She warned that the amendment jeopardized all remedial and protective legislation for women in regard to marital and property rights. Mrs. Charles Heming, state president of the New York League of Women Voters, also opposed ERA because the chief discrimination against women was caused by custom not prejudice in the law and would create "endless confusion in the courts."[6]

In spite of this opposition, a modified ERA amendment was approved in 1950 by the Senate 63 to 19. During debate over the ERA, Senator Carl Hayden (D-AZ) attached a rider stating that "the provisions of this article shall not be construed to impair any rights, benefits, or exemptions conferred by law upon the persons of the female sex." ERA supporters opposed the Hayden rider because of the restrictions it placed on the amendment and as a result the bill failed to come to the House floor for a vote.

The emergence of a new women's movement in the late 1960s imparted new life to the ERA. In October 1967 the newly formed National Organization for Women (NOW) voted overwhelmingly to endorse the Equal Rights Amendment. In Congress, the liberal chairman of the House Judiciary Committee, Emanuel Celler, who supported women's protective labor legislation, held up the ERA in his committee. In the summer of 1970, Representative Martha Griffiths (D-MI) rallied a majority of her House colleagues to have the ERA discharged from the Judiciary Committee. On August 10, 1970, after only one hour of debate, the House approved the amendment by a vote of 352 to 15. Senate sponsor Birch Bayh (D-IN) and Majority Leader Mike Mansfield (D-MT) brought the House-approved ERA directly to the Senate floor. Democratic North Carolina Senator Sam Ervin's attempt to attach a series of riders to the amendment protecting women from the military draft, alimony, child custody rights, and protective labor laws failed to gain support in the Senate. Differences arose as to limiting the time for state ratification, and the 91st Senate adjourned without taking action.

The House again passed ERA on October 12, 1971, after rejecting the Wiggins Amendment to exempt women from "compulsory military service" and to preserve other laws "which reasonably promote the health and safety of the people." An overwhelming majority of the House, 354, supported ERA, while only 23 members voted "No," including the senior female member, pro-labor Representative Leonor Sullivan (D-MO). In the Senate, Ervin proposed nine separate amendments to ERA to protect the traditional rights of women. Every one was defeated on roll-call votes on March 21 and 22, 1972, and ERA then passed the Senate by 84 to 8. Congress granted seven years for the amendment to be ratified by three-fourths of the states. Then on January 22, 1973, the U.S. Supreme Court legalized abortion, a decision that was to have profound implications in debates over women's rights in the 1970s and 1980s.

Within the first year after passage by Congress on March 22, 1972, thirty states ratified the ERA; only eight more states were needed for ratification. ERA appeared headed for speedy ratification when Phyllis

Schlafly organized the STOP ERA movement in September 1972. Her involvement came about serendipitously in December, 1971, when she was invited to a debate sponsored by a conservative forum in Connecticut. She suggested that the debate focus on national defense, but was told the club wanted to address the Equal Rights Amendment, then pending in the U.S. Senate. Claiming she did not know much about ERA, she asked for material to be sent to her. After reading the material, she decided she was against the amendment.

Prior to this Schlafly had not taken much interest in feminism. This turn to feminism, or more exactly, antifeminism, reflected a turn in grassroots conservatism to social issues that would be no longer linked to communism or defense. In the 1960s, the Supreme Court's ban on prayer in school sparked the first signs of Christian political mobilization. Some Republicans joined in this opposition, as seen when Senator Everett Dirksen (R-Illinois) proposed legislation to allow prayer in school. Schlafly had supported this legislation, but her major interest remained defense. Schlafly's response to the ERA initiated a direct response to the feminist challenge from Christian women who saw traditional culture under attack. The ERA issue introduced large numbers of Christian women to politics and tapped into their fears that their values were being threatened by the secular Left.

Schlafly took the lead in rallying this festering opposition when she published "What's Wrong with 'Equal Rights' for Women?" in the *Phyllis Schlafly Report* in February 1972.[7] In this antifeminist manifesto, Schlafly articulated the basic principles that would guide the anti-ERA forces for the next ten years. In doing so, she laid out fundamental reasons for opposing the women's liberation movement, arguing that the family is "the basic unit of society, which is ingrained in the laws and customs of our Judeo-Christian civilization [and] is the greatest single achievement in the history of women's rights." The family, she argued, "assures a woman the most precious and important right of all—the right to keep her own baby and to be supported and protected in the enjoyment of watching her baby grow and develop." This opening declaration was a direct challenge to feminist Betty Friedan, who had argued in her bestselling book, *The Feminine Mystique* (1963), that American women had been taught to accept traditional, middle-class gender roles of homemakers and housewives, and that kept them from pursuing self-fulfillment in the workplace, largely out of social pressures and fears of being labeled an "improper mother." To the contrary, Schlafly argued that women benefited from the "Christian tradition of chivalry," which obligated men to support and protect their wives and children. Furthermore, she continued, American women were the beneficiaries of the technological advances of the late nineteenth and twentieth century. She wrote that the real liberation of women from backbreaking drudgery of prior centuries is "the American free enterprise system which stimulated inventive geniuses" to provide women with labor-saving devices.

Continuing, she called ERA a direct threat to the protection that mothers and working women enjoyed in American society. Specifically, she argued that the ERA would "abolish a woman's right to child support and alimony," and would "absolutely and positively make women subject to the draft." The issue, she claimed, was not whether women should be given better employment opportunities, equal pay for equal work, appointments to high position, or gain more admission to medical schools. Such goals were desirable and she supported "any necessary legislation" to fulfill these goals. But the feminists, she said, were claiming these goals as their own in order to sugar coat with "sweep syrup" an agenda that was "anti-family, anti-children, and pro-abortion." Actually, "women libbers view the home as a prison, and the wife and mother as a slave. . . . The women libbers don't understand that most women want to be a wife, mother and homemaker—and are happy in that role."[8] In making this argument, her language was direct, unqualified, and bound to infuriate feminists.

SHAPING THE ANTIFEMINIST MOVEMENT

A month after publishing "What's Wrong with 'Equal Rights' for Women?" Schlafly received a phone call from an excited subscriber in Oklahoma, Ann Patterson, who told her that the Oklahoma state legislature had defeated ERA after her report had been circulated to them. Schlafly knew immediately that she had found an issue to rally the grassroots.[9] Yet, even after the Oklahoma defeat, few believed that ERA could be stopped. The very day that the U.S. Senate passed the ERA, Hawaii became the first state to ratify, followed in the next few days by Delaware, Nebraska, New Hampshire, Idaho, and Iowa.[10] By mid-1973, 30 states had ratified the ERA, but then ratification slowed; three more states ratified in 1974, one in 1975, and another in 1977, bringing the total to thirty-five states of the needed thirty-eight.[11] Schlafly entered the ERA fight as an experienced organizer with a network of supporters throughout the country, but political observers believed that chances for defeating the ERA were nil.[12]

The national campaign against ERA began on July 7, 1972, when Schlafly called a small meeting of Illinois supporters to a one-day meeting at the O'Hare Airport Inn. Most of these women had been with her in the National Federation of Republican Women (NFRW) battle. They were mostly women in their 40s and 50s, but in the course of the fight they brought in many young women. They agreed there was a need to form a national organization against ERA ratification. The group felt that the name for the new organization needed to zero-in on the ERA. When Kate Hoffman, who would head the anti-ERA effort in Illinois, suggested STOP ERA (Stop Taking Our Privileges), the group had its name and its mission.[13] On September 26, 1972, Schlafly held the first national conference of STOP ERA when over 100 women from throughout the country gathered in St. Louis to discuss anti-ERA strategy. By this time five states had defeated ERA: Oklahoma, Illinois, Ohio, Nevada, and Louisiana. At the conference, Ann Patterson spoke on how ERA was defeated in Oklahoma, Irma Donnelson on Ohio, Kate Hoffman on Illinois, and Charlotte Felt on Louisiana. All had been involved in Schlafly's NFRW race except for Felt, whom Schlafly knew from her anticommunist activities. These women brought their organizing experience to the ERA campaign. At this two-day strategy meeting, it was decided to organize under a national coordinating committee called STOP ERA, using the stop sign as its logo.[14] Little did they realize how prolonged the battle would be, as some states continued to bring up ratification year after year.

There was some discussion of working with Pro America, a longtime conservative organization, but Schlafly decided it would be a political mistake to align the movement directly with another political group. She understood that the new organization would have its greatest success as a single-issue group with one goal—defeating ERA. Some at the meeting wanted to transform the ERA issue into a larger debate about the United Nations or socialism, but that was contrary to Schlafly's vision of the mission.[15] By focusing on the social and legal ramifications of ERA, Schlafly allowed a broad coalition to be formed that included conservatives and establishment Republican women such as Mrs. Edgar Eisenhower, the former president's sister-in-law,

Senator Sam J. Ervin's wife, Senator Paul Fannin's wife, and the wives of Congressmen from Mississippi, North Carolina, Utah, Texas, Pennsylvania, California, and Arizona.

By early 1973, STOP ERA organizations existed in twenty-six states and were especially strong in states critical to the ratification of ERA—Arizona, Florida, Illinois, Louisiana, Missouri, Ohio, Oklahoma, Utah, Nevada, North and South Carolina, and Virginia.[16] As Schlafly told one state director, STOP ERA is the "most loosely organized organization you will ever be associated with." Schlafly appointed state directors, but state organizations developed their own campaign tactics and raised their own funds. STOP ERA was joined by a variety of other ad hoc groups such as Women Who Want to Be Women and the Family Preservation League. More established organizations such as the National Council of Catholic Women provided considerable support against the ERA. Until it changed its position in 1975, the AFL-CIO opposed ERA. Senator Erwin's office provided initial support.

At first, Schlafly drew activists from her network of conservative Republican women across the country, particularly women who had traveled to Washington, D.C., in 1967 to vote for her as president of the National Federation of Republican Women, and those who had distributed copies of *A Choice Not an Echo* in 1964. As the campaign grew, she effectively reached out to women not previously involved in politics, especially younger, evangelical Christian women. One television producer remarked in filming a television special on ERA, "I've been surprised at the variety of women who oppose it. There are many young, attractive mothers who feel threatened by ERA, for instance, because they believe it would deprive them of special protection they now have."[17] These evangelical Christians tended to be stay-at-home mothers, but many worked outside the home as well. What they shared were organizational and speaking skills acquired in their churches.[18] These women brought an evangelical enthusiasm that energized the entire anti-ERA movement and impressed state legislators with their commitment to stop ERA from being ratified. Evangelical women were drawn from the Church of Christ, Southern Baptist, and fundamentalist independent churches, but Mormons, Orthodox Jews, and Roman Catholic women were effectively mobilized as well. For the first time, these women were brought into the larger conservative movement by social issues, rather than anticommunism. What held these groups together was Schlafly's personal leadership plus their organ of communication, the *Phyllis Schlafly Report*, which each month presented news and new arguments against ERA, kept a running tally of votes by the states, and advised on campaign strategies and tactics. The establishment of these chapters encouraged Schlafly to broaden her political base. In November 1975, she established Eagle Forum, calling it "the alternative to women's lib." By the end of the ERA battle, Eagle Forum members no longer viewed themselves as "the alternative"; believed they were mainstream, even though their membership of 60,000 paled in comparison to the National Organization for Women with its 220,000 members.[19]

Overall, anti-ERA activists mirrored pro-ERA activists, although with important differences. Both pro- and anti-activists drew largely from white, middle-class women. For example, charter members of the National Organization for Women (NOW), the leading pro-ERA group, were 50 percent over the age of thirty, 66 percent held bachelor's degrees, with approximately half of the college graduates also possessing advanced degrees.[20] Surveys showed that support for ERA was greatest among highly educated and divorced women who did not attend church services regularly. Many ERA supporters were young, unmarried, and employed outside the home.[21] While anti-ERA activists tended to be married women, over half in one survey reported above-average family incomes and many had college educations and worked outside the home. The fundamental distinction between anti-ERA activists and pro-ERA activists lay in their different value systems, as indicated by religious affiliations. A remarkable 98 percent of anti-ERA supporters claimed church membership, while only 31 to 48 percent of pro-ERA supporters did. Studies done at the time consistently showed that anti-ERA activists were motivated by a strong belief in the tenets of traditional religion.[22] ERA supporters tended to welcome the new morality of sexual liberation and reproductive rights, and identified with progressive causes. For antifeminist activists, ratification of the ERA and legalization of abortion symbolized threats to the traditional nuclear family. They saw themselves as upholding the ideal of the two-parent family—a father, a mother working at home, and children—which they feared was being replaced in the 1970s by single-parent families and cohabitating couples, both heterosexual and homosexual. Anti-ERA activists identified themselves as politically conservative, committed to the old morality, and supporters of traditional gender roles. For fundamentalist and evangelical Protestant women, beliefs about the place of wives in the family and women in society came from biblical injunctions to uphold the authority of husbands and fathers.

Yet, many of the empirical studies of anti-ERA activists showed that these women, like their counterparts on the other side of the debate, believed that they could control their own lives and were heavily involved in the political system.[23] As one study concluded, females who were opposed to equal rights for women were "high achievers, but closed-minded." While anti-ERA females denied significant gender discrimination, they supported equal pay for equal work, knowing that federal law already outlawed such discrimination.[24] Such evidence suggested that anti-ERA activists were not motivated by any sense of alienation from society, urbanization, industrialization, or status anxiety caused by declining social positions—a case frequently made by later feminist scholars. On the contrary, as one study noted, "the personal and political characteristic of its members [in this case, anti-ERA activists in North Carolina] do not fit most of the hypothesized characteristics ascribed to opponents of women's liberation."[25] Moreover, while many of the anti-ERA activists held conservative beliefs that were anti-big government, anti-egalitarian, and fearful about moral disorder in society, they never had contact with the segregationist Right—the Ku Klux Klan, the Minutemen, or white separatist groups. While one study suggested that this was due to class differences, a more likely explanation could be found in the belief system of anti-ERA activists, many of whom were religious conservatives who accepted equal opportunity for all groups.[26]

The anti-ERA movement reflected the character of the diverse localities from which its members were drawn. In Oklahoma, many of the local activists belonged to the Church of Christ; in Utah, Nevada, and Arizona, many of the key activists were Mormon; the Southern states drew heavily from Southern Baptists, the Church of Christ, and smaller fundamentalist churches. Illinois attracted many Roman Catholics, and orthodox rabbis played an important role in the Chicago campaign. The South Dakota STOP ERA chairman was an Austrian immigrant, a refugee from the Nazis and the Communists. The North Dakota STOP ERA chairman was one of twelve children born to Hispanic parents. The Vermont STOP ERA chairman was a twenty-something who had voted for George McGovern in 1972. STOP ERA's legal adviser was a single woman practicing law in Indianapolis. The head of the North Carolina STOP ERA campaign, Dorothy Slade, was a member of the

John Birch Society.[27] The diversity and commitment of these women were not something easily captured in a statistical survey.

For the most part, the women who joined Schlafly were middle-American women, down-to-earth and not given to airs of sophistication. They called one another "dear" and "honey" and referred to themselves as "girls." Even in their political correspondence they often spoke of their children and might share a recipe for banana bread. What they brought to the anti-ERA movement was an ability to talk to state legislators, many of whom they knew as neighbors or as members of their congregations, without appearing threatening. These were women who would send a thank-you card to their legislators for voting "No" on ERA with a drawing of an adoring woman with her head tilted and her laced fingers under her chin, surrounded by floating hearts with a caption reading, "For Recognizing the Difference, You are Terrific, Fantastic, and Marvelous."[28]

Typical was Shirley Curry, the wife of a Church of Christ minister, who with anti-ERA material under one arm and the *Congressional Record* under the other, joined with "other informed Christian women to tour this state [Tennessee] talking to ladies Bible classes, telling each group which representative they need to influence" because ERA was "a vital issue for the church and the nation." In Alabama, Peggy Alston phoned Eunice Smith to tell her that she had given birth to twin babies a month early, but "this little series of events did not interfere with her plans for attending the ERA hearings." Her fellow Alabamian Chris Collins reported to Phyllis Schlafly that she gave five speeches before the leading women of Anniston, including black church groups—"all enthusiastic. I have really stirred up the town. All are agog regarding your coming to Alabama for two days." In Michigan, Elaine Donnelly, described by a local newspaper as "young, pretty, happily married" with two young children, declared that the feminists "reject the values that the majority of women hold . . . they have a very negative attitude toward the family and I don't think they understand the nature of commitment to the family." Many STOP ERAers came to the movement as political novices, so they took pride when they were able to debate effectively with a local professor or testify at legislative hearings. Anna Graham wrote Schlafly in the summer of 1973 about one such hearing, "We anticipated the proponents accurately and matched them point by point and person to person—youth, blacks, a lawyer, a housewife, a working gal, elderly, etc. . . . . Really I was so pleased that we did so well, considering the lack of political experience most of the opposing women have."[29]

These women were the backbone of the anti-ERA movement. To ensure that they were prepared for the battle ahead, Schlafly conducted workshops on how to debate and testify at a public hearing. Schlafly talked about the importance of good grooming and what kind of makeup to wear, what colors looked good on television, and how to be poised and smile when attacked. Above all, Schlafly emphasized the importance of conducting oneself as a lady. The president of the Florida Women for Responsible Legislation summarized the attitude of these grassroots activists when she told a local reporter that "looking feminine is important" in winning support against ERA.[30] Schlafly encouraged this use of femininity to win over state legislators. "Get Maud Rogers and that pretty young girl who had the baby and the nice looking redhead," she told her leaders in Arkansas, "to commit themselves to talk personally with ten legislators. That would be thirty. Pick the ones who are wavering and go for it."[31] However much feminists deplored these tactics, they knew that in the battleground states, located largely in the South and the Midwest, such tactics were well suited to win over the middle-aged white male legislators who dominated the state legislatures.[32] The women who joined the anti-ERA campaign became unrelenting in their political activity. These were local women whom most politicians feared to alienate, because these women talked politics, volunteered in political campaigns, and wore political buttons when they came to meetings. They placed ERA as the most important issue in their political world.[33]

In organizing against ERA, opponents portrayed the ERA as elitist, an amendment promoted by leftist feminists out of touch with and hostile to stay-at-home mothers. Typical was an anti-ERA letter, hand-typed and mimeographed, which was distributed to Ohio state legislators: "We are a group of wives, mothers and working women vitally concerned with how the Equal Rights Amendment will affect the status of women and the fundamental respect for the family as a basic unit of our society." The letter went on to say, "Those women lawyers, women legislators, and women executives promoting ERA have plenty of education and talent to get whatever they want in the business, political, and academic world. We, the wives and working women, need you, dear Senators and Representatives to protect us. We think this is the man's responsibility, and we are dearly hoping you will vote NO on ERA."[34] Feminists were repulsed by this language that appealed to the paternalistic instincts of male legislators and they were even more disgusted when anti-ERA women showed up at state capitols, of course wearing dresses, to deliver home-baked bread and pies to their legislators. These tactics probably did not change many votes, but they did generate publicity for the STOP ERA cause.

STOP ERA women had another advantage—a capacity to attack the amendment from a variety of directions, which kept their opponents off balance. The anti-ERA movement was unified politically, even though its participants opposed the amendment for different reasons. This allowed STOP ERA to bring together women from different social backgrounds, different religious denominations, different careers, and different beliefs. Pro-ERA women were more ideologically homogeneous in that they considered themselves feminists, even though they differed on the political and legal consequences of ERA. The abortion issue was especially divisive, and many ERA leaders tried to separate reproductive rights from ERA. On the other hand, leaders in NOW and some local American Civil Liberties Union lawyers tried to further reproductive rights by bringing suit under state ERA laws. In Hawaii and Massachusetts, pro-abortion activists filed briefs claiming that their state ERAs provided the right to use tax funds for abortions based on the doctrine that "equality of rights under the law shall not be denied or abridged by the state on account of sex." Such actions allowed Schlafly to link abortion with ERA by arguing that the federal ERA was a way for feminists to push abortion-on-demand and homosexual rights surreptitiously into the U.S. Constitution.[35] These kinds of arguments fed into Schlafly's larger point that the ratification of ERA would have unforeseen consequences when activist courts began to interpret the amendment. The Alabama STOP ERA made this point exactly in a long letter sent to each legislator: "There is no way for anyone to say positively how the Supreme Court will apply the ERA to conscription, combat duty, alimony, child support, wife support, divorce, homosexuality, public restrooms, separate gym classes and athletic teams, single sex education, sexual crimes, and prostitution. . . . It is these women's liberationists—a well-financed and vocal minority wishing to reconstruct the American family—who have the money and are eager to bring cases to court under the ERA which would force the changes in our lives which they desire."[36]

Schlafly argued that the amendment was also unnecessary because Congress had already enacted the Equal Pay Act (1963) and Title VII of the Civil Rights Act (1964); equal opportunity found expression in the Equal Employment Opportunity Act (1972); educational opportunity for women was ensured by Title IX of the Education Amendments Act (1972); and credit protection for women was guaranteed in the Depository Institution Amendments Act of 1974. Feminists argued that problems of inequality existed in other areas that could not be addressed through piecemeal legislation and, furthermore, without a constitutional amendment, this legislation could be repealed. As Karen De-Crow, president of the National Organization for Women, asserted in a debate with Schlafly, "Congress gave us the right to equal pay for equal work, but Congress can take it away. Congress gave us Title IX, and Congress can take it away."[37] This kind of argument suggested, however, that progress had been made, even though it might be tenuous. The fact is that opponents of ERA had mixed views on the meaning of social equality, which feminists might have exploited but did not. For example, many Christian anti-ERA activists believed that women held a special, yet subordinate, position to their husbands in the family. Illinois State Representative Monroe Flinn wrote anti-ERA activist Kathleen Sullivan, "I have always stated that I have no opposition to women having equal rights in every respect, but we must also respect the fact that God created us differently. To pass a law or constitutional amendment saying that we are all alike in every respect, in my opinion, flies in the face of what our Creator intended."[38]

Too often feminists in debating Schlafly—their main opponent—instead of exploiting inconsistencies in the anti-ERA movement, turned to personal attacks on her.[39] In battling Schlafly over ERA, many feminists manifested a personal antagonism that never emerged with the other opponents she had energetically fought, such as the anti-anticommunists and the Rockefeller Republicans. The bitter antagonism that emerged in the ERA fight reflected a politics-is-personal style that emerged in the 1970s and the fact that the ERA fight went to the heart of deeply philosophical issues over the meaning of life and lifestyle in America. Schlafly was experienced in these kinds of appeals to emotion, so as a result, these debate tactics usually backfired by allowing her to portray her opponents as the actual extremists. For example, at a debate with Schlafly in 1973 at Illinois State University, an angry Betty Friedan declared, "I consider you a traitor to your sex, an Aunt Tom" and said what became an oft-repeated line: that she would like to burn Schlafly at the stake. Schlafly calmly replied, "I'm glad you said that because it just shows the intemperate nature of proponents of ERA."[40] By making Schlafly the sole target of their attacks, feminists inadvertently enhanced her prominence as a media star. Schlafly became a regular guest on daytime television talk programs such as the Phil Donahue and the Mike Douglas shows. In 1975, Schlafly started a five-year engagement as regular commentator on the nationally syndicated CBS radio program, *Spectrum*. In 1976, the Associated Press named Schlafly as one of the ten most influential *people* in Illinois, and in 1978 the *World Almanac* selected her as one of the 25 most influential women in the United States. Starting in 1977, *Good Housekeeping's* reader poll regularly listed her as one of the ten most admired women in the world. Feminists helped make Schlafly into a national figure and perhaps even a cultural icon. Making Schlafly into a primary target allowed the anti-ERA movement to appear more unified ideologically than perhaps it actually was.

Problems within Pro-ERA Ranks

While the anti-ERA movement appeared unified, the pro-ERA movement was factious. The two principal organizations involved in the pro-ERA ratification movement, the National Organization for Women (NOW) and ERAmerica, often found themselves at loggerheads over general strategy and tactics. ERAmerica was formed in 1976 after proponents of the amendment realized they had been caught off guard by Schlafly's STOP ERA movement. ERAmerica was an umbrella organization representing 120 groups including labor unions, the American Civil Liberties Union, and religious and political organizations. Based in Washington, D.C., ERAmerica advised state coalitions on techniques of legislative lobbying, presentation of research, testimony at hearings, contacts by constituents, and public education campaigns. The premier feminist organization, the National Organization for Women (NOW), however, refused to join ERAmerica and conducted separate fundraising and political activities over a range of issues of which ERA was one.

The two groups disagreed on strategy, tactics, and even some issues. Especially problematic was NOW's insistence, as the battle for the amendment continued, on linking ERA to legalized abortion and gay rights. ERAmerica leaders believed that NOW was exploiting the ERA issue for fundraising and to increase its membership. The fact was that NOW did increase its membership and its financial coffers during the ERA fight, but whether this opportunism explains NOW's refusal to join ERAmerica is debatable. NOW reflected the radicalization of the feminist movement in the late 1960s as it turned to issues such as lesbian rights, reproductive rights, and social change. As a new generation of women entered NOW, they challenged the older leadership that had come of age in the 1950s. These younger women drew their inspiration from the civil rights struggles and antiwar protests in the late 1960s. As a consequence, this younger generation of feminists saw the ERA fight as part of a larger struggle over reproductive rights, lesbian rights, and patriarchal control of American society.

The division between ERAmerica and NOW reflected the contentious nature of the feminist movement itself in the 1970s, as feminists splintered into liberal, socialist, separatist, and other tendencies.[41] Many feminist women in the late 1960s and 1970s were angry and alienated from American politics and society. This sense of alienation on the part of feminists led many to look down on day-to-day politics. Large numbers of ERA activists traveled to their state capitals to knock on legislators' doors, but for many, especially members of NOW, political struggle meant merely attending rallies, marching, and carrying signs. Only too late did the pro-ERA movement realize that political tactics based on mass protest were counter-productive in winning ratification of a constitutional amendment. Reflecting on the state of ERA in 1977 after five years of struggle, one leader representing the American Civil Liberties Union observed that when ERA was first passed in 1972, "civil rights was still a popular cause. . . . The women's movement was burgeoning, focused and effective. The difference is captured in one Florida anti-ERA rally placard, 'Send the ERA back to Russia.' We have become a more conservative society."[42]

By 1978 it had become evident that ERAmerica and the National Federation of Business and Professional Women's Clubs had developed skills in targeting and defeating state legislators, while local NOW activists often insisted on marches and rallies.[43] As a result, ERAmerica leaders believed that NOW activists actually hurt lobbying efforts by their radical demeanor and appearance and their open hostility to the older white male politicos who dominated state legislatures in the 1970s. For example, an ERAmerica lobbyist in Illinois complained to the national office, "You can imagine how the hard-nosed

Cook County pols that inherited Mayor Daley's power have looked upon the flower-hatted League of Women Voters ladies and the braless loud-mouthed NOW women."[44] The problem in reconciling these two approaches was that the radical feminist movement had rejected a strategy that emphasized working within the political system.[45] In 1975, Karen DeCrow won election as the NOW president on the slogan "Out of the Mainstream: Into the Revolution," arguing that NOW should be fighting for jobs and for homosexual rights.[46]

Schlafly exploited this public image of radicalism within NOW by suggesting that while ERA appeared ostensibly to be innocuous, it actually contained the seeds of a revolutionary social transformation that the feminists were seeking. She republished at her own cost a NOW handbook, *Revolution: Tomorrow Is NOW* (1973) and distributed it to STOP ERA members, state legislators, and the general public. Schlafly believed that the thirty-odd page handbook revealed the radical mentality of NOW. *Revolution: Tomorrow Is NOW* criticized women's voluntarism and community service as "in essence housekeeping on a large scale. . . . Volunteering for women is yet another form of activity which serves to reinforce the second-class status of women . . . which is antithetical to the goals of the feminist movement and thus detrimental to the liberation of women." In addition, *Revolution: Tomorrow Is NOW* demanded the ordination of women in all religious denominations and "the end of the sexist bias in compulsory military service," although NOW resolved "that as feminists, we seek to bring a universal end to war and create a society in which feminist, humanist values will prevail." The booklet welcomed the sexual revolution, declaring, "the lesbian is doubly oppressed both as a woman and as a homosexual [and] she must face the injustice and degradation common to all women, plus endure additional social, economic, legal and psychological abuses as well."[47] For some young women in the 1970s such rhetoric did not seem extreme, but for the average American housewife such talk was jarring.

ERAmerica leaders found such rhetoric counter-productive in the campaign to ratify ERA, but whatever their ideological differences, ERAmerica and NOW shared similar organizational problems that went beyond ideological divisions. Both ERAmerica and NOW were top-down organizations lacking the strong grassroots infrastructure needed to organize statewide campaigns if ERA were to be ratified. The ERA movement tended to be run out of Washington, unable to respond to immediate local needs necessary to win a state-level campaign. Lacking grassroots organizational strength, the pro-ERA campaign relied on paid lobbyists and high-priced media experts to organize ratification campaigns in key battleground states. This led Sheila Greenwald, political director of ERAmerica, to resign in 1976 after informing the board, "you must face and respond to the problems of financial disaster, lack of state organizations and complete lack of management. It is my opinion that ERAmerica should be shut down."[48]

ERA supporters believed that their opponents were better organized because they were financed by corporate interests and supported by right-wing organizations. This belief that insurance corporations and the Far Right were the puppet-masters behind STOP ERA was found in a detailed 100-page report produced by the Nebraska state NOW chapter, "The Insurance Connection with Stop ERA Forces: A Report." Although based on hearsay and guilt by association, this report was used by opponents to charge that Schlafly was being supported by the insurance industry and the John Birch Society.[49] Nonetheless, the charges that the insurance industry (or the John Birch Society, Ku Klux Klan, or Communist party) were supporting or colluding with Schlafly appear unfounded. Financial statements prepared by certified public accountants provide a detailed portrait of STOP ERA funding. In 1973 and 1974, STOP ERA spent $2,865.93 and $16,664.08, respectively. In 1975, the organization's expenditures rose to $25,579.00. In 1976, STOP ERA spent $17,346.29 and in 1977 expenditures were $53,813.60. STOP ERA spending reached a high mark in 1978, with $110,640.52. In its final years, 1979, 1980, 1981, and 1982, STOP ERA spent $58,250.45, $95,280.19, $49,774.00, and $96,229.00, respectively.[50] In addition, Schlafly raised funds to support state legislators who voted "No" on ERA. Reports to the Illinois State Board of Elections show that STOP ERA's political action committee spent $79,636.01 during the primary and general elections of 1978; $118, 687.65 during the primary and general elections of 1980; and $110,767.20 during the primary election in 1982, the last election before ERA expired. Of this total sum, 74 percent came in small contributions under $150. In addition, Schlafly formed a federal political action committee to support state legislative candidates outside of Illinois. For the elections of 1978, the federal STOP ERA PAC donated $40,076 to state legislative candidates, $7,999.21 for the 1980 elections, and $2,000 for the elections of 1982.[51]

Although ERAmerica leaders complained of a shortage of operating funds, its expenditures reached hundreds of thousands of dollars, and by 1980, the organization was spending millions of dollars in an intense media campaign in key states. Although a full financial record was not found in the archival record, correspondence indicates the amount of money that was spent in the pro-ERA campaign. For example, in the 1976 elections, ERAmerica contributed hundreds of thousands of dollars to pro-ERA candidates. In Missouri alone, ERAmerica budgeted $180,000 for the election of pro-ERA candidates.[52] In 1981 and 1982, ERAmerica concentrated its effort in a few key states voting on ERA. For radio advertising alone in 1981, $250,000 was raised for a five-state campaign that included Florida, Georgia, Missouri, Oklahoma, and Virginia.[53] In 1982, in its final push to ratify the ERA, ERAmerica raised over $200,000 for advertising of which $70,000 was spent in Florida, $85,000 in Illinois, $33,000 in North Carolina, and the remainder in the other key states.[54] In short, the pro-ERA side spent more for advertising than the entire STOP ERA budget combined. In raising funds for this campaign, ERAmerica received direct financial contributions from the American Association of University Women, American Women in Radio and Television, National Federation of Business and Professional Women's Clubs, League of Women Voters, National Education Association, National Woman's Party, National Women's Political Caucus, National Organization for Women, United Methodist Church, and Women in Communications, Inc. In addition, many of these groups contributed directly to pro-ERA lobbying efforts.

The broad support the pro-ERA movement enjoyed was a great strength, but it tended to make, at least initially, ERA activists overconfident and to underestimate Schlafly's ability to mobilize an effective counter-movement to ratification. ERA was actively supported by the major women's organizations in the country. Although the AFL-CIO initially opposed the ERA, it changed its position in 1975 and then provided significant financial support to the ERA movement. The ERA was also aided by an impressive list of celebrities, including television actor Alan Alda, comedians Lily Tomlin and Carol Burnett, producer Norman Lear, former sit-com star and wife of Phil Donahue, Marlo Thomas, actress Candice Bergen, cartoonist Garry Trudeau ("Doonesbury"), columnists Ann Landers and Erma Bombeck, Maureen Reagan, and Christie Hefner, daughter of *Playboy* publisher Hugh Hefner. Indeed, the list of celebrities who came out in support of ERA, contributing

time and money, seemed endless. Joining the celebrity list were ac-
tresses Jean Stapleton (*All in the Family*) and Patty Duke Austin. Singer
Helen Reddy, whose hit song "I Am Woman" captured the mood of
feminist women in the 1970s, enlisted in the ERA crusade. Stars of popular television programs of the day also were found at fundraisers and
political rallies, including Tyne Daly Brown, Valerie Harper, Henry
Winkler, Ed Asner, and Jack Klugman. Even columnist Abigail Van
Buren of "Dear Abby" advised supporting ERA. These celebrities attended fundraisers, testified at hearings, spoke at ERA rallies, and appeared in television and radio spots on behalf of ERA. Not all feminists
welcomed these celebrities, however, in their ranks.[55]

Joining the pro-ERA fight was another unusual ally, the mainstream
women's magazines. Although feminists complained that women's
magazines perpetuated the feminine mystique that imprisoned women
as materialistic sex objects or witless housewives, the editors of these
magazines came together in 1974 under the leadership of *Redbook* editor Sey Chassler and all agreed to run articles in support of ERA. In the
course of the next year, pro-ERA articles appeared with titles such as
"What You Should Know about the Equal Rights Amendment" (*Good
Housekeeping*) and "10 Myths about the Equal Rights Amendment"
(*Family Circle*).[56] In an effort to intensify the ERA campaign in its final
stages, thirty-two magazine editors in 1979 again met to plot a strategy
of coordinating the publication of more pro-ERA articles. Once again, a
series of articles promoting ERA appeared in *Redbook, Parents Magazine,
Good Housekeeping, Modern Bride, Viva, Family Circle, Woman's Day, Cos-
mopolitan, Time,* and *Playgirl.*[57]

FORD ADMINISTRATION SUPPORTS ERA

The ERA had the support of the American political establishment, including the endorsement of both political parties. Eisenhower endorsed
the passage of the ERA in his message to Congress in 1957, although
Schlafly pointed out that ERA then included the Hayden provision
that protected rights previously conferred on women by law. Although
Nixon's support for the ERA was opportunistic, in 1971, prodded by
White House counsel John W. Dean and White House aide John
Ehrlichman, Nixon publicly reaffirmed his earlier endorsement of ERA;
he declined to campaign for ratification, however, even though White

House staffer Anne Armstrong urged him to do so. After he won re-election in 1972, Nixon allowed Armstrong to lobby state legislators to ratify ERA, although White House support was superfluous in the rush to ratification by the first thirty states in 1972 and 1973. Afterward, Nixon's support of ERA was lost in the Watergate scandal that eventually forced Nixon from office.[58]

Reversing Nixon's phlegmatic policy toward ERA, Gerald Ford threw full White House backing into ERA ratification. Ford's enthusiasm for the ERA stemmed from a calculated decision to position himself as a political centrist. Although the momentum for ratification had begun to slow in 1974, few believed it could be stopped, so it made good political sense from Ford's point of view to endorse ERA. Ford had voted for the amendment as House minority leader in 1970, although after his office was flooded with negative mail from his constituents because they feared the ERA meant drafting women, he was absent when the vote came to the floor the following year. Still, there was no reason for him to reverse course on ERA when it had been endorsed by the Republican National Platform since 1940. In addition, former New York model and First Lady Betty Ford was a vigorous supporter of ERA. In one of her first interviews with the press, Betty Ford shocked conservatives when she said her views on abortion were similar to those held by vice-presidential nominee Nelson Rockefeller, and that she would accept a decision by her daughter to have an abortion if that was what she wanted. She also surprised many when she told an interviewer that she did not think smoking marijuana was terrible. On the ERA issue, she was especially adamant and declared she was going to actively campaign for its ratification.[59] She kept her promise, appearing at rallies and fundraisers, and she wrote letters and telephoned state legislators in South Dakota, Florida, Georgia, Arizona, Nevada, North Carolina, Illinois, and Missouri, often to the consternation of state representatives who complained publicly about undue White House influence. The Los Angeles Times reported, "Not since Eleanor Roosevelt has there been a First Lady so willing to take an unequivocal position on controversial and highly emotional political issues."[60]

Modeling oneself after Eleanor Roosevelt was not a way to propitiate the Republican Right. In fact, the White House reported that mail ran 3 to 1 against her stance on the ERA, but Betty Ford refused to back down, telling reporters, "I'm going to stick to my guns on this. I expected this.

And I'm not bothered by it." The Ford White House let her go her own way, realizing that she was not a woman easily controlled. She told the press that she was "only following her own conscience" and not doing the President's bidding. "Besides, he's a male chauvinist," she added. White House staffers were often kept on edge wondering what Betty Ford was going to say next to the press, even though they tried to script her remarks beforehand. At the signing of the declaration for International Women's Year, President Ford turned to his wife for a comment, and instead of delivering remarks carefully prepared for her by the staff, she ad-libbed, "I just want to congratulate you, Mr. President. I am glad to see you have come a long, long way."[61] When Phyllis Schlafly and a group of women picketed the White House in protest against Betty Ford's active involvement in ERA, Betty Ford dismissed the protesters: "I know Mrs. Schlafly and I know her arguments." Instead, Mrs. Ford sent a memo to the White House staff notifying them of a briefing to be held in the White House Theater by ERA paid consultant John D. Deardourff.[62] Her attempts to present herself as a liberated woman did not always have the effect she hoped. She could attend a benefit luncheon where she modeled a $1,500 Gloria Sachs dress, and then tell a reporter from Good Housekeeping that she recognized "the low status of the homemaker in today's society and would like to find ways to raise it."[63]

The White House saw Betty Ford's activism as a political benefit, representative of centrist political views and a symbol of a moderate Republican party working for equal opportunity and social justice for all Americans. President Ford upheld the Republican tradition of fiscal conservatism, but he deliberately distanced himself from the right-wing of the GOP. Ford sought to put the past behind the nation and look to the future. To fulfill this aspiration, Ford downplayed divisive social issues such as abortion and school prayer, while at the same time he pursued a foreign policy intended to ease Cold War tensions with the Soviet Union. Ford, like other Republicans in the moderate branch of the party, believed this made good political sense. Such policies, though, assumed that the GOP Right had been extirpated and did not pose a threat to his nomination for a second term. This was evident when he decided to keep Henry Kissinger as his Secretary of State and selected Nelson Rockefeller as his vice president. Ford believed Rockefeller was a safe bet; it tightened his relationship with the liberal wing of his party.[64] Yet as soon as it was announced, the Right exploded in anger. Nobody could rattle the cages of the Right like Nelson Rockefeller, although this appeared not to matter to Gerald Ford.[65] While Congress held up Rockefeller's confirmation hearing for three months to conduct hearings on Ford's pardon of Richard Nixon, the Right railed against Rockefeller.[66] While it would be a mistake to conclude from the Rockefeller nomination that that the inner circles of the Ford administration showed flagrant disregard for the conservative wing of his party, there was a cavalier, even flippant, attitude about the GOP Right within the administration.[67] It was easy to underestimate the Republican Right, if only because most Republicans in Congress tended to be aligned with the moderate and liberal wings of the party. Moreover, in the 1974 elections following Nixon's resignation from office, Democrats gained 46 seats in Congress and controlled the House 290–145; in the Senate, they picked up four seats, adding to their already large majority. Ford seemed tone-deaf to the stirrings of the grassroots that marked the revival of the conservative movement.[68]

LOBBYING ERA AT STATE CAPITOLS

Aware of the growth of the anti-abortion movement and concerned about alienating the Catholic vote, Ford sought to avoid a direct confrontation on the abortion issue. On the ERA issue, however, he stood ready to engage Phyllis Schlafly and the STOP ERA movement. The fight for ratification was waged in key states. In 1974, STOP ERA showed that it had become a movement to be reckoned with as it defeated ratification in critical battles. By 1974, seventeen state legislatures had voted and rejected ratification of the ERA.[69] Proponents won in Maine, Ohio, and Montana, bringing the total of ratifying states to 33. With only five more states needed to ratify the ERA, the battle took on a ferocity that left many state legislators stunned and angry at both sides. Illinois, where the ERA amendment was introduced every year until the time limit ran out for ratification, became the most hard-fought state. By 1975, STOP ERA in Illinois had a coordinator in all 59 legislative districts. Furthermore, STOP ERA had mobilized evangelical Christian women through appeals to their religion. Typical was a widely circulated leaflet by Rosemary Thomson called "A Christian View of the Equal Rights Amendment" (1975), which declared, "As Christians, we ought to support laws that provide equal opportunity for women, but we must oppose a sweeping Constitutional change that would take away their individual choices and alter Americans' lifestyle. Jesus cautioned us about wolves in sheep's clothing . . . of Satan coming as an angel of light so even the elect will be deceived."[70]

In addition, Schlafly drew upon the support of traditional Catholic women by enlisting the support of the National Council of Catholic Women and the Illinois Federation for Right to Life.[71] Schlafly also drew the support of African-American ministers, Lutherans, and Orthodox Jews.[72] Not all of her supporters were religious groups; after a debate at a statewide meeting of the Illinois Federation of Women's Clubs, this largest women's social group refused to endorse ERA. Schlafly flooded the state with literature and kept active pressure on the state legislature when it was in session. Over 600,000 copies of an anti-ERA pamphlet, "STOP ERA," were passed out by these women at supermarkets in Illinois and excerpts printed on half-page ads in every major paper in the state.

STOP ERAers came to the state capital in carloads every week to lobby state legislators to vote against ERA. They descended, as one local newspaper described it, "to wage holy war against the Equal Rights Amendment. Neatly dressed teenage daughters with scrubbed faces and frilly blouses cried, 'Please Don't Draft Me,' while their mothers carried signs reading 'Send the Libbers to Siberia. We'll Stay Home and Keep the Beds Warm.' "[73] Such slogans were intended to portray the pro-ERA activists as extremists while humorously mocking feminists. Feminists coming to Springfield to lobby in favor of ERA found Schlafly's imprint everywhere. Following a massive demonstration in favor of ERA in 1975, State Senator Dawn Clark Netsch, a leading ERA supporter, was asked whether these kinds of major demonstrations had any effect on the vote. She replied, "No, not really. I think because Phyllis Schlafly has her people here so often the proponents were kind of nervous."[74]

In 1975, the pro-ERAers staged their biggest rally when an estimated 8,000 women from 30 states showed up in Springfield in support of what one speaker called "the second American Revolution." The demonstrators chanted, "Hey, hey, what do you say. Ratify ERA" and waved signs reading, "Lactators for ERA," and "A Middle Class Housewife is a Husband Away from Welfare." Demonstrators represented church groups, housewives, labor unions, as well as lesbians, the Trotskyist Socialist Workers party, the Maoist Progressive Labor party, and other militant groups. During the rally, a plane overhead trailed a STOP ERA banner reading, "Illinois women oppose ERA—libbers go home." Schlafly won the public relations war that day.

Grassroots activism defeated ERA in Illinois, but the anti-ERA forces were helped by a provision of the Illinois State Constitution that requires a three-fifths majority in both houses of the state legislature to ratify a constitutional amendment. When ERA passed the Illinois House, the three-fifths requirement prevented it from passing the Senate. Although pro-ERA attorneys challenged this rule in court, the federal court ruled that the state legislature had the right to adopt it. Schlafly was also helped by the politics of the Illinois Democratic party. Many regular Democrats who appeared to support ERA actually opposed it in private for a variety of reasons. Some Democratic legislators concluded that voting for ERA would cost them more than they would gain politically. As one Democratic legislator candidly told a group of ERA lobbyists, "If I felt this issue were strong enough and important enough to commit political suicide, I would change my position."[75] Votes were arranged to allow legislators to vote "Yes" on the amendment knowing that ratification would be defeated. This saved embarrassment for legislators from liberal districts. As one legislative insider observed, many legislators voted for ERA "to get the feminists off their backs," knowing that the bill would fail. These political games left pro-ERA legislators embarrassed by their inability to predict the vote. Esther Saperstein, a state senator from Chicago, announced at the beginning of the 1975 session that ERA was going to pass easily, only to find at the end of the session that once again it failed in a close vote. Accurate counting is an important measure of a politician's skill and miscounts eroded confidence among pro-ERA legislators.[76]

Many Democrats resented the condescending and threatening attitude of NOW and ERA activists, and rivalries within the Democratic party often divided the ERA vote. One of the first sponsors of ERA in the Illinois House, Rep. Eugenia Chapman, had alienated Chicago Mayor Richard Daley in 1972 when she backed his rival, Adlai Stevenson, to head the Illinois delegation to the Democratic Convention that year. When ERA came up a second time in the Illinois House, Daley ordered seven Democrats to pull support for the bill, which then failed. When Chapman declared herself a candidate for Speaker of the House in 1973, she again angered machine Democrats who retaliated by not supporting ERA. This led feminists to denounce publicly the

Democratic leadership in Springfield, including Illinois Senate leader, Senator Cecil Partee, a black legislator from Chicago and sponsor of ERA, who was accused by pro-ERA feminists as being "personally responsible for blocking passage of the amendment."[77] Schlafly believed that Partee resented this accusation that he had double crossed ERA supporters, and this contributed to seven black legislators withholding their votes for ERA in a later critical vote.[78] Threats by pro-ERA activists of political retaliation at the polls hardened positions and made it difficult to change votes, especially when legislators who voted "No" were warmly treated by their supporters. Following his negative vote in 1973, Rep. John Edward Porter, representing a liberal district in Evanston, wrote Phyllis Schlafly, "I had a very large volume of mail on this matter [ERA], some being very shrill and even threatening. I want you to know that your letter was without question the nicest one that I have received."[79]

ERA divided the Republican party, but the division was largely between Republicans on the national level and state levels. When Betty Ford told a fundraiser sponsored by Republican Women Power in 1974 that she hoped her efforts would help pass ERA in Illinois, she learned the next day in the newspaper that one of the candidates being supported by the group was State Representative Mary Lou Kent, a staunch opponent of ERA in the Illinois House.[80] Intervention by the White House led to resentment on the part of Republican legislators who received phone calls from Mrs. Betty Ford. When State Senator Donald E. Deuster from Mundelein, outside of Chicago, received a phone call from Mrs. Ford in 1975, he issued a press release admonishing her to "immediately desist" her "long distance telephone lobbying campaign from the White House" to Illinois legislators in support of the "Sex Equality Amendment to the U.S. Constitution." He sarcastically extended her an invitation to Springfield to testify so "all members of the General Assembly—not just a secretly selected few—could benefit from her thinking on the subject of Sex Equality."[81]

While the ERA fight raged in Illinois, Schlafly coordinated the anti-ERA fight in all the other states, too. The *Phyllis Schlafly Report* remained the principal means of keeping anti-ERA activists in touch with what was happening in other states, as well as providing intellectual ammunition against ERA.[82] In 1975 and 1976, Schlafly maintained an exhausting speaking schedule; it was not unusual to find Schlafly testifying at a legislative hearing and meeting with legislators, and then traveling the next day to speak at a couple of different locations in another state. Given this arduous schedule, the Schlafly family was stunned one evening at dinner in April 1975, when Phyllis Schlafly announced she was going to enter law school at Washington University. She was fifty-one years old at the time; she entered law school in the fall of 1975, taking the standard first year courses in Contracts, Property, Torts, and Constitutional Law. In her second year she won the prize as the best student in Administrative Law, and when she graduated in the spring of 1978, she ranked 27th in a class of 186 and passed the Illinois Bar a few months later.[83]

Ford Under Attack in 1976

In 1976, as Schlafly continued her studies in law school and carried the anti-ERA banner to state after state, a clear mobilization of the GOP Right was evident. While the Ford administration was not impervious to the threat from the Right, there still was a tendency to underestimate it. The backlash caused by Betty Ford's persistent phoning of Republican state legislators caused discontent in the ranks. In 1975, Ford tried to shore up his right flank by proposing tax cuts to restrain the budget overloads. While social issues were motivating the grassroots Republicans, trouble began to brew over Ford's foreign policy. By the end of 1975, as conservative historian Steven Hayward later observed, only about two dozen genuine multiparty democracies were left in the world, while six new pro-Soviet regimes could be counted. Inevitably there was talk that democracy had failed; Robert Moss's *The Collapse of Democracy* became a best seller in both England and the United States.[84] Not only did democracy appear to be failing, there were warnings that the United States had fallen dangerously behind the Soviet Union in military preparedness.[85] U.S. intelligence estimates showed that the Soviet Union had five times as many tanks as the United States. 2.5 times the manpower, twice the submarines and aircraft, and an elaborate antimissile defense system. The Central Intelligence Agency estimated the annual Soviet defense spending at 12 percent of per annum GDP, while the Defense Intelligence Agency estimated 30 percent. (After the collapse of the Soviet Union in the 1990s, estimates placed Soviet military spending as high as 70 percent of GDP in the 1970s.) It was not just the Right that was critical of the Ford-Kissinger policies. AFL-CIO

President George Meany told the Senate Foreign Relations Committee, "Détente means ultimate military superiority over the West." Paul Nitze, who had been critical of SALT I, resigned from the SALT II negotiating team because he felt the United States was negotiating away its ability to defend itself against Soviet threats. He joined with others in forming the influential bipartisan Committee on the Present Danger which called for an arms buildup and opposition to SALT II. The controversy became further heated when Admiral Elmo Zumwalt in his memoir *On Watch: A Memoir* (1976) claimed that Kissinger had confided to him in 1970 that America was headed downhill and that his job was to persuade the Russians to give us the best deal possible. Kissinger denied this accusation, but the view that the administration was either being hoodwinked or was willingly accepting a superior Soviet Union extended beyond the ideological Right.

Schlafly found Zumwalt's accusation about Kissinger confirmation of what she had written a year earlier in her second to last book coauthored with Admiral Chester Ward, *Kissinger on the Couch* (1975). This was Schlafly's most ambitious book, running over 800 pages. Published by Arlington House Publishers, a conservative press located in New Rochelle, New York, *Kissinger on the Couch* came out in 1975 at the height of the ERA fight and the year Schlafly entered law school. Although the hardback sold only about 25,000 copies—the smallest sale of any of the Schlafly-Ward books—*Kissinger on the Couch* presented their most sophisticated analysis of American defense policy. Like their previous books, *Kissinger on the Couch* remained polemical and was written for a conservative audience, but it was not written as a campaign handout. They explained Kissinger's foreign policy as a manifestation of his megalomania and defeatism. Kissinger, they argued, believed he was smarter than anybody else and that he had an understanding of mega-history. This led him to conclude that American civilization was on the wane and the Soviet Union was emerging as the dominant superpower as the twentieth century drew to a close.

Also, there was a tendency to see greater agreement within the administration than existed. For example, they spoke throughout the book of the "Kissinger-Schlesinger suicidal policies," even though after the book's publication it became known that Secretary of Defense James Schlesinger expressed deep reservations within the Nixon and Ford administrations and, after resigning from office, emerged as one of the major critics of SALT I and SALT II. The book recognized that the

Sino-Soviet split was real, but Schlafly and Ward believed the Soviet Union's military power posed the most serious threat to American national security. Schlafly and Ward believed that the Soviet Union's object was to achieve world conquest through arms control treaties. Because leaders such as Kissinger had developed an "obsessive, pervasive fear of nuclear war," they were dismantling U.S. nuclear capability, so that the Soviets would believe they did not need to launch an attack. Schlafly and Ward argued that United States leadership needed "courage and dedication" to initiate a massive defensive buildup. They called for a new satellite early warning system, which would allow the United States to "reconstruct our strategic superiority" and "give us time to develop an advanced defense system against Soviet super missiles." The book was an open criticism of the Nixon and Ford administrations and it conveyed unreserved opposition by the GOP Right to the Ford-Kissinger policies. The book concluded, "Henry, say some who know him well, has no God. Does he have a country?"[86] These were words from an opposition with which there could be no compromise. The election of 1976 was shaping up to be a fight for the soul of the party, just as it had been in 1964.

Despite the resurgence of the Right, President Ford refused to take the threat to his nomination seriously. The Ford campaign believed that Schlafly and the STOP ERA movement were unrepresentative of Republican women, so he invited Elly Peterson, co-chair of ERAmerica, and Schlafly's nemesis in the National Federation of Republican Women battle, to join his campaign staff. Even when the Right began to coalesce around a Ronald Reagan challenge to the GOP nomination, the Ford campaign dismissed the threat, with the assurance by Ford administration official Dick Cheney that the president had an "enthusiastic following among grassroots conservatives," so he did not need to worry about the nomination.[87] A campaign memo further reassured Ford that many voters considered Reagan as "too slick" and "too much of being a politician."[88] That was wishful thinking, but in the early primaries it appeared to be an accurate assessment of Reagan's chances. Only when Reagan began to denounce giving ownership of the Panama Canal to the government of Panama did his campaign come to life. His phrase, "we built it, we paid for it, its ours, and we should tell Torrijos [Panama's dictator] and company we are going to keep it." Reagan lost Florida (barely), Illinois, Massachusetts and Vermont, but then he won North Carolina with Senator Jesse Helms's help and his campaign gained momentum. By the time of the Republican National Convention in Kansas City, neither Ford nor Reagan had enough delegates for a first-ballot victory. Reagan campaign strategist, John Sears, thought that Reagan could win over enough delegates by declaring Pennsylvania Senator Richard Schweiker, a moderate Republican, as his running mate.[89]

When Southern delegates headed by Clarke Reed deserted Reagan, Ford won the nomination with a slim 117-vote margin. Conservatives lost the nomination, but it was a landmark turn to the right when the 1976 Republican National Convention repudiated Ford's foreign policy and adopted the platform advocated by North Carolina Senator Jesse Helms. Before the convention convened, Helms decided to lead the battle to adopt a platform based on what he called a "morality in foreign policy" plank that criticized the giveaway of the Panama Canal, détente with the Soviet Union, and unilateral concessions on nuclear testing. Conservatives saw it as a tremendous victory when the convention adopted the Helms plank. At the same time, the platform called for ending federal meddling in schools, abolishing the Department of Education, and teaching "chastity until marriage as the expected standard of behavior." In addition, the convention voted to "protest the Supreme Court's intrusion into the family structure" and pledged to "seek enactment of a constitutional amendment to restore protection of the right to life for unborn children." When the Republican Subcommittee on Human Rights and Responsibilities met to vote on ERA, the committee voted 8 to 7 not to endorse the Equal Rights Amendment. Instead, it approved language recognizing the ERA as a matter for individual states to decide. Pro-ERA Republicans were stunned by the defeat, including Betty Ford, who denounced it as "incredible." After heavy political pressure by the Ford campaign, the full Platform Committee overturned the subcommittee decision by a narrow 51 to 47 vote. A petition of 27 signatures would have allowed the ERA plank to come to a floor vote, but Schlafly decided not to make a floor fight on this issue because she expected Reagan to lose the nomination and did not want to be blamed for his defeat.[90]

In November, Jimmy Carter defeated Gerald Ford, but as biographer Steven Hayward concluded, Reagan had won the soul of the Republican party. The stage was set for Ronald Reagan to win the GOP nomination in 1980.

This illustration appeared in Phyllis Schlafly's *Safe—Not Sorry*. The illustrator was Vic Vac, a supporter of Phyllis Schlafly in her race for the presidency of the National Federation of Republican Women in 1967. The picture captures resentment of grassroots women against the Republican establishment. Courtesy of Eagle Forum Archives.

Schlafly ran for Congress from Illinois a second time in 1970, losing narrowly after a vigorous and expensive campaign. Courtesy of Eagle Forum Archives.

The battle over the Equal Rights Amendment often appeared as a clash of irreconcilable worlds. Photo shows unidentified pro-ERA signs in Springfield, Illinois. Courtesy of Eagle Forum Archives.

Reverend Henry Mitchell (on right), an African-American conservative, with unidentified staff from his Black Star Mission in Chicago, planning anti-ERA activities. Courtesy of Eagle Forum Archives.

Schlafly speaks at "The End of an E.R.A." banquet in Washington, DC, on March 2, 1979. Courtesy of Eagle Forum Archives.

Throughout her career in politics, Schlafly met with many Republican leaders including President Richard Nixon, Vice President Spiro Agnew, President Gerald Ford, and Vice President Nelson Rockefeller. All photos courtesy of Eagle Forum Archives.

President Ronald Reagan and Phyllis Schlafly at a White House reception during the 1980s.

Schlafly speaks at Harvard Law School in 1984 about the ten-year battle of ERA.

This portrait shows the entire Schlafly family in 1981. Seated at the piano are Anne and John. Standing from left to right: Phyllis, Andrew, Liza, Bruce, Fred, and Roger.

By 1988 Eagle Forum had become a major grassroots organization with chapters in most states. Its national meetings drew national conservative speakers. Pictured from left to right are Senator Phil Gramm (R-Texas), Mrs. Jack Kemp, Jack Kemp, Phyllis Schlafly, Mary Ellen Bork, and Judge Robert Bork.

CHAPTER TEN

The Triumph of the Right

In 1978, WHILE attending a conference of historians in Washington, D.C., four academics with Midwestern connections, Zane Miller, a leading urban historian, and three junior scholars, Alan Marcus, Judith Spraul-Schmidt, and Ellen Cangi decided to go to the Shoreham Hotel for some after-dinner drinks. The four settled themselves in the lounge when suddenly the band struck up, as Alan Marcus recalls, "I Enjoy Being a Girl," and in walked Phyllis Schlafly. Out came the signs, STOP ERA. The assembled women and men got up and gave her a standing ovation. Schlafly went from table to table greeting people who were there to lobby against a time extension for ratification of the Equal Rights Amendment (ERA). The two male historians were bemused by being in the same room with Schlafly, but the two women were "livid" and thought it was their duty to confront Schlafly. After being urged caution about causing a scene, the two women decided it was best to finish their drinks and "hightail" out of the place while they could contain themselves.[1]

The fight about ERA was not over, however, and Congress extended the deadline for its ratification until 1982. Nonetheless, many feminists felt themselves in retreat under the onslaught of a growing conservative movement, as many tradition-minded voters began to abandon the Democratic party. Economic liberalism was perceived by many as having failed, and they were repulsed by the cultural excesses of liberalism. The erosion was gradual, beginning in the border states and then the suburban South and in some ethnic neighborhoods in the North, but this movement accelerated in the waning years of the 1970s as economic conditions worsened and the cultural left became more emboldened. A stagnant economy, high inflation, and a hostage crisis in Iran accelerated this erosion. The extent and full power of the collapse of liberalism would not be fully known until the 1980 presidential election when Ronald Reagan, an avowed conservative, won the White House. Activists such as Phyllis Schlafly had set the stage for one of the most dramatic turnabouts in American political history.

THE INTERNATIONAL WOMEN'S YEAR CONFERENCE

In 1977, when Carter stepped into the White House, few people realized that the political tides would shift so suddenly away from liberalism, even the moderate form that Carter represented. No doubt, many of Carter's problems were connected to the peculiarities of the mid-1970s, a time of high inflation, stubborn unemployment, oil crises, international economic instability, and the emergence of Islamic extremism in the Middle East. Many of his problems came from within the left wing of his own party, as Carter found himself in an ideological riptide from which there was no natural escape. Typical of his problems were his relations with the feminists. Whatever he did, it seemed he could not do enough to win the confidence of the left wing of his party, especially feminists, homosexuals, and those who supported unrestricted reproductive rights and abortion. He committed the White House to ratification of the ERA, but feminists accused him and his wife, Rosalynn, of not doing enough even though, like Betty Ford before her, Rosalynn Carter attended ERA fundraisers, met with ERA leaders at the White House, telephoned state legislators, and spoke on behalf of ERA. Although many legislators resented her intervention, she played an important role in winning Indiana for ERA ratification in 1977. When U.S. Senator Birch Bayh (D-IN) phoned the White House to say that the Indiana Senate was deadlocked 25-25, Rosalynn Carter telephoned Senator Wayne Townsend to persuade him to switch his vote.[2] Indiana became the thirty-fifth, and the last, state to ratify the ERA.

Furthermore, the Carter administration supported the appropriation of federal funds for the International Women's Year Commission. The United Nations had proclaimed 1975 the International Women's Year (IWY), and President Ford showed American support for this proclamation by appointing a U.S. Commission on International Women's Year. This commission subsequently issued a report recommending a plan to hold fifty-six state and territorial conferences to elect delegates to a national conference to be held in Houston, Texas.[3] IWY became an immediate lightning rod for the anti-ERA movement after the *Phyllis Schlafly Report* in January 1976 urged its readers to write their congressmen to defeat the $5 million appropriation for these conferences. She described the IWY as a federally funded effort to rally support for ERA, publicly proclaiming it "a front for radicals and lesbians". Although Congress voted the appropriation, the fight over IWY continued. State conferences were held to debate resolutions and elect delegates to the national convention. Schlafly appointed Rosemary Thomson, a Republican activist from Morton, Illinois, as national chairman of the International Women's Year Citizen's Review Committee. Thomson organized similar committees in other states to challenge feminists within state conventions. Critical in organizing grassroots opposition was an audio cassette, produced by Dianne Edmondson of Oklahoma, that made a direct appeal to traditional Christian women to stand up against the "evil that is inherent within the so-called women's liberation" movement and show "how as Christians we must do good as the Lord commands by opposing this evil."[4] Anti-ERA activists challenged the core list of resolutions put forward by the National Commission for the IWY Conference in its "National Plan of Action." In particular, STOP ERA activists targeted resolutions calling for abortion rights, ERA, government funded daycare centers, sex education, and gay rights. At the first state conventions, feminists were caught off guard when large numbers of antifeminists showed up to elect delegates to the Houston convention. Mormons were particularly active among the antifeminist forces in Hawaii, Washington, Montana, Idaho, and Utah. In the end, antifeminists were able to elect a majority in at least fourteen state delegations to the Houston conference, but this added up to only 25 percent of the total.[5]

Realizing that the Houston conference would be controlled by feminists, Schlafly agreed to sponsor a counter-conference, the Pro-Family Rally. The idea for a counter-rally was first proposed by Lottie Beth Hobbs, a fifty-seven-year-old single woman who had formed an anti-ERA organization called the Four Ws (Women Who Want to be Women). She became the principal organizer for the Pro-Family Rally. Hobbs audaciously decided to rent the Astro-Arena in Houston and fill it with women from all over the country. Uncertain that the arena could be filled, or might provide an occasion for unwelcome organizations to opportunistically attend, thereby causing embarrassment to STOP ERA, several women in Schlafly's inner circle voiced opposition to this rally.[6] However, Schlafly gave the go-ahead to support the counter-rally. This was a major gamble for STOP ERA because if the Houston counter-rally failed, it might suggest that the anti-ERA movement lacked popular support.

Feminists organizing the IWY Conference in Houston also took a gamble, although a lesser one, by proposing two very sensitive resolutions supporting abortion-on-demand and gay rights. The Reproductive Freedom resolution called for federal and private insurance funding for abortion, family planning for teenagers, sex education in all schools, including elementary schools, and publicly supported child care. The resolution also opposed involuntary sterilization. The Sexual Preference resolution called for federal, state, and local legislation to eliminate discrimination on the basis of sexual or affectional preference and to repeal state laws that restrict private sexual behavior between consenting adults.[7] These issues had divided the modern women's movement since its inception. For some feminists an affirmation of reproductive rights and gay rights went to the very core of what the women's movement was all about—the right to control their bodies.

When the International Women's Year Conference convened in Houston on November 18, 1977, over 1,000 delegates and over 10,000 supporters from across the nation came, as their official report declared, to "voice their needs and hope for the future"[8] The Reproductive Freedom plank easily passed the conference, although Ann O'Donnell, an anti-abortion activist from Missouri, denounced the plank as oppressive to "the less powerful [the unborn]."[9] When the Sexual Preference plank came before the floor, all eyes turned to Betty Friedan, who earlier had castigated other feminists for taking up the cause of gay rights. Recognized by the chair, she now spoke in behalf of the resolution. Referring to her recent divorce from her husband, she declared, "As someone who has loved men too well, I have had trouble with this issue. Now my priority is passing the ERA. And because there is nothing in it that will give any protection to homosexuals, I believe we must help the women who are lesbians."[10] Friedan's endorsement of gay rights marked a significant turning point and the delegates cheered wildly. The only dissent came from pro-family delegates who turned their backs on the podium during the vote. The plank won overwhelmingly. Lesbians in the gallery released pink and yellow balloons reading, "We are everywhere."[11]

While the official IWY Conference met at the Albert Thomas Convention Center, 20,000 women gathered at the other side of Houston to attend the Pro-Family Rally at the Astro-Arena. They came from across America in cars and chartered buses, often driving all night; many left immediately after the rally in order to attend church services with their families on Sunday. Most were middle-aged, white women and many came from fundamentalist or evangelical Christian churches. There was a revival atmosphere to the rally. Hobbs opened the rally asking for a show of hands from each of the state delegations attending the rally. Then she presented the pro-family petitions with 300,000 signatures to be sent to Congress—the boxes filled the stage. There were speeches against abortion by Mildred Jefferson, a Harvard-educated black surgeon, and Nellie Gray, president of the March for Life. Elisabeth Elliot, well-known Christian author and wife of Christian missionary Jim Elliot who had died in the jungle of Ecuador, spoke on "Let Me Be a Woman." Clay Smothers, a black Texas state legislator, declared "I want to segregate my family from these misfits and perverts." Phyllis Schlafly stepped to the stage and opened with her standard line, "First of all, I want to thank my husband Fred, for letting me come—I always like to say that, because it makes the libs so mad!" She went on to berate ERA as an attack on the family. Finally, Robert Dornan, a former conservative radio commentator who had just been elected a first-term Congressman from California, brought the crowd to its feet with his flamboyant rhetoric, "Let Your Voice Be Heard in Washington."[12]

Because of its enormous media coverage, the IWY Conference provided a rich opportunity for Phyllis Schlafly and the pro-family movement to air their differences with feminists in a national forum. Following the IWY Conference, Schlafly and other social conservatives adroitly exploited the conference as an organizing tool to bring new supporters into the anti-ERA movement and the emerging conservative movement. The IWY Conference in Houston turned out to be a defeat for feminists. It did not reach beyond its narrow circle of feminists into Middle America, critical to winning the ERA battle. The Conference did mark a victory for gay rights and helped mobilize gay and lesbian activists. Arguably this had long-term social and political consequences, but in the short term the anti-ERA side won the public relations contest between the two rallies at Houston.

For Schlafly, Houston became the "Midway" battle, the decisive turning point in the ten-year ERA struggle. Writing after the conference, Schlafly declared that there now was no question which side was going to win. ERA was dead. The war was not over yet, she wrote, but the "Women's Lib movement has sealed its own doom by deliberately hanging around its own neck the albatross of abortion, lesbianism, pornography and Federal control." For the rest of the ERA fight until 1982, antifeminists highlighted the IWY Conference resolutions on abortion and lesbianism. As one activist declared, "It's the best recruiting tool I've ever had. I just spend twenty minutes reading the Houston resolutions to them. That's all I have to do."[13] During the conference a STOP ERA member collected several boxes from the exhibitor's tables, including lesbian and Marxist groups, and then prepared an exhibit filling more than sixty sheets of poster board. This display was shown in more than thirty states by the time the ERA fight was over.[14]

In the three months following the Houston Conference, ERA continued to lose: on January 12, 1978, the Georgia State Judiciary Committee unanimously voted against ERA; on January 31, 1978, Alabama Senate voted "No," 24 to 8; on February 7, 1978, the South Carolina Senate voted "No" 23 to 18; on February 22, 1978, Florida announced it would not vote on ERA. With the ERA deadline set for March 22, 1979, time was running out. On October 20, 1977, as a hedge against failure, Rep. Elizabeth Holtzman introduced a resolution to extend the ERA ratification deadline another seven years. This unprecedented strategy had been devised by two California law students who were members of NOW. After an 18-month intensive lobbying effort including a march of a reported 100,000 people to Washington, D.C., Congress approved a 39-month extension to June 30, 1982.[15]

THE DEATH THROES OF ERA

During the time extension period, both sides concentrated their efforts on five critical states: Illinois, Florida, North Carolina, Missouri, and Oklahoma. Both sides pursued a take-no-prisoners strategy. NOW voted to conduct boycotts of states that refused to ratify ERA, and while over 350 political and professional organizations, including most academic associations, joined in supporting this boycott, its political effects were unclear. NOW's strategy was to wage a national campaign to get ERA ratified. While there is evidence that some state legislators became more intransigent in the face of these economic boycotts, this national strategy ignored (as one leading scholar of the history of ERA later observed) the need to build strong state organizations in battleground states. Coalitions needed to be built with moderate to centrist groups and politicians, but NOW's radical image worked against such alliances.[16] Not a single state ratified the ERA during the extension period; indeed, two states, Kentucky and South Dakota, rescinded their previous ERA votes, bring the total to five states that overturned their previous affirmative votes.[17] By 1978, opposition to ratification of the ERA had become arguably insurmountable, especially given the strong organization, sophisticated electoral strategy, and effective use of campaign funds developed by Schlafly and her supporters on the state level.

Blocked at every turn by Schlafly, ERA proponents became increasingly frustrated. The general feeling in the anti-ERA ranks was that pro-ERA feminists knew they were in a lost cause. North Carolina STOP ERA chairman, Alice Wynne Gatsis, reported that "The pro-people are desperate and the more desperate the more dangerous."[18] Reports began to drift into Schlafly from various states that pro-ERA feminists had become threatening. At the mass demonstration in Washington, D.C., in support of extending the deadline, Gloria Steinem told the crowd of an estimated 100,000 women that "the lawful and peaceful state of our revolution may be over. It's up to the legislators. We can become radical if they force us. If they continue to interfere with the ratification of the ERA they will find every form of civil disobedience possible in every state."[19] Steinem's prediction was realized as militant women, usually independent of mainstream pro-ERA organizations, undertook nonviolent civil disobedience demonstrations. Women chained themselves to the Republican party headquarters in Washington, D.C. In 1982, a hunger strike by several women began in Springfield, Illinois, with less than two months remaining for ratification. These actions often cut at cross purposes from lobbying by ERAmerica and NOW. When Eleanor Smeal approached the ERAers who had chained themselves to the door of the Senate Chamber at the Illinois state capitol to try to dissuade them from continuing their protest, which NOW felt was bad publicity for the movement, the women shouted obscenities at her. She told Elly Peterson that these women were "not part of the women's movement," and kept them out of the NOW parade and off the ERA rally platform.[20]

Thus, with the extension providing an additional three plus years to secure three states, the pro-ERA side found itself in the awkward situation of restraining its own militant women while trying to employ many of Schlafly's methods to win over state legislators. These efforts included more effective lobbying of state legislators, and targeting specific state races to protect pro-ERA legislators or to defeat anti-ERA legislators. Mass advertising campaigns on television and radio were also initiated in battleground states. NOW and ERAmerica became politically skillful in this uphill battle. But, things did not always go quite right. One Illinois NOW activist was convicted in 1980 of trying to bribe a state legislator to cast a pro-ERA vote. ERA supporters charged that the bribery conviction was part of a "right wing effort to defeat the ERA," but this defense seemed rather hollow after a court conviction.[21]

NOW brought considerable financial resources to the final stages of the campaign. In 1980, at its national meeting, NOW pledged total mobilization for ERA. ERA Walkathons across the country raised impressive amounts of money for the campaign. NOW receipts rose from $150,000 to $1 million in 1981, as membership grew from 55,000 to 220,000 in this same period. By 1981, NOW employed a full-time staff of 300, as well as 6,700 full-time volunteers, and claimed to have the ability to raise $1 million a month.[22] Huge coffers, however, were not enough to win the ERA fight.

The legislative battle in Florida presents a case study in the problems faced by pro-ERA activists and the bitterness that came with defeat. ERA was first defeated in Florida in 1974 at the height of Watergate. Following this defeat, both sides targeted Florida as a key state. In Florida, the anti-ERA forces were well organized under the leadership of Shirley Spellerberg, the founder of Women for Responsible Legislation in South Florida. Spellerberg was a successful real-estate broker in Dade County who started her organization in Miami with only 20 members, but it grew to 500. Spellerberg's group networked with other anti-ERA groups that had sprung up across the state, including Happiness of Women and the Christian Family Movement.[23] During the course of the long campaign to defeat ERA, these groups found that evangelical Christian women were natural allies. Some of these evangelical and fundamentalist Christian women had been mobilized earlier by singer Anita Bryant's campaign in 1977 against a gay rights ordinance in Dade County.

The anti-ERA women in Florida found their greatest friend in the state's most important power broker, Dempsey Barron, the Democratic Senator from Panama City. He opposed ERA because he thought the amendment was unnecessary and also because the amendment was being promoted by political rivals in the Democratic party.[24] The power Barron exerted was evident in the 1979 Senate vote when ERA lost 21-19. The pro-ERA side thought that they had won the vote, but at the last minute Senator Ralph Poston switched his vote to "No." Shocked by the turn of events, pro-ERA supporters claimed that he had been pressured into doing so when he was exonerated two days earlier by the Senate Rules Committee on ethics charges.[25] Poston was not the only senator who voted "No," however. Senator Alan Trask told the press that as a recently reborn Christian, he abhorred "homosexuality, and anyway I want to see women on a pedestal."[26] Other negative votes were defended with more substantive statements.

Senator Vernon C. Holloway (D-Miami) delivered a reasoned defense of his opposition to ERA. Holloway was an old-time labor Democrat who had served in the state senate twelve years. In a speech given on the senate floor, he told his colleagues that "I can honestly say that I am in favor of equal rights for all persons regardless of race, creed, color, or sex." Yet he feared that the federal ERA would override federal and state legislation that had been enacted to protect women. He was an old-fashioned liberal who voted his conscience and who believed from polling in his district that his constituents opposed ERA. He knew that by voting "No" he would disappoint supporters of ERA who considered him a swing vote. He was not prepared, however, for the wrath the vote brought down on him; his office was flooded with letters from throughout the country personally attacking him. In what appears to have been a concerted campaign, enclosed in dozens and dozens of these letters were used sanitary napkins and obscene clippings from homosexual pornography magazines.[27] Although Schlafly tried to rally support for him when he came up for reelection, Holloway was defeated by a pro-ERA candidate, former Senator Dick Renick. Other anti-ERA incumbents were also defeated, although sometimes for reasons other than ERA. Dan Scarbrough (D-Jacksonville) lost to developer Dan Jenkins in the primary because of a liquor license scandal. Schlafly also tried to help George Williamson (R-Ft. Lauderdale), another anti-ERA incumbent, but he lost in the primary.[28] Despite these victories for the Florida ERA campaign, when the vote came up in 1980, ERA was again defeated in the Florida senate.

ERA activists began to explain their legislative defeats by blaming a right-wing conspiracy and Jimmy Carter's White House. Accusations against Schlafly being linked to a Far Right conservative design to defeat the ERA were heard throughout the ERA battle. As the battle heated up in trying to win more states, attacks against Schlafly intensified. Typical of the rhetoric was that of Elly Peterson, who told the *Detroit Free Press* that the ERA was being attacked by "a well-financed conspiracy of wealthy white 'super patriots and super Christians' to give the New Right control of the U.S." Their target is not the ERA, Peterson said, but "welfare mothers, opportunities for the poor, the blacks, foreign borns, Jews, women." Audrey Rowe Colom, chair of the National Women's Political Caucus, told the press that many feminist leaders suspected that "the John Birch Society, the American Nazi Party, the Ku Klux Klan, and the Conservative Caucus are part of the organized opposition."[29]

These attempts to link Schlafly with the Ku Klux Klan were especially vicious. Jo Ann R. Horowitz, representing the Chicago League of Women Voters, told Schlafly in a debate that "you are going down in history as a friend to the KKK and the Communist Party."[30] A NOW member warned at an ERA workshop in Detroit that while it was likely that the Nazi party and the KKK were involved in the anti-ERA movement, it is certain that behind STOP ERA was an unnamed "highly extremist right wing group. . . . Nobody who is a good American is against equality."[31] Writing in the Illinois Education Association's *Advocate*, Arnie Weissman warned in an article, "The New Klan? The New Right?" that the KKK and Phyllis Schlafly had "made the leap to respectability." The front cover of the magazine had pictures of Phyllis Schlafly and Larry Hicks, president of the Ku Klux Klan, as if they were allies. Vera Glaser from the Washington, D.C., office of the *Detroit Free Press* made this association between the Klan and Schlafly more direct when she said that the Ku Klux Klan, the John Birch Society, and militant groups of Catholics, Mormons, and Baptists belong to "an informal coalition which supports Phyllis Schlafly." The article quoted George Higgins, Jr., Grand Dragon of the Mississippi Knights of the Ku Klux Klan, saying he had advised and helped fund Schlafly and her followers.[32] Nonetheless, this accusation that Schlafly and her followers were linked to the racist right continued to be heard, even though Schlafly and her followers were mostly middle-and upper-class, white-gloved Republicans whose only knowledge of the KKK would have been from history books. In 1977, Doonesbury cartoonist Garry Trudeau placed one of his characters, Joanie Caucus, in a debate with Phyllis Schlafly. As Schlafly speaks to the crowd, Joanie Caucus thinks, "Hey Phyllis your sheet is showing."[33]

These representations of Schlafly as a racist and part of an organized right-wing cabal sometimes took a sinister turn when some opponents, carried away with their rhetoric, suggested that violence was the best way to stop Schlafly. On August 27, 1974, activist attorney Florence Kennedy, author of *Abortion Rap* (1971), appeared on CBS radio affiliate WKAT in Miami to promote ratification of ERA. During the course of the conversation she denounced Schlafly as a "pigocrat" and exclaimed, "I just don't see why some people don't hit Phyllis Schlafly in the mouth." Later, when asked about her remarks by *Parade Magazine*, she explained, "I don't think she [Schlafly] should be damaged seriously, but I don't think it would hurt if somebody slapped her. We're arguing with people [like Schlafly] who obviously aren't speaking from a rational perspective. Instead of so much argument people should slap."[34] Florence Kennedy was not the only one who spoke of violence. She was joined by science fiction writer Harlan Ellison, perhaps best known for his scripts for the cult television classic "Star Trek," who had become an activist for ERA after declaring himself a feminist. Appearing on the "Tomorrow Show" with host Tom Snyder on May 18, 1980, Ellison spouted, "Imbeciles like Phyllis Schlafly—if Phyllis Schlafly walked into the headlights of my car, I would knock her into the next time zone." Snyder appeared stunned and replied, "No. Come on," to which Ellison answered. "I would do it. I would do it. That woman is mischievous. She's a mischievous woman. She says terrible things."[35] Shortly after this, a hired demonstrator walked up to Schlafly at a Women's National Republican Club reception at the Waldorf-Astoria in New York and threw an apple pie in her face. A photographer captured the incident and it appeared the next day in many newspapers. It left Schlafly with a painfully scratched eye and her family worried about the potential for more serious attacks.[36]

Carter's Problems

Phyllis Schlafly bore the brunt of feminist frustrations, but President Jimmy Carter also came under sharp criticism for what feminists believed was his ambivalent support for their cause. Carter was not vilified by feminists, but he was not liked either. During the 1976 campaign, Carter's moderate stance on abortion left many in the women's movement unhappy. Matters did not get better when word got out that Carter believed that Betty Ford's strong pro-abortion views had helped the Democrats win the White House. From the outset Carter's relations with feminists were fragile, and over the course of time broke down completely, leading NOW and other women's organizations not to endorse him for reelection. Some of the problems lay in the high expectations feminists placed on the first Democratic administration in office since 1968. A deeper problem lay in the changing expectations of the women's movement. While ERA was the major priority of NOW, ERAmerica, the Women's Equity Action League, and the National Women's Political Caucus, the women's movement had so "broadened and diversified," as one historian has observed, that "no single issue could begin to satisfy feminist aspirations."[37]

Although his support for ERA intensified as the 1980 election approached, Carter had shown his support for ERA early in his administration. Carter's wife Rosalynn later joined the ERA campaign, traveling to states to support the amendment. Key state representatives were singled out for special treatment through invitations to the White House, where they were wined and dined, even though politically Carter was criticized for involving himself in local and state politics.[38] In the fall of 1978, Carter and Vice President Walter Mondale changed seven congressional votes to enable the extension of the ERA deadline to pass, and Rosalynn Carter held a White House briefing for key administrative officials on the importance of the extension.[39] Carter made a media event out of signing the congressional resolution extending the deadline. Carter told the press it was well known that such a resolution did not require a presidential signature, but "I particularly wanted to add my signature to demonstrate as strongly as I can my full support for the Equal Rights Amendment."[40]

Carter's problems with the feminist movement were further strained in his dealings with the President's Advisory Committee for Women, which he had formed on June 22, 1978. Against the urging of his political advisers, Carter appointed Bella Abzug to serve as co-chair with Carmen Delgado Votaw.[41] Carter was uneasy about appointing Abzug, but he was anxious to mend fences with feminists. Once onboard, she began openly criticizing Carter's anti-inflationary policies that she believed hurt women. The committee caused other problems when it used a State Department mailing permit to send out a newsletter that compared the Mormon Church's policies on race to the Ku Klux Klan. At a meeting on January 11, the committee had prepared a ten-page memorandum to be given to the President, "The First 18 Months:

A Status Report of the Carter Administration Action on International Women's Year Resolutions." Before the meeting, the commission had prepared a press release critical of President Carter's commitment to women's issues. At the meeting, all hell broke lose when Carter told Abzug that he disliked her "confrontational style." Sharp words were exchanged on both sides. Abzug then met with the press to express her dismay with Carter. Within moments after the press conference, she was summoned to the office of presidential aide Hamilton Jordan, where she was requested to resign. Others on the commission and within the administration rallied to Abzug by resigning as well. In May, Carter reconstituted the President's Advisory Committee for Women and named Lynda Johnson Robb as its chair. Later, Carter claimed that the mail had run two to one in his favor for firing Abzug, but clearly this marked a breaking point in his relations with the feminist movement.[42]

Carter was livid at the turn of events, but he continued to press forward on ERA. He appointed his eldest son's wife Judy to serve as White House troubleshooter on the amendment, with ERAmerica agreeing to pay for her travel to lobby state legislators.[43] On Oct. 23, 1979, Carter sponsored a "Presidential Salute to the ERA," drawing more than 800 people to the White House. This was followed by a strategy session on December 13, 1979, and a second strategy session on January 30, 1980, shortly after he had called for the ratification of ERA in his 1980 State of the Union Message. Later he hosted a White House reception for 500 people in conjunction with a NOW fundraiser.[44] Still, the damage done by firing Abzug was not easily overcome, and it further weakened Carter with the left-wing of his party.[45] In a college lecture tour, Abzug continued to criticize the administration. She told her audiences that when Carter fired her, "it was as though every woman in this country was fired." Women had made a mistake, she said, in trusting Carter and the establishment to ratify ERA. In explaining the failure of ERA to one student who asked why it had failed, she replied, "We left it to those in power. We have sent in only our nicest ladies. . . . Right now women have no power. We are on the fringes of democracy looking in."[46]

CARTER, THE GOP RIGHT, AND THE PANAMA CANAL

While Carter was having problems with feminist issues, grassroots conservatives, including Schlafly's Eagle Forum, attacked him on foreign policy, specifically his proposed turnover of the Panama Canal and arms control with the Soviet Union.[47] While the SALT II treaty was being negotiated in 1979, Carter ran into a buzz-saw when the Panama Canal treaties were brought before the Senate. The Panama Canal turnover and the SALT II Treaty convinced the GOP Right that Carter was leading an American retreat in military power and status in the world. The proposed Panama Canal turnover became a flashpoint in the confrontation between the Carter administration and the GOP Right. While Carter saw the turnover as an important step toward improving relations with Central and Latin America, a path that had been started by previous administrations, the canal became for many Americans a symbol of whether the United States was going to remain a world power or gradually decline into a second rate power.

Two treaties were concluded between the Carter administration and the strongman government of Omar Torrijos—one transferring legal title of the American Canal Zone to Panama and a second protocol declaring the right of the United States to defend the canal's neutrality against external threats.[48] When Carter signed the treaties in Washington, D.C., in September 1977, he was exhilarated by his success.[49] Yet polls taken in August 1977 showed that 78 percent of the American people opposed the treaty. Schlafly and other conservatives sought to tap the public's opposition to the turnover to apply pressure on the Senate to defeat the treaty.[50] Realizing the importance of this treaty to his administration and to the Torrijos government, the Carter administration encouraged a coordinated pro-treaty effort. The U.S. Chamber of Commerce, banking interests, shipping companies, and large multinationals with investments in Panama joined the campaign to get the treaty through Congress. The Panamanian government hired F. Clifton White (Reagan's presidential campaign manager in 1968) and Lawrence F. O'Brien (former Democratic party chairman) to conduct a public relations campaign in the media and universities.[51]

In 1977, Phyllis Schlafly, still embroiled in the ERA fight, turned her copious energy to the Panama Canal Treaty. Schlafly took aim at the treaties in her syndicated column, her regularly featured CBS editorials on *Spectrum*, and her monthly newsletter, which by 1977 had reached a circulation of nearly 30,000. Her first attack came in the February, 1977, newsletter that declared, "Don't Surrender the U.S. Canal!" but for her the Panama Canal was not a new issue. She had warned in the 1950s that Alger Hiss in his opening address to the United Nations in 1945 had called for the internationalization of the Panama Canal, and the first issue of the *Phyllis Schlafly Report* (August 1967) attacked a treaty drafted by the Johnson administration to turn over the canal to Panama. "Don't Surrender the U.S. Canal!" picked up this anticommunist theme by declaring that "Torrijos is part of a Marxist military junta operating in close collaboration with Communist Cuba and the Soviet Union. . . . The real issue is U.S. control versus Communist control!"[52]

Schlafly was not unique in pressing this anticommunist message. This theme was also found in other conservative attacks on the turnover, including Denison Kitchel, *The Truth about the Panama Canal* (1978) and long-time anticommunist Isaac Don Levine's 98-page booklet, *Hands Off the Panama Canal* (1976). Jeffrey Hart, a conservative English professor at Dartmouth College, wrote in the *National Review* that the debate was not "United States v. Panama, but the United States v. the Soviets."[53] Denison Kitchel, in trying to persuade his former boss Barry Goldwater to oppose the treaty, warned that once the United States withdrew from the Canal Zone as the treaty required in 1999, "it seems inevitable that the Soviets, not directly, but through the Cuban surrogate, would move quickly to fill it."[54] This fear of a Soviet takeover of the canal was heightened by what conservatives perceived as Soviet adventurism in Angola (where Cuban troops had been sent to support a pro-Soviet government), the anti-American, pro-Soviet revolutionary Sandinista government in Nicaragua, and the stationing of Soviet combat troops in Cuba.

Schlafly took the issue beyond communism when she accused the Carter administration of complicity in a rigged financial bonanza for multinational corporate interests. Writing in *Phyllis Schlafly Report* (October 1977), she charged that "ten of the largest banks in the United States joined with several foreign banks in lending $135 million to Panama." She pointed out that Sol M. Linowitz, the chief American negotiator of the treaty, was a director and member of the executive committee of Marine Midland Bank in New York, which had loaned money to Torrijos. The Federal Reserve had placed Midland on a list of problem banks that had overextended themselves.[55] In raising this argument, Schlafly expressed the traditional grassroots conservative distrust of Eastern financial elites and banking interests.[56]

The fight over the canal turnover was a pivotal point in the history of the American Right. Not since Franklin Roosevelt's court packing scheme had a political issue aroused such powerful emotions on the

Right. Newspaper publisher Gene Pulliam displayed this emotion when he told Goldwater, "I think Kissinger's position on Panama is almost treasonable and we will have to hit it with everything we've got as long as we live."[57] Emotions ran high during the canal debate and created fissures within the Right itself. When William F. Buckley, Jr., endorsed the treaty—and forcefully argued his position in debates with Ronald Reagan and Phyllis Schlafly on his weekly PBS television program, *Firing Line*, the *National Review* was flooded with letters canceling their subscriptions to the magazine. So serious was the problem that publisher William Rusher tried to plug the dam by sending a mass mailing to subscribers saying, "You and I believe Bill Buckley was wrong about the Canal treaties. But I hope you will agree with me, on reflection, that this kind of occasional disagreement is inevitable among spirited personalities. . . ."[58]

Schlafly and her fellow conservatives lost their battle when the Senate ratified the treaty on March 16, 1978, by 68–32, but the canal fight was a major factor in building conservative strength in the Republican party. By tapping into the wellspring of popular opposition against the treaty, the GOP mobilized its own base, fanned the fires of popular discontent with the Carter administration, and extended its political reach to a larger public. As pioneers in political direct mailing, the Right used the Panama Canal to fill its campaign coffers. It was reported that during the peak of the fight over the Panama Canal treaty, a direct-mail campaign by the American Conservative Union brought in $15,000 a day and built its donor list by tens of thousands. A fundraising letter by the Republican National Committee bearing Reagan's signature brought in $700,000 to fund an antitreaty campaign.

The canal treaty made conservatives fighting mad and imparted a populist tone to their complaints against the liberal establishment. William Rusher captured this sense of frustration and anger when he wrote a grassroots activist in California, "Personally, my mood of identification with some of the populist tendencies we see around us is beginning to deepen . . . I am thoroughly fed up with our bipartisan foreign policy establishment, which coolly shoved two noxious measures (the Panama Canal treaties and the Peking recognition) down the throats of the American people despite polls showing that the people consistently opposed both steps by substantial margins." He added by way of qualification, "I am not saying the people are always right; but I am damned if I see much point in letting such important matters as

American foreign policy be run by a handful of multinational corporations, their lawyers, and their government friends."[59] This anger found further expression in the ratification fight over the SALT II treaty that came soon after the Panama Canal treaty.

CARTER AND SALT II

Phyllis Schlafly squared off against SALT II even before it reached the Senate in 1979. The occasion for Schlafly's preemptive strike came when President Gerald Ford and Soviet leader Leonid Brezhnev met in Vladivostok in 1974. Out of this meeting came an interim treaty setting the "framework" for a final SALT II treaty. The framework limited the United States and the Soviet Union to 2,400 strategic missiles and bombers, but allowed for multiple independently targeted reentry vehicles (MIRVs) to continue. America had capitulated on its demand that the Soviets reduce their "heavy missiles," while leaving ambiguous the issues of the American cruise missile system and the new Soviet strategic bomber, the Backfire.[60]

This interim SALT II agreement suffered a blast of criticism from Democratic hawks and the GOP Right. Phyllis Schlafly and Chester Ward brought the issue to grassroots conservatives in *Ambush at Vladivostok*, published in 1976 by Schlafly's Pere Marquette Press. Like their previous books, this one was written to provide grassroots activists with basic information about strategic arms control policy and to encourage them to apply pressure to induce their elected representatives and the Republican party to support "peace through strength" defense policies. The book was a clarion call for the Reagan wing of the GOP to claim control of the party. They concluded that the "crisis confronting America in our Bicentennial year is not a crisis of technology, or a crisis of resources, or a crisis of production, or even a crisis of funding. It is a crisis of leadership. . . . Gerald Ford has been put to the test and found wanting."[61]

In challenging Ford's leadership of the Republican party, Schlafly and Ward took issue with the administration's claim that it had maintained the "highest-in-history" defense budget. They charged that the Ford defense budgets were high only in inflated paper dollars, quoting from a report from the Foreign Policy Task Force chaired by Eugene V. Rostow (once criticized by Schlafly as an appeaser) that Ford's "defense budget is an invitation to disaster."[62] American defenses, which had deteriorated since the Johnson administration, needed to be rebuilt, but the first step was to accept a launch-on-verfication-of-warning strategy. New satellite technology enabled the United States to detect a missile launch from the Soviet Union even before the missiles arrived in the United States. Such a policy, contrary to "the alarmist cries of the disarmament elites," would "avert the causes of a nuclear crisis."[63] *Ambush at Vladivostok* was contentious and at times caustic in its appraisal of the Ford administration, but the authors were not alone in their criticisms.

Hawks in both parties were appalled by the Vladivostok agreement. Even before Carter became President, opposition to SALT II was evident on both sides of the aisle in Congress. To many critics, the Soviet Union's power seemed to be on the rise, while American power was in decline.[64] Especially worrisome was Carter's appointment of Cyrus Vance as Secretary of State and Paul Warnke as chief negotiator in arms talks with the Soviet Union. Hawks took some reassurance in the appointment of Zbigniew Brzezinski as Carter's National Security Adviser, but it was clear that Carter was pushing for an arms control agreement based on the Vladivostok framework. An early indication of coming troubles came when Albert Wohlstetter published a series of articles in *Foreign Policy* magazine showing that American intelligence had been systematically underestimating Soviet strategic offensive capabilities.[65] Shortly after the appearance of this article, Paul Nitze, Eugene Rostow, and David Packard organized the Committee on the Present Danger to open a public debate on the proposed SALT II negotiations.[66]

The final SALT II Treaty concentrated on offensive capabilities. It imposed a ceiling of 2,400 aggregate strategic nuclear launch vehicles and a subceiling of 1,200 intercontinental ballistic missiles (ICBMs) and submarine launched ballistic missiles (SLBMs) that could be converted to MIRV launchers. This favored the Soviets, whose missiles were substantially larger than the United States and could carry substantially larger payloads in megatonnage, although the United States led in bombers and nuclear submarines. Critics of the treaty furthermore argued that the Soviets were allowed to have modern large ballistic missiles (their SS-18s), while the United States was to have none. At the same time, the treaty, in effect, granted the Soviet Union superiority in heavy bombers.[67]

Especially revealing was the testimony of Henry Kissinger before the Senate Committee on Foreign Relations on July 31, 1979. Kissinger opened his testimony by declaring that the "ideology of the Soviet leaders does not make them content to practice their preferred social system at home; they strive for its victory worldwide." Kissinger noted that while he had helped design SALT I and was involved in the negotiations of the Vladivostok accord in 1974, he had concluded that the "military balance is beginning to tilt ominously against the United States in too many significant categories of weaponry" at a time when the Soviets had undertaken the use of "proxy" wars in Africa, the Middle East, and Southeast Asia. "It is imperative," he declared, "that we recognize without illusion the dangerous trends that are emerging. It is crucial that we begin now to rectify them." Apologizing for his own complacency in this imbalance, he declared that the American intelligence communities had underestimated the Soviet buildup. By the time Lyndon Johnson came into office, Kissinger testified, the Soviets had reached nuclear parity with us, but instead of stopping the buildup, "as the Johnson Administration expected, the Soviets continued their missile buildup."[68] Much of Kissinger's testimony sounded like the Schlafly-Ward warnings a decade earlier.

In the end, however, the Senate Foreign Relations Committee approved the treaty in a 9 to 6 vote. Realizing the treaty was in trouble in the Senate, Carter responded by promising to raise defense spending 4.5 percent for five years. This increase was intended to reverse the slowdown in American strategic defense programs initiated under Secretary of Defense McNamara. Carter further proposed a counter-deployment of intermediate-range missiles in Europe to counter the Soviet SS-20. Carter's proposals failed to persuade hawks in the Senate that SALT II was safe. The Senate Armed Services Committee voted on December 20, 1979, 10–0 with 7 abstentions that SALT II was "not in the national security interests of the United States." A few days later, when the Soviet Union invaded Afghanistan, Carter withdrew the treaty.

1980: The Triumph of the GOP Right

Even as his foreign policy lay in shambles, and economic problems appeared intractable, Carter believed that he would win a second term, especially if the GOP decided to go with its frontrunner, Ronald Reagan.

Carter welcomed the rise of the Right that had become evident since the midterm elections in 1978. Witnessing the success of Schlafly's ability to mobilize evangelical Christians and grassroots conservatives, Republican operatives seized the opportunity to energize the grassroots by tying social issues such as abortion and prayer in schools to long-standing Republican causes—free-market economics and hard-line military and foreign policies. Republican strategists channeled cultural frustrations felt by evangelical and traditionalist Christians into the political arena. No single event sparked this religious eruption, but evangelical and traditionalist Christians concluded that the place of traditional values in the larger society was under attack and, moreover, their own ability to pass their values on to their children was threatened. Social and political secularism appeared to be replacing traditional religious values; traditional morality had been repudiated by the entertainment industry; and the Supreme Court had removed religion from the public schools, banned state restrictions on abortion, and protected pornography as freedom of speech.[69]

A growing cultural cleavage raised questions about the proper role of government in arbitrating cultural values. In the past, cultural issues around prayer in school, flag-burning, the pledge of allegiance, and legalized abortion, while arousing intense emotions, had not led to changes in party affiliation or voting patterns. As more Americans accepted secularist values, these issues seemed to initiate a culture war. Conservative strategists sought to mobilize evangelical Protestants and traditionalist Catholics against both the Democratic party and the dominant liberal-moderate wing of the GOP. As a minority within a minority party, conservatives had nothing to lose by introducing volatile cultural and religious issues into the political arena. In order to gain control of the GOP, conservatives realized they needed to bring a new constituency into Republican politics, so they fastened on these social issues as a political weapon to defeat their opponents in both parties.[70]

Conservative operatives brought their political skills into the congressional election of 1978 by using these social issues as a wedge to separate liberal Democratic Congressional representatives from their more socially conservative constituents. Conservative strategists took advantage of the post-Watergate election reform laws to establish PACs, as well as larger fundraising conduits such as the National Conservative Political Action Committee. The strategy paid off in 1978, when

Democratic seats declined from 292 to 277 in the House, and from 61 to 59 in the Senate. The marginal loss in numbers was politically significant. The midterm elections also revealed Democrats losing support where Carter had run well in 1976, in rural and small-town areas. Tradition-minded voters in 1976 had turned toward Carter, a Southern Baptist, and away from a veteran politician, Gerald Ford, whose wife supported ERA, abortion, and women's liberation. By 1978, Carter's equivocation on abortion and his support of the Panama Canal "give-away" were turning voters toward the Republican party. The 1978 midterm elections showed that the Democrats had lost a core constituency, white evangelical voters in both the South and the North. The 1978 election also revealed that Republican moderates were no longer safe from the GOP Right.[71]

The election also proved a warning sign for the political establishment in both the Democratic and Republican parties: The emergence of the pro-family movement, consisting of evangelical Protestants and Catholics, and a revitalized conservative movement in the Republican party, set the stage for the 1980 contest between Carter and the hero of many conservatives, Ronald Reagan. The Right stood resurgent, ready to take complete control of the GOP and win the next presidential election. This time there was little dissension in the ranks over rival candidates or talk of forming a third party. Success in the midterm elections in 1978 propelled an activated Right to try to elect Ronald Reagan to the White House and conservatives to Congress.[72] The label New Right was promoted by Paul Weyrich, founder of the Committee for the Survival of a Free Congress, to identify a group of Republicans operating inside Washington, D. C., who employed new techniques of coalition building, direct mail campaigns, and fundraising. This group included fundraiser Terry Dolan, a master at slashing negative campaigns against liberal incumbent Senators; Howard Phillips, founder of The Conservative Caucus; and Richard Viguerie, a pioneer in computer-assisted direct mail campaigns. The press sometimes identified Phyllis Schlafly as part of the New Right, but while she associated with them at conservative gatherings such as C-PAC, the annual conservative conference, her pro-family movement had its own identity and was grassroots-oriented. Other groups also became components of the Reagan coalition, such as the Moral Majority headed by Baptist preacher Jerry Falwell. Although Falwell's Moral Majority never extended much beyond Baptist churches in the South, he played a major role in getting evangelical Christians involved in politics by registering to vote. In the late 1980s, Pat Robertson formed the Christian Coalition, which further encouraged evangelical Christian participation in politics.

New Right activists such as Paul Weyrich teamed with anti-abortion activists to prepare for the 1980 elections. Typical was the call issued by the National Pro-Life Political Action Committee in its September 1979 newsletter, which declared "1980 Elections Start Now!" The Pro-Life Action Committee reported that it had sent fourteen "specially selected" men and women from campaign staffs to a week-long day training school run by the Committee for the Survival of a Free Congress to learn "every aspect of political management."[73] The antiabortion movement became a juggernaut on the grassroots level in a direct counter-assault against the feminists. In this counterattack, feminists found themselves stranded, cut-off from grassroots organizational support on the local and state levels. Writing in the *Saturday Review* a year before the election, journalist Roger Williams reported that the feminists had advanced their agenda so quickly on the abortion issue and the ERA that they had outstripped their supply lines.[74]

During the Republican primaries, Reagan focused on the economic failures and foreign policy debacles of the Carter administration, and at the same time he reassured his right-wing base in the party that he was one of them on social issues by advocating a constitutional amendment to prohibit all abortions except when necessary to save the life of the mother. Feminists within the Republican party tried to rally behind a third-party challenge from Illinois congressman John Anderson, but Reagan swept the primaries. At the Republican National Convention in Detroit in July 1980, pro-ERA and pro-abortion Republicans were pounded into defeat by STOP ERA and pro-life activists. The battle was one-sided from the outset. The CBS poll of delegates reported 62 percent opposed ERA, and the *Washington Post* reported 70 percent opposed. In the Women's Rights section of the platform, the Republican party reaffirmed its "historic commitment to equal rights and the equality for women," but for the first time since 1940 did not endorse the Equal Rights Amendment. Support for the ERA was removed, and activists inserted declarations in support of a constitutional amendment against abortion and in support of the family. The language of these two planks showed the power the GOP Right now exerted in the party. The plank on abortion declared, "While we recognize differing views on this [the abortion] question among Americans in general—and in our own Party—we affirm our support of a constitutional amendment to restore protection of the right to life for unborn children. We also support the congressional efforts to restrict the use of taxpayers' dollars for abortion."

The plank on families also conveyed the strong feelings of conservative Republican activists. "Unlike the Democrats," the platform asserted, "we do not advocate new federal bureaucracies with ominous power to shape a national family order. Rather, we insist that all domestic policies, from child care and schooling to Social Security, and the tax code, must be formulated with the family in mind."[75] Mary Dent Crisp, co-chairman of the Republican party, tried to rally pro-abortion moderates within the party to defeat these planks, but they were adopted by the Human Resources Subcommittee by a vote of 14 to 1, and then by the entire platform committee, representing delegates from every state, by a vote of 90–9.

While the general campaign focused primarily on economic and foreign policy issues, Reagan's commitment to the conservative social agenda assured him of the support of the newly mobilized Christian Right and traditionalist women. During the campaign, Reagan appointed a Family Policy Advisory Committee to establish campaign links with the pro-family organizations. Chairman of the 25-person board was Mrs. Connaught Marshner, editor of the *Family Protection Report*. The board, including representatives of right-to-life, STOP ERA, and Christian school and pro-family groups, supported Reagan's campaign, the Human Life Amendment, school choice, and dismantling the Department of Education. At the same time, the Committee for the Survival of a Free Congress and the Eagle Forum sponsored several training programs for campaign volunteers involved in critical Senate campaigns in Iowa, Idaho, Indiana, South Dakota, Florida, North Carolina, Oklahoma, and Alaska.[76]

By boldly linking economic and social issues into a populist attack on federal bureaucrats, out-of-touch politicians, and an arrogant cultural elite, Reagan overwhelmed Carter at the polls, receiving 51 percent of the vote to Jimmy Carter's 42 percent (7 percent went to John Anderson who ran as an Independent). Exit polls showed that women for ERA gave Carter 63 percent of their vote, while women opposing the ERA supported Reagan, 69 percent to 31 percent.[77] Republican candidates for Senate and House ran essentially even with Reagan nationwide.[78] The GOP Right claimed much of the credit for this success at the polls. Taking advantage of a loophole in the campaign finance reform law that allowed unlimited "independent expenditures" by political action committees, Terry Dolan's National Conservative Political Action Committee (NCPAC) targeted six liberal Democratic Senators with hard-hitting ads and defeated four of them—Birch Bayh (Indiana), John Culver (Iowa), George McGovern (South Dakota), and Frank Church (Idaho). During the 1980 campaign, NCPAC spent nearly $1 million in independent expenditures, primarily for negative radio and television ads. A NCPAC target often faced as many as 72 negative radio ads a day and 200 television ads per week. In later elections, this loophole would be exploited by liberal PACs.

In the House, Republicans gained 33 seats. In congressional races, Republicans won more votes outside the South than the Democrats for the first time since 1968. Tip O'Neill, who was elected speaker in January 1977, was left with such a thin margin of control that any desertion by Southern Democrats meant that the Republicans could score legislative victories. In the Senate, Republicans gained 12 seats and won control of that body for the first time since 1952 and only the third time since Hoover's defeat in 1932. This was the largest net gain in the Senate for any party since 1958, when the Democrats took over 15 seats. The Senate was not only more Republican, but more conservative because leading liberal Democrats were defeated.[79]

Reporting on the results of the 1980 election, Cable News Network (CNN) concluded that the outcome was a tremendous defeat for the feminist movement.[80] Joyce Miller, president of the Coalition of Labor Union Women, was quoted by the *New York Times* as declaring that the election was a "total disaster" for advocates of women's rights. Some tried to explain away the results of the election as a "a national convulsion of discontent" having to do with inflation, although Senator George McGovern, one of the casualties of the election, explained, "People were reluctant to come right out and admit they wanted to put women in their place, but there was a strong current of that running through much of what happened."[81] Consolation could be found in the fact that feminism still stood as a strong force in the Democratic party and in American culture, but in November 1980, feminism stood battered as so many liberal Democrats who had been staunch advocates of feminist goals went down in defeat. Anti-ERA activists relished, in particular, the defeat of Birch Bayh of Indiana, the Senate sponsor of ERA.

The election of Warren Rudman in New Hampshire and Arlen Specter in Pennsylvania showed that it was not a complete sweep for the GOP Right, but conservatives were nevertheless ecstatic. Whatever doubts they might have had about Reagan were swept away by his overwhelming victory. His election, they declared, was a victory for conservative ideology. Phyllis Schlafly, who had been selected to serve on Reagan's Defense Policy Advisory Board during the campaign, spoke for movement conservatives when she declared in her December 1980 newsletter, later reprinted in the January issue of the *Conservative Digest*, that Reagan won by riding "the rising tides of the Pro-Family Movement and the Conservative Movement. Reagan articulated what those two separate movements want from government, and therefore he harnessed their support and rode them into the White House."[82] While Reagan won by mobilizing social and economic conservatives, as well as an electorate fed up with the Carter administration, Schlafly claimed that the pro-family movement had been especially important to the election. Post-election analysis showed that evangelical Christians and social conservatives played crucial roles in winning the South for Reagan and were significant in many congressional races.

In making this claim for the pro-family movement, Schlafly was less interested in setting the historical record straight than in shaping the policy agenda for the incoming administration.[83] Furthermore, she maintained that STOP ERA had introduced "something entirely new in American politics—a coalition of Catholics, Protestants, Mormons, and Orthodox Jews working together to defeat the Equal Rights Amendment." By 1980, she said, STOP ERA had become part of a larger pro-family movement consisting of different segments including "the right-to-life movement, the religious-schools movement, the prayer-in-school movement, the antipornography movement, and the evangelical Christians who are motivated by a cluster of moral issues including homosexuality." The anti-ERA forces and the pro-family movement had been critical in helping Reagan win New Hampshire and Illinois primaries. When the polls said that George Bush would carry New Hampshire, STOP ERA leaders, including Phyllis Schlafly, went to the state the week before the primary and worked to give Reagan a "surprise victory." Schlafly reported that Reagan had phoned her a week before the March primary in Illinois to ask for her help after polls predicted that Illinois Congressman John Anderson would win the state. Anti-ERA forces went to work "around the clock" for the next five days to enable Reagan to win Illinois.

She boasted that in the general election the STOP ERA movement dealt a deadly blow to Carter and other Democrats. During a White House election strategy meeting, Carter had a premonition that "I am afraid the anti-ERAers will defeat me," and he had been proved correct. (A *New York Times*-CBS News poll conducted in late September and mid-October before the election showed surprisingly that more men—55 percent—supported the Equal Rights Amendment than women—47 percent.[84]) Furthermore, two of the leading female senatorial candidates who were supporters of ERA were defeated in 1980, Elizabeth Holtzman in New York and Mary Buchanan in Colorado, while Paula Hawkins, an opponent of ERA, won her Senate race in Florida.

However accurate Schlafly's claims for the success of the pro-family movement, she understood that the Reagan campaign had tapped a wellspring of moral conservatism that ran deep in the American electorate.[85] She set forth the principles of these moral conservatives, shortly before Reagan took office, when she declared that "separation of church and state is a time-honored pillar of our American Constitution and culture. . . . but it never meant that religion should be excluded from public life or from our schools and colleges." She predicted that the fight against liberalism had become a war of two moralities, a cultural divide between fundamentally and irreconcilably different moral visions of the meaning of human life and the purpose of state and church. "The real reason the liberals are so upset," she found, "is because they have made secular humanism our de facto state religion in government and education, and they realize that those who believe in the external verities and the Ten Commandments of the Judeo-Christian culture are starting to exercise their inalienable political rights."[86] This was a declaration that the war against liberal political culture would continue and that while Reagan's election marked an apotheosis for the GOP, beware those who sought to backslide on the moral questions of the day because a nation organized as a bold experiment in republican government was at stake.

On the eve of the inauguration, William Rusher, a scion of the conservative movement, captured the mood of the GOP Right when he wrote President-Elect Ronald Reagan, "I honestly don't know whether there is still time to turn this country around, but I know that the man Americans elected on November 4th intends to try. And that is the best news in many, many years."[87]

CHAPTER ELEVEN

Ideology and Power in a Divided Nation

ON JANUARY 30, 2003, over 3,000 conservative leaders and grassroots activists attended a banquet, hosted by the prominent umbrella group C-PAC, to honor Phyllis Schlafly as the "conservative movement's founding mother" and the founder of the pro-family movement who rallied millions of religious voters for Ronald Reagan in 1980.[1]

Introduced by long-time conservative friend and former U.S. Representative Bob Dornan (R-California), Schlafly was hailed as the woman who has opposed "every evil that threatened our children."[2] Other conservatives joined in acclaiming Schlafly's contribution to the conservative cause. Paul Weyrich held that Schlafly had been critical in the revival of the Right declaring, "Phyllis dressed the conservative movement for success at a time when absolutely no one thought we could win. She taught us that sheer dogged determination can reverse the odds."[3] Conservative firebrand Ann Coulter introduced Schlafly to a new generation of conservatives in her best seller *Slander* (2002) when she wrote, "Schlafly is one of the most accomplished and influential people in America. . . . She is a senior statesman in the Republican Party."[4] Pro-life activist Caia Hoskins affirmed Coulter's assessment, "Phyllis Schlafly is responsible for the pro-life plank being in the [Republican] platform—period," adding that the "pro-abortion side didn't have enough people to start a floor fight. All they had was the media. Phyllis Schlafly had the grassroots."[5]

Much of this praise came from activists who represented the right of a conservative party. Establishment GOP leaders were more reticent in their praise of Schlafly. These mainstream party leaders and intellectuals—the Pharisees of the GOP—recognized Schlafly as a leader who had led the multitude to the gates of the temple, but they were not anxious to allow her into the inner sanctum. Perhaps her followers were too observant in their belief of what constitutes principled conservatism, or perhaps party leaders feared that Schlafly might try to drive the money-changers and compromisers out of the temple; whatever the case, party leaders cautiously kept their distance, even while carefully not dismissing her influence among many party loyalists. In a closely divided political culture, both parties seek to capture the center without alienating their activist bases. As a consequence, party leaders could not ignore Schlafly, who had become a symbol of a grassroots activism that had transformed the Republican party. She played a leadership role in defeating ERA, was a critical force in keeping an antimissile defense as a front-burner issue among the grassroots conservatives, helped revive the conservative movement at its nadir following the Watergate scandal, thwarted conservative plans for a constitutional convention during the Reagan administration, kept a strong pro-life plank in the GOP platform, and authored books that sold millions of copies. Through radio commentaries, syndicated columns, and a monthly newsletter, Schlafly kept up a steady call to the grassroots Right to keep the GOP on the right track on the economic, education, defense, legal, and moral issues of the day.

There was a continuity in Schlafly's activities that could be traced back to her early days as a grassroots anticommunist in the 1950s. The collapse of the Soviet Union in the early 1980s, however, set a new context for these issues. For nearly thirty years, the threat of the Soviet Union and communism had framed Schlafly's discussion of political issues. Schlafly and the Republican Right maintained that America must remain strong domestically and militarily against a formidable, perhaps even indomitable, foe—the Soviet Union. With the demise of the Soviet Union, the moorings that had held in place the Right's political agenda had come loose. At the same time, the end of the Cold War enabled the Democratic party to free itself—at least momentarily—from having to insist that it, too, was strong on national defense. In 1992, the first nonveteran in the post–World War II era was elected to the White House, Bill Clinton. In this context, Democrats were allowed what turned out to be a brief window to focus on social and economic issues, although even here they were constrained by the Reagan legacy of smaller government, fiscal restraint, and social conservatism. Following the victorious Republican midterm election in 1994, Clinton Democrats turned to a centrist program and threatened to usurp the GOP agenda. The Republican Right denounced the Democrats as disingenuous liberals, but at the same time they confronted their own internal problems that had grown since Reagan won in 1980.

When Reagan came into the White House, the GOP Right showed the tensions that came with an out-of-power faction becoming part of a governing coalition. This tension was revealed in the debate over pragmatism versus principle within the GOP. The GOP Right itself was not of one mind on this question, and divisions also arose over simple difference of opinion. Such was the case in the call for a constitutional convention to enact a balanced budget amendment put forward by a group of conservatives. Schlafly led the opposition that defeated this proposal. The debate over principles was more apparent in convention fights over a pro-life plank in the party platform. As founder of the Republican National Coalition for Life, Schlafly was deeply involved in protecting the pro-life plank from being watered down. Similarly, profound and nearly irreconcilable divergence emerged in the GOP Right over social and cultural issues such as immigration, free trade, and same-sex marriage. This gave the GOP the appearance of being as divided as ever.

For Phyllis Schlafly, transition into the new post-Cold War era was made easier by the Equal Rights Amendment. From her struggle against feminism she concluded that America faced an enemy within that threatened the traditional order of a Christian-based society. Although Schlafly would never admit it, her opponents also drew from a powerful sentiment in American republican thought derived from the eighteenth-century Enlightenment. That was a secular outlook emphasizing individual rights, personal liberation, the advancement of worldly knowledge over what was considered religious superstition and custom, and a conviction that mankind was basically good. These strains in American thought had clashed at critical points in American history, but a careful balance had always been struck, or at least appeared to have been struck. With the erosion of religious faith among a significant segment of the population, especially among the educated classes, in the late twentieth century, American culture appeared to be in disequilibrium, which was reflected in its politics. Debates over abortion, stem-cell research, and same-sex marriage placed these opposing outlooks, the secular and the religious, into sharp relief.

In arguing their case, the GOP Right employed populist rhetoric that appealed to the public against the elites. The GOP Right saw political advantage in such rhetoric, but this was a sincere expression of their belief that they represented the common person against the liberal elite. Schlafly had used such oratory from her first days as an anticommunist, and fifty years later she still carried a populist message to the grassroots. In her *The Supremacists* (2004), she called for the American people to rally against the abuses of activist judges who time and again thwarted the will of the people through wrong-headed inter-pretations of the Constitution.[6] She represented a moral populism within the GOP, a voice that persisted in the cacophony of compromise poli-tics in Washington. For moral populists such as Schlafly, victory did not mean merely winning political power, but ensuring moral order in the American Republic.

RONALD REAGAN AND THE REPUBLICAN RIGHT

Ronald Reagan's presidency (1981–88) was a seminal event in the his-tory of American conservatism. Reagan transformed the Republican party and changed the direction of American politics. Yet in the cele-bration of his presidency, tensions within the administration and with grassroots conservatives tended to be overlooked. Once in office, Rea-gan appeared to place cultural issues on the back burner in order to pursue his agenda of tax cuts and a military buildup, but his alleged backsliding on social issues can be overstated.[7]

Although Reagan gave highest priority to economic and defense is-sues, he did not turn his back on social issues such as abortion. Reagan was motivated by a genuine ideological opposition to abortion and to the banning of prayer in schools, but politically he needed to maintain support among social conservatives such as Schlafly, evangelical Chris-tians, and pro-life activists. His staff reminded him that "these people could help a great deal in providing grassroots support for your eco-nomic program."[8] As a consequence, when Reagan spoke at the annual dinner of the Conservative Political Action Conference (C-PAC), he de-clared, "Because ours is a consistent philosophy of government, we can be very clear: We do not have a separate social agenda, a separate eco-nomic agenda, and a separate foreign policy agenda. We have one agenda." He added, "Just as surely as we seek to put our financial house in order and rebuild our Nation's defenses, so too we seek to protect the unborn."[9] Such rhetoric, while applauded by conservatives, did not make the GOP Right fall lockstep behind every Reagan proposal and, in-deed, tensions with the ideological Right were already evident in the presidential campaign and the transition period before Reagan entered the White House.

The rejection of the Equal Rights Amendment in the 1980 Republican platform and Reagan's opposition to ERA and to *Roe v. Wade* made the pragmatists in his administration believe that he needed to do something to get the women's vote. The Reagan-Bush presidential campaign announced on September 11, 1980, the formation of a Women's Policy Board to give Reagan "substantive policy advice on defined issues so the concerns of women are strongly represented and articulated."[10] The chair and vice-chair of this committee were Mary Louise Smith and Bobbie Kilberg, both pro-ERA and pro-abortion supporters. Kilberg was especially offensive to conservatives because she was on the advisory board and had served as the vice-chair of the National Women's Political Caucus (NWPC). The twenty-seven other women appointed to the panel were members of the NWPC and were pro-ERA, a fact proudly noted in the Reagan-Bush campaign press-release.[11] Not a single anti-ERA or pro-life activist was appointed to the committee. In response, Phyllis Schlafly sent out an emergency telegram to STOP ERA activists and Eagle Forum members to protest through phone calls, letters, and telegrams to the Reagan campaign.[12]

Within days of Schlafly's rallying call to the grassroots, Reagan personally phoned Schlafly at her home to apologize for the establishment of this committee staffed by pro-ERA women. He told her that he had not been consulted about the list of appointments to the committee or the press release before it was released. At a conference with Schlafly and other pro-family leaders on September 22, Reagan's campaign director William Casey and Reagan's chief of staff Edwin Meese agreed to establish a Family Policy Board to be headed by conservative Connie Marshner, a family policy analyst at Paul Weyrich's Free Congress Research Foundation. Eagle Forum was well represented on this new panel by Tottie Ellis of Tennessee, Kathleen Sullivan and Rosemary Thomson of Illinois.[13] The board issued policy papers supporting the Human Life Amendment, school choice, and the dismantling of the Department of Education. Meanwhile, Reagan invited Schlafly to serve on the National Security Task Force, headed by Reagan's defense advisor Richard Allen.

Schlafly and other social conservatives welcomed Reagan's willingness to bring them on board as advisers during the campaign, but Reagan's transition into the White House reopened concerns about the future direction of the administration. At issue was pragmatism versus principle as the incoming administration began to think about appointments to government. As president of the United States and leader of the Republican party, Ronald Reagan remained steadfast in his conservative convictions, but his aides believed they had to call on the services of men and women with a long history of service to the government. This inevitably meant calling on people who had served in the Nixon and Ford administrations. This excluded many conservative activists from top positions in the administration. In reality, many conservatives ultimately won appointments in the administration, both on the White House staff, as well as in governmental agencies, especially in Health and Human Services, Education, and Treasury. Reagan sought to balance the moderate and conservative wings of his party, while pressing forward with his conservative political agenda in the Democratic-controlled Congress. At the same time, grassroots conservative activists applied steady pressure on the administration to move more quickly on conservative issues such as abortion, downsizing government, and budget cuts.

Throughout Reagan's first term, grassroots activists were sensitive to any sign that the administration would backslide into moderate Republicanism. Reagan's close political adviser, Senator Paul Laxalt (R-Nevada), told the *Wall Street Journal* that many grassroots conservatives were "a little afraid" of Reagan, and the selection of George Bush as his running mate had confirmed these fears. Laxalt reported that if President Reagan were like Governor Reagan, he would be a political pragmatist pursuing policies more moderate than his rhetoric. He added, "Opposing the ERA and abortion is important, but we've got bigger issues to worry about."[14]

This pragmatic side to Reagan's approach to governing was represented during the transition by E. Pendleton James, Reagan's chief talent-hunter for the new administration, as well as former deputy director of Gerald Ford's Domestic Council James Cavanaugh and Washington attorney Peter McPherson. This transition team came under heavy criticism from Reagan's Kitchen Cabinet leaders Joseph Coors and businessman Bill Wilson for recommending former Nixon and Ford appointees.

The conservative *Washington Inquirer*, published by the Council for the Defense of Freedom, expressed shock when Defense Secretary Casper Weinberger, no favorite of grassroots conservatives to begin with, appointed Frank Carlucci as his deputy secretary of defense. The *Inquirer* noted that the list of "missing persons" not being appointed to the administration included Dr. William Van Cleave, Howard Phillips, black economists Walter Williams and Thomas Sowell, and "women's leader,

Phyllis Schlafly."[15] The failure to appoint Dr. William Van Cleave, a University of Southern California professor and Reagan's defense advisor for the previous six years, was especially disappointing to Phyllis Schlafly, who had worked with Van Cleave on the campaign's defense advisory board. Following the announcement that Van Cleave was returning to Southern California, Schlafly joined the criticism of the drift of the administration in her syndicated column, "Reagan's Appointments" (January 8, 1981).

Shortly before the election, Schlafly met with Edwin Meese to talk about her involvement in the campaign, which had included traveling to 15 states and her mailgrams and letters to her followers urging them to vote for Reagan. She warned that Richard Nixon's failure to pursue conservative policies had begun with the transition into the White House.[16] Following Reagan's victory, conservatives such as South Carolina Republican Roger Milliken and Amway founder Jay Van Andel wrote to Reagan promoting her appointment as Deputy Secretary of Defense or Deputy Secretary of Education.[17] She also helped organize the Coalition for Change in Government, an ad-hoc group of conservative women seeking to influence future Reagan appointments. The group lobbied for direct involvement in remaining administration appointments. A number of the women in this group received appointments in the new administration, but Phyllis Schlafly was not one of them.[18] In 1981 and 1982, Schlafly's preoccupation was the final defeat of the Equal Rights Amendment and building her Eagle Forum in the new era of Reagan conservatism. However, Schlafly enjoyed excellent relations with the administration and was invited to the White House on many occasions. Furthermore, Reagan spoke via video to the annual Eagle Forum Leadership Conference year after year, praising the Eagle Forum for setting high standards of volunteer participation in the political and legislative process.

THE DEATH THROES OF ERA

The election of Ronald Reagan signaled the landmark shift of the American electorate to the right. ERA supporters were still confident that victory could be theirs, but private correspondence of some ERA leaders indicated that they knew ERA was dying.[19] Time was running out on the amendment. The time extension won in Congress in 1978 had backfired, turning many state legislators against ERA. As one Illinois state legislator declared, "I've seen corpses in the morgue that looked livelier [than the ERA]."[20] The legislators wanted to rid themselves of this divisive issue once and for all. They were tired of activists on both sides who lobbied them on an issue that had become a no-winner politically.[21] Fierce battles were still fought in Illinois, Florida, and North Carolina as pro-ERAers made a last desperate attempt to save a dying cause. Both sides threw resources into a referendum on an Iowa state ERA, but it was defeated overwhelmingly by a 55 percent vote in November 1980.[22] By 1982, John Leonard, writing in the *New York Times* concluded, "The 'backlash' against feminism looks more like a tidal wave."[23]

ERA's death was ugly and comical at the same time. Frustrated and angry by the impending defeat of ERA, pro-ERA activists spared no wrath in accusing Schlafly of having hoodwinked American women. The court's upholding of the conviction of pro-ERA activist Wanda Brandstetter for attempting to bribe an Illinois state legislator only fueled this anger. ERA supporters became the ones portrayed in the press as zealots, fighting a lost cause in a society that had turned its back on them. The *New York Times* described NOW president Eleanor Smeal as exuding "the ardor of a religious preacher."[24] When Phyllis Schlafly appeared in 1981 before the Senate Labor and Human Resources Committee to testify against the Equal Employment Opportunity Commission guidelines on sexual harassment in the workplace—declaring that men seldom made passes at virtuous women—feminists responded with a moral fervor that captured headlines across the country. She was denounced in editorials and letters to the editor as a "diabolical genius," a women with "a secret agenda to dismantle protections for all working women," and "obsolete."[25]

Other pro-ERA tactics came across as intolerant and even bigoted. When U.S. District Court Judge Marion Callister was assigned to hear a case involving the constitutionality of Idaho's rescission of ERA ratification, ERA demonstrators in January 1981 set effigies of Ronald Reagan and Judge Callister on fire. Around the judge's neck was a sign saying, "Mormon Judge Callister." ACLU lawyers filed suit attempting to bar Callister from hearing the suit because he was a Mormon. Such logic would have prevented Catholic judges from hearing cases on abortion or family planning, or female judges from hearing cases on ERA. The protest against a Mormon judge by ERA supporters projected an image of religious intolerance. This position drew criticism from newspaper editors across the country who saw the inconsistency of the position.[26] Actually, the Carter Justice Department filed a motion to disqualify Callister from the case, but he refused to step down. In December 1981, Judge Callister ruled that Congress had exceeded its constitutional authority when it voted in 1978 to extend the deadline for ERA ratification and ruled that states that had ratified the ERA had the right to rescind ratification prior to the deadline. The decision was a tremendous blow to ERA supporters in the waning days of ERA.

On appeal, the U.S. Supreme Court delayed its decision until the deadline granted by the time extension expired and then declared the issue "moot." The Court did not have to rule on the validity of the time extension or rescissions because ERA had failed to win thirty-eight states even by the extended deadline.[27]

One of the more ugly occasions in the backlash against Schlafly came in an episode of the CBS television series, "Cagney and Lacey," aired on August 9, 1982. Originally scheduled to be aired on June 28th, two days before the ERA extension ran out, the episode was pulled at the last minute because of its explosive nature. The episode had the two female detectives assigned to guard an anti-ERA leader (with Schlafly mannerisms, such as taking off her left earring to make a phone call) whose life is threatened by a psychotic. Within the context of the recent murder of rock and roll star John Lennon, and the attempted assassination of Ronald Reagan, Schlafly supporters protested to CBS that the show was socially irresponsible.[28]

As New Age religion became trendy in the late 1970s, some feminists turned to more esoteric strategies to defeat Schlafly. While not typical, some responses imparted a comic light to feminism when reported by the press. For example Zsuzanna Budapest, the self-acclaimed high priest of the Susan B. Anthony Coven #1 in Los Angeles, told a conference of "wimmin" attending the Witches and Amazons Conference in South Bend, Indiana, how to cast a victory spell for ERA. She told the hundred or so participants at the conference that when the moon is full, go to a place "wild and lone [sic] (or your own backyard)" and place on the ground a map with the not-ratified states outlined in red. Form a circle holding hands and chant "I invoke those Goddesses of all beginnings Ea, Astare, Ishtar, Lilith. Come and witness our rites in the name of the righteousness for wimmin! Let there be a new beginning for the ERA—a beginning with victory." No less bizarre was a NOW-ERA fundraiser in Wheaton, Illinois, which offered for auction a voodoo doll in the image of Phyllis Schlafly, "complete with pins." Jan Seblick, local president of the NOW chapter, upon purchasing the doll, told the *Chicago Tribune* that she would "be glad to loan it to any interested person."[29]

Only a few ERA supporters, it seemed, were able to offer detached assessments of Schlafly's abilities in light of the defeat of ERA. One of the more insightful strategies to counter Schlafly's skill on the debate platform appeared in a small four-page handout produced by graduate students in Speech Communications at Indiana University. The booklet declared, "To counteract her power and success, certain steps must be taken. . . . Don't sound antagonistic or hostile. . . . Realize that disruptive audience behavior works for her rather than against her. She is cool under attack; she's good at it. . . . Don't ask her to justify herself (e.g., Why is she on the road when she 'belongs' at home?). She knows all the answers."[30] Elaine Kindall, writing a review of Carol Felsenthal's recent biography of Schlafly, *The Sweetheart of the Silent Majority* (1979), echoed a similar assessment of the nemesis of feminism, when she observed, "The Schlafly Fog Machine—or charm—turns everything it touches into putty. Once the fog machine has done its work, you can caulk windows with your objectivity." She added that Schlafly was "exemplary. She's ingratiating, intelligent, uncorrupted, energetic, determined, magnificently organized—conservatives tend to be gently bred, well mannered, splendidly educated, and perfectly groomed."[31] Kindall was critical of Schlafly and her anti-ERA followers, but she contrasted their image with the image that had been projected by the pro-ERA side.

With ERA approaching its demise, the Reagan administration sought to repair some of the political damage the ERA defeat had caused among women voters. The administration understood that while ERA had been pushed by feminists, many supporters of ERA were average American women who simply wanted the equality of women recognized in the Constitution. Although Reagan had won a landslide election against Carter in 1980, Republican strategists understood that some of this vote had been simply anti-Carter. As a consequence, the Reagan White House continued to reach out to diverse constituencies to bring them into the fold. Task forces were established on African-American, Hispanic, Roman Catholic, evangelical Protestant, and gay voters. Given the gender gap—in which single women overwhelmingly voted Democratic—women were a special concern for the administration.

During the presidential campaign, Reagan spoke against the Equal Rights Amendment, thereby reversing his earlier support for ERA.[32] By 1980 he was opposed to the ERA because he feared how the courts might interpret the amendment, but declared that he was dedicated to eliminating discrimination against women. He also promised to appoint a woman to the Supreme Court. Having won election, the Republican administration began to consider specific measures to fulfill campaign promises to eliminate gender discrimination in the federal government. Some discussion arose about resurrecting a modified equal rights amendment that would exempt women from military conscription. Proposed by Barbara Honegger, a special assistant to presidential adviser Martin Anderson, a call for resurrecting the ERA was tone-deaf politically. Fearing the occurrence of such a proposal, Phyllis Schlafly fired a strongly worded memorandum to her political friends that quickly made its way to the White House. She wrote that "it would be politically irresponsible to give a dead issue an artificial life . . . to the detriment of real issues and real problems."[33]

Instead, Reagan announced that Judy Peachee would serve as a White House special assistant with the responsibility of launching a Fifty States Project "to ferret out any remaining discriminatory laws at the state level." He also established through an executive order the Task Force on Legal Equity for Women to ensure that current and future federal regulations did not discriminate against women. The panel included senior officials from federal departments and agencies.[34] Prior to the announcement of the panel, Phyllis Schlafly had telephoned Elizabeth Dole, White House Assistant for Public Liaison, to voice her opposition to the panel, but emphasizing that if it went forward, the pro-family movement wanted input on appointments. Schlafly also lobbied Wendy Borcherdt and Morton Blackwell to ensure that the panel stayed on course.[35]

Schlafly opposed a review of all federal laws, arguing that feminists such as Ruth Bader Ginsburg, later appointed to the Supreme Court by Bill Clinton, sought to accomplish what ERA had failed to do by changing all federal laws to make them gender-neutral. She specifically attacked a study written by Ruth Bader Ginsburg and Brenda Feigen-Fasteau, *Sex Bias in the U.S. Code: A Report of the U.S. Commission on Civil Rights* (April 1977). She maintained that *Sex Bias in the U.S.*

Code proved that "the social and political goals of the ERA are radical, irrational, and unacceptable to Americans." She undertook a detailed critique of the book on employment policy, women in the military, family, moral standards, education, social security, and language. She quoted the report as arguing for "a comprehensive program of government-supported child care"; lowering the age of sexual consent for females by finding "a person is guilty of an offense if he engages in a sexual act with another person, not his spouse, and . . . the other person is, in fact, less than 12 years old"; and legalizing prostitution because "prostitution, as a consensual act between adults, is arguably within the zone of privacy protected by women." Schlafly also pointed out that *Sex Bias* called for the sex integration of the Boy Scouts and Girl Scouts. About 750 out of the 800 changes in the federal laws demanded by the book had to do with specific language changes. She said that out of the 800 laws allegedly discriminating against women, only about a half dozen changes were worthwhile. She stated in a letter to presidential assistant Elizabeth Dole that "Our policy should be to eliminate discrimination *against* women and to achieve *equity* for women without sacrificing *traditional* women's rights."[36]

The time extension for ERA expired on June 30, 1982. That evening, Schlafly hosted a celebratory dinner in Washington, "The Rainbow Dinner." Proponents made an effort to reintroduce ERA into Congress in January 1983. After the House Judiciary Committee showed support for nine amendments to ERA, Speaker of the House Tip O'Neill (D-Massachusetts) called for a suspension of the rules that barred a floor vote on any amendments. In a dramatic roll call on November 15, 1983, ERA lost by a six-vote margin. Politically, ERA was dead.

The battle over culture appeared to have just begun, however, and this was evident in the politics of abortion, which had become closely tied to the anti-ERA campaign. The anti-abortion vote had been important in carrying Reagan into the White House. Reagan's stance against abortion was more than political calculation. By appointing anti-abortion advocates into his administration, he assured that abortion would be placed on the policy agenda. By supporting even a limited anti-abortion agenda, Reagan and his staff knew that this carried political costs, especially among single women. Reagan strategists noted the "gender gap" among unmarried women in the 1980 returns, but the Reagan administration pursued a limited program of restricting government involvement in family planning whenever possible. This also entailed supporting pro-life appointments.[37] Under Otis R. Bowen, who became head of Health and Human Services in 1985, the agency placed a ban on federal funding of organizations that performed or counseled abortion; this administrative fiat became known as the "gag rule" and led pro-abortion and feminist activists to accuse Reagan of waging war on women.[38] Reagan believed he was making pro-life appointments to the Supreme Court.[39] He shared the conservative belief that the federal courts had become too activist and by doing so had undermined the separation of powers between the legislative and the judicial functions. Nevertheless, Reagan's record of appointments on the Supreme Court proved mixed from the point of view of the anti-abortion wing of his party. Reagan's first nominee to the Supreme Court, Sandra Day O'Connor, in 1981 drew immediate opposition from anti-abortion groups because of her earlier support of a family planning bill in Arizona that would have replaced an existing state law banning abortions.[40]

The anger that the O'Connor nomination elicited led White House official Morton Blackwell, serving as the liaison with the conservative movement, to meet with Paul Weyrich, Connie Marshner, and Dick Dingman, as well as fifty other leaders of the conservative and pro-family organizations, including representatives of Schlafly's Eagle Forum. Following the meeting, Blackwell informed the White House that these leaders opposed O'Connor's nomination and that there was a growing concern among these groups that the President and his senior advisors "don't think this coalition contributed significantly to his election."[41] Reagan immediately sought to prevent a brushfire in the ranks of social conservatives by sending a widely circulated response to the number of letters that came into the White House opposing the O'Connor nomination.[42] O'Connor easily won appointment to the court as its first female justice. As a justice, O'Connor shifted the legal foundation for regulating abortion away from the trimester approach of *Roe* to the doctrine of "undue burden."[43] In his second term, the Reagan administration continued to maintain its anti-abortion policies, although a Democratic-controlled Congress restrained Reagan initiatives.[44]

While continuing to denounce the ERA as a pro-abortion measure, Schlafly did not become directly involved in the abortion policy debate. Instead, she continued to focus on ERA and wrote extensively on national defense and education issues through her *Phyllis Schlafly Report*, which reached a high mark of nearly 40,000 subscribers.[45] In 1992, however, when Mary Dent Crisp (who had supported third-party presidential candidate John Anderson in 1980) started an effort to delete the GOP's pro-life platform plank at the Republican National Convention, Schlafly organized the Republican National Coalition for Life to support the party's anti-abortion position.[46] In the meantime, Schlafly proved to be a strong supporter of Reagan's domestic program to cut taxes and his program to strengthen the nation's military capability. Other social conservatives, however, were less sanguine about Reagan's policies. Indeed, early in Reagan's presidency, Richard Viguerie and his *Conservative Digest* publicly attacked Reagan for backing away from conservative principles, leading Reagan to privately write John Lofton, editor of the *Digest*, "I believe that the July *Conservative Digest* is one of the most dishonest and unfair bits of journalism I have ever seen."[47]

Schlafly Defends the Constitution against Conservatives

Other divisions between religious conservatives and economic conservatives emerged in the Reagan administration, and the Republican Right was divided over tactics as well. Most significant was the call to enact a Balanced Budget Amendment by calling for a federal constitutional convention, popularly known at the time as "Con Con." Under the leadership of conservative activist Lewis Uhler, twenty-six states had passed resolutions calling for a constitutional convention. Uhler had served as chairman of the California Tax Reduction Task Force under Governor Ronald Reagan in 1972, before he organized the grassroots National Tax Limitation Committee. By 1982, the movement to call a constitutional convention was only two states short of the thirty-four states specified in Article V as the trigger for a convention. Initially financed through his own funds, Uhler's organization grew into a multimillion dollar organization, claiming tens of thousands of members, and had become a national crusade supported by most conservatives—with a notable exception, Phyllis Schlafly.[48] She stepped forward to oppose the Con Con movement, much to the surprise and chagrin of conservatives who had endorsed the Balanced Budget Amendment.

Writing in the *Phyllis Schlafly Report* in December 1984, she attacked Con Con as playing Russian roulette with the U.S. Constitution. Given her opposition to the Equal Rights Amendment, her opposition to the Con Con appeared consistent, and her argument against Con Con drew upon a similar theme of the potential for damaging unintended consequences if a convention were held. She observed that a balanced budget was may be "a desirable thing," but she warned that the call for a constitutional convention was no guarantee that the Balanced Budget Amendment would be passed. Instead, she feared that liberals would take over a constitutional convention to press their own agenda such as repealing the Second Amendment. She pointed specifically to the Committee on the Constitutional System, chaired by C. Douglas Dillon, former Secretary of the Treasury under John F. Kennedy, and Lloyd N. Cutler, former counsel to President Jimmy Carter. This group had met at a conference held at the Woodrow Wilson Center in Washington, D.C., in 1983 to discuss their goals, including elimination of the Electoral College, the two-thirds requirement for ratification of treaties, and the Twenty-Second Amendment; allowing the President to dissolve Congress for new elections; publicly funding political campaigns; and increasing the terms of U.S. House members from two to four years. Such an agenda, she wrote, "could put our entire Constitution on the bargaining table to be torn apart by the media, political factions, and special interest groups." She concluded that "the intemperate language and *ad hominem* attacks against anyone who opposes Con Con are offensive to fair-minded people."[49]

Schlafly organized against the call for a constitutional convention by using many of the tactics of the Stop ERA campaign. Employing the slogan, "Can the Con Con," and using a Campbell Soup-like logo, Schlafly targeted the four remaining states that were to vote on the call for a constitutional amendment—New Jersey, Kentucky, Michigan, and Montana. In the course of the next couple years, Schlafly testified in state legislatures in Trenton, Lexington, Lansing, and Helena. Appearing before the Montana Senate in March 16, 1987, she maintained, "Even assuming that a Balanced Budget Amendment is a good end, it does *not* justify plunging our nation into the constitutional chaos, confusion, and controversy of an unprecedented Constitutional Convention."[50] In Michigan, former Stop ERA activist Elaine Donnelly headed efforts that thwarted the Con Con resolution in the state legislature.[51] At the same time, Schlafly's articles against the call for a constitutional convention appeared in conservative publications such as *Daughters of the American Revolution Magazine*, *The New American*, and her syndicated newspaper column warning about the unintended consequences of Con Con. Much like her anti-ERA campaign, Schlafly's articles were reprinted by local groups and sent out in mass-mailings to targeted conservatives. State leaders of the DAR and the Sons of the American Revolution in Kentucky mailed 5,000 reprints of Schlafly's "Con Con: A Threat to the U.S. Constitution" to Michigan members shortly before the vote by the state legislature.[52] Her debate with Congressman Larry Craig (R-Idaho) held in Washington, D.C., in 1985 was republished and circulated in conservative circles, as was her address to the American Bar Association's Section on Individual Rights and Responsibilities during the ABA's 1987 Annual Convention in San Francisco. Schlafly produced one of her most effective anti–Con Con pieces when she convinced former Chief Justice Warren Burger to write a one-page letter opposing a constitutional convention.[53] Burger had left the Supreme Court to allow Reagan to appoint William Rehnquist as the new Chief Justice and Antonin Scalia, another conservative, to replace Rehnquist. Reagan appointed Burger chairman of the Presidential Commission on the Bicentennial of the U.S. Constitution, on which Schlafly also served as a Reagan-appointee from 1985–91.

Schlafly's campaign against Con Con replicated the Stop ERA campaign with one notable exception—her opponents this time were mostly conservatives. In organizing against Con Con, Schlafly's Eagle Forum members formed a grassroots coalition that included liberal groups such as the American Civil Liberties Union, Common Cause, the National Education Association, the National Association for the Advancement of Colored People, Americans United for Separation of Church and State, People for the American Way, the AFL-CIO, as well as Republicans such as Senator Nancy Kassebaum (R-Kansas) and U.S. Representative Jack Kemp (R-New York).[54] On the other hand, prominent Republicans such as Senator Robert Dole (R-Kansas) and most conservative organizations favored Con Con. Schlafly's opposition to having a Balanced Budget Amendment enacted through a constitutional convention outraged many on the GOP Right, including Dennis DeConcini (R-Arizona), Phil Gramm (R-Texas), and the Reagan White House.[55] Lewis Uhler, director of the National Tax Limitation Committee, accused Schlafly of spreading "widespread misinformation and misunderstanding" about Con Con.[56]

The defeat of convention resolutions in New Jersey, Kentucky, Michigan, and Montana killed the Con Con by 1988, much to the consternation of fiscal conservatives who largely blamed Schlafly for the defeat.[57] They were correct; not a single state passed a Con Con resolution after Schlafly entered the battle.

STRENGTHENING GRASSROOTS CONSERVATISM

Phyllis Schlafly joined with Representative Henry Hyde (R-Illinois) in 1984 as the Illinois delegates on the Republican Platform Committee to place a stronger pro-life plank in the National Platform. The platform in 1980 had moved the party to the Right on this issue by calling for "a constitutional amendment to restore protection of the right to life for unborn children." The 1984 abortion plank called for specific action: "The unborn child has a fundamental individual right to life which cannot be infringed. We therefore reaffirm our support for a human life amendment to the Constitution, and we endorse legislation to make clear that the Fourteenth Amendment's protections apply to unborn children." The plank also affirmed the party's opposition to publicly funded abortion and the elimination of funding for organizations that advocate or support abortion, e.g., Planned Parenthood. Such language gained the overwhelming support of a convention with an unusually high percentage of delegates who identified themselves as evangelical Christians.[58]

The growing strength of the religious Right in the GOP was further indicated by the strong moral language found in the party platform in 1984. The platform denounced "Washington's governing elite" for trying to "build a brave new world by assaulting our basic values. . . . They attacked the integrity of the family and parental rights. They ignored traditional morality. And they still do." Attacks on Washington's liberal elite were not new in Republican party platforms—such language dated back to at least the 1948 convention. What was new was the emphatic language defending the family and traditional values in schools. The 1984 platform also called attention to the physical and sexual abuse of children and spouses, which was attributed in part to "gratuitous sex and violence in the entertainment media" and the pornography industry. The platform called for the "vigorous" enforcement of "constitutional laws to control obscene materials which degrade everyone, particularly women, and depict the exploitation of children." Reagan was applauded in the platform for creating a commission on pornography, which had led to new child pornography legislation.[59]

The platform also called for the enforcement of the Protection of Pupil Rights Amendment (PPRA) that "prohibited requiring any pupil to reveal personal or family information as part of any federally supported program, test, treatment, or psychological examination unless the school obtains written consent of the pupil's parents."[60] Schlafly had supported this legislation because she believed that government and school officials were infringing on the privacy rights of parents to teach their own moral values to their children. The Pupil Rights Amendment had been passed by Congress in 1978, but the U.S. Department of Education did not enforce it. Eagle Forum and other conservative pro-family organizations began pressuring the Department of Education in the Reagan administration to issue regulations enforcing the amendment. Schlafly's involvement in the Pupil Rights Amendment combined her belief in parental rights and her distrust of federal involvement in public education programs. Schlafly's persistent demand for PPRA enforcement resulted in the Department of Education regulations posted in the *Federal Register* on February 22, 1984, with public hearings held in Seattle, Pittsburgh, Kansas City, Phoenix, Concord, Orlando, and Washington, D.C., March 13–27, 1984. At these hearings, hundreds of parents, teachers, and conservative activists turned up to testify about alleged violations of parents' and pupils' rights in the classroom by federally funded guidance and counseling programs, sex-education classes, social studies courses, inappropriate questions about relations with parents and siblings, and personal family and individual behavior about sex, drugs, and suicide. The National Education Association (NEA) vigorously opposed the Pupil Rights Amendment and its 1984 Department of Education regulations. More than 1,300 pages of testimony were collected at the hearings, but the NEA did not testify at any of them.

When the Department of Education refused to publish the hearings, Schlafly received a copy of the transcript of the hearings from a supporter in the Department of Education. On August 13, 1984, Schlafly published *Child Abuse in the Classroom*, a 434- page book that excerpted verbatim testimony from the hearings. Endorsed by conservative Thomas Sowell and Ronald Reagan, *Child Abuse in the Classroom* sold over a quarter-million copies.[61] Shortly after publication of the book, the Department of Education issued strong regulations that protected students from "psychiatric or psychological examination or tests pertaining to attitudes, habits, traits, opinions, beliefs or feelings," or "psychiatric or psychological treatment" that was "designed to affect behavioral, emotional, or attitudinal characteristics of an individual or group," without prior written parental consent.[62] The Eagle Forum took much of the credit for this victory, which encouraged local and state members to continue their involvement in education curricula and parent rights issues.

By the early 1980s, the Eagle Forum operated on local, state, and national levels through a membership that reached about 50,000 members by the end of the ratification period for ERA.[63] In 1981, Schlafly established the Eagle Forum Education & Legal Defense Fund, a tax-exempt 501(c) (3) organization, to serve as a research and education affiliate of the Eagle Forum. Prior to Reagan's coming into office, the National Organization for Women had gained tax-exempt status for its Education and Legal Defense Fund, so Schlafly decided to establish her own tax-exempt organization. With Republicans in the White House, she began to consider opening an Eagle Forum office in the District of Columbia. Surprisingly, for one of the few times in their thirty-two-year marriage, Fred Schlafly took serious issue with his wife's plans to open an office in the nation's capital because he worried that Phyllis might spend too much time away from home, but in the end he agreed that Eagle Forum needed a presence in Washington, D.C. In the spring of 1981, the 56-year-old Phyllis Schlafly opened a Washington office, consisting of four barely furnished rooms on Capitol Hill. She announced that Noreen Barr would serve as her legislative aide in Washington and that she would support the Reagan economic agenda.[64] Further expansion of Eagle Forum came in 1993 when Phyllis Schlafly purchased an elegant two-story brick building in the upscale St. Louis suburb and county seat of Clayton, Missouri. The building houses the national offices of Eagle Forum Education & Legal Defense Fund, as well as the Cardinal Mindszenty Foundation that continued to operate under her sister-in-law Eleanor Schlafly. In 1994, following the death of her husband Fred Schlafly from a degenerative disease, Phyllis Schlafly moved from Alton to the affluent St. Louis suburb of Ladue.

By 2003, the Eagle Forum and the Eagle Forum Education & Legal Defense Fund had combined total revenues of $2,382,000 and net assets of $15,085,000. Both the Eagle Forum and the Eagle Forum Education & Legal Defense Fund operate from private contributions.[65] Schlafly also established Eagle Forum PAC to provide financial contributions to political candidates representing pro-family values. When it started it was the only political action committee among pro-family organizations. From an office in Alton, Illinois, the monthly *Phyllis Schlafly Report* (published continuously from 1967) is produced and distributed, along with the monthly *Education Reporter*, education videos and materials such as her reading instruction books for young children, *First Reader* and *Turbo Reader*.

Schlafly maintains organizational stability through a centralized managerial structure in which she provides strategic direction to Eagle Forum members, while state and local chapters undertake their own projects. Local and state chapters vary in strength and grassroots participation. For example, the Texas Eagle Forum has active chapters throughout the state, while other state chapters tended to be dominated by a few activist leaders who rely on rallying a loosely tied grassroots network to specific political causes. Eagle members gather for annual Eagle Leadership Conferences that alternate meeting in St. Louis and Washington, D.C. Many of the leaders of Eagle Forum are involved in Republican politics in their states, serving as state and national committee members and as delegates to state and national Republican conventions. In these positions they support Republican candidates who are moral and fiscal conservatives. The Eagle Forum maintains strong ideological positions, often to the Right of the regular Republican party. In doing so, the Eagle Forum seeks to keep the party on a conservative path on issues such as national defense, education, health care, abortion, feminism, and immigration.

Journalists and scholars of the Right in America often describe Eagle Forum as part of the Christian Right, but in fact the pro-family movement, the pro-life movement, and the Christian Right represent various strains of moral conservatism. Each of these groupings is composed of different organizations, loosely affiliated by an ideological concern to protect what they consider the traditional moral and religious foundations of the American Republic. In the 1980s, hundreds of organizations emerged around a plethora of specific issues, including school choice, school prayer, opposition to the feminist and homosexual agenda, antipornography, anti-abortion, sex education, and public school curricula. While these groups often join in a campaign around specific legislation, they differ in their loyalty to the Republican party and support of GOP candidates. For example, Pat Robertson's Christian Coalition, established in 1989 and claiming more than 2 million members by 1997, became closely tied to the Republican party. Indeed, its support of Republican candidates led the IRS to reject its application for tax-exempt status.

Concerned Women for America (CWA), founded in 1979 by Beverly LaHaye during the ERA battle, shares similar policy concerns with the Eagle Forum, but is strongly evangelical Protestant in its orientation. The CWA organizes prayer circles for its 600,000 members, while calling them to become involved in social issues including opposition to humanism in public schools, support of the Contras in Nicaragua in the mid-1980s, and opposition to the United Nations, abortion, and homosexuality. Through its monthly publication, *Family Voice*, the CWA attacks abortion, calls for abstinence/sex education, denounces special rights for homosexuals, and is involved in local curricula issues. Although LaHaye stepped down as president of CWA in 2001, the organization continues its energetic involvement in pro-family issues. Dr. James Dobson organized Focus on the Family shortly after the International Women's Year Conference in Houston in 1977 to "teach the scriptural principles of marriage and parenthood and to help preserve and strengthen families." Dobson also organized the Family Research Council in 1980 as a pro-family research center. Under Gary Bauer, a former policy adviser in the Reagan administration, the Family Research Council became the premier pro-family research organization in Washington, D.C. In 1992, the Family Research Council severed its ties with Focus on the Family to become legally independent.

HOW THE REPUBLICAN REVOLUTION SPUTTERED
AND THEN TRIUMPHED

Whatever difficulties Reagan experienced with anti-abortion activists and evangelical Protestants, he left office a hero of conservatives. Reagan has become the standard under which all other conservatives are to be judged.[66] It was the dramatic end of the Cold War, "without firing a shot," as Lady Margaret Thatcher later said, that solidified Reagan's status as a permanent hero of the conservatives. The grassroots who had worked for so many years to alert Americans about the dangers of, first, communist infiltration into the U.S. government, and then to the awesome danger of the Soviet nuclear missile force, had hardly dared to believe that the Soviet threat would disappear in their lifetime. They saw in Reagan the leader who would pursue an aggressive strategy against the Soviet arms buildup. Schlafly saw Reagan's televised speech about the Soviet military threat on March 23, 1983, as finally explaining to the nation what she and the late Admiral Ward had been saying for years. She supported Reagan's call for a missile defense system through the Strategic Defense Initiative, which Senator Edward Kennedy promptly ridiculed as Star Wars. Although Ward had passed away in

1977, Schlafly continued to write on defense issues in her monthly newsletter.[67] She threw her full energies into battling the nuclear freeze movement of 1982, and she made it a personal mission to refute the U.S. Catholic Bishops' call for a nuclear freeze in their pastoral letter on nuclear war.[68]

When Reagan scheduled a summit with Mikhail Gorbachev in Geneva in the fall of 1985, actress Jane Alexander and feminist Bella Abzug announced they would go to Geneva to demand that Reagan abandon SDI. Schlafly responded by organizing a counter-demonstration through forming an ad hoc Coalition of Women for a Real Defense. She led a delegation of forty (mostly women) heads of organizations from America and Europe to appear in Geneva in support of Reagan.[69] On November 17, 1985, they staged an American-style demonstration with pro-SDI signs and SDI balloons. The next day a crowded news conference was held at the Geneva Hilton Hotel. Later, Reagan personally telephoned Schlafly to thank her for her expedition.

Under Reagan, a seismic shift in American politics had occurred by the transformation of the Republican party into a party of conservatism. The Democrats were on the defensive on national security and social issues. As the 1988 presidential election approached, Democrats sought to regain ground on the social issues. In the summer of 1987, the *New York Times* announced that the Democratic left had decided to "fight for custody of the 'family issue.'" Noting households headed by unmarried women were now common, liberals claimed that conservatives were projecting a "Leave It to Beaver" (a 1950s television program) model on the family. Marian Wright Edelman, head of the advocacy group the Children's Defense Fund, declared "There is a new recognition that someone has to do something about families and soup kitchens, and the homeless . . . Government clearly has a role." Asked for a response, Schlafly replied, "Liberal policies all require government to take over the functions of the family and reduce family rights."[70]

Social conservatives such as Schlafly were suspicious of George H. W. Bush's position on conservative issues and were reluctant to endorse him as the rightful heir of the Reagan presidency, even though he had served eight years as Reagan's Vice President. Bush claimed to have changed his views on abortion, federal family planning, and world population control, but as a Republican Congressman from Texas he had played a leading role in pushing this agenda in the House. Conservative

Representative Vin Weber (R-Minnesota) told the *Wall Street Journal*, "Bush does like us and his people don't like us."[71] Schlafly and other conservatives came out for Jack Kemp (R-New York) in the 1988 primaries, but his race for the presidency faltered, as a journalist noted, under the weight of his "ego, slack-self discipline, and his logorrheic way with words."[72] Schlafly and other conservatives had switched their support to Bush before the Republican convention in New Orleans. Still, relations between Bush and the Republican Right were never warm. Behind closed doors Bush adviser James Baker referred to these people as "the full-moon bayers of the Republican Right."[73] Tensions between social conservatives and the Bush campaign remained evident in a series of meetings the Bush campaign held with conservative women's groups, including representatives of the Eagle Forum, in the summer of 1988. Caroline More, representing Eagle Forum, alerted Schlafly that the Bush campaign appeared to be pushing federal day care. She also reported that Bush staffer Lindsay Johnson had declared at one meeting that Bush favored a pro-life amendment, outlawing abortion "with the exception of rape, incest, or illness of the mother." When anti-abortion activist Mary Powell attempted to correct her by saying she meant "life of the mother," another Bush staffer replied, "No, now it's illness. . . . that has been changed." Johnson added, "Since it's not a clean-cut issue, it doesn't pick up anybody . . . so we won't discuss it within any coalition. . . . We want a broad base and we don't want to lose anybody."[74] Discussions such as this tempered grassroots conservatives' enthusiasm for Bush.

Whatever reservations Schlafly may have had about Bush, she played a critical, behind-the-scenes role in mobilizing support for his election in 1988. Her involvement came through what became a benchmark of the campaign—the issue of an African-American named Willie Horton, who had been convicted of first-degree murder for the brutal slaying of a seventeen-year-old gas-station employee during an armed robbery on the night of October 26, 1974, in Lawrence, Massachusetts. Horton was sentenced to life in prison, but under a program established under Republican Governor Francis W. Sargent, Horton was given an unguarded 48-hour furlough from prison on June 6, 1986. He did not return. Instead on April 3, 1987, he broke into the home of Clifford Barnes, a 28 year-old, in Oxon Hill, Maryland. For the next seven hours Horton tortured Barnes, and when Barnes' fiancée, Angela Miller, returned home from a wedding party, Horton attacked her, raping her twice over a four-hour period. Horton was arrested and returned to prison. Massachusetts governor Michael Dukakis came under immediate criticism for allowing the program to furlough prisoners convicted of murder. In 1986, he had pocket-vetoed a bill to ban furloughs for first-degree murderers, declaring that it would "cut the heart out of efforts of inmate rehabilitation."

Following the Horton crime, legislation was introduced to ban furloughs for first-degree murderers, but the bill was stalled in committee by legislative allies of Governor Dukakis. In the face of growing opposition, Governor Dukakis made modest revisions in the program, but this failed to stop a referendum being placed on the ballot in November 1987. Two reporters for the Lawrence *Eagle-Tribune* began an investigation of the furlough system; their nearly 200 articles later won the Pulitzer Prize. Under immense public pressure, Dukakis capitulated and agreed to legislation banning furloughs for convicted murderers.

During the New York Democratic party primary, presidential hopeful Senator Albert Gore, Jr. (D-Tennessee) raised the Willie Horton case in an effort to prevent Dukakis from winning the nomination. Bush strategists quickly picked up the issue. In mid-June at the Illinois Republican convention, Bush charged Dukakis with allowing first-degree murderers out on weekend passes, even after one of them had brutally raped a woman and stabbed her husband. In July, when Bush strategist Lee Atwater overheard black women at a local restaurant in Luray, Virginia, talking about an article on Willie Horton they had just read in *Reader's Digest*, he knew that Bush had an issue that could be used against Dukakis. (The black women had not mentioned that Horton was black, but the entire restaurant had gotten angrily involved in a discussion on how criminals were being let loose to commit crimes on innocent citizens.)[75]

Reading the same article, Phyllis Schlafly decided to bring this issue to the grassroots. She had seen a video that had been crucial in removing Justice Rose Bird from the California Supreme Court. She thought this same technique could be used against Dukakis. In July she commissioned a 28-minute video to be made based on the *Reader's Digest* article. Costing approximately $44,000 to make and selling at $19.95, *Justice on Furlough* gained the support of Congressman Newt Gingrich (R-Georgia) and conservative Grover Norquist.[76] In announcing the video for sale, Schlafly described the video as "not political. No political candidate is mentioned. It is a straight documentary, depicting the facts of what occurred in the state of Massachusetts under Governor Dukakis." The video presented interviews with the Maryland victims of escaped killer Willie Horton, as well as interviews with the victims of violent crimes and their repeated attempts to get Governor Dukakis to revoke the furlough program. The video shows, Schlafly said, "how Dukakis was more compassionate toward murderers and rapists than to their victims."[77]

The video gained wide circulation with the grassroots Right. Representative Newt Gingrich (R-Georgia) promoted the video in his "special orders" speeches at the end of House sessions broadcast live on C-Span, and gave the telephone number in Alton to order the tape.[78] In September, the Republican National Committee placed a large order for the video and offered it for sale. A letter from the chairman of the Republican National Committee urged the video to be shown to "every editorial board in your district," to "rallies, fundraisers, and coffees," and to college and teenage Republican meetings. Republican congressional candidates were urged to purchase the tape and show it at their events. The video drew the attention of USA Today, which quoted Schlafly as saying that the film showed how innocent victims become "just acceptable losses in a liberal social program."[79] By the end of the campaign, sales of the video reached the $100,000 mark.[80]

In October, the Bush campaign released a thirty-second television ad, "Weekend Passes," that targeted the Dukakis furlough program. Placed on the defensive, the Dukakis campaign responded poorly to the issue. His campaign manager claimed that the Massachusetts prison furlough program was only one of forty other such programs found in other states. She failed to note that Massachusetts was unique in that it was the only one that did not ban convicted murderers from participating in its program. Jesse Jackson, who had made a bid for the nomination, attacked the campaign ad as racist, "designed to create the most horrible psychosexual fears." Atwater responded, "Race has nothing to do with the issue. I would condemn in any way, shape or form the issues used in this way," he told the Washington Post. Columnist Charles Krauthammer quoted Representative Richard Gephardt (D-Missouri) saying about the Bush campaign, "Hitler would have loved these people." Krauthammer pointed out that the liberals' attack on Robert Bork's nomination to the Supreme Court a year earlier had "far clearer racial code words than 'furlough' could ever hope to be." He pointed to a powerful television ad that showed actor Gregory Peck implying that

Bork favored poll taxes and literacy tests.[81] Clearly, Republicans saw the Horton issue as crime, while Democrats saw the issue as race. The public controversy about the Willie Horton issue was concentrated exclusively on two television ads; the critics never discovered Schlafly's powerful *Justice on Furlough* video, which was distributed under campaign radar. In the short run, Dukakis's inability to deal with these issues allowed the Bush campaign to paint him as a fuzzy-minded, indecisive liberal. Bush easily won the election in November.

The Bush administration left conservatives frustrated. Bush supported the Clean Air Act Amendments of 1989 and the Americans with Disabilities Act in 1990. When Bush agreed to tax hikes in the 1990 budget (repudiating his "read my lips" campaign promise), the rupture appeared complete. Bush's appointment of Clarence Thomas to the Supreme Court regained the support of conservatives. Yet, shell-shocked by the hostile media reception of Patrick Buchanan's speech at the Republican Convention in Houston in which he declared America was in a culture war, the 1992 Bush campaign stayed away from social issues, unlike his campaign four years earlier. This allowed his Democratic opponent, Bill Clinton, to keep the presidential race focused on economic issues. It cost Bush the election, even though the economy was in recovery.

The first two years of Clinton's administration aided the conservative movement in unexpected ways. Clinton's ill-fated plan for national health insurance frightened Republicans and independents alike. It also energized southern Republicans and conservative activists, such as Schlafly, to set the stage for the approaching midterm elections. When the first leaks about Clinton's health care plan appeared, Schlafly warned that "Hillary's Health Care proposals, if enacted, meant poorer service, longer waits, tighter controls, and higher taxes," and the Eagle Forum mobilized to defeat it. When it was officially released in the fall of 1993, Schlafly charged that it meant the rationing of health care, offering "a financial windfall to big business and pushing small business to the edge of bankruptcy. It is a plan to dump onto the taxpayers the financial burden of big corporations' mistakes in making unrealistic commitments for generous health benefits to retirees." She called for Republicans to fall in line to support a proposal by U.S. Senator Phil Gramm (R-Texas) to establish individual medical savings accounts combined with catastrophic health insurance. Using the populist rhetoric of the Republican Right, she asserted, "The contrast between these two plans provides conclusive proof that the Democratic Party does the bidding of Big Business, while the Republican Party is the friend of small business, entrepreneurs, workers, and taxpayers."[82] Schlafly repeatedly called for the establishment of medical savings accounts, maintaining that such accounts, owned by individuals, were a necessary step toward solving all problems connected with health care: "portability, affordability, preserving your right to choose your own doctor, pre-existing conditions, job lock, uninsured Americans, co-payments, paperwork, long-term care, Medicare going bankrupt, and even the decline in real wages."[83] Congress finally passed a plan with health savings accounts in 2004.

In the 1994 midterm elections, Republicans seized on the perceived dangers of the Clinton health care plan, the effects of the 1990 reapportionment, the unusually large number of Democratic retirements in 1992–94, the recruitment of excellent Republican candidates, and the Gingrich-inspired legislative covenant with the voters, "Contract with America." The strategy paid off: Republicans captured both houses of Congress with a 230–204 majority in the House and eight new Senate seats. More importantly, voters who called themselves conservative constituted a larger share of the electorate than in 1992, and they were voting Republican. The new Republican majority initiated bills concerning crime, congressional term limits, welfare reform, the federal budget, social security, defense, illegal drugs, and taxation. In a well-orchestrated counterattack coordinated from the Clinton White House, Social Security and Medicare became flash points in the battle over the national budget for fiscal 1996.

The resilience of the Clinton administration to withstand Republican attacks deepened fissures within the Republican party, now out of the White House for the first time in twelve years. These divisions were not simply over principle versus pragmatism, social conservatives versus economic conservatives, or even conservatives versus moderates within the GOP. In 1996 these differences were personified in two candidates who sought the GOP nomination: long-time party loyalist Senator Robert Dole (Kansas) and Patrick Buchanan. Buchanan represented an Old Right sentiment that had lain dormant in the party since the end of the Second World War. He articulated a program of a nationalist foreign policy, protection of American jobs, immigration restriction, and an unqualified social conservatism on cultural issues. Schlafly won election as a Buchanan delegate from Missouri to the national convention. Buchanan won the New Hampshire primary, but his campaign sputtered in South Carolina, where Pat Robertson mobilized his Christian base in the state to vote for Dole.

When the Republican convention convened in San Diego in 1996, Dole had enough votes for the nomination. Anxious to project himself as "mainstream," Dole kept a tight rein on the convention, making sure that Buchanan delegates were not given an opportunity to demonstrate for their candidate. Only Dole or Dole-Kemp signs were allowed on the floor and the aisles were blocked to avoid spontaneous demonstrations. Buchanan's name was prevented from being placed into nomination. Behind the scenes, heated negotiations took place between the anti-abortion wing of the party, represented by Phyllis Schlafly, and the Dole campaign staff. After having announced to the press that he had not read the platform and was not bound by it anyway, Dole personally insisted on a "tolerance" statement in the party platform that welcomed a diversity of views in the party. Schlafly and others saw this plank as a way for Dole to back away from the strong anti-abortion plank of the party. Schlafly helped keep the strong pro-life plank in the party platform unchanged.[84] In November Clinton was reelected with a little less than 50 percent of the vote, while his Republican opponent, Senate Majority Leader Robert Dole, received only 42 percent of the vote, and Reform party candidate Ross Perot garnered 8 percent of the vote.

In the presidential election of 2000, the conservative wing of the party rallied around George W. Bush. All factions of the party rallied behind Bush, who declared himself a "compassionate conservative." While differences in the GOP were buried, the presidential election of 2000 intensified further partisanship when Al Gore demanded a recount in Florida after Bush appeared the winner by only a few hundred votes. The Florida State Supreme Court ordered a recount, after which a divided U.S. Supreme Court confirmed Bush the winner. Although Bush called for an end to partisanship, neither Democrats nor Republicans were in the mood to settle their differences. The terrorist attacks on the New York World Trade Center and the Pentagon in Washington, D.C., on September 11, 2001, briefly modulated partisan rhetoric, but Bush's war on terrorism—including military interventions in Afghanistan and Iraq, as well as antiterrorist legislation such as the Patriot Act—quickly reignited partisan fires between Democrats and Republicans and within the Republican party itself.

PHYLLIS SCHLAFLY, THE GOP RIGHT, AND POLITICS
IN A NATION DIVIDED

Many of the Right, including Phyllis Schlafly, held deep reservations about Clinton's military interventions and the globalization of American foreign and trade policies. Shortly before the 1994 election, she called the proposed World Trade Organization (WTO) a "direct attack on American sovereignty, independence, jobs, and economy. . . . Any country that must change its laws to obey rulings of a world organization has sacrificed its sovereignty."[85] In another article on the WTO, she unsuccessfully urged Congress to reject WTO in order to ensure that America remains "an independent nation with the sovereign power to write our own laws and make our own decisions about our own livelihood."[86] Similarly, she opposed the North American Free Trade Agreement (NAFTA), quoting historian Alfred E. Eckes that protectionism was the traditional Republican policy.

These long-standing fears over the loss of national sovereignty were consistent with her denunciations of internationalism, the U.N., and the Korean War fifty years earlier. With the collapse of the Soviet Union in the late 1980s, international communism no longer remained a threat, but the erosion of American sovereignty by treaties and international organizations alarmed conservatives such as Schlafly. Opposition to American military intervention when a direct threat to national security was not clearly evident continued to characterize Schlafly's politics, as well as that of others in the GOP Right. Her anxieties about the nation's loss of sovereignty found expression in her denunciation of the United Nations on its fiftieth anniversary. Having as a college student applauded the founding of the United Nations, Schlafly now characterized the anniversary as "a cause for mourning not celebration. It is a monument to foolish hopes, embarrassing compromises, betrayal of our servicemen, and a steady stream of insults to our nation. It is a Trojan Horse that carries the enemy into our midst and lures Americans to ride under alien insignia to fight and die in faraway lands." In her polemic against the United Nations, she revealed the strain between the GOP Right and the first Bush administration when she observed, "Unfortunately, President George [H. W.] Bush rehabilitated the UN's reputation with his Gulf War and his rhetoric about the "New World Order."[87] Such sentiments led Schlafly in 1996 to criticize Clinton's decision to send 20,000 troops to

Bosnia in early 1996. Noting that Balkan nations have fought each other for 500 years, she declared that "U.S. servicemen are not policemen and should not be forced to assume that role."[88]

Schlafly was a Bush alternate delegate at the 2000 Republican National Convention in Philadelphia, but nonetheless, she was critical of President George W. Bush because of large increases in domestic spending, such as for federal control of education, and of Bush's forays into global and hemispheric integration, such as signing the Declaration of Quebec City. Schlafly opposed the Bush Administration's immigration policy and deplored its apparent unwillingness to control U.S. borders from illegal crossings, which she saw as a major threat to national security.

On the other hand, Schlafly cheered loudly when Bush withdrew from the 1972 ABM Treaty, a decision she had urged for nearly thirty years, and cheered again when Bush "unsigned" the International Criminal Court Treaty and refused to push for ratification of the Kyoto Protocol. Bush invited her to be present at the White House when he gave his speech against human cloning. Schlafly was given credit by the *New York Times* for the reduction of the "marriage penalty" tax in Bush's $674 billion tax-cut plan. Described as "the indefatigable foe of feminism," the *New York Times* observed, Schlafly has "fought for years to ensure that marriage-penalty relief flows to families with stay-at-home moms as well as two-income households."[89]

By 2004, Phyllis Schlafly had become the *grand dame* of the conservative movement. Schlafly continued an active writing and public speaking schedule before college campuses and conservative groups. She made over 300 television and radio appearances concerning her *Feminist Fantasies* (2003), a collection of her essays published over thirty years. Her weekly radio broadcast "Phyllis Schlafly Live," was heard on forty radio (primarily Christian) stations across the country. Her three-minute-a-day, five-days-a-week editorial series, running since 1983, are heard on 460 radio stations. The issues she continues to address remain much the same as when she had first entered politics fifty years before—national security, education, immigration, and cultural values. Yet the world was much different in the twenty-first century. The Soviet Union had collapsed and the United States was no longer threatened by international communism. While Schlafly and other conservatives warned about what they perceived as the growing dangers from U.N treaties and mainland China, the major threats to international stability came from renegade states armed with nuclear weapons and Islamic terrorists.

Cultural issues loomed of much greater importance than they had fifty years earlier when Schlafly first entered politics. Indeed, the cultural issues emerging in the 1970s provided the impetus for a revived conservative movement. As Schlafly told the *U.S. News and World Report* for its cover story on the decade of the 1970s, "We saw an attack on marriage, the family, the homemaker, the role of motherhood, the whole concept of different roles for men and women. What we did was take these cultural issues and bring into the conservative movement people who had been stuck in the pews. We taught 'em politics."[90] *U.S. News* described Schlafly as having led "a counter-revolution" against the feminists. Schlafly and her supporters believed that the battle was far from over and that opponents of traditional culture have continued to advance their agenda, even while the nation appeared to have moved politically to the Right. The persistent pace of changing sexual mores and practices was no better evidenced for Schlafly and cultural conservatives than in the advance of gay rights and the demand for same-sex marriage licenses.

While Schlafly's written materials during the ERA battle had warned that the amendment, if ratified, would lead to taxpayer funding of abortion and same-sex marriage, she had usually shied away from controversies over homosexual rights. When the Massachusetts Supreme Judicial Court ruled 4 to 3 to legalize same-sex marriages in *Goodridge v. Department of Public Health* in late 2003, Schlafly felt compelled to address the issue. Denouncing the four judges who had overturned nearly 400 years of Massachusetts history and law, Schlafly declared that "the issue won't go away, and every candidate" should be prepared to provide a coherent answer to the challenge. She maintained that the real issue was not same-sex marriage *per se*, but forcing the "rest of us to accept a public judgment that personal desire outweighs the value of traditional marriage and outweighs the need of children for mothers and fathers." She warned that the result of legalizing same-sex marriage would be to legitimize marriage for those who want to marry a child, or a sibling, or more than one wife. "If a 13-year old girl can exercise 'choice' to 'control her body' and get an abortion," Schlafly asked rhetorically, "why can't she have the choice to marry?"[91]

In her testimony to the Subcommittee on the Constitution of the House Judiciary Committee on June 24, 2004, Schlafly proposed a counter-strategy to defeat what she saw as the judiciary's attack on marriage. Citing Congress's constitutional power in Article III, she called on congress to withdraw jurisdiction from the federal courts over marriage, so activist judges would be unable to invalidate federal or state Defense of Marriage Acts. She detailed the historical record of federal statutes in which Congress has successfully restricted the jurisdiction of the courts and she asked, "Isn't the protection of marriage just as important as any of [those] issues?" She added, "The very idea that unelected, unaccountable judges could nullify both other branches of government and the will of the American people is an offense against our right of self-government that must not be tolerated."[92] It was clear that the seventy-nine-year-old Phyllis Schlafly still had the capacity to inflame her opponents through her rhetoric that painted issues black and white.

Her 2004 book, *The Supremacists: The Tyranny of Judges and How to Stop It*, is a bid to rally the grassroots to challenge the conventional wisdom that "the Constitution is whatever the Supreme Court says it is." The book received endorsements from former Attorney-General Edwin Meese, former judges Robert Bork and William P. Clark, and economist Thomas Sowell in its demand to restore constitutional balance to the Republic. In the book, Schlafly describes how, as she sees it, activist judges (the supremacists) have overturned laws and the will of the people in areas of the Pledge of Allegiance, the Ten Commandments, prayer in schools, marriage, pornography, criminal justice, and elections. Aimed at a grassroots audience, she maintains that judges should not be permitted to have disproportionate power over the other two branches of government. She calls for a change in Senate rules to facilitate confirmations of federal judges, new legislation to prohibit judicial activism in specific types of cases, and legislation to prohibit federal courts from relying on foreign laws, administrative rules, or court decisions. While a constitutional amendment defining marriage as a union between a man and a woman failed in the Senate, the House passed HR 3313, introduced by Republican John Hostettler (Indiana), removing the jurisdiction of federal courts from the Defense of Marriage Act (1996) signed by president Clinton. Schlafly claimed that Eagle Forum members were a driving force behind this vote. The Hostettler bill sought to protect the 49 other states from having to recognize the Massachusetts Court decision in *Goodrich* that legalized same-sex marriage licenses.

In a certain sense, American politics in the late twentieth century had become black and white for many people.[93] Religious and cultural polarization spilled over into American politics, intensifying partisan politics, while at the same time alienating voters who disdained what they perceived as partisan bickering. Nonetheless, religious and cultural polarization of the political parties appeared to have become the outstanding feature of American politics well into the millennium.[94] Phyllis Schlafly played a critical role in mobilizing moral and cultural traditions for the Grand Old Party. In doing so, she contributed to the shift to the Right within the Republican party, the erosion of public support for New Deal economic liberalism, and the deepening divide between the two parties. Her rhetoric fueled the flames of partisanship, and her ability to tap into the frustration of traditionally minded religious people revived a conservative movement that had been weakened by the anti-anticommunism in the early 1960s, the failure of the Goldwater campaign in 1964, and Nixon's and Ford's disdain for the Republican Right in the 1970s. While neither she nor her followers accomplished this alone, Schlafly played a critical role in this conservative victory in the Republican party and the shift to the Right in American politics. Whether her organization sustains itself in the future remains uncertain, although she has established an endowment and a team of state leaders to continue the organization after she steps down as its leader.

In June 2004, Phyllis Schlafly attended her fourteenth Republican National convention as an active participant. She went to the New York City convention as a Bush delegate, but like many conservatives, she felt uneasy about the administration's big government policies and involvement in a war in Iraq. As an experienced hand in convention politics, she was again the leader in forcing platform changes to reflect particular concerns of the GOP Right. While Schlafly and her allies did not succeed in getting all the changes they sought, they were able to insert strong wording in several sections of the platform, including those on immigration and judicial activism. For example, on immigration, conservatives succeeded in inserting amendments to strengthen the Border Patrol, to apply stiff punishment to those smuggling illegal aliens into the United States, and to enforce tough penalties against employers and employees who violate immigration laws. Conservatives also added strong language to condemn "judicial supremacy" and to endorse congressional legislation to withdraw jurisdiction from the federal courts over the Defense of Marriage Act, the Pledge of Allegiance, and depictions of the Ten Commandments. Still, many conservatives believed that, contrary to most previous Republican platforms that were the product of grassroots initiatives, the 2004 Platform was largely a tightly controlled administration-written document. Significantly, the Bush-written platform did include the pro-life plank that Schlafly and Rep. Henry Hyde had inserted in the 1984 platform and was retained in all subsequent platforms.

Schlafly endorsed Bush in his bid for reelection, but she focused her election efforts in congressional races and state amendments to lock traditional marriage into state constitutions. In the last weeks of the campaign, she gave a leave of absence to a staff member to work with the John Thune campaign in South Dakota in his challenge to Senate minority leader Tom Daschle. Throughout the campaign, Schlafly felt confident that George W. Bush would win reelection against his Democratic challenger John Kerry, a U.S. Senator from Massachusetts, but the size of the Republican victory was a welcome surprise. While Bush's victory was not a landslide, it was a clear confirmation that the country had moved to the center-right. In an election that turned out record numbers of voters (about 105.4 million voted, which was over 54 percent of eligible voters), President Bush strengthened his support in counties he won in 2000, while winning New Mexico and Iowa, states that he lost to Democratic nominee Al Gore in 2000. Furthermore, Bush increased his share of the vote among women, African Americans, Hispanics, and older voters into a 3.6 million popular vote victory. Especially disheartening for Democrats, Tom Daschle was defeated by challenger John Thune in South Dakota, enabling Republicans to pick up four seats in the Senate. Democrats were further shaken as Republicans increased their majority in the House, while extending their number of state governors to twenty-nine. In the 2004 election, voters in eleven states overwhelmingly passed ballot initiatives upholding traditional marriage. Since these ballot initiatives passed by larger margins than the Bush vote in all but one of the eleven states, commentators believed that the key to Bush's victory lay in his strategy to appeal to social conservatives who felt alienated from the popular culture.[95]

The 2004 election showed that the Right will remain a force within American politics into the foreseeable future. Yet, conservatives confront the dilemma posed by a democratic system given to political compromise. If the Republican party is driven by Bush's victory to accept policy gestures large and small that add up to an affirmation of big government at home and empire-building abroad, how long can conservatives continue as a viable force in politics?[96] Conservatives have arguably brought down "this thing called liberalism"—as William Buckley, Jr., demanded in the first issue of *The National Review*—but as yet they have not confirmed that conservatism is viable in an age of rights unrestrained by obligation, of Wilsonian promises of international transformation, and of unbridled demands on government spending. Conservatives—intellectuals such as William Buckley, Jr., activists such as Phyllis Schlafly, and politicians such as Ronald Reagan—turned the GOP to the Right and in doing so shifted the political debate in a conservative direction. They issued a call for a political revolution to overturn the New Deal order, and enjoyed much success in doing so, but the ideological and cultural civil war continues unabated as the United States enters the twenty-first century.

Manuscript Collections

ARIZONA STATE UNIVERSITY, TEMPE, ARIZONA

Barry Goldwater papers
Eleanor D. Higgins papers
Theodore Humes papers
Roy Rosenzweig papers

CHICAGO HISTORICAL SOCIETY, CHICAGO, ILLINOIS

Clarence Manion papers

EAGLE FORUM, ST. LOUIS, MISSOURI

Schlafly Book files
Campaign (1952) files
Campaign (1970) files
Communism files
Daughters of the American Revolution files
ERA files
Republican files
NFRW files
Pre-1972 Subject files
Fred Schlafly Personal papers
Phyllis Schlafly pre-1948 files
Phyllis Schlafly Report Subject files
Chester Ward files

GERALD FORD LIBRARY, ANN ARBOR, MICHIGAN

Foster Chanock files
Richard Cheney files
Betty Ford papers
President Ford's Committee Records,
    Administrative Office (Marik) files
    Chairman's Office files
    Correspondence topical files
    Roy Hughes files
    People for Ford files

Congressional Relations Office (Max L. Friedersdorf) files
Michael Raoul-Duval files
Patricia Lindh and Jeanne Holm files
Office of the Press Secretary
   Wanda M. Phelan files
   Paul A. Miltic files
Elizabeth O'Neill files
President Ford Committee Records
White House Central Files

JOHN F. KENNEDY LIBRARY, BOSTON, MASSACHUSETTS

John F. Kennedy Presidential papers
National Security files
Arthur Schlesinger, Jr. papers
Walter Rostow papers
Adam Yarmolinsky papers
Paul Warburg papers

LIBRARY OF CONGRESS, WASHINGTON, D.C.

Richard Dudman papers
ERAmerica papers
Curtis LeMay papers
Claire Booth Luce papers
Paul Nitze papers
Herbert Philbrick papers
Edward Rickenbacker papers
William Rusher papers
Robert A. Taft papers
James Wadsworth papers

RONALD REAGAN LIBRARY, SIMI VALLEY, CALIFORNIA

Linda Arey papers
Mariam Bell papers
Morton Blackwell papers
Robert Bonitat papers
Wendy Borcherdt papers
Elizabeth Dole papers
Dee Jepsen papers
Edwin Meese papers

Mary Quint papers
Faith Whittlesey papers
WHORM, Alpha File (SA-SD)

ROCKEFELLER FAMILY, TARRYTOWN, NEW YORK

Graham Molitor papers
Nelson Rockefeller papers

PHYLLIS SCHLAFLY, LADUE, MISSOURI

Personal Correspondence
Scrapbooks

UNIVERSITY OF ARKANSAS, FAYETTEVILLE, ARKANSAS

John D. Bale papers
William Fulbright papers

UNIVERSITY OF MICHIGAN, ANN ARBOR, MICHIGAN

Elly Peterson papers

UNIVERSITY OF OREGON, EUGENE, OREGON

T. Coleman Andrew papers
Lee J. Adamson papers
Tom Anderson papers
Lucille Cardin Crain papers
Augereau Gray Heinsohn, Jr. papers
Howard E. Kershner papers
Willford I. King papers
Willis S. Stone papers

Notes

INTRODUCTION

1. Geoffrey Layman, *The Great Divide: Religious and Cultural Conflict in American Party Politics* (New York), p. 1.

2. For a good example of this interpretation of the conservative movement, see Jonathan Schoenwald, *Time for Choosing: The Rise of Modern American Conservatism* (New York, 2000); Lee Edwards, *The Conservative Revolution: The Movement that Remade America* (New York, 1999); Godfrey Hodgson, *The World Turned Right Side Up: A History of the Conservative Ascendancy* (Boston, 1996); Mathew Dalek, *The Right Moment: Ronald Reagan's First Victory and the Decisive Turning Point in American Politics* (New York, 2000); and Gregory Schneider, *Cadres for Conservatism: Young Americans for Freedom and the Rise of the Contemporary Right* (New York, 1999).

3. The use of the term "grassroots conservatives" is intended to distinguish local activists from the Republican Establishment and conservative intellectuals and writers. This book uses the term interchangeably with grassroots activists, grassroots anticommunists, the grassroots Right and, at times, the Hard Right. These were the rank and file in the conservative anticommunist movement and the Republican party, and later the anti-ERA campaign and the anti-abortion campaign. Grassroots conservatism tended to be further to the Right than the mainstream of the Republican party, although the difference was less in the early 1950s. The grassroots Right believed that political change could occur through the democratic process and had nothing in common with the extremists, who called for revolutionary change through violence. Historian Lisa McGirr makes this important distinction about right-wing views of the democratic process. For this reason, she consciously avoids using such terms as "ultraconservatism," "Radical Right," or "Far Right" to describe grassroots conservatives, or labels such as "white supremacist, paramilitary and fascist fringe groups like the Ku Klux Klan, and the Minute Men, groups that stepped outside the Democratic political process to achieve their goals." Two other qualifiers should be added to this clarification of right-wing extremism. The nondemocratic Right holds an absolutist view of what the world is and should be, and this absolutism is usually derived from a gnostic belief that it possesses a secret knowledge or special empowerment unique to its cause. For example, the conspiratorial belief that the world is controlled by the Bavarian Illuminati, whose purpose and plans are only understood by a select few, is typical of nondemocratic extremism. Lisa McGirr, *Suburban Warriors: The Origins of the New Right* (Princeton, NJ, 2000), p. 10.

4. William F. Buckley, Jr., *Up from Liberalism*, (New York, 1959), p. 18.

5. Richard Carwardine, *Evangelicals and Politics in Antebellum America* (New Haven, Conn., 1993).

6. Rev. John Hall and Rev. William E. Moore, *Presbyterians: A Popular Narrative of Their Origin, Progress, Doctrines and Achievements* (New York, 1892), xiv.

7. Rebecca Klatch, *Women of the New Right*, (Philadelphia, 1985), p. 25.

8. David Hume, "Abstract, *Treatise of Human Nature*," in *Theory of Knowledge*, edited D.C. Yalden-Thomson (New York, 1951) p. 246.

CHAPTER ONE
THE MAKING OF A GRASSROOTS CONSERVATIVE

1. This discussion of Betty Friedan relies on Daniel Horowitz, *Betty Friedan and The Making of The Feminine Mystique: The American Left, the Cold War, and Modern Feminism* (Amherst, Mass., 1998), and an earlier essay by Horowitz, "Rethinking Betty Friedan and *The Feminine Mystique:* Labor Union Radicalism and Feminism in Cold War America," *American Quarterly*, 48:1 (1996), pp. 1–42. For additional details of Friedan's life not found in Horowitz, see Judith Hennessee, *Betty Friedan: Her Life* (New York, 1999).

2. For an interesting discussion of progressive women in Queens, New York, where Friedan settled as a young adult, see Sylvie Murray, *The Progressive Housewife: Community Activism in Suburban Queens, 1945–1965* (Philadelphia, 2003), especially pp. 133–52.

3. Patricia Springborg, ed. "Introduction," *Astell: Political Writings*, (Cambridge, 1996), pp. xi–xxxvi.

4. This discussion of the republican motherhood draws from Rosemarie Zaggari, "Morals, Manners, and the Republican Mother," *American Quarterly*, 44:2 (June, 1992), pp. 192–215. Also, useful is Jan Lewis, "The Republican Wife: Virtue and Seduction in the Early Republic," *The William and Mary Quarterly*, 44 (October, 1987), pp. 689–721. Ruth Bloch maintains that in the nineteenth century, feminine allusions to virtue became more prominent due to the influence of American evangelical religion and Anglo-American literary sentimentalism. See Ruth Block, "The Gendered Meanings of Virtue in Revolutionary America," *Signs* 12 (Autumn 1987) and "American Feminine Ideals in Transition: The Rise of the Moral Mother, 1785–1815," *Feminist Studies*, 4 (June 1978), pp. 101–26. These studies qualify and challenge Linda K. Kerber, *Women of the Republic: Intellect and Ideology in Revolutionary America* (Chapel Hill, NC, 1980).

5. This discussion of women's participation in the Federalist party is informed by Rosemarie Zagarri's engaging essay, "Gender and the First Party System," Doron Ben-Atar and Barbara B. Oberg, *Federalists Reconsidered* (Charlottesville, 1998), pp. 118–35. For the Whig party, see Elizabeth R. Varon, "Tippecanoe and

the Ladies, Too: White Women and Party Politics in Antebellum Virginia," *Journal of American History* 82 (1995), pp. 494–521.

6. This discussion of evangelical participation in Whig politics relies heavily both in concept and language on Richard Carwardine, *Evangelicals and Politics in Antebellum America* (New Haven, 1993), pp. 32–34. Also, of particular usefulness, see Paul Goodman, *Towards a Christian Republic: Antimasonry and the Great Transition in New England, 1826–1836* (New York, 1988).

7. Richard Carwardine, *Evangelicals and Politics in Antebellum America*, pp. 20–21.

8. Feminist historians Sonya Michel and Robyn Rosen insightfully examine how this "essentialist maternalist ideology"—a concept in gender history that finds women's unique capacity to mother translated to the political world— bridged the Right and Left in the early twentieth century. Kim E. Nielsen maintains that conservative women did not accept this maternalist ideology. See Sonya Michel and Robyn Rosen, "The Paradox of Maternalism: Elizabeth Lowell Putnam and the American Welfare State," *Gender and History* 4 (Autumn, 1992), pp. 364–86.; and Kim E. Nielson, *Un-American Womanhood: Antiradicalism, Antifeminism, and the First Red Scare* (Columbus, OH, 2001), especially pp. 51–52. Also useful for understanding women reformers in this period is J. Stanley Lemons, *The Woman Citizen: Social Feminism in the 1920s* (Urbana, IL, 1973).

An important study of antisuffrage opposition to the Nineteenth Amendment is found in Susan E. Marshall, *Splintered Sisterhood: Gender and Class in the Campaign against Woman Suffrage* (Madison, Wisconsin, 1997). Marshall located this opposition in what she describes as "gendered class interests" in which antisuffragists opposed suffrage to protect their own privileged position. Marshall shows, however, that female opposition to suffrage was often expressed in terms, although elitist, of protecting the family, bettering society, and promoting moral reform. There is an extensive literature on the suffragists, including Nancy Cott, *The Grounding of Modern Feminism* (New Haven, 1987); Ellen Carol DuBois, *Feminism and Suffrage: The Emergence of an Independent Women's Movement in America, 1984–1869* (Ithaca, NY, 1978); Nancy Schrom Dye, *As Equals and As Sisters: Feminism, the Labor Movement, and the Women's Trade Union League of New York* (Columbia, MO, 1980); and two classics, Eleanor Flexner, *Century of Struggle: The Women's Rights Movement in the United States* (Cambridge, MA, reprinted 1975) and Aileen S. Kraditor, *The Ideas of the Woman's Suffrage Movement, 1890–1930* (New York, reprinted 1981).

9. Geoffrey Layman, *The Great Divide: Religious and Cultural Conflict in American Party Politics* (New York, 2001), pp. 4–5. Also, see Robert Wuthnow, *The Struggle for America's Soul: Evangelicals, Liberals, and Secularism* (Grand Rapids, MI, 1989).

10. Odile (nicknamed Dadie) Stewart's family tree included the Jean Baptiste Pratte family and General Ernest Dodge, commander in the Black Hawk

War, Civil War general, and first U.S. Senator from the State of Wisconsin. His son, Augustus Dodge, was elected to Congress as a representative from Iowa; the father sat in the Senate and the son in the House. Dadie took pride in the intellectual side of the family. Dadie's great-grandfather on her father's side, the Reverend Adiel Sherwood, D.D., was the president of Shurtleff College in Alton, Illinois. He was a scholar of considerable religious learning who knew Latin, Greek, Hebrew, and Assyrian. See "Additional Manuscript Containing the Roger Heriot Branch," and Notation and Clipping, "Funeral Service Tomorrow for E.C. Dodge Lawyer," Scrapbook, 13–15 years, Phyllis Schlafly Home Papers, St. Louis Missouri. Also, Carol Felsenthal, *The Sweetheart of the Silent Majority: The Biography of Phyllis Schlafly* (New York, 1981).

11. Her sister Odile Mecker, however, does remember her father and mother complaining about the Franklin Roosevelt administration at the dinner table. When Phyllis Schlafly told Odile she did not remember this, Odile replied, "Oh, you were probably off in your room doing your homework." Author's interview with Odile Mecker, November 11, 2003.

12. These conclusions were reached by Carol Felsenthal who undertook extensive interviews with family, friends, and acquaintances of the Stewart and Schlafly families. Felsenthal, *Sweetheart of the Silent Majority: The Biography of Phyllis Schlafly* (New York, 1981).

13. Quoted in Carol Felsenthal, *Sweetheart of the Silent Majority,* p. 18. She quotes Bruce Stewart's brother-in-law, Carl Pfeifer.

14. In 1940, the total population of St. Louis City was 816,048, with 440,000 Roman Catholics. In 1940, Franklin Roosevelt received 233,338 votes to Wendell Willkie's 168,165 votes. In 1944, Roosevelt received 204,687 votes to Dewey's 134, 411. See, Dwight H. Brown, *State of Missouri: Official Manual, 1940* (Jefferson City, MO, 1940); and Wilson Bell, *State of Missouri: Official Manual, 1944* (Jefferson City, MO, 1944).

15. See "Scrapbook, 13–15 years," Personal Papers. Phyllis Schlafly Home papers, St. Louis, Missouri; also quoted in Carol Felsenthal, *The Sweetheart of the Silent Majority: The Biography of Phyllis Schlafly,*

16. Notation, June 3, 1938, 13–15 Years of Age Scrapbook, Personal Papers of Phyllis Schlafly.

17. "Student Memories" Scrapbook, Personal Papers of Phyllis Schlafly.

18. "June 1, 1941," Notebook, Began June 6, 1940, Personal Papers of Phyllis Schlafly.

19. "May 19, 1942," "June 6, 1942," "Scrapbook, June 6th–October 3, 1944," Personal Papers of Phyllis Schlafly.

20. In his letter of recommendation Lien wrote, "Miss Stewart is a person of very unusual attainments. Her intellectual capacity is extraordinary and her analytical ability is distinctly remarkable. I have no hesitation in saying that Miss Stewart is the most capable woman student we have had in this department in

ten years. Add to this the possession of a very attractive personality and a ge-
nial approach to life, the result is altogether remarkable." Arnold Lien to Dean
Bernice (n.d.), June 27, 1944, Personal Papers of Phyllis Schlafly.

21. April 3, 1944, "Scrapbook, June 6th–October 3, 1944," Personal Papers of
Phyllis Schlafly.

22. June 27, 1944, "Scrapbook, June 6th 1941–October 3, 1944," Personal Papers of Phyllis Schlafly.

23. Entry, "Student Memoirs Scrapbook, Personal Papers of Phyllis Schlafly.

24. The importance of Hayek's *Road to Serfdom* is discussed in Paul Gottfried
and Thomas Fleming, *The Conservative Moment* (Boston, 1988), pp. 1–14.

25. Phyllis Bruce Stewart, "The Controversy Concerning the Division of Economic Research of the National Labor Relations Board, 1940," paper for Public
Administration, April 25, 1945; "Integration," paper for Government, January
4, 1945; "Better Public Personnel," paper for Government, November 30, 1944;
and "Detailed Analysis of *Cloverleaf Butter Co. v. Patterson 315 U.S. 148, 1942*,"
paper for Constitutional Law course, May 1945; pre-1949 Office File, Eagle
Forum Archives.

26. In a similar vein, she declared in a term paper for her course on International Law, "A strong and prosperous United States is the most important contribution that Americans can make to the economic reorganization
of the world. But we cannot be prosperous unless we share actively in re-
organizing prosperity and strength in the other countries." Phyllis Bruce
Stewart, "Does the Dumbarton Oaks Proposal Provide Effective Military
Sanctions to Enforce International Peace?" paper for International Law, February, 1945; and "American Economic Policy in International Relations,"
paper for American Foreign Policy, May 1945, Pre-1949 Office File, Eagle
Forum Archives.

27. One of her disappointed professors wrote, "It was a pleasure to have you
around last year and I am sorry that you won't be here in September, even
though I agree that you aren't cast for the role of a female professor." Benjamin
Wright to Phyllis Stewart, August 11, 1945, Scrapbook for the Year at Radcliffe
College, 1944–45.

28. Dad to Phyllis, June 10, 1945; "Stewart Rotary Engine," *Southern Power
and Industry*, December, 1945, pp. 8 and 28.

29. The essay is not available in her papers, but discussed in a letter James
Daniel to Phyllis Schlafly, November 3, 1945, Scrapbook Washington, D.C.,
Phyllis Schlafly Home Files.

30. For insight into some of the anti-Semitic cranks in the 1930s such as Eliz-
abeth Dilling, Grace Wick, Catherine Curtis, and Agnes Waters, see June Melby
Benowitz, *Days of Discontent: American Women and Right-Wing Politics, 1933–1945*
(DeKalb, IL, 2002) and Glen Jeansonne, *Women of the Far Right: The Mother's
Movement and World War II* (Chicago, 1996).

31. The mothers' antiwar movement is discussed in detail by Glen Jeansonne, *Women of the Far Right: The Mother's Movement and World War II*. For the pre–World War II Right, see William Rusher, *The Rise of the Right* (New York, 1984); Michael Miles, *The Odyssey of the Right* (New York, 1980); George Wolfskill, *The Revolt of the Conservatives: A History of the American Liberty League, 1934–1940* (Boston, 1962); and Ronald Radosh, *Prophets on the Right: Profiles of Conservative Critics of American Globalism* (New York, 1975). The prewar, noninterventionist Right is explored in the informative Justin Raimindo, *Reclaiming the American Right: The Lost Legacy of the Conservative Movement* (Burlingame, CA, 1975) and briefly in Paul Gottfried and Thomas Fleming, *The Conservative Movement* (Boston, 1988). The flavor of prewar conservatism is found in Gregory L. Schneider, ed., *Conservatism in America Since 1930* (New York, 2003), pp. 5–68. John T. Flynn is especially important in linking the pre–World War II Right and the postwar Old Right. Included in his publications are *As We Go Marching* (New York, 1944); *Country Squire in the White House* (New York, 1940); *The Roosevelt Myth* (New York, 1956); *The Decline of the American Republic* (New York, 1955); *The Road Ahead: America's Creeping Revolution* (New York, 1949); and *While You Slept, Our Tragedy in Asia and Who Made It* (New York, 1951).

32. American Enterprise Association, "A Statement of Purposes: Extracts from an Address by Lewis H. Brown, June 1, 1945.

33. Lewis Harold Brown, "Using Business Agencies to Achieve Public Goals in the Postwar World," *American Economic Review*, Supplement (1943) pp. 71–81; and idem, "How to Get the Country Back to Work," *Vital Speeches* (March 15, 1946), pp. 342–5; and "The Brown Plan," *Business Week* (October 25, 1947), p. 25. On Brown see "Lewis Harold Brown," *Current Biography, 1947* (New York, 1948), pp. 68–70. An interesting letter that reveals his influence on business thinking of the time is found in an exchange of letters in the Rockefeller Foundation Archives: see Virgil Jordan to John D. Rockefeller, Jr. June 8, 1944; John Spargo to William Allen White, June 29, 1938; and John Spargo to George Houston, July 15, 1938, John D. Rockefeller, Jr. papers, Rockefeller Foundation Archives.

34. James Smith, *The Idea Brokers: Think Tanks and the Rise of the New Policy Elite* (New York, 1991); and Donald T. Critchlow, "Think Tanks, Antistatism, and Democracy: The Nonpartisan Ideal and Policy Research in the United States, 1913–1987," Michael J. Lacey and Mary O. Furner, *The State and Social Investigation in Britain and the United States* (Cambridge, 1991), pp. 279–319.

35. She received a certificate from the club declaring, "Phyllis B. Stewart is a member of the United Nations Club and endorses the principles which are to foster through the media of educational pursuits and common fellowship a truer understanding among the peoples through the world." "Enrollment Card, United Nations Club," Scrapbook, 1945–46, Personal Papers of Phyllis Schlafly.

36. *Redbook Magazine* to Miss Phyllis B. Stewart, January 17, 1946; and Kathleen Toner to Ms. Stewart, January 14, 1946, Scrapbook, 1945–46, Personal Papers of Phyllis Schlafly.

37. Dadie Stewart to Phyllis Stewart, (n.d.) Scrapbook, 1945–46, Personal Papers of Phyllis Schlafly.

38. OEM to Phyllis Stewart, April 28, 1946, Scrapbook, 1945–46, Personal Papers of Phyllis Schlafly.

39. Quoted in Carol Felsenthal, *The Sweeheart of the Silent Majority: The Biography of Phyllis Schlafly* (New York, 1981), p. 77.

40. Speeches written for Bakewell included, "Veteran Housing," "America at the Crossroads," "The Housing Confusion," "A Year of Confusion," "Labor and Labels," "A Square Deal for Veterans," "Communist Infiltration," "Republican Labor Policy," "Crisis Government," "The Local Machine," "Beer and the New Deal," "Military Justice," and "Tolerance and Liberalism." Pre-1949 files, Eagle Forum Archives.

41. Phyllis B. Stewart to Frances Spivy, September 26, 1949, Pre-1949 Office Files, Eagle Forum Archives.

42. Typical articles in the newsletter included "England's Financial Crisis and the American Dilemma" (supporting limited foreign aid to England); "Congressional Investigations" (critical of the "vulgar sensationalism" of HUAC, although "it has uncovered a great mass of evidence of communist activists"); "Henry Wallace and Communist Tactics" (warning against "forced equalization of wealth"); "What to Do about Inflation," (capital gains tax cuts); "The Influence of Communism upon Political Thinking in the United States" (Ludwig von Mises denouncing "interventionist progressivism").

43. Conservative women have attracted considerable attention, much of it tied to the antiwar movement. See June Melby Benowitz, *Days of Discontent: American Women and Right-Wing Politics, 1933–1945* (DeKalb, IL, 2002); Glen Jeansonne, *Women of the Far Right: The Mother's Movement and World War II* (Chicago, 1996); and Laura McEnaney, "He-Men and Christian Mothers: The America First Movement and the Gendered Meanings of Patriotism and Isolationism," *Diplomatic History*, 18 (Winter, 1994), pp. 47–57. Also, useful for understanding Republican women in this period is Catherine Elaine Rymph, "Forward and Right: The Shaping of Republican Women's Activism, 1920–1967," (Ph.D. diss., University of Iowa, 1998) and Michelle M. Nickerson, "Domestic Threats: Women, Gender, and Conservatism in Los Angeles, 1945–1966," (Ph.D. diss. Yale University, 2003). Antifeminist conservative women during the Red Scare after the First World War are explored by Kim E. Nielsen, *Un-American Womanhood: Antiradicalism, Antifeminism, and the First Red Scare* (Columbus, 2001). For a comparative perspective of right-wing women, heavily theoretical in its approach, see Paola Bacchetta and Margaret Power, eds., *Rightwing Women: From Conservatives to Extremists around the World* (New York, 2002). Of particular

interest is Kathleen M. Blee, "The Gendered Organization of Hate: Women in the U.S. Ku Klux Klan," pp. 101–115, and Ronnee Schreiber, "Playing 'Femball': Conservative Women's Organizations and Political Representation in the United States," pp. 211–25; and Brownwyn Winter, "Pauline and Other Perils: Women in Australian Right-Wing Politics," pp. 197–211.

44. For the speeches she wrote for bank officers, see Herbert F. Boettler, Speech before Conference of Bank Correspondents, November 4, 1948; and Speech, William A. McDonnell (n.d.), Pre-1949 Office Files, Eagle Forum Archives.

45. "It Takes a Will to Fill the Bill," *St. Louis Globe-Democrat* (n.d.), Scrapbook September 1947–August 1948, Personal Papers of Phyllis Schlafly. For speeches see, Phyllis Stewart, "The Trust Company: Its Development and Function," "Women's Financial Problems," "Wives and Wills," "The Marital Deduction," "Minor Beneficiaries," "Living Trusts," and "Estate Planning," in Eagle Forum Office File, Pre-1949, Eagle Forum.

46. Towner Phelan, "Housing in St. Louis," manuscript (1947), Pre-1949 Files, Eagle Forum Archives.

47. "Citizens Council Urges Bond Issue as Step to Big Housing Projects," *St. Louis Post-Dispatch* (October 17, 1948), 1; and Clipping, "Phyllis Stewart Makes Front Page of *Post*," *St. Louis Junior League* (November 1948), p. 1.

48. Phyllis Stewart told her suitor, "I have never been able to sympathize very much with Republican campaign oratory about Roosevelt's statement in regard to sending our boys to fight in foreign wars. . . . He did not send any boys to fight in foreign wars until after Pearl Harbor, and then it certainly was our war." Fred Schlafly had found his match. A typical missive read, "My goodness gracious, what an essay sagacious, from one so young and pretty; to have to dispute it, even refuse it, is truly a pity." The next stanzas revealed their shared abhorrence of liberals and their distrust of Roosevelt: "Liberals have such a generous paw; He'll spill your blood to have his war. [Republicans of the 1940s understood that F.D.R.'s accent made war rhyme with paw.] He's so liberal with your money and life, he will even expropriate your wife. Scratch a liberal and you'll find a man, panting to get and keep all that he can. Pursuing riches and spouse with crude élan. Take not my word, look at the Roosevelt clan." Phyllis Stewart to Fred Schlafly, August 1, 1949 and Fred Schlafly to Miss P. B. Stewart, June 10, 1949, SP Scrapbook, Personal Papers of Phyllis Schlafly.

49. Jane Clark, "Phyllis Schlafly: Outspoken Advocate of Peace through Military Strength," *St. Louis Globe-Democrat*, November 19, 1965, Box 1965–66, Personal Papers of Phyllis Schlafly.

50. See Fred Schlafly's letter to former isolationist activist (later turned anti-McCarthyite in the 1950s) Father John A. O'Brien. Schlafly wrote, "I have long admired your wisdom and courage, first manifested to me when you joined with Colonel Lindbergh and General Robert E. Wood in warning of a foreign

policy which could only help Communism and hurt Western Civilization." Fred Schlafly, Jr. to Rev. Father John A. O'Brien, July 13, 1953, John F. Schlafly Papers, Folder 1953, Eagle Forum Archives (unprocessed).

51. Typical was a letter he wrote Captain Robert A. Winston, author of *The Pentagon Case* (1958), to ask the name of the naval officer who allegedly had been given a lobotomy by the military to prevent his revealing the true Pearl Harbor story. Writing under the pseudonym Colonel Victor J. Fox, *The Pentagon Case* (New York, 1958), he presents his case as a novel. For the exchange of letters between Fred Schlafly and Winston see Schlafly to John G. Scott and George S. Montgomery, Jr., May 12, 1960; R.A. Winston to Fred Schlafly, April 30, 1960; FS to R.A. Winston, May 9, 1960, John Fred Schlafly Correspondence Unmarked Box 1, Fred Schlafly Papers Folders 1960 (unprocessed).

52. William F. Buckley, "A Dilemma of Conservatives," *Freeman* (August, 1954), quoted in Sheldon Richman, "New Deal Nemesis: The 'Old Right' Jeffersonians," *The Independent Review* (Fall, 1996), I:2, 201–37.

One of the problems of this discussion is that the prewar Right has not been fully explored by scholars, other than studies of congressional conservative opposition to the New Deal and studies of noninterventionists. For congressional conservatism, see James T. Patterson, *Congressional Conservatism and the New Deal: The Growth of the Conservative Coalition in Congress, 1933–1939* (Lexington, 1967); also James T. Patterson, *Mr. Republican: A Biography of Robert A. Taft* (Boston, 1972). The best study of noninterventionists is Justus D. Doenecke, *Storm on the Horizon: The Challenge to American Intervention, 1939–1941* (Lanham, MD, 2000), but also important are Wayne S. Cole, *America First: The Battle against American Intervention, 1940–1941* (New York, 1953); Wayne S. Cole, *Charles A. Lindbergh and the Battle against Intervention in World War II* (New York, 1983); also Robert James Maddox, *William E. Borah and American Foreign Policy* (Baton Rouge, 1969); and Ronald Radosh, *Prophets on the Right: Profiles of Conservative Critics of American Globalism* (New York, 1975).

53. Leo P. Ribuffo, *The Old Christian Right: The Protestant Far Right from the Great Depression to the Cold War* (Philadelphia, 1983); Justin Raimondo, *Reclaiming the American Right: The Lost Legacy of the Conservative Movement* (Burlingame, CA, 1993); and Paul Gottfried and Thomas Fleming, *The Conservative Movement* (Boston, 1988).

54. Both quoted in Justus D. Doenecke, *Storm on the Horizon: The Challenge to American Intervention, 1939–1941* (Lanham, MD, 2000), pp. 212 and 219. The following discussion of anti-interventionists relies heavily on this study.

55. Writing to Senator James Wadsworth in 1935 about the recent establishment of the anti-Roosevelt Liberty League, oilman J. Howard Pew observed that monopoly in business and monopoly in government were equal threats. J. Howard Pew to James W. Wadsworth, January 4, 1935, James W. Wadsworth papers, Box 26, Library of Congress.

56. Typical in this regard was Fred Schlafly's friend, Clarence E. Manion. In the 1930s, Manion emerged as a powerful figure in the Indiana Republican party and a national leader in the America First movement. Pushed out of the deanship by Theodore Hesburgh, the new president of Notre Dame, who had taken up the university's seemingly perennial quest for the holy grail of academic respectability, Manion launched a radio program in 1954, the "Manion Forum," that made him one of the leaders of the emerging conservative movement. Manion brought to the conservative movement a distrust of economic concentration that first found expression when he and a group planned to launch the *Independent Citizen*, a monthly magazine devoted to the interests of the "little fellow" in business and politics in early 1929. Through this magazine, which never got off the ground because of the Crash of 1929, Manion sought to denounce big government, chain stores, and the "pagan" statist philosophies of fascism and communism. Clarence Manion to Senator Brookhard, February 12, 1929; and Manion to Hon. Gifford Pinchot, February 12, 1929, Clarence Manion papers, Box 1, Chicago Historical Society.

57. John Fred Schlafly to D. M. Ellinwood, September 1, 1961, John F. Schlafly Papers, 1961 Folder, Eagle Forum Archives (unprocessed).

58. "The Left Wing and the Bill of Rights," *St. Louis Union Trust Company Letter* (October 1949), p. 38.

CHAPTER TWO
IDEOLOGY AND POLITICS IN 1952

1. Ronald Reagan, "Creators of the Future," March 8, 1985, Presidential Papers of Ronald Reagan (Washington, D.C., 1986).

2. "About Books," *American Legion Magazine*, October 1956, Phyllis Schlafly to Editor, *Our Sunday Visitor*, April 20, 1958 in Scrapbook, 1957–58, Personal Papers of Phyllis Schlafly.

3. Herbert Philbrick, *I Led Three Lives: Citizen, "Communist," Counterspy* (New York, 1952); James Burnham, *The Web of Subversion: Underground Networks in the U.S. Government* (New York, 1954); J. Edgar Hoover, *Masters of Deceit: The Story of Communism in America and How to Fight It* (New York, 1958); Robert Morris, *No Wonder We Are Losing* (New York, 1958); and Ralph de Toledano, *Seeds of Treason* (Chicago, 1962).

4. John Earle Haynes, *The American Communist Movement: Storming Heaven Itself* (Chicago, 1992).

5. Elinor Lipper, *Eleven Years in Soviet Prison Camps* (Chicago, 1951); and John Noble, *I Was a Slave in Russia: An American Tells His Story* (New York, 1962). Also see, Anne Applebaum, *Gulag: A History* (New York, 2003); and Donald T. Critchlow and Agnieszka Critchlow, *Enemies of the State: Personal Stories from the Gulag* (Chicago, 2002).

6. Whittaker Chambers, *Witness* (New York, 1952); and Benjamin Gitlow, *I Confess: The Truth about Communism* (New York, 1940). Sam Tanenhaus, *Whittaker Chambers: A Biography* (New York, 1998).

7. The best book on the conservative intellectuals remains George Nash, *The Conservative Intellectual Movement since 1945* (New York, 1976). For a depiction of anticommunist hysteria as a cyclical pattern of repression, see James Morone, *Hellfire Nation: The Politics of Sin in American History* (New Haven, 2003).

8. Phyllis Schlafly, "The Moral Obligations of Citizenship," *The Mindszenty Report*, October 15, 1963, Home Correspondence Files, Box 1963, Schlafly Home Archives.

9. Phyllis Schlafly, "We Invite You to Join a Cardinal Mindszenty Speakers Club," 1960, Schlafly Annual Correspondence, Home Files, Box 1959–60.

10. For understanding the relationship between intellectual Catholics and political conservativism, see Patrick Allitt, *Catholic Intellectuals and Conservatives in America, 1950–1985* (Ithaca, NY 1993).

11. An important and generally overlooked book that reveals the Republican party perspective on these past defeats is James L. Wick, *How NOT to Run for President: A Handbook for Republicans* (New York, 1952).

12. Fred Schlafly captured the complaint of the Right's views of the UN when he described the body as "a ruthless instrument of power politics to enforce the outrageous status quo that resulted from the agreements of Teheran, Yalta, and Potsdam." The "status quo" in this case was Soviet control of Eastern and Central Europe; the subjugation of these people; and the brutal repression of political and religious dissidents in the Soviet Union. Fred Schlafly warned that the draft United Nations Covenant on Human Rights would "give us world government through the back door." Other critics, given more to eschatological interpretation, went further than the Schlaflys in denouncing the UN as a "secular and anti-Christian" organization whose agenda was to move the "USA closer to a world secular pattern. . . . [Promoters of the United Nations] hate Christians" and will "tie up with godless Red China sooner than most think." Phyllis Schlafly, "Why the United States Should Reject the UN Covenant on Human Rights," Schlafly Office Files, 1949 Drawer, Eagle Forum Archives (unprocessed). Also, William Fleming, "Danger to America: The Draft Covenant of Human Rights," Schlafly Office Files, 1949 Drawer, Eagle Forum Archives (unprocessed).

13. Useful for understanding Truman's relations with the 80th Congress are Robert J. Donovan, *Conflict and Crisis* (New York, 1987), pp. 257–66, 299–305; Alonzo Hamby, *Man of the People: Harry S. Truman* (New York, 1995); Hamby, *The Imperial Years* (New York, 1976), pp. 147–48; James T. Patterson, *Grand Expectations: The United States, 1945–1974* (New York, 1996), pp. 134–64; Patterson, *Mr. Republican: A Biography of Robert A. Taft* (Boston, 1972), pp. 407–72.

14. Patterson, *Mr. Republican*, pp. 409–18.

15. Quoted in Donovan, *Conflict and Crisis*, pp. 399, 401, 417.

16. W. A. Stubblefield to Editorial Department, May 29, 1952, Robert Taft Papers, Box 410, Library of Congress.

17. Fred Schlafly to Senator Robert A. Taft, March 8, 1952, Fred Schlafly Personal Papers, Folder 1951, Eagle Forum Archives (unprocessed).

18. William J. Reardon to Robert Taft, May 21, 1952, Robert Taft Papers, Box 110, Library of Congress.

19. Quoted in Patterson, *Mr. Republican*, p. 515.

20. Historian James Patterson offers a detailed account of the 1952 campaign in his majestic biography of Taft, *Mr. Republican*, pp. 517–87.

21. Republican National Committee, *Proceedings of the Republican National Convention, Chicago, July 7–11, 1952* (Washington, D.C., 1952), p. 178. Edward L. Schapsmeier and Frederick H. Schapsmeier, *Dirksen of Illinois: Senatorial Statesman* (Urbana, 1985), pp. 78–79.

22. Patterson, *Mr. Republican*, p. 557, and for an analysis of the convention, pp. 558–65.

23. George S. Milnor to Fred Schlafly, December 16, 1954, Box 1, Folder 1954, Personal Papers of Fred Schlafly.

24. Byron Shafer, "Economic Development, Racial Desegregation, and Partisan Change," paper presented at Policy History Conference, St. Louis, May 21, 2004.

25. "Mrs. J. F. Schlafly Jr. Seeks GOP Nomination," *Alton Evening Telegraph*, January 22, 1952, Green Scrapbook I, Schlafly Personal Files.

26. "Alton Housewife Enters Race for Congress," *St. Louis Globe-Democrat*, January 23, 1952, Schlafly Personal Files.

27. Coincidentally, across the river in St. Louis, the Democrats nominated a female candidate for Congress, Mrs. Leonor Sullivan, running against the incumbent whom Schlafly had helped elect in 1946, Claude Bakewell. Sullivan went on to win her race and in 1971 spoke eloquently on the House floor against the Equal Rights Amendment.

28. "Fall Housecleaning Needed in Capital, Mrs. Schlafly Says," *Belleville News-Democrat*, October 3, 1952, Green Scrapbook, 1952, Schlafly Personal Files.

29. "Mrs. Schlafly Places Morality in Office above Intelligence," *Wood River Journal*, April 8, 1952, Green Scrapbook, 1952.

30. "Young Alton Housewife in District Race for GOP," *East St. Louis Journal*, February 22, 1952, Green Scrapbook, 1952.

31. "GOP Faction Lists Endorsements," *East St. Louis Journal*, March 26, 1952, Green Scrapbook, 1952.

32. "Candidate with Ideas of Her Own—Alton's Phyllis Stewart Schlafly," *Highland News*, March 5, 1952, Green Scrapbook.

33. "Alton Housewife Attracting Unusual Political Reaction," *Community Press*, February 28, 1952, Green Scrapbook.

34. "She's Running for Congress and Not Just on Face Value," *St. Louis Globe-Democrat*, March 3, 1952, Green Scrap Book, Schlafly Personal Papers.

35. "Housewife Who's Running for Congress," *St. Louis Post-Dispatch*, February 28, 1952, Green Scrapbook.

36. "Punishing Infractions of Youth Unfair in Light of Official Knavery, Says Mrs. Schlafly," *Wood River Journal*, February 28, 1952, Green Scrapbook.

37. The view that the Soviet Union had lured the United States into a war in Korea was plausible at the time, and archival material later found in the Soviet archives shows that Stalin had concluded that Truman would not intervene in Korea.

38. "Republican Elephant Exhibits Signs of Being Revitalized," *Wood River Journal*, February 14, 1952, Green Scrapbook.

39. She won 8,171 votes in Madison County to Godlewski's 1855 votes, and 7757 votes in St. Clair County to Godlewski's 9,532 votes.

40. "Mrs. Schlafly, Price Answers Voter Queries," *Alton Evening Telegraph*, September 26, 1952, 1952 Green Scrapbook.

41. Fred Schlafly to Mr. Samuel Wade, October 17, 1952, 1952 Box, Personal Papers of Phyllis Schlafly.

42. H.L. Hunt's contribution came out of the blue. He had never met, corresponded with, or spoken to Schlafly before or after sending the check. For a detailed list of contributors and expenditures, see "Campaign Contributions of Phyllis Stewart Schlafly" and "Campaign Expenditures of Phyllis Schlafly," November 15, 1952, loose-leaf three-page report, Green Scrapbook, Schlafly Personal Papers.

43. "Nixon Analyzes Adlai; Jones Scores Carter; Mrs. Schlafly Blasts Blunder," *Belleville Daily Advocate*, October 21, 1952, Green Scrapbook.

44. After one of Bliss's speeches in East St. Louis, a Polish American came up to Schlafly to tell him, "Too bad Roosevelt didn't live. If he had, Poland would be free today." Fred Schlafly to John G. Scott (undated, October 15, 1952?), Personal Correspondence Box 1, Folders 1952, Fred Schlafly Papers.

45. "Mrs. Schlafly Hits Price Vote Record," *Alton Evening Telegraph*, October 28, 1952; "Advertisement," *East St. Louis Journal*, October 28, 1952, Green Scrapbook II, Personal Papers of Phyllis Schlafly.

46. "McCarthy Is Due, Phyllis Is Surprised," *East St. Louis Journal*, Sept. 23, 1952, Green Scrapbook, Schlafly Personal Papers.

47. "Mrs. Schlafly-Price Debate Foreign Policy," *Belleville News-Democrat*, October 22, 1952, Green Scrapbook

48. "Mrs. Schlafly, Melvin Price Tell Views to BPWC Members," *Alton Evening Telegraph*, October 22, 1952, 1952 Box, Schlafly Personal Files.

49. "What Caused the Korean War," (advertisement) *Belleville Advocate*, July 30, 1952; "Calls for Real Get Tough in Korea Policy," *Belleville Advocate*, June 24, 1952; Mrs. Schlafly Asks Bombing of Korean Plants," *Alton Evening Telegraph*, June 24, 1952, Green Scrapbook

50. "Mrs. Schlafly Hits Price on Defense," *Alton Evening Telegraph*, October 28, 1952, 1952 Green Scrapbook.

51. "10,000,000 Youth Face Draft If New Dealers are Reelected," *Alton Evening Telegraph*, October 20, 1952, 1952 Box; "Korean Draft Hit by Schlafly," *Alton Evening Telegraph*, November 1, 1952, Green Scrapbook II.

52. "Women Must Stand to Protect Family: Schlafly," *Belleville Advocate*, September 9, 1952, Green Scrapbook.

53. This position was strikingly similar to prewar Tory policy in England, which called for a rearmament program confined to the defense of the home islands by air and naval power, which would minimize economic and political disruption.

54. For an excellent discussion of Tory prewar policy, see Brendan Evans and Andrew Taylor, *From Salisbury to Major: Continuity and Change in Conservative Politics* (Manchester, 1996), pp. 52–57.

55. "Why Our District Needs a New Congressman," Political Advertisement, 1952 Box, Schlafly Personal Files; "Price and Mrs. Schlafly Talk to Wood River Woman's Club," *Belleville News Democrat*, October 11, 1952, 1952 Green Scrapbook II.

56. " 'Price Misled Veterans on VA Loans,' Mrs. Schlafly," *Belleville News Democrat*, October 4, 1952; "VA Treats Veterans 'Way Knetzer Treated Customers,'" *East St. Louis Journal*, October 5, 1952 in 1952 Green Scrapbook, Schlafly Personal Papers.

57. "Labor Betrayed by New Deal, Says Congress Nominee," *Belleville Advocate*, August 30, 1952; "Mrs Schlafly Says Labor 'Betrayed,'" *Alton Evening Telegraph*, August 30, 1952, 1952 Green Scrapbook.

58. "Mrs. Schlafly Flays Democratic Policies," *Alton Evening Telegraph*, October 15, 1952, 1952 Green Scrapbook.

59. "Price Spurs Lady's Call for Debate in District," *East St. Louis Journal*, September 12, 1952; "Mrs. Schlafly Asks Debate with Price," *Alton Evening Telegraph*, September 12, 1952, 1952 Green Scrapbook.

60. "Price, Mrs. Schlafly Cannot Agree on Campaign Issues," *Belleville News-Democrat*, September 25, 1952, 1952 Green Scrapbook.

61. "Mrs. Schlafly, Price Answer Voter Queries," *Alton Evening Telegraph*, September 26, 1952), Green Scrapbook II.

62. Phyllis Schlafly Says Korean War Can End Quickly," *Belleville Advocate*, September 26, 1952.

63. "Congressional Race," *St. Louis Post-Dispatch*, October 26, 1952, Green Scrapbook II.

64. James O. Monroe, "Double-Edge Sword," *Collinsville Herald*, June 27, 1952, 1952 Green Scrapbook.

65. "Half Truths Are the Biggest Lies," *Collinsville Herald*, August 22, 1952, 1952 Green Scrapbook.

66. Lee Brashear, "Our Two Ladies for Congress," *St. Louis Post-Dispatch*, October 19, 1952, Green Scrapbook II.

67. "The County Campaign," *East St. Louis Journal*, November 2, 1962, Green Scrapbook II.

68. Just a year earlier Fred Schlafly had written Illinois Senator Everett Dirksen to compliment him on his recent vote against extending the draft. "My wife and I congratulate you on your courageous vote against extending the draft. . . . [O]ur country should not furnish a standing army for Europe, particularly when the latter is unwilling to draft many of its own boys." Fred Schlafly to Senator Everett Dirksen, May 29, 1951, Fred Schlafly Personal Papers, Unmarked Box 1, Folder 1951, Eagle Forum Office.

69. Her reference compared Dean Acheson's practice of wearing formal morning attire to Alger Hiss' wearing a prisoner's uniform. "Mrs. Schlafly Delivers Keynoter for GOP Convention in Springfield," *East St. Louis Citizen*, June 27, 1952, in 1952 Campaign Green Scrapbook I, Phyllis Schlafly Personal Papers.

70. Ibid.

CHAPTER THREE
ANTICOMMUNISM: A YOUNG WOMAN'S CRUSADE

1. Phyllis Schlafly, "What Can One Individual Do for Freedom?" draft, Annual Correspondence, Box 1960, Personal Papers of Phyllis Schlafly.

2. "Is this Tomorrow, America Under Communism," Catechical Educational Guild Society (1947).

3. The importance of race and anticommunism in the South is captured in Jeff Woods, *Black Struggle Red Scare: Segregation and Anti-Communism in the South, 1948–1968* (Baton Rouge, 2004); and for another perspective, Neil R. McMillen, *The Citizen's Council: Organized Resistance to the Second Reconstruction, 1954–64* (Urbana, 1971), especially pp. 189–206.

4. Phyllis Schlafly to Vincent P. Ring, July 4, 1959, Box 1959–60, Personal Papers of Phyllis Schlafly.

5. A critical account of past historical treatments of communist espionage in the American government is found in John Earl Haynes and Harvey Klehr, *In Denial: Historians, Communism and Espionage* (San Francisco, 2003).

6. Information drawn from Bentley interviews became known in Fr. John F. Cronin, *The Problem of American Communism in 1945: Facts and Recommendations* (Baltimore, 1945), based on secret information given to him by J. Edgar Hoover, director of the FBI.

7. A good summary of these spy cases can be found in John Earl Haynes, *Red Scare or Red Menace? American Communism and Anti-Communism in the Cold War Era* (Chicago, 1996), pp. 50–63. For an evaluation of these spy cases in light of later documents drawn from American intelligence and the Soviet archives, see Harvey Klehr and John Earl Haynes, *The Secret World of American Communism* (New Haven, 1995), pp. 309–313; Haynes and Klehr, *Venona: Decoding Soviet Espionage in America* (New Haven, 1999); Allen Weinstein, *The Haunted Wood: Soviet Espionage in America—The Stalin Era* (New Haven, 1999); and Herbert Romerstein and Eric Breidel, *The Venona Secrets: Exposing Soviet Espionage and America's Traitors* (Washington, D. C., 2000). Of interest is Elizabeth Bentley's autobiography, *Out of Bondage* (New York, 1988). This reissue of her earlier memoir includes an extensive afterword by Hayden Peake, which rebutted attacks on her testimony, especially by David Caute, *The Great Fear: the Purge under Truman and Eisenhower* (New York, 1978). For the Rosenberg case, see Ronald Radosh and Joyce Milton, *The Rosenberg File* (New York, 1983). For an earlier attempt to exonerate the Rosenbergs, see Walter and Miriam Schneir, *Invitation to an Inquest* (New York, 1973). The Chamber-Hiss affair is discussed in Allen Weinstein, *Perjury: The Hiss-Chambers Case* (New York, 1978). Sam Tanenhaus offers a superb biography in *Whittaker Chambers: A Biography* (New York, 1997).

8. Quoted in M. J. Heale, *American Anti-Communism: Combating the Enemy Within, 1830–1970* (Baltimore, 1990), p. 148.

9. Useful works include David Oshinsky, *A Conspiracy So Immense: The World of Joe McCarthy* (New York, 1983); Michael J. Ybarra, *Washington Gone Crazy: Senator Pat McCarran and the Great American Communist Hunt* (Hanover, NH 2004); Arthur Herman, *Joseph McCarthy: Reexamining the Life and Legacy of America's Most Hated Senator* (New York, 2000). Although Herman's book received many unfavorable reviews, it contains a wealth of information not found in earlier accounts of McCarthy.

10. Historical evidence reveals that the North Korean invasion was approved by Josef Stalin. See John Gaddis, *We Now Know: Rethinking the Cold War* (New York, 1997).

11. Congressional criticism of McCarthy certainly did not mean opposition to investigating communist infiltration into government. Senator John McClellan (D-Arkansas), who led Democratic opposition to McCarthy in the Committee on Government Operations and later replaced McCarthy as chair of that committee, remained staunchly anticommunist and continued to argue for outlawing the Communist party.

12. A Gallup poll taken immediately after the hearings showed that McCarthy was still viewed favorably by 34 percent of the American people. George H. Gallup, *The Gallup Poll, Public Opinion 1935–1971 Volume II* (New York, 1971), p. 1247.

13. This observation and term is found in Richard Gid Powers, *Not Without Honor*, p. 248. The examples of popular anticommunism are drawn from this book, see pp. 229–33; 245–55.

14. An excellent study of the anticommunist mindset is found in Michelle M. Nickerson, "Women, Gender, and Conservatism in Cold War Los Angeles, 1945–1966," Ph.D. Dissertation, Yale University, 2003. Also, see Philip Jenkins, *The Cold War at Home: The Red Scare in Pennsylvania, 1945–1960* (Chapel Hill, 1999); M. J. Heale, *American Anti-Communism: Combating the Enemy Within, 1830–1970* (Baltimore, 1990); and for liberal anticommunism, Richard Gid Powers, *Not Without Honor* (New York, 1995).

15. "Mrs. Schlafly Says Price Partly Right in Communist Claim," *Belleville Advocate*, September 19, 1952; "Red Spies Had a Field Day Here: Mrs. Schlafly," *Belleville News-Democrat*, October 9, 1952 in Green Scrapbook II; "Mrs. Schlafly Hits Price Vote Record," *Alton Evening Telegraph*, October 25, 1952, 1952 Correspondence; "Advertisement," *East St. Louis Journal*, October 28, 1952, Green Scrapbook II, Phyllis Schlafly Personal Papers.

16. Peter H. Irons, "American Business and the Origins of McCarthyism: The Cold War Crusade of the United States Chamber of Commerce," in Robert Griffith and Athan Theoharis, eds., *The Specter: Original:Essays on the Cold War and the Origins of McCarthyism* (New York, 1974).

17. These examples are drawn from Kenneth D. Durr, *Behind the Backlash: White Working-Class Politics in Baltimore, 1940–1980* (Chapel Hill, 2003) pp. 45–55; Becky M. Nicolaides, *My Blue Heaven: Life and Politics in the Working-Class Suburbs of Los Angeles, 1920–1965* (Chicago, 2002), pp. 280–85; and Philip Jenkins, *Cold War at Home: The Red Scare in Pennsylvania, 1945–1960* (Chapel Hill, 1999), pp. 142–62.

18. Quoted in M. J. Heale, *American Anti-communism: Combating the Enemy Within, 1830–1970* (Baltimore, 1990), p. 171. This discussion of Protestant anticommunism draws heavily from Heale's study.

19. Fred Schlafly subsequently appeared as a frequent lecturer in Schwarz schools across the country, speaking on Supreme Court decisions, communism, and civil liberties.

20. Powers, *Not Without Honor*, discusses Catholic anticommunism, especially on pp. 275–76.

21. First proposed by economics professor Lev E. Dobriansky in the mid-1950s, Captive Nations Week was designed to focus national attention on Soviet imperialism and educate the American people about the plight of the enslaved peoples of Eastern Europe. American Friends of Captive Nations was formed in April 1956 to pressure the Republican party to endorse this proposal in its party platform. In 1958, it was introduced in Congress by Rep. Albert Cretella (R-Connecticut) and became public law in January 1960. It revealed the deep involvement of Catholics in the anticommunism movement. Catholics

also saw Captive Nations Week as a vehicle to gain greater recognition of the plight of Catholic countries under communist control. For the importance the Right placed on Captive Nations, see Bernard Bailey, *The Captive Nations: Our First Line of Defense* (Chicago, 1969). Richard Nixon's blurb on the front cover read, "We will never write off the millions of people enslaved behind the Iron Curtain. Their freedom shall always be our objective." Also, Powers, *Not Without Honor*, pp. 275–276. Also, see "Testimony of Christopher Emmet, Chairman, American Friends of Captive Nations, Republican Platform Committee, July 10, 1960" (mimeograph copy); and "Dr. Lev E. Dobriansky," *The Manion Forum* (November 12, 1961); Lev. E. Dobriansky to Member of Captive Nations Week Observance Committee, June 8, 1960; "Captive Nations Week Credited to Professor," *Chicago Tribune*, July 25, 1959, in Communism Office Files, Eagle Forum Archives.

22. There is a large literature on the history of tensions between American pluralism and Catholics. A good starting point is Philip Gleason, *Speaking of Diversity: Language and Ethnicity in Twentieth-Century America* (Baltimore, 1992). Also see John Courtney Murray, *Religious Liberty: Catholic Struggles with Pluralism* (Louisville, 1993). An excellent discussion of secular liberalism and Catholics is found in Philip Gleason, "American Catholics and Liberalism, 1789–1960," in R. Bruce Douglass and David Hollenbach, eds., *Catholicism and Liberalism: Contributions to American Public Philosophy* (Cambridge, MA, 1994). Also, see John T. McGreevy, *Catholicism and American Freedom: A History* (New York, 2003).

23. Phyllis Schlafly to T. Coleman Andrews, February 19, 1957, Box 6, T. Coleman Andrews Papers, University of Oregon.

24. The American Legion's All-American Conference provided an umbrella for the gathering of groups. These meetings were not intended to create a unified movement with a shared program, but instead provided opportunities to hear major speakers of the day. The John Birch Society (JBS), founded by candy-manufacturer Robert Welch in 1958, was the first organization with a national membership and a centrally directed program, but many conservatives and grassroots leaders and activists shied away from it. Moreover, the establishment of the JBS occurred at a time when organized anticommunism was being subsumed into the larger Goldwater for President campaign.

25. Dr. Fred Schwarz, *Beating the Unbeatable Foe* (Washington, D.C. 1996).

26. K. H. Donavine, "The Fight against Communism, Socialism, and Other Menaces to Our Liberty and Welfare: An Estimate of the Situation," in Hubbard Russell to New Deal Friend, July 4, 1955, Schlafly Office Subject Files pre-1972, Eagle Forum Archives.

27. Cited in Arnold Forster and Benjamin R. Epstein, *Danger on the Right*, p. 11.

28. Major George Racey Jordan, *From Major Jordan Diaries* (New York, 1952). However, Jordan collected a $10,000 check from NBC for libeling him.

29. Daughters of the American Revolution of Illinois, *Proceedings of the Sixty-First Annual State Conference, March 11–12–13, 1957* (Chicago, 1957), pp. 112–13.

30. Betty Shaw, "Report of America Wake Up Radio Committee" (1962), DAR, Wake Up America Program, Schlafly Home Files.

31. Daniel Bell, "The Dispossessed," *The Radical Right*, pp. 14–45.

32. Writing in 1962, sociologist Seymour Lipset provided some hard data to his examination of the Right in his *Politics of Unreason*, but even this study reached conclusions that with hindsight appear surprisingly unwarranted.

33. Friedrich A. von Hayek, *The Road to Serfdom* (Chicago, 1944).

34. Richard Gid Powers, *Not Without Honor* (New Haven, 1998 edition) provides an excellent survey of liberal anticommunism, from which this discussion draws heavily.

35. This summary of Schlesinger draws heavily from Richard Gid Power's discussion of the *Vital Center* in *Not Without Honor*, pp. 203–207, but only reading *The Vital Center* itself captures its full power. See Arthur Schlesinger, *The Vital Center: The Politics of Freedom* (Boston, 1949).

36. Roger Kimball, "The Power of James Burnham," *New Criterion* (September 2002), p. 4–11.

37. On the fringe of the anticommunism movement were those such as the Liberty Lobby (no relation to the anti-New Deal Liberty League), founded in 1957 by Willis Carto, given to elaborate conspiracy theories that placed communists within a larger, more tangled network with origins extending back to the ancient Babylonians.

38. Richard Gid Powers maintains that the primary difference between liberal ("respectable") and grassroots ("counter-subversive") lay in their attitudes toward the American Communist party. The above discussion relies on Powers in distinguishing liberal and grassroots attitudes toward domestic subversion, but takes exception to limiting differences only to domestic policy. See *Not Without Honor*, pp. 214–15.

39. Phyllis Schlafly, "The Economic Failure of Communism," America Wake Up Program, January 13, 1963, Annual Correspondence, Box 1963, Personal Papers of Phyllis Schlafly.

40. Schlafly used this theme in a number of speeches and writings, but it is fully developed in a private letter, Phyllis Schlafly to Vincent P. Ring, Knapp Monarch Company, July 44, 1960, Annual Correspondence, Box 1959–60, Personal Papers of Phyllis Schlafly.

41. Ibid.

42. Christian Anti-Communism Crusade, "What Is the Christian Anti-Communism Crusade?" (1963).

43. Merrill Root, "The Battle for the Mind," speech delivered at DAR National Defense Dinner, Abe Lincoln Hotel, March 9, 1960, where he was introduced by State Chairman Schlafly, Annual Correspondence, Box 1960, Personal Papers

of Phyllis Schlafly. Root's books were highly recommended and often cited in grassroots conservative literature. He later became a founding member of the John Birch Society. See E. Merrill Root, *Brainwashing in the High Schools* (New York, 1959); and *Collectivism on the Campus: The Battle for the Mind in American Colleges* (New York, 1955).

44. Phyllis Schlafly, Notes on Dr. Fred Schwarz's Speech, Naval Air Station, May 2, 1960, Subject Files Communism, Eagle Forum Archives.

45. Taylor Caldwell, *The Devil's Advocate* (New York, 1952), p. 30.

46. See Phyllis Schlafly, "Notebook," Greater St. Louis School of Anti-Communism, April 24–28, 1961, Subject Files, Communism, Eagle Forum Archives. An extensive literature critiquing the educational establishment appeared in the 1950s. See Augustin G. Rudd, *Bending the Twig: The Revolution in Education and Its Effort on Our Children* (Chicago, 1957); Mary L. Allen, *Education or Indoctrination* (Caldwell, ID, 1956); Paul W. Shafer and John Howland Snow, *The Turning of the Tides* (New York, 1956); and George N. Allen, *Undercover Teacher* (Garden City, New York, 1960).

47. C. S. Lewis, *The Screwtape Letters* (New York: Time Inc., 1967 edition), p. 1.

48. In this regard, she drew the same conclusions as Mary L. Allen, who concluded, "Basically the Dewey pragmatic philosophy is materialist, recognizing no permanent truths or values." See, *Education or Indoctrination*, p. 28. Dewey remained the enemy of conservatives into the twenty-first century.

49. Schlafly often wrote and spoke about American education throughout the 1950s. A summary of her views is found in her speech, "What's Happened to Our Schools," in Annual Correspondence, Box 1960–62, Personal Papers of Phyllis Schlafly.

50. Fred Schwarz, "Introduction to Major William E. Mayer," Chicago Seminar (n.d.) Cassette, Eagle Forum Archives.

51. Daughters of the American Revolution, *Textbook Study* (Washington, D.C. 1964); Jenkin Lloyd Jones, "Time to Get New Schoolbooks," *U.S. News and World Report*, (March 25, 1963), in Subject Files, Public School, Eagle Forum Archives.

52. Quoted in Phyllis Schlafly, "Fred C. Schwarz Lecture Notes, April 30, 1957, Subject Files, Communism, Eagle Forum Archives.

53. More tempered in tone and substance, Arthur S. Trace, Jr. wrote in *The Bookman* that American children were not able to learn from their textbooks that their country was "great and beautiful" and had produced many great men and women in the past. Trace declared that conservatives did not believe that "our schools should launch a program to instill in our students a raging jingoism or which will exhort them to flag-waving demonstrations, nor to adopt a systematic and relentless, even brutal indoctrination program, which is the Communist program." Arthur S. Trace Jr., "Patriotism in Soviet and American Textbooks," in *The Bookman* (Winter 1962), pp. 27–35. Also, see Medford

Evans, "Are School Textbooks Aiding in the Destruction of the American Republic?" *News and Views* (September 1961), pp. 8–11; E. Merrill Root, "Let's Review a Textbook," *Human Events*, (April 18, 1954), p. 17; Mary Barclay Erb, "National Defense Committee," *DAR Magazine* (September 1957), pp. 1071–74; Elizabeth Chestnut Barnes, "How Government Agencies Changed Our History Textbooks," *DAR Magazine* (December 1960), pp. 701–702, in Subject Files, Communism, Eagle Forum Archives.

54. Phyllis Schlafly, "How Many More Christmases?" Mindszenty Foundation Press Release, December 15, 1961, Annual Correspondence, Box 1961, Personal Papers of Phyllis Schlafly.

55. Phyllis Schlafly, "Patriotism Protects the Constitution," Speech before the Division Meetings of the Illinois State Society of DAR: Danville, September 15, 1959; Chicago, September 16; Rockford, September 17; Mount Vernon, September 19; East St. Louis, September 30; Quincy, October 1; Roseville, October 2, 1959; Box 1959, Personal Papers of Phyllis Schlafly.

56. Fred Schlafly to Clarence Manion, January 3, 1957, Unmarked Box 1, Fred Schlafly Personal Papers, Eagle Forum Archives.

57. Fred Schlafly served as legal counsel for the Manion Forum. The Schlaflys attended several Notre Dame football games as the Manions' guests, and Manion stayed at the Schlafly home in Alton the night after he delivered a nationwide radio broadcast for Eisenhower just before the 1952 election. Manion and the Schlaflys saw the world in similar terms. Manion built a national reputation as a constitutional authority for the conservative anticommunist movement and an opponent of internationalism. Clarence Manion's rise to national prominence was one of many Catholic success stories that occurred in the first half of the twentieth century. Born into a working class family in Henderson, Kentucky, the precocious Manion attended a local Catholic college, St. Mary's, and then Catholic University in Washington, D.C., where he received an M.A. in Philosophy. He took a position teaching history and government at the University of Notre Dame in Indiana. In 1941 he became Dean of the Law School. A superb discussion of Hesburgh's removal of Manion at Notre Dame is found in Robert E. Burns, *Being Catholic, Being American: The Notre Dame Story, 1934–1952*, Volume II (Notre Dame, Indiana, 2000), pp. 428–36.

58. For Schlafly's role in drafting the report, see Fred Schlafly to Emmet Glore, October 15, 1958, Personal Correspondence, Folders 1957, Unmarked Box 1, Fred Schlafly papers.

59. For a discussion of cases in context of the ABA report see, Harry W. Kirwin, *The Inevitable Success: Herbert R. O'Conor* (Westminster, MD, 1962), pp. 533–35.

60. Specifically, the report called attention to *McGrain v. Daugherty* (1927), which categorically upheld the power of Congress to investigate and its power to order the arrest of a material witness. The report also pointed to published

articles by Justices Felix Frankfurter and Hugo Black, written before they came to the bench, supporting congressional investigations. Writing for *Harper's* in 1936, Black had called for congressional investigations to destroy "by rays of pitiless publicity the abuses of special privilege." The report concluded that if it were proper to "investigate businessmen, it is surely proper to investigate Communists." Hugo L. Black, "Inside a Senate Investigation," *Harper's Monthly*, 127 (February 1936), pp. 275–86, quoted in Kirwin, *The Inevitable Success*, p. 536. Frankfurter spoke in the context of the Teapot Dome scandal.

61. Geo S. Montgomery Jr. to Pres. Walter E. Craig, ABA, March 2, 1964; Fred Schlafly to Clarence Manion, February 25, 1964; and Fred Schlafly to Clarence Manion, July 16, 1965, Box 79, Manion papers.

62. Fred Schlafly remained on the ABA committee for two more years and in 1958 and 1959 (under the chairmanship of Peter Campbell Brown) submitted substantially identical reports criticizing the Warren Court's decisions. The above discussion of the writing and reception of the report is found in Kirwin, *The Inevitable Success*, pp. 529–45. For Fred Schlafly's perspective on the case, see Herbert R. O'Conor to Fred Schlafly, March 28, 1958, Folders 1957, and Correspondence Unmarked Box 1, Fred Schlafly papers.

63. Fred Schlafly, "Communism and the Constitution," in "Communism on the Map and the Greater St. Louis School of Anti-Communism," April 1961, prepared by the St. Louis Civil Liberties Committee, St. Louis, 1962. Mimeograph, Dudman papers, Box 17, Library of Congress.

64. Dr. Fred Schwarz, *Beating the Unbeatable Foe: One Man's Victory over Communism, Leviathan, and the Last Enemy* (Washington, D.C., 1996), pp. 165–67.

65. Phyllis Schlafly's involvement in organized anticommunist education began in the summer of 1956 when she hosted a weekend anticommunist seminar at Pere Marquette Lodge in Grafton, Illinois, featuring Louis Budenz, a former Communist party official and editor of the *Daily Worker* who broke with the party to testify before Congress on the Communist threat inside America. The two-day seminar drew 40 participants from Wisconsin, Illinois, and Missouri. The following year she brought the Australian physician, Dr. Fred Schwarz, to St. Louis for a series of four lectures on communism at the St. Louis Medical Society. In 1958 she organized a week-long anticommunist school held at Tower Grove Baptist Church in St. Louis, which featured Dr. Fred Schwarz as the principal speaker, as well as Richard Arens on "The Psychology of Communists," and William B. Strube on "Communism and Business." Following the school, Schwarz recommended that the Schlaflys establish a Catholic anticommunist organization. Fred Schlafly to Eleanor Schlafly, July 6, 1956; and Fred Schlafly to Karl Hess, May 11, 1956; and Karl Hess to Fred Schlafly, Personal Correspondence, Unmarked Box I, Folder 1953, Fred Schlafly Papers (unprocessed), Eagle Forum Archives.

66. Council members included Fr. C. Stephen Dunker, C.M., a missionary in China when the communists took over; Bishop Cuthbert O'Gara and Bishop Rembert Kowalski, who both spent time in Chinese prisons; Fr. John A. Houle, S.J., assistant director of the American Jesuits in China; Fr. Harold W. Rigney, S.V.D., who was imprisoned by the Chinese Communists and later worked in a leper colony in the Philippines; Fr. John Kelly, who escaped from Castro's Cuba; Fr. Warren DiCharry, Fr. Vincent Loeffler, and Fr. Robert Crawford, who had been missionaries in China and imprisoned by the Communists; Fr. Ismael Teste, an exiled Cuban priest; and Fr. L. K. Parker, O.Praem, who experienced communism in Hungary.

67. Harold William Rigney, *Four Years in Red Hell* (Chicago, 1956), p. 157.

68. Press Release, Cardinal Mindszenty Foundation, June 15, 1959, Schlafly Annual Correspondence Box 1959, Personal Papers of Phyllis Schlafly.

69. Most of the key texts promoted by the movement were hardly page-turners. Even Frank Meyer's insider's account of the Communist party, *The Moulding of a Communist* (1961), made for dry reading. Most such books provided long didactic passages describing Marxist dialectics, Soviet history, and Communist tactics.

70. Phyllis Schlafly, "The Big Things Are Done by Little People," draft, February 15, 1960, Schlafly Annual Correspondence, Box 1959, Personal Papers of Phyllis Schlafly.

71. Duncan Stewart, "America's Freedom Fighters," *Priest Magazine* (August 1961), Box 196, Personal Papers of Phyllis Schlafly; also, a report of Mindszenty activities is found in a pamphlet, Mindszenty Foundation, "Handbook to Combat Communism" (St. Louis, 1961).

72. For example, see Mrs. L. Helen Krippendorf to Phyllis Schlafly, March 11, 1963, Schlafly Office Subject Files, pre-1972 Mindszenty Foundation.

73. When the Cardinal Mindszenty Foundation finished conducting a two-day seminar in 1960 for social science teachers in the Archdiocese of St. Louis, the alumnae of Villa Duchesne, a prestigious girls' high school, hosted a dinner for 1,432 people to thank the Mindszenty Foundation. Among the dignitaries attending was the Archbishop of St. Louis, the auxiliary bishop of the city, the president of the local Jesuit college, Saint Louis University, the superintendent of schools for the archdiocese, and the chancellor of Washington University. Phyllis Schlafly, "Teaching Communism in Catholic Schools," Annual Correspondence, Box 1959–60, Personal Papers of Phyllis Schlafly.

74. Phyllis Schlafly, "Communism Is an Iceberg," speech to Senior Citizens Club, Alton, Illinois, Annual Correspondence, Box 1959, Personal Papers of Phyllis Schlafly.

75. Phyllis Schlafly, "Teaching Communism in Catholic Schools;" Schlafly, "The Cold War inside America," "The Red Trap of Disarmament," "The Magic

of Words," and "Don't Fall for the Fallout Falsehoods," draft for Cardinal Mindszenty Newsletter (January, 1960) Box 1959–60, Personal Papers of Phyllis Schlafly. On consumerism from a different perspective, see Lizabeth Cohen, *A Consumer's Republic: The Politics of Mass Consumption in Postwar America* (New York, 2003).

76. Admiral C. Turner Joy, *How Communists Negotiate* (New York, 1955), p. xi.

77. The extent of this grassroots mobilization on behalf of the Bricker amendment is detailed in the Clarence Manion papers, especially Voters USA, Maryland Branch to William L. McGrath, President, Foundation for the Study of Treaty Law, January 4, 1953; W. L. McGrath to Arnold Kruckman, December 28, 1953; Elizabeth E. Shannon, St. Paul Archdiocese of St. Paul, to Clarence Manion, November 18, 1953; Mrs. Dorothy Dreiling to Clarence Manion, December 4, 1953; Walter A. Knerr to Clarence Manion, Edward A. Rumley, Executive Secretary, Committee for Constitutional Government, to Clarence Manion, January 14, 1954; Theodore G. Hollinshead, President, Buffalo Freedom Club, to Clarence Manion, January 24, 1954; and Manion to Pierre Champion, Champion Rivet Company, January 25, 1954, in Clarence Manion papers, Box 62, Chicago Historical Society.

78. Author interview with Schlafly, September 25, 2002.

79. "GOP Women to Hear Mrs. Schlafly," *Alton Evening Telegraph*, October 15, 1953, Scrapbook, 1953–57, Schlafly Personal Papers.

80. When President Eisenhower's cabinet met in January 1954, most cabinet members supported the Bricker amendment and Secretary of Defense Charles Wilson spoke on behalf of it. Lee Edwards, *The Conservative Revolution: The Movement that Remade America* (New York, 1999), pp. 73–74; and William Manchester, *The Glory and the Dream: A Narrative History of America, 1932–1972* (Boston, 1973), I:824–25.

81. The amendment also caused rancor in the lower levels of his administration, although Eisenhower vehemently denied that the division over the amendment was simply conservatives versus liberals. Dwight D. Eisenhower, *Mandate for Change: The White House Years* (New York, 1963), pp. 278–85, quoted on p. 280.

82. E. E. Townes to Clarence Manion, March 16, 1954, Box 62, Manion papers.

83. Merwin K. Hart to Earl Harding, March 26, 1954, Box 62, Manion papers.

84. John W. Bricker to Clarence Manion, November 14, 1978; John W. Bricker to Clarence Manion, August 14, 1979, Box 62, Manion Papers.

85. Khrushchev did not discuss the widespread arrests and executions against nonparty members or the continued existence of Soviet labor camps. David J. Dallin, *Soviet Foreign Policy after Stalin* (Philadelphia, 1961), pp. 369–82.

86. For example, Radio Free Rakoski broadcast these words. "Attention, attention! We ask you to forward our call for help to President Eisenhower. We

ask for immediate intervention, immediate intervention." Later a freedom fighter was quoted as saying, "We didn't expect arms—we knew that was impossible. We wanted moral support." Quoted in an eyewitness account of the Soviet invasion, Noel Barber, *Seven Days of Freedom: The Hungarian Uprising, 1956* (New York, 1974), pp. 200 and 210.

87. "Right or Wrong: Our Share in Hungary's Tragedy," *Our Sunday Visitor*, December 9, 1956, Black Scrapbook, 1953–57, Personal Papers of Phyllis Schlafly.

88. Schlafly, Report of National Defense Committee (1961) Box 1959–60, Personal Papers of Phyllis Schlafly.

89. Peter Deriabin's revelations as to KGB spy activities, as well as Soviet military and foreign policy strategy, made for exciting reading, confirming many of the worst fears of the grassroots. See, Peter Deriabin and Frank Gibney, *The Secret World: The Terrifying Report of a High Officer of Soviet Intelligence Whose Conscience Finally Rebelled* (Garden City, New York, 1959); also, Peter Deriabin, *The Spy Who Saved the World: How A Soviet Colonel Changed the Course of History* (New York, 1992). Phyllis Schlafly, "Culture as a Cover" (1959) Box 1959, Personal Papers of Phyllis Schlafly. Fred Schwarz, "The Meaning of Cultural Exchanges," Speech before the Illinois DAR Convention (1959), in Box 1959, Personal Papers of Phyllis Schlafly.

90. For one example see, Robert Morris, *Disarmament: Weapon of Conquest* (New York, 1963).

91. Phyllis Schlafly, "Don't Fall for the Fallout Falsehoods," (draft), *Cardinal Mindszenty Newsletter* (January 15, 1960), Annual Correspondence, Box 1959–60, Personal Papers of Phyllis Schlafly.

92. Phyllis Schlafly, "The Red Trap of Disarmament," Speech at Illinois DAR State Conference, Chicago, March 3, 1961, Box 1959, Personal Papers of Phyllis Schlafly.

93. Seymour Martin Lipset and Earl Raab, *The Politics of Unreason: Right-Wing Extremism in America, 1790–1970* (New York, 1970). Also, for a more limited scholarly study published three years earlier, see John H. Bunzel, *Anti-Politics in America* (New York, 1967) and in 1971, Davis Brion Davis's *The Fear of Conspiracy: Images of Un-American Subversion from the Revolution to the Present* (Ithaca, 1971).

CHAPTER FOUR
THE REPUBLICAN RIGHT UNDER ATTACK

1. For example, Arnold Forster and Benjamin R. Epstein warned that the Radical Rightists "constitute a serious threat to our democratic process." Arnold Forster and Benjamin R. Epstein, *Danger on the Right: The Attitudes, Personnel, and Influence of the Radical Right and Extreme Conservatives* (New York, 1964), p. xvii.

2. Author discussion with Phyllis Schlafly, January 7, 2003.

3. Dr. Fred Schwarz said that the thousands of people who had flocked to his anticommunist schools in the late 1950s suddenly stopped coming in 1961 and 1962. Similarly, Herbert Philbrick, author of *I Led Three Lives* and a regular on the anticommunist lecture circuit, found fewer and fewer speaking engagements, finally forcing him to take a minor position in the federal government to support his family. Fred Schwarz, *Beating the Unbeatable Foe* (Washington, D.C. 1996), pp. 250–73. The Herbert Philbrick papers in the Library of Congress chart the decline in his speaking engagements in the 1960s. The rest of his career became one of trying to make a living on the fringes of conservative politics.

4. John Earl Haynes, *Red Scare or Red Menace? American Communism and Anti-Communism in the Cold War Era* (Chicago, 1996). For the Rosenberg case, see Ronald Radosh and Joyce Milton, *The Rosenberg File* (New Haven, 1997).

5. Phyllis Schlafly, "Don't Fall for the Fallout Falsehoods," (draft) *Cardinal Mindszenty Newsletter*, January 15, 1960; Phyllis Schlafly, "Communism in the Movie Industry," *DAR Bulletin* (January 1961); Phyllis Schlafly, "Television— Battleground of the Cold War," (draft), *The Mindszenty Report*, September 15, 1962, Box 1959–60, Personal Papers of Phyllis Schlafly.

6. Shute's position fell within a strong antinuclear sentiment within the Tory party. Shute's political views are captured in *Slide Rule: The Autobiography of an Engineer* (1955).

7. Right-wingers disliked both the plot and the authors—Eugene Burdick, a political scientist from the University of California, Berkeley, and Harvey Wheeler, a Harvard-trained political scientist then teaching at Washington and Lee University. Burdick had been acclaimed the "new Jack London" for his first novel *The Ninth Wave* (1956) and his second novel *The Ugly American* (1958). The idea for *Fail-Safe* came from a short-story, "Abraham, '58," written by Wheeler in 1957 when he was on a sabbatical at the Center for the Study of Democratic Institutions in Santa Barbara—a hotbed of radicals, pacifists, and appeasers in the eyes of many conservatives. The book was a natural for Hollywood. Eugene Burdick and Harvey Wheeler, *Fail-Safe* (New York, 1962).

8. Sidney Hook, *The Fail-Safe Fallacy* (New York, 1963).

9. Allen Winkler, *Life under a Cloud: Anxiety about the Atom* (New York, 1993).

10. Phyllis Schlafly, "Don't Fall for the Fallout Falsehoods," Ibid; Phyllis Schlafly, "Communist Master Plan for 1961," *Cardinal Mindszenty Newsletter*, February 15, 1961, Box 1960–61, Personal Papers of Phyllis Schlafly.

11. William Rorabaugh captures the optimism and tensions of the early 1960s in *Kennedy and the Promise of the Sixties* (New York, 2002); also see Godfrey Hodgson, *America in Our Time* (Garden City, New York, 1976).

12. Especially useful on these changes are Morris Dickstein, *Gates of Eden: American Culture in the Sixties* (New York, 1977); William Brandon, *Age of Aquarius: Technology and the Cultural Revolution* (Chicago, 1970); and James T. Patterson, *Grand Expectations: The United States, 1945–1974* (New York, 1996), especially pp. 442–57.

13. Quoted in Michael Beschloss, *The Crisis Years: Kennedy and Khrushchev, 1960–1963* (New York, 1991), p. 25; also, Herbert Parmet, *JFK: The Presidency of John F. Kennedy* (New York, 1980); David Burner, *John F. Kennedy and a New Generation* (Boston, 1988); and James Giglio, *The Presidency of John F. Kennedy* (Lawrence, 1991).

14. Cardinal Mindszenty Foundation, "Has the New President a Plan of Action?" Mindszenty Foundation, November 15, 1961, Box 1960–61, Schlafly Personal Files.

15. In his memoirs Khrushchev recalled, "I won't hide it, this was a happy time for me. . . . At the same time we were still conducting arrests. It was our view that these arrests served to strengthen the Soviet state and clear the road for the building of socialism on Marxist-Leninist principles." Quoted in William Taubman, *Khrushchev: The Man and His Era* (New York, 2002), p. 139, also see pp. 114–46.

16. Conservatives acted on past precedent and their understanding of the nature of communism; liberals acted on faith in their ability to change the course of history. Khrushchev had embarked on new diplomacy that broke with Stalinist foreign policy and called for détente. Yet, as Khrushchev's major biographer notes, there was another side to Khrushchev's call for peaceful coexistence. He writes that the Soviet leader believed that "reducing tensions could undermine Western resistance to Communist gains, tempt capitalists to increase East-West trade, and project a friendlier image in the Third World." William Taubman, *Khrushchev: The Man and His Era*, p. 348.

17. Phyllis Schlafly, "Are You a Sucker for Slogans?" America Wake Up Transcript, March 31, 1963, Box 1963, Phyllis Schlafly Personal Papers.

18. Mrs. J. F. Schlafly, Jr. to Mrs. Edwin Tait, May 4, 1959, Box 1959 Home Files; and "Statement Made to the Platform Committee of the Republican National Convention, July 21, 1960, Schlafly, President, Illinois Federation of Republican Women, Box 1960, Personal Papers.

19. In making this announcement, Castro revealed that he had developed a "parallel" Marxist government, kept secret even from his own cabinet. In developing this parallel government, Castro had worked with Cuban Communist party intellectual Carlos Rafael Rodríguez and his brother Raul Castro to train a disciplined Marxist cadre to take over the administrative reins of the new state. Tad Szulc, *Fidel: A Critical Portrait* (New York, 2000 edition), p. 541. Also, Georgie Anne Geyer, *Guerrilla Prince: The Untold Story of Fidel Castro* (Boston, 1991).

20. "Castro: In the Image of Lenin-Marx," *National Review*, September, 1959, p. 1; "Cuba–Reds' New Colony," *U.S. News and World Report*, December 7, 1959, p. 23; "Publisher Says Castro is Out and Out Red," *St. Louis Globe-Democrat*, July 20, 1959, p. 1; and "Cuba Air Force Chief Describes Castro, Brother, and Others as Communists," *Wall Street Journal*, July 15, 1959, p. 1.

21. Thomas Freeman (pseudonym), *The Crisis in Cuba* (New York, 1963), pp. 80–102.

22. William F. Buckley, Jr. "Herbert Matthews and Fidel Castro: I Got My Job through the *New York Times*," *Rumbles Left and Right* (New York, 1963), pp. 60–70. Former American ambassador to Cuba, Earl E. T. Smith charged that officials in the State Department had hindered his efforts to oppose Castro before he came to power. Phyllis Schlafly to Reverend John B. Sherrin, February 8, 1961, Box 1960–61, Personal Papers of Phyllis Schlafly. Also, Earl E. T. Smith, *The Fourth Floor* (New York, 1962).

23. The Committee to Defend Cuba was a broad-based conservative group that included people such as liberal anticommunist Sidney Hook, physicist Edward Teller, foreign policy expert Robert Strausz-Hupé, and others. Reflecting more of a grassroots effort was the Committee for the Monroe Doctrine that called for the protection of the Western Hemisphere from Soviet intrusion. For a perspective on grassroots organizing efforts among student and anticommunist groups in Boston see Charles A. Steele to Herbert Philbrick, June 16, 1963, Box 5, Herbert Philbrick Papers. The New Left drew inspiration from Fidel Castro. See, Van Gosse, *Where the Boys Are: Cuba, Cold War America and the Making of the New Left* (London, 1993).

24. Tad Szulc, *Fidel*, pp. 548–49. The flaws in overall strategy of the Bay of Pigs invasion are discussed in Peter Wyden, *Bay of Pigs: The Untold Story* (New York, 1979). Also, see Michael Beschloss, *The Crisis Years: Kennedy and Khrushchev, 1960–1963* (New York, 1991), pp. 144–46.

25. Adding to conservatives' belief that the State Department was pro-Castro were charges made by the American Ambassador to Costa Rica, Whiting Willauer, that he had been relieved of duties in planning the Bay of Pigs operation by Secretary of State Dean Rusk in order to prevent air support being provided to the invasion force. The State Department vehemently denied these charges, maintaining that Willauer was removed because he was not a military planner. For Phyllis Schlafly's view of the Bay of Pigs debacle and Willauer's role, see Schlafly, *The Betrayers*, pp. 34–40.

The atmosphere became even more charged when Otto F. Otepka was removed from his post as Deputy Director of Security at State. Furthermore, he claimed that his unwillingness to give security clearances to Kennedy appointees to the State Department, including Walt Rostow, had engendered the animosity that led to his removal from State. Otepka became a *cause célèbre* in conservative circles and the case led to a long drawn out legal battle between the State Department and Otepka. Conservatives rallied to Otepka's defense, including Phyllis Schlafly, who gave $105 to the legal fund. Eventually Otepka won a settlement from the U.S. government, which was taken by grassroots conservatives as a confirmation that Otepka's charges were true after all. Otto F. Otepka to Mrs. Schlafly, December 4, 1968, *The Betrayers* Box, Phyllis Schlafly Personal Papers. For a conservative view of the Otepka case, see William J. Gill, *The Ordeal of Otto Otepka* (New Rochelle, NY, 1979).

26. B. Bruce-Briggs, *The Shield of Faith: A Chronicle of Strategic Defense from Zeppelins to Star Wars* (New York, 1988), pp. 161–65. Also, Gregg Herken, *Cardinal Choices: Presidential Science Advising from the Atomic Bomb to SDI* (Stanford, 2000); Marc Trachtenberg, *History and Strategy* (Princeton, 1991); Glenn Seaborg, *Kennedy, Khrushchev, and the Test Ban* (Berkeley, 1981).

27. Transcript, "Close the Truth Gap on Cuba," America Wake Up Broadcast Number 7 (1962), Box 1962–63, Personal Papers of Phyllis Schlafly.

28. Phyllis Schlafly and Chester Ward, *The Gravediggers* (Alton, Illinois, 1964), p. 102.

29. Fred Schwarz, "The Meaning of Cultural Exchanges," March 11, 1959, Box 1959, Phyllis Schlafly Personal Papers.

30. Gregory L. Schneider, *Cadres for Conservatism: Young Americans for Freedom and the Rise of the Contemporary Right* (New York, 1999); and John A. Andrews, *The Other Side of the Sixties: The Rise of Conservative Politics* (New Brunswick, 1997).

31. The rebellious side of the student Right is captured in Niels Bjerre-Poulsen, *Right Face: Organizing the American Conservative Movement, 1945–65* (Copenhagen, 2002), especially pp. 163–84; and Rebecca E. Klatch, *A Generation Divided: The New Left, the New Right, and the 1960s* (Berkeley, 1999), although it should be noted that as informative as Klatch's study is in showing the similarity between students on the Right and Left, too much is made of this apparent similarity. William Rusher captures the excitement of the growth of the early conservative movement in *The Rise of the Right* (New York, 1984).

32. M. Stanton Evans, *Revolt on the Campus* (Chicago, 1961).

33. Welch maintained in his two-day seminar on communism, later reprinted in *The John Birch Society Blue Book*, that following the Second World War, communism took Eastern Europe, turned to Asia where China fell, and then brought Tibet, North Vietnam, and North Korea under control. In addition, Welch warned that in Syria, Lebanon, Egypt, Libya, Tunisia, Algeria, Morocco, "the Communists either already have control, however disguised, or are rapidly acquiring control." Finland, Iceland, and Norway were "for all practical purposes" in the hands of communists, and in the Western Hemisphere, he found communists were in "complete control" in British Guyana, Bolivia and Venezuela. John Birch Society, *The Blue Book of the John Birch Society* (Belmont, MA, 1961), pp. 12–21.

34. Gerald Schomp, *Birchism Was My Business* (New York, 1970), pp. 46–62.

35. For Welch's retraction of the Eisenhower accusation, Gordon Hall, "Birch Society Head Now Says Ike Was No Communist . . . Only," *Boston Globe*, March 24, 1963, p. 33. Welch noted that journalist Joseph Barnes, named as a communist in a congressional hearing, had been selected personally by Eisenhower to write his memoirs, *Crusade in Europe*. Joseph Barnes' association with the Communist party is discussed in Herbert Romerstein and Eric Breindel, *The Venona Secrets: Exposing Soviet Espionage and America's Traitors* (Washington, D.C., 2000), pp. 403, 433–34. It should be noted that evidence against Barnes remains circumstantial. For Phyllis Schlafly's views of Welch see Dean Sauer to Fred M. Switzer, January 1962, Box 1962, Phyllis Schlafly Personal Papers.

36. Clare Boothe Luce to William F. Buckley, Jr. October 30, 1961, Box 220, Clare Boothe Luce papers, Library of Congress.

37. Carol Felsenthal, a Chicago journalist and biographer of Schlafly, undertook extensive research into this charge, only to conclude that she could find no evidence to support it. Carol Felsenthal, *Phyllis Schlafly: The Sweetheart of the Silent Majority* (Garden City, New York), pp. xvii, xviii, 186, 265. Fred Schlafly wrote Robert Welch, "I know of no other more patriotic or dedicated group than your council. I regret, however, that I must decline your invitation for a number of reasons, the principal one being I am already committed as to time to various anti-communist organizations and causes." Fred Schlafly to Robert Welch, March 21, 1962, Folder 1962, Fred Schlafly Papers (unprocessed); Phyllis Schlafly, "Notes of Speech, Robert Welch, August 14–15, 1959, John Birch Society," Subject Files, Eagle Forum Archives. Typical of the attacks on Schlafly as a Bircher, or at least a fellow-traveler of the Birch Society, is Barbara Ehrenreich, *The Hearts of Men: American Dreams and the Flight from Commitment* (Garden City, NY, 1993), pp. 152–58.

38. Robert Welch to Fred Schwarz, September 6, 1960, and Fred Schwarz to Robert Welch, September 19, 1960, Box 173, Herbert Philbrick Papers.

For example, Herbert Philbrick, the most popular lecturer on the anticommunist circuit in the 1950s, wrote a secret memorandum to the FBI in which he described "the cloak and dagger" atmosphere of a Welch seminar he attended in August, 1959. Philbrick was shocked by Welch's "constant emphasis of 'treason' on the part of our present national leaders, including President Eisenhower." He warned that if the Birchers reached a membership of a million or more and fell into the "wrong hands" that "we would have a rather highly explosive force." Yet, Philbrick became an active supporter of the Birch Society in public and became a member at large of the Society. See Herb Philbrick to Frank Willette, May 28, 1959; Box 129; Philbrick to Robert Welch, August 4, 1959; Welch to Philbrick, August 6, 1959; Philbrick to Welch, August 10, 1959; Welch to Philbrick, September 14, 1959; Philbrick to Welch, December 31, 1959, Box 173.

Also, see Frank E. Holman to Stuart Thompson, September 16, 1959; Stuart G. Thompson to Clarence Manion, Box 70, Clarence Manion Papers.

39. Much of the discussion of communist infiltration into the civil rights movement is found in pamphlets, a good deal of it produced by the Citizens' Council, but not all of it. For example, see Zygmund Dobbs, with forward by Archibald B. Roosevelt, *Red Intrigue and Race Turmoil* (New York, 1958); Herbert Ravenel Sass, *Mixed Schools and Mixed Blood* (Greenwood, MI, 1958); Reverend G. T. Gillespie, *A Christian View on Segregation* (Greenwood, MI, 1954); Mississippi State Junior Chamber of Commerce, *Oxford: A Warning for Americans* (Jackson, MI, 1962); Lloyd Wright and John Satterfied, *Blueprint for Total Federal Regimentation; Analysis of the Civil Rights Act of 1963* (Washington, D.C., 1963); and The Fact Finder, *Will Negroes Give Their Votes to the Communists?* (Chicago, 1965).

40. Welch publicly and privately denounced anti-Semitism and racism. When reports reached Welch that Robert DePugh, a member at large in Missouri, was preaching armed resistance and had formed a militant group called the Minutemen, Welch removed him from the membership lists. He issued a public statement saying that the Society "does not in any way engage in, or even condone, the possession of any weapons which it is illegal for private citizens to own such as machine guns, or other weapons which will fire more than once from one pull of the trigger." We are opposed to any "armed resistance" program. Phyllis Schlafly, "Notes of Speech, Robert Welch, August 14–15, 1959," John Birch Society Folder, Subject Files, Eagle Forum Archives.

Welch forced the resignation of founding member Revilo P. Oliver, following his anti-Semitic remarks and denial of the holocaust in a speech given at the New England Rally for God, Family, and Country in 1966. Robert Welch to Mrs. W. B. McMillan, July 13, 1964, Box 61, Manion papers. "A Birch Society Founder Quits: Pressure by Welch Is Reported," *New York Times*, August 16, 1966 (copy), Box 173, Herbert Philbrick papers. On DePugh, see Robert Welch to Mrs. W. B. McMillan, July 13, 1964, Box 61, Clarence Manion papers. Also, of particular importance on the relationship between the Citizens' Council and the John Birch Society, see Neil R. McMillen, *The Citizens' Council: Organized Resistance to the Second Reconstruction, 1954–65* (Urbana, 1971), pp. 189–204, especially 200–201; and James Graham Cook, *The Segregationists* (New York, 1962), pp. 77, 80–81, 263–65.

41. "The New Right: Populist Revolt or Moral Panic," introductory essay in Francis G. Courvares, Martha Saxton, Gerald N. Grob, and George Athan Billias, *Interpretations of American History: Patterns and Perspectives* (New York, 2000, seventh edition), pp. 392–405.

42. Fred J. Cook, "The Ultras: Aims, Affiliations and Finances of the Radical Right," *The Nation*, June 23, 1962, pp. 565–95.

43. Alan Barth, "Report on the 'Rampageous Right'" *New York Times Magazine* (November 26, 1961), pp. 1–4.

44. Framing this "paranoid-style" argumentation within a psychology of "status resentment," Richard Hofstadter argued that during episodic times of social adversity, certain groups under duress expressed a sense of "powerless and victimization" that fed resentments against established politicians, bureaucrats, intellectuals, and other "experts." His account allowed him to group the Ku Klux Klan, Prohibitionists, nativists, and ordinary grassroots anticommunists in the 1950s into a tradition of anti-intellectualism. See Richard Hofstadter, *The Paranoid Style in American Politics and Other Essays* (New York, 1967) and his *Anti-Intellectualism in American Life* (New York, 1963).

45. Arnold Forster and Benjamin R. Epstein, *Danger on the Right*, p. 263.

46. An excellent discussion of this literature is found in Richard Gid Powers, *Not Without Honor: The History of American Anticommunism* (New York, 1995; reprinted New Haven, 1999), pp. 273–318. Also, see Lisa McGirr, *Suburban Warriors: The Origins of the New Right* (Princeton, NJ, 2000), pp. 9–10.

In his etiological study of the Right, *The Strange Tactics of Extremism* (1964), Harry Allen Overstreet diagnosed right-wing thinking as a mental disease. The titles of the books told their readers what to expect: The *Challenges of Democracy: Consensus and Extremism in American Politics* by Murray Havens; *The American Ultras: The Extreme Right and the Military Industrial Complex* (1965) by Irwin Suall; *The Christian Fright Peddlers* (1962) by Brooks Walker. St. *Louis Post-Dispatch* reporter, Richard Dudman, restricted the title of his exposé of the Right to a single gender, *Men of Fear* (1963), even though he showed a particular dislike for Phyllis Schlafly. Other books of this period include Mark Sherwin *The Extremists* (New York, 1963); and Donald Janson *The Far Right* (New York, 1963).

47. When liberal millionaire and peace advocate Cyrus Eaton sent a memorandum to presidential aide Walt W. Rostow that the "anti-Soviet propaganda" campaign against "East-West accommodation" had led to "new war psychosis sweeping the United States," Rostow forwarded the memo to higher officials in the administration. While many in the administration believed Eaton had been hyperbolic in his talk of a "war psychosis," there was little doubt within the Kennedy administration that the Right was on the rise and had to be taken seriously. The expansion of communism was widely discussed at anticommunist meetings, classes, seminars, and dinner parties. For these letters, see Cyrus Eaton to Walt Rostow (June 15, June 19, July 24, August 24, August 28, 1961) and Betty Ryan (Eaton's personal secretary) to Walt Rostow, October 31, 1961 in Walt W. Rostow papers, Box 1, John F. Kennedy Library. Similar sentiments were echoed when in 1962, Adam Yarmolinksy in the Defense Department warned that there was a "greater belligerence from the radical right." He felt especially upset because he had warned his superiors a year earlier that

"it seems to me we have to step on this sort of thing [right-wing attacks] vigorously and publicly whenever it crops out in order to avoid it getting out of hand." Adam Yarmolinsky to Professor Richard H. McCleery, March 8, 1962; Adam Yarmolinksy to Sec. Stahr, April 21, 1961, Box 10, Adam Yarmolinsky papers, John F. Kennedy Library.

48. Under Defense Department Directive 5122, Eisenhower had ordered commanding officers to alert troops to national defense issues.

49. "New Drive Against the Anti-Communist Program," Hearing before the Subcommittee to Investigate the Administration of the Internal Security Act and Other Internal Security Laws, July 11, 1961, Eighty-Seventh Congress, 1st Session (Washington, D.C., 1961), pp. 26–29.

50. Cabell Philips, "Right-Wing Officers Worrying Pentagon," New York Times, June 18, 1961, p. 1.

51. "General Edwin Walker, 83, Is Dead; Promoted Rightest Causes in 60s," New York Times, November 2, 1993, p. B10.

52. J. W. Fulbright to John F. Kennedy, June 28, 1961, Box 277, National Security Files, Papers of President John F. Kennedy, John F. Kennedy Library.

53. "The New Drive Against the Anti-Communist Program," Hearing before the Subcommittee to Investigate the Administration of the Internal Security Act and Other Internal Security Laws, Committee of the Judiciary, 87th Congress, First Session, July 11, 1961, pp. 1–82; Strom Thurmond, "Military Anti-Communist Seminars and Statements," Congressional Record, July 20, 1961, 87th Congress, 107:128; Monday, July 31 1961, 107:129; August 2, 1961, 107:131; August 3, 1961, 107:138; August 15, 1961, 107:104; August 25, 1961, 107:15989–997; 15998–16003.

54. Willard Edwards, "Reveal Censors Cut Speeches of 79 High Officers," Chicago Tribune, January 26, 1962, p. 1.

55. "The Right to Know Our Enemy," Strom Thurmond Reports to the People, July 1961.

56. By singling out Walker for being excessive in his anticommunist troop indoctrination program, the administration was taking on a genuine World War II war hero. In fact, the New York Times had praised him for command of the Arkansas National Guard during the Little Rock school integration crisis. Acting on the advice of McNamara, President Kennedy decided to stay clear of the Fulbright memorandum controversy and let the U.S. Senator from Arkansas fend for himself. McNamara felt that "Senator Fulbright has gotten himself into a somewhat untenable position with this matter and has given his political opponents quite an opening." The Fulbright papers are full of letters protesting the memorandum and the Walker Affair. In particular see Box 28, William Fulbright Collection, University of Arkansas Archives. C. V. Clifton to John F. Kennedy, August 9, 1961, Box 277, National Security Files, Papers of President Kennedy.

57. "What Price Glory," *Dan Smoot Report* (August 28, 1961), pp. 1–8; "Complete Disarmament of American People Now Planned Through the U.N.," *The Manion Forum* (January 7, 1962, pp. 1–4; "Strategic Consequences of the Fulbright Memorandum," Washington Report, October 11, 1961, pp. 1–8. Also, "Inquiry on Muzzling," *America's Future* (January 19, 1962), pp. 1–3 and Hannah Marie Haug, "The Fulbright Memorandum," *American Mercury* (November, 1961), pp. 17–25.

58. Phyllis Schlafly, "President's Note," *Federation Fanfare* (September 1961), pp. 1–6; "Muzzling the Military Resolution" (draft); and Arch E. Roberts to Phyllis Stewart Schlafly, November 10, 1961, Muzzling the Military Folder, Subject Files, Eagle Forum Archives.

59. "Text of Walker's Statement to Senate Panel and Request to Resign from Army," *New York Times*, November 3, 1961, p. 22; Edwin A. Walker, "The American Eagle is not a Dead Duck," Press Release, February 9, 1962, Muzzling the Military Folder, Subject Files, Eagle Forum Archives. Robert Welch to Members of Our Council, October 8, 1962, Box 61, Manion papers.

Further difficulty came when Walker was arrested on federal charges for having incited a riot at Oxford, Mississippi in October 1962. Under Robert Kennedy's orders, Walker was transported to a mental institution in Missouri, where he was held for observation without consultation with his lawyers. He was charged with four counts of insurrection and seditious conspiracy, but a federal grand jury failed to indict him. Walker undertook a legal defense, suing newspapers across the country for libel in charging him with having incited the riot. Fred Schlafly, working through an organization he had been instrumental in creating, Defenders of American Liberties, participated in filing libel suits. Walker won a total of $23 million in libel damages, including an $800,000 jury award in Fort Worth against the Associated Press. A Louisiana jury awarded Walker another $3 million in damages in another libel suit. On June 12, 1967, the Supreme Court overturned the Associated Press award by 9–0 on the ground that public figures were the same as public officials and therefore the media deserved protection for mistakes made without malice. Walker made news again when Lee Harvey Oswald tried to assassinate him using the same rifle that later was used in the Kennedy assassination. This provided fodder for conspiratorial theorists on both the left and the right, although the best evidence is that Oswald acted alone in both cases and sought to assassinate Walker because of his anti-Cuban statements. On June 23, 1976, Walker was again in the news when he was arrested on a charge of public lewdness at a restroom in a Dallas park after he made sexual advances to an undercover officer. In 1982, the army restored Walker's pension rights as a major general, which he had relinquished when he resigned his commission under Kennedy. He died on November 2, 1992.

60. Perhaps most prominent among conspiratorial authors was Victor Fox (a pseudonym), whose novel, *The Pentagon Case* (1961), revealed communist

infiltration in the Defense Department. Edward F. Burns to Dear Folks, February 27, 1963, Subject Files: Communism, Eagle Forum Archives.

61. John A. Andrew III, *The Other Side of the Sixties: Young Americans for Freedom and the Rise of Conservative Politics* (New Brunswick, 1997) and Andrew, *Power to Destroy: The Political Use of the IRS from Kennedy to Nixon* (Chicago, 2002). Also, Rick Perlstein, *Before the Storm: Barry Goldwater and the Unmaking of the American Consensus* (New York, 2001), p. 151.

62. John F. Kennedy, Speech before Democratic Party Dinner, Los Angeles, November 18, 1961, *Public Papers of the Presidents of the United States: John F. Kennedy* (Washington, D.C., 1962), pp. 733–36; Tom Wicker, "Kennedy Asserts Far Right Groups Provoke Disunity," *New York Times*, November 19, 1961, p. 1.

63. Quoted in Jonathan M. Schoenwald, *A Time for Choosing: The Rise of American Conservatism*, pp. 96–97.

64. Quoted in Schoenwald, p. 97.

65. Alan Barth, "Report on the 'Rampageous Right,'" *New York Times Magazine*, November 26, 1961, pp. 1–4.

66. T. George Harris, "The Rampant Right Invades the GOP," *Look* Magazine, July 16, 1963, p. 14.

67. NCWC News Services, "Social Action Conference Leaders Ask Facts on U.S. Reds from Government to End Controversies," May 28, 1962, Communism in the Churches Folder, Subject Files, Eagle Forum Archives.

68. Reverend Edward Duff, S. J. "There Is a Conspiracy," April 1962, "Communism," Subject Files, Eagle Forum Archives.

69. Phyllis Schlafly, "Communism: The Threat to Freedom by John F. Cronin," *The Tablet*, March 24, 1962 (reprint), Communism in the Church Folder, Subject Files, Eagle Forum Archives.

70. "Editorial Comment: About a Controversial Booklet," *The Priest*, 18:5, May 1962, pp. 393–397; Richard Ginder, "Right or Wrong: Communism at Home," *Our Sunday Visitor*, December 17, 1961, p. 2; Letters to the Editor (full page on Cronin controversy), *The Wanderer*, June 14, 1962.

71. The *National Review* declared that the distinction between an external and internal threat was "old fashioned" because "the distinction between the internal and the external threat is unreal: the scope of the Communist effort transcends conventional barriers, and therefore the conventional vocabulary is anachronistic." See "Fr. Cronin's Pamphlet," *National Review*, April 10, 1962, pp. 236–38. Also, see William F. Buckley, Jr., "Conservatives and Anti-Communism," *Ave Maria*, April 7, 1962, pp. 5–8.

72. For example, see Phyllis Schlafly to Most Reverend Cuthbert O'Gara, May 7, 1962; Phyllis Schlafly to Reverend Thomas K. Gorman, Bishop of Dallas-Fort Worth, March 23, 1962; Phyllis Schlafly to Editor, *The Alamo Messenger*, March 21, 1961 (ms.); Phyllis Schlafly to William E. Cousins, April 25, 1962; Janet McLaughlin to Editor, *The Tablet*, April 4, 1962; Eleanor Schlafly

(Phyllis Schlafly) to Very Rev. Daniel Moore, *St. Louis Review*, April 2, 1962, Box 1962, Personal Papers of Phyllis Schlafly.

73. Phyllis Schlafly to Editor, *Our Sunday Visitor*, December 11, 1961; Phyllis Schlafly to Editor, *The Register* (Denver), *The Tablet*, *Chicago Daily News*, *The Wanderer*, December 7, 1961, Box 1961, Schlafly Personal Files.

74. Dale Francis, "Is Fidel Castro a Communist? *Our Sunday Visitor*, May 3, 1959, Phyllis Schlafly to Mr. Francis (n.d. 1962?), Communism in Cuba. Dale Francis Folder, Subject Files, Eagle Forum Archives.

75. Rev. John F. Cronin to Editor, *Ave Maria Press*, July 7, 1962, p. 3.

76. Francis wrote Schlafly that he had done more than just publish about communism in Cuba: He informed Schlafly that "throughout 1959–60–61, I filed a series of reports with the CIA, again at my own expense but at the request of the CIA, giving many facts I did not dare print which I believe were extremely valuable, among them the names of foreign nationals collaborating with the Castro regime." Dale Francis to Ms. Schlafly (n.d.), Phyllis Schlafly to Dale Francis, February 4, 1962; Dale Francis to Phyllis Schlafly, January 22, 1962; Phyllis Schlafly to Dale Francis, Jan 9., 1962, Box 1962, Personal Papers of Phyllis Schlafly.

77. Phyllis Schlafly to Msgr. James R. Hartnett, July 16, 1962, Box 1962, Personal Papers of Phyllis Schlafly.

78. Mr. and Mrs. George H. Wegener to Mrs. Phyllis Schlafly, July 12, 1962; Mrs. Leota Scherer to Phyllis Schlafly, July 21, 1960, Subject Files "Letters from Supporters," Schlafly Archives.

79. Jack E. Ison to Fred Schlafly, February 2, 1961, Office Subject Files, ASC, Eagle Forum Archives.

80. Schlafly read conservative defense strategists Stefan Possony; Robert Strausz-Hupé, who had introduced geopolitical theory to Americans during the Second World War and was the author of *A Forward Strategy for America* (1961); and Earl H. Voss, best known for his polemic, *Nuclear Ambush: The Test Ban Treaty* (1963). She was much influenced by General Thomas S. Power, former head of the Strategic Air Command, who inscribed his book *Design for Survival* (1965) and a photograph to her. Thomas S. Power, *Design for Survival: A Crucial Message to the American People Concerning Our Nuclear Strength and Its Role in Preserving Peace* (New York, 1964).

81. Phyllis Schlafly to Nicholas Shuman, October 6, 1960, Box 1960–61, Schlafly Personal Correspondence.

82. Phyllis Schlafly to Miss Eleanor Schlafly, January 10, 1964, Box 1964, Personal Papers of Phyllis Schlafly.

Chapter Five
The Goldwater Campaign

1. Fred Schlafly to Mother, August 12, 1964, Folder 1964, Unmarked Box, Fred Schlafly Papers.

2. T. Coleman Andrews, Eisenhower's IRS Commissioner, made a losing third-party effort in 1956 under the States Rights banner. Edgar C. Bundy to Phyllis Schlafly, July 19, 1956, Abraham Lincoln folder, Subject Files, Eagle Forum Archives. Also, for further criticism of Eisenhower, see Herbert Philbrick to Mr. Panzieri, October 19, 1963, Box 5, Herbert Philbrick papers.

3. Bill Rusher to Bill Buckley, October 10, 1960, Box 121 William A. Rusher papers.

4. Thomas J. Anderson, "Straight Talk," Speech before the Free Electors Meeting, Jackson, Mississippi, June 17, 1960, Subject Files, Communism, Eagle Forum Archives.

5. Quoted in Michael Kramer and Sam Roberts, "I Never Wanted to Be Vice-President of Anything!": An Investigative Biography of Nelson Rockefeller (New York, 1976), p. 221.

6. Earl Harding to Clarence Manion, March 26, 1954, Box 62, Clarence Manion papers.

7. Although Manion remained a Democrat until 1939, he was a southern conservative Democratic, not a big-government liberal as one historian described him. In Before the Storm: Barry Goldwater and the Unmaking of the American Consensus, Rick Perlstein portrays Manion as a New Dealer who supported big government liberalism. Perlstein cites Manion's textbook, Lessons in Liberty: A Study of American Government (South Bend, IN, 1939), which he describes as an argument for activist government to provide a decent standard of living for all Americans. Contrary to Perlstein, Manion was hardly a liberal. Manion drew upon Roman Catholic social teaching in arguing for a "living wage," but this book was mostly a polemic against communism and "the pagan all powerful state." For Perlstein's discussion of Manion, see Before the Storm, pp. 6–7.

Also, see Clarence Manion, Lessons in Liberty: A Study of American Government (South Bend, IN, 1939); The Education of an American (South Bend, IN, 1939).

8. Included in the group were General Bonner Fellers representing For America; publisher and rancher Hubbard Russell; New York lawyer George Montgomery; South Carolina Republican committeeman and textile manufacturer Roger Milliken; L. L. Smith of the Kohler company of Wisconsin; Brent Bozell, Jr., brother-in-law of William F. Buckley, Jr.; Texas activist and historian Evetts Haley; Robert Welch, founder of the newly organized John Birch Society; and Illinois attorney Fred Schlafly.

9. He felt that his Jewish name was a handicap, and that he was unqualified for the job of president because he had only one year of college. He was convinced that the race within the GOP was between Nixon and Rockefeller and only a miracle could "draw lightning his way." Minutes, Conference on Goldwater, May 15, 1959, Box 69, Manion Papers.

10. Clarence Manion to William F. Buckley, Jr. September 28, 1959, Box 62; Jim Johnson to Dean Clarence Manion, March 24, 1954, Box 69; and Frank

C. Hanighen to Clarence Manion, Box 70, Manion papers. Also, J. Evetts Haley to Hugh Grant, A. G. Heinsohn, R. A. Kilpatrick, Box 70; William Jennings Bryan Dorn to Manion, October 28, 1959; Manion to Hon. William Jennings Bryan Dorn, October 22, 1959, Box 70, Clarence Manion papers.

11. Manion to James L. Wick, November 27, 1959, Box 70, Manion papers.

12. Robert E.Wood to Clarence Manion, April 13, 1959, Box 70, Manion papers.

13. William F. Buckley, Jr. to Manion, September 24, 1959, Box 70, Manion papers. On Fulton Lewis, see James I. Wick to Clarence Manion, December 2, 1959, and Clarence Manion to Hubbard Russell, December 4, 1959, Box 70, Clarence Manion papers.

14. Clarence Manion to Hon. J. Bracken Lee, September 21, 1959; Dan Smoot to Hubbard S. Russell, October 13, 1959; and Frank E. Holman to William H. MacFarland, October 15, 1959, Box 70, Manion papers.

15. Turned down by the major presses, Manion decided that he would publish and distribute the book himself by forming a nonprofit publishing company, Victor Publishing. Clarence Manion to William F. Buckley, Jr. September 28, 1959; Clarence Manion to Roger Milliken, January 29, 1960, Box 62; and Clarence Manion to Frank Brophy, July 28, 1959, Box 70, Manion papers.

16. For a discussion of the publication of *The Conscience of a Conservative*, see Rick Perlstein, *Before the Storm*, pp. 60–68.

17. Barry Goldwater, *Conscience of a Conservative* (New York, 1961, 1st edition, 13th printing), pp. 14–15.

18. The following account of the 1960 convention draws on many sources, including newspaper clippings found in Subject Files: Goldwater, Eagle Forum Archives, as well as many excellent secondary accounts of the convention, including Theodore White, *The Making of the President, 1960* (New York, 1961); Robert Alan Goldberg, *Barry Goldwater* (New Haven, 1995); Lee Edwards, *Goldwater: The Man Who Made a Revolution* (Washington, D.C., 1995); Michael Kramer and Sam Roberts, *"I Never Wanted to Be Vice-President of Anything!" An Investigative Biography of Nelson Rockefeller* (New York, 1976).

19. Kramer and Roberts, *"I Never Wanted to Be Vice-President of Anything!"* p. 227.

20. Ibid., p. 227.

21. This discussion relies heavily on Kramer and Robert, Ibid., pp. 230–42.

22. When Schlafly became president of the Illinois Federation it boasted 150 chapters and some 27, 000 members. Still, Schlafly's plan to host a luncheon at the National Convention was bold. The IFRW had only $2,359 in its treasury when Schlafly made her proposal. She estimated the luncheon would cost about $10,000. She had a lot riding on the success of the event. Minutes, IFRW Executive Committee, February 17, 1959, Subject files, NFRW, Eagle Forum Archives.

23. The luncheon committee under Schlafly's direction selected a Hawaiian theme for the event. Hawaii had recently been admitted to the Union and the

state was an exotic attraction. The luncheon was billed as a Hukilau with a Hawaiian fashion show sponsored by a Chicago store, island music, and Hawaiian food (pork roast with a special Polynesian sauce and a macadamia nut dessert). Ventriloquist Edgar Bergen and Charlie McCarthy provided entertainment. Hawaii's new Republican Governor William Quinn, originally from St. Louis where he had been a star of high school musicals, sang for the occasion. Dignitaries and public officials sat at a head table and VIP tables. Mrs. Nelson Rockefeller was seated at VIP table #14.

24. Phyllis Schlafly, "Opening Remarks to Hawaiian Hukilau Luncheon, July 26, 1960," Subject Files: NFRW, Eagle Forum Archives.

25. Proceedings of the 27th Republican National Convention, 1960, p. 291. Also see Robert Alan Goldberg, *Barry Goldwater* (New Haven, 1995). This is a superb biography of Goldwater.

26. During the 1960 campaign, Goldwater gave 126 speeches for the Nixon-Lodge ticket. Following the election, Goldwater made another 225 appearances on behalf of the GOP.

27. Names of potential candidates floated in and out of the news—New York City mayor, John Lindsay; former vice-presidential candidate Henry Cabot Lodge; former American Motors chief and Michigan Governor George Romney; and Pennsylvania Governor William Scranton.

28. Graham T. Molitor, Position Paper on Communism, August 31, 1963, Graham T. Molitor Papers, Rockefeller Family Archives.

29. Quoted in Kramer and Roberts, *"I Never Wanted to Be Vice-President of Anything,"* pp. 274–76.

30. One strange aspect of the 1964 campaign was that the great enthusiasm for the Goldwater candidacy was not shared by the candidate himself. Following Kennedy's assassination in November 1963, Goldwater's eagerness for a presidential race vanished. He had looked forward to a race against Kennedy, whom he had known in the Senate and personally liked. Recalling his mood in 1963, he later recorded in his private diary that he and Kennedy had talked about running an "old fashioned" cross-country debate on the issues of the day "without Madison Avenue, without any makeup or phoniness, just the two of us traveling around on the same airplane, but when he was assassinated that ended that dream." Barry Goldwater, Diary Entry, March 18, 1977, Box 8/3 Personal and Political Series III, Barry Goldwater Papers, Arizona State University Archives.

31. Phyllis Schlafly to Goldwater, December 13, 1963, Box 1964, Personal Papers.

32. Nichol C. Rae, *The Decline and Fall of the Liberal Republicans: From 1952 to the Present* (New York, 1989).

33. As the nation mourned Kennedy's death, Schlafly felt it was inappropriate to continue with her standard speeches lambasting the Democrats. Phyllis

Schlafly to Mrs. Carl S. Winters, February 12, 1964, Box 1964, Phyllis Schlafly Personal Papers.

34. Phyllis Schlafly, *A Choice Not an Echo* (Alton, IL, 1964, 3rd edition), p. 6.

35. Ibid., pp. 23–29.

36. Ibid., pp. 65, 69.

37. Ibid., pp. 103–116, especially pp. 115 and 116 for quotations.

38. C. Wright Mills, *The Power Elite* (New York, 1956). For an engaging history of the transformation of grassroots populism in the nineteenth century to conservative populism in the late twentieth century, see Michael Kazin, *The Populist Persuasion: An American History* (Ithaca, 1995; rev. 1998).

39. There is a rich literature on conspiracy in America. A good place to begin to read this literature is David Brion Davis, "Some Themes of Counter-Subversion: An Analysis of Anti-Masonic, Anti-Catholic, and Anti-Mason Literature," *The Mississippi Valley Historical Review*, 47: September, 1960, pp. 205–224. On the political nature of conspiracy theory in the early Republic, a good, but much overlooked study is Joseph W. Phillips, *Jedidiah Morse and New England Congregationalism* (New Brunswick, 1983). A good sense of this early conspiratorial literature can be gained from reading John Robison, *Proofs of a Conspiracy*... (New York, 1798).

40. Schlafly, *A Choice Not an Echo*, p. 103.

41. Naturally, the book's critics singled out the conspiratorial tone and description of the Bilderbergers—pointing out that the *New York Times* had reported on the group before the publication of *A Choice Not an Echo*, albeit without the wealth of detail spelled out in the Schlafly book. Actually, the *New York Times* in reporting on the Bilderbergers in May and June 1954 and February 1957 (and later in May 1964 after the publication of *A Choice*) described the Bilderbergers as a "secret group," listing only a handful of the important American participants.

42. For a particularly misleading critique of Schlafly's conspiratorial views by a sociologist who seems to have his own view of "a power elite" dominating American politics and policy, see G. William Domhoff, *The Higher Circles* (New York, 1970). Domhoff inaccurately lumps Dan Smoot, Phyllis Schlafly, and William S. McBirnie together. He falsely suggests that Schlafly saw David Rockefeller as a communist (p. 291); and that she believed such far-fetched notions as that Dean Acheson alone could have prevented China from going communist (p. 300), and that the Bay of Pigs invasion was purposely designed to fail (p. 301).

43. "The Bilderberger Conference," May 29–31, 1954, Box 58, Paul Nitze Papers, Library of Congress; see also extensive material found in Box 58 and 59 concerning other differences within the Bilderbergers.

44. Buckley to Rusher, May 11, 1976, William A. Rusher Papers, Box 121, LC.

45. Phyllis Schlafly to Chester Ward, August 23, 1968, *The Betrayers* File, Eagle Forum Archives.

46. *None Dare Call It Treason* encapsulated in 254 pages the extensive corpus of grassroots anticommunist writings, beginning with chapters on the origins of world communism and its growth, and then moving on to communist influence in government, education, the churches, the media, the mental health profession, organized labor, and economics. Most important, Stormer said, Americans must make a spiritual commitment. Too many Americans, he warned, attend man-centered rather than God-centered churches. Fundamentalist Christian Stormer told his readers that without a belief in God, nothing could be accomplished and demoralization in the fight against communism was inevitable.

47. Phyllis Schlafly to Clarence Manion (Dear Friend), undated, Box 79, Clarence Manion papers.

48. Fred Schlafly to George Crocker, April 26, 1964; Fred Schlafly to John Ashbrook, May 4, 1964; Fred Schlafly to Patrick Frawley, April 27, 1964; Fred Schlafly to Rogers Follansbee, April 1 1964; Fred Schlafly to Henri Salvatori, April 11, 1964, Unmarked Box 1, Folder 1964, Fred Schlafly Papers.

49. Phyllis Schlafly, Interview with author, November 29, 2000. Also, Clarence Manion to Phyllis Schlafly, April 4, 1964, Box 79, Manion Papers; Fred Schlafly to Horace, August 24, 1964, Folder 1964, Fred Schlafly Correspondence (unprocessed).

50. Phyllis Schlafly to Clarence Manion, August 24, 1964, Box 79, Manion Papers.

51. These responses came from Iowa delegates after receiving copies of the widely distributed book. See Richard D. Verstegen to Mr. A. Von Boeselager, June 22, 1964; I. H. Wentzeien to Mr. A. Von Boseselager, June 20, 1964; Charles E. Wittenmeyer to Mr. A. Von Boesleager, June 19, 1964; and William R. Ruther to A. Von Boeselager, June 20, 1964, Box 3, Personal and Political Series III, Barry Goldwater Papers, Arizona State University Archives.

52. Schlafly, *A Choice Not an Echo.*

53. The following discussion of the Republican party and the 1964 primary campaign draws heavily on John Howard Kessel, *The Goldwater Coalition: Republican Strategies in 1964* (Indianapolis, 1968), pp. 25–28.

54. Phyllis Schlafly to Barry Goldwater, November 19, 1963, Box 1964, Personal Papers.

55. Howard Kessel, *The Goldwater Coalition: Republican Strategies in 1964,* p. 60.

56. A useful study on California conservatism is Kurt Schuparra, *Triumph of the Right: The Rise of the California Conservative Movement, 1945–1966* (Armonk, NY, 1998).

57. Author unknown, Memorandum, March, 1964, Box 173, William A. Rusher Papers.

58. Quoted in Kessel, *The Goldwater Coalition: Republican Strategies in 1964,* p. 89.

59. Clarence Manion to Fred Schlafly, July 27, 1964, Box 79, Clarence Manion Papers.

60. Fred Schlafly to Gerry and Patrick Frawley, June 4, 1964, Unmarked Box 1, Folder 1, Fred Schlafly Papers.

61. Quoted in Kessell, *The Goldwater Coalition: Republican Strategies in 1964,* pp. 103–104.

62. Her race created some tensions within the 24th District. She had offered not to run if her principal rival, an Alton neighbor, would declare in advance for Goldwater. When he did not, she declared and easily defeated him. Fred Schlafly to Mary Dell Olin, February 28, 1964, Folder 1964, Unmarked Box, Fred Schlafly Papers; also, Press Release, March 23, 1964, Phyllis Schlafly Personal Papers; and Fred Schlafly to Clarence Manion, April 16, 1964, Box 79, Manion Papers.

63. Charles Percy had been embarrassed when the Illinois delegation refused to elect him co-chair of the delegation. He then decided to stay in line with the rest of his state delegates. He was running for governor of Illinois so he wanted to avoid a split within the state. Illinois Delegate Report, June 23, 1964, Box 3, W Series, Barry Goldwater Papers.

64. Fred Schlafly to Mr. and Mrs. John C. Newington, Folder 4, Unmarked Box, Fred Schlafly papers.

65. Perlstein, *Before the Storm,* p. 366.

66. Schorr's CBS report is quoted in Perlstein, *Before the Storm,* p. 375.

67. This description of press reaction and the convention is drawn from Robert Alan Goldberg, *Barry Goldwater,* pp. 108–209, especially p. 201.

68. An excellent discussion of the 1964 platform and the fight over it is found in Robert Alan Goldberg, *Barry Goldwater,* pp. 202–204.

69. Quoted in Ibid., p. 204.

70. Interview, Charles Lichenstein with Author, Washington, D.C., August 12, 2001.

71. Delegate Report/Schlafly, 1964 G. Series, Box 5, Barry Goldwater Papers.

72. Phyllis Schlafly to Barry Goldwater, January 6, 1964, Box 1964, Personal Papers of Phyllis Schlafly.

73. Volunteers for Goldwater, Newsletter (n.d.), Box 1964, Personal Papers of Phyllis Schlafly.

74. He began by congratulating her on the success of the book. "Your book is every place I go in Honolulu. Everybody's reading it and talking about it. The newsstands can't keep it in stock." Quoted in Carol Felsenthal, *Sweetheart of the Silent Majority* (Garden City, NY, 1981), pp. 214–15.

75. Raymond H. Wagner to Phyllis Schlafly, September 19, 1964; Raymond H. Wagner to Otto Otepka, September 19, 1964; Raymond H. Wagner to Phyllis Schlafly, August 19, 1964, Subject Files: Communism, Eagle Forum Archives.

76. Interview, Charles Lichenstein with Author, Washington, D.C., August 12, 2001.

77. This description of the 1964 election relies on Robert Alan Goldberg, *Barry Goldwater*, pp. 233–35, especially p. 233.

CHAPTER SIX
THE ESTABLISHMENT PURGES SCHLAFLY

1. Phyllis Schlafly to Mrs. John T. Salmon, October 12, 1965, Box 1965, Personal Papers of Phyllis Schlafly.

2. Bliss's charges of extremism in the GOP were specifically directed toward members of the John Birch Society, but many Goldwater supporters saw the attack as aimed at them. Ray Bliss, "Statement of extremism by Republican National Chairman Ray C. Bliss," November 5, 1965, NFRW Files, Eagle Forum Office Files. For a favorable account of Bliss, John F. Bibby and Robert J. Huckshorn, "Out-Party Strategy: Republican National Committee Rebuilding Politics, 1964–1966," in Bernard Cosman and Robert J. Huckshorn, eds., *Republican Politics: The 1964 Campaign and Its Aftermath for the Party* (New York, 1968), pp. 205–233. Also, for an overview of Bliss, see William Rusher, *The Rise of the Right* (New York, 1985).

3. National Federation of Republican Women, "Statistical Report, 1960–61," and "Beatrice Rumple to Phyllis Schlafly, August 12, 1962, National Federation of Republican Women, Eagle Forum Archives.

4. In 1962, for example, the Illinois Federation spent a total of $7,896, including $1,200 incurred for travel expenses for the president. Illinois Federation of Republican Women, "Financial Report, 1962," Subject Files, NFRW, Eagle Forum Archives.

5. Schlafly's booklist reveals what grassroots conservatives were reading in the early 1960s. Listed in order, they included M. Stanton Evans, *The Fringe on Top*; Barry Goldwater, *Why Not Victory*; Frank Kluckhohn, *America: Listen*; George Crocker, *Roosevelt's Road to Russia*; John T. Flynn, *The Roosevelt Myth*; Ralph de Toledano, *Seeds of Treason*; Veritas Foundation, *Keynes at Harvard*; Earl E. T. Smith, *The Fourth Floor*; Max Rafferty, *Suffer, Little Children*; Bryton Barron, *Inside the State Department*; W. Cleon Skousen, *The Naked Communist*, and Rosalie Gordon, *Nine Men Against America*. Phyllis Schlafly, "Planning Political Programs" (1956), National Federation Office Files, Eagle Forum Archives. Also, Phyllis Schlafly, "Planning Programs for IFRW Chapters," (1962) Box 1962, Personal Papers of Phyllis Schlafly.

6. Phyllis Schlafly, "Christmas and the Lost Four Freedoms" (manuscript), December 15, 1962, Box 1962, Personal Papers.

7. Phyllis Schlafly, "Report of the President and Legislative Chairman of the Tenth Biennial Convention of the Illinois Federation of Republican Women, November 30, 1960, Box 1960–1961, Schlafly Personal Files.

8. Phyllis Schlafly, "Women in Politics" (manuscript), September, 1960; Phyllis Schlafly to Shirley S. Ferchaud, National Editor, Phi Gamma Nu Magazine, September 27, 1960, Shirley S. Ferchaud to Mrs. J. Fred Schlafly, September 27, 1960, Box 1960–61, Personal Papers of Phyllis Schlafly.

9. In 1963 when Schlafly received the Woman of Achievement Award from the *St. Louis Globe-Democrat*, she was given a sterling silver plate and publisher Richard Amberg said, "Phyllis Schlafly stands for everything that made America great and for those things which will keep it that way." Hundreds of letters across Missouri and Illinois poured in congratulating her. Most of these letters were not perfunctory congratulations, but lengthy, heartfelt expressions of shared joy and achievement. Mrs. Earl Edward Clark to Phyllis Schlafly, July 29, 1960, NFRW files, Eagle Forum Archives. These letters are found in Phyllis Schlafly's personal papers. As a matter of policy, Schlafly saved only "important" correspondence. It is revealing, therefore, that these letters were saved as an expression of respect for these women. See Box 1963, Personal Files; also, "Phyllis Schlafly, Woman of Achievement," *Globe-Democrat*, December 28–29, 1963.

10. A review of correspondence sent to Schlafly during her presidency of the Illinois Federation of Women and her race for the presidency shows that many young professional women with careers supported Schlafly. She also drew support from young mothers. A conclusion that can be adduced from this correspondence is that her supporters in the NFRW were ideologically conservative and mostly younger women.

11. Mrs. Nancy Elder to Phyllis Schlafly, November 26, 1961, NFRW Files, Eagle Forum Archives.

12. Dorothy Thompson to Phyllis Schlafly, December 15, 1961, NFRW, Eagle Forum Archives.

13. Phyllis Schlafly to Mrs. Carl S. Winters, February 12, 1964, Box 1964, Personal Papers.

14. Phyllis Schlafly to Virginia (Becker?), May 28, 1962, Box 1962, Personal Papers.

15. Dorothy A. Elston, "Report of the NFRW President" (1964), NFRW Files, Eagle Forum Archives.

16. Elly Peterson to Mary Brooks, Febuary 15, 1966, Box 7, Elly Peterson papers.

17. The victory in Michigan is described in Elly Peterson to Dorothy McHugh (New York), Rosemary Ginn (Missouri), Mary Lou Smith (Iowa), Dorothy Stanislaus (Oklahoma), June Honeman (Pennsylvania), Dorothy Goodnight (California), September 30, 1965, Box 14, Elly Peterson papers, Bentley Library, University of Michigan.

18. Katherine K. Neuberger to Elly Peterson, May 9, 1966, Box 7, Elly Peterson papers.

19. Janet L. [last name unclear] to Elly Peterson, May 10, 1966, Box 7, Elly Peterson papers.

20. On the selection of O'Donnell, see Gladys O'Donnell to Elly Peterson, March 19, 1966, Box 7; Rhoda Lund to Elly Peterson, October 10, 1965, Box 6; and Janet [?] to Elly Peterson, May 29,1966; Elly Peterson to Katherine Neuberger, May 31, 1966, Box 7, Elly Peterson papers.

21. Wilma C. Rogalin to New York Federation Club Presidents, March 1967, Box I, NFRW Files, Personal Papers of Phyllis Schlafly.

22. "Fanatics in GOP Blasted," *Long Beach Independent*, May 16, 1965; "Hopeful Moves by GOP Conservatives," *Los Angeles Times*, May 16, 1965; "GOP Women Lead the Way, *Independent Press Telegram*, May 16, 1965, Box 1, NFRW files, Personal Papers of Phyllis Schlafly.

23. Phyllis Schlafly to Gladys O'Donnell, June 14, 1965; O'Donnell to Schlafly, May 30, 1965, Box 1, NFRW files, Personal Papers of Phyllis Schlafly.

24. "GOP Group Hits Phone Slanders," *Los Angeles Times*, May 14, 1965, Box 1, NFRW files, Personal Papers of Phyllis Schlafly.

25. Cecil Kenyon to Phyllis Schlafly, June 22, 1965, Box 1, NFRW files, Personal Papers of Phyllis Schlafly.

26. Elly Peterson to Mrs. George Anna Theobald, November 11, 1966; Mrs. George Anna Theobald to Elly Peterson, December 3, 1966, Box 7, Elly Peterson papers.

27. Phyllis Schlafly to Chester Ward, December 2, 1965, NFRW Files, Eagle Forum Archives.

28. Resolutions Committee Report, August 13, 1965, NFRW Files, Eagle Forum Archives.

29. Phyllis Schlafly to Chester Ward, December 2, 1965, NFRW Files, Eagle Forum Archives.

30. Lucile Hosmer to Phyllis Schlafly, August 28, 1965; and Mrs. W. Glenn Suthers to Phyllis Schlafly, August 26, 1965, NFRW Files, Eagle Forum Archives.

31. Phyllis Schlafly to NFRW Board of Directors, November 1966, NFRW Files, Eagle Forum Archives.

32. Lahoma Dennis to Katharine Kennedy Brown (n.d. 1966); Dorothy Elston to NFRW Board Members, November, 1966, NFRW Files, Eagle Forum Archives.

33. Included on the list were Mrs. Dorothy Camp of Iowa, Ginny Pearson of Texas, Mrs. Virginia Kirk of Rhode Island, Mrs. Ruth Parks of Colorado, Mrs. Leona Troxell of Arkansas, Mrs. Dorothy Goodknight of California, and Wilma Rogalin of New York. "Predict Floor Fight for Head of GOP Women," *Chicago Tribune*, January 26, 1967, NFRW Files, Eagle Forum Archives.

34. "Mrs. Schlafly Charges GOP Is Purging Her," *Washington Post*, March 9, 1967; also, "Fight Shaping Up Among GOP Women," *Long Island Press*, March 12, 1967, Box 1, NFRW Files, Personal Papers of Phyllis Schlafly.

35. Clipping, "Prediction of Floor Fight for Head of GOP Women," *Chicago Tribune*, January 26, 1967, Box 1, NFRW Files, Personal Papers of Phyllis Schlafly.

36. Lucille Young, "The Other Side" (undated mimeograph, 1967), NFRW Files, Eagle Forum Office Files.

37. Mrs. Jean Canion to Mrs. Power, March 23, 1967, Box I, NFRW Files, Personal Papers of Phyllis Schlafly.

38. "Adversity Will Make Governor Reagan Stronger, Daughter Predicts," *San Diego Union*, March 15, 1967; and Press Release, "Schlafly Announces Candidacy," April 5, 1967, NFRW Files, Eagle Forum Office Files.

39. William Rusher, *The Plot to Steal the GOP* (New York, 1967).

40. Clipping, David Broder, "Who Runs the Republican Party," *Washington Post*, May 9, 1967, in NFRW Files, Eagle Forum Office Files.

41. Clipping, Richard Dudman, "Mrs. Schlafly Shunted from a Top GOP Job," *St. Louis Post-Dispatch*, September 23, 1965, NFRW Files, Eagle Office Files.

42. In an essay appearing just a year after the NFRW presidential fight, "The Role of Conservative Women in Politics," she wrote, "The trouble is that conservative women do not carry the political clout in the Republican party to which their tremendous work entitles them. . . . This leaves the power to choose candidates and determine policies in the hands of Party payrollers and political technicians. . . . Women will continue to be ignored in the centers of political power until they hold a substantial percentage of public offices and are elected to party positions." Phyllis Schlafly, "The Role of Conservative Women in Politics" (ms.) Box 1968–69, Personal Papers of Phyllis Schlafly.

43. Quoted in Marie Smith, "Mrs. Schlafly Charges GOP Is Purging Her," *The Washington Post*, March 9, 1967, Box 1, NFRW files, Personal Papers of Phyllis Schlafly.

44. Mrs. George Mizer, "Letter to Presidents of Republican Women," March 3, 1967, Box 1, NFRW Files, Personal Papers of Phyllis Schlafly.

45. Lucille Young, "The Other Side" (mimeographed letter) (n.d. 1967).

46. Phyllis Schlafly, "Notes on Call to John Ashbrook," July 3, 1967, Box 1, NFRW Files, Personal Papers of Phyllis Schlafly; William Loeb to Mrs. William D. Leetch, June 12, 1967, Box 1, NFRW Files, Personal Papers of Phyllis Schlafly.

47. "GOP Women Should Pick Mrs. Schlafly," *Dixon Telegraph*, March 21, 1967; Karl E. Mundt to Sanford J. Bowyer, March 28, 1967, Box 1, NFRW Files, Personal Papers of Phyllis Schlafly.

48. Thomas A. Lane, "Republican Party's Left Aims at GOP Women," *Jefferson City Post Tribune*, April 10, 1967, Box 1, NFRW Files, Personal Papers of Phyllis Schlafly.

49. Clipping, "Mrs. Schlafly Charge Denied by Goldwater," *St. Louis Post-Dispatch*, April 6, 1967, NFRW Files, Eagle Forum Office Files.

50. Ridiculous charges of Schlafly being a member of the Minutemen were repeated in a letter, Pauline (?) to Schlafly, June 6, 1967, NFRW Convention Files, Eagle Forum Office Files. For an investigation of these charges that Schlafly was a member of the John Birch Society, see Carol Felsenthal, *The Sweetheart of the Silent Majority*, pp. xviii–ix, 185–86.

51. Mrs. Jean Canion to Mrs. Power, March 23, 1967, Box I, NFRW Files, Personal Papers of Phyllis Schlafly.

52. Phyllis Schlafly to Mrs. Ginny Kenney, September 12, 1967, Box 5, NFRW Files, Personal Papers of Phyllis Schlafly.

53. Clipping, "Moderate-Conservative GOP Women Prepare for a Showdown," *The Grand Rapids Press* (May 1, 1966); for divisions in the California NFRW, see Grace Thackeray to Barry Goldwater, copy of letter in NFRW Files, Eagle Forum Office Files.

54. Elly Peterson to Federation Board Members, July 15, 1965, NFRW Files, Eagle Forum Archives.

55. Dorothy Punches to Dorothy Benton, July 19, 1965, NFRW Files, Eagle Forum Archives.

56. "Moderate-Conservative GOP Women Prepare for Showdown," Box 2, NFRW Files, Personal Papers of Phyllis Schlafly.

57. Dorothy A. Elston to Mrs. Beverly Climer, December 27, 1966; "Petition to NFRW Executive Committee" (1966), NFRW Files, Eagle Forum Archives.

58. Louis Boehn and Jan Jacobs, "Wisconsin Club Story," October 7, 1968, NFRW Files, Eagle Forum Archives.

59. NFRW, Executive Committee Minutes, January 23–25, 1967, NFRW Files, Eagle Forum Archives.

60. Phyllis Schlafly to Mrs. Grace Thackeray, July 24, 1967; Grace Thackeray to Phyllis Schlafly, July 20, 1967, Box 1 NFRW Files, Personal Papers of Phyllis Schlafly.

61. Lucile Hosmer to Dorothy A. Elston, May 5, 1963; Lucile Hosmer to Phyllis Schlafly, April 16, 1965; Lucile Hosmer to Elizabeth Fielding, August 27, 1965, NFRW Files, Eagle Forum Archives.

62. "Mrs. Schlafly Invades GOP," *Washington Evening Star*, March 23, 1967, Box 1, NFRW Files, Personal Papers of Phyllis Schlafly.

63. Mrs. Audrey R. Peak to Robert Greenway, April 22, 1967, NFRW Files. Robert Greenway, the publisher of the *DeKalb Daily Chronicle* (Illinois) surveyed party officials as to their positions in the NFRW fight. These responses were sent by Greenway to Schlafly. See NFRW files, Eagle Forum.

64. Angela Bryce, Arizona *Eagle*, May 25, 1967, NFRW Files, Eagle Forum Office Files.

65. "Barry Denies Mrs. Schlafly Purge Cry," *Chicago Tribune*, April 6, 1967, Box I, Personal Papers of Phyllis Schlafly.

66. Everett McKinley Dirksen to Mrs. R. H. Daniel, April 6, 1967, Box 1, NFRW Files, Personal Papers of Phyllis Schlafly.

67. These letters are found in Phyllis Schlafly's personal papers. See Donald Rumsfield to Robert F. Greenaway, April 16, 1967; and Charles Percy to Robert T. Green, Box I, Personal Papers of Phyllis Schlafly.

68. Mrs. F. Woodrow Bush to Phyllis Schlafly, January 23, 1968, Box 1, NFRW Files, Personal Papers of Phyllis Schlafly. Also, James H. Hatch III to Rosalind Frame, May 16, 1967; Katharine Kennedy Brown to Phyllis Schlafly, May 16, 1967, Box 4, NFRW Files, Personal Papers of Phyllis Schlafly.

69. Mary Ann Dunbar to Mrs. Phyllis Schlafly, July 11, 1968, Box I, NFRW Files, Eagle Forum Archives.

70. "Storm Centers on Credentials," *Washington Post*, May 6, 1967, NFRW Files, Personal Papers of Phyllis Schlafly.

71. Savannah, Georgia, "Protest Presented to the NFRW Convention, May 6, 1967; Ohio State NFRW, "Protest to National Office of NFRW," May 6, 1967; Bobbie Ames, "A Federation State President Protests the Unfair and Divisive Tactics Being Employed by the Nominating Committee" (1967); Box 1, NFRW Files, Personal Papers of Phyllis Schlafly.

72. Ohio Republican Woman's Club, *Newsletter*, June 1967, Box I, Personal Papers of Phyllis Schlafly.

73. "Storm Centers on Credentials," *Washington Post*, May 6, 1967, NFRW Files, Personal Papers of Phyllis Schlafly.

74. Phyllis Schlafly to Iris F. Maloney, July 11, 1967, Box 1, NFRW Files, Personal Papers of Phyllis Schlafly.

75. Irene Peshel, "Report of the 14th Biennial Convention," June 1967, Box 1, NFRW Files, Personal Papers of Phyllis Schlafly.

76. For a detailed summary of these charges, see Phyllis Schlafly, *Safe—Not Sorry* (Alton, Illinois, 1968). For her concession speech, Phyllis Schlafly, "Note on Defeat" (1967), NFRW Files, Eagle Forum Office Files. The NFRW Files provide a detailed record of this fight.

77. Phyllis Schlafly to Ray Bliss, June 6, 1967; "Mrs. Schlafly Assails Bliss, Calls his Office Un-Neutral," *St. Louis Post-Dispatch*, June 8, 1967, Box I, Personal Papers of Phyllis Schlafly.

78. Richard Bergholz, "GOP Woman Foresees End to Bloodletting," *Los Angeles Times*, June 30, 1967, Box 1, NFRW Files, Personal Papers of Phyllis Schlafly.

79. Elly Peterson, "Report of NFRW's Convention, May 8, 1967, Box 1, NFRW Files, Personal Papers of Phyllis Schlafly.

80. "Discouraged by Polls, Romney Talks of Quitting," *Cleveland Press*, January 6, 1968, Box 5, NFRW Files, Personal Papers of Phyllis Schlafly.

81. "Important Roles for GOP Women," *Oakland Tribune*, September 30, 1967, Box 5, NFRW Files, Personal Papers of Phyllis Schlafly.

82. Phyllis Schlafly, "Memo on Conservation with Frederick Sontag," Box 1974, Personal Papers of Phyllis Schlafly.

83. Phyllis Schlafly to Dear and Loyal Friend, May 10, 1967, National Federation of Republican Women Files, Eagle Forum Archives.

84. "3 Nebraska Clubs Quit GOP Women's Group, *Omaha World Herald*, May 26, 1967; "GOP Officials Quit," *Champaign Gazette*, June 6, 1967; Lola Reese Holl to Phyllis Schlafly, June 9, 1967, Box 1, NFRW Files, Personal Papers of Phyllis Schlafly.

85. Anne Brine, "Why We Need a New Organization," Doris Dickens, "Against Remaining in the National Federation," Box 4, NFRW Files, Personal Papers of Phyllis Schlafly.

86. Wilma (?) to Phyllis, July 11, 1967, Box 1, NFRW Files, Personal Papers of Phyllis Schlafly.

87. Mrs. F.S. Frierband, to Phyllis Schlafly, June 29, 1967, Box 1, NFRW Files, Personal Papers of Phyllis Schlafly.

88. David S. Broder, "Who Runs the Republicans," *Washington Post*, May 9, 1967, Box 5, NFRW Files, Personal Papers of Phyllis Schlafly.

89. Factional struggles within the GOP occurred between moderates and conservatives, as well as among conservatives. Some right-wing conservatives such as Mike Djordjevich, a California activist, accused William F. Buckley, Jr., Clifton White, and William Rusher of forming a clique to control the Young Republicans. See Mike Djordjevich to Glenn Campbell, August 15, 1965; Djordjevich to William F. Buckley, July 7, 1965; Djordjevich to William A. Rusher, June 7, 1967; NFRW Files, Personal Papers of Phyllis Schlafly.

CHAPTER SEVEN
CONFRONTING THE SOVIETS IN A NUCLEAR AGE

1. Phyllis Schlafly to John T. Salmon, June 1, 1966, Box 1965–66, Personal Papers of Phyllis Schlafly.

2. Jane Clark, "Phyllis Schlafly: Outspoken Advocate of Peace through Military Strength," *St. Louis Globe-Democrat*, November 19, 1965, Box 1965–66, Personal Papers of Phyllis Schlafly.

3. These sales figures were provided by Phyllis Schlafly in an interview with the author, April 29, 2003. The author was not granted access to her financial records, so there was no way to verify these figures, but based on correspondence between Schlafly and her co-author, Chester Ward, which discussed sales of books, these figures seem accurate. See Chester Ward to Phyllis Schlafly, November 6, 1968, *The Betrayers* Box, Eagle Forum Archives.

4. Rear Admiral Chester Ward, September 8, 1960, Box 100, Disarmament Subject File, John F. Kennedy Papers, John F. Kennedy Library.

5. Strom Thurmond, *The Faith We Have Not Kept* (San Diego, 1967), especially pp. 54–121.

6. Phyllis Schlafly, "The Cry Is Peace" (ms.), *Mindszenty Foundation Newsletter*, December 15, 1965, Box 1965–66, Personal Papers of Phyllis Schlafly.

7. Phyllis Schlafly, "Are We for the Captive Nations or Their Captors," America Wake Up, Number 178 (1966), Box 1965–66, Personal Papers of Phyllis Schlafly.

8. Msgr. Charles Owen Rice, China, *Pittsburgh Catholic*, October 6, 1966 (facsimile reproduction), Legion of St. Michael, Godfrey, Illinois, 1966, in "Catholics," Communism files, Eagle Forum Archives.

9. She also quoted James Burnham, whose influence on conservative thinking about the Soviet Union cannot be overestimated: "The liberal's arm cannot strike with consistent firmness against Communism, either domestically or internationally, because the liberal dimly feels that in doing so he would be somehow wounding himself." Phyllis Schlafly, "Lining Up the Liberals" (script), America Wake Up, Number 135, Box 1964–65, Personal Papers of Phyllis Schlafly.

10. Phyllis Schlafly to John T. Salmon, June 1, 1966, Box 1965–66, Personal Papers of Phyllis Schlafly.

11. Ibid.

12. In their professional writings, liberal economists such as Walt Rostow and Robert Heilbroner argued that centralized, authoritarian regimes enabled less advanced countries to accelerate the stages of modernization through rapid capital accumulation, commanded-economic resource development, and state-directed production. W. W. Rostow outlined this argument for the efficiency of authoritarian-command economic development in *An American Policy in Asia* (New York, 1955) and developed it further in *The Economics of Take-Off into Sustained Growth* (London, 1963). This argument was also evident in Robert Heilbroner, *The Quest for Wealth: A Study of Acquisitive Man* (New York, 1956) and fully articulated in his widely used classroom textbook, *The Great Ascent: The Struggle for Economic Development in Our Time* (New York, 1963).

13. Unbeknownst to Ward or Schlafly, as early as the mid-1950s a group of Democratic party foreign policy intellectuals began to meet regularly at Thomas K. Finletter's apartment in New York. Included in the group were Paul Nitze, W. Averell Harriman, Joseph Alsop, George Kennan, Burt Marshall, Chester Bowles, and Arthur Schlesinger, Jr. The group outlined its program in a lengthy, 20-page memorandum drafted by Thomas Finletter. Dated January 19, 1954, "The Broad Program of the Group" declared its primary assumption that the Democratic party should continue its role as the leading advocate of "getting rid of war." The only way to get rid of war was to develop a "foolproof enforceable system for controlling the weapons of war." The report concluded that tensions between the Soviet Union and the United States could be reduced through U.S. reduction in arms. In other words, they proposed to turn arms

diplomacy on its head: it was not necessary to reduce tensions between the United States and the Soviet Union before securing an arms control treaty; instead, secure the arms control treaty first and this would led to a reduction of tensions.

Six months later on July 21, 1954, Arthur Schlesinger, Jr. wrote in another memorandum that he had concluded after discussions with Paul Nitze and Joseph Alsop that it was apparent the United States was losing its weapons superiority and that the United States was also losing "our economic superiority" as the "rate of economic expansion in the Soviet world has been markedly greater since the end of the war than the free world." He said the United States must maintain "enough military strength to deter external aggression," but American negotiators must be willing to negotiate with the Soviet Union and make concessions including admission of Red China into the United Nations. Thomas K. Finletter, "The Broad Program of the Group," Janaury 19, 1954, Box 99, Paul Nitze papers, Library of Congress. Nitze claimed that he attended the meetings irregularly. Paul Nitze, *From Hiroshima to Glasnost*, pp. 169–70.

14. This characterization of the Kennedy administration by Schlafly and Ward was one sided. Although liberals did predominate the administration, one of the problems of the Kennedy administration was its internal incoherence and constant shifting of policy. Moreover, within the administration there were a number of hard-liners including Secretary of State Dean Rusk, Adolf Berle, Averell Harriman, and Allen Dulles. McGeorge Bundy, a Harvard political scientist, became national security advisor. His deputy Walt Rostow came from MIT. Presidential Science Adviser Jerome Wiesner, also from MIT, was recruited by Harvard Law professor Abram Chayes, who got a job at State. Robert McNamara, a one-time Harvard business professor and Ford Motor Company president, became Secretary of Defense despite his lack of defense experience. Adam Yarmolinsky, whom conservatives claimed had edited a Communist newspaper when he was a student at Harvard University in the 1930s, was appointed to a top position in the Defense Department. Paul Nitze was not an academic, but was a known supporter of restricted nuclear warfare. For the complicated nature of the Kennedy administration and its policies, see W. J. Rorabaugh, *Kennedy and the Promise of the Sixties* (New York, 2002). For more recent understandings of the Cold War, see H. W. Brands, *The Devil We Knew* (New York, 1993); John L. Gaddis, *The United States and the End of the Cold War* (New York, 1992); and Richard N. Lebow and Janice G. Stein, *We All Lost the Cold War* (Princeton, 1994).

15. In his speech, Nitze developed a step by step argument that the United States should not develop a "Class A" capacity to enable the United States to win a nuclear war if deterrence fails, but instead should pursue a "Class B" capability, i.e., "a variety of secure, purely retaliatory systems." Paul Nitze, *From Hiroshima to Glasnost*, p. 173. For an understanding of peace efforts such as

Pugwash, see Militon S. Katz, *Ban the Bomb* (Westport, CT, 1986); and Joseph Rotblat, *Scientists in the Quest of Peace* (Cambridge, MA, 1986).

16. Robert S. McNamara, *In Retrospect: The Tragedy and Lesson of Vietnam* (New York, 1995); and Michael Beschloss, *The Crisis Years: Kennedy and Khrushchev, 1960–1963* (New York, 1991). For a highly critical account from the political left of Nitze, David Callahan, *Dangerous Capabilities: Paul Nitze and the Cold War* (New York, 1990). Also, Joseph M. Grieco, *Paul H. Nitze and Strategic Stability: A Critical Analysis* (Ithaca, NY, 1976); and Strobe Talbott, *Master of the Game: Paul Nitze and Nuclear Peace* (New York, 1988).

17. Phyllis Schlafly and Chester Ward, *The Gravediggers* (Alton, Illinois, 1964), pp. 43–45.

18. Phyllis Schlafly, Notes of Admiral Ward's Visit to Alton, July 29–August 2, 1965, *Strike from Space* Folders, Eagle Forum Archives.

19. Phyllis Schlafly, "Has the New President a Plan of Action?" Press Release, Mindszenty Foundation, Box 1960–61, Annual Correspondence, Personal Papers of Phyllis Schlafly.

20. David Holloway, *The Soviet Union and the Arms Race* (New Haven, 1983).

21. McGeorge Bundy, "Notes on Discussion of the Thinking of the Soviet Leadership," Cabinet Room, February 11, 1961, Box 405, National Security Files, John F. Kennedy Library.

22. In a lengthy memorandum to President Kennedy in June 1961, Walt Rostow described how he suggested to U.S. arms negotiator John McCloy that two fundamental principles should be considered in our relations with the Soviet Union. "First," he said, "we should be prepared to proceed by steps toward general and complete disarmament in which the degree of effective international control would be proportioned to the degree of disarmament actually achieved." Second, he felt, Americans should emphasize that "general and complete disarmament does demand effective international rules of law." Also, we should not spend time debating "what the end of the road would be like," but instead "propose principles for moving along that road."Walt W. Rostow, Memorandum to the President," June 12, 1961, Box 401, National Security Files.

23. *Freedom from War* declared that nations of the world should begin to direct their attention to the "disbanding of all national armed forces other than those required to preserve international order and for contributions to a United Nations Peace Force." The statement proposed a three-stage process for disarmament. The first stage would be to prohibit the testing of nuclear weapons, the reduction of strategic delivery vehicles, and the reduction of the United States and Soviet Union arms. The next stage began with the creation of a United Nations Peace Force and a substantial reduction in arms, especially strategic weapons. The final stage would retain only nonnuclear armaments to

maintain internal order. Department of State, *Freedom from War: The United States Program for General and Complete Disarmament in a Peaceful World* (Publication 7277), (Washington, D.C.: Government Printing Office, 1961), p. 2.

24. An internal memorandum in 1962 from Secretary of Defense McNamara reported that if a comprehensive test ban were reached at this point, "the United States and the Soviet Union would have approximate parity in the absence of all further tests. It is assumed they will have larger weapons and that we have higher ratios in light warheads, and greater variety in weapons with low yields." Gerald W. Johnson, Assistant to Secretary of Defense to Leland J. Haworth, Atomic Energy Commissioner, "Memorandum on Relative Technical and Military Advantages of Testing or Non-Testing Under Various Testing Constraints," July 29, 1962, Box 256, National Security Files, Papers of President Kennedy.

25. The Soviets proved to be exceptionally tough negotiators, forcing the United States to retreat step-by-step. After on-site inspections were rejected by the Soviet negotiators, the United States proposed internationally manned inspection sites. After this was rejected, the United States proposed automatic seismic stations. By the time this was rejected, arms negotiators in the Kennedy administration were assured by its scientists that seismic stations were not necessary after all because of new seismic technology. A chronological summary of the negotiations is found in "Signing the Test Ban Treaty, August 1, 1963," Box 266, National Security Files, John F. Kennedy Library. An excellent inside account of treaty negotiations and the treaty's ratification is found in Glenn T. Seaborg, *Kennedy, Khrushchev, and the Test Ban* (Berkeley, 1981). A context for the treaty is found in John Newhouse, *War and Peace in the Nuclear Age* (New York, 1989), pp. 192–195. Also, Robert Divine, *Blowing in the Wind: The Nuclear Test Ban Debate, 1954–1960* (New York, 1978).

26. "Testimony of Phyllis Schlafly on the Nuclear Test Ban Treaty, U.S. Senate Committee on Foreign Relations, *Hearings*, August 12–27, 1963 (Washington, D.C., 1963), pp. 906–916.

27. Quoted in William W. Prochnau and Richard Larsen, *A Certain Democrat: Senator Henry M. Jackson* (Englewood Cliffs, NJ, 1972), p. 217.

28. The Kennedy administration's efforts for the Test Ban Treaty are found in Frederick Dutton to Mr. Theodore Sorenson, "Public Campaign to Support the Test Ban Treaty," August 16, 1963, Box 100, President's Office Files, John F. Kennedy Library.

29. The Test Ban Treaty allowed enough ambiguity to provide room for legitimate debate. In his memoirs, Paul Nitze wrote that a few years later he reexamined the verification issues in light of technological developments, only to conclude that the Kennedy administration was "wide of the mark" on some issues of verification capabilities at the time, but in most ways we were more successful than we had "originally anticipated." Whatever the merits of

the treaty—and most observers at the time believed that the ratification was an important first step toward achieving later arms control treaties—Senate ratification was an important political victory for Kennedy. Paul Nitze, *From Hiroshima to Glasnost*, p. 193.

30. In their willingness to think in new ways about defending the nation, Kennedy defense experts introduced two new themes to defense policy: "flexible response" and "second-strike nuclear capacity." Both these concepts, "flexible response" and "second-strike nuclear capacity," had profound consequences for arms control and military procurement over the next decade. The first concept concerned conventional military strategy. Kennedy strategists argued that the United States military needed to develop a flexible response capability to fight "limited wars" against communist-led insurgencies and hot spots that might flare up in the new post-colonial world. The second concept—second-strike deterrence—involved nuclear strategy. This concept emerged from studies at the RAND Corporation conducted by William W. Kaufmann, Albert Wohlstetter, and later Thomas Schelling. In 1959, Albert Wohlstetter, in "The Delicate Balance of Terror" in *Foreign Affairs*, argued that contrary to common sense, a weak strategic force *invulnerable* to a preemptive strike was in a better position than a stronger strategic force *vulnerable* to a preemptive strike. Similarly, a nation with the capacity to launch a massive counter-strike or second strike against an enemy was in a stronger position than its enemy. Wohlstetter maintained, therefore, that the key to deterrence lay in a nation's capacity to take a first-strike, not have its delivery weapons wiped out, and launch a second retaliatory (counterforce) strike against its adversary. Wohlstetter and his colleagues at RAND concluded that the first-strike strategy—followed by the Eisenhower administration—was inherently provocative and dangerous in that an adversary such as the Soviet Union might launch a surprise preemptive strike if it felt threatened.

This concept of second-strike deterrence suggested another critical concept—the need for arms control between the two nations. If a clear balance of terror could be found through arms control treaties preventing one side from having a clear advantage over the other, then nuclear war could be avoided. (This perspective also assumed conventional confrontations between the United States and the Soviet Union would be fought through surrogates in developing nations or in limited wars.) Thomas Schelling and Morton Halperin in *Strategy and Arms Control* extended the logic of Wohlstetter's argument to arms control by arguing that negotiations between the superpowers should not necessarily be used to reduce arms—such a result might actually be dangerous if one side came out ahead in such a negotiation. Instead arms control negotiations should aim to "stabilize" nuclear forces by specifically building second-strike capabilities on both sides. They argued that nuclear parity between the United States and the Soviet Union created a mutual interest in avoiding a nuclear war. Henry Kissinger, after attending Schelling's arms control seminar in Cambridge, came out in favor of this new concept of arms control in "Arms Control, Inspection, and Surprise Attack" in *Foreign Affairs* in the summer of 1960. As historian Patrick Glynn later observed, "Indeed, nearly all the first-rank defense and foreign policy officials and consultants of the Kennedy administration had been exposed to arms control theory by the time they joined the administration." This discussion of Kennedy-Johnson defense policy relies on Patrick Glynn, *Closing Pandora's Box: Arms Races, Arms Control, and the History of the Cold War* (New York, 1987). Also, useful are Fred M. Kaplan, *Wizards of Armageddon* (New York, 1983); B. Bruce-Briggs, *The Shield of Faith* (New York, 1988); and Lawrence Freedman, *The Evolution of Nuclear Strategy* (New York, 1982). Also, Henry A. Kissinger, "Arms Control, Inspection, and Surprise Attack," *Foreign Affairs* 38 (July 1960): 555–75. Paul H. Nitze, *From Hiroshima to Glasnost: At the Center of Decision,* (New York, 1989), pp. 195–96.

31. Stewart Alsop, "Our New Strategy: The Alternative to Total War," *Saturday Evening Post*, December 1, 1962, p. 18, quoted in Patrick Glynn, *Closing Pandora's Box*, p. 199.

32. Patrick Glynn, *Closing Pandora's Box*, p. 200. For a different and important alternative view of McNamara and his policies, see Deborah Shapley, *Promise and Power: The Life and Times of Robert McNamara* (Boston, 1993) and William A. Kaufman, *McNamara Strategy* (New York, 1964). Also, a sympathetic view of McNamara is found in Henry L. Trewhitt, *McNamara* (New York, 1971). Important to understanding strategic nuclear policy is William H. Baugh, *The Politics of Nuclear Balance: Ambiguity and Continuity in Strategic Policies* (New York, 1984).

33. Because of its inaccurate guidance system, the Titan carried a heavy load, which would have destroyed everything around the target, including countryside and population. Strobe Talbott, *Endgame: The Inside Story of Salt II* (New York, 1990), pp. 23–26.

34. Strobe Talbott, *Endgame: The Inside Story of Salt II*, pp. 27–28.

35. When Khrushchev was removed from office in October 1964, the Soviet Union lagged behind the United States in intercontinental ballistic forces. The Soviet Union had given priority to the deployment of the intermediate range SS-4 and SS-5 missiles. Nearly 750 of these missiles were produced between 1959 and 1965, but only four SS-6 ICBMs were deployed in these years and the development of the next generation of Soviet ICBMs came only in 1962. In the mid-1960s, after the Kennedy administration, the Soviet Union began a rapid buildup of its ICBM force. By 1969, two years after McNamara left office, the Soviet Union surpassed the United States in the number of ICBM launchers. Moreover, the Soviets had developed the SS-9 that carried a warhead with a yield of 25 megatons, and a smaller SS-11 with a 1–2 megaton warhead. As U.S. defense analysts watched the SS-9 rumble into deployment, they reached the obvious conclusion: The SS-9 was not a retaliatory weapon, but a first-strike

weapon designed to knock out the American land-based ICBM force in a *pre-emptive strike*. This extraordinary buildup that continued throughout the 1970s revealed that Soviet leaders were not willing to accept inferiority to the United States nuclear arsenal. The Soviets claimed they were seeking nuclear parity—an ambiguous measurement by any standard—but critics of the McNamara strategy believed that the rapid Soviet buildup had reduced America to an inferior position. By 1972, five years after McNamara stepped down as Secretary of Defense, the Soviet Union had outdistanced the United States in numbers of ICBMs and was gaining in SLBMs (submarine launched ballistic missiles). Defenders of the McNamara strategy argued that American missiles were more accurate and therefore more deadly. This discussion of Soviet strategic development and defense strategy relies heavily on David Holloway, *The Soviet Union and the Arms Race* (New Haven, 1983), pp. 45–93.

The rapid buildup of Soviet nuclear forces is evident in this table.

Soviet-American Strategic Balance

	USA		Soviet Union
1969 November-SALT begins	1054	ICBMs	500
	656	SLBMs (submarine launched missiles)	110
	525	Bombers	145
	2,235	Total	1470
1972 May-SALT Signed	1054	ICBMs	1527
	656	SLBMs	459
	430	Bombers	156
	2,140	Total	2142
1974 November Vladivostok Accord	1054	ICBMs	1567
	656	SLBM	655
	390	Bombers	156
	2100	Total	2378

Source: David Holloway, *The Soviet Union and the Arms Race*, pp. 58–59.

36. Khrushchev's speeches made it clear that peaceful coexistence did not mean the end of competition with the United States, politically, economically, or ideologically. As Khrushchev declared in a speech in 1961, "In the conditions of peaceful coexistence favorable opportunities are provided for the development of the class struggle in the capitalist countries and the national-liberation

of the peoples of the colonial and dependent countries." Khrushchev remained firmly convinced the United States could be severely wounded through wars of national liberation. Quoted in Paul Nitze, *From Hiroshima to Glasnost*, p. 165. Also, David Holloway, *The Soviet Union and the Arms Race*, pp. 84–85. William Taubman, *Khrushchev: The Man and his Era* (New York, 2003), pp. 529–620.

37. *Proceedings of the Twenty-Seventh Republican National Convention, Chicago,* July 1960, p. 234; *Proceedings of the Twenty-Eighth Republican National Convention, San Francisco,* July 1964, p. 284; *Proceedings of the Twenty-Ninth Republican National Convention, Miami Beach, Florida,* August, 1968, p. 265.

38. Phyllis Schlafly, "Notes of Admiral Ward's Visit to Alton, July 20–August 2, 1965," *Strike from Space* Folder, Eagle Forum Archives.

39. Some critics at the time later charged Schlafly and Ward with calling for a preemptive strike against the Soviet Union. Writing in 2002, journalist Frances FitzGerald described the "Curtis LeMay-Phyllis Schlafly school of strategy" as viewing "no essential difference between nuclear and conventional weapons" and believing that in a nuclear exchange with the Soviet Union, the United States could protect 90 percent of its population if proper policies were implemented. Schlafly and LeMay never met or corresponded. Linking LeMay and Schlafly as bogeymen and placing them together in a school of thought is inaccurate, and pretending that they did not know the difference or assume a difference between nuclear and conventional weapons is partisan. Frances FitzGerald, *Way Out There in the Blue* (New York, 2000), p. 122.

40. Phyllis Schlafly and Chester Ward, *The Gravediggers* (Alton, IL, 1964), pp. 13–16 and Schlafly and Ward, *Strike from Space* (Alton, IL, 1965), pp. 84–85.

41. Schlafly and Ward, *The Gravediggers*, p. 17.

42. Desmond Ball, *Politics and Force Levels: The Strategic Missile Program of the Kennedy Administration* (Berkeley, California, 1980), pp. 183–85.

43. Phyllis Schlafly, "Should We Have an Anti-Missile Defense?" America Wake Up (transcript), Number 183 (1966), Box 1966 Annual Correspondence, Personal Papers of Phyllis Schlafly. B. Bruce-Briggs provides a readable summary of weapon and strategic debate in *The Shield of Faith* (New York, 1988), pp. 149–61.

44. A succinct discussion of the ABM and MIRV issues is found in John Newhouse, *War and Peace in the Nuclear Age*, pp. 199–208. Also see, Lawrence Freedman, *The Evolution of Nuclear Strategy* (New York, 1982).

45. He met immediate opposition within the Pentagon, later recalling that "almost everyone in that the building was for ABM, except [Deputy Secretary of Defense] Cy Vance and me." Quoted in John Newhouse, *War and Peace in the Nuclear Age*, p. 203.

46. U.S. Congress, "The Changing Strategic Military Balance: U.S.A. vs. U.S.S.R.," Committee on Armed Services House of Representatives, Ninetieth Congress, First Session, July 1967 (Washington, D.C., 1967).

47. John Newhouse, *War and Peace in the Nuclear Age,* pp. 200–203.

48. U.S. Congress, "The Changing Strategic Military Balance: U.S.A. vs. U.S.S.R.," Committee on Armed Services House of Representatives, Ninetieth Congress, First Session, July 1967 (Washington, D.C., 1967), pp. 29, 53, and 58.

49. Phyllis Schlafly, *Safe Not Sorry* (Alton, IL, 1967), pp. 133–34.

50. Schlafly and Ward, *Strike from Space,* pp. 185–87.

51. Schlafly and Ward, *The Gravediggers,* pp. 202–203.

52. Arthur Lee Harper to Paul Nitze (n.d.); Frank Eiklor to Paul Nitze, April 5, 1962, Box 49, Paul Nitze papers.

53. For example, Lawrence McQuaide at the Defense Department was specifically assigned to answer these letters against Paul Nitze. In a typical letter, McQuaide wrote, "Nitze is invariably one of the hard-headed sensible people in the policy formulating echelons around Washington. It's ridiculous to equate him with the weak-fibred folk who are the primary source of concern" in the minds of the right-wing. McQuade's responses are found in Nitze papers. Typical is Lawrence McQuade to Donald C. Fitch, June 11, 1963, Box 49, Nitze papers.

54. Paul Nitze, *"The Gravediggers*: Memoranda for Mr. Joseph Califano," March 22, 1965, Box 142, Nitze papers.

55. Paul H. Nitze, *From Hiroshima to Glasnost,* pp. 170–174.

CHAPTER EIGHT
NIXON BETRAYS THE RIGHT

1. "Cong. Ashbrook Says U.S. in Conservative Mood," *Phyllis Schlafly Report,* May 1969.

2. John Ashbrook, "The Nixon Administration's First 1000 Days," reprinted, *PSR,* December 1971.

3. Joan Hoff, *Nixon Reconsidered* (New York, 1994).

4. This discussion of the 1968 election is drawn in part from Michael Barone, *Our Country: The Shaping of America from Roosevelt to Reagan* (New York, 1990), pp. 417, 425–26; and James T. Patterson, *Grand Expectations: The United States, 1945–1974* (New York, 1996), pp. 679–709.

5. Kenneth D. Durr, *Behind the Backlash: White Working Class Politics in Baltimore, 1940–1980* (Chapel Hill, 2003), p. 147.

6. This discussion should begin with Gareth Davies, *From Opportunity to Entitlement: The Transformation and Decline of Great Society Liberalism* (Lawrence, KS, 1996); Hugh Davis Graham, *The Civil Rights Era: Origins and Development of National Policy, 1960–1972* (New York, 1990); and Lawrence Friedman, *The Republic of Choice: Law, Authority, and Culture* (Cambridge, MA, 1990).

7. Kenneth D. Durr, *Behind the Backlash: White Working Class Politics in Baltimore, 1940–1980* (Chapel Hill, 2003), pp. 138–39; 113.

8. Governor George Wallace of Alabama attempted to direct this populist impulse toward his presidential bid in 1968, but most conservatives saw Wallace as an old time Southern Democrat. He was not antigovernment, but was critical of the excesses of the executive and judicial branches of government. Indeed, as one historian of right-wing populism wittily observed, Wallace "favored a government that aided the common folk—as long as it stayed out of their schools, unions, and family lives." Quote from Michael Kazin, *The Populist Persuasion: An American History* (New York, 1995), p. 236; and Kenneth D. Durr, *Behind the Backlash: White Working Class Politics in Baltimore, 1940–1980* (Chapel Hill, 2003), pp. 33, 122.

9. Phyllis Schlafly's major statement on this issue was "Crisis in Law and Order," *Phyllis Schlafly Report* (May 1968), which was a discussion of the recently published congressional report, Subcommittee on Investigations of Government Operations Committee hearings, chaired by Senator John L. McClellan, *Riots, Civil and Criminal Disorders* (Washington, D.C., 1967). The major focus of Schlafly's summary of the report was the increase in urban riots. She wrote, "The only solution to the present rise in crime and riots is to *elect to office this November public officials who will enforce the law*" [original italics]. She pointed out that the get-tough policy during the Miami riot had been "fully supported by Negroes there." While Phyllis Schlafly did not speak against busing, she did reprint a transcript from a Manion Forum program in which Fred Schlafly appeared to criticize the recent 1971 Burger Court decisions, *Swann v Charlotte-Mecklenburg* and *Davis v Board of School Commissioners of Mobile County.* Fred Schlafly felt that these decisions overstepped the Civil Rights Act of 1964. To remedy the "confusion" over busing, he felt that a constitutional amendment was too slow. Instead, he called for Congress to enact legislation declaring the Federal courts shall not have jurisdiction to require the assignment of students based on race. Such a proposal excluding the Supreme Court from judicial oversight is especially interesting in that Phyllis Schlafly later made the same proposal to exclude Supreme Court oversight over a range of social issues. See Schlafly, *The Supremacists: The Tyranny of the Judges and How to Stop It* (Dallas, 2004). For Fred Schlafly's opposition to busing, see Fred Schlafly, "How to Stop Busing Now!" *Phyllis Schlafly Report* (October 1971).

10. For a contrary view, Dan T. Carter, *The Politics of Rage: George Wallace, the Origins of New Conservatism, and the Transformation of American Politics* (Baton Rouge, 1995). Also, of importance is Earl Black and Merle Black, *The Rise of Southern Republicanism* (Cambridge, MA, 2003). For another view, see Joseph Aistrup, *The Southern Strategy Revisited: Republican Top Down Advance in the South* (Lexington, KY, 1995) and Gerald Alexander, "The Myth of the Racist Republicans," *Claremont Review of Books* (Spring, 2004).

11. The Right's antipathy toward Romney is found in Antoni E. Golan, *Romney: Behind the Image* (Arlington, Virginia, 1967). M. Stanton Evans'

introduction offers a keen analysis from the right of Romney's presidential ambitions.

12. Hugh Scott lost his bid to become chairman of the Republican Senatorial Campaign Committee in late 1967 to conservative George Murphy (California) in large part because of his endorsement of Romney.

13. He later joined the Nixon administration as Secretary of Housing and Urban Development; he resigned in 1973, much to Nixon's relief.

14. Nixon knew that some on the Republican Right distrusted him because of his role in the 1952 convention as part of the deal to win the nomination for Dwight D. Eisenhower. Furthermore, he had promoted the Khrushchev visit to the United States in 1959, and during his gubernatorial race in 1962 he had sought to expel the John Birch Society from the California Republican party. On the other hand, he was the young congressman who had caught Alger Hiss in his lies; the vice president who had debated Khrushchev at the American exhibit in Moscow; and one of the few prominent Republicans who had vigorously campaigned for Barry Goldwater in 1964 when so many abandoned him.

15. Phyllis Schlafly, *Safe—Not Sorry* (Alton, Illinois, 1967), pp. 5–36; and Phyllis Schlafly, "Pornography and Pro-Communism" (manuscript), America Wake Up, Number 145, Box 1965–66, Phyllis Schlafly Personal Papers.

16. Phyllis Schlafly, "Ambush: A One-Hour Television Show," Box 1966, Personal Papers of Phyllis Schlafly.

17. It was assumed that communists were exploiting the civil rights movement for political purposes, and some conservatives such as John Bales warned that Martin Luther King, Jr. was surrounded by communists and perhaps might be one himself. See, "Martin Luther King, Jr. File," John Bales papers (unprocessed), University of Arkansas.

18. Phyllis Schlafly, *Safe—Not Sorry*, pp. 23–24.

19. Reagan drew considerable support among conservatives, as seen in a sixty-page booklet, M. Stanton Evans, *The Reason for Reagan* (LaJolla, CA, 1968). Also, see Stephen Hayward, *The Age of Reagan: The Fall of the Old Liberal Order, 1964–1980* (Roseville, CA, 2001).

20. Phyllis Schlafly to Admiral Chester Ward, November 8, 1968, *Betrayers* Box, Eagle Forum Files.

21. She wrote Ward, "Writing books is like having babies . . . one night I never went to bed at all, but worked right through the night and through the next day. Several other nights it was only two or three hours sleep. But we had to make the schedule if we wanted to be in the swim of the election." Phyllis Schlafly to Admiral Chester Ward, September 22, 1968, *Betrayers* Box, Eagle Forum Files.

22. Admiral Chester Ward to Phyllis Schlafly, August 31, 1968, *Betrayers* Box, Eagle Forum Files.

23. Phyllis Schlafly to Admiral Chester Ward, September 22, 1968, *Betrayers* Box, Eagle Forum Files.

24. Phyllis Schlafly to Admiral Chester Ward, October 23, 1968, *Betrayers* Box, Eagle Forum Files.

25. Richard Nixon to Phyllis Schlafly, October 27, 1968. For other comments on the book, see Strom Thurmond to Phyllis Schlafly, October 10, 1968; Edith Kermit Roosevelt to Phyllis Schlafly (n.d.); Mrs. Merwin Kimball Hart, November 21, 1968, *Betrayers* Box, Eagle Forum Files.

26. Shortly after the book's publication, Schlafly wrote to John Mitchell and Maurice Stans at the Nixon campaign headquarters urging them to distribute the book as part of their campaign literature. Schlafly received a reply to her letter in the final two weeks of the campaign when Maurice Stans phoned her to say that the letter had been misplaced. Although he had read the book and found it "very interesting," it was too late to use it in the campaign. In repeating the conversation to Ward, Schlafly observed that Stans seemed stunned when I told him, "Oh, that's all right, we have already sold 100,000 and are on our second 100,000." Phyllis Schlafly to Admiral Chester Ward, November 8, 1968, *Betrayers* Box, Eagle Forum Files.

27. Phyllis Schlafly to Admiral Chester Ward, November 8, 1968, *Betrayers* Box, Eagle Forum Files.

28. Phyllis Schlafly, Memo Re. Visit by Charles Percy to Alton, January 31, 1970, 1970 Campaign File, Eagle Forum Archives.

29. During her 1970 congressional campaign she wrote her campaign manager, James Brady, "Sometime, somewhere, a similar question might come up about Percy. The answer is that I fully supported Percy each time he was the Republican nominee, that is, for governor in 1964 and for Senator in 1966. I support the straight Republican party ticket always, and Percy had my full support both times he ran." Phyllis Schlafly to Jim Brady, January 8, 1970, 1970 Campaign File, Eagle Forum Archives.

30. Mrs. Donald E. Bateman to Republican Friend, July 1, 1968, Box 1968, Personal Papers of Phyllis Schlafly.

31. Phyllis Schlafly to Chester Ward, July 16, 1968, *Betrayers* File, Eagle Forum Files.

32. Phyllis Schlafly to Supporters, July 19, 1968; Phyllis Schlafly to Ruth, Kate, Mary, Grace, and Louise, July 17, 1968, Box 1968, Personal Papers of Phyllis Schlafly.

33. At the time the Gallup poll showed that in a Nixon-Humphrey race, Nixon would win 40–38 percent with 16 percent for Wallace, while Rockefeller stood even with Humphrey, 36–36 percent with 21 percent going to Wallace. Ronald Reagan showed the most upward potential as the convention opened. Michael Barone, *Our Country*, pp. 441–42. Useful on Reagan's background in California politics is Matthew Dallek, *The Right Moment: Ronald*

Reagan's First Victory and the Decisive Turning Point in American Politics (New York, 2000).

34. Schlafly could not understand why smart conservatives deferred to White's doomed strategy. Phyllis Schlafly to Chester Ward, August 12, 1968, *Betrayers* file, Eagle Forum Files. Phyllis Schlafly to Neil McCaffrey, November 20, 1968, Box 1968, Personal Papers of Phyllis Schlafly; Phyllis Schlafly, "Why Reagan Was Not Nominated," *Phyllis Schlafly Report*, August 1968.

35. Phyllis Schlafly, "Phyllis's Confidential Notes of the Republican National Convention, 1968," Box 1968–69, Personal Papers of Phyllis Schlafly.

36. Phyllis Schlafly to John Mitchell, October 1, 1968, Box 1968–69, Personal Papers of Phyllis Schlafly.

37. Phyllis Schlafly to John Mitchell, August 29, 1968; and Phyllis Schlafly to Richard Nixon, November 11, 1968, Box 1968–69, Personal Papers of Phyllis Schlafly.

38. Dan T. Carter, *The Politics of Rage: George Wallace, the Origins of the New Conservatism, and the Transformation of American Politics* (Baton Rouge, 1995) argues that the origins of the American Right, specifically, the New Right, can be found in the Wallace campaign and the race issue. It is clear that most conservatives did not support George Wallace in 1968 or 1972.

39. Phyllis Schlafly, "Nixon Wins Without the Help of Liberals," *Phyllis Schlafly Report*, November 1968. For the 1968 election, see Lewis Gould, *1968: The Election that Changed America* (Chicago, 1993) and Gould, *Grand Old Party: A History of the Republicans*, pp. 374–82.

40. For example, Patrick Buchanan became a speech writer, and conservative activist Howard Phillips became head of the Office of Economic Opportunity. When Nixon tried to appoint Clement Haynsworth, a judge from Thurmond's home state of South Carolina, the Senate rejected his nomination 55 to 45. Nixon expected his replacement nominee, Judge Harrold Carswell from Florida, to find easy confirmation from a Senate that had just gone through a bitter confirmation fight. Nixon was wrong; Led by Senator Birch Bayh (D-Indiana) Carswell was defeated 51–45 in April 1970. For the Nixon administration, there are a number of excellent books on various policies, but overviews can be found in Joan Hoff, *Nixon Reconsidered* (New York, 1994); Stephen Ambrose, *Nixon* (New York, 1987); and Herbert S. Parmet, *Richard Nixon and His America* (New York, 1990).

41. William Rusher to Michael Djorjevich, January 7, 1969, Box 26, William Rusher papers.

42. Michael Barone, *Our Country: The Shaping of America*, (New York, 1990), pp. 457–59.

43. Kennedy's failure to call the police immediately and his changing stories ruined his presidential chances. The American Right saw in Chappaquiddick a symbol of the moral decline in American society, encouraged by a liberal elite

54. Phyllis Schlafly, "Congressional Candidate Questionnaire," November 1970, 1970 Campaign File, Eagle Forum Files.

55. "Congressional Candidate Questionnaire," November 1970; "Fed Dems Blamed by Mrs. Schlafly for Money Crisis," *Alton Evening Telegraph*, July 28, 1970, 1970 Campaign File, Eagle Forum Files. For a critical account of Nixon's economic policies, Allen J. Matusow, *Nixon's Economy: Booms, Busts, Dollars, and Votes* (Lawrence, 1998).

56. Schlafly for Congress Campaign, "We've Been Short-Changed Too Long" (1970), 1970 Campaign File, Eagle Forum Files.

57. Phyllis Schlafly Campaign, "Roads" and "Social Security" scripts (1970), 1970 Campaign File, Eagle Forum Files.

58. Phyllis Schlafly Campaign, "Opening Questions for Television Campaign," 1970 Campaign File, Eagle Forum Files.

59. Schlafly unsuccessfully tried to get one of these celebrities or a country and western star to come to her district to campaign for her. Phyllis Schlafly to W. Clement Stone, August 20, 1970, 1970 Campaign Files, Eagle Forum Files.

60. "Key State Race in 23rd District," *Chicago Tribune*, October 11, 1970, 1970 Campaign File, Eagle Forum Files.

61. "Mrs. Schlafly Gains in Representative Shipley's District," October 29, 1970, *St. Louis Globe-Democrat*, 1970 Campaign File, Eagle Forum Files.

62. Phyllis Schlafly, Memorandum, August 18, 1970, 1970 Campaign File, Eagle Forum Files.

63. "What We Think about Phyllis for Congress," *Alton Evening Telegraph*, October 26, 1970, 1970 Campaign File, Eagle Forum Files.

64. David Nathan, "A Race with Spice in Illinois," *St Louis Globe-Democrat*, October 16, 1970, 1970 Campaign File, Eagle Forum Files.

65. George E. Shipley to Mrs. Ruby Etcheson, May 19, 1970, 1970 Campaign File, Eagle Forum Files.

66. "George Shipley Reports" (n.d., October 1970?), 1970 Campaign File, Eagle Forum Files.

67. David Nathan, "A Race with Spice in Illinois," *St Louis Globe-Democrat*, October 16, 1970, 1970 Campaign File, Eagle Forum Files.

68. "What We Think about Phyllis for Congress," *Alton Evening Telegraph*, October 26, 1970, 1970 Campaign File, Eagle Forum Files.

69. "Mrs. Schlafly Gains in Rep. Shipley's District," *Chicago Tribune*, October 29, 1970, 1970 Campaign Materials, Personal Papers of Phyllis Schlafly.

70. John Beckler, "Alton Hawk Challenges Shipley," *Alton Evening Telegraph*, October 22, 1970, Box 2, 1970 Campaign Materials, Personal Papers of Phyllis Schlafly.

71. For example, see Confidential Letter to Phyllis Schlafly, August 21, 1970, Box 2, 1970 Campaign Materials, Personal Papers of Phyllis Schlafly.

that eschewed traditional values in favor of self-indulgence ι
of humanism. The Right took immediate advantage of this tra
cism of Chappaquiddick continued for years. The John Birch ξ
Western Islands, published Zad Rust, *Teddy Bare* (Belmont, 1971
were certainly not the only ones who criticized Kennedy. In 1988
Senatorial Privilege (New York, 1988) became a best-seller. For a
spective of Chappaquiddick, see Michael Barone, *Our Country: 1
America*, p. 467.

44. David Nathan, "A Race with Spice in Illinois," October 16, 1ξ
Globe-Democrat, October 16, 1970, 1970 Campaign Files, Eagle Foru:

45. "Alton Hawk Challenges Shipley," *Alton Evening Telegraph*,
1970, 1970 Campaign Files, Eagle Forum Files.

46. John Camper, "Stylish Phyllis Trying to Charm Those Coun
Chicago Daily News, October 12, 1970, 1970 Files, Eagle Forum Archiv

47. Patrick J. Gorman to Phyllis Schlafly, April 10, 1970; Patrick (
Phyllis Schlafly April 7, 1970; Phyllis Schlafly to Patrick Gorman,
1970, 1970 Campaign Files, Eagle Forum Files.

48. Large contributors included W. Clement Stone who gave over
Robert Pabst, $5,000; Arthur C. Nielson, $4,000; Mr. and Mrs. DeWitt
$2,000; Rogers Follansbee, $3,000; and Roger Milliken, $3,000. The fu
contributors is found in "Contributions to Phyllis Schlafly's 1970 Congrι
Campaign," Campaign File, Eagle Forum Archives.

49. Phyllis Schlafly to Arthur C. Nielson, November 13, 1970, 197(
paign Files, Eagle Forum Files.

50. Phyllis Schlafly to Dear Friend, July 10, 1970, 1970 Campaign Files,
Forum Files.

51. "Phyllis Speaks Out for Youth" (brochure), Box 2, 1970 Campaign Ν
rials, Personal Papers of Phyllis Schlafly.

52. During the Cambodia protest, a SIU professor led a small group of
dents into the Selective Service office where they ripped to shreds a portra
Richard Nixon and then lowered the American flag at the local post office
short time later, four SIU students carrying handguns drove a univers
sedan to Springfield for a Black Panther rally. Such shenanigans did not pl
well with voters, but they were minor compared to violence occurring on oth
campuses.

53. She gave a number of speeches on the scandal of the TFX aircraft, a fightε
plane that had run into cost overruns under the McNamara Defense Depart
ment, but while her speech was placed in the *Congressional Record*, she founc
that her audiences' eyes glazed over when she went into any detail about the
plane. Phyllis Schlafly, "The F-111 Debacle," *Congressional Record-Senate*, S12520,
July 31, 1970, Schlafly Home Correspondence, Box 1971–72; Speech, Dinner
Kiwanis Club, Bunker Hill, May 27, 1970, 1970 Campaign File, Eagle Forum Files.

72. Phyllis Schlafly to Arthur C. Nielson, Sr., November 13, 1970, 1970 Campaign Materials, Personal Papers of Phyllis Schlafly.

73. Nixon's support of the Family Assistance Plan, in effect a guaranteed national income proposal (although first proposed by libertarian Milton Friedman in *Capitalism and Freedom* in 1962), drew heavy opposition from conservatives. By 1971 this proposal was all but dead in Congress, only to be replaced by the two other programs: the Supplemental Security Income program and a food stamp program.

74. Excellent studies of FAP are Vincent J. Burke and Vee Burke, *Nixon's Good Deed: Welfare Reform* (New York, 1974); Kenneth M. Bowler, *The Nixon Guaranteed Income Proposal: Substance and Process in Policy Change* (Cambridge, 1974); and Daniel P. Moynihan, *The Politics of a Guaranteed Income: The Nixon Administration and the Family Assistance Plan* (New York, 1973). A good discussion of Nixon's social policies is found in Joan Hoff, *Nixon Reconsidered* (New York, 1994).

75. Nixon took the first step toward implementing an affirmative action program for minorities. Conservatives reacted in horror at Nixon's support of the Philadelphia Plan. William Rusher warned that if Nixon got away with this one, he would be able to impose racial quotas on any business involved in interstate commerce. Rusher's prediction proved accurate: William Rusher to Priscilla Buckley, January 12, 1970, Box 123, William Rusher Papers.

76. See Dean J. Kotlowski's superb *Nixon's Civil Rights* (Cambridge, MA, 2001), pp. 232–40.

77. Schlafly and Ward, *Strike from Space*, chapter 3. Young Americans for Freedom prowar activities are discussed in John Andrew, *The Other Side of the Sixties: Young Americans for Freedom and the Rise of Conservative Politics* (New Brunswick, 1997); and Gregory L. Schneider *Cadres for Conservatism* (New York, 1999).

78. Phyllis Schlafly, "The Calley Case: How the Reds View It," *The Red Line*, April 1971, Personal Papers of Phyllis Schlafly.

79. Phyllis Schlafly, "Will Ping Pong Propaganda Erase History?" *Phyllis Schlafly Report*, May 1971.

80. Phyllis Schlafly, "Notes on Meeting with Senator Barry Goldwater," November 20, 1971, Box 1971–72, Personal Papers of Phyllis Schlafly.

81. The growing estrangement between the Republican Right and the administration was expressed in a letter that Lawrence J. Meisel, a major GOP contributor, wrote to the Republican finance committee in 1971, later reprinted in the *Phyllis Schlafly Report*. Lawrence J. Meisel to Jeremiah Milbank, Jr. Republican National Finance Committee, August 6, 1971, *Phyllis Schlafly Report*, November 1971.

82. Liberal thought at the time is found in John Kenneth Galbraith, *How to Control the Military* (Garden City, NY, 1969), p. 43; McGeorge Bundy, "To Cap

the Volcano," *Foreign Affairs* (October 1969). See also Patrick Glynn, *Closing Pandora's Box: Arms Races, Arms Control, and the History of the Cold War* (New York, 1992), pp. 234–37.

83. Opposition to ABM deployment took three major lines of argument: (1) the Safeguard was ineffective; (2) the United States could survive a first-strike nuclear attack and be able to retaliate, so the Safeguard was unnecessary; and (3) the continuation of the arms race would provoke a nuclear mishap. For an understanding of the liberal opposition to ABM, see Abram Chayes and Jerome B. Wiesner, editors, *ABM: An Evaluation of the Decision to Deploy an Antiballistic Missile System* (New York, 1969).

84. Phyllis Schlafly to Dear Ken (no last name), June 11, 1969, Box 1969, Personal Papers.

85. Phyllis Schlafly, "Should We Build the Sentinel," *PSR*, March 1969.

86. Everett Dirksen to Phyllis Schlafly, June 6, 1969, Box 1969, Personal Papers.

87. "Political Fallout from the ABM Treaty," *PSR*, September 1969.

88. Phyllis Schlafly "What SALT Means to America," *Testimony before the Senate Foreign Relations Committee, June 29, 1972*, reprinted by National Association of Pro America, "What SALT Means" (1972).

89. Phyllis Schlafly, "SALT Freezes US as Poor Second," *PSR*, June 1972; "Number 2 Tries Harder," *PSR*, July 1972.

90. Paul Nitze, *From Hiroshima to Glasnost* (New York, 1989), pp. 328–29.

91. Schlafly never seriously entertained joining a third-party effort, but she accepted an invitation to meet with George Wallace in early December 1971, arranged through her friend Bobbie Ames. At the meeting, Wallace made it clear he was going to make another try for the presidency. He told Schlafly that 150,000 votes properly distributed in North and South Carolina and Tennessee would have denied Nixon a majority of electoral votes, but that Strom Thurmond's strenuous campaign on behalf of Nixon had held the South. Phyllis Schlafly "Notes on Conference with Governor Wallace, December 4, 1971," Box 1971–72, Personal Papers of Phyllis Schlafly.

92. "Ashbrook Tells UROC He Won't Back Nixon," *San Francisco Examiner*, August 27, 1972, p. 3, Box 26, William Rusher papers.

93. Michael Barone, *Our Country*, pp. 525–34.

94. William Rusher to William F. Buckley, Jr. February 19, 1973 and February 21, 1973, William Rusher to William Buckley, March 13, 1975, Box 121, William Rusher Papers.

95. Board of Directors of the American Conservative Union Foundation, "The Conservative Century Dinner" (2000), pp. 4–5.

96. Howard Phillips, "Conservatives Should Help Remove Nixon (press release), July 30, 1974, Box 71, William Rusher papers.

97. For a contrary view of ideology and American politics, see John Gerring, *Party Ideologies in America, 1828–1996* (Cambridge, 1998).

98. Michael Schaller and George Rising, *The Republican Ascendancy: American Politics, 1968–2001* (Wheeling, IL, 2002).

99. Ruth Rosen, *The World Split Open: How the Modern Women's Movement Changed America* (New York, 2000) pp. xi–xvii.

CHAPTER NINE
THE ERA BATTLE REVIVES THE RIGHT

1. ABC Radio and Television, Transcript *Issues and Answers*, Sunday, February 25, 1973, ERA Files, Eagle Forum Archives.

2. "Senate Committee Heat Singes ERA," *Alton Evening Telegraph*, June 14, 1975, Illinois Action Folder, ERA File, Eagle Forum Archives.

3. Jerry Rubin, *Growing Up at Thirty-Seven* (Philadelphia, 1976). The theme that the liberal society had degenerated into a narcissistic and self-indulgent culture found expression in books such as cultural historian Christopher Lasch's *The Culture of Narcissism* (1975).

4. Sylvia Ann Hewlett, *A Lesser Life: The Myth of Women's Liberation in America* (new York, 1986), p. 211, quoted in Steven Hayward, *The Age of Reagan: The Fall of the Old Liberal Order, 1964–1980*, (Roseville, CA, 2001), p. 310.

5. The ERA was first introduced in Congress in 1923 by Republican Senator Charles Curtis through the efforts of Alice Paul, a militant feminist leader of the National Woman's Party. In the Senate, pro-labor Democrats led by Thomas Walsh (D-MA) defeated the amendment. For divisions within feminists, see William Chafe, *The American Woman: Her Changing Social, Economic and Political Roles, 1920–1970* (New York, 1972). For a more sophisticated understanding of these divisions, see Jane J. Mansbridge, *Why We Lost the ERA* (Chicago, 1986), pp. 8–19; J. Stanley Lemons, *The Woman Citizen: Social Feminism in the 1920s* (Urbana, 1973); and Susan D. Becker, *The Origins of the Equal Rights Amendment: Feminism between the Wars* (Westport, CT, 1981). Particularly useful in understanding the earlier feminist movement, see Steven Buechler, *Women's Movements in the United States: Woman Suffrage, Equal Rights, and Beyond* (New Brunswick, New Jersey, 1990); Lee Ann Banaszak, *Why Movements Succeed or Fail: Opportunity, Culture, and the Struggle for Woman Suffrage* (Princeton, NJ, 1997). See also Margaret Finnegan, *Selling Suffrage: Consumer Culture and Votes for Women* (New York, 1999); Nancy Cott, *The Grounding of Modern Feminism* (New Haven, 1987).

6. Cecilia Yawman to James W. Wadworth, September 27, 1945; James Wadsworth to Cecilia M. Yawman, October 1, 1945; Mrs. Charles E. Heming to James Wadsworth, March 15, 1944; Jane H. Todd to James W. Wadsworth, March 18, 1947, Box 24, James W. Wadsworth papers, Library of Congress.

7. Phyllis Schlafly, "What's Wrong with 'Equal Rights' for Women?" *Phyllis Schlafly Report* (February 1972).

8. The description of the social conservative view of the family is taken from Rebecca E. Klatch, *Women of the New Right* (Philadelphia, 1987), pp. 22–24.

9. Detailed arguments against ERA are found in nearly a hundred issues of the *Phyllis Schlafly Report* from 1972 to 1982. Schlafly's first articulation of her opposition to ERA appeared in "What's Wrong with 'Equal Rights' for Women?" *Phyllis Schlafly Report*, February 1972. She soon followed this with "The Fraud Called the Equal Rights Amendment," *Phyllis Schlafly Report*, May 1972; and "The Right to be a Woman," *Phyllis Schlafly Report* November 1972. Also of importance in understanding the legal opposition to ERA is Paul Freund, "The Equal Rights Amendment Is Not the Way," *Harvard Civil Rights-Civil Liberties Law Review*, March 1971.

10. This history of the ERA draws heavily from Jane J. Mansbridge, *Why We Lost the ERA*, pp. 8–20.

11. As the deadline for ERA approached, ERA activists were admitting that they had failed to win over the average homemaker. The view that women's groups had failed to connect with "homemakers" is found in Bonnie Cowan to Jane Wells (National Coordinator ERAmerica) March 19, 1976 ERAmerica, Box 1, Library of Congress, Washington, D.C.

12. As author of *A Choice Not an Echo*, a campaign book that had played a critical role in winning the Republican nomination for Barry Goldwater in 1964, Schlafly carried a national following into the campaign. Moreover, she brought to the campaign grassroots organizing skills not found among her opponents. She had run for Congress in 1952 and 1970, served as President of the Illinois Federation of Republican Women from 1960–1964, and later as vice president of the National Federation from 1964–1967. Carol Felsenthal, *The Sweetheart of the Silent Majority: The Biography of Phyllis Schlafly* (New York 1981).

13. Phyllis Schlafly to Dear Eagles Who Met Last Week at the O'Hare Inn, July 7, 1972, ERA Office Files, Eagle Forum Archives.

14. Phyllis Schlafly proposed the name "Why Lib" for the organization, but Kate Hoffman, who would head the anti-ERA effort in Illinois suggested STOP (Stop Taking Our Privileges) ERA.

15. Only gradually did STOP ERA activists accept Schlafly's strategy to keep the fight focused on the social and legal ramifications of ERA. Phyllis Schlafly, interview with author, July 20, 2001. Also, Margaret Stacy Kling, "In My Opinion," *Cincinnati Post*, January 8, 1973, Ohio ERA Action, ERA Files, Eagle Forum Archives.

16. Ruth Murray Brown, *For a 'Christian America': A History of the Religious Right*, (Amherst, New York, 2002), pp. 52–53.

17. John Archibald, "TV Comment," *St. Louis Post-Dispatch*, October 21, 1976, Box 18, Elly Peterson papers, University of Michigan, Ann Arbor.

18. A useful study of anti-ERA activists is found in David Brady and Kent Tedin, "Ladies in Pink: Religion and Political Ideology in the Anti-ERA Movement," *Social Science Quarterly* 57 (March 1976): 72–82.

19. Ruth Murray Brown, *For a 'Christian America': A History of the Religious Right*, (Amherst, NY, 2002), pp. 52–54.

20. Jo Ann Freeman, *The Politics of Women's Liberation* (New York, 1975), pp. 911–92; Ethel B. Jones, "ERA Voting: Labor Force Attachment, Marriage, and Religion," *The Journal of Legal Studies* (January 1983), 12:1, 157–168, especially p. 158. Also, Janet K. Boles, *The Politics of the Equal Rights Amendment: Conflict and the Decision Process* (New York, 1975).

21. Val Burris, "Who Opposed the ERA? An Analysis of Judicial Support for Gender-Based Claims," *Social Science Quarterly* (June 1983), 64:2, pp. 305–317, especially pp. 306–397.

22. Kent L. Tedin, David W. Brady, Mary E. Buxton, Barbara M. Gorman, and July L. Thompson, "Social Background and Political Differences Between Pro- and Anti-ERA Activists," *American Politics Quarterly* (July 1977), 5:3, pp. 395–404. Also, see Carol Mueler and Thomas Dimieri, "The Structure of Belief Systems among Contending ERA Activists," *Social Forces* (March 1982), 60:3, pp. 657–76.

23. Pamela Johnston Conover, "The Mobilization of the New Right: A Test of Various Explanations," The *Western Political Quarterly* (December 1983), 36:4, pp. 632–49, especially, pp. 633–34 and 644–45.

24. Theodore S. Arrington and Patricia A. Kyle, "Equal Rights Amendment Activists in North Carolina," *Signs*, 3:3 (Spring 1978), pp. 666–80.

25. Theodore S. Arrington and Patricia A. Kyle, "Equal Rights Amendment Activists in North Carolina," *Signs*, 3:3 (Spring 1978), pp. 666–80, quoted p. 678.

26. David W. Brady and Kent L. Tedin, "Ladies in Pink: Religion and Political Ideology in the Anti-ERA Movement," *Social Science Quarterly* (March 1976), 56:4, pp. 564–75.

27. While some state leaders agreed with an Ohio activist who told Schlafly that being identified with the Birch Society limited effectiveness in forming a broad coalition, Dot Slade was an exception. She was a natural leader, a single woman who worked full-time for a modest salary as a secretary. She supplemented her income through Tupperware parties so she could devote herself to what proved to be a ten-year, hard-fought battle, which, as one activist said at the end of it, "no one could have reasonably believed that ERA could be stopped in North Carolina when Dot Slade started the battle." Mrs. Daisy McWhorter to Phyllis Schlafly, February 6, 1973, Beth Hartsook to Phyllis Schlafly, May 13, 1986, ERA Action in North Carolina files ERA files, Eagle Forum Archives.

28. "Thank you Card," Illinois folder, ERA Files, Eagle Forum Archives.

29. Mrs. Shirley Curry to Ruth Ann Howell, October 22, 1974; "Peg Alston," *Alabama STOP ERA Newsletter*, September-October, 1974; "ERA Foe Charges Lib Movement Has Distorted View of Women," *Birmingham News*, February 5, 1975; and Anna Graham to Phyllis Schlafly, June 4, 1973, Drawer 1, ERA Files, Eagle Forum Archives.

30. Dorothy Clifford, "Mrs. Spellerberg in Forefront, Anti-ERA Not Just a Pretty Face," *Tallahassee Democrat*, December 7, 1973, ERA Drawer I, ERA Files.

31. Phyllis Schlafly to Rachel and Mary, January 24, 1973, Arkansas folder, ERA Files, Eagle Forum Archives.

32. Style was important, but in the end politics mattered. Anti-ERA women had deep roots in their communities, having been active in their local churches, parent-teacher clubs, and local community volunteer groups. They knew how to win their neighbors and local communities to their side. Furthermore, anti-ERA women tended to vote, if only because a higher proportion of anti-ERA women were married and a larger proportion of pro-ERA women were single. Specifically, in any given election, about two-thirds of married women will vote, while two-thirds of single women will not vote. The leading scholar of ERA believes these community roots are critical to understanding the success of STOP ERA. See Jane J. Mansbridge, *Why We Lost the ERA* (Chicago, 1986) pp. 49–55.

33. Surveys revealed that on a Left-Right spectrum, ERA activists placed themselves further on the liberal side than anti-ERA activists who considered themselves to be at the political center, even though they identified themselves as conservative. As a result, pro-ERAers perceived themselves as being further removed from the political center than did anti-ERAers. Kent L. Tedin, David W. Brady, Mary E. Buxton, Barbara M. Gorman, and July L. Thompson, "Social Background and Political Differences Between Pro-and Anti-ERA Activists," *American Politics Quarterly* (July 1977), 5:3, pp. 395–404. Also David W. Brady and Kent L. Tedin, "Ladies in Pink: Religion and Political Ideology in the Anti-ERA Movement," *Social Science Quarterly* (March 1976), 56:4, pp. 564–75. Jane L. Mansbridge, *Why We Lost the ERA* (Chicago, 1986), pp. 14–19.

34. Mrs. Paul Theroux to Dear Senators and Representatives, March 5, 1973, ERA Topical Files, Eagle Forum Archives.

35. Schlafly corresponded with the National Right to Life attorneys in the Hawaii case. See James Bopp to Rep. L. Michael Getty (December 71, 1978), ERA files, Eagle Forum Archives.

36. Miss Olive Spann to Dear State Legislator, March 10, 1975, ERA file, Eagle Forum Archives.

37. Lois Brown, "Schlafly-DeCrow ERA Debate Draws 750," *The Oxford Press*, April 19, 1978, ERA Defeat-Pro-ERA Defeat Files, Eagle Forum Archives.

38. Monroe Flinn to Mrs. Kathleen M. Sullivan, August 4, 1981, Illinois Action #2 Folder ERA, Eagle Forum Archives.

39. Writing at the time of the ERA campaign, sociologist Andrew Hacker observed, "With Phyllis Schlafly always in the limelight, many people concluded that ERA was a one woman operation." Andrew Hacker, "ERA-RIP," *Harper's*, September 1980, Family Lib Folder, ERA files, Eagle Forum. This point is also made by Jane Mansbridge, *Why We Lost the ERA* (Chicago, 1984).

40. "Feminist Derides ERA Foe," *Kansas City Star*, May 3, 1973, IWY Material, ERA Files, Eagle Forum Archives.

41. Alice Echols, *Daring to Be Bad: Radical Feminism in America, 1967–1975* (Minneapolis, 1989).

42. Patricia Beyea, "ERA's Last Mile," *The Civil Liberties Review* (July/August 1977), 4:2, pp. 45–49.

43. Janet K. Boles, "Building Support for the ERA: A Case of Too Much, Too Late," *PS*, Fall 1982, XV, 4, pp. 572–578; and Janet K. Boles, *The Politics of the Equal Rights Amendment* (New York, 1979).

44. Shelia Greenwald to Liz Carpenter, October 6, 1977, Box 18, Elly Peterson papers; and on Illinois, Marie Bass to Stewart Mott, April 28, 1978, Box 1, ERAmerica papers, Library of Congress.

45. Representing this shift, journalist Gloria Steinem found herself at odds with Betty Friedan, one of the founders of NOW. Trouble between the two women began when Steinem declared at a news conference in 1971, "We are all lesbians now." Following this remark—which was a play on Nixon's "We are all Keynesians now," Friedan began warning about radicalism within the feminist movement. Matters came to a head between the two women leaders at the 1973 National Women's Political Caucus, when Friedan lost her race for a seat on the national steering committee in a nasty election, which she claimed was rigged. Ruth Rosen, *The World Split Open: How the Modern Women's Movement Changed America* (New York, 2000); Carol G. Heilbrun, *The Education of a Woman: The Life of Gloria Steinem* (New York, 1995); and a superb study by Daniel Horowitz, *Betty Friedan and the Making of the Feminine Mystique: The American Left, the Cold War, and Modern America* (Amherst, 1998).

46. Patricia O'Brien, "Friedan Leads Rift in NOW," *Los Angeles Times*, November 27, 1975, IV:10; Joan Zyda, "Internal Struggle Jeopardizes NOW," *Chicago Tribune*, November 20, 1975; Pam Protor, "Has the Feminist Movement Reached a Turning Point," *Parade*, February 15, 1976; and "Lesbian Rights Get Top Billing," *Kansas City Times*, October 28, 1975; "NOW Presidency Karen DeCrow By Narrow Margin," *The Philadelphia Inquirer*, October 27, 1975; and Lauri Johnston, "Feminists Score Friedan Article Assailing Movement Disrupters," *New York Times*, March 8, 1973, Betty Friedan folder and NOW folder, ERA Files, Eagle Forum Archives.

47. National Organization for Women, *"Revolution: Tomorrow Is NOW"* (New York, 1973), pp. 2 (veteran benefits); 4–5 (voluntarism); 9–10 (education); 17–18 (religion); 18–20 (war and violence), 21–23 (sexual revolution).

48. Shelia Greenwald to Elly Peterson, July 22, 1976; and Elly Peterson to Shelia Greenwald, October 24, 1976, Box 18, Elly Peterson papers.

49. Also, Ann K. Justice, Editor, NOW, Lincoln, Neb. Chapter, "The Insurance Connection with Stop ERA Forces, A Report Published, September 1974." Box 120, ERAmerica Papers. Eileen Shanahan, "Opposition Rises to Amendment on Equal Rights," *New York Times*, 14 January, 1973; Lisa Cronin Wohl, "Phyllis Schlafly: Sweetheart of the Silent Majority," *Ms.* (March

1974), and Jo Freeman, *The Politics of Women's Liberation*, (New York, 1975), pp. 220, 55ff.

50. Scheffel and Company, "STOP ERA Financial Statements" (1973, 1974, 1975, 1976, 1977, 1978, 1979, 1980, 1981, and 1982), Eagle Forum Vault. Correspondence in the ERA files shows that most donations were in modest amounts and many contributors were evangelical women who tithed in support of the anti-ERA movement.

51. See "Report of Campaign Contributions or Annual Report of Campaign Contributions and Expenditures," 6/3/77–6/30/78; 7/1/78–6/30/79; 7/1/79–6/30/80; 7/1/80–6/30/81; and 7/1/81–6/30/82 and "Report of Receipts and Expenditures for a Candidate or Committee Supporting any Candidates(s) for Nomination or Election to Federal Office, Election Year 1978, 1979, 1980 (corrected 1981), ERA PAC Contribution Forms, Eagle Forum Archives.

52. Shelia Greenwald to Co-Chairs, October 19, 1975, Box 8, ERAmerica papers.

53. Deborah Meyers to Kathleen Currie, December 22, 1981, Box 140, ERAmerica papers.

54. Deborah Meyers to Ms. Faith Taylor, Feb. 16, 1982, ER, Box 140; Meyers to Faith Taylor, March, 4, 1982, ER, Box 140.

55. Alan Alda's television character "Hawkeye" in his television hit "M*A*S*H" was criticized for the way he treated women in the show, and some feminists felt uncomfortable receiving large financial contributions from the Playboy Foundation. Anne Marie Lipinski, "Playboy's Strange Playmates," *Chicago Tribune*, March 30, 1980, ERA-Playboy folder, ERA Files, Eagle Forum Archives.

56. Phyllis Schlafly, "Pro-ERA Propaganda in Women's Magazines," *Phyllis Schlafly Report* (August 1976).

57. Suone Cotner to William Glover, Jr. December 14, 1979, Box 1; Suone Cotner to ERAmerica Co-Chairs, October 16, 1979, Box 3, ERAmerica papers.

58. Dean J. Kotlowski, *Nixon's Civil Rights* (Cambridge, MA, 2001), pp. 232–40.

59. Helen Thomas, "Betty Ford Backs ERA," *Columbus Citizen Journal*, September 15, 1974, Ohio ERA Action Folder, ERA Files, Eagle Forum Archives.

60. "First Lady Sticks to Her Guns on ERA, *Los Angeles Times*, February 18, 1975, Ford Folder, ERA Files. Eagle Forum Archives.

61. "Remarks of the President on Signing an Executive Order," January 9, 1975, Box 2, Elizabeth O'Neill Files, Gerald Ford Presidential Library, Ann Arbor, Michigan.

62. "First Lady Sticks to Her Guns on ERA," *Los Angeles Times*, February 18, 1975, Ford Folder, ERA Files.

63. Winzola McLendon, "Betty Ford Talks about Homemaking," *Good Housekeeping* (August 1976); "Mrs. Ford Phones ERA Passage," *Washington Post*, February 15, 1975, Box 4, Elizabeth O'Neill Files.

64. He did not expect much controversy, although many Republicans had pushed George Bush for the position. William F. Buckley, Jr. had recommended Bush to Ford because he combined "deep understanding of Republican principles with an ability to communicate to the jaded ears of the old . . . and the cynical ears of the young." Herbert Parmet, *George Bush: The Life of a Lone-Star Yankee* (1978), p. 165. William F. Buckley, Jr. to President Gerald Ford, August 14, 1974, White House Central Files, Box 434, Subject Files, Buckley, Ford papers.

65. Steven F. Hayward, *The Age of Reagan: The Fall of the Old Liberal Order, 1964–1980* (Roseville, CA, 2001), p. 398; and John Robert Green, *The Presidency of Gerald R. Ford* (Lawrence, 1995), p. 30.

66. When the confirmation hearings finally started, Rockefeller found himself answering charges that he had bribed the head of the state New York Republican party. At the hearings, a resentful Rockefeller was forced to disclose his financial holdings, but in the end he won confirmation 90–7 in the Senate and 298–128 in the House, with conservative Republicans joining liberal Democrats in opposition. For JBS opposition to Rockefeller, Gary Allen, *The Rockefeller File*, (Seal Beach, CA, 1976). For an insider account of the nomination, see Robert T. Hartman, *Palace Politics: An Inside Account of the Ford Years* (New York, 1980), p. 235.

67. David Broder in the *Washington Post* observed that the Rockefeller nomination was seen by many GOP leaders as "an opportunity to overcome its [the Republican party's] status as a permanent minority in American politics." R. W. Apple declared in the *New York Times* that the new President "hasn't made a wrong move yet." With the exception of *New York Times* columnist William Safire, who warned that Rockefeller's appointment was a grave political mistake that would come back to bite the Ford administration, most political observers praised it.

Even as late as 1975, Richard Cheney joked with his boss, White House assistant Donald Rumsfeld, that he should try using Cheney's credentials to crash an upcoming convention of Howard Phillips's Conservative Caucus. Neither Cheney nor Rumsfeld took any conservative organization seriously and it would not have occurred to either of them at the time to establish better relations with the Right. Instead, they were convinced that the emerging Reagan wing of the party would be exposed as "really a front for Joseph Coors." Dick Cheney to Donald Rumsfeld, May 1, 1975, Box 19, Dick Cheney Papers, Ford Library.

68. There are many books on the New Right and the Christian Right. Especially useful are Clyde Wilcox, *God's Warriors* (Baltimore, 1992); Wilcox, *Onward Christian Soldiers? The Religious Right in American Politics* (Boulder, CO, 1996), Steve Bruce, *The Rise and Fall of the Christian Right* (New York, 1988), Oran P. Smith, *The Rise of Baptist Republicanism* (New York, 1997). Also, see Steve Bruce, Peter Kivisto, and William H. Swatos, Jr. *The Rapture of Politics* (New York, 1995);

Matthew Moen, *The Christian Right and Congress* (Tuscaloosa, 1983); Robert Liebman and Rother Wuthnow, *The New Christian Right* (New York, 1991); and David Bromley and Anson Shupe, *New Christian Politics* (Macon, GA, 1984). For the New Right, see Alan Crawford, *Thunder on the Right* (New York, 1980). Also, useful within this context is Nicol C. Rae, *The Decline and Fall of the Liberal Republicans: From 1952 to the Present* (New York, 1989).

69. Alabama, Arizona, Arkansas, Florida, Georgia, Illinois, Indiana, Louisiana, Mississippi, Missouri, Nevada, North Carolina, North Dakota, Oklahoma, South Carolina, Utah, and Virginia.

70. Rosemary Thomson, "A Christian View of the Equal Rights Amendment," Illinois Action Folder, ERA Files, Eagle Forum.

71. See for example, Mrs. Felicia Goeken, Illinois Federation for Right to Life, to Richard Daley, Illinois Action #2 Folder, ERA Files, Eagle Forum.

72. Reverend Henry Mitchell of the North Star Mission Church in southside Chicago, well known for its extensive social programs, rallied his predominately African-American congregation to oppose the ERA because of its pro-abortion implications. Missouri Synod Lutherans were mobilized through the efforts of Otto Hintze, a professor at Concordia Theological Seminary in St. Louis to send anti-ERA mass mailings to Lutherans throughout Illinois and Missouri. She worked with Chicago Rabbi Yitzchok Bider to alert the Daughters of Israel, whom Schlafly described after talking with them as "enthusiastic, smart, and family oriented," to set up a legislative committee to work against ERA. Bider proved especially important in getting representatives in District 15 in northside Chicago to vote against the ERA. Phyllis Schlafly to Otto Hintze, April 24, 1975; Rabbi Yitzchok Bider to Phyllis Schlafly, June 20, 1977; and Phyllis Schlafly to Rabbi Yitzchok Bider, June 28, 1977, Illinois Action #2 Folder, ERA Files, Eagle Forum.

73. Lisa Wohl, "Final Tribute," *New Times* (n.d. 1975), Illinois Action #2 Folder, ERA Files, Eagle Forum.

74. Bud Farrar, "ERA Supporters Bring Battle to Springfield," *Edwardsville Intelligencer*, April 10, 1975, Illinois Action Folder #2, ERA Files, Eagle Forum.

75. "Representative Rolland Tipsword Resists Pro-ERA Pressure," *Springfield Herald*, June 12, 1974, Illinois Action Folder, ERA Files, Eagle Forum Archives.

76. Jane J. Mansbridge, *Why We Lost the ERA*, (Chicago, 1980), p. 162.

77. Ibid. pp. 160–63; and "Tell Daley to Pledge to Pass ERA," *St. Louis Post-Dispatch*, March 24, 1975, Illinois Action Folder #2, ERA Files, Eagle Forum Archives.

78. "Senate Committee Heat Singes ERA," *Alton Evening Telegraph*, June 14, 1975, Illinois Action #2 Folder, ERA Files, Eagle Forum Archives. Phyllis Schlafly, Conversation with author, September 23, 2003.

79. Representative John Edward Porter to Phyllis Schlafly, April 18, 1973, Illinois Action #2 Folder, ERA Files, Eagle Forum.

80. Eleanor Randolph, "Mrs. Ford Keeps Peace at Party Here," *Chicago Tribune*, September 25, 1974, Illinois Action #2 Folder, ERA Files, Eagle Forum Archives.

81. Donald E. Deuster, "Deuster Admonishes First Lady to Stop Telephone Lobbying from White House" (press release), February 15, 1972, Illinois Action #2 Folder, ERA Files, Eagle Forum Archives.

82. Typical of Schlafly's articles that appeared in the *Phyllis Schlafly Report* in 1974 and 1975 were "Effect of ERA on Family Property Rights," "How ERA Will Hurt Divorced Women," "Why Virginia Rejected ERA," "ERA and Homosexual Marriages," "ERA Means Abortion and Population Shrinkage," "Will ERA Make Child-Care the State's Job?"

83. "Schlafly, Phyllis Stewart," Washington University School of Law Transcript, Personal Papers of Phyllis Schlafly.

84. Steven Hayward, *The Age of Reagan*, p. 413.

85. "Soviet Navy Plans Better than U.S., Zumwalt Says," *Washington Post*, July 28, 1975, p. AI, quoted in Hayward, *The Age of Reagan*, p. 420. The following discussion of détente and defense policy relies on Hayward, Patrick Glynn, *Closing Pandora's Box: Arms Races, Arms Control, and the History of the Cold War* (New York, 1992); and Paul H. Nitze, *From Hiroshima to Glasnost: At the Center of Decision* (New York, 1989).

86. Phyllis Schlafly and Chester Ward, *Kissinger on the Couch* (New Rochelle, NY, 1975), pp. 781–85.

87. Richard Cheney, Memo, November 13, 1975, Box 1, Richard Cheney Papers.

88. Foster Chanock, "Key Issues Difference," June, 1976, Box 1, Foster Chanock papers, Gerald Ford.

89. Steven Hayward, *The Age of Reagan*, pp. 473–77.

90. Initially Reagan had supported the ERA, but in 1976 he came out against it. When asked about the issue, Reagan gave a stock answer: "I do not believe that a simple amendment, the Equal Rights Amendment, is the answer to the problem. I think it opens a Pandora's Box, and could in fact militate against the very things that women are asking for. I believe the answer is by statute. . . . I would hate to see a nation that's going to rely on women in the combat forces." See "Press Conference by Ronald Reagan Announcement of Candidacy, November 20, 1975, Subject File, Box 2, President Ford Committee Records. For the decision not to fight over ERA at the Republican convention, see "ERA and the Republican Platform," *Phyllis Schlafly Report*, September 1976.

CHAPTER TEN
THE TRIUMPH OF THE RIGHT

1. Alan I. Marcus to Author, November 24, 2003.

2. "Rosalynn Carter Helps Pass Equal Rights in Indiana," *The Loraine Journal*, January 19, 1977. For criticism, "An Unwise Intrusion" (editorial), *Tampa Tribune* (n.d. 1978), ERA Carter Folder, ERA Files, Eagle Forum Archives.

3. A good summary of the IWY and its state conferences is found in Ruth Murray Brown, *For a "Christian America"* (Amherst, NY, 2002), pp. 104–121.

4. Quoted in Ruth Murray Brown, *For a "Christian America"* (Amherst, NY, 2002), p. 107.

5. The number of delegations controlled by the antifeminists is given by Ruth Murray Brown, in *For a "Christian America,"* p. 107, but she does not cite a source.

6. Elaine Donnelly to Rosemary Thomson, Alternate Strategies for Houston, Sept. 7, 1977 (Confidential), IWY Material/ IWY Lesbians Folder, ERA Office Files, Eagle Forum Archives.

7. Verbatim resolutions are found in Caroline Bird and National Commission on the Observance of International Women's Year, *What Women Want: From the Official Report to the President, the Congress and the People of the United States* (New York, 1979), pp. 160–64 and 167–69.

8. Quoted in National Commission on the Observance of International Women's Year, *The Spirit of Houston: An Official Report to the President, the Congress, and the People of the United States* (Washington, D.C., 1978), p. 3.

9. Quoted in Ruth Murray Brown, *For a "Christian America,"* p. 115.

10. Quoted in National Commission on the Observance of International Women's Year, *The Spirit of Houston: An Official Report to the President, the Congress, and the People of the United States* (Washington, D.C., 1978), p. 167.

11. Ruth Murray Brown, *For a "Christian America,"* pp. 114–21.

12. "Pro-Family Rally Attracts 20,000," and "What Really Happened in Houston," *Phyllis Schlafly Report*, December 1977.

13. Quoted in Ruth Murray Brown, *For a "Christian America,"* p. 117.

14. Opponents claimed that most of the material did not come from the conference at all, but had been purchased at an adult bookstore. While this accusation appears highly unlikely, this literature was not representative of most of the women attending the IWY Conference. The Socialist Workers party (pictured in the display) was a small, sectarian Trotskyite party. Estimates place the percentage of lesbian delegates at about 10 percent (but the resolutions they put forward were overwhelmingly adopted). Whether representative or not, the material was shocking to Middle America. And, while the claim made by anti-ERA forces that federal monies had paid for the off-beat booths was false, the U.S. Civil Rights Commission published the pamphlets on lesbian rights that were included in the material STOP ERA put on display. Ruth Murray Brown, *For a "Christian America,"* p. 119.

15. Janet K. Boles, "Building Support for the ERA: A Case of Too Much, Too Late," *Political Science*, Fall 1982, XV, 4, pp. 572–78; and Janet K. Boles, *The Politics of the Equal Rights Amendment* (New York, 1979).

16. Ibid., pp. 572–78.

17. Kentucky rescinded its ratification on March 16, 1978, and South Dakota on March 1, 1979. The three previous states were Nebraska (March 15, 1973), Tennessee (April 23, 1974), and Idaho (February 8, 1977).

18. Alice Wynne Gatsis to Phyllis Schlafly, March 13, 1978, IWY Folder, ERA Files, Eagle Forum Archives.

19. Grace Marie Arnett, "ERA Fight Continues," *Columbus Citizen Journal*, July 5, 1978, Feminism Folder, Eagle Forum Archives.

20. Elly Peterson, "Diary Notes," June 6, 1982, Box 19, Elly Peterson Papers, University of Michigan.

21. "NOW Worker Indicted on ERA Bribe Charge," *Cleveland Plain Dealer*, June 6, 1980; "ERA Bribe Conviction Called Right Wing Plot," *The Seattle Times*, August 25, 1980, Bribery Folder, ERA Files, Eagle Forum Archives.

22. These figures are cited in Janet Boles, "Building Support for the ERA: A Case of Too Much, Too Late," *Political Science* (Fall 1982), XV, 4: pp. 572–78; and see Paul Taylor, "NOW Seeking $3 Million War Chest to Oust ERA Foes, Fight New Right," *Washington Post*, 27 August 1982, A2, and they are confirmed in Elly Peterson's diary, "Diary Notes," June 6, 1982, Box 19, Elly Peterson Papers, University of Michigan.

23. Dorothy Clifford, "Mrs. Spellerberg in Forefront of Anti-ERA; Not Just a Pretty Face," *Tallahassee Democrat*, December 7, 1973, Florida Action Folder, ERA Files, Eagle Forum Archives.

24. Eight years after the ERA fight, he was quoted in the press as saying, "Women don't need any more help. They've already got 50 percent of the money and 100 percent of the other things men need." Bill Cottrell, "From the Peak of Power: Dempsey Barron's Defeat Ends 32 Year Era of Senate History," *Tallahassee Democrat*, September 11, 1988, Florida Action Folder, ERA Files, Eagle Forum Archives.

25. Poston denied the charge, claiming in a nonsequitur that he voted against ERA because he had trouble with women getting married and not taking their husband's name.

26. Jane O'Reilly, "Only Nine Votes Could Have Meant a Victory for ERA," *Washington Star*, May 8, 1978, Box 145, ERAmerica papers.

27. Many of these shocking letters were sent to Phyllis Schlafly as a sample of the kind of mail he received pertaining to his vote. Vernon C. Holloway to Phyllis Schlafly, December 26, 1979, Florida Action Folder, ERA Files, Eagle Forum Archives.

28. Phyllis Schlafly to Dear Florida Friend, September 3, 1980, Florida Action Folder, ERA Files.

29. "Fight New Right, Women Told," *Detroit Free Press*, November 30, 1979, Cheryl Arvidson, Women Leaders Fear Right Wing Sabotage," *Cleveland Press*, October 5, 1977, IWY Folders; and Iris F. Mitgang, National Chair, Women's

Political Caucus to Caucus Member, March 25, 1981, Lib Tactics Folder, ERA files; Jean Whitter, "NOW Legal Defense and Education Fund Letter," April 11, 1977, NOW Tactics Folder, ERA Files, Eagle Forum Archives.

30. Miss Jo Ann Horowitz to Phyllis Schlafly, March 31, 1974; Phyllis Schlafly to Miss Jo Ann Horowitz, April 10, 1974, ERA-Rebuttals, ERA files.

31. Transcript, ERA Workshop, NOW Detroit Chapter, April 1977, NOW Folders, ERA Files, Eagle Forum Archives.

32. When Phyllis Schlafly phoned the press to complain about the article, the editor replied in a letter that "we have no evidence to show that you have sought or received the support of the Ku Klux Klan itself. . . . We are prepared, however, to publish a letter to the editor signed by you, disavowing any relationship between you and the Ku Klux Klan." Responding, Schlafly thanked the editor for "the kindly tone" of his letter, but said that a "self-serving letter from me to the editor" saying that I am not associated with the KKK "does not remedy the wrong of a news story falsely indicating that I am so funded." She asked for an interview with an objective reporter, but when this was refused she ended up publishing a letter to the editor denying this association. See Kurt Luedtke to Phyllis Schlafly, December 20, 1977; Phyllis Schlafly to Kurt Luedtke, January 9, 1978; For KKK articles, see Arnie Weissmann, "The New Klan? The New Right?" *Illinois Education Association Advocate*, March 1981, 15:5 pp. 11–14; Vera Glaser, "Women's Year Meeting Anti-Feminists," *Detroit Free Press*, August 25, 1977, ERA Smears Folder, ERA Files.

33. See Liz Carpenter and Elly Peterson to Garry Trudeau, January 6, 1977, Box 18, Elly Peterson papers.

34. "Transcript, Talk of the Town," August 21, 1975; Bill Smith (Program Director WKAT) to Phyllis Schlafly, PSR Files, June 1975 Report, Eagle Forum Archives; Pam Proctor, "Phyllis Schlafly: She Thinks Women Are Better Off than Men," *Parade, St. Louis Post-Dispatch*, May 25, 1976, p. 15. Also, "Big Money and Tough Tactics to Ratify ERA," *Phyllis Schlafly Report*, June 1975.

35. "Transcript of the Tomorrow Show," May 18, 1980, ERA Smears Folder, ERA Files.

36. Carol Felsenthal, *The Sweetheart of the Silent Majority*, p. 7.

37. For an informed and judicious assessment of the Carter presidency and the women's movement, see Susan Hartmann, "Feminism and Public Policy," *The Carter Presidency: Policy Choices in the Post-New Deal ERA* (Lawrence, KS, 1998), pp. 224–43. This discussion of the Carter administration draws on Hartmann's essay.

38. Paul Scott, "White House's ERA Problem," *The Washington New Intelligence Syndicate*, June 27, 1979, in ERA Topic Files, Schlafly Office Files, Eagle Forum; White House, "President's Advisory Committee for Women, Monday, May 14, 1979, *Weekly Compilation of Presidential Documents*, vol. 5:19, pp. 789–843;

Jack Germond and Jules Witcover, "Battle for ERA May Be Finished," *Newark Star Ledger*, December 9, 1978, in ERA Office Files, ERA Democrats, Eagle Forum Office.

39. President's Advisory Committee on Women, "Fact Sheet, Passage of the ERA: A Summary of the Efforts of Jimmy Carter" (June 30, 1980), Carter Folder, ERA Topic Files, Eagle Forum Archives. For a view that Carter was not consistent in his support of women, see Emily Walker Cook, "Women White House Advisers in the Carter Administration: Presidential Stalwarts or Feminist Advocates?" (Ph.D. dissertation, Vanderbilt University, 1995), and Mary Frances Berry, "*Why ERA Failed: Politics, Women's Rights, and Amending the Constitution* (Bloomington, Indiana, 1986).

40. "Carter Signs Extension of ERA," *Chicago Tribune*, October 21, 1979, Carter Folder, ERA Files.

Carter's difficult relations with feminists were personified by his troubles with Midge Costanza, whom he had appointed to the White House staff as director of the Office of Public Liaison. Carter met Costanza after her unsuccessful run for Congress in Rochester, New York, in 1974. Impressed with her political savvy, he asked her to co-chair his New York campaign and then second his nomination at the 1976 Democratic convention. Following the election, he appointed her as one of his top six policy advisors. In this position she vowed to support such controversial issues as gay rights, abortion, and the decriminalization of marijuana. The first months went well, but troubles began when she hosted a fundraiser to pay off her campaign debt from her unsuccessful campaign for Congress in 1974, which led some critics to ask about Carter's highly touted ethical guidelines for the White House staff. Her public opposition to Bert Lance, director of the Office of Management and Budget, began a downward slide in Costanza's position in the Carter administration. The next step downward came when Carter endorsed the Supreme Court decision in *Harris v. McRae*, which upheld congressional restrictions on funding for abortions through Medicaid. Costanza and other women in the administration let it be known to the press that they disagreed with the President's position. Things did not get better when Carter signed legislation that banned federal funds for abortions except to protect the life of a mother or in cases of rape and incest. Although Costanza retained her title, she stood in disfavor within the administration. In April 1978 Carter appointed Anne Wexler, a former Deputy Undersecretary of Commerce, to take over some of Costanza's duties. For divisions in the Carter administration, see Clark R. Mollenhoff, *The President Who Failed: Carter Out of Control* (New York, 1980), pp. 162–64; Joseph Califano, *Governing America: An Insider's Report from the White House and the Cabinet* (New York, 1981).

41. After being elected to Congress in 1972 as an antiwar Democrat, Abzug gave up her New York seat to run for the U.S. Senate seat in 1976. In the primary,

she lost to Daniel Moynihan who went on to win the general election. She tried to reenter Congress in 1978, but was readily beaten by her Republican opponent.

42. "Washington Report of the President's Advisory Committee for Women, January 20, 1979," Office Files, ERA Office Files, President's Advisory Committee on Women. This report was sent to Phyllis Schlafly by an unknown supporter on the National Women's Advisory Commission.

43. "Women Exerting a Lot of Energy Says Judy Carter," *Atlanta Journal*, February 22, 1978; Marguerite Sullivan, "Judy Carter on the Campaign Trail for ERA," *Herald News*, November 9, 1977 ERA President Carter Folder, ERA Files, Eagle Forum Archives.

44. Fact Sheet, Passage of the ERA: A Summary of the Efforts of Jimmy Carter (June 30, 1980), Carter Folder, ERA Files, Eagle Forum.

45. President's Advisory Committee on Women, "Report on the National Committee for Women," Abzug Folder, Eagle Forum Archives.

46. Carolyn Cole, "Bella Abzug, a Dedicated Activist," *Waterloo Courier*, September 17, 1978; Leslie Bennetts, "The New Bella Abzug: She's Down but Not Out," *Chicago Tribune*, December 10, 1978; "Bella: An Old Fashioned Woman Removes Her Political Kid Gloves for ERA," *Everett Herald*, March 24, 1978 in Abzug Folder, ERA File, Eagle Forum Archives.

47. Various views of Carter's foreign policy are found in Gaddis Smith, *Morality, Reason, and Power: American Diplomacy in the Carter Years* (New York, 1986); Donald S. Spencer, *The Carter Implosion: Jimmy Carter and the Amateur Style of Diplomacy* (New York, 1988); and Timothy P. Maga, *The World of Jimmy Carter: U.S. Foreign Policy, 1977–1981* (New Haven, 1995).

48. Walter LaFeber, *The Panama Canal: The Crisis in Historical Perspective* (New York, 1978). Also, J. Michael Hogan, *Panama Canal in American Politics: Domestic Advocacy and the Evolution of Policy* (Carbondale, IL, 1986); and James Cockcroft, *Latin America—History, Politics, and U.S. Policy* (Chicago, 1996).

49. Attending the ceremony, his National Security Adviser Zbigniew Brzezinski recalled, "Carter clearly enjoyed his role as the political emancipator of a downtrodden people. For him, this occasion represented the ideal fusion of morality and politics: he was doing something good for peace, responding to the passionate desires of a small nation and yet helping the long range national interest." Zbigniew Brzezinski, *Power and Principle: Memoirs of the National Security Adviser, 1977–1981* (New York, 1983), p. 137; also Erwin C. Hargrove, *Jimmy Carter as President: Leadership and the Politics of the Public Good* (Baton Rouge, 1988), p. 124. For the context of the Panama treaty in the Carter presidency, see Richard C. Thornton, *The Carter Years* (New York, 1991), pp. 357–81.

50. Petitions, letters, and resolutions flooded Congress. The Veterans of Foreign Wars came out against the treaty. The Conservative Caucus organized a mass letter-writing campaign. In California, Phillip Harmon organized the Canal Zone Non-Profit Public Information Corporation that became a major conduit

for antitreaty literature. Americans living in the canal submitted an antitreaty petition to the sympathetic House Subcommittee on the Panama Canal. U.S. Senator Adlai Stevenson III (D-Illinois) reported that in 1977 he received 5,600 letters opposing the treaty and only 5 in favor. The *St. Louis Globe-Democrat* reported similar numbers with over 2,000 letters against and only 29 in favor.

51. Walter LaFeber, *The Panama Canal*, pp. 212–16.

52. "Final Issues in the Panama Canal Giveaway," *Phyllis Schlafly Report*, April 1978; "The Moral Issues in the Panama Treaties," November 1977; "Defeat the Panama Canal Treaty!" October 1977; and "Don't Surrender the U.S. Canal!" February 1977.

53. Jeffrey Hart, "Panama Illusion," *National Review*, October 9, 1977.

54. Denison Kitchel to Barry Goldwater, November 28, 1977, Box 9, Personal and Political, Series II, Barry Goldwater Papers.

55. In particular, Schlafly targeted the financial ties between American bankers and the Torrijos government. In a series of columns arguing against ratification of the treaties, she noted that the Torrijos's regime was pushing hard for the treaty to pass in order to get the loans promised by the U.S. government as part of ratification plus the projected revenues from the canal as specified in the treaty. In 1974, Torrijos had turned to an international consortium of bankers to alleviate his country's financial problems caused by his failed economic programs. A five-year, $45 million loan was provided by a consortium organized by Citicorp (First National City Bank of New York). The Continental Bank of Chicago formed a group to extend a $17.5 million loan for sugar production. Torrijos also gave Texasgulf Corporation the rights to develop Cerro Colorado, one of the richest copper deposits in the world. The Panama Canal treaty thus offered a financial life-line to the Torrijos government. Revenues from the canal promised to pay $40 to $50 million annually, along with an American loan package promised by Carter of $295 and an additional $50 million in military assistance. Steven F. Hayward, *The Age of Reagan: The Fall of the Old Liberal Order, 1964–1980* (Roseville, CA, 2001), pp. 546–47.

56. Alan Crawford in *Thunder on the Right* (New York, 1980) suggests that the New Right represented a populist uprising caused by class resentment. Also, Kenneth D. Wald, Dennis E. Owen, and Samuel S. Hill, Jr., "Evangelical Politics and the Status Issue, *Journal for the Scientific Study of Religion*, 28:1 (1989). Steve Bruce argues against this status argument in *The Rise and Fall of the Christian Right* (Oxford, 1988); and Clyde Wilcox, *God's Warriors* (Baltimore, 1992).

57. Gene C. Pulliam to Goldwater (1975), Box 5 / 1, Political and Personal, Series III, Barry Goldwater Papers.

58. William Rusher to Subscribers, May 5, 1978, Box 119, William Rusher papers.

59. William Rusher to Michael Djordjevich, October 16, 1978, Box 26, William Rusher papers.

60. Patrick Glynn, *Closing Pandora's Box: Arms Races, Arms Control, and the History of the Cold War* (New York, 1999), pp. 269–70.

61. Phyllis Schlafly and Admiral Chester Ward, *Ambush at Vladivostok* (Alton, Illinois, 1976), p. 153.

62. Schlafly and Ward did not explain how Nitze and Rostow had become defense hawks. Phyllis Schlafly and Admiral Chester Ward, *Ambush at Vladivostok* (Alton, Illinois, 1976), p. 140.

63. *Ibid*, pp. 153–55.

64. These negative views of SALT II were set within the context of the fall of Saigon in April 1975, when the North Vietnamese forces captured the city. That same month the communist Khmer Rouge came into power in Cambodia and the communist Pathet Lao in Laos. In Africa, Cuban troops openly poured into Angola to aid the communist resistance forces trying to gain power in the former Portuguese colony. Shortly after Carter came into office, Ethiopia fell to a pro-Soviet government. Patrick Glynn, *Closing Pandora's Box: Arms Races, Arms Control, and the History of the Cold War*, pp. 268–72.

65. Paul H. Nitze, *From Hiroshima to Glasnost* (New York, 1989), pp. 351–53.

66. When Nitze learned that Carter had nominated Paul Warnke to be director of the Arms Control and Disarmament Agency and chief negotiator of SALT II, the Committee on the Present Danger challenged the appropriateness of Warnke for the position, given Warnke's reputation as a well-known dove who his critics thought wanted an arms-control treaty with the Soviets at any cost. Nitze prevailed upon the Senate Foreign Relations Committee to use its confirmation hearings on Warnke to debate the administration's posture toward the Soviet Union and arms control in general. At the hearings, Senator Henry Jackson (D-Washington), representing the pro-defense wing of the Democratic party, showed that Warnke had opposed the building of the B-1 bomber, the Trident submarine and Trident II missile, the submarine-launched cruise missile, the mobile ICBM, and MIRV deployment. When Paul Nitze appeared before the committee, he questioned the "inconsistent and misleading testimony by Mr. Warnke." The Democratic-controlled Senate approved Warnke as director of the Arms Control and Disarmament Agency by 70 to 29, but the vote confirming him as chief SALT negotiator was approved by only 58 to 40. With this vote, progress toward concluding a SALT II agreement was uncertain. Nitze, *From Hiroshima to Glasnost*, pp. 354–55.

67. Limitations of SALT II are described by Nitze, *From Hiroshima to Glasnost*, p. 362.

68. Kissinger's appraisal of the Soviet nuclear program was alarming. He said that there was now "general agreement" that Soviet improvement in missile accuracy and warhead technology would place the Soviet Union "in a position to wipe out our land-based forces of Minuteman ICBMs by 1982." While

he doubted that the Soviets would exercise this capability, he warned that the United States had been caught with its guard down. "Rarely in history has a nation so passively accepted such a radical change in the military balance. If we are to remedy it we must first recognize the fact that we have placed ourselves at a significant disadvantage voluntarily." The Soviets, he maintained, had not lived up to the spirit of SALT I when they developed a new generation of ICBMs. He warned that there had been "an unprecedented Soviet assault on the international equilibrium." Nonetheless, he recommended that the treaty be ratified, but only after two stipulations were implemented. First, he urged the Senate to make it clear that "Soviet expansionism threatens the peace and that coexistence depends above all on restrained conduct." Second, the Senate should give its advice and consent to ratification of the SALT II treaty only after the administration submitted and Congress authorized a supplemental defense budget to overcome the appalling neglect of the nation's defense. Henry Kissinger, "The Strategic Arms Limitation Treaty (SALT II), July 31, 1979," in Henry Kissinger, *For the Record: Selected Statements, 1977–1980* (Boston, 1981), pp. 191–230. For a different perspective of SALT II, see Cyrus Vance, *Hard Choices: Critical Years in America's Foreign Policy* (New York, 1983); Strobe Talbott, *Endgame: The Inside Story of SALT II* (New York, 1978); Jimmy Carter, *Keeping Faith: Memoirs of a President* (Toronto, 1982); and John Newhouse, *Cold Dawn: The Story of SALT* (New York, 1974).

69. Geoffrey Layman, *The Great Divide: Religious and Cultural Conflict in American Party Politics* (New York, 2001), pp. 10–11. Also Duanne M. Oldfield, *The Right and the Righteous: The Christian Right Confronts the Republican Party* (Lanham, MD, 1996).

70. Geoffrey Layman, *The Great Divide: Religious and Cultural Conflict in American Party Politics*, pp. 23–52. Also, pertinent to this discussion of party realignment on issues is James L. Sundquist, *Dynamics of the Party System: Alignment and Realignment of Political Parties in the United States* (Washington, D.C., 1983); and E. E. Schattschneider, *The Semisovereign People: A Realist's View of Democracy in America* (New York, 1960).

71. Typical was the case of Charles Percy, the Republican Senator from Schlafly's home state of Illinois. Following the primary, which Percy won, Schlafly told the *St. Louis Post-Dispatch* that Percy had personally phoned her to ask for support. "I gave him the same consideration he gave me when I asked him to vote against the ERA extension. He wants ERA, and he'll do anything to get it." She added, "I certainly will not vote for him because I think he has been insulting to Illinois." Percy prevailed on civil rights activist Jesse Jackson and former heavyweight boxer Muhammad Ali to campaign for him to try to shore up his vote in the African-American community as some compensation for defections from the right wing of the Republican party. Percy

won reelection, but the race left him severely damaged, and he lost his seat in 1984. See Phyllis Schlafly to Friend, October 27, 1978, Box 124, ERAmerica papers; and Bill Lambrecht, "Percy Says He's Underdog, Seeks Help from Ford," *St. Louis Post-Dispatch*, November 1, 1978, IWY Folder, ERA Files, Eagle Forum Archives.

72. A rich literature has emerged on the Christian Right. Among works useful for this study see David H. Bennett, *The Party of Fear: From Nativist Movements to the New Right in American History* (Chapel Hill, NC, 1988); Steve Bruce, Peter Kivisto, and William H. Swatos, Jr. *The Rapture of Politics* (New York, 1995); Mathew Moen, *The Christian Right and Congress* (Tuscaloosa, AL, 1992); Robert Liebman and Robert Wuthnow, *The Christian Right* (New York, 1983); James Davison Hunter, *Cultural Wars: The Struggle to Define America* (New York, 1991); Clyde Wilcox, *Onward Christian Soldiers? The Religious Right in American Politics* (Boulder, CO, 1996); Michael D'Antonio, *Fall from Grace: The Failed Crusade of the Christian Right* (Boston, 1989); and David Bromley and Anson Shupe, *New Christian Politics* (Macon, GA, 1984).

73. "1980 Elections Start Now!" *The Pro-Life Political Reporter*, September 1979, I:4, in Dee Jepsen papers, Box I, Ronald Reagan Library; and Michael Margolis and Kevin Neary, "Pressure Politics Revisited: The Anti-Abortion Campaign," *Policy Studies Journal* 8 (Spring 1980): pp. 698–716.

74. Roger Williams, "The Power of Fetal Politics," *Saturday Review* (June 9, 1979), pp. 12–15.

75. "The Republican Party Platform," *Phyllis Schlafly Report*, August, 1980.

76. "1980 Elections Start Now!" *Pro-Life Political Reporter* 1 (September 1979): 4, Box 1, Dee Jepsen Papers, Ronald Reagan Library.

77. For mobilization of the New Right see Pamela Johnston Conover, "The Mobilization of the New Right: A Test of Various Explanations," *Western Political Quarterly* 36 (December 1983): 632–49; Carol Mueller, "In Search of a Constituency for the 'New Religious Right,' " *Public Opinion Quarterly* 47 (Summer 1983): 213–29; and Clyde Wilcox and Leopoldo Gomez, "The Christian Right and the Pro-Life Movement: An Analysis of Sources of Political Support," *Review of Religious Research* 31:4 (June 1990): 380–88. Also, "Reflecting on Feminism, Politics, and the Democratic Party," *Washington Post*, December 9, 1980, in ERA Office Files, ERA Democrat, Eagle Forum Office.

78. Gillian Peel, *Revival and Reaction: The Right in Contemporary America* (New York, 1984).

79. Moreover, Republicans introduced a new class of dedicated conservatives including Dan Quayle (Indiana), Charles E. Grassley (Iowa), Steven D. Symms (Idaho), James Abdnor (South Dakota), Robert W. Kasten, Jr. (Wisconsin), and John P. East (North Carolina). Republican conservatives also replaced GOP liberal senators with conservatives: Alfonse M. D'Amato replaced Jacob Javits in New York, and Don Nickles, backed by fundamentalist groups, took Henry Bellmon's seat in Oklahoma.

80. "ERA Election Results" (transcript), Cable News Network, November 6, 1980, ERA History Folder, ERA Files, Eagle Forum Archives.

81. Leslie Bennetts, "Feminists Dismayed by the Election and Unsure of What the Future Holds," *New York Times*, November 7, 1980, p. A.16.

82. Phyllis Schlafly, "Does Reagan Know Who Elected Him?" *Phyllis Schlafly Report*, December 1980.

83. The pro-family movement had helped war hero Admiral Jeremiah Denton win his Senate race in Alabama; Don Nickles' election in Oklahoma was due primarily to STOP ERA and Moral Majority support; and Congressman Robert Dornan withstood a major challenge from Hollywood actor Gregory Peck's son. Antiabortion activists, she continued, had "proved their mettle in knocking off Senator Dick Clark in Iowa in 1978," and on November 4th, they "collected an impressive list of scalps," including pro-abortion Senators Birch Bayh, Frank Church, John Culver, George McGovern, Warren Magnuson, Gaylord Nelson, and Robert Morgan. Abortion was not the only issue, but she pointed to exit polls in Iowa showing that 10 percent of the voters chose Charles Grassley over Culver because of his anti-abortion stance. Iowa voters also defeated a proposed state equal rights amendment that was on the 1980 ballot.

84. Leslie Bennetts, "Women May Hold Key to Election in Pivotal States," *New York Times*, October 17, 1980, p. A.22.

85. This view of American history as a moral epic is explored in James Morone, *Hellfire Nation: The Politics of Sin in American History* (New Haven, 2003).

86. Phyllis Schlafly, "Mixing Religion and Politics," *Phyllis Schlafly Report*, (December 1980).

87. William Rusher to Ronald Reagan, August 3, 1979, Box 75, William Rusher Papers, Library of Congress.

CHAPTER ELEVEN
IDEOLOGY AND POWER IN A DIVIDED NATION

1. Quoting David Keene, C-PAC President, "CPAC's Presidential Banquet Will Honor Phyllis Schlafly on the 20th Anniversary of the Defeat of ERA," November 14, 2003, www.cpac.org.

2. Carl Limbacher, "Schlafly, Sen Kyl Honored at C-PAC," NewsMax.com, January 31, 2003, www. Newsmax.com., January 7, 2004; and Keith Barton, "Conservatives Give Tribute to Phyllis Schlafly," ChronWatch, February 2, 2003, http://www.chronwatch.com.

3. Karla Dial, "Founding Mother," *Citizen Magazine*, November 2002.

4. Ann Coulter, *Slander: Liberal Lies about the American Right* (New York, 2002), pp. 36 and 38.

5. Karla Dial, "Founding Mother," *Citizen Magazine*, November 2002.

6. The message of *The Supremacists* was a far cry from those conservatives who had defended the Supreme Court against Roosevelt's New Deal in the 1930s. Phyllis Schlafly, *The Supremacists: The Tyranny of Judges and How to Stop It* (Dallas, 2004).

7. Lou Cannon, *President Reagan: The Role of a Lifetime* (New York, 1991), p. 112. This discussion of Reagan's relations with conservatives draws from Donald T. Critchlow, "Mobilizing Women: The Social Issues," in W. Elliot Brownlee and Hugh Davis Graham, *The Reagan Presidency: Pragmatic Conservatism and Its Legacies* (Lawrence, KS, 2003), pp. 293-327.

8. Letters urging Reagan to meet with anti-abortion leaders are seen in Orrin G. Hatch to the President, May 28, 1981; William L. Armstrong to Hon. Edwin Meese III, May 29, 1981, Morton Blackwell papers, Box 8, Ronald Reagan Library.

9. Presidential Papers of Ronald Reagan, 1981, "Conservative Political Action Conference, March 20, 1981, pp. 327–28, in Box 1, Abortion folder, Elizabeth Dole papers, Ronald Reagan Library.

10. Quoted in "Armstrong Picks Pro-ERA Women's Panel for Women," *Human Events*, September 27, 1980, p. 3.

11. Reagan-Bush Campaign, News Release, September 11, 1980, Reagan, Women's Policy Board folder, Post-1970 Box, Eagle Forum Archives.

12. Phyllis Schlafly, Telegram, September 11, 1980, Reagan, Women's Policy Board folder, Post-1970 Box, Eagle Forum Archives.

13. Phyllis Schlafly, Telegram, September 19, 1980; Phyllis Schlafly, Handwritten notes on telephone conversation with Connie Marshner (n.d.), Reagan, Family Policy Advisory Board folder, Post-1970 Box, Eagle Forum Archives.

14. Dennis Farney, "Reagan and the Conservatives," *Wall Street Journal*, July 28, 1980, Al.

15. John D. Lofton, Jr., "Carlucci Appointment Disturbs Conservatives," *Washington Inquirer*, January 16, 1981, pp. 1–2; Donald Lambro, "Reagan Loyalists Fight Transition Team Choices," *Washington Inquirer*, January 23, 1981, pp. 1, 3; and Karen McKay, "Van Cleave Sent Packing by Weinberger," *Washington Inquirer*, January 23, 1981, p. 3.

16. Phyllis Schlafly, "Notes on Conference with Ed Meese, Arlington, VA, October 29, 1980, Reagan, Transition Folder, Post-1970 Box, Eagle Forum Archives.

17. Roger Milliken to Phyllis Schlafly, November 19, 1980; Roger Millikin to Edwin Meese, November 19, 1980.

18. Included on the Executive Committee of the Coalition for a Change in Government were Lorelei Kinder, Betty Heitman, Nancy Chotiner, Leora Day, Phyllis Schlafly, Bob Baldwin, Connie Marshner, Louise Ropog, Jo Ann Gasper, Jo Ann McMurray, Ginny Martinez, Allen Martin, and Marilyn Thayer. See Phyllis Schlafly, "Notes on Coalition for Change in Government,"

December 19, 1980, Reagan, Transition folder, Pre-1970 Box, Eagle Forum Archives.

19. These sentiments, for example, were expressed in a private letter of resignation from Elly Peterson to her co-chair of ERAmerica, Liz Carpenter, Elly Peterson to Liz Carpenter, November 2, 1978, Box 18, Elly Peterson papers.

20. Mike Feinsilber, "ERA Appears Doomed in Anti-Ratification States," *Miami Herald*, August 30, 1981, ERA Topic Files, Eagle Forum Archives.

21. Especially good on this point is Jane J. Mansbridge, *Why We Lost the ERA* (Chicago, 1986), pp. 149–64.

22. Other referenda on State ERAs included Wisconsin, November 1973 (60,000 majority against); New York, November 1975 (420,000 majority against); New Jersey, November 1975 (52 percent against); Nevada, November 1978 (66 percent against); and Florida, November 1978 (60 percent against). The Iowa vote was 55 percent against, and the vote on a state ERA in November 1984 in Maine was 64 percent against. Vermont narrowly defeated a state ERA in 1986. See "A Brief History of ERA," *Phyllis Schlafly Report*, September 1986.

23. John Leonard, "Books of the Times," *New York Times*, October 30, 1981.

24. "NOW Funds Soar in Amendment Bid," *New York Times*, May 30, 1982, ERA Topic Files, ERA 1981–82, Eagle Forum Archives.

25. "Mrs. Schlafly's Absurdities," *Palm Beach Post*, April 23, 1981; "Obsolete Crusade for a Wrong Cause: Mrs. Schlafly in the Museum, Not in the Kitchen," *Louisville Times*, April 27, 1981; Carol Ashkinaze, "Schlafly Stirs Virtuous Indignation," *Atlanta Journal*, May 2, 1981; "Schlafly, Nice Girls Escape Sex Harassment," *Philadelphia Daily News*, April 22, 1981; Rusty Brown, "Women Won't Quit Fighting for Rights," *Mobile Suburban Register* (n.d.), ERA Smears folder, ERA Topic Files, Eagle Forum Archives.

26. Carol Felsenthal, "How Feminists Failed," *Chicago Magazine* (June 1982), pp. 139–42, 154–58, especially 156.

27. *Idaho v. Freeman* (1981) was an important decision. The ruling stated that the congressional time extension from 1979 to 1982 was unconstitutional, and that states did have a right to rescind their ERA ratifications prior to the deadline. When the Supreme Court declared the issue "moot," Schlafly claimed victory because the Court ruled in effect that ERA was dead. Letter quoted in "U.S. Stance Further Jeopardizes ERA," *Washington Post*, January 6, 1982; Wendy Borcherdt to Elizabeth Dole, "ERA," January 8, 1982; and Morton Blackwell to Diana Lozano for Elizabeth Dole, January 12, 1982, Box 6, Wendy Borcherdt papers, Ronald Reagan Library.

28. Judy Flander, "TV Highlights: 'Cagney and Lacey' Tackle Subject of ERA," *Chicago Tribune*, June 28, 1982; Ron Alridge, "CBS Puts on Rare Display of Social Responsibility," *Chicago Tribune*, June 30, 1982; Elizabeth Clarke to

William S. Paley, August 10, 1982, Cagney Lacey Folder, ERA Topic Files, Eagle Forum Archives.

29. "Hex for Sex Equality," *Chicago Tribune*, Suburban edition, December 17, 1981, Guy Christopher, "Letters to Editor," *The Weekly* (Champaign-Urbana), April 10–16, 1981; Z. Budapest, "A Spell for ERA," *Allegheny Feminists* (ERA Special Issue), July 1978, pp. 1, 7.

30. Graduate Students in Speech Communications, "A Briefing Book on Phyllis Schlafly," February 24, 1982, ERA Topic Files, ERA 1981–82, Eagle Forum Archives.

31. Elaine Kindall, "The Sweetheart of the Silent Majority," *Des Moines Register*, February 1, 1981.

32. Ronald Reagan to Miss Doris K. Steward, May 11, 1972 (copy), Box 19, Elly Peterson Papers.

33. Barbara Honegger, "Memorandum for Elizabeth Dole," June 17, 1980, Phyllis Schlafly, "Is There Life for E.R.A. After June 30th" (n.d.), Box 6, Wendy Borcherdt papers, Ronald Reagan Library.

34. White House Press Release, "Remarks of the President at Signing Ceremony for Executive Order Establishing Task Force on Legal Equity for Women," December 21, 1981, Reagan, Women's Equity Task Force folder, Post-1970 Box, Eagle Forum Archives.

35. Elizabeth H. Dole to Phyllis Schlafly, December 5, 1981; Phyllis Schlafly to Elizabeth Dole, April 3, 1981; Phyllis Schlafly to Elizabeth Dole, November 8, 1981; Diana Lozano to Elaine Donnelly, November 9, 1981; and Judy Peachee to Phyllis Schlafly, October 2, 1981; Phyllis Schlafly to Judy P. Peachee, November 6, 1981; Reagan, Women's Equity Task Force, Post-1970 Box, Eagle Forum Archives.

36. "How ERA Would Change Federal Laws," November, 1981; Phyllis Schlafly to Elizabeth Dole, November 9, 1981, Box 2, Dee Jepsen papers, Ronald Reagan Library.

37. Reagan selected Dr. C. Everett Koop, a Philadelphia surgeon, evangelical Christian, and anti-abortionist as surgeon general in charge of programs administered by the Centers for Disease Control, the Population Research Center, and the National Institutes of Health. In addition, he appointed Marjory Mecklenburg, president of American Citizens Concerned for Life, to head the Office of Adolescent Pregnancy Programs, which gives grants to aid teenage mothers and counsels them on birth control. A number of other appointments within the administration were made to people with well-known anti-abortion credentials including Gary Bauer, Morton Blackwell, and Dee Jepsen in the Public Liaison Office, and Michael Uhlmann in the Attorney General's office.

38. This perspective is expressed in Michele McKeegan, *Abortion Politics: Mutiny in the Ranks of the Right* (New York, 1992), pp. 1–23; and Tanya Melich, *The Republican War against Women: An Insider's Report from Behind the Lines* (New York, 1998).

39. Steve Alumbaugh and C. K. Rowland, "The Links Between Platform-Based Appointment Criteria and Trial Judges' Abortion Judgments," *Judicature* 74:3 (October/November 1990): 153–62.

40. Charles Fried, *Order and Law: Arguing the Reagan Revolution—A Firsthand Account* (New York, 1991), p. 58.

41. Morton Blackwell to Elizabeth H. Dole, "Conservative Organization Reaction to Sandra O'Connor Nomination," July 8, 1981, Conservative File, Box 2, Elizabeth Dole papers, Ronald Reagan Library.

42. Ronald Reagan to Mrs. Marie Craven, August 3, 1981, Prolife file, Box 8, Morton Blackwell papers.

43. In her first major abortion case on the Court, Justice O'Connor joined dissenters in *Akron v. Akron Center for Reproductive Health, Inc.* (1983) that struck down most restrictions on abortion legislated by the Akron City Council. In her dissent O'Connor noted that *Roe* was "on a collision course with itself" because the trimester approach was "unworkable" in light of changing medical technology that lengthened viability. She echoed U.S. Solicitor's General Rex E. Lee's *amicus* brief that asserted that the test for state regulation for abortion should rest on the principle of "undue burden." This marked an important shift in the Court's thinking on the subject. Karen O'Connor, *No Neutral Ground?* pp. 94–102; and McKeegan, *Abortion Politics*, pp. 173–91.

44. Author interview with Jo Ann Gasper, September 3, 2001; "Anti-Abortion War Resumed by Reagan," *The Washington Times*, July 31, 1987, AI, 12. Press Release, "Remarks by the President in Briefing for Right to Life Leaders," July 10, 1997, Abortion file, Box 1, Gary Bauer papers, Ronald Reagan Library. For example, see Douglas Johnson, National Right to Life Legislative Director, to Board of Directors and State Offices, "Enactment of prohibition on funding of abortions by the government of the District of Columbia," October 5, 1988, Prolife File, Box 1, Mariam Bell papers.

45. In the July 1982 *Phyllis Schlafly Report*, she spoke out in favor of prayer in school.

46. A full record of the Republican National Coalition for Life can be found in the Eagle Forum Archives.

47. In his handwritten draft, Reagan had added, "not excepting *Pravda* and *Tass* that I have ever seen." Richard Darman, reviewing the draft letter, convinced Reagan to delete the phrase. Ronald Reagan to John Lofton, July 30, 1982, Draft, Ronald Reagan to John Lofton, n.d. Box 3, Presidential Handwritten File, Series II, Presidential Records, Ronald Reagan Library. I thank historian Robert Collins for calling attention to this exchange.

48. Lewis K. Uhler, *Setting Limits: Constitutional Control of Government* (Washington, D.C., 1989). A good summary of the call for a constitutional convention to pass a balanced budget amendment is found in "Support Growing for Spending Ban: Need 34 States for Change," *Washington Times*, January 25, 1985, p. 1.

49. Phyllis Schlafly, "Con Con: Playing Russian Roulette with the Constitution," *Phyllis Schlafly Report*, December 1984. Political scientist James L. Sundquist evaluated the various proposals for structural reform of government through constitutional amendments in *Constitutional Reform and Effective Government* (Washington, D.C., 1986).

50. Phyllis Schlafly, "A Call for a Constitutional Convention: Statement to the Montana Senate" (ms.), March 16, 1987; and Citizens to Protect the Constitution, "Should We Have a Constitutional Convention to Enact a Balanced Amendment?" and Helena Eagle Forum, *Oppose Federal Constitutional Convention Newsletter* (1987), Con Con Documents 1984 Folder, Con Con Files, Eagle Forum Archives.

51. See material in Con Con Action in Michigan, 1985–1987, Con Con Files.

52. Phyllis Schlafly to Warren E. Burger, April 4, 1986, Warren E. Burger to Phyllis Schlafly, April 8, 1986; Marshall Peters to Phyllis Schlafly, August 14, 1985, Action in Michigan folder.

53. Phyllis Schlafly to Warren E. Burger, August 18, 1986; Warren E. Burger to Phyllis Schlafly, August 23, 1986; Con Con Action, 1986 folder.

54. For example, see the brochure, Americans United for Separation of Church and State, "Warning: A Constitutional Convention May Be Hazardous to Your Religious Freedom."

55. Conservative Patrick Buchanan, assistant to Ronald Reagan, denied to Schlafly that Reagan had endorsed the constitutional convention. Nonetheless, Reagan in his speeches suggested he was in favor of a Balanced Budget Amendment, and key personnel including Edward Rollins and the Office of Management and Budget supported the call for a constitutional convention. See Patrick J. Buchanan to Phyllis Schlafly, April 16, 1985; Phyllis Schlafly to Patrick Buchanan, March 28, 1985; Phyllis Schlafly to Donald Regan, March 28, 1985; and Donald Regan to Phyllis Schlafly, April 15, 1985, Action in Michigan Folder; also see, Phyllis Schlafly to Ed Rogers, Office of Political Affairs, White House, April 3, 1986 and Ed Rogers to Phyllis Schlafly, April 3, 1986, Action in 1986 folder.

56. Lewis K. Uhler to Mr. and Mrs. Raymond F. Babb, April 29, 1987, Con Con Action in Montana 1987 Folder, Con Con Files.

57. Jonathan Fuerbringer, "Budget-Balancing Change for Constitution Loses," *New York Times*, March 26, 1986, p. 11.

58. In 1980, the percentage of evangelical Christian first-time delegates was 6.76 percent, while in 1984 the percentage had increased to 9.68 percent. Geoffrey Layman, *The Great Divide: Religious and Cultural Conflict in American Party Politics* (New York, 2001), pp. 100–110, especially p. 106. For the entire wording of the GOP National Platforms on abortion in 1980 and 1984, Republican National Committee, *Thirty-Second Republican National Convention* (1980), p. 255; Republican National Committee, *Thirty-Third Republican National Convention* (1984), p. 308.

59. Republican National Committee, *Thirty-Third Republican National Convention* (1984), pp. 304–305. For a feminist view of these changes in party policies, see Tanya Melich, *The Republican War against Women* (New York, 1996).

60. *Thirty-Third Republican National Convention*, p. 293.

61. Author conversation with Phyllis Schlafly, January 10, 2004.

62. For a discussion of the hearings, education regulations, and publication of the book, see Phyllis Schlafly, "Foreword," *Child Abuse in the Classroom* (Alton, IL, 1984), pp. 11–24.

63. Ruth Murray Brown, *For a "Christian America," A History of the Religious Right,* (Amherst, NY, 2002). Also, Jerome L. Himmelstein, *To the Right: The Transformation of American Conservatism* (Berkeley, 1990); Alan Crawford, *Thunder on the Right* (New York, 1980); William B. Hixson, *The Search for the American Right Wing* (Princeton, 1992); William C. Martin, *With God on Our Side* (New York, 1996); James L. Guth and John C. Green, *The Bible and the Ballot Box: Religion and Politics in the 1988 Election* (Boulder, 1991).

64. Bill O'Brien, "Schlafly Moves to Other Causes," *St. Louis Globe-Democrat,* March 4, 1981.

65. Scheffel & Company, "Independent Audit Report for FY 2002" (compilation), Eagle Forum, Alton, Illinois. In 1997 the Eagle Forum received $473,279 or 73 percent of its revenue from contributors and $71,908 or 11 percent from membership dues; the Eagle Forum Education & Legal Defense Fund in 1997 received $872,286 or 64 percent of gross revenue from contributions and grants (including $25,000 from the John M. Olin Foundation and $5000 from the Richard and Helen DeVos Foundation); $274,199 or 20 percent from the sale of books and videos; $109,537 or 8 percent from interest on savings and temporary cash investments; and $99,444 or 7 percent from dividends and interest from securities. These figures are found in Derk Arend Wilcox, *The Right Guide: A Guide to Conservative, Free Market, and Right-of-Center Organizations* (Ann Arbor, 2000), pp. 132–33.

66. The following discussion of fissures within the Republican party draws heavily on Donald T. Critchlow, "When Republicans Become Revolutionaries: Conservatives in Congress, 1976–2001," in Julian Zelizer, ed., *The Reader's Companion to the American Congress* (New York, 2005).

67. See *Phyllis Schlafly Report* January 1982, May 1982, October 1982, April 1983, May 1983, November 1984, March 1985, and October 1985.

68. See *Phyllis Schlafly Report*, January 1983.

69. Members included Sarah King, president general of the DAR; Beverly LaHaye, president of Concerned Women for America; Joan Hueter, president of Pro America; Illinois State Rep. Penny Pullen; Helen Marie Taylor, vice president of the Eagle Forum Education & Legal Defense Fund; Nina May, president of Renaissance Women; Nancy Gree, president of the Women's Institute of Strategic Analysis; Cynthia Haeberle, Dallas Public Affairs Club; Captain

Red McDaniel, American Defense Institute; Lady Olga Maitland, president of Women and Families for Defense; Evelyn Lecheme, president of British Women for Defense; Ada Boerma and Attie Soels, Dutch Interfaith Groundswell for Bipartisan Disarmament; and representatives from state Eagle Forums in Texas, Michigan, South Dakota, and Indiana. See "Coalition of Women for a Real Defense Meets in Geneva," *News and Notes* (November 15, 1985).

70. This debate over the family issue was framed by both Republicans and Democrats in the knowledge that in 1980 Reagan received 53 percent of the male vote and 49 percent of the female vote, and in 1984 this increased to 63 percent and 56 percent, respectively. "Left and Right Fight for Custody of 'Family Issue,'" *New York Times*, August 30, 1987.

71. "GOP's Right Wing, Bitter Over Bush's Triumph, Debates Whether to Support Him in November," *Wall Street Journal*, April 26, 1988, p. 62.

72. Peter Goldman and Tom Mathews, *The Quest for the Presidency 1988* (New York, 1989).

73. Peter Goldman et al., *Quest for the Presidency 1992* (College Station, Texas, 1994), p. 404.

74. Caroline More, "Bush Organizational Meeting Women Groups," June 9, 1988, Campaign, 1988 folder, Box 16, Post 1970 Files, Eagle Forum Archives.

75. This discussion of Republican strategy on the Horton issue draws from Jack W. Germond and Jules Witcover, *Whose Broad Stripes and Bright Stars: The Trivial Pursuit of the Presidency 1988* (New York, 1989), pp. 92, 157-163. A more favorable view of Dukakis on this issue is found in Peter Goldman and Tom Mathews, *The Quest for the Presidency: The 1988 Campaign* (New York, 1989, pp. 354–65. The report that made this a national issue was Robert James Bidinotto, "Getting Away with Murder," *Reader's Digest* (July 1988), pp. 1–7.

76. The exact number of sales could not be found in the records, and when asked, Phyllis Schlafly did not recall the number of sales, but said that overall the video broke even, although a Spanish version of the tape lost money. One handwritten count of sales for September and October had sales at 5,000, but this might not be indicative of total sales since this appears to be an unofficial count. Geoffrey Botkin to Phyllis Schlafly, October 16, 1988, and Phyllis Schlafly to Geoffrey Botkin, December 8, 1988 Campaign, 1988 Justice on Furlough, Box 16, Pre-1970, Eagle Forum Archives.

77. Phyllis Schlafly to Arnaud de Borchgrave, *The Washington Times*, August 30, 1988, Campaign 1988 folder, Box 16, Post 1970, Eagle Forum Archives.

78. "Gingrich Plugs Video Attacking Dukakis," *Washington Times Insight* (October 24, 1988), p. 9.

79. Frank J. Fahrenkopf, Jr., chairman, Republican National Committee, September 30, 1988; Joseph R. Gaylord to All Congressional Candidates, September 23, 1988; "A Closer Look: Issues Storm," *USA Today*, October 27, 1989. Campaign 1988 folder, Box 16, Post-1970, Eagle Forum Archives.

80. Although records do not reveal how many copies the Republican National Committee purchased, receipts show that the order was in the amount of $38,000. In addition, quantity-orders of less than 500 were placed by Young America's Foundation, Reed Irvine of Accuracy in Media, and Newt Gingrich. Author Telephone Conversation with John Schlafly, June 14, 2004.

81. Sidney Blumenthal, "Willie Horton and the Making of an Election Issue," *Washington Post* (October 28, 1988), pp. D1, D8; Charles Krauthammer, "The Last Refuge: Cries of Racism," *The Washington Post* (October 28, 1988).

82. Phyllis Schlafly, "Hillary's Health Plan: Medicaid-Style Care for All Americans," *Phyllis Schlafly Report* (July 1993); and "Clinton's Totalitarian Health Care Plan," *Phyllis Schlafly Report* (November 1993). Schlafly continued to write on health care in her newsletter. See "Save Freedom—Defeat Phony Health 'Reform,'" (July 1994); "Health Care 'Compromises' Go From Bad to Worse" (August 1994) "Will Health Care Defeat Republicans in 1996," *Phyllis Schlafly Report* (June 1995).

83. Phyllis Schlafly, "We Need Medical Savings Accounts Now."

84. Her role in the 1996 convention is discussed in Phyllis Schlafly, "The Kingmakers," (unpublished book manuscript), Personal Papers of Phyllis Schlafly.

85. Phyllis Schlafly, "What's So Wrong About GATT/WTO?" *Phyllis Schlafly Report* (October 1994).

86. Phyllis Schlafly, "New World Order, Clinton-Style," *Phyllis Schlafly Report* (June 1994).

87. Phyllis Schlafly, "The United Nations—An Enemy in Our Midst," *Phyllis Schlafly Report* (November 1995); also, see "Free Trade, Protectionism, NAFTA, and GATT," Phyllis *Schlafly Report* (February 1996).

88. Phyllis Schlafly, "America Has No Business in Bosnia," *Phyllis Schlafly Report,* (January 1996).

89. Edmund L. Andrews, "A Marriage Penalty, Except When It Isn't," *New York Times* (January 19, 2003), p. 1.

90. "The 1970s," *U.S. News and World Report,* July 2, 1970, p. 18.

91. Phyllis Schlafly, "Marriage Must Be Protected from the Judges," *Phyllis Schlafly Report* (December 2003).

92. "How to Stop Judges's Mischief about Marriage," *Phyllis Schlafly Report* (July 2004).

93. As political scientist Geoffrey Layman shows in *The Great Divide: Religious and Cultural Conflict in American Party Politics* (2001), the GOP became "a party of religious conservatives with traditional moral and cultural values," while the Democratic party "witnessed an influx of religious liberals and secularists." In a detailed analysis of party delegates and activists, Layman showed that the divide in American politics between the Democrats and Republicans reflects deep-seated religious and moral divisions. "On one side of the contemporary

cultural divide," he writes, "are individuals with orthodox religious beliefs and affiliations with high levels of religious commitment." These traditionalists believe in nonnegotiable moral truths that they see as the backbone of American society. By the twentieth century, these traditionalists had reached a consensus that Catholics, Protestants and Jews who held that Judeo-Christian beliefs and teachings should be "the backbone of society." On the other side are secularists and religious liberals who see "moral authority as changing within the boundaries of human knowledge and circumstances of human experience." By the late 1960s, he finds, secularism found growing social and political influence with "the desertion of traditional morality by the entertainment industry, and Supreme Court decisions removing religion from public schools, banning state restrictions on abortion rights, encompassing pornography under freedom of speech, and threatening government aid to religious schools." Geoffrey Layman, *The Great Divide: Religious and Cultural Conflict in American Party Politics* (New York, 2001), pp. x, 10, 17, 19, 35, 101–27, 326–41.

94. For a view of the declining influence of the Christian Right vote in the 2000 election, see Clyde Wilcox, "Wither the Christian Right? The Elections and Beyond," Stephen J. Wayne and Clyde Wilcox, ed. *The Election of the Century* (Armonk, NY, 2002), pp. 107–24; Geoffrey Layman, *The Great Divide,* p. 341.

95. For an overview of the conservative movement leading to the presidency of George W. Bush, see John Micklethwait and Adrian Woolridge, *The Right Nation: Conservative Power in America* (New York, 2004). Conservative opposition to the Bush administration was voiced in Patrick J. Buchanan, *Where the Right Went Wrong: How Neoconservatives Subverted the Reagan Revolution and Hijacked the Bush Presidency* (New York, 2004). Changes in the Republican platform are described in "What Do the Two Parties Stand For?" *Phyllis Schlafly Report* (October 2004). Also, Jon Sawyer and Kevin McDermott, "Conservatives Feel Left Out of Spotlight," *St. Louis Post-Dispatch,* September 1, 2004; Ralph Z. Hallow, "Bush Team Keeps Conservative Agenda in Check," *Washington Times,* August 27, 2004; and John Micklethwait and Adrian Wooldridge, "For Conservatives, Mission Accomplished," *New York Times,* May 18, 2004. For the mobilization of religious voters in 2004, Laurie Goodstein and William Yardley, "President Benefits from Efforts to Build Coalition on Religious Voters," *New York Times,* November 5, 2004, A19. An opposing view on the significance of moral values in the election is found in James Q. Wilson, "Why Did Kerry Lose? (It Wasn't 'Values')," *Wall Street Journal,* November 8, 2004.

96. This question is posed by Steven F. Hayward, "Hillary's Makeover," *The Claremont Review of Books* (Fall, 2003).

Index

Abdnor, James, 392n. 79
ABM and the Changed Strategic Military Balance, 166
ABM Treaty (1972), 206, 299
abortion: and Carter, 263; and the ERA, 225, 227; and Betty Ford, 233, 263; and Gerald Ford, 235; legalization of, 217, 221, 225; as mobilizing issue for conservatives, 2, 4, 15, 214, 234; and Reagan, 273, 281–82; Phyllis Schlafly on, 202, 218, 393n. 83. *See also* National Pro-Life Action Committee and Republican National Coalition for Life and *Abortion Rap* (Kennedy), 253
Abzug, Bella, 254–55, 291, 387n. 41
Acheson, Dean, 169, 348n. 42; conservative criticism of, 53, 100; Phyllis Schlafly on, 60, 323n. 69
ACLU, 225, 227, 228, 277, 285
ACU. *See* American Conservative Union
AEA. *See* American Enterprise Association
affirmative action, 373n. 75
AFL-CIO, 240; and ERA, 220, 231
African Americans, 252; and civil rights movement, 63, 99; and electoral politics, 119, 195, 279, 303; and the ERA, 223, 238, 382n. 72; and local politics, 31; in the National Federation of Republican Women, 152; professional, 186, 236, 247, 275; in public office, 53, 238, 247; and public schools, 186; and state politics, 21, 95, 391n. 71; women, 293
Agnew, Spiro, 192, 206
Akron v. Akron Center for Reproductive Health, Inc., 397n. 43
Alabama: ERA, defeat of, 248
Alda, Alan, 213, 231, 380n. 55
Alsop, Joseph, 358n. 13
Alsop, Stewart, 174

Alton (Illinois), 31, 32, 33, 45, 48, 50, 51, 52, 58, 60, 65, 68, 71, 109, 116, 138, 146, 160, 164, 195, 288, 294, 312n. 10, 329n. 57, 350n. 62
Alton Evening Telegraph, 52, 201
Ambush at Vladivostok (Schlafly and Ward), 164, 259–60, 390n. 62
Amerasia (journal), 64
America First Committee, 25, 26, 46, 318n. 56
American Bar Association, 79–80, 83, 85, 285
American Civil Liberties Union. *See* ACLU
American Conservative Union, 209, 258
American Council of Christian Churches, 67
American Enterprise Association, 25–27, 29, 41, 49
American Federation of Labor and Congress of Industrial Organizations. *See* AFL-CIO
American Jewish League, 66
American Legion Magazine, 39
American Liberty League, 25
American Magazine, 27
American Mercury (magazine), 78
American Security Council, 107, 166
Americans with Disabilities Act, 295
Andrews, T. Coleman, 68–69
antiballistic missile system, 163; and Johnson, 177–79; Phyllis Schlafly on, 179, 205–6; Phyllis Schlafly and Ward on, 176–77; in Soviet Union, 178, 206
Antiballistic Missile Treaty. *See* ABM Treaty
anti-Catholicism, 9, 25
anticommunism: activists, 71, 82; American opinion of, 89; in books and films, 66, 89, 100; and the Catholic Church, 67–68; and civil rights opposition,

POLITICS AND SOCIETY IN TWENTIETH-CENTURY AMERICA

Series Editors:

William Chafe, Gary Gerstle, Linda Gordon, and Julian Zelizer

Civil Defense Begins at Home: Militarization Meets Everyday Life in the Fifties
by Laura McEnaney

Cold War Civil Rights: Race and the Image of American Democracy
by Mary L. Dudziak

Divided We Stand: American Workers and the Struggle for Black Equality
by Bruce Nelson

*Poverty Knowledge: Social Science, Social Policy, and the Poor in
Twentieth-Century U.S. History*
by Alice O'Connor

Suburban Warriors: The Origins of the New American Right
by Lisa McGirr

The Politics of Whiteness: Race, Workers, and Culture in the Modern South
by Michelle Brattain

State of the Union: A Century of American Labor
by Nelson Lichtenstein

Changing the World: American Progressives in War and Revolution
by Alan Dawley

Dead on Arrival: The Politics of Health Care in Twentieth-Century America
by Colin Gordon

*For All These Rights: Business, Labor, and the Shaping of America's
Public-Private Welfare State*
by Jennifer Klein

*The Radical Middle Class: Populist Democracy and the Question of Capitalism
in Progressive Era Portland, Oregon*
by Robert D. Johnston

American Babylon: Race and the Struggle for Postwar Oakland
by Robert O. Self

*The Other Women's Movement: Workplace Justice and
Social Rights in Modern America*
by Dorothy Sue Cobble

Impossible Subjects: Illegal Aliens and the Making of Modern America
by May M. Ngai

More Equal than Others: America from Nixon to the New Century
by Godfrey Hodgson